The Story of Sea Island Cotton

The Story of SEA ISLAND COTTON

Richard Dwight Porcher and Sarah Fick

GIBBS SMITH
TO ENRICH AND INSPIRE HUMANKIND

© Gibbs Smith, Publisher, 2010

All contents © 2005 The Charleston Museum

All rights reserved. No part of this book may be reproduced by any means whatsoever without written permission from the publisher, except brief portions quoted for purpose of review.

Published by Gibbs Smith, Publisher

P.O. Box 667
Layton, Utah 84041

Orders: 1.800.748.5439
www.gibbs-smith.com

Designed by Gil Shuler Graphic Design, Inc.
Printed and bound in The United States of America

Library of Congress Control Number: 2005 931934

ISBN 13: 978-1-4236-1763-1
ISBN 10: 1-4236-1763-0

Contents

List of Illustrations — ix

Foreword — xv

Preface — xvii

Acknowledgements — xxiii

Chronology — xxiv

Part I. Sea Island Cotton

CHAPTER ONE — 3
The Natural Landscape of the Sea Islands

CHAPTER TWO — 39
The Cotton Plant (*Gossypium* spp.)

CHAPTER THREE — 64
The Science of *Gossypium barbadense* L.

CHAPTER FOUR — 73
The Worldwide Dispersal of *Gossypium barbadense* L.

CHAPTER FIVE — 89
The Origin of Sea Island Cotton

CHAPTER SIX — 101
The Geographical Distribution of Long-Staple Cotton in South Carolina, Georgia and Florida

CHAPTER SEVEN — 133
The Culture of Sea Island Cotton

CHAPTER EIGHT — 173
The Market Preparation of Sea Island Cotton

CHAPTER NINE — 185
The Ginning of Sea Island Cotton

CHAPTER TEN
The Fones McCarthy Roller Gin and Sea Island Cotton — 219

CHAPTER ELEVEN
The Textile Industry and Sea Island Cotton — 238

CHAPTER TWELVE
The Insect Pests and Diseases of Sea Island Cotton — 283

CHAPTER THIRTEEN
The Sea Island Cotton Trade — 298

CHAPTER FOURTEEN
The Kinsey Burden Family and Sea Island Cotton — 341

Part II. Sea Island Cotton Plantation Architecture

The Dwelling Houses	359
The Sea Island Plantation Landscape	370
Brick House, Edisto Island	381
Head Quarters (Fenwick Hall), Johns Island	383
Tom Seabrook's House, Edisto Island	386
Laurel Bay, Port Royal Island	389
Old Fort (Smith's) Plantation, Port Royal Island	391
Baynard's Old Place, Edisto Island	393
Tombee, St. Helena Island	396
Unidentified House, St. Helena Island	399
Coffin Point, St. Helena Island	400
Vanderhorst House, Kiawah Island	404
William Edings House (Seaside), Edisto Island	407
Myrtle Bush, Port Royal Island	410
Hopkinson's, Edisto Island	413
Coggins Point, Hilton Head Island	414
William Seabrook House, Edisto Island	417
Mary Jenkins House, St. Helena Island	421
Seaside, St. Helena Island	423
Frogmore, Edisto Island	425
Peter's Point, Edisto Island	429
The Launch/Middleton's, Edisto Island	433
Prospect Hill, Edisto Island	436
Oak Island, Edisto Island	441
Woodward, Port Royal Island	445
Brick House/Stanyarne Hall, Johns Island	448
Brookland, Edisto Island	451

Fish Hall, Hilton Head Island	454
Tom Fripp House, St. Helena Island	457
Oakley Hall (Bloody Point), Daufuskie Island	459
Melrose (Salt Pond), Daufuskie Island	461
Crawford's, Edisto Island	465
William J. Jenkins House, St. Helena Island	467
Cassina Point, Edisto Island	470
McLeod, James Island	473
The Oaks, St. Helena Island	477
Youghal, Christ Church Parish	479
Ashe's/Little Edisto/Windsor, Edisto Island	481
Rose Hill, St. Luke's Parish	483

Appendices

1. PATENTS	487
2. SCIENTIFIC NAMES OF PLANTS	489
3. PLANTATION FAMILIES	491

Bibliography 503

Index 521

Illustrations

Part I
Figures

1-1. Ice sheets in North America during the Pleistocene Epoch	5
1-2. Location of the Southeast Georgia Embayment	6
1-3. Map of the sea islands	7
1-4. Map of the barrier islands of the Georgia coast showing Holocene and Pleistocene islands	10
1-5. Long Island, Charleston County	12
1-6. Formation of barrier islands	13
1-7. Edingsville and Edingsville Beach, 1851-1852	16
1-8. Formation of ebb-tidal and flood-tidal deltas	20
1-9a-c. Origin of erosion-remnant islands	22
1-10. Average length of growing season in days	32
1-11. Average date of last freeze in the spring	32
1-12. Average date of the first freeze in the fall	33
1-13. Annual average rainfall for coastal zone	33
1-14. July average maximum and minimum temperatures for coastal zone	34
1-15. January average maximum and minimum temperatures for coastal zone	35
2-1. Mature leaf of *G. barbadense* and *G. hirsutum*	41
2-2. Monopodial and sympodial branching on cotton plant	42
2-3. Flowering pattern on a sympodial branch	44
2-4. Ideal form of sea island cotton plant	44
2-5. Longitudinal section of flower of *G. barbadense*	47
2-6. Structure of the cotton seed	48
2-7. Laminations of cellulose fibrils that comprise a cotton fiber	51
2-8. As cotton fibers mature, they collapse and twist	55
2-9. The principal commercial types of cotton, showing the variation in length of staple	55
3-1. Plukenet's drawing of *G. barbadense* L.	66
3-2. Diagram of the origin of allotetraploid in *Gossypium*	68
3-3. Geographical distribution of the six New World allotetraploid species of *Gossypium* prior to 1492	71
4-1. *Barbadense* cotton in the West Indies	77
4-2. Development of Egyptian and American-Egyptian cultivars through 1949	86
5-1. Burden's Island, St. Paul's Parish, Colleton District, 1825	97
5-2. Location of Kinsey Burden's plantation on Johns Island	98
6-1. Geographical distribution of market classes of long-staple cotton	102
6-2. Plantation homes and planters of the Santee long cotton region	109
6-3. Porcher Embankment	112

ILLUSTRATIONS

6-4. Map showing East Florida, Middle Florida and West Florida	122
6-5. Map of Florida and Georgia interior sea island cotton and Carolina sea island cotton	126
7-1. Salt marsh cotton fields	141
7-2. Method of seed selection as practiced on James and Edisto islands	147
7-3. Ditch and bed system on level land	149
7-4. Ditch and bed system on hilly land	150
7-5a-d. Construction of beds	156
7-6. Double roller used on the sea islands	157
7-7. Plan of the mode of laying the planks	161
7-8. Sowing cotton seed in holes on beds	167
8-1. Sorting sea island cotton	176
8-2. Whipping sea island cotton	178
8-3. McCarthy's "Endless Return Cotton-Whipper"	179
8-4. Moting	181
8-5. Packing sea island cotton	182
8-6. Bag of sea island cotton ready for shipping	182
9-1. Single-roller gin	189
9-2. Reproduction of a churkha gin	191
9-3. Worm gear of churkha gin	191
9-4. Tooth-geared roller gin	194
9-5. Double-crank hand gin	194
9-6. Foot gin	197
9-7. Foot gin with iron flywheels	197
9-8. James Harvie's patent	199
9-9. Reconstruction of a barrel gin	201
9-10. The Eve gin	203
9-11. Sea island cotton cleaner by Jesse Reed, 1827	206
9-12. Whittemore's gin	208
9-13. Cross-section of Model 1838 Carver roller cotton gin	210
9-14. Whittemore's leather and roughened-metal rollers	211
9-15. Roller gin, 1844, of Richard Reynolds of Beaufort, South Carolina	211
9-16. 1845 roller cotton gin by T. Ely	212
9-17. Kokemuller's gin	212
9-18. Steam-powered gin	214
9-19. Foss double-roller gin	216
9-20. Boesch Model 1910 roller gin	217
10-1. Fones McCarthy roller gin	220
10-2. The McCarthy gin, Reissue No. 262, April 18, 1854	223

10-3. Principle of the McCarthy roller gin	224
10-4. Cross-section of the 1840 McCarthy roller gin	224
10-5. Ginning roller, stationary knife, and stationary brush doffer	225
10-6. Roller covered with walrus hide and stationary brush doffer	225
10-7. Israel F. Brown's doffer	227
10-8. Townsend's "Attachment for Roller Cotton Gins"	228
10-9. McCarthy Patent No. 67,327	231
10-10. Wauklyn's roller	232
10-11. McCarthy roller gin	234
10-12. Double action McCarthy gin	235
10-13. Principle of the rotary-knife roller gin	236
11-1a. Spindle and whorl	242
11-1b. Vase spinning	242
11-2. Spinning on the Jersey wheel	244
11-3. The spinning position	244
11-4a-b. The Saxony wheel	246
11-5. Lewis Paul's carding machine	247
11-6. Spinning jenny reconstructed from James Hargreaves's patent of 1770	247
11-7. Hargreaves's improved spinning jenny	251
11-8. Arkwright's water frame	254
11-9. Working elements of Crompton's mule	258
11-10. Detailed technical aspects of Crompton's mule, 1774-79	258
11-11. Horizontal weaving	262
11-12. Warp-weighted loom from Iceland	264
11-13. Primitive two-barred loom from Peru	264
11-14. Standard hand loom	266
11-15. Cartwright's power loom	268
11-16. Salt House Dock in Liverpool	272
12-1a-b. Cotton caterpillar	286
12-2. Spread of the boll weevil	290
12-3a-c. Life stages of the boll weevil	291
12-4. Mature boll cut open showing full-grown larva	291
12-5. Anthracnose	295
13-1. Sea island cotton being loaded on steamer at Port Royal, ca. 1861	309
13-2. Sea island cotton plantations in South Carolina in 1824	316
14-1. Map of Johns Island by Kinsey Burden, 1826	347
14-2. Plat of Oakvale Plantation, 1873	349

Plates

1-1. Edingsville	16
1-2. North end of Bull Island, Charleston County, with characteristic ridge-swale topography	17
1-3. Pig Island Shell Complex, Edisto River, Charleston County	23
1-4. Maritime shell forest on Hutchinson Island, Colleton County	27
2-1. Flower of *G. barbadense*	45
2-2. Unripe capsule with glands	48
2-3. Capsule splitting at maturity	52
2-4. Seashore mallow	59
2-5. Swamp rose mallow	59
7-1. Abandoned salt marsh fields, Prospect Hill Plantation, Edisto Island	142
7-2. Remains of subsoil tile drainage system, Dill Wildlife Sanctuary, James Island	153
7-3. Remains of Native American shell mound on Edisto Island	162
11-1. Sea island cotton lace	280
14-1. Oakvale Plantation by Portia Trenholm	349
14-2. Ruins of tabby structure, 3405 Kemway Road, Stono Point, Johns Island	352

Tables

2-1. Average analysis of sea island cotton seed kernels	49
2-2. Average analysis of sea island cotton seed coats	50
5-1. Exports of sea island cotton from South Carolina, 1789-1801	96
6-1. Major islands where sea island cotton was grown in South Carolina	103
6-2. Cotton production on Brunswick Plantation, St. John's Parish, in 1837	114
6-3. Monetary value of Santee long cotton in St. John's Parish, 1838-40	115
6-4. Production in bales of long-staple cotton from 1909 to 1918 for Florida, Georgia and South Carolina	120
6-5. Production of Florida interior sea island cotton from 1900 to 1922	128
9-1. Pounds of cotton ginned a day with different types of roller gins	188
13-1. Sea island cotton exported from the United States, 1805-60	310
13-2. Weekly quotations in the Charleston cotton market, 1816-25	311
13-3. Prices of cotton at Liverpool, 1844 and 1845	312
13-4. Sea island cotton prices, 1819-25	312
13-5. Prices of all descriptions of cotton wool at Liverpool	312
13-6. Annual averages of monthly prices of sea island cotton in Charleston, 1800-1860	313
13-7. Average price per pound of sea island cotton and Georgia and Florida interior sea island cotton, 1910-21	313
13-8. Historical values of sea island cotton exports, 1805-18	317
13-9. Historical values of sea island cotton exports, 1820-34	318

13-10. Historical values of sea island cotton exports, 1835-60 — 322
13-11. Historical values of sea island cotton crop for South Carolina, 1867-1920 — 332
13-12. Exports of sea island cotton from South Carolina, 1790-1801 — 334
13-13. Exports of bales of sea island cotton from the United States, 1825-57 — 335
13-14. Exports of sea island cotton from Charleston and Georgia to England and France, 1843 and 1844 — 337
13-15. Exports of bales of sea island cotton from Charleston, 1906-07 to 1919-20 — 337

Part II

[NOTE: *Date indicates photo date, not date of construction.*]

Vanderhorst House, 2003 — 360
Ashe's/Little Edisto, view north across Russell Creek, 2003 — 361
Floor plan, Head Quarters Plantation House — 363
Floor plan, McLeod Plantation House — 363
Floor plan, Cassina Point Plantation House — 364
Floor plan, Vanderhorst House — 364
Floor plan, Prospect Hill Plantation House — 365
Floor plan, Crawford's Plantation House — 365
Floor plan, William Seabrook House — 366
William Seabrook House, entry hall, 1978 — 367
Oak Island Plantation House, hallway and stair, 1978 — 368
William Edings House, drawing room cornice detail, 1978 — 369
McLeod Plantation House, first floor drawing room, 1990 — 369
Preparing cotton for the gin, Old Fort Plantation, 1862 — 371
Sorting cotton, Fish Hall Plantation, 1862 — 372
Cotton gin building, Edisto Island, ca. 1862 — 372
Old Fort Plantation, 1862 — 373
Water garden at Oak Island Plantation, 1862. Cassina Point House is seen at upper left. — 373
Outbuilding on Swallow's Bluff Plantation, Edisto Island, 1991 — 375
Ice house at Bleak Hall Plantation, 1971 — 376
The library at Oak Island Plantation, 1862 — 376
The grounds at Oak Island Plantation, 1862 — 377
Gazebo at Melrose Plantation, ca. 1910 — 377
Slave cabins at McLeod Plantation, 1990 — 378
Slave chapel, Old Fort Plantation, 1862 — 379
Slave cabins on unnamed plantation, Port Royal Island, 1862 — 379
Brick House, 1928 — 381
Head Quarters Plantation House and Outbuilding, ca. 1910 — 383
Tom Seabrook's House, 1930. — 386

ILLUSTRATIONS

Laurel Bay Plantation, 1862	389
Old Fort (Smith's) Plantation, 1862	392
Baynard's Old Place, ca. 1930. Rear of house viewed from Russell Creek	393
Tombee Plantation House, 1975	397
Unidentified house on St. Helena Island, 1920	399
Coffin Point Plantation House, ca. 1880	401
Coffin Point Plantation House, 1985	401
Vanderhorst House, 2003	405
William Edings House, 1978	408
Myrtle Bush Plantation House, 1862	411
House on Hopkinson's Plantation, 1862	413
Coggins Point Plantation House, 1862	414
William Seabrook House, 1928	418
Mary Jenkins House, 1862	422
Seaside Plantation House, 1997	423
Frogmore Plantation House (rear view), 1991	426
Peter's Point Plantation House, ca. 1960	430
The Launch Plantation House, ca. 1930	433
Prospect Hill Plantation House, 2005	437
Interior doorway, Prospect Hill Plantation House, 2005	438
Oak Island Plantation House, 1862	442
Interior doorway, Oak Island Plantation House, 1978	442
Woodward Plantation House, 1862	446
Brick House/Stanyarne Hall, ca. 1930	448
Brick House Interior, ca. 1930	449
Brookland Plantation House, 2003	451
Fish Hall Plantation House (land side), 1862	454
Tom Fripp House, ca. 1863	457
Oakley Hall Plantation House, ca. 1890	459
Melrose Plantation House, ca. 1894	461
Garden at Melrose Plantation, ca. 1890	463
Crawford's Plantation House, 1992	465
William J. Jenkins House, ca. 1863	467
Garden at William J. Jenkins House, ca. 1863	468
Cassina Point Plantation House, ca. 1930	471
McLeod Plantation House, 1990	473
The Oaks Plantation House, ca. 1863	477
Youghal Plantation House, 1952	479
Ashe's/Little Edisto Plantation House, 2003	481
Rose Hill Plantation House, 1986	483

FOREWORD

Cotton was a major enterprise in South Carolina by the early 1800s. Exceeded in volume by short-staple upland cotton, sea island cotton was nonetheless preferred in international markets for its long, silky fibers. It was a distinctive commodity which grew only along the coast in limited quantity, brought premium prices, and contributed substantially to the antebellum prosperity of Charleston and the Palmetto State.

Inspired by the late Mr. Hugh C. Lane, a former trustee of The Charleston Museum, this carefully researched volume is the most comprehensive study of sea island cotton to date. Co-authors Dr. Richard D. Porcher and Sarah Fick present its multifaceted story in a readable and richly illustrated text. Porcher, Professor Emeritus of Biology at The Citadel, focuses on the natural history, production and commerce of sea island cotton. Historian and preservationist Fick discusses the nineteenth century architectural legacy of the sea island plantations and the families who owned them.

Founded in 1773, The Charleston Museum preserves the cultural and natural heritage of the South Carolina lowcountry. We are proud to publish this important contribution to South Carolina history and are deeply grateful to Mr. Lane and the Mills B. Lane Memorial Foundation for making it possible.

John R. Brumgardt, Director
The Charleston Museum

PREFACE

This is the story of sea island cotton—the luxury staple that profoundly influenced the agricultural, social, economic, and environmental history of the sea islands of Georgia, Florida and South Carolina and the lowcountry of South Carolina. Although the story of sea island cotton is a story of the three states in which it was grown, it centers on the South Carolina sea islands where its culture reached its zenith and where the highest quality fiber was produced. Sea island cotton was one of the two great crops that contributed to the wealth of the sea islands and the lowcountry of South Carolina (Carolina gold rice was the other). One cannot adequately tell the history of the sea islands and the lowcountry without including the history of sea island cotton. By all accounts, it was the finest quality of cotton ever grown—anywhere or at any time. It gained a reputation in Great Britain and the European continent, and was a major export from the states from its beginning in 1786 until its demise in 1920.

This book is divided into two parts: a history of the sea island cotton industry and a study of the architecture of the plantation dwellings. Richard D. Porcher, a field botanist and ecologist, documented the crop from the viewpoint of its growers, incorporating discussions of plant genetics, agricultural practices, processing and marketing. Sarah Fick, an architectural historian, researched the planters' country seats from the perspectives of architecture and family life.

PART I. SEA ISLAND COTTON

The story of sea island cotton is the story of thousands of years of evolution of the genus *Gossypium*; of enslaved Africans who toiled in the fields; of cloth made of sea island cotton that clothed the royalty and aristocracy of England and France; of vast wealth accumulated by sea island planters; of planters who served in local and state governments and were the most influential men of their times; of a world of ease and wealth dashed with the end of the Confederacy; of a history of Great Britain and the Industrial Revolution; of Charleston and Savannah's growth into world-class ports; of a period after the Civil War when young men returning from the war tried to revive sea island cotton on the sea islands, but ultimately failed; and of the natural history of the sea islands that was changed forever.

I view this book as a celebration of the planters and slaves who produced the finest cotton ever grown and added so much to the rich history of the sea islands and the lowcountry. Although this is the first book written on sea island cotton, it does not address all aspects of sea island cotton history. Certain topics were out of my expertise; others have been covered so thoroughly in other works I felt I could add nothing significant. I tended to focus on areas that have not been adequately covered, or in which new material has become available. I did not address topics such as overseers and drivers, political history, or the relative economic standing of sea island planters to others. I felt I could add nothing to the social history of the sea islands that has not been covered in books such as Guion Johnson's *A Social History of the Sea Islands*, Willie Lee Rose's *Rehearsal for Reconstruction: The Port Royal Experiment*, and T. J. Woofter's *Black Yeomanry: Life of St. Helena Island*, among others. More recently, Charles F. Kovacik and Robert E. Mason covered changes in the sea islands since the end of sea island cotton in their article "Changes in the South Carolina Sea Island Cotton Industry."

Sea island cotton enjoyed only a brief period of production compared to other cotton and agricultural crops worldwide, many of which were cultivated for thousands of years. Still, during its brief period from 1786 to 1920, it had a significant influence on the sea islands, on the South Carolina lowcountry, and overseas. Sea island cotton came into being in the first decade after the American Revolution, at a time when the colonies were looking for crops to export. Sea island cotton was the perfect crop. Its importance rose in concert with the Industrial Revolution overseas, without which sea island cotton may not have attained the significance it did. Regrettably, it also contributed to the enslavement of Africans and to the American Civil War. Sea island cotton survived the war, but never reached the peak it had occupied before the war. Planters had to change their methods of growing and adjust to a different labor and financial system during Reconstruction and the immediate aftermath. But it survived. Later, World War I gave planters renewed hope that sea island cotton would be a viable crop, but this was not to be. Sea island cotton's brief crop history ended with the coming of the boll weevil in 1920.

In detailing the sea island cotton industry, quotes from planters like Whitemarsh Seabrook and William Elliott have been used throughout the text. These men planted sea island cotton, but more importantly, they were students and innovators of its culture. Their words are the story of sea island cotton. I decided to tell this story as much as possible through their written works rather than substitute my interpretation. I also relied extensively on prints, diagrams and photographs; over a hundred are included. Some of the diagrams and figures have been produced just for this book; however, the majority have come from private sources, and from the literature and archives.

To fully understand the history of sea island cotton, one must consider many fields of endeavor. Natural history is one. The unique natural history of these sea islands—principally, their soils and climate—proved to be the ideal setting for this luxury staple to reach its fullest potential. The differences in soils and climate inland from the sea islands are one of the reasons why long-staple cotton grown inland (called Santee long and mains) never equalled the quality of sea island cotton. In chapter 6, I present evidence which explains this disparity.

The modern science of molecular systematics has added much to the knowledge of the origin of *Gossypium barbadense* L., the species of cotton to which all long-staple cottons belong, including sea island cotton. Once believed to be a native of Persia and listed as such in many early accounts, *G. barbadense* has had its origin confirmed through modern molecular systematics to be in Peru and Ecuador around a million years ago. Likewise, molecular systematics has traced the route of *G. barbadense* on its journey into the Caribbean and on to Georgia, where it was developed into sea island cotton. This complex new theory in the origin of *G. barbadense* and sea island cotton is a vital part of its history, yet questions still remain. Future research in molecular systematics will undoubtedly answer them.

The culture and market preparation of sea island cotton, as practiced by the planters of the sea islands, was unquestionably advanced for the times. This is, perhaps, one of the most notable aspects of the story. The early planters had no history as a guide; they were the first to grow sea island cotton. They had to create their own support system, and, through trial and error, develop the tools and techniques to produce the staple that would gain worldwide renown. That they succeeded is a testimony to their resolve and ingenuity.

The story of sea island cotton is also the story of the Industrial Revolution in Great Britain. Here were invented the marvelous machines to spin and weave cotton, especially Samuel Crompton's "mule" or muslin wheel which produced the fine, high-count cotton yarns which were woven into the softest laces and muslins. Without these machines, and other aspects of the Industrial Revolution, the market for sea island cotton would never have materialized, and the sea islands may never have been a "sea of cream blossoms" from one end to the other.

Part I closes with a history of Kinsey Burden and his family. Burden, more than anyone else, was responsible for bringing sea island cotton to its highest quality. His seed selection process created the luxury staple that was prized in England and the continent. Many legends and stories are passed among the descendants of Kinsey Burden. Research for this book has solved one of the enduring mysteries of sea island cotton history: the location of Oakvale Plantation and the plantation house where Burden and wife Mary lived on Johns Island and where he practiced his seed selection. A second mystery was whether and where Burden kept a locked seed barn where he protected his seed so it could not be used by other planters. Research for this book suggests that he did have such a seed barn, and that a ruin near the site of the former Oakvale house was this barn.

Artifacts of the industry are scarce, and their absence has made it difficult to adequately write about certain aspects of the sea island cotton story. No intact gin houses remain in the sea islands. The gins and power sources are long gone; most of the structures are gone. The few buildings that exist have been turned into homes or storehouses and add nothing to the understanding of the ginning process. Several McCarthy roller gins are still present in museums or are being restored, but no types of gins used before the McCarthy gin were found. An extensive search here and abroad produced only a few articles of clothing or cloth made of sea island cotton (and some of these are of questionable authenticity). For reasons unknown, it appears that no serious attempt was made to preserve articles of clothing or other items made from sea island cotton. Fortunately, a rich written record of the culture has survived from the planters themselves.

Cotton production today has advanced to a state that sea island planters would not recognize. Genetically modified cotton seeds produce transgenic plants resistant to herbicides so that an entire cotton field can be sprayed and the cotton plants not killed; the same modified seeds produce insect-resistant plants that need no insecticides. Fixed-wing aircraft fly over a farm and produce digital images that analyze the moisture level, nitrogen content, and elevation of the soil in minute detail. The data is then downloaded into a computer that color-codes a map to reveal the health of individual plants in the field. This data is transferred to an on-board computer in a tractor that directs a computerized feeder-sprayer to apply the correct amount of chemicals to each of thousands of individual plants. But this high-tech agriculture should not lessen our appreciation of the skill of the planters and the work of the enslaved Africans that caused the lint of this plant to be admired and sought after on both shores of the Atlantic.

The last seeds having been lost, sea island cotton as grown on the Carolina sea islands is gone forever, although its genetic base survives in the many long-staple cottons grown in other parts of the world today. It might be argued that it is theoretically possible, by obtaining seeds of *G. barbadense* and growing crops similar to the way they were grown on the sea islands, to produce a crop with fiber quality similar to the original sea island cotton. However, I argue that it would not be true sea island cotton. For it to be considered sea island cotton, seed from crops grown on the sea islands must be used, and these seeds no longer exist. The only seeds secured from crops grown on the sea islands were sent to the USDA Bureau of Plant Industry's Pee Dee Experiment Station in Florence, South Carolina. From here, in 1934, the seeds were sent to Georgia and Florida to revive the Georgia and Florida interior sea island cotton crop. When this failed in the 1940s, the seeds were not saved. Thus, the continuous genetic line from the last crops of Carolina sea island cotton was lost, and cannot be replaced.

But even if a long-staple cotton with fiber quality similar to sea island cotton could be produced, conditions in the sea islands today make it impractical to grow cotton on a scale large enough to be commercially feasible. The sea islands of South Carolina are a different world from when the last crop of sea island cotton was planted. Urbanization has made most of the land too valuable to return to agriculture on a large scale. More importantly, the amount of cotton produced would be so small that it would not be profitable for a mill to change its machines to handle the longer lint.

Sea island cotton is now history. Part I tells the story of that history.

PART II. SEA ISLAND COTTON PLANTATION ARCHITECTURE

The houses on sea island cotton plantations hold a mystique that developed from their inaccessibility and from generations of legends about their occupants. With each telling, the planters become wealthier, their daughters more beautiful, and their dwelling houses larger, finer, and more lushly furnished. The purpose of this survey was to investigate the buildings as they were, through photographic and documentary research.

While a number of the properties included in this study have previously been discussed in books about South Carolina architecture, before now there has not been a focus on the particular architecture of the sea islands. That became the goal of this study: to review as many of the sea island residences as possible, and to evaluate whether there was a distinctive architectural style unique to sea island cotton plantations.

Too many of the dwellings have been lost, and others have been significantly altered during the century and a half since their construction. Visual records are essential to understanding architecture, so, early in the research the focus narrowed to only those houses for which photographs could be located. Although experience in urban areas confirms that the houses of prominent citizens are most likely to have been photographed, the culture of the sea islands assured that almost every plantation proprietor was considered a man of substance. However, the isolation of the sea island plantations hampered photographic documentation. Only in post-Civil War Beaufort County were there many itinerant photographers. Otherwise, the plantation houses were rarely photographed until the 1920s. Therefore, it was impossible to locate images of the houses of such prominent planters as John Townsend at Bleak Hall, Kinsey Burden at Oakvale, or William Pope at Cotton Hope.

The record is even more limited with respect to the dwellings of slaves. Here too, it is for Beaufort County that the collections left by northern photographers proved invaluable.

From the available photographs an idea emerges of the general architecture of the sea island cotton plantations. The houses built from about 1790 until the early 1860s were not the carefully studied designs of nineteenth-century Charleston, Beaufort, and Savannah, nor were they the sprawling mansions of twentieth-century hunting plantations. The sea island cotton planters' residences were restrained in scale and simple in plan, most often a rectangular form, two stories in height with a one-story porch. Most had a central-hall plan, four rooms at the principal level, two or four above, and a raised basement level. The grandeur perceived by the planters' contemporaries and later observers frequently came from the bold scale of the rooms, sometimes from the elegance of the finishes or furnishings, but most often from the setting. It was their locations that afforded the sea island dwellings a prominence far beyond that provided by the architecture. Whether a house was approached by land or water, it stood out from a background of carefully managed gardens and neatly kept service buildings like the figure in a portrait.

The search for photographs was accompanied by research into land records and personal histories. Property records, wills, and estate papers for Charleston County are readily available, but the destruction of Beaufort County's records during the Civil War removed a great store of information. Even when papers were protected and deposited in a courthouse or research institution, the habit of transferring property within a family often involved descriptions that must have been clear to the parties involved, but are obscure today. For plantations that were openly sold, particularly when part of a court-supervised estate settlement, newspaper advertisements provide important details about land, buildings, and previous ownership.

PREFACE

Once the question of ownership of a given property has been answered, other documents illuminate its occupancy. Census records supply information about households, slave ownership, and crop production. Estate inventories list property (personal, chattel, and financial) held at the time of death. Wills clarify family relationships, property acquisitions, and plantation names. Genealogical resources place plantation families on the historical calendar, and investigating individual families also allows the identification of some buildings whose locations and names had been unrecorded.

This architectural study is only one component of a full understanding of the sea island plantation culture. A planter's education, his city life and public career, even his family's notions about their place in society, might have influenced his architectural choices, but that subject is outside the scope of this book.

In studying these photographs, the reader gains a new awareness of the power of place. Just as the cities and villages of the lowcountry each developed a distinctive architectural vocabulary, there came into being in South Carolina a house type recognizable as the sea island cotton plantation residence.

ACKNOWLEDGEMENTS

The Story of Sea Island Cotton could not have been told without the assistance and resources of many persons and organizations. The authors appreciatively thank these sources for helping to bring the book to fruition.

Hugh C. Lane, Sr. was the genesis of this book. He initiated the idea and funded the book through the Mills B. Lane Memorial Foundation. This book is just one of many projects Mr. Lane has conceived and supported. The history of the lowcountry will always be indebted to the Charleston Museum under the guidance of director John R. Brumgardt, who assembled the team of the authors and Wyrick & Company, the publisher.

We are also indebted to special friends who willingly and ably gave of their time. Father John Seiler spent countless hours on the internet searching for books and related documents that contributed greatly; William Robert Judd allowed us to reproduce his drawing of the barrel gin; Annie Caroline and George Marion Reid loaned their painting of Oakvale and material on the Burden family; David L. Lybrand of Edisto Island shared his map collection; Elizabeth Rhodes of the geology department at the College of Charleston provided suggestions on the natural history chapter; and we especially thank Laura Moses, who worked with us on a daily basis to refine the manuscript. All these contributions were beyond the reach of normal research facilities and added greatly to the completion of the book.

We are indebted to many local organizations and their staffs who so willingly assisted with our research: the South Carolina Room at the Charleston County Public Library; the Charleston Library Society; Special Collections at the College of Charleston Library and college archivist Gene Waddell; the South Carolina Historical Society, director Eric Emerson, and staff members Nicholas Butler, Mike Coker, Matthew A. Lockhart, and Pat Kruger; Hayden Smith, who did research on cotton prices and scanned the many documents that were used in the book; image consultant Kevin L. Metzger of the ITS Multimedia Services of The Citadel; Daniel Library at The Citadel, director Angie Whaley LeClercq, and staff members Debbie Causey and David Hessen; and director Karen Nickless of the Edisto Island Historic Preservation Society.

We also acknowledge the staffs of numerous research institutions in the United States and Great Britain where we located documents that contributed to the completion of the book: Jan Comfort, government documents reference librarian of the R. M. Cooper Library at Clemson University, who located numerous patents; Ed Hughs, research director of the Southwestern Cotton Ginning Research Laboratory in Mesilla Park, New Mexico, who contributed valuable material on the McCarthy gin; the South Caroliniana Library of the University of South Carolina; the Georgia Historical Society; the Rhode Island Historical Society; the Southern Historical Collection at the University of North Carolina; the British Museum of Natural History; and the Roger Milliken Textile Library.

Richard Dwight Porcher and Sarah Fick
Charleston, South Carolina 2005

CHRONOLOGY

ca. 25 mybp — The seeds from an Old World A-genome diploid cotton undergo a transoceanic dispersal to what will become South America in the New World.

ca. 25-1 mybp — Several diploid D-genome cottons evolve in the New World from the ancestral Old World A-genome.

ca. 2 mybp — The Ice Age begins.

ca. 1-2 mybp — Six New World allotetraploid cottons, including *G. barbadense*, the progenitor of sea island cotton, evolve from the initial allotetraploid ancestor.

ca. 1 mybp-100,000 ybp — Seeds of a second Old World diploid A-genome *Gossypium* disperse into South America via a trans-oceanic route from Asia and hybridize with a diploid D-genome New World species, producing the allottraploid ancestor of all six New World allotetraploid species.

ca. 120,000 ybp — In North America, the last major glacial, called the Wisconsinan, starts and lasts for more than 100,000 years.

ca. 18,000 ybp — The Wisconsin Glacier advances to its furthest point in North America.

ca. 16,000 ybp — The Wisconsin Glacier begins to retreat from North America.

ca. 4400 BC — The first archeological evidence of a two-barred loom, found in an Egyptian tomb, dates to this era.

ca. 3500-3000 BC — *G. barbadense* from the Real Alto site on the coast of Ecuador dates to this era.

ca. 2500 BC — Seeds of *Gossypium barbadense* first appear in the archeological record, in Peru and Ecuador.

ca. 1800-1700 BC — The heddle makes its first appearance in the archeological record of the New World.

1800 BC - AD 1492 — Dooryard *G. barbadense* is carried by Native Americans from Peru and Ecuador into middle America and the Caribbean.

CHRONOLOGY

1492	Christopher Columbus lands in the West Indies and observes a dooryard cotton, likely *G. barbadense*, growing among the Lucayo of the Bahamas and the Arawak of the Greater Antilles. He carries the cotton with him on his return trip, and Europe gets its first look at long-staple cotton from the New World.
ca. 1519	The Saxony spinning wheel is invented.
ca. 1600	Cotton textile production begins in England.
1700	In England, the first law forbidding the use of cotton (in the interest of wool producers) is enacted.
Late 1700s	Long-staple perennial *barbadense* cotton is a major commercial crop of the West Indies.
1711	Thomas Newcomen first harnesses the power of steam to drive an engine.
1736	Carolus Linnaeus visits the Plukenet Herbarium in London and observes Plukenet's specimen on which he bases his description of *Gossypium barbadense*.
1738	John Kay of Bury in Lancashire, England invents the flying shuttle. Lewis Paul invents the carding machine. Lewis Paul patents a roller spinning machine invented by John Wyatt.
1746	A French colonist in Louisiana, Moulin du Sr. Prat, replaces the worm gear of roller gins with toothed gears.
1753	Carolus Linnaeus publishes *Species Plantarum* which establishes the taxon *Gossypium barbadense* L.
1769	Richard Arkwright of Cromford, England patents the water frame for spinning yarn.
1770	James Hargreaves of Stanhill, England patents the spinning jenny.
ca. 1770	The barrel gin is introduced into the colonies.

CHRONOLOGY

1774	William Bartram, in his *Travels*, describes a perennial *G. barbadense* growing in Georgia.
1777	Kinsey Burden Sr. constructs a roller gin made of burnished gun barrels, reportedly the first roller gin made in South Carolina.
1779	Samuel Crompton of Bolton, England invents the spinning mule.
1783	The first cloth made entirely of cotton is manufactured in Lancashire, England.
1785	A steam engine is first used to drive an English cotton mill.
	August 24, the Agricultural Society of South Carolina is founded in Charleston.
	Seeds of a perennial form of *G. barbadense* from Anguilla in the Caribbean are sent to Georgia.
1786	Some plants from the seeds planted in Georgia in 1785 survive the mild winter and flower in the spring of 1786. The annual, day-neutral plant that will become sea island cotton is established from these plants.
	Edmund Cartwright of Nottingham, England patents the power loom.
1788	Portia Ash Burden, widow of Kinsey Burden Sr., plants Bourbon cotton on Burden's Island. Although the crop fails, it is the first attempt to raise a crop of long-staple cotton in South Carolina.
	Alexander Bisset introduces a foot-treadle roller gin in St. Simons Island, Georgia.
1790	Joseph Eve, a resident of the Bahama Islands, introduces into Georgia his modified foot-treadle gin.
	William Elliott of Hilton Head Island produces the first commercial crop of sea island cotton in South Carolina, selling the crop for 10.5 cents per pound.
	Samuel Slater emigrates from England and builds a factory at Pawtucket, Rhode Island that embodies the coveted English inventions for spinning yarn.
1792	Richard Arkwright dies.

CHRONOLOGY

1793	The first cotton sewing thread is made by a Mrs. Slater in Rhode Island.
	General William Moultrie plants the first Santee long cotton at Northampton Plantation, St. John's Parish, Berkeley County, South Carolina.
1794	Eli Whitney patents the wire-tooth gin that gins short-staple upland cotton.
1798	Kinsey Burden plants his first crop of long-staple cotton on Burden's Island, St. Paul's Parish.
1799	Captain Peter Gaillard of the Rocks Plantation in St. John's Parish, Berkeley averages sales of $340.00 per hand for his Santee long cotton crop.
1801	Judge William Johnson commences the practice of using salt-marsh mud as a soil ameliorating agent.
1802	The cotton caterpillar is first reported in the sea islands.
1803	December 6, Joseph Eve is granted a patent for a "Machine for Separating Seed from Cotton." This gin is the one he introduced in Georgia in 1790.
1804 or 1805	According to his own records, Kinsey Burden is the first planter in the sea islands to attempt to improve the fineness of black-seed (long-staple) cotton by seed selection.
1805	Kinsey Burden marries Mary Legaré and moves to Oakvale Plantation on Johns Island.
1806	The sea island cotton crop of William Elliott sells for 30 cents per pound.
1807	The Embargo Act of 1807 is implemented.
1820	Louis Alexis Jumel's tree cotton is introduced into small-scale cultivation in Egypt.
	James Harvie of Berbice obtains a patent for a brush to remove cotton from the rollers of a roller gin.
1823	Egyptian long-staple cotton of an excellent quality (superior to any other kind except sea island) begins to be exported to England from Egypt.

1825	Edward Barnwell of Beaufort, South Carolina begins reclamation of salt marsh to plant sea island cotton.
	Kinsey Burden Sr. dies.
1826	Kinsey Burden sells his sea island cotton for $1.10/pound ($19.89 in today's value).
1827	Kinsey Burden sells his sea island cotton for $1.25/pound ($22.41 in today's value).
	Kinsey Burden's "Letter to Whitemarsh Seabrook," read before the Agricultural Society of St. John's Colleton, appears in an article by Seabrook published by A. E. Miller.
1828	The *Southern Agriculturist* begins publication.
	Kinsey Burden sells two bags of sea island cotton for $2.00/pound ($37.75 in today's value), the highest price yet recorded.
	William Elliott publishes "On the cultivation and prices of sea island cotton" in the *Southern Agriculturist*.
1829	Whitemarsh B. Seabrook publishes "Remarks on the advantage of marsh mud as a manure for cotton" in the *Southern Agriculturist*.
1830	The planters of Santee long cotton begin obtaining seeds from sea island planters.
1831	James King Sr. of Little Britain Island, St. Paul's Parish, publishes "The best mode of applying Cotton-Seed as a Manure" in the *Southern Agriculturist*. This is the first recorded description of the practice.
	Thomas Spalding publishes "On the Introduction of Sea-Island Cotton into Georgia" in the *Southern Agriculturist*.
1834	William Whittemore Jr. of New Cambridge, Massachusetts is granted a patent for a roller gin.
1835	William H. Capers publishes "The Culture of Sea-Island Cotton" in the *Southern Agriculturist*.
	Thomas Spalding publishes "Cotton—its Introduction and Progress of its

Culture, in the United States" in the *Southern Agriculturist*.

1836   Fire destroys the U.S. Patent Office in Washington, DC.

1840   James King Sr. dies.

Fones McCarthy of Demopolis, Alabama patents the McCarthy Roller Gin, which revolutionizes the ginning of long-staple cotton.

1844   Kinsey Burden publishes "Introduction of Black and Green Seed Cotton into South Carolina" in the *Southern Agriculturist*.

Thomas Spalding publishes "The Cotton Gin, and Introduction of Cotton" in the *Southern Agriculturist*.

R. Reynolds of Beaufort, South Carolina patents a hand-operated triple-roller gin.

Henry William Ravenel publishes "On the Santee long cotton crop" in the *Southern Agriculturist*.

1847   Whitemarsh Seabrook publishes "Memoir on Sea Island Cotton."

1853   William Seabrook gins the first crop of sea island cotton with a McCarthy Roller Gin.

1854   Fones McCarthy is reissued a patent for the McCarthy Roller Gin.

Robert F. W. Allston of Chicora Wood Plantation in Georgetown County, South Carolina publishes his *Essay on Sea Island Crops*.

1859   Kinsey Burden dies.

1860   Early Ashmouni cotton is developed in Egypt.

1861   August 5, the U.S. Congress imposes a war tax of $363,570 ($7,379,798 in today's value) on South Carolina.

November 7, the Union is victorious in the Battle of Port Royal. Union forces occupy St. Helena Parish and Hilton Head; most of the white population flees the sea islands.

November, the Confederate Army orders the sea islands from Charleston south evacuated as indefensible.

The U.S. Treasury takes over supervision of picking the 1861 cotton crop on the sea islands.

The planting of sea island cotton on the sea islands of South Carolina ceases due to the Civil War, except by freedmen in St. Helena Parish.

1862

January, first school for former slaves opens on Hilton Head Island.

Union forces occupy Edisto and Kiawah islands.

February, call for agents to operate abandoned plantations and for teachers to educate former slaves.

March, Port Royal Experiment begins. Dozens of northern teachers and clergy sail for South Carolina to assist former slaves in growing cotton, and to educate them.

Spring, northern volunteers arrive on the sea islands of Charleston and Beaufort.

June 7, Congress authorizes tax to be collected on all occupied land, under threat of forfeit. Rebels are given 60 days to pay. Most taxes go unpaid.

June, U.S. War Department takes over responsibility for refugees and abandoned lands. Union troops withdraw from Edisto Island; 1,600 freedmen evacuate to St. Helena Island.

1863

February 4, William Elliott of Hilton Head Island dies.

March 9, first auction sales occur in Beaufort District.

March, 76,775 acres in St. Helena Parish are seized for non-payment of taxes and sold by U.S. government.

Israel F. Brown of New London, Connecticut receives U.S. Patent No. 39,767 for an "Improvement in Cotton-Gins."

1865

January 16, General William Tecumseh Sherman's Field Order 15 orders land on the sea islands to be sold only to freedmen. Most land in Beaufort District is unaffected by this order as the area is under the 1862 Direct Tax Laws, but thousands of freedmen settle on the Charleston sea islands.

March 3, the Freedman's Bureau Act is passed.

April 9, the Civil War ends with the surrender of General Robert E. Lee.

May 29, President Andrew Johnson pardons all those formerly in rebellion against the Union.

The Freedmen's Bureau initiates land reform on Wadmalaw, Johns and James islands.

October, the head of the Freedmen's Bureau informs freedmen on Edisto Island that Field Order 15 will not be honored.

The U.S. government announces plans to allow former rebels to reclaim their land by pledging allegiance to the Union. Planters begin swearing oaths and reclaiming land, but most plantations in the Beaufort area have been sold.

1866   The U.S. Congress, over a veto by President Johnson, votes an extension of the Freedman's Bureau Act. Freedmen's Bureau and U.S. Army supervise labor contracts between plantation owners and their former slaves.

1867   The war over, sea island cotton is again planted on Edisto, Wadmalaw, Johns, and James islands.

1872   Redemption Act allows owners to reclaim land by paying the war tax plus interest.

The first attempt at subsoil drainage is initiated by the planters of the sea islands.

July 4, the James Island Agricultural Society is organized.

E. J. Donnell publishes *Chronological and Statistical History of Cotton*.

1882   Long-staple Egyptian Mit Afifi cotton is developed.

1885   Jennie Haskell publishes "Cotton, in the Coast and Upland Fields of South Carolina" in *Frank Leslie's Popular Monthly*.

1889   Final reclamations are made of land seized for non-payment of taxes.

1892   The Mexican cotton-boll weevil crosses the Rio Grande near Brownsville, Texas.

1893   The Sea Island Hurricane destroys the village of Edingsville and kills around two thousand inhabitants of the adjacent sea islands. Another thousand or so die from injury, dehydration, starvation, or illness.

1899	Elias L. Rivers finds one healthy plant in a James Island field of sea island cotton attacked by wilt, leading to the development of the Rivers cultivar of sea island cotton.
1901	Egyptian long-staple Sakel cotton is developed.
1902	The wilt-resistant Rivers sea island cotton cultivar is made available to cotton planters.
	David Fairchild of the USDA brings the Mit Afifi cultivar of *G. barbadense* from Egypt to the United States.
	Seeds of Rivers sea island cotton are sent to the West Indies to start the West Indian sea island cotton industry.
1903	Leland L. Foss of Manassas, Georgia invents the Foss Double-Roller Gin.
1904	Carolina sea island planters terminate the sale of seed to the West Indies, to Georgia and Florida, and to their fellow planters, resulting in a degradation of the crop in all three areas.
1907	Sir George Watt publishes *The Wild and Cultivated Plants of the World*.
	W. A. Orton publishes "Sea Island Cotton: Its Cultivation, Improvement, and Diseases."
1908	The Yuma cultivar of *G. barbadense* is segregated from a stock of Mit Afifi seed.
1910	A new cultivar of long-staple cotton, Pima, is developed from a single outstanding plant in a field of Yuma cotton.
	J. C. Boesch and J. H. G. Von Oven of Charleston invent the Boesch Gin, which features a metal ginning roller.
1912	The Yuma cultivar is released for commercial production in the Salt River Valley in Arizona and in the Imperial Valley in California.
1914	William R. Meadows publishes "Economic Conditions in the Sea Island Cotton Industry."

CHRONOLOGY

1915	The Mexican cotton-boll weevil reaches Georgia.
1916	Experimental (but ultimately unsuccessful) plantings of Meade cotton, a long-staple upland cotton, are made in the Carolina sea islands.
1917	Nicholas Turnbull publishes "The Beginning of Cotton Cultivation in Georgia" in the *Georgia Historical Quarterly*.
	The Agricultural Society of South Carolina offers a prize of $10 a bushel for the earliest sea island cotton produced in Charleston County.
1918	The Mexican cotton-boll weevil reaches South Carolina.
	The Pima cultivar, developed from Yuma, has become the dominant long-staple cotton in the Salt River Valley in Arizona.
1920	The last commercial crop of sea island cotton is planted in South Carolina.
1922	Egyptian long-staple Giza 7 cotton is developed.
1924	M. D. C. Crawford publishes *The Heritage of Cotton: The Fibre of Two Worlds and Many Ages*.
	James S. Townsend of Charleston, South Carolina receives a patent for a rotary doffer for roller gins.
1925	The Agricultural Society of South Carolina purchases 160 acres on James Island; 100 acres are made available to the USDA to establish the Cotton Experiment Station to determine the possibility of producing sea island cotton under boll weevil conditions.
1928	G. S. Zaitzev publishes "A contribution to the classification of the Genus *Gossypium* L." in the *Bulletin of Applied Botany & Plant Breeding*.
1930	T. J. Woofter publishes *Black Yeomanry: Life on St. Helena Island*.
	Guion G. Johnson publishes *A Social History of the Sea Islands*.
1934	The USDA closes the Cotton Experiment Station on James Island. Leftover seeds of the Seabrook strain are sent to the Pee Dee Experiment Station in Florence, South Carolina for storage.

Seeds of the Seabrook strain from the Pee Dee Experimental Station at Florence are shipped to Florida to revive the Florida interior sea island cotton industry.

1936 — The last of the Seabrook seeds from the Pee Dee Experimental Station are shipped to Georgia to revive the Georgia interior sea island cotton industry.

1940 — J. O. Beasley publishes "The origin of the American tetraploid *Gossypium* species" in *American Naturalist* and "The production of polyploids in *Gossypium*" in the *Journal of Heredity*.

1940s — The attempt to revive the Georgia and Florida interior sea island cotton fails.

1941 — The long-staple cultivar S x P, a cross between Sakel and Pima, replaces Pima as the dominant long-staple cotton of the American Southwest.

1945 — J. B. Hutchinson and H. L. Manning publish "The Sea Island Cottons" in *Empire Journal of Experimental Agriculture*.

1955-63 — The rotary-knife roller gin is developed to gin long-staple cotton.

1958 — Lewis Cecil Gray publishes *History of Agriculture in the Southern United States to 1860*.

1959 — Y. I. Prokhanov publishes "What is *Gossypium barbadense* Linnaeus?" in *Taxon*.

1967 — G. K. Brizicky publishes "Nomenclatural notes on *Gossypium* (Malvaceae)" in the *Journal of the Arnold Arboretum*.

1968 — Paul A. Fryxell publishes "The typification and application of the Linnaean binomials in *Gossypium*" in *Brittonia*.

J. W. Purseglove publishes *Tropical Crops: Dicotyledons*.

1974 — S. G. Stephens and M. E. Mosely publish "Early domesticated cottons from archeological sites in central coastal Peru" in *American Antiquity*.

1976 — S. G. Stephens publishes "The Origin of Sea Island Cotton" in *Agricultural History*.

1979 — Paul A. Fryxell publishes *The Natural History of the Cotton Tribe*.

1985	Charles F. Kovacik and Robert E. Mason publish "Changes in the South Carolina Sea Island Cotton Industry" in *Southeastern Geographer*.
	J. E. Endrizzi, E. L. Turcotte and R. J. Kohel publish "Genetics, cytology, and evolution of *Gossypium*" in *Advances in Genetics*, firmly establishing that the progenitor genomes of the allotetraploid species are most similar to the genomes existing in the Old World *G. herbaceum* and in *G. raimondii* of the New World.
1986	Theodore Rosengarten publishes *Tombee: Portrait of a Cotton Planter*.
1989	J. F. Wendel publishes "New World tetraploid cottons contain Old World cytoplasm" in *Proceedings of the Natural Academy of Science, U.S.A.*
1990	R. G. Percy and J. F. Wendel publish "Allozyme evidence for the origin and diversification of *Gossypium barbadense* L." in *Theoretical and Applied Genetics*. They conclude that Peru and Ecuador are the ancestral home of *G. barbadense* L.
1992	J. F. Wendel and V. A. Albert publish "Phylogenetics of the cotton genus (*Gossypium*): Character-state weighted parsimony analysis of chloroplast-DNA restriction site data and its systematic and biogeographic implications" in *Systematic Botany*.
1995	Mary R. Bullard publishes *Robert Stafford of Cumberland Island: Growth of a Planter*.
	G. L. Wang, J. M. Dong and A. H. Paterson publish "The distribution of *Gossypium hirsutum* chromatin in *G. barbadense* germ plasm: molecular analysis of introgressive plant breeding" in *Theoretical Applied Genetics*.
2002	Martha L. Keber publishes *Seas of Gold, Seas of Cotton*.
2003	Angela Lakwete publishes *Inventing the Cotton Gin: Machine and Myth in Antebellum America*.
2005	Richard Dwight Porcher and Sarah Fick publish *The Story of Sea Island Cotton*.

mybp = million years before present
ybp = years before the present

Part I. Sea Island Cotton

by Richard Dwight Porcher

The Natural Landscape of the Sea Islands

Sea island cotton was a product of the unique geology and climate of the sea islands of Florida, Georgia and South Carolina; the highly advanced (for its time) seed selection practiced by the sea island planters; cultivation methods practiced by these island planters; and millions of years of evolution of the genus *Gossypium* to which all cottons belong. This chapter presents aspects of the natural history of the sea islands that, in part, contributed to the uniqueness of sea island cotton.

This book recognizes eight different landforms that occur along the South Carolina coast. In the broadest meaning, "sea islands" refers to these eight different landforms; this is how the term is used in the present chapter. In subsequent chapters, "sea islands" will refer to the erosion-remnant and beach-ridge barrier islands where sea island cotton was actually cultivated. The erosion-remnant islands include James, Johns, Edisto, Wadmalaw, St. Helena, Lady's and Port Royal. Of the beach-ridge barrier islands, sea island cotton was grown on Bull, Kiawah and Capers in Charleston County and on Hilton Head and Daufuskie in Beaufort County.

EARLY GEOLOGICAL HISTORY OF THE SEA ISLANDS

The natural history of the sea islands began with the formation of the Atlantic Coastal Plain about 180 million years ago when its ancestral continent, Pangaea, broke apart along a line parallel to the present eastern seacoast. The soon-to-be land bodies of Africa, Europe and America drifted apart; the Atlantic Ocean formed between. Shallow marine and near-shore sediments were deposited on the margin of the old continental crust, which was comprised of ancient igneous and metamorphic rock.

Approximately 130 million years ago, during the Cretaceous Period,[1] and lasting until the beginning of the Ice Age (2 million years ago), the ocean stood at the base of the piedmont. Rivers flowing down to the new shore began laying down a thin wedge of sediments offshore that ultimately became the coastal plain. These sediments were weathered from rock of the Appalachian highlands. The wedge of sediments is thousands of feet thick at the continental shelf, but tapers to a shallow layer at its westward edge where it abuts the piedmont. Where the sandy sediments of the submerged coastal plain met the piedmont, igneous and metamorphic rocks of the piedmont formed a distinct boundary, revealed as a line of falls and rocky rapids along the streams that flowed eastward to the coastal plain. This "fall line" is present today as rocky rapids in the Savannah, Broad and Catawba rivers.

Some of the sediment brought down from the mountains and piedmont to the edge of the ocean was spread laterally between the river mouths by ocean currents, forming an ancient shoreline. This former shoreline became the fall-line sandhills as the ocean retreated during the beginning of the Ice Age. Today, the fall-line sandhills lie in a discontinuous belt some five to fifteen miles wide through the center of the midlands, roughly paralleling the coast, and form a distinctive ecological area (Porcher and Rayner 2001, 86).

During the Quaternary Period,[2] two million years ago to the present, sea level changed very rapidly compared to most times in the history of the Earth. The cause of the changes in sea level during this period was the advance and retreat of the polar ice caps and extensive glaciers. The vast quantities of water required to create these ice caps and glaciers caused a lowering of the world's oceans. Then, as the glaciers retreated and polar ice caps melted, the oceans rose. Previously, there were thought to have been four major glacial cycles. However, recent studies of sediment cores in the ocean basins suggest that there were many more glacial cycles. As stated by Davis and Fitzgerald (2004, 65), "The evidence for these numerous glacial cycles has been masked on land by deposits of the four larger and longer-lasting glacial cycles."

Although the ice sheets and glaciers never reached the coastal plain, they shaped the face of today's Atlantic Coastal Plain. Periods of glaciation were followed by inter-glaciation. Each time the ice crept south, the ocean level dropped; each time the ice retreated, the ocean level rose. The topography of the coastal plain was formed during these retreats and advances. Each time it rose and retreated, the ice produced a pattern of ridges or scarps that were once coastal beaches. Unconsolidated sands and clays that comprise the coastal plain were laid down as the shoreline shifted back and forth. The shells of dead marine organisms were transformed into marl and limestone formations which today underlie the sands and clays. With each fall in sea level, the rivers eroded deeply into the bed of the coastal plain, gouging out wide valleys, leaving escarpments, and exposing the marl and limestone formations. With each new rise, the river valleys flooded again, creating estuaries. Streams winding across the coastal plain filled with sediment and became low-lying swamps.

CHAPTER ONE

The Pleistocene Epoch of the Quaternary Period, also called the Ice Age, came to a close 10,000 years ago. During the Late Pleistocene (circa 170,000 years ago), cooler global temperatures resulted in the creation of greatly expanded polar ice caps and a series of several continental-sized glaciers. In North America, the last major glacial era, called the Wisconsinan, started about 120,000 years ago and lasted for more than 100,000 years. (The time of 120,000 years ago is generally considered the most recent time sea level was where it is today.) The ice sheets of the Wisconsinan glacier reached their maximum extent around 18,000 years ago (fig.

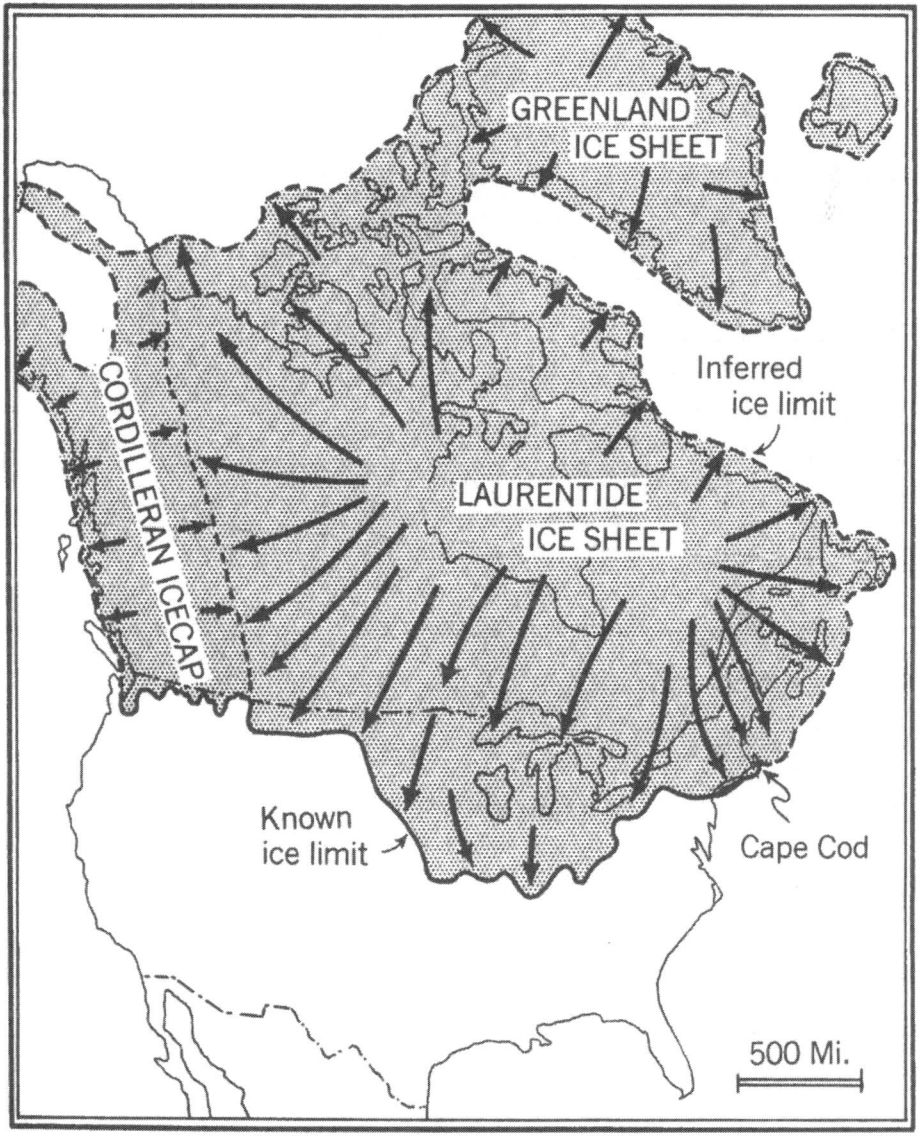

Figure 1-1. The shaded area represents the maximum extent of the ice sheets in North America during the Pleistocene Epoch. (Strahler 1966, 6)

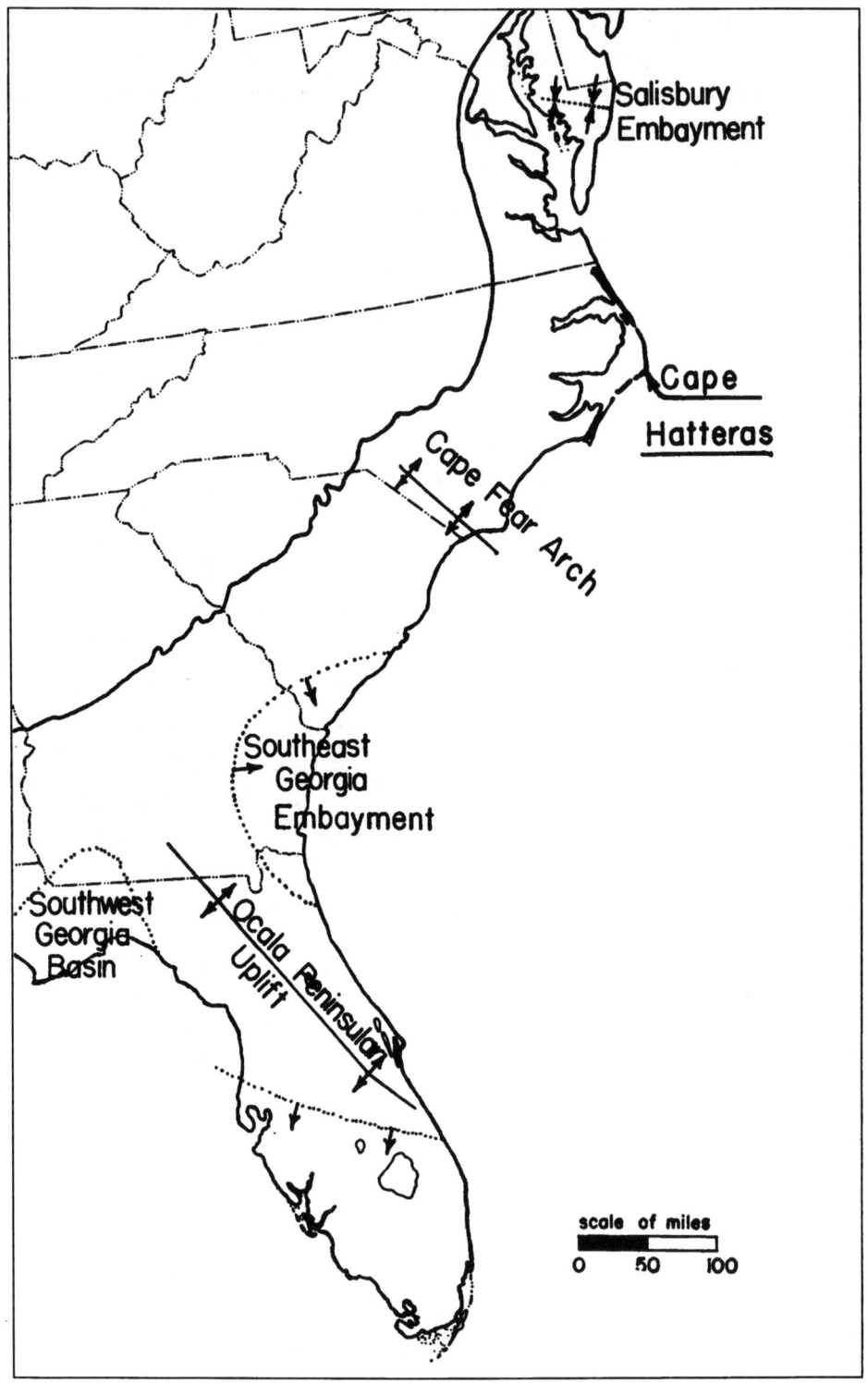

Figure 1-2. Location of the Southeast Georgia Embayment (H. E. LeGrand 1961, 1559)

CHAPTER ONE

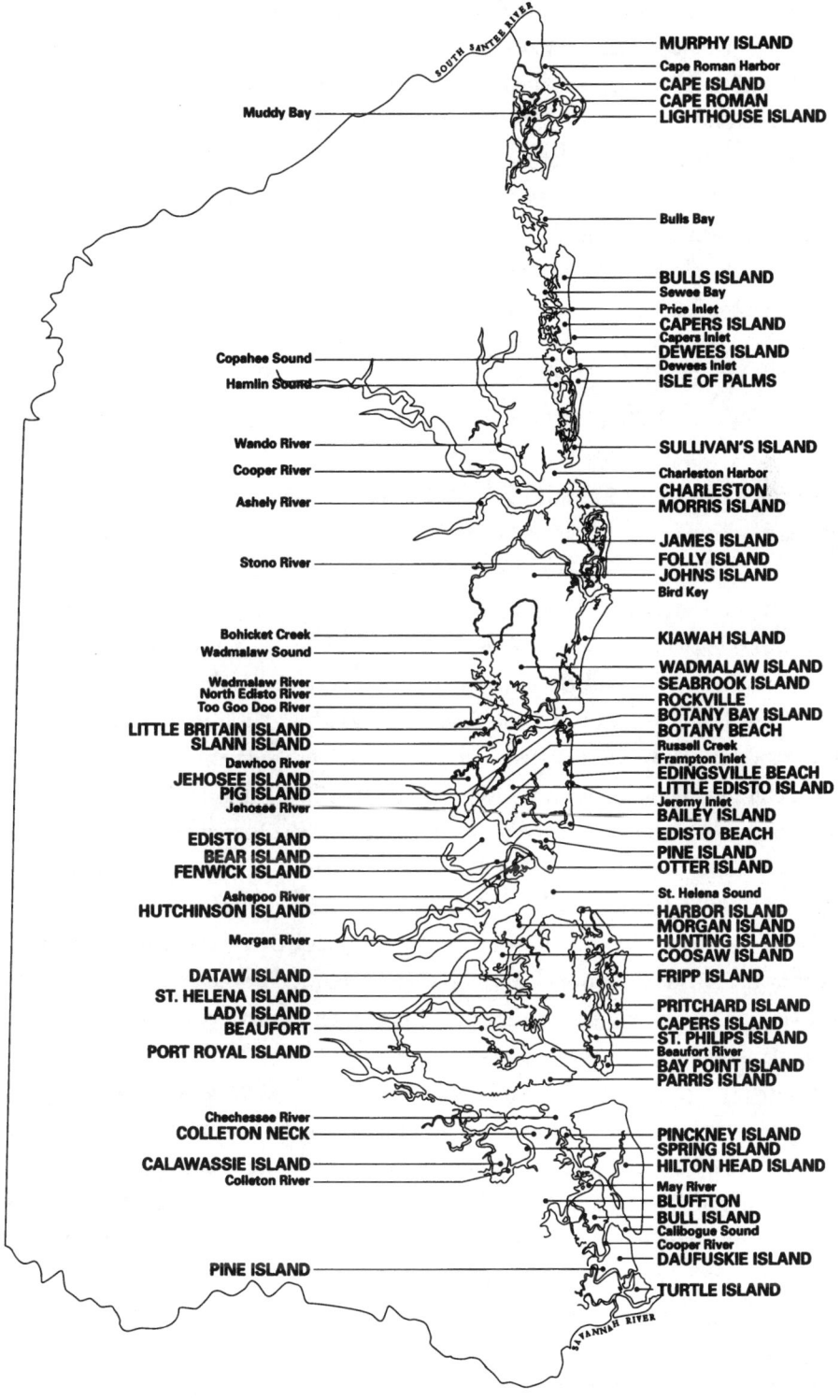

Figure 1-3. Map of the sea islands

1-1). Sea level dropped until it stood at the continental shelf, fifty miles from today's shoreline, about 150 feet lower than today.

About 16,000 years ago, the onset of warmer temperatures led to a world-wide reduction of these ice fields (often referred to as "the great warming"). In North America, the Wisconsinan glacier began its retreat and sea level rose. This initial rise was rapid and continued through the Holocene Epoch up until about 5,000 years ago. During this period of rapid rise in sea level, the shoreline moved so quickly landward that barrier islands along the coast had no time to build vertically. Then, 5,000 years ago, the rate of sea level rise slowed down considerably. The Holocene barrier islands were born during this slower rate of sea level rise.

PHYSIOGRAPHY OF THE SEA ISLANDS

The emerged part of the Atlantic Coastal Plain today extends from Cape Cod to the tip of the Florida peninsula. The section between Virginia and Florida is classified into three separate regions: the Embayed Section, the Arcuate Section and Southeast Georgia Embayment. The Embayed Section occurs from Cape Henry, Virginia, to Cape Lookout, North Carolina. South of the Embayed Section is the Arcuate Section, stretching southwest from the Embayed Section to northeast of Cape Romain. The third section, the Southeast Georgia Embayment (fig. 1-2), runs from northeast of Cape Romain to south of Cumberland Island in Georgia. The sea islands of South Carolina occur in this Georgia Embayment.

The general physiography of the South Carolina sea islands (fig. 1-3) consists of a series of Holocene barrier islands fronting the ocean. Landward of the barrier islands are either sounds or tidal marshes reaching to either the Pleistocene depositional terraces of the coastal plain (that is, the mainland), or to Pleistocene erosion-remnant islands. From Charleston north, landward of the barrier islands (for example, Capers and Bull), extensive tidal marshes or sounds abut the mainland. From Charleston south, landward of the barrier islands (for example, Kiawah and Seabrook), the marshes and sounds abut Pleistocene erosion-remnant islands (for example, Johns and Edisto islands).

The sea island coast is punctuated by numerous estuaries, some with significant freshwater discharge (brownwater rivers) and some with minor amounts of freshwater discharge (blackwater rivers). The brownwater rivers occupy drowned river valleys and originate in the mountains and piedmont. The Savannah and Santee are brownwater rivers; their brown color is due to the clay carried from erosion in the mountains and piedmont. These rivers have broad alluvial floodplains with meandering channels, oxbow lakes, extensive sands along the edge and typically cut straight across the Pleistocene depositional terraces of the coastal plain. They produce large deltas where they enter the ocean.

The blackwater rivers, which arise in the coastal plain and are generally sediment-free, get their color from the presence of organic acids derived from decaying leaves. They have narrow floodplains and do not have sand dunes along their edges. The blackwater rivers are generally deflected in their course to the ocean by Pleistocene depositional terraces and often run parallel to the coast. They enter the ocean at estuaries located behind the Holocene barrier islands. Charleston Harbor is an example of an estuary fed by two blackwater rivers, the Ashley and the Cooper.

In addition to estuaries, the coast is indented by many tidal inlets separating barrier islands. Price Inlet between Dewees Island and Capers Island is an example.

The sea island region is quite complex in respect to geology and ecology. The islands and marshes are unstable because of tides, winds and ocean currents. Not to be overlooked are the man-made structures and disturbances that altered the natural environment of the sea islands. Harbor jetties and rivers that were dammed to create lakes (for example, the Santee River dammed to create Lake Marion) changed water flow and robbed deltas of sand and silt, and seawalls, breakwaters and groins caused significant alteration of natural movements of sand. Spoil areas created in marshes caused significant alteration of these valuable wetlands. But through it all, the sea islands retained much of their natural integrity.

Nine types of landforms comprise the Carolina and Georgia coast: marsh islands, marsh hummocks, beach-ridge relict islands, barrier islands, flood and ebb tidal deltas, erosion-remnant islands, natural shell deposits, Native American shell deposits and composite barrier islands. The first eight occur in both South Carolina and Georgia and their origins are described below. Composite barrier islands occur primarily in Georgia; geologists differ on whether they occur in South Carolina. A composite barrier island is comprised of a Pleistocene barrier island, seaward of which is a Holocene barrier island (Pilkey and Fraser 2003, 243-248). The chain of large Pleistocene islands along the Georgia coast (fig. 1-4) was formed around 120,000 years ago during the Ice Age. At that time, the ancient shoreline remained stationary long enough for the islands to form vertically. As the ocean retreated, the chain of islands was left behind. Then, during the Holocene, as the ocean rose, Holocene barrier islands were formed seaward to the Pleistocene barrier islands. In the case of Cumberland Island, the Holocene island is much reduced and attached to the front of the older island, forming one composite island. At the north end of the Georgia coast, the Holocene islands are widely separated by marsh from the Pleistocene islands. For example, Skidaway Island, Pleistocene in formation, is separated seaward from Wassaw, a Holocene island, by a wide expanse of marsh.

One source states that Hilton Head Island in South Carolina is a composite island, with the beach-ridge portion southwest of Broad Creek a Pleistocene formation. If this is true, the Holocene island must be much reduced or completely eroded away. Other sources do not confirm this theory, and local geologists believe that the geology of barrier islands south of Edisto Beach have not been studied extensively enough to make this determination.

THE NATURAL LANDSCAPE OF THE SEA ISLANDS

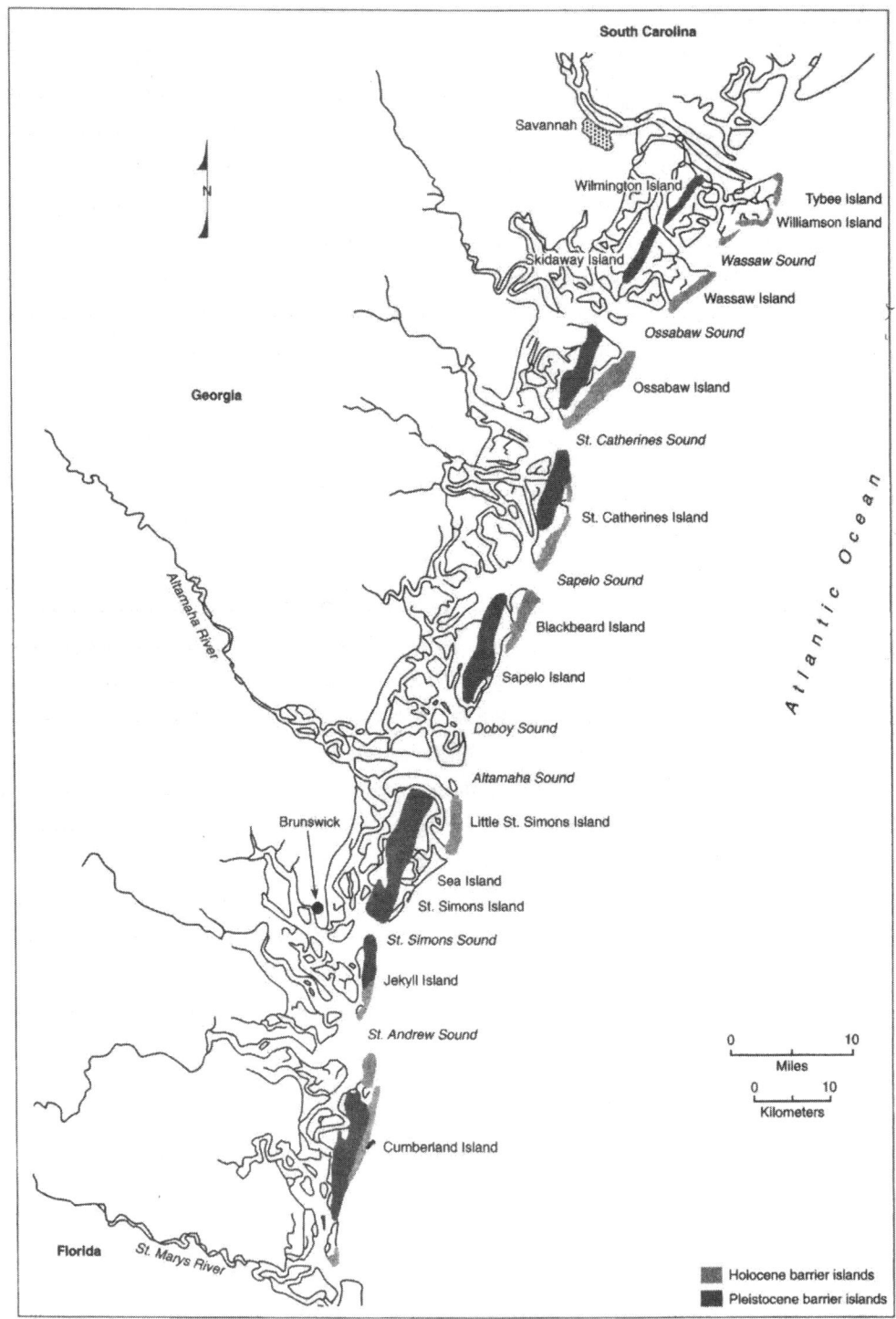

Figure 1-4. Map of the barrier islands of the Georgia coast showing Holocene and Pleistocene islands (Pilkey and Fraser 2003, 245)

CHAPTER ONE

Marsh Islands

Marsh islands develop behind barrier islands between them and the mainland or erosion-remnant islands. Here, protected from wave action, various plants (predominately smooth cordgrass, *Spartina alterniflora* Loiseleur), become established on sand or mud flats exposed at low tide. Silt and clay, moved and carried by the tides, are trapped by the emerging stems, and the soil level is raised. A major source of these initial sediments were from the erosion of the developing erosion-remnant islands. Over the years, as the sea level rose, the marsh islands kept up growth by deposition of silt and clay trapped by the vegetation. Although this is a simplified explanation of marsh island formation and other factors are involved, this is, in general, how the marsh islands of the sea islands were formed and are still forming.

Marsh islands were the source of salt-marsh mud used for a soil ameliorate in the cotton fields (see chapter 7).

Marsh Hummocks

Approximately 2,500 marsh hummocks occur along the Carolina coast, varying in size from an acre to hundreds of acres. Marsh hummocks are raised areas above the level of the marsh islands and generally support some type of woody vegetation. In general, they occur between the barrier islands and the mainland or the erosion-remnant islands, and in the marshes that extend up the rivers and sounds.

The origin of marsh hummocks has not been well documented. Most maps indicate that they are Pleistocene in origin. Whether they were formed like the marsh islands or erosion-remnant islands or by other means is unclear.

Some of the hummocks appear to have been used for agriculture and/or have been timbered. Cotton Island, a small forested marsh hummock located opposite Rockville along Bohicket Creek, has visible former agricultural ridges where sea island cotton was grown. Remains of house sites and agricultural fields can also be seen on some of the larger marsh hummocks. At the same time, however, many of these hummocks appear in a pristine condition, their remoteness having precluded significant disturbance. Marsh hummocks were also the site of Native American camps or villages.

Marsh hummocks are a significant ecological formation in the sea islands. Hummocks have been and are still sites for native wildlife, especially birds, and the diamondback rattlesnake.

Beach-Ridge Relict Islands

Beach-ridge relict islands are located between the mainland or erosion-remnant islands and the barrier islands. Put another way, they are located behind the barrier islands and are surrounded by salt marsh. Unlike the marsh hummocks, they consist of a series of ridges

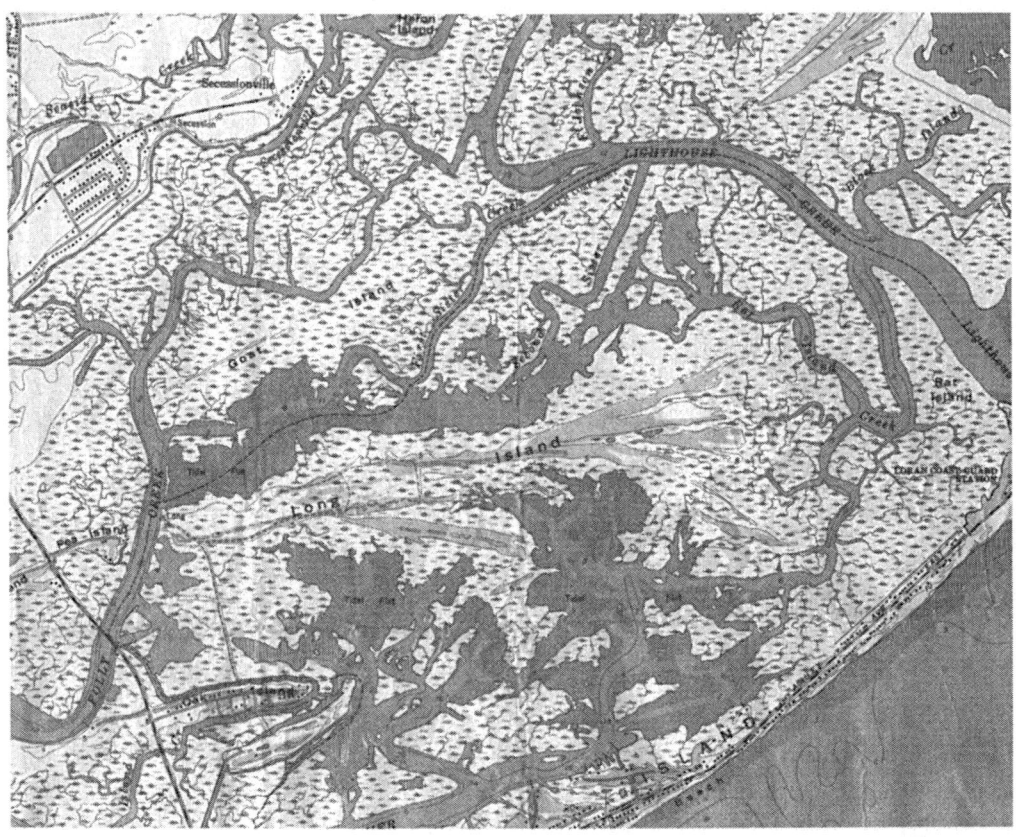

Figure 1-5. Long Island, Charleston County (U.S. Department of the Interior Geological Survey, James Island Quadrangle, 1959)

CHAPTER ONE

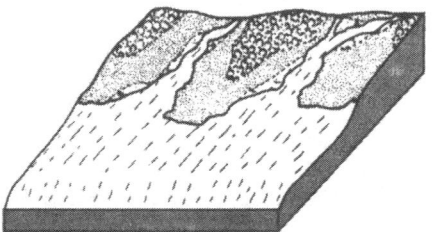

Stage 1) Flooding of river valleys

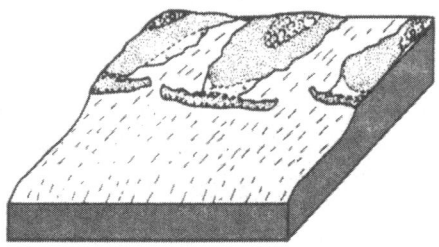

Stage 2) Formation of spits along lead lands

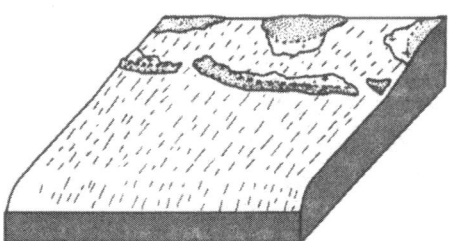

Stage 3) Separation of barrier from mainland

Figure 1-6. Formation of barrier islands (Lennon et al. 1959, 15)

and swales with an orientation parallel to the coast (fig. 1-5). Two examples are Long Island, behind Folly Beach in Charleston County, and Old Island, behind Fripp Island in Beaufort County.

The position of these islands indicates they are Pleistocene in origin and were formed by wind and wave action as the ocean retreated. (It would have been impossible for these beach-ridge relict islands to have formed during a rising sea level since the Holocene barrier islands would have blocked wind and wave action from the areas behind them where the relict islands are located.)

The author found no direct evidence that any of the beach-ridge relict islands were planted in sea island cotton. However, many of them show past human activity and it is likely that, like the marsh hummocks, some were sites of sea island cotton cultivation.

Barrier Islands

The barrier islands (so named because they form a barrier to the marsh and mainland against storms and hurricanes) along the South Carolina coast were formed during the Holocene Epoch. During the first half of the Holocene, sea level rise was rapid. The shoreline moved landward so quickly that barrier islands had no time to build vertically. (For barriers to develop, it is necessary for the shoreline either to be stable or to move very slowly in order for waves and currents to have enough time to construct barriers.) Then, about 5,000 years ago, the rate of sea level rise slowed and the shoreline became more stable in position. The Carolina barrier islands were formed during this stable period.

The origin of barrier islands has been debated by scientists for 150 years. Most agree that any theory of origin must address the following phenomena (Davis and Fitzgerald 2004, 144):

1. Barrier islands are aligned parallel to the coast.
2. Most have formed in a regime of slow worldwide sea-level rise.
3. They are separated from the mainland by shallow lagoons, marshes, and/or tidal flats.
4. Tidal inlets separate individual barriers along a chain.
5. They are composed of sand (some contain gravel).
6. They formed during periods of sand abundance.

Numerous theories have been postulated to explain the origin of barrier islands. Most scientists agree that no one theory can explain the development of all barriers worldwide. In many cases, it is impossible to explain how a barrier formed because natural processes such as rising sea level modified the barriers after they were formed, and man subsequently altered the barriers with groins, seawalls, etc.

The theory that best seems to explain the formation of the barrier islands along the Carolina coast was outlined in Lennon et al. (1959, 15) and described in more detail by Orrin H. Pilkey (1990) as depicted in figure 1-6.

CHAPTER ONE

About 16,000 years ago, the Carolina shoreline was located fifty miles offshore of its current position. Then the sea level began to rise; former river valleys were flooded. What were once ridges separating the valleys became headlands protruding out to sea (stage 1). These headlands were vulnerable to attack by waves. Their erosion began to produce sand spits extending across the mouths of the newly drowned river valleys (stage 2). As the sea level continued to rise, the low-lying land behind the spits became flooded and the spits were cut off from the mainland (stage 3). As the sea level rose even further, the islands migrated rapidly landward as the front beach eroded and the landside widened from overwash, incorporating flood-tidal deltas. The flooding of the headlands by the rising sea behind the barriers kept the barriers separated from the mainland.

Then, about 5,000 years ago, sea level rise slowed considerably. When the sea elevation slowed, the islands stopped migrating. Since they remained in position, they began to widen seaward by the addition of dune ridges one by one to the seaward side. This is what gives barrier islands their ridge-and-swale topography. They also built vertically.

The relative stability of the islands lasted until the 1930s. Around 1930, sea level rise again accelerated to more than a foot a century. Many of the barrier islands along our coast are entering a thinning phase for their eventual migration landward.

Davis and Fitzgerald (2004, 148-153) classify barrier island into three types: aggrading; retrograding (commonly called thin, retreating barrier islands); and prograding (commonly called beach-ridge barrier islands).

Aggrading barrier islands. Aggrading barrier islands formed vertically through time in a rising sea level, and occupy approximately the same location as they did when first formed. There are no aggrading barriers along the South Carolina coast.

Retrograding barrier islands. Davis and Fitzgerald (2004, 149-50) described retrograding barriers:

Retrograding barriers form when the supply of sand is inadequate to keep pace with relative sea-level rise and/or with sand losses. Stated in terms of a sediment budget, a barrier becomes retrogradational when the amount of sand contributed to the barrier is less that the volume transported away from the barrier. The sand may be lost offshore during storms, moved along shore in the littoral system, or transported across the barrier by overwash. The end result is erosion to the front of the barrier, causing a decrease in width of the beach and ultimately destruction of the foredune ridge. Eventually, a narrowing and lowering of the barrier profile produces a retreat of the barrier across the adjacent bay, lagoon, or marsh system. This landward migration of the barrier, termed barrier rollover, is accomplished primarily during storms by overwash. Overwash is a cannibalistic process whereby storm waves transport sand from the beach through the dunes, depositing it along the landward margin of the barrier. In this way the barrier is preserved by retreating landward.

Four islands among the Carolina sea islands represent retrograding barrier islands: Edingsville Beach[3] (Edings' Bay), Botany Beach,[4] Morris Island and Bay Point. These islands

THE NATURAL LANDSCAPE OF THE SEA ISLANDS

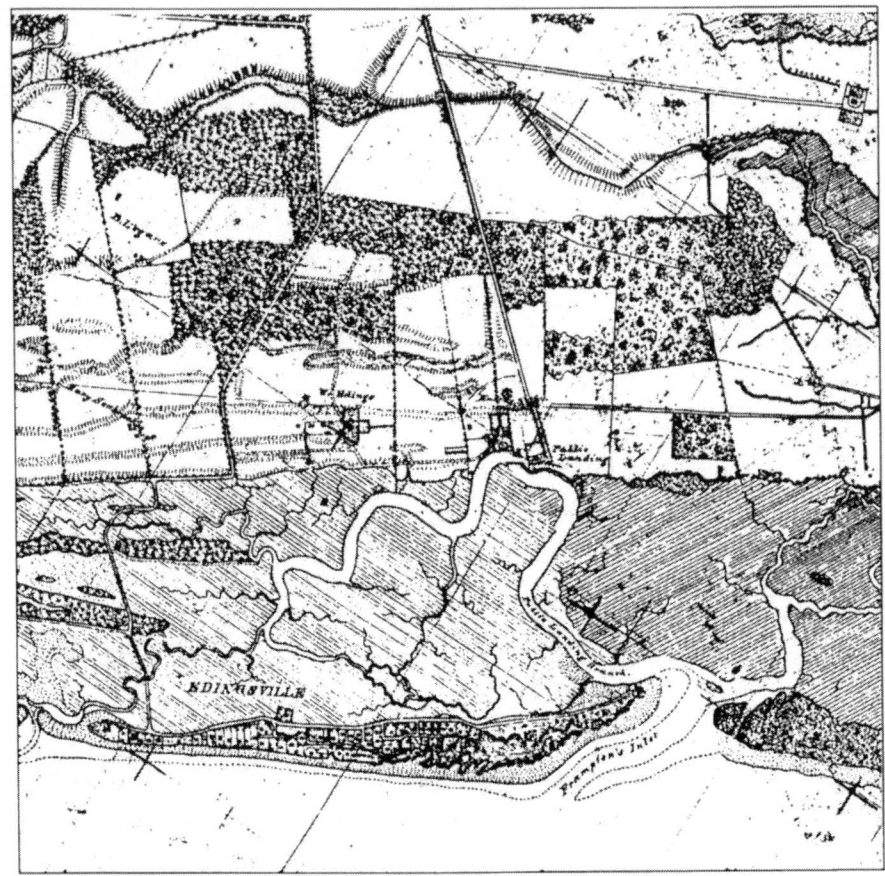

Figure 1-7. Edingsville and Edingsville Beach, 1851-52
(Courtesy of David Lybrand of Edisto Beach)[6]

Plate 1-1. Edingsville (Courtesy of the Edisto Island Historic Preservation Society)

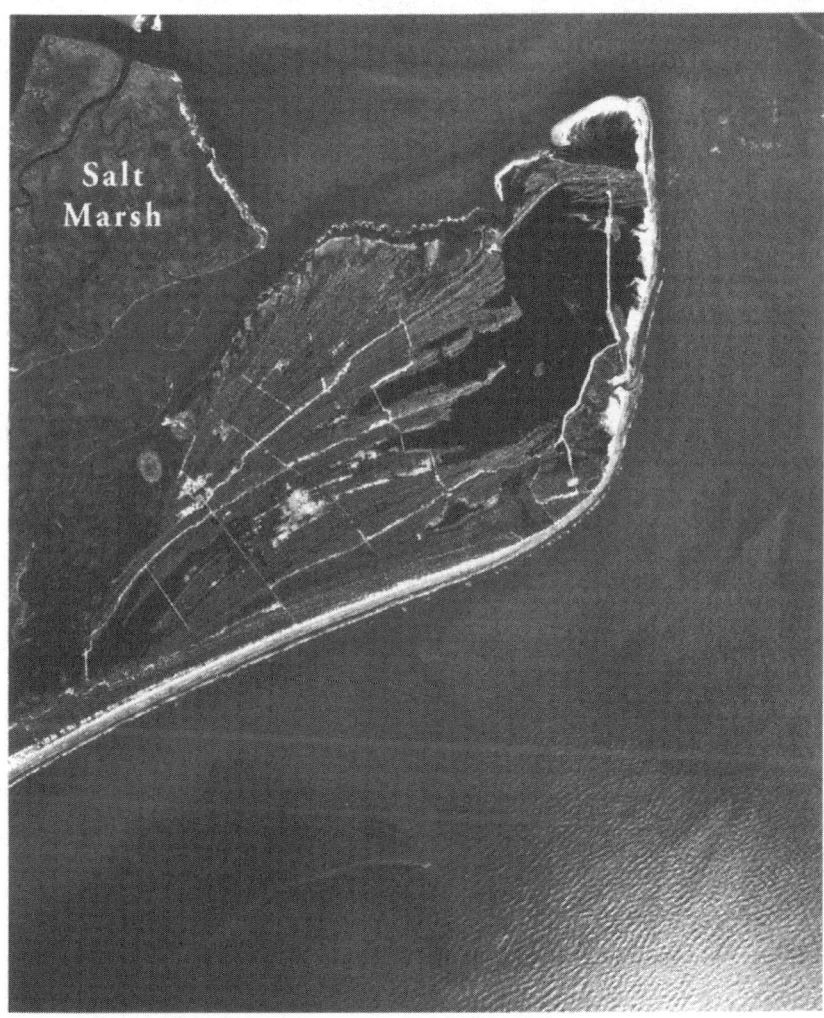

Plate 1-2. North end of Bull Island, Charleston County, with characteristic ridge-swale topography (Source: www.dnr.sc.state.us)

are thin strips of sand that are rapidly migrating landward. Wave action continually causes overwash. Since there are no dunes to prevent overwash, these islands migrate rapidly as the front erodes and the back side builds.

Edingsville Beach (Edings' Bay) is a classical example of a retrograding barrier island. Edingsville Beach, bounded by Jeremy Inlet (where Scott Creek enters the ocean) on the south and Frampton Creek (where Public Landing Branch enters the ocean) on the north (fig. 1-7), was the site of the village of Edingsville (plate 1-1), the summer resort and a refuge from malaria for the sea island planters of Edisto and neighboring islands. The island harbored about fifty dwellings and about 600 people during the summer months. Nineteenth-century maps indicate that it was a beach-ridge barrier island at that time (fig. 1-7).

Lewis R. Gibbes (1857, 241-48)[5] described Edingsville Beach in 1847: It was "not more than a mile and a quarter in length, and scarcely a quarter of a mile in breadth." Access to the island was by a causeway from Edisto Island. Even at the time of Gibbes's article, there was severe erosion on the island. When speaking of the stumps of palmetto and barrels from old wells on the front beach, he stated: "All these remains indicate the encroachment of the ocean…" If one walks the beach of Edingsville at low tide today, one can see oyster shells and roots of marsh grass, evidence that this part of the beach was once on the back side of the island.

The Sea Island Hurricane of 1893 contributed to reducing Edingsville Beach to today's retrograding barrier island. The storm's rising waters flooded the causeways and evacuation routes, trapped the residents and destroyed the village. As many as 2,000 inhabitants of Edingsville and the surrounding sea islands may have perished during the hurricane and another 1,000 may have died afterward from injury, dehydration, starvation, or illness.

Prograding barrier islands. Prograding barrier islands (beach-ridge barrier islands) commonly build in spurts during a period of abundant sand supply and during a period of stable or slowing sea level rise. Their beaches build in a seaward direction, widening the berm and separating the foredunes from the ocean by an enlarging expanse of sand. This seaward addition of sand produces the characteristic ridges and swales that characterize a barrier island. The ridges are the former dunes, each ridge marking a former shoreline (plate 1-2). As the ridges are further and further removed from the shore and the effects of salt spray, they become vegetated, first by grasses and other herbs, then by shrubs, and finally by a maritime forest. One can determine from the pattern of the beach ridges how the island was formed and evolved over time.

There are probably no true *prograding barrier islands* along the South Carolina coast. All the beach-ridge barrier islands along the coast show some degree of erosion.[7] However, they are large enough at present not to be classified as retrograding islands. The major barrier islands, from Cape Romain south, are (fig. 1-3): Murphy, Bull, Capers, Dewees, Isle of Palms, Sullivans, Folly Beach, Kiawah, Seabrook, Edisto Beach, Otter, Hunting, Fripp, Pritchard's, Hilton Head and Daufuskie. Bull, Capers, Kiawah, Hilton Head and Daufuskie were sites of sea island cotton cultivation.

A primary reason that the barrier islands along the South Carolina coast are eroding is human alteration of the environment which changed the sediment supply. Reduced flow of freshwater down the Santee River deprived the Santee Delta of a sediment source that ordinarily would have been carried down the coast by longshore currents and deposited on the islands. The Charleston jetties deprived Morris Island and Folly Beach of sediments to replace normal loss, contributing to erosion. Seawalls have been placed in front of barrier islands to "protect" and stabilize the beach. Unfortunately, these seawalls actually cause erosion. Waves that hit directly on the seawalls cause scouring at the base, and sediment is removed from the island. And groins alter sand flow, depositing it offshore so it is not available to nourish the beach. Further complicating the status of barrier islands is the process of beach renourishment. Islands that have experienced erosion now have more sand on the shoreline, although temporarily, and have been changed to a "prograding" island.

One last note on barrier islands: Carolina's coastal barrier islands are not expanding in size. Barrier islands grow in size by widening in a seaward direction, not by migrating (during migration they stay the same size). The major barrier islands along the Carolina coast are shrinking in size.

Flood-Tidal and Ebb-Tidal Deltas

Inlets between barrier islands generally have large bodies of sand associated with them called flood-tidal and ebb-tidal deltas (fig. 1-8). Flood-tidal deltas are fan-shaped lobes of sediment carried by currents and deposited to the landward side of the inlet. Longshore currents move fast enough to carry the sediments. As the tidal currents enter the inlet, the narrowing channel further speeds up the current, allowing the sediment to be carried through the inlet into the landward sound. Once past the inlet channel, the current of water spreads laterally, slowing down. At the slower speed, the sediments settle out, forming the delta.

As inlets migrated laterally between the barrier islands, the flood-tidal deltas also moved. Barrier islands that migrated inland in response to rising sea levels eventually encountered these flood-tidal deltas and incorporated them into their landward sides. (This is one way barrier islands grow in size.) Flood-tidal deltas are also preserved in sounds when the inlets close and the deltas eventually become part of the barrier island. The part of Hilton Head Island (fig. 1-3) northeast of Broad Creek is a classic example of a flood-tidal delta that was formed by sediment moving landward up Port Royal Sound. It became attached to the beach-ridge portion of Hilton Head. Harbor Island, located behind Hunting Island (a beach-ridge island), is also a flood-tidal delta formed from sand transported up St. Helena Sound. Like the beach-ridge islands, flood-tidal deltas are comprised primarily of well-sorted, fine sands.

An ebb-tidal delta, formed by outgoing tides, is a delta-shaped body of sand extending seaward of the mouth of the inlet. When the inlet closes, ocean waves quickly disperse the sand of the delta.

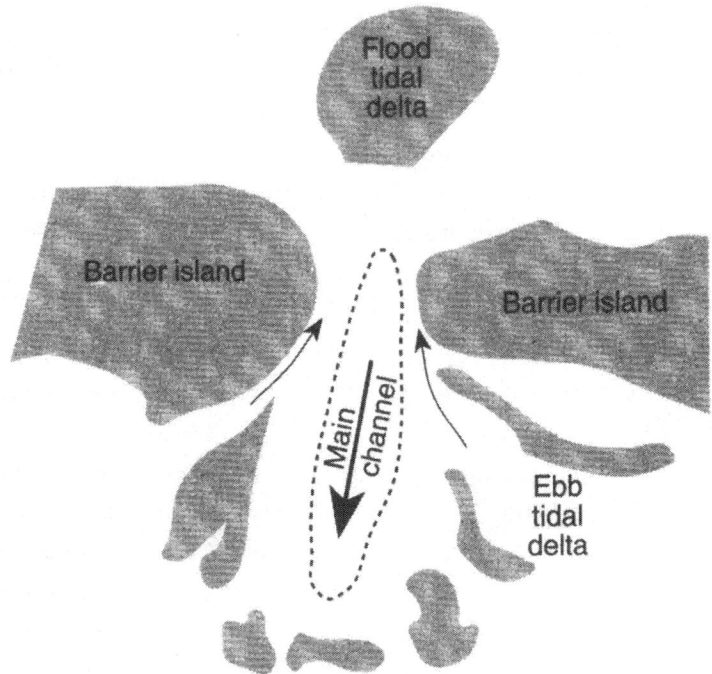

Figure 1-8. Formation of ebb-tidal and flood-tidal deltas
(Lennon et al. 1996, 19)

A classical example of an ebb-tidal delta on the South Carolina coast is Bird Key in the mouth of Stono Inlet. Bird Key is a State Heritage Preserve.

Erosion-Remnant Islands

Erosion-remnant islands date from the Pleistocene Age, and include the major sea islands where sea island cotton was grown. The principal erosion-remnant islands of South Carolina are Johns, James, Edisto, Wadmalaw, St. Helena, Lady's and Port Royal.

Zeigler (1959, 225-234) gives an account of the formation of erosion-remnant islands. He proposes that the erosion-remnant islands have a lithology (rock formation) similar to the mainland and not to the barrier islands, for these two reasons: (1) the topography of the erosion-remnant islands resembles the mainland and does not resemble the beach-ridge island topography, and (2) the beach-ridge islands are composed of well-sorted sands while the erosion-remnant islands are comprised of sands and clayey or limy sands with scattered pockets of clay similar to the mainland.

The formation of the erosion-remnant islands by the rising sea is illustrated in figure 1-9a-c. The islands have conspicuously reticulate outlines formed during their origin from the Pleistocene coastal plain. At the time of lowest sea level, the present-day erosion-remnant islands were part of the divides between the watersheds of rivers that drained the emerged portion of the coastal plain (fig. 1-9a). As sea level rose, the rivers were flooded and the edge of the submerging mainland was eroded, creating incipient marshes. At the same time, part of a developing drainage system followed the strata of less-resistant sediments roughly parallel to the present-day coast, truncating the major divides (fig. 1-9b). The characteristic irregular outline of the erosion-remnant islands resulted from the variable resistance of the sediments to stream erosion. Continued sea level rise flooded the river valleys between the divides and the drainage systems behind the truncated divides. St. Helena Sound, Port Royal Sound, and Charleston Harbor are flooded river valleys. Erosion from all sides of the truncated divides added sediment to the surrounding waters, helping to create a marsh between the truncated divides and the mainland, and to the seaward side. The land around the cuestas[8] of the divides finally became drowned and the isolated cuestas became the erosion-remnant islands (1-9c).

Natural Shell Deposits

Natural shell deposits are a result of wave action and currents depositing banks of shells along the edge of tidal creeks. These deposits occur throughout the maritime zone and are especially prominent along inlets that dissect barrier islands.

Natural shell deposits were probably the source Native Americans used to build shell rings and shell mounds (see next section).

THE NATURAL LANDSCAPE OF THE SEA ISLANDS

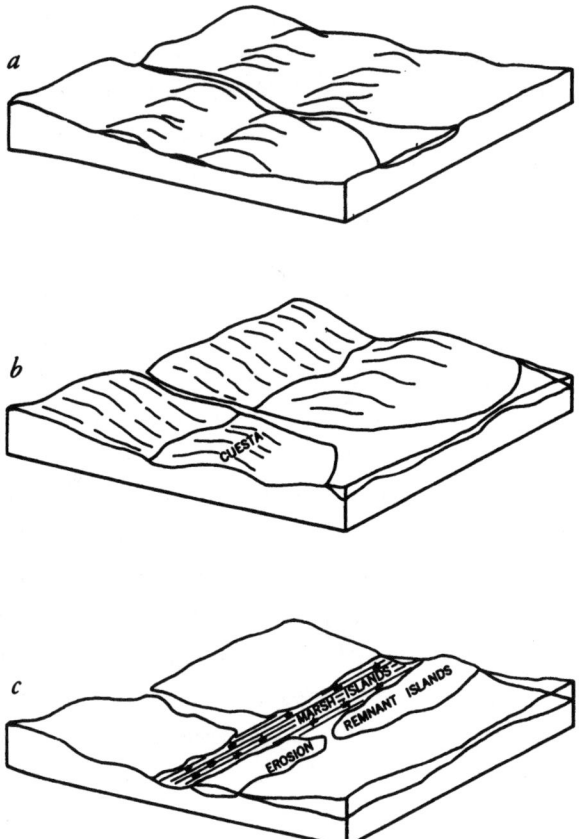

Figure 1-9 a-c. Origin of erosion-remnant islands
(Zeigler 1959, 233)

Plate 1-3. Pig Island Shell Complex, Edisto River, Charleston County (Photograph by author)[9]

Native American Shell Deposits

Sometime around 13,000 BC, Native Americans entered South Carolina and arrived on the coast soon thereafter. Around 3,000 to 4,000 years ago, during the cultural period archaeologists refer to as Late Archaic, they left shell deposits along the coast on marsh islands, marsh hummocks, tips of land masses within estuaries, and on the uplands of the erosion-remnant islands and barrier islands. It is probably safe to say that virtually all presently inhabitable coastal areas have had some type of Native American shell deposits.

Native American shell deposits are of three types: rings, mounds and middens (Porcher and Rayner 2001, 105-106). Plate 1-3 shows a shell ring with an associated shell mound and midden. The ring is a circular deposit of shells raised several feet above the marsh; the mound is a mass of shells raised considerably higher than the shell ring (from 10 to 30 feet high); shell middens are shells deposited in piles or in sinuous formations as refuse around a camp site or village.

Considerable debate exists about the origin of these Native American shell deposits, and irrefutable evidence of their function has eluded archaeologists to this day. Latest reports, however, suggest that the rings and mounds were purposely built, probably for ceremonial uses, and the middens were the result of gradual accumulation of shells discarded around camp sites or villages.

The source of shells used by Native Americans to construct shell rings and mounds was likely the natural shell banks. Drayton (1802) described the shell accumulations on Fort Johnson which he attributed to Native Americans:

...a mound of oyster shells... of a circular form... measuring around two hundred and forty paces... as they were not possessed of proper tools for breaking the earth... They could, however, carry on their heads these shells from neighboring shores; and by continual additions raise this curious structure.

Virtually all the shell deposits on the uplands of the sea islands were destroyed by human activities. The main destruction occurred from agriculture; the shell deposits were leveled during construction of fields (mostly for sea island cotton). Many deposits were destroyed when the shells were used for their lime content as fertilizer on fields or for home construction by early colonists. Another source of destruction was the use of the shells to build county roads (Bierer 1972, 92).

The majority of extant pristine shell deposits occur on marsh islands and marsh hummocks where their isolation precluded significant disturbance. The South Carolina Heritage Trust Program has taken steps to buy or obtain easements on some of the remaining shell deposits. One example is Green's Shell Enclosure Heritage Preserve along Jenkins Creek adjacent to Hilton Head. The enclosure represents a midden. Another preserve, Daws Island Heritage Preserve in Port Royal Sound, Beaufort County, protects a midden, a ring and a mound.

CHAPTER ONE

Buzzard Island on Copahee Sound is a shell ring purchased by the Heritage Trust Program.

The greatest concentration of shell middens occurs on the southern portion of Hutchinson Island in Colleton County. Botanists in the late 1990s identified ten marsh hummocks on Hutchinson Island with shell middens.

VEGETATION OF THE SEA ISLANDS

A brief description of the vegetation of the sea islands, both today and historically, is important to an understanding of the natural world as it existed when the sea island planters began their experiment with agriculture. [Porcher (1995) in *Wildflowers of the Carolina Lowcountry and Lower Pee Dee* and Porcher and Rayner (2001) in *A Guide to the Wildflowers of South Carolina* give descriptions of the plant communities and flora of the coastal area of South Carolina.]

Commercial and residential development, and a long history of agriculture, have removed virtually all of the original vegetation of the sea islands, and today secondary vegetation dominates. The vegetation today of the erosion-remnant islands bears little resemblance to the historical vegetation. Only along the immediate coast where the maritime communities occur does today's vegetation approach that of the historical flora.

Of the nine landforms described earlier, only the erosion-remnant islands occur outside Porcher and Rayner's maritime strand. In the maritime strand, the salt environment (salt water and salt spray) is the primary parameter that shaped vegetation. The larger erosion-remnant islands, such as Edisto and Wadmalaw, are shaped by the salt influence only along the tidal creeks and where they front the large salt-marsh sounds. Their interiors are too far removed from the salt influence to be primarily affected by maritime forces. In this way, they are more similar to the mainland, as is their vegetation.

Marsh Islands

Salt Marsh Community

The marsh islands are dominated by smooth cordgrass (*Spartina alterniflora*) that forms the salt marsh community. Salt marshes occur on regularly flooded substrates along tidal inlets and behind barrier islands (plate 1-2) and spits, and extend to the front side of the erosion-remnant islands, forming wide expanses. In general, the marsh islands developed as smooth cordgrass became established on sand or mud flats exposed at low tide. Silt and clay were trapped by the roots of cordgrass, raising the soil level. As sea level rose, the soil level rose as well, but did not exceed the rate of sea level rise. Smooth cordgrass grows only in environments that are flooded daily by the sea; cordgrass marshes, then, do not generally occur on soil much above the average sea level.

This community is species-poor, often supporting pure stands of smooth cordgrass; however, it is one of the most productive communities in the world.[10] It is the dominant marine wetland in the coastal zone of South Carolina, comprising approximately 150,000 acres. As cordgrass dies, it is washed into the inlets and ocean, where it forms the basis of the estuarine food chain. Large "racks" of cordgrass wash to the front of barrier islands or along the high tide line of the marsh, where it ultimately decomposes.

Three forms of smooth cordgrass occur: tall, medium and short. Tall cordgrass grows next to the tidal creeks in relatively deep water where it receives an energy subsidy of water and nutrients. Away from the creek, the tall cordgrass grades into the medium, then the medium grades into the short cordgrass which occurs at the highest elevation where it is flooded daily, but only to a depth of a few inches to a foot or so.

In the elevated zone, two species that also occur in the adjacent salt shrub thickets intermix with the short cordgrass: sea lavender and saltmarsh aster.

Salt Flat Community

Salt flats are formed in salt marshes where tidal waters drain incompletely and the soil becomes hyper-saline as the water evaporates, leaving behind the salt, which often forms a white crust on the soil. Even the most salt-tolerant species cannot survive in these hypersaline areas, and the centers of salt flats are often barren. However, as salinity decreases toward the margins, a variety of fleshy halophytes, salt-loving grasses and other herbs appear. Closest to the center are perennial glasswort and saltwort, obligate halophytes that tolerate the highest salinity. Salt flats grade into either salt marshes or salt shrub thickets. Intermixed with saltwort and glasswort are diminutive forms of species associated with the salt marshes and salt shrub thickets: sea ox-eye, marsh-elder, smooth cordgrass, sea lavender, saltmarsh aster and seaside goldenrod.

Salt flats most often form in the high salt marshes behind the barrier islands and where the erosion-remnant islands front the sounds.

Marsh Hummocks

Marsh hummocks vary considerably in substrate, elevation and age. Accordingly, they harbor a variety of vegetational types. Three forest communities occur on the larger, relatively undisturbed hummocks of the sea islands. Most common are hummocks that harbor a maritime forest. Others harbor an oak-hickory forest which some botanists believe may be similar to the oak-hickory forests that occurred on the interiors of the erosion-remnant islands. These forests occur in the center of the hummocks. Here the higher elevation and central loca-

CHAPTER ONE

Plate 1-4. Maritime shell forest on Hutchinson Island, Colleton County
(Photograph by author)

tion removes the area from salt influence. On disturbed hummocks, loblolly pines are seeded in after disturbances, and on many hummocks they form the dominant tree canopy. Other elements of the maritime forest community are established subsequently, and will ultimately replace the loblolly forest after the pines die of old age.

Some marsh hummocks harbor a rare community, the maritime shell forest, that occurs where Native Americans discarded the shells of marine organisms they used for food.

Beach-Ridge Relict Islands

The more undisturbed beach-ridge relict islands support a characteristic maritime forest. On their edges, a zone of salt shrub thicket separates the maritime forest from the adjacent salt marsh. Scattered through the salt marsh are salt flats.

Beach-ridge relict islands that have had significant human disturbance are dominated by loblolly pine that became established after the disturbance. However, maritime forest species occur as a common component of the islands. In time, as the loblolly pines die out from natural causes, the maritime forest community will prevail.

Natural Shell Deposits

Natural shell deposits provide habitat for numerous birds, such as the American oystercatcher, that feed on animals from the creek. Shrubs such as yaupon, wax myrtle, sea ox-eye, marsh-elder and groundsel-tree initially populated these shell sites, followed by trees of the maritime forest community if the site was stable and large enough.

Native American Shell Deposits

Native American shell deposits (rings, mounds and middens) have only recently been studied botanically along the Carolina coast. The studies indicate that the shell deposits are floristically unique. They combine a cultural site and a natural site and are high on the list to be protected. The key environmental parameters determining the floristic composition of the Native American shell deposits are the presence of calcium from the shells and their elevation above the highest tide. These sites harbor numerous calcicoles,[11] many of them rare, and a rare community described as a "maritime shell forest."[12]

Shell rings are either isolated in the marsh or attached to a land mass. The isolated shell rings (plate 1-3) harbor few calcicoles, with only tough bumelia and shell-mound buckthorn being common. The shell rings attached to an adjacent land mass, however, harbor many of the rare calcicoles found on the high mounds and shell middens. The Sewee Shell Ring, attached to the mainland along the edge of Bull's Bay in Charleston County, harbors tough bumelia, basswood, dwarf buckeye, hackberry, Carolina buckthorn, shell-mound buckthorn, rough-leaved dogwood, and crested coral-root.

The shell mounds and shell middens harbor a true maritime shell forest (plate 1-4). This is a rare coastal forest community comprised of a variety of woody trees, shrubs and herbs that thrive in calcium-rich soils. The trees and shrubs include tough bumelia, basswood, dwarf buckeye, hackberry, Carolina buckthorn, shell-mound buckthorn, roughleaved dogwood, the rare southern sugar maple, and Godfrey's forestiera. Rare herbs include mottled trillium, Indian midden morning-glory and crested coral-root. In the marsh hummocks, the shell forest is confined to the interior of the hummock. Here Native Americans located their camps in the center and cast shells around the campsite, forming a midden and creating the conditions for the shell forest to develop. Around the rim of the hummock is generally found a typical maritime forest. Sites with southern sugar maple are the most spectacular. In the fall their leaves turn a distinctive red, and the community can be located from the air.

Barrier Islands

Prograding Barrier (Beach-Ridge) Islands

The Carolina beach-ridge barrier islands have been stable long enough that forest communities have developed. The following communities occur on the prograding barrier islands: *coastal beach, coastal dune, maritime shrub thicket, maritime forest,* and *salt shrub thicket.*

Coastal Beach: If there is no erosion or retreating, barrier islands are fronted on the ocean side by a beach, a thin strip of sand just in front of the foredunes. Ocean currents and waves deposit sand below the high tide line, picked up by the waters from offshore coastal sites or brought down the rivers from inland areas. At low tide, winds blowing across the beach pick up sand and carry it along the beach. When the wind hits plants of the beach community, the sand it carries is dropped, beginning the formation of dunes, which are mounds of unconsolidated sand.

Two hardy species, sea rocket and Carolina saltwort, are generally the first (and often the only) species to become established in this harsh environment. Another plant that sometimes becomes established with sea rocket and Carolina saltwort is the rare and endangered seabeach amaranth, which occurs in South Carolina from upper Charleston County to North Carolina.

Coastal Dune: Coastal dunes front the Carolina barrier islands just above the beach. Dunes are the first line of defense for the interior against hurricanes and winter storms.

Coastal dunes form as follows: If the beach is accreting seaward, the incipient dunes that formed in the beach community become farther removed from the effects of salt spray. Now numerous other plants become established which act as windbreaks, and more sand is added to the dunes, increasing their height. In the process, the pioneer species are eliminated because they become covered with sand.

The plant most associated with building coastal dunes in the southeast is sea oats. Other grasses that help build the dunes are seaside panicum and dune sandbur. These grasses can survive the increase in dune height and not be covered up because they have the ability to grow faster than the sand accumulates.

Once the dunes become fairly stable, the following forbs become established and help further stabilize the dunes: beach pea, horseweed, beach evening-primrose, dunes evening-primrose, camphorweed, seaside pennywort, among others, and two species of cactus, prickly-pear and devil-joint.

Between the dunes develop the swales, low-lying areas protected from the salt-laden winds where a fresh-to-brackish system may develop as rainwater forms a layer above the heavier salt water. In the dune swales, but also on the sandy tips of bars and on the back side of the barrier islands, grows sweetgrass, used to make sweetgrass baskets.

Maritime Shrub Thicket: On barrier islands where dunes are building seaward and the inner dunes become protected from salt-laden winds, or where the shoreline has been stabilized for years, the dune communities may be replaced by maritime shrub thickets. These thickets occur in the swales between and on the tops of stabilized dunes, seaward of the maritime forests. On top of the dunes, a pronounced stunted, shrubby growth occurs due to the effects of salt-laden winds that sweep the dune tops. Dominant plants here are shrubs and vines. Shrubs include wax myrtle, yaupon, and groundsel tree. Vines include dune greenbrier, poison ivy, Virginia creeper and the non-native Japanese honeysuckle.

Maritime Forest: The dominant forest community of the Carolina barrier islands is the maritime forest. Maritime forests also occur as a fringe on the ocean side of the erosion-remnant islands where it grades into the upland vegetation of the island, and on many of the marsh hummocks.

On barrier beaches, where accretion is occurring and the dunes are more removed from the ocean's edge and the effects of salt spray, maritime forests replace the maritime shrub thickets as live oak and other maritime trees become established. The characteristic species here are a variety of salt-tolerant evergreen trees and shrubs. There is little herbaceous cover except when natural breaks occur in the canopy, or in disturbed areas.

On the ocean side, maritime forests closest to the ocean's edge are shaped—literally—by the effects of salt spray. The wind blowing from the sea carries salt, depositing it on the windward branches and leaves. These leaves and branches die from the salt, while those on the leeward side, protected from the salt spray, continue growing. The result is a "shearing" effect of the trees and shrubs. Inland, away from the effects of salt spray, the trees assume a typical appearance.

The characteristic evergreen trees of maritime forests are live oak, bull bay, loblolly pine and laurel oak. The subcanopy includes the evergreen trees cabbage palmetto, American holly, red bay, Hercules'-club, and, in more open sites, wax myrtle, yaupon, wild olive and southern red cedar. Herbaceous wildflowers are sparse because of the dense canopy, but two species can be found in more open sites: prickly-pear cactus and trailing bluet. In the southern area of the state (Beaufort and Jasper Counties), saw palmetto and slash pine become important components of maritime forests. Otherwise, the species are the same.

The maritime forests along the Atlantic coast have been extensively timbered since colonial times. No original growth stands exist along the South Carolina coast, with the possible exception of the interior of St. Phillips Island in Beaufort County where low swales prevented timbering. Islands such as Capers Island in Charleston County and Daufuskie Island in Beaufort County once had extensive sea island cotton fields in their interior; their present forests are secondary growth. Abandoned agricultural rows can still be seen. However, the secondary maritime forests that have reclaimed these barrier islands are remarkably similar in composition and structure to the original vegetation.

Timbering began in the maritime forests in the 1700s, mainly for live oak to build wooden sailing vessels. After the War of 1812, "live oak mania" began as expeditions were sent from the northern shipyards to the Atlantic and Gulf coasts to harvest live oak. The curved branches of the live oak were used as ribs of the hull. The wood of live oak is one of the densest known, and the branches were shaped into curved ribs. After the shift to iron and steel ships in the early 1900s, live oak was given a reprieve. Timber companies then began to harvest the pines of the maritime forests. Maritime forests of the lowcountry today are secondary forest; the large live oaks were either spared from harvest or arose from seedlings. The live oak is a fast-growing tree on a good site and can reach an impressive size in fifty years.

Salt Shrub Thicket: Salt shrub thickets occur on the back side of the barrier islands in a narrow zone between the salt marshes and the maritime forests. This distinct zonation exists because of the differential degree of tidal flooding: the lowest zone floods only at extreme high tides, and the highest only during storms or hurricanes.

The two indicative species of the salt shrub community are sea ox-eye and marsh-elder. Needle rush generally forms a dense growth at the lowest zone. Above the needle rush is a zone of perennial glasswort, sea lavender and salt grass. The highest zone is a shrub border of sea ox-eye, marsh-elder, sea myrtle and yaupon. Mixed in with the shrubs, or landward of them, occurs a variety of trees including cabbage palmetto and southern red cedar. Other species may include wax myrtle, sand-vine, seaside goldenrod and salt grass.

Retrograding (Retreating) Barrier Islands

This island type (thin, retreating barrier islands) is migrating so quickly landward that a forest community does not have time to become established. The beach and dune communities are nonexistent because of the erosion of the front beach. The thin strip of highland supports a scattered stand of grasses, forbs and shrubs of the communities listed above for beach-ridge islands.

Erosion-Remnant Islands

Based on the evidence available, it is difficult to determine much about the original vegetation of the Carolina erosion-remnant islands. Native Americans certainly had an impact on the face of the islands and altered much of the original vegetation. However, their impact was minor compared to the changes brought about by agricultural practices of the early colonists

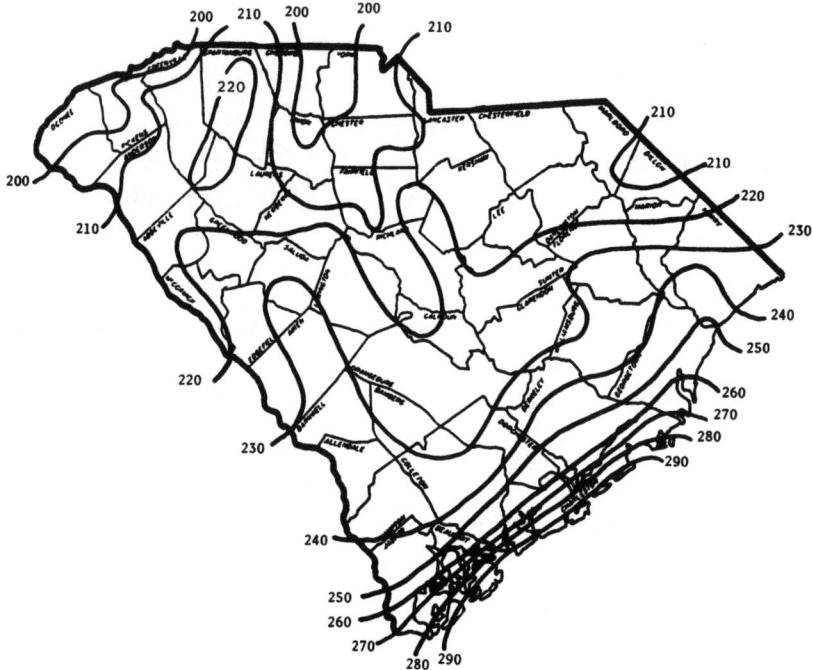

Figure 1-10. Average length of growing season in days (Kish, Wayne and Toler 1976, 5)

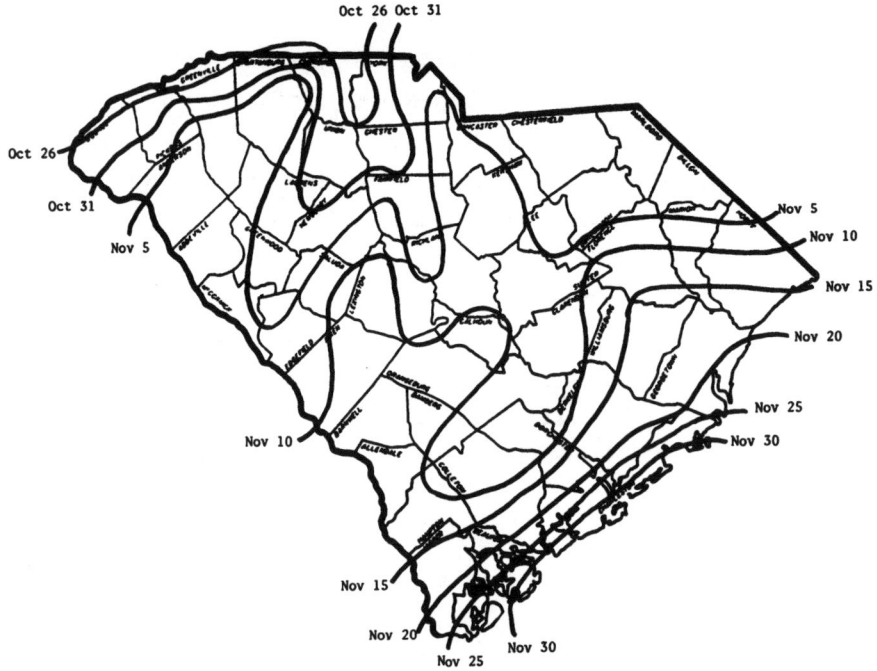

Figure 1-11. Average date of last freeze in the spring (Kish, Wayne and Toler 1976, 6)

CHAPTER ONE

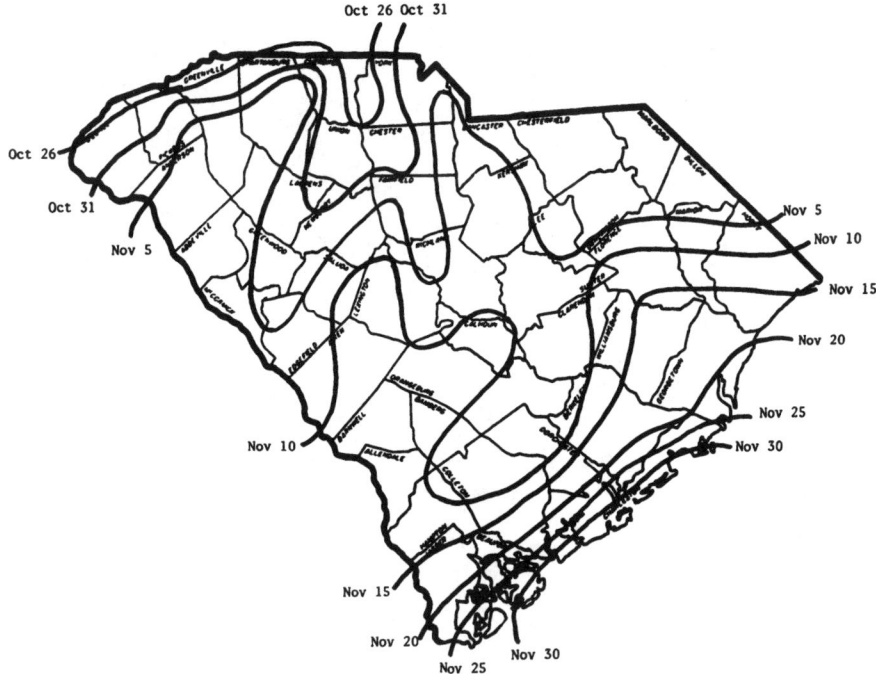

Figure 1-12. Average date of the first freeze in the fall (Kish, Wayne and Toler 1976, 7)

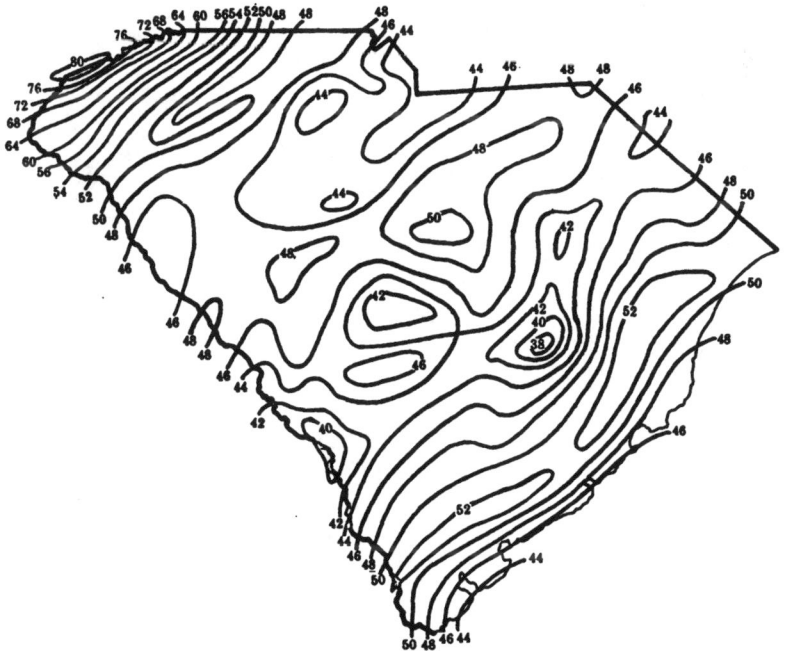

Figure 1-13. Annual average rainfall for coastal zone (U.S. Weather Bureau, 1935-64)[14]

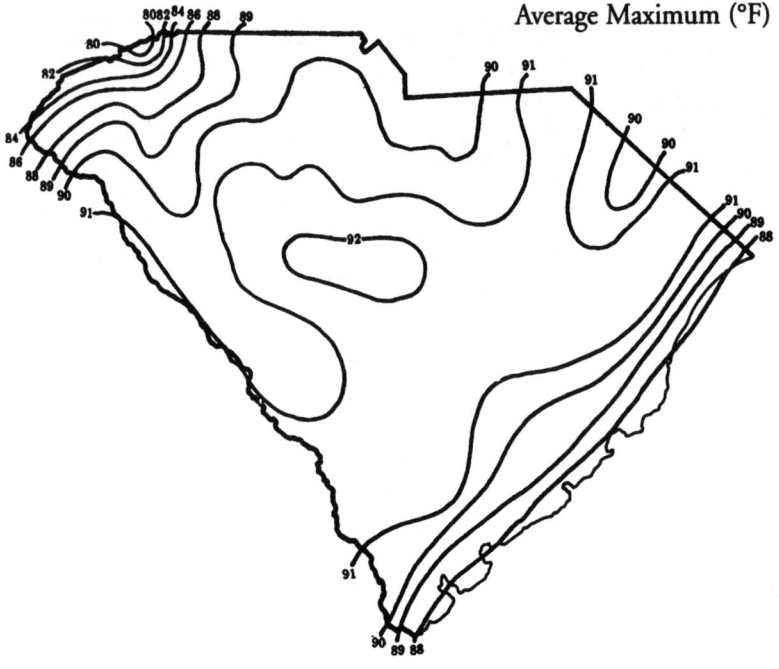

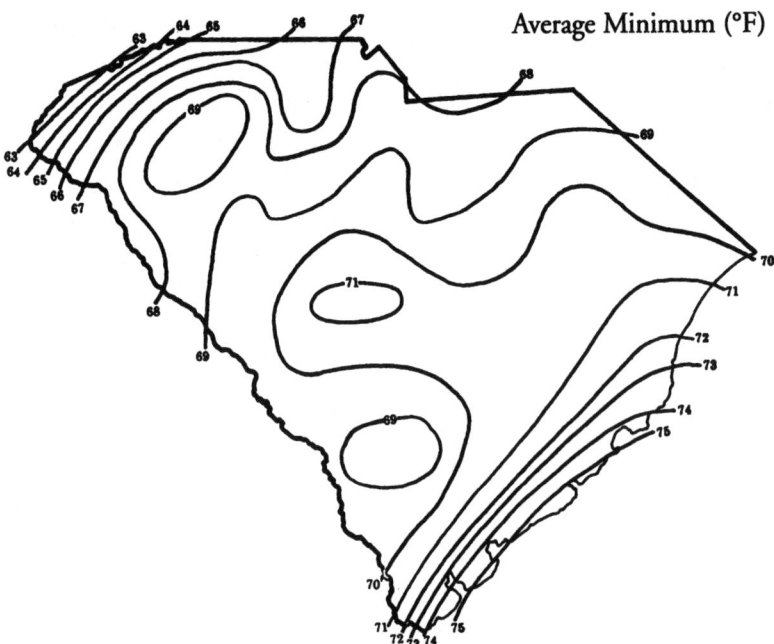

Figure 1-14. July average maximum and minimum temperatures for coastal zone (U.S. Weather Bureau, 1935-64)

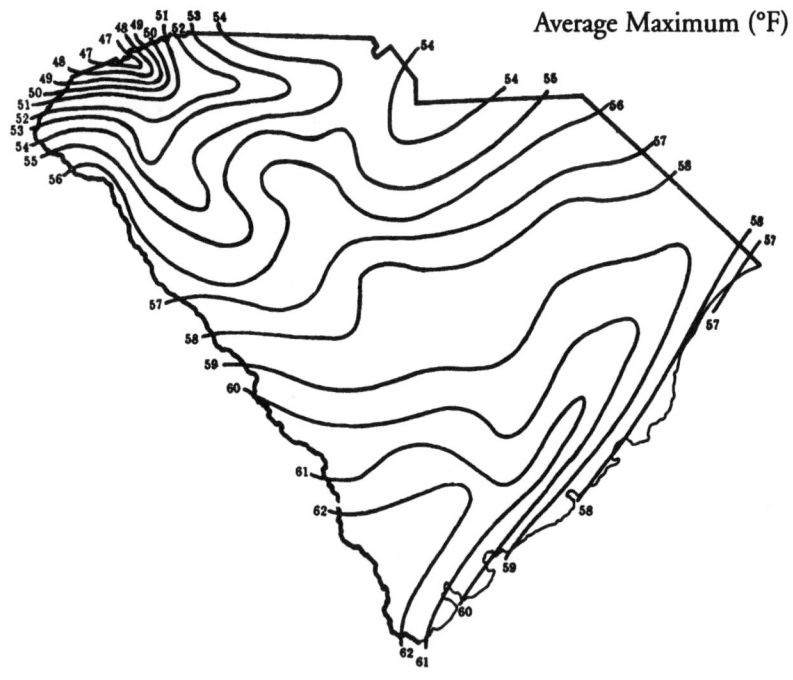

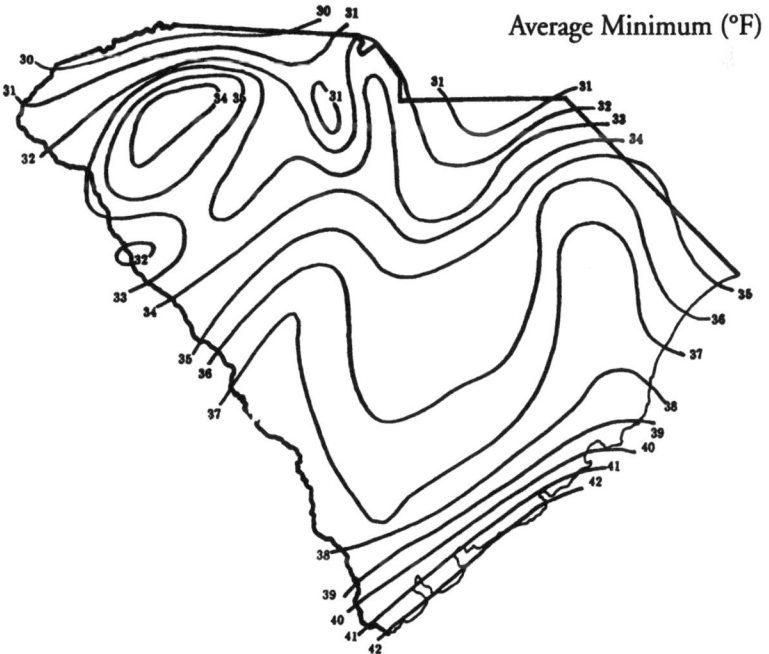

Figure 1-15. January average maximum and minimum temperatures for coastal zone (U.S. Weather Bureau, 1935-64)

beginning in the late 1600s. Couple this with other human activities for 300-plus years, and it should be apparent to the most casual observer that the vegetation today of the erosion-remnant islands is all secondary.

Only scattered clues appear in the literature relating to the original vegetation that greeted the early settlers. It was obviously a land of great beauty and diversity; however, their descriptions are few and not of the breadth and detail to reconstruct an adequate vegetational map. Even the few maps found of the sea islands do not give meaningful clues. Terms such as woodlands that are seen on some maps are too vague to determine, for example, whether the woodland was an oak-hickory or a beach forest.[13]

CLIMATE OF THE SEA ISLANDS

The Carolina sea islands are located in a humid subtropical climate. This climate is modified considerably by the islands' proximity to oceanic influences. This modification is most noticeable during the winter months when island temperatures are 10 to 15 degrees higher than temperatures inland. The ocean proximity also influences moisture levels, the time of early frost and late frost, and the length of the growing season. These climatic differences between the sea islands and the mainland are identified by the author in chapter 6 as one of the factors that produced sea island cotton, and that made the difference between the quality of sea island cotton and the other two market classes of long-staple cotton, mains and Santee long.

Length of the Growing Season. Figure 1-10 shows that the growing season in the sea islands is about 30 days longer than on the adjacent mainland.

Average Dates of First and Last Freezes. Figures 1-11 and 1-12 indicate that the last freeze in the spring on the sea islands is about two weeks earlier than on the mainland, and the first freeze in the fall is about two weeks later on the sea islands than on the mainland.

Annual Average Rainfall. Rainfall on the immediate coast where the sea islands are located averages about six inches less than on the adjacent mainland (fig. 1-13).

July Average Maximum and Minimum Temperatures. The sea islands differ slightly from the mainland in the average maximum and minimum temperatures for the month of July (fig. 1-14a-b). The maximum temperature is approximately 2° F cooler than the mainland and the minimum temperature is approximately 3° F warmer.

January Average Maximum and Minimum Temperatures. The sea islands also differ slightly from the mainland in the average maximum and minimum temperatures for the month of

CHAPTER ONE

January (fig. 1-15). The sea islands' average maximum temperature is about 3° F cooler than the mainland and the average minimum temperature is about 2° F warmer.

1. The Cretaceous Period ran from 135 million to 65 million years before the present.
2. The Quaternary Period runs from 2 million before the present to the present. It is divided into the Pleistocene Epoch, which ran from 2 million years before the present to 10,000 years before the present, and the Holocene Epoch (sometimes referred to as the Recent Epoch) which runs form 10,000 years ago to the present. The Pleistocene was marked by the alternate appearance and recession of northern glaciation and by the arrival of humans to the New World.
3. The island today most often appears on maps as Edingsville Beach; older maps and charts identify it as Edings' Bay. There is also some confusion regarding Edingsville Beach and today's Edisto Beach. In the 1820 map surveyed by Vignoles and Ravenel and included in the Mills *Atlas* of 1826, today's Edisto Beach is identified as Edings' Island, and today's Edingsville Beach is called Edings' Bay.
4. Botany Beach has had a variety of names applied to it over the years. It seems best to use the name Botany Beach to distinguish it from the island immediately adjacent and north which is referred to today as Botany Bay Island. Botany Bay Island abuts the North Edisto River where it enters the ocean. The confusion between Botany Bay Island and Botany Beach comes from the fact that in the 1800s the two islands were one island referred to as Botany Bay Island. Erosion resulted in an inlet connecting with Townsend Creek forming and separating the original island into two. Further erosion reduced the southern end to a thin, retreating island, now best called Botany Beach. The name Clark's Island has also been used for the original Botany Bay Island. In the 1820 map surveyed by Vignoles and Ravenel and included in the Mills *Atlas* of 1826, the name Clark's Island appears. Today's Jeremy Inlet on the same map is called Clark's Inlet.
5. Gibbes's "Botany of Edings' Bay" was included in its entirety in David Taylor's *South Carolina Naturalists*, published in 1998 by the University of South Carolina Press.
6. The map of Edingsvilllle is taken from three U.S. Coast Surveys in the possession of David Lybrand of Edisto Realty on Edisto Beach. The three maps were made into a composite by Mr. Lybrand, and it is hard to tell which map the section of Edingsville came from. One map is dated 1852, another 1851.
7. In this book, the term "erosion" is used when there is a net loss of sediment from an island, and the island is reduced in size. Storm-generated washover, where sediment is carried from the front of the island to the backside, is not considered erosion since the sediment stays on the island, and the island remains essentially the same size. Here the shoreline is considered as retreating and not eroding.
8. A cuesta is a land elevation with a gentle slope on one side and a cliff on the other.
9. Pig Island Shell Complex is a state Heritage Preserve. Visitors should contact the South Carolina Heritage Trust Program in Columbia to determine what type of access, if any, is permitted on this preserve.
10. Productivity of the salt marsh refers to the ability during photosynthesis to convert light energy into chemical energy. During decomposition of dead smooth cordgrass, energy in the form of organic compounds and minerals becomes the basis of the food chain of the marsh and adjacent seas.
11. Calcicoles are plants that cannot tolerate acid soils, and instead thrive in circumneutral to basic soils. The calcium in sea shells makes soil basic.
12. "Maritime shell forest" is a term coined by botanists Richard D. Porcher and Patrick D. McMillan,

and first used in *Wildflowers of South Carolina* (Porcher and Rayner 2001:105).

13. The author (a botanist by profession) did travel throughout the sea islands to see what clues remained to arrive at a rudimentary description of the early erosion-remnant islands. In final consideration, it was decided that there was not enough material, either historically or presently in the field, to develop an adequate description of the original vegetation. A description of the present-day secondary forests and associated communities of the erosion-remnant islands will serve no purpose in this book in relation to sea island cotton. In chapter 7, "The Culture of Sea Island Cotton," a brief description is given about the major vegetation types that were best suited for the production of sea island cotton.

14. Figures for rainfall and temperature during years that sea island cotton actually was grown (1786-1920) are not available. Although these data may vary from the figures used here (1935-64), the variation would not be significant.

The Cotton Plant (*Gossypium* species)

No attempt will be made in this chapter to give a comprehensive account of the cotton genus (*Gossypium*). However, the author believes that for the reader to understand the processes of cultivation and market preparation of sea island cotton, a basic understanding of the ecology, morphology and physiology of the cotton plant will be helpful. The following material applies in general to all species of commercial cottons. Significant features that apply only to wild cottons and sea island cotton are noted.

The English word "cotton" is derived from the Arabic *katán* (or *qutn, kuteen*), though it is claimed the name originally denoted flax (the source of linen). The word "linen" was itself at one time used to denote cotton, and even today we speak of the cotton fibers after ginning as "lint." In earlier times, "linen" was used to denote a particular texture rather than to describe a distinct fiber.

Ecology of the Cotton Plant

Wild species of *Gossypium* grow in frost-free areas in tropical and subtropical areas. Commercial cottons in the New World extend from 37°N to 32°S. Wild cottons and dooryard[1] and landrace[2] cottons are perennial, photoperiodic short-day plants; commercial sea island cotton and upland cotton were converted to annual, day-neutral plants (see chapter 5). Cotton is a sun-loving plant and cannot tolerate shade, particularly in the seedling stage. Anything that increases shade to the plant, such as cloudy days or shading from nearby plants, reduces flowering and fruiting and causes boll shedding.

Wild cottons are xerophytes (plants which grow in a moisture-deficient environment) and will not tolerate very heavy rainfall. The ability to withstand drought has persisted in modern cultivated cottons so that they recover from a dry spell and resume growth and fruiting. Adequate but not excessive moisture is necessary for early vegetative growth; however, the first flowering period requires relative dryness, or excessive boll shedding will ensue. Moisture increase is required for proper boll development; however, dry conditions are required for ripening and harvest. Up to 15% more bolls are shed on days when rain falls during flowering. Although cotton has been adapted to more mesic conditions, it grows best in hot, dry conditions.

Morphology of the Cotton Plant

Gossypol Glands. The genus *Gossypium* is characterized by the presence of glands throughout the above-ground parts of the plant, especially on the calyx, where they are large and prominent. The glands produce gossypol, a terpenoid aldehyde pigment that is toxic to nonruminant animals.[3] It is an undesirable constituent found in the oil extracted from the kernel of the seeds and in the nutritionally valuable meal (cake) that remains as a byproduct after oil extraction. Most of the gossypol is rendered harmless by union with a protein during the crushing or heating phases of commercial preparation. The meal left after removal of the oil may still contain minute quantities of gossypol to which pigs and chickens (nonruminants) are sensitive. Gossypol is not toxic to ruminants such as cattle, and the meal is a valuable cattle feed.

The natural role of gossypol was unknown for years, but may recently have been discovered. The presence or absence of the gossypol glands is under genetic control. The production of strains relatively free of gossypol once appeared to be economically significant. Glandless types (although not completely gossypol-free) of *G. hirsutum* (upland cotton) were created through selective breeding and transgressive segregation. These glandless cultivars, however, were attacked by many nontraditional insect pests such as bollworm and tobacco budworm, leading to the conclusion that gossypol may have evolved as a natural protection. Other research produced cultivars that processed high gossypol gland densities to reduce crop destruction by these pests; however, gossypol's general biocidal properties greatly complicated the use of highly glanded cottonseed as food for nonruminant animals.

Roots. The normal root system in cotton is a typical tap root that penetrates deeply into the soil (about two to three feet in fertile, well-drained soils), while at the same time, lateral roots are forming. If the soil becomes saturated around the tap root during the flowering season, the flowers will drop off. Should the growing tip of the tap root be killed, an immediate flush of growth of secondary branch roots occurs behind the necrotic area. One of these secondary roots may assume a dominant growth pattern and penetrate downward as would the tap root. Most often, however, branch roots proliferate to form a lateral root system, normally from two to four inches below the surface, which never penetrates deep into the soil as would the original tap root.

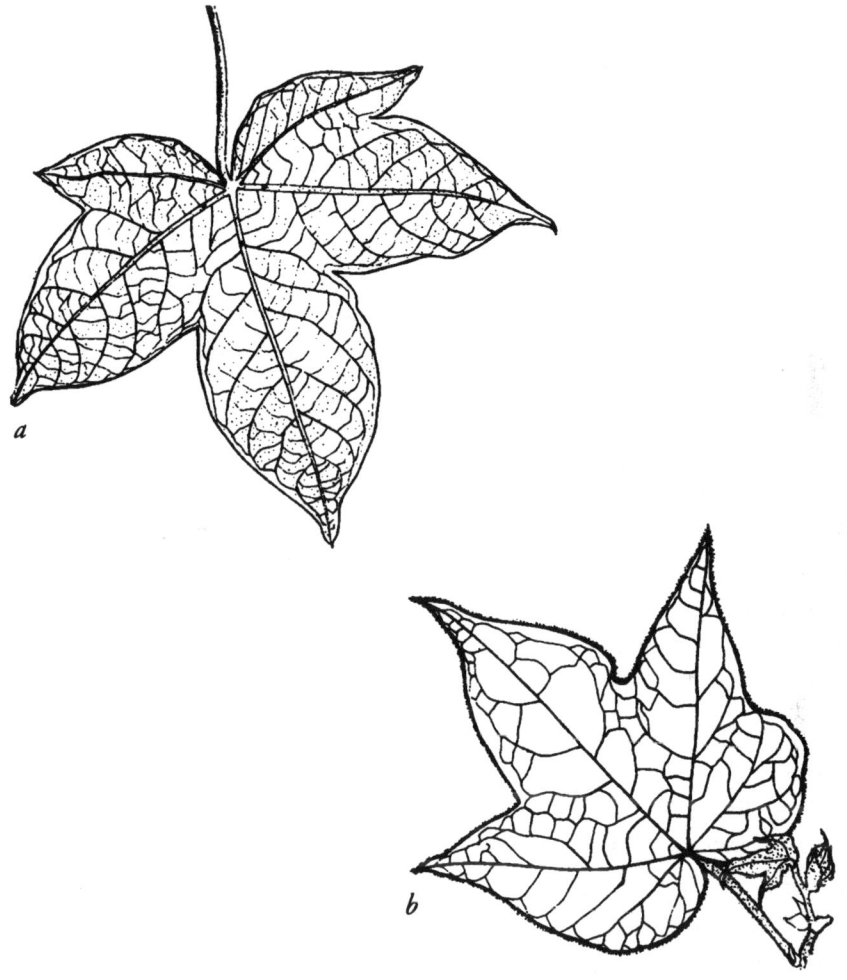

Figure 2-1. Mature leaf of *G. barbadense* (a) and *G. hirsutum* (b) (Purseglove 1968, 350 and 352)

THE COTTON PLANT (*GOSSYPIUM* SPECIES)

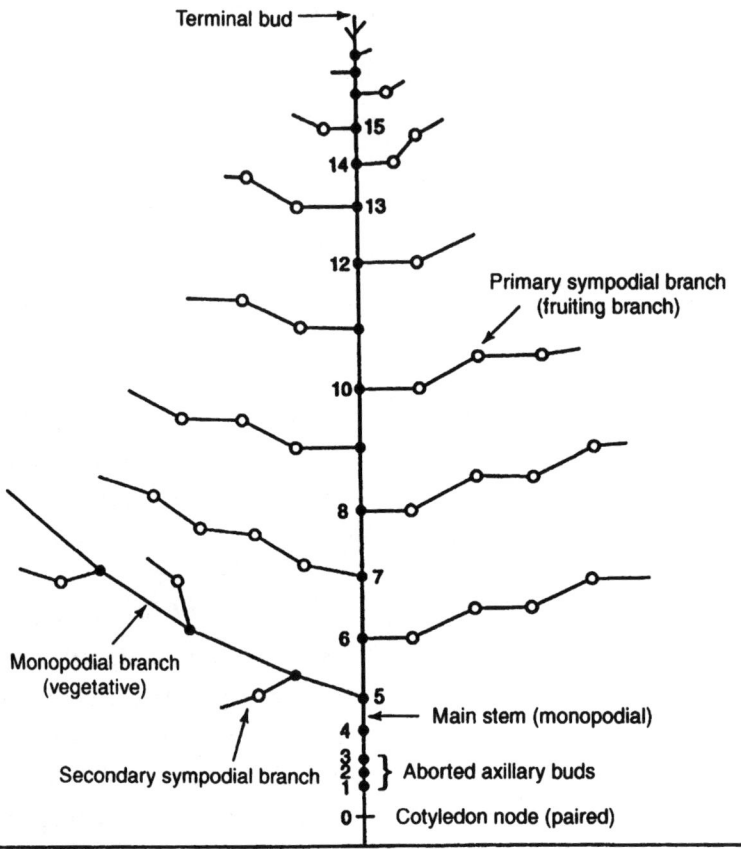

Figure 2-2. Monopodial and sympodial branching on the cotton plant
(Smith and Cothren 1999, 199)

Leaves. The leaves of *G. barbadense* (fig. 2-1) are cut 2/3 of their length into 3-5 lobes as compared to *G. hirsutum* which are cut 1/2 their length or less, usually into three lobes.

Monopodial and Sympodial Branching. Two types of branches may develop on a cotton plant (fig. 2-2): a monopodial (or vegetative) branch and a sympodial (flowering and fruiting) branch. The vegetative branch is morphologically similar to the main stem and arises from the main stem. The main stem is vegetative and produces no flowers. Monopodial branches tend to grow upright and do not produce flowers or fruits: however, they may bear sympodial branches which do bear flowers and fruits. Sympodial branches arise from a monopodial branch as well as from the main stem. Sympodial branches are generally horizontal in orientation. Once a plant begins producing sympodial branches, only under unusual environmental conditions will it revert to producing a monopodial branch above a sympodial branch.

Upland cottons generally begin to produce fruiting branches at lower joints on the main stem, commonly at node six or seven; the first fruiting branches of sea island cotton are usually formed at node eight or nine, or even further up the main stem.

The number of vegetative branches produced by a particular plant depends primarily on the environment (rain, temperature, etc.) and on plant spacing. Optimum plant spacing was effected by thinning (see chapter 7). Obviously, the number of sympodial branches produced in a growing season greatly determined the harvest yield, and consequently, the profits.

Flowering Pattern. Cotton's flowering pattern is distinctive. Flowers open first at the lower main-stem nodes, usually node six or seven, and at the first position along the sympodial branch (figs. 2-3 and 2-4). On a sympodial branch a second flower (and the ones thereafter) open about six days later, referred to as the "horizonal flowering interval." About three days lapse between the opening of a flower on one branch and the opening of a flower on the branch above. This is referred to as the "vertical flowering interval." Flowering then occurs spirally upward and outward. Flowers will continue to be produced until frost.

Flower. A flower (plate 2-1) begins as a small bud (fig. 2-3) called a "square." Each flower is on a peduncle (stalk) with three nectaries near the top of the peduncle. The square is enclosed by three large green bracteoles called the eipcalyx which protect the flower bud (fig. 2-5). The bracteoles persist throughout fruit development, unlike the leaves, which are shed. The bracteoles are a major source of trash in seed cotton.

The internal parts of the flower are best seen in a longitudinal cut (fig. 2-5). The calyx is reduced to a cup-shaped structure with five lobes, with a ring-shaped nectary inside and three nectaries outside near the base. The cup-shaped calyx encloses the bases of the petals. The corolla is large and showy, about 5 cm. in diameter, composed of five petals joined at their bases. The petals open, but are not widely expanding after flowering (plate 2-1). The flower

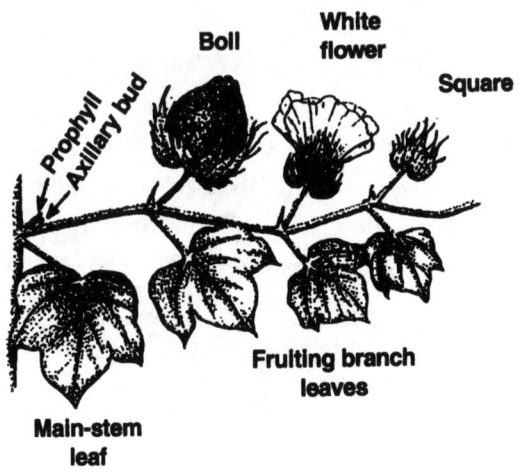

Figure 2-3. Flowering pattern on a sympodial branch (Smith and Cothren 1999, 191)

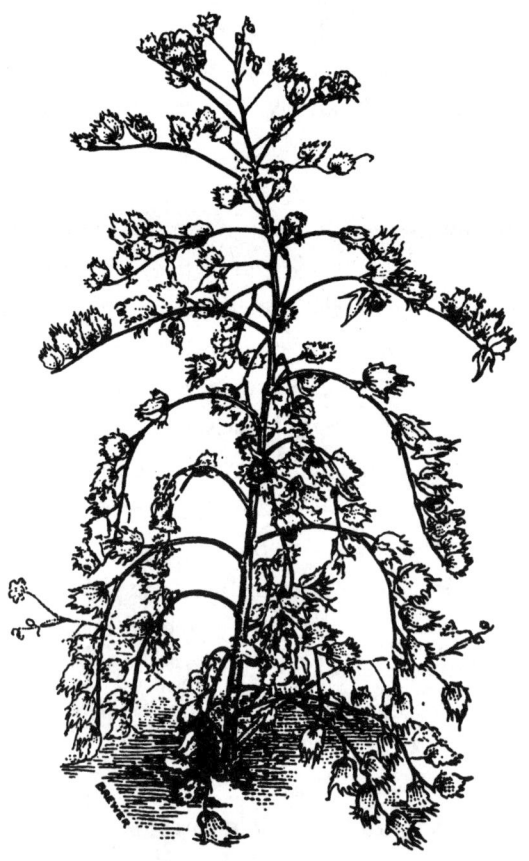

Figure 2-4. Ideal form of sea island cotton plant; leaves have been removed to show manner of branching. (Orton 1907, 35)

CHAPTER TWO

Plate 2-1. Flower of *G. barbadense* (Photograph by author)

of sea island cotton is creamy yellow with a red or purple spot at the base of each petal. The proximal ends of the filaments of the individual stamens are united to form a tube, the staminal column, which surrounds the style and is fused to it (fig. 2-5). The distal end of each filament projects from the staminal column, and each ends in a small anther. In *G. barbadense* the anthers are closely packed on short filaments which are all about the same length. The pistil (female structure) is composed of the ovary, style and stigma. The stigma is exerted above the end of the staminal column. The ovary has 3-5 locules, each locule containing 8-15 ovules, the number varying with species, variety and growth conditions. In *G. barbadense* the ovary is generally trilocular with 5-8 seeds per locule. Only about eight ovules in each locule mature into seeds.

Flowering in sea island cotton began in July. The flowers opened at or near dawn and remained open for a single day. As the flower faded, it turned from a cream color to rose pink. Pollination occured shortly after the flower opened.

Shedding of Squares and Young Bolls. Premature shedding of squares and young bolls significantly reduced cotton yield. Even during the early years of sea island cotton cultivation, planters were aware of the problem, and to some degree, understood the causes. Where they could take corrective measures, they were successful in increasing yields.

The causes of premature shedding were numerous, and included shading, insects, disease, water stress, nutrition and temperature. Shedding was common in reclaimed salt marshes because storms often drove salt water over the banks, and the excess water caused shedding of the leaves, squares, flowers, and fruits. Here, the planters resorted to building higher banks. To alleviate water overflow, drainage systems were installed.

Nectaries. In the genus *Gossypium*, nectar-secreting glands may be developed at four sites: (a) on the leaf veins; (b) outside and (c) inside the involucral whorl; and (d) between the calyx and corolla (floral nectary).

Pollination. As soon as the flower opened, the stigma was receptive to pollen, but for only one day. Pollen was shed at the same time the flower opened, so the majority of flowers were self-pollinated.[4] However, some degree of cross-pollination[5] did occur, normally about 6-25%, but it could have been as high as 50-80% when pollinators such as species of *Bómbus*[6] were present. Since no insecticides were available and the native habitat prevailed, there was an abundant supply of bees and other insects to effect cross-pollination. Bees are attracted to the flower by the nectar in the nectaries. The large size of the cotton flower facilitated cross-pollination. In *G. hirsutum*, the percentage of cross-pollination at 100 meters is 0.1%, so this is the minimum distance required to prevent cross-hybridization with upland cotton. In other words, bee pollinators did not cover a distance of over 100 meters between plants to effect cross-hybridization. No figures are available for *G. barbadense*, but it is probably similar. Thus, to prevent

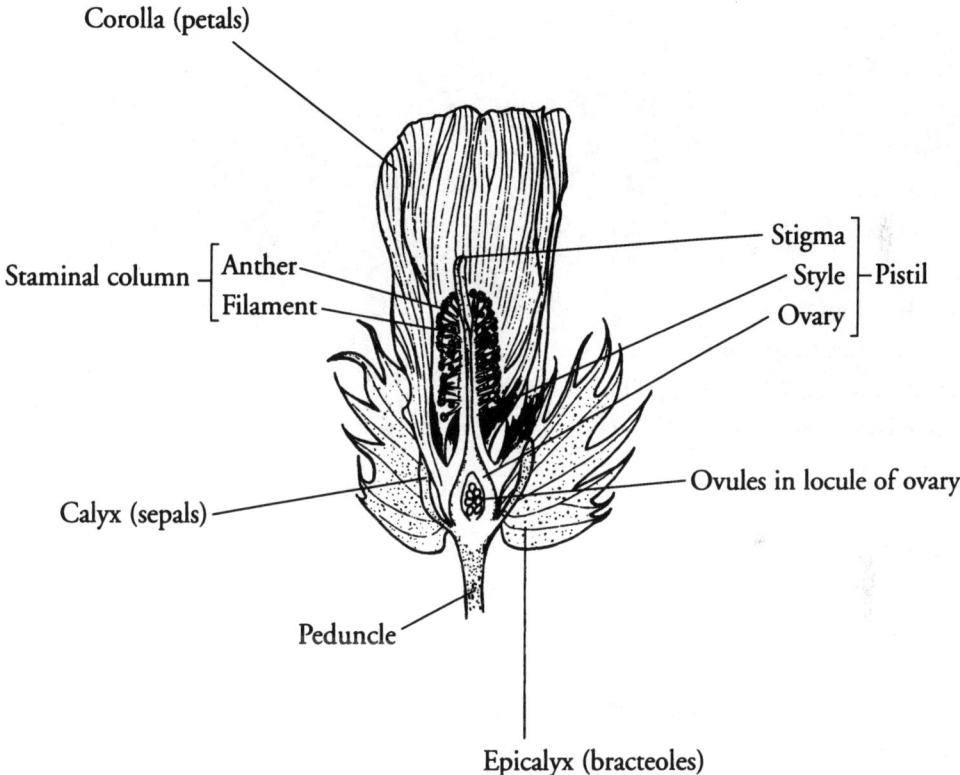

Figure 2-5. Longitudinal section of flower of *G. barbadense* (Purseglove 1968, 351)

Plate 2-2. Unripe capsule with glands (Photograph by author)

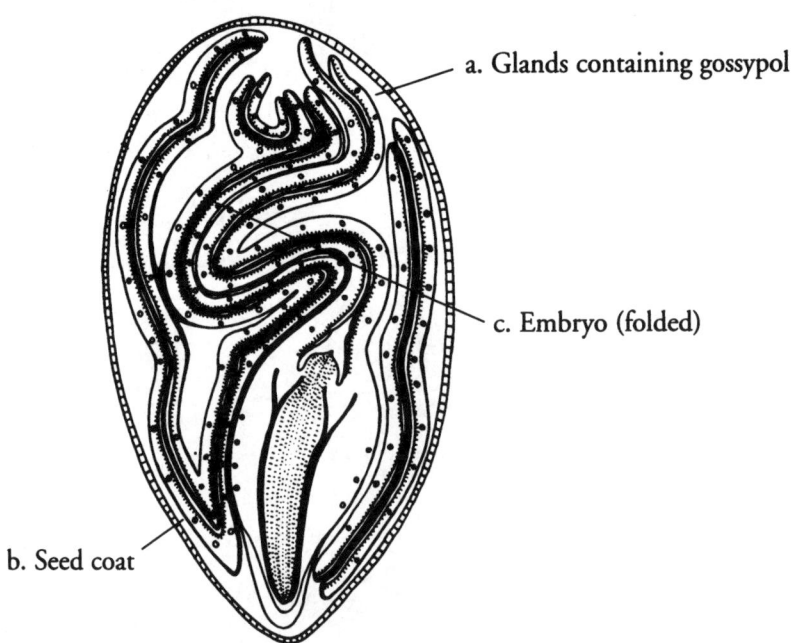

a. Glands containing gossypol

c. Embryo (folded)

b. Seed coat

Figure 2-6. Structure of the cotton seed (Simpson and Ogorzale 1995, 339)

hybridization[7] between plants of a field of sea island cotton and plants of a field of upland cotton, the fields were separated over 100 meters apart.

Hybridization between different genome groups[8] does not produce fertile progeny; however, hybridization between different species of the same genome group (in this case, between *G. barbadense* and *G. hirsutum*, both from the AD genome) produces fertile progeny. Since hybridization between different species resulted in inferior plants in regard to fiber quality (which degenerated), to keep a pure cultivar, sea island cotton planters kept their fields away from upland cotton. Hybridization between upland and sea island cotton on the mainland was the major reason that long-staple cotton (mains and Santee long) grown on the mainland never equalled the quality of sea island cotton.

Fruit. The fruit of the cotton plant is a capsule, commonly called a boll. Bolls of *G. barbadense* are dark green (plate 2-2), pitted with abundant oil glands, usually trilocular with 5-8 seeds per locule. The bolls grew to full size in about 25 days after the flowers opened; the seeds generally developed for another 25 days before the boll opened.

Seed. The cotton seed (fig. 2-6) is composed of a multilayered seed coat surrounding the embryo, called the kernel. The seed coat, also called the hull, enables the seed to withstand physical forces on the seed during harvesting, ginning and conditioning operations. If the seed coat is broken during these operations, seed viability is reduced. It is from the surface of the seed coat that the cotton fibers originate (see next section).

F. S. Shiver (1902) did extensive research on the chemical composition of sea island cotton seeds. The seed coats accounted for roughly 40% of the weight of a seed, and the kernel roughly 60%. The chemical composition for the kernels in given in table 2-1 and for the seed coats in table 2-2.

	Ash of Kernel	Water-free Kernels	Air-dried Kernels
Moisture			6.47
Crude Ash		6.17	5.77
Nitrogen (N)		5.82	5.44
Phosphoric Acid (P_2O_5)	46.37	2.861	2.676
Potash (K_2O)	30.02	1.852	1.782
Lime (CaO)	6.48	0.400	0.374
Magnesia	15.69	0.068	0.905
Insoluble Water	0.89	0.055	0.050

Table 2-1. Average analysis of sea island cotton seed kernels.
Figures represent mean percentages. (Shiver 1902, 16)

From these data, Shiver concluded that sea island kernels possessed considerable fertilizing value since they contained nitrogen, phosphorus (phosphoric acid) and potassium (potash).

	Ash of Seed Coats	Water-free Seed Coats	Air-dried Seed Coats
Moisture			10.29
Crude Ash		3.36	3.01
Nitrogen (N)		1.19	1.07
Phosphoric Acid (P_2O_5)	12.83	0.431	0.387
Potash (K_2O)	44.64	1.500	1.346
Lime (CaO)	7.92	0.266	0.239
Magnesia	10.98	0.369	0.331
Insoluble Water	1.67	0.056	0.051

Table 2-2. Average analysis of sea island cotton seed coats. Figures represent mean percentages. (Shiver 1902, 21)

From the data in this table, Shiver concluded that the seed coats, compared to the kernels, with the possible exception of potash, were poor in fertilizing constituents. But when the seeds were used whole, they were excellent as a crop fertilizer.

The kernels of *Gossypium* are the source of cottonseed oil. With the invention of Eli Whitney's wire-toothed gin in 1793, a large supply of cotton seed from the upland cotton crop (*G. hirsutum*) became available, and experiments with its use and extraction were initiated. Indeed, it was the excess of seed, not the demand for its products, that stimulated interest in cottonseed oil. Sometime before 1802, a South Carolinian, Benjamin Waring, was the first American to produce cottonseed oil commercially from a mill he built in Columbia (Wrenn 1995, 3). From the beginning, the oil was used in a variety of products: paint, lamp oil, the manufacture of woolens, machine lubricants, and as a substitute for lard. But it was not until David Wesson in 1900 developed a way to purify the oil that it became an important food. At this point, oil from the seed of upland cotton became a major industry, and a wide variety of new products were made available.

The use of sea island cottonseed oil is not well documented. Indeed, the author found no specific mention of their oil being used commercially during the period of cultivation prior to the Civil War. Part of the reason may be that, compared to other cottons, *G. barbadense* has the highest kernel content of gossypol.

Seed Hairs. All species of *Gossypium* have at least some seed hairs. In the case of cultivated cottons, the seed hairs have been strikingly modified, becoming longer, heavier, and more abundant through a long history of human selection, and have lost any original function that

Figure 2-7. Laminations of cellulose fibrils that comprise a cotton fiber; dark mass in center is residual protoplasm. (Klein 1979, 356)

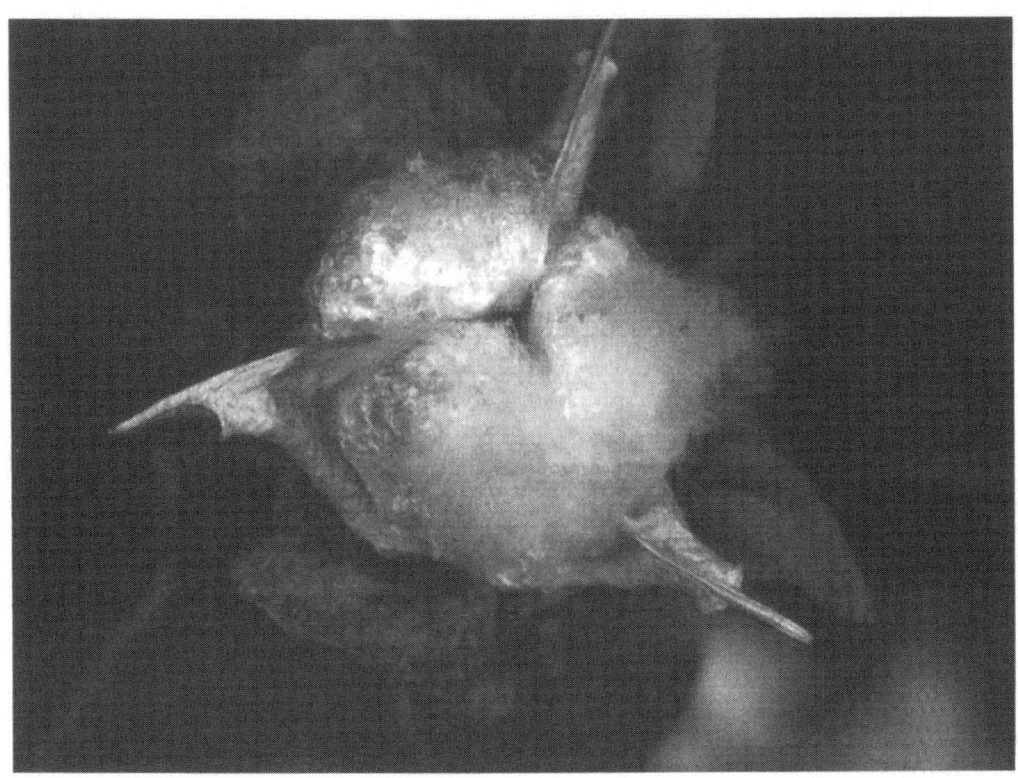

Plate 2-3. Capsule splitting at maturity (Photograph by author)

they might have once possessed. What the initial adaptive value of lint was is unknown. Seed dispersal by birds taking the lint for nesting material is one possibility. But whatever the original function of the seed hairs, this seemingly trivial characteristic had profound consequences for human history.

Seed hairs vary considerably in length and diameter, but they are all unicellular outgrowths of the epidermis of the seed coat, and are therefore morphologically equivalent. In wild plants, they may be so short as to escape notice, or they may be up to 1/2 inch long, and more or less appressed to the seed. In cultivated plants, lengths of 2 1/2 inches have been obtained.

The primary use for species of *Gossypium*, historically both as wild plants and as cultivated plants, was for the seed hairs. Each seed hair (or fiber) is a single, long cell that grows from the epidermis (surface layer of cells) of the seed coat. In a pound of cotton there are some 90 million seed hairs. Depending on the species and cultivar, the cells range from 1000 to 6000 times as long as wide, with a narrow cavity (lumen) running the length. The cavity represents where the living part of the cell, the protoplast, was located. The protoplast dies at maturity and appears as a dark mass in cross section (fig. 2-7). The seed hair first attains maximum length, which occurs in the first twenty days after bloom. *Low temperatures reduce the rate of elongation so total length is reduced.* (This is one reason that sea island cotton had such a long fiber—nighttime temperatures were mild enough to allow significant elongation.) Then, for the next 20-30 days, the cell wall daily increases in thickness. The cell wall is made almost entirely of cellulose and is laid down during growth as concentric laminations of cellulose fibrils (fig. 2-7). Wall thickness, and hence fiber quality, is partially influenced during this period by weather or growing conditions.

In addition to the protoplasm, there are found in the fiber during its development and its maturity minute microscopic bodies, the endochrome. The endochrome is found more or less in every class of cotton. It does not, except in a few cases, permeate the cell wall of the fiber, but becomes coagulated as the fiber matures, and forms a central core in the fibril cavity. It is this endochrome core which imparts to the fiber its color by reflection through the transparent cell wall. The endochrome imparts the deep brown color of "brown Egyptian" cotton and the deeper color of "red Peruvian."

The presence of the endochrome is more emphasized in wild cottons than in cultivated species. On this note, the fiber of all wild cotton plants has a deep rusty tint. The presence of the endochrome in wild cottons in the field may be accepted as an almost certain indication of a low-grade plant, defective cultivation, unsuitable environment or reversion to an ancestral condition

As the seed ripens, the drying hair collapses into a twisted filament (fig. 2-8). The marked cohesiveness caused by the twisting and staple length, plus the durability, strength, and pliability, lend these seed hairs extremely well to spinning. At maturity, the boll splits open (plate 2-3) and the cotton fibers expand, covering the plant with white "snowballs."

In many cultivated cottons there is a second layer of short fuzzy hairs underneath the fibers, called "linters," that apparently evolved under domestication. The linters are firmly attached to the seed and are too short to be spun. Linters of upland cotton are removed when cottonseed oil is processed from the seeds and are employed for papermaking, cotton batting and gumcotton.

Sea island cotton, however, is generally spoken of as "lintless." Strictly speaking, this is not correct, since the seeds of sea island cotton always have a small amount of linters. But the linters from sea island cotton did not possess any considerable economic importance, since, even with the largest mills, only a few bales were obtained from a season's work.

Fiber Quality. The quality of the cotton fiber depends not only on the species, but on the seed, soil, mode of cultivation and climatic conditions. For commercial use, cotton fiber is classified as follows (Purseglove 1968, 357):

1. Length: the normal staple length is the average length of the longest fibers (fig. 2-9).
2. Maturity: fiber showing immaturity contains 25% or more of thin-walled fibers, which results in neppiness (knotting) and other manufacturing difficulties.
3. Fineness: associated with long hairs with small cell diameter and properly thickened cell walls, and is an indication of maturity and strength. The relative fineness of the fiber seems to vary directly with staple length; the shorter staples have the coarsest fiber.
4. Fiber strength: depends partly on the cross-sectional thickness of the fiber wall and is measured by determining the breaking strain.
5. Yarn strength: depends partly on fiber strength and partly on the efficiency with which the individual fibers twist about each other and cling together in spinning, which depends upon fiber strength, fineness and convolutions.
6. Uniformity of lint: depends upon growing pure strains or cultivars, sorting before ginning, efficient ginning and classification of the fiber into standard grades before ginning.
7. Absence of faults: includes no foreign matter (leaves, bracteoles or seed-coat fragments); good color (no staining or spotting from insect or fungal damage); and no neps (small tangled knots due to immaturity) or motes (aborted ovules or immature seeds).

The first four characteristics—length, maturity, fineness and fiber strength—are natural aspects of the fiber; yarn strength depends on a combination of the fiber strength and the spinning process; uniformity of lint and absence of faults depend primarily on the cultivation and market preparation methods.

By all standards, sea island cotton exceeded all other long-staple cottons in fiber length, as well as maturity, fineness, and strength. Sea island cotton varied little in length or twist, and immature fibers were not frequent. Its color was of a light, creamy tint. The reasons for the high quality of sea island cotton fiber are discussed in subsequent chapters.

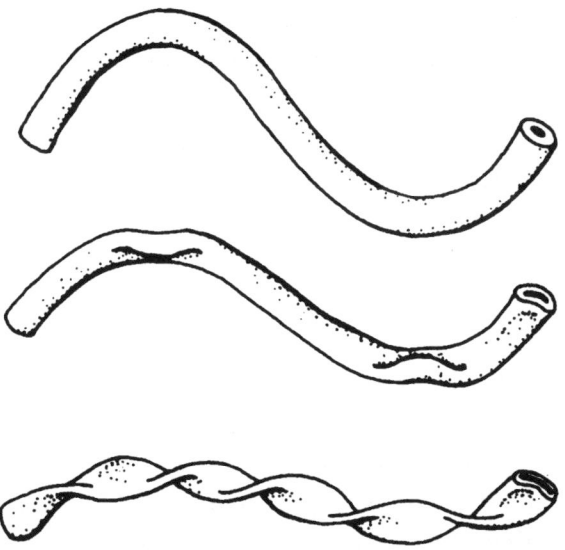

Figure 2-8. As cotton fibers mature, they collapse and twist. (Klein 1979, 356)

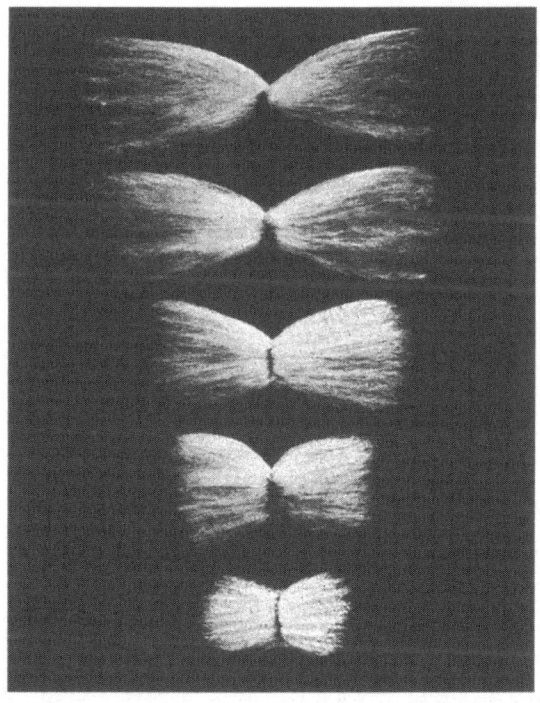

Figure 2-9. The principal commercial types of cotton, showing the variation in length of staple. From top: sea island, American-Egyptian, upland long-staple, upland short-staple, and Asiatic. (Hill, 1952)

Commercial Classification of Cottons by Staple Length

The International Cotton Advisory Committee classifies commercial cottons based on staple length. Two staple lengths are pertinent to this book:

Extra-long staple: 1 3/8 inches and longer
Long-staple: 1 1/8 to 1 5/16 inches

Extra-long staple (ELS) cottons are all *barbadense* cottons and include sea island cotton (no longer grown) and modern cultivars of *barbadense* grouped as American-Egyptian (for example, Pima) grown in the American Southwest; Egyptian (grown in Egypt and Sudan); and cultivars grown today in Australia, Peru, and in the Committee of Independent States (Tajikistan, Turkmenistan and Uzbekistan, formerly part of the USSR). Cultivars once grown in the West Indies which derived from sea island cotton also were extra-long staple. ELS cottons comprise about six percent of world cotton today and are characterized not only by their length of fiber, but also by fineness and high fiber strength.

Long-staple cottons include cultivars of *G. hirsutum* referred to as upland long-staple cottons and some cultivars of *G. barbadense* grown today. It would also have included cottons that Lewis Gray (1958) reported were classified as Santee long and mains. Gray stated that the staple length for Santee long and mains was 1 1/8 to 1 1/2 inches long. Georgia and Florida interior cottons, with the same staple length, would also have been classified as long-staple cottons.

An obvious problem arises if this book uses the term "extra-long staple cotton". The designation was not used in the cotton trade until 1907, when an attempt was made at standardization. However, since this book generally covers the history of sea island cotton and the cotton industry prior to 1907, most of the quotes and references use the term "long-staple cotton." When reference was made to upland cotton that had a staple length similar to some *barbadense* cottons, it was referred to as "upland long-staple cotton." To avoid confusion between today's ELS cottons and the use of "long-staple" in the historical literature, this book will not use the term ELS. The reader knows, however, that ELS is used today for all *barbadense* cottons with a staple length over 1 3/8 inches long. In this book, "long-staple" will refer to all *barbadense* cottons.

Physiology of the Cotton Plant

Flowering and Fruiting. Fruiting in wild, perennial short-day cottons is controlled by three factors: (1) photoperiodicity: wild cotton is a short-day plant and only sets flowers (and therefore fruits) in the short days of fall; (2) water supply: the flower buds shed if the plant is subjected to copious amounts of water. This insures that the fruit is brought to maturity only in dry weather which favors seed dispersal; and (3) branching: fruiting is controlled by the node at which the first sympodial fruiting branch appears, irrespective of the external environment, thus determining the onset of the reproductive phase in the first season. When tropical wild, short-day perennial cottons are taken to temperate regions, they become highly vegetative and produce few or no fruiting branches when grown under long days.

The conversion of perennial short-day cottons to annual, day-neutral commercial cottons (*G. barbadense* and *G. hirsutum*) required the loss of all periodicity controls, and gaining control of the water supply. A detailed discussion of the loss of periodicity is presented in chapter 5 and of control of the water supply in chapter 7.

Mineral Requirement. (a) nitrogen: sea island cotton required less nitrogen than most crops, especially on low or moist soils. Excess use of nitrogen stimulated vegetative development, resulting in tall, coarse, and relatively unproductive plants; a lack of nitrogen resulted in small plants; (b) potassium: a liberal supply of potash was very important for sea island cotton. Potassium influences the formation of starches and sugars and is indispensable for protein formation; (c) phosphorus: phosphorus in the form of phosphoric acid was indispensable to the sea island cotton plant for general development, especially for the seed and lint; (d) lime: lime, as a rule, was not used by sea island cotton growers since the soil of the sea islands had a shell component.

Tolerance to Salinity. Mauney and Stewart (1986, 111) stated: "The physiology of cotton response and adaptation to salinity is relatively unexplored. The high salt tolerance of most varieties of cotton evaluated suggests that this factor in itself may be the reason why the physiology of salt adaptation in cotton and the specific effects of salinity on cotton functions have not been studied more thoroughly." In particular, they state that American-Egyptian varieties have consistently good salt tolerance. Although not stated by Mauney and Stewart, or any other source known to the author, sea island cotton undoubtedly also had a good tolerance to salinity and explains, in part, why sea island cotton could thrive on the barrier islands, marsh islands and areas of the erosion-remnant islands close to the ocean or salt creeks.

The Cotton Family, Malvaceae

The mallow family, Malvaceae,[9] to which cotton belongs, is a family of about 100 genera and some 1500 species, widely distributed in tropical and temperate areas of the Old World and the New World. The family includes herbs, shrubs and (rarely) small trees. The stems of the herbs are often fibrous. Members of the family are generally adapted to special local habitats rather than dominating regional vegetation formations. They generally grow in thin, scattered populations and rely on insect and bird pollination—hence, they have showy flowers to attract pollen vectors. One genus, *Gossypium*, includes all major commercial crop species (New

World species *Gossypium barbadense* L.,[10] long-staple cotton, and *G. hirsutum* L.,[11] short-staple cotton; and Old World species *G. arboreum* L. and *G. herbaceum* L.). The family name, Malvaceae, is derived from the genus name *Malva*, an old Latin name, from the Greek *malache*, or *moloche*, indicating the emollient leaves of some genera of the family.

A key characteristic that identifies the mallows and their relatives is an unusual feature of their flowers: the numerous stamens are joined to make a cylinder around the style. This feature is readily seen in seashore mallow (*Kosteletskya virginica* (L.) Presl, plate 2-4).

Malvaceae is divided into two tribes: Hibisceae with schizocarpous fruits such as *Althaea* and *Modiola*, and Gossypieae with capsular fruits such as *Hibiscus* and *Gossypium*. The fruits of both groups are composed of one to many (often five) parts (the carpels), these often forming a ring and each containing one to several seeds. In the schizocarpous species, the fruits at maturity separate into indehiscent (not splitting open to release seeds), one-seeded segments. In the capsular species, the fruit at maturity forms a capsule, a dry, dehiscent (splitting at maturity to release seeds) fruit. The fruit of cotton (plate 2-3) and okra are typical capsular species.

There is considerable difference in the literature on whether these two tribes are natural divisions within the Malvaceae, and if they are natural divisions, whether the Gossypieae belongs to the Malvaceae family or the Bombacaceae[12] family. Fryxell (1968a) made a strong argument for the division into two well-defined tribes, obsreving that the two groups are clearly distinct and both tribes have closer affinities with the Malvaceae than the Bombacaceae. The two main features that characterize the tribe Gossypieae are: (1) the presence of pigment glands in various parts of the plant, but especially in the cotyledons (of the seed embryo), with the capacity to synthesize gossypol (derived from the genus name, *Gossypium*); and (2) the structure of the embryo of the seeds (conduplicate[13] in Gossypieae and bent in Hibisceae). The glands and their pigments appear to be unique to the Gossypieae. Gossypol has economic importance as an undesirable discoloring constituent found in the oil extracted from cottonseed, and as a toxic contaminant in the protein-rich meal that remains as a byproduct after oil extraction from the cottonseed.

Representative genera of the family include *Althaea* (with 12 species, including hollyhock and marshmallow); *Malva* (40 species, including mallow); *Sida* (200 species); *Abutilon* (100 species, including flowering maple and Indian mallow); *Hibiscus* (300 species, including okra, rose mallow and flower-of-the-hour); *Modiola*; and *Gossypium* (cotton, with 34 species).

Except for the cotton plant, the family is not economically important. Numerous species, however, are valued for cultivation worldwide. In the southeast United States, three commonly cultivated species are the shrubby Rose-of-Sharon (*Hibiscus syriacus* L.), a native of east Asia; hollyhock (*Althaea rosea* Cavanilles); and high mallow (*Malva sylvestris* L.), the latter two introduced from Europe.

The only species of Malvaceae important commercially in the South, except for the cotton plant, is okra (*Hibiscus esculentus* L.). Okra is a native of tropical Africa believed to have orig-

Plate 2-4. Seashore mallow (Photograph by author)

Plate 2-5. Swamp rose mallow (Photograph by author)

inated in the northeast African center of domestication, and is reportedly found wild in the upper Nile watershed. It spread to the Far East and Europe in Christian times, and was brought to the New World in the 1600s. Okra found exceptional popularity in the French cookery of Louisiana. They referred to okra by its African name, *gumbo*. The green pods, when quite young, are sliced in soups and similar dishes, to which they impart a thick, viscous or gummy consistency due to the mucilaginous coating of the seeds. Okra has maintained its place in southern agriculture because it can tolerate even the hottest southern months (much like cotton) and still produce a substantial crop at the end of the long growing season.

In the sea islands and adjacent mainland of South Carolina, four members of the mallow family are highly conspicuous elements of the native flora (Porcher, 1995). In freshwater tidal marshes, roadside ditches and edges of ponds and lakes grow three common species: seashore mallow (*Kosteletskya virginica* (L.) K. Presl, plate 2-4), swamp rose mallow (*Hibiscus moscheutos* L., plate 2-5), and halberd-leaved marsh mallow (*Hibiscus militaris* Cavanilles). Another colorful native hibiscus, pineland hibiscus (*H. aculeatus* Walter), grows in longleaf pine savannas and longleaf flatwoods in more inland sites.

A native species that is relatively inconspicuous is bristly-mallow (*Modiola caroliniana* (L.) G. Don), found in lawns, roadsides, disturbed areas and pond shores. One species of the mallow family that has become naturalized in the sea islands is arrowleaf sida (*Sida rhombifolia* L.), naturalized from the tropics. It is common along roads, in fallow fields, yards, pastures and vacant lots.

Besides the economic use of the species of cotton for fibers, cottonseed meal, and cottonseed oil, the economic value of the family is limited. There are, however, some interesting documented uses of members of the family. *Abutilon theophrasti* Medicus, or velvet leaf, cultivated in China, is the source of a fiber called China jute. Other malvaceous species yielding fiber include kenaf (*Hibiscus cannabinus* L.), roselle (*H. sabdariffa* L.), and majagua (*H. tiliaceus* L.). The roots of *Althaea officinalis* L. were once an ingredient in marshmallow confections. Francis P. Porcher (1869) stated that in the South, the parched seeds of okra were used as a substitute for coffee.

Classification of *Gossypium*

After Linnaeus described five or six species of *Gossypium*, further attempts to study *Gossypium* taxonomy led to great controversy. Parlatore recognized seven species, Todaro 54, while Sir George Watt (1907), who provided the most complete and detailed classification at that time, recognized 29 species and 13 varieties. Classifications after Watt's work again produced variation in the number of cotton species and varieties. No classification is accepted by all scientists, and different classifications appear as new species are described when new genetic or molecular information is presented. Accordingly, the classification below from J. W. Purseglove (1968, 335-341) is certainly not accepted by all scientists. However, it will suffice for this book since it is easily understood and concise. The author has modified it based on information published by Paul A. Fryxell (1979) and Wendel & Albert (1992). Thirty-four species, segregated into six genome groups, are represented in the classification.

A. Wild Lintless Cottons
Section I: Sturtiana (Diploid Chromosome Number = 26)   C Genome
   About 9 species in Australia.

Section II: Erioxyla (Diploid Chromosome Number = 26)   D Genome
   Three species: *G. aridum* in western Mexico, *G. armourianum* on San Marcos Island in the Gulf of California, and *G. harknessii* in Baja California and adjacent islands.

Section III: Klotschiana (Diploid Chromosome Number = 26)   D Genome
   Two species: *G. klotzschianum* var. *klotzschianum* endemic in the Galapagos Islands and *G. klotzschianum* var. *davidsonii* in Baja California and adjacent islands; and *G. raimondii* in northern Peru (probably the DD ancestor of the New World allotetraploids).

Section IV: Thurberana (Diploid Chromosome Number = 26)   D Genome
   Four species: *G. thurberi* from Arizona to Mexico, and *G. gossypioides*, *G. trilobum* and *G. lobatum* in Mexico.

Section V: Anomala (Diploid Chromosome Number = 26)   B Genome
   Three African species.

Section VI: Stocksiana (Diploid Chromosome Number = 26)   E Genome
   Five species centering in the Arabian peninsula.

B. Old World Linted Cottons
Section VII: Herbacea (Diploid Chromosome Number = 26)   A Genome
   Two commercial species with a number of cultivated races in Asia and Africa.
   1. *G. herbaceum* L. Perennial and annual shrubs or subshrubs with rounded capsules which are usually smooth with a few oil glands. Five races are recognized.
   2. *G. arboreum* L. Much-branched perennial shrubs to two meters high or annual subshrubs; capsules tapering, profusely pitted with oil glands. Six races are recognized.

C. New World Linted Cottons
Section VIII: Hirsuta (Tetraploid Chromosome Number = 52)   AD Genome
   Six species of allotetraploids[14, 15] containing one diploid set of chromosomes from an Old World linted cotton (A Genome, probably *G. herbaceum*) and a diploid set of chromosomes from a New World species (D Genome, probably *G. raimondii*). Two species, *G. barbadense*

and *G. hirsutum*, are the commercial cottons in cultivation and have spread to every cotton growing country in the world.

1. *G. barbadense* L. Perennial shrubs or annual subshrubs 1-3 meters high. Seeds with a copious, even coat of seed hairs; fuzz (linters) may cover the seeds, form a tuft at one end, or be absent. The center of origin is west of the Andes in southwest Ecuador and northwest Peru. Wild forms are found north and south of the Guayas Estuary in Ecuador and on an island offshore from Manta. Dooryard plants occur scattered throughout South and Central America and the Caribbean. The annual habit and day-neutral flowering was established when seeds from the West Indies were introduced into Georgia in 1785, and gave rise to four market classes of long-staple cottons along the Atlantic Coast, including sea island cotton. Modern improved cultivars include Pima and its many derivatives.

One variety of *G. barbadense* is recognized (Fryxell 1979, 10): var *brasiliense*. It is commonly called "kidney seed" cotton because the seeds of one locule are fused into a solid mass that is somewhat kidney-shaped. The solid mass allows the seeds to be ginned more readily by hand and to be planted in holes by hand more readily (the "mass" has the seeds oriented in one direction that allowed for optimum emergence). These traits were selected for under primitive agricultural conditions. However, when cotton culture moved from primitive agriculture dooryard culture to field production after the Industrial Revolution, these traits were no longer valuable. Today, var. *brasiliense* persists as "only a remnant of a more primitive type of cotton agriculture" in the Amazon Basin.

Percy and Wendel (1990) did not consider var. *brasiliense* distinct from *G. barbadense* and considered it a geographically restricted domesticated from of *G. barbadense* rather than a distinct taxon.

2. *G. hirsutum* L. Perennial small trees and shrubs and small annual subshrubs. Indigenous to Central America and the Caribbean and in certain Pacific islands. Cottons referable to *G. hirsutum* show a broad range of variation, from highly specialized cultivars (upland cottons) to fully wild forms. The wild forms occur on beaches rimming the Gulf of Mexico, to some extent in the Caribbean, and extend to various localities in Polynesia. The lint of wild forms is sparse and fine. Dooryard *G. hirsutum* is found widely through Central America and to some extent also in northern America and West Africa. Domestication in *G. hirsutum* was for selection for increased quantity of seed fiber, and for the annual habit to give upland cotton, which now forms the basis of much of the world's commercial upland, short-staple cotton.

3. *G. darwinii* Watt, Wild & Cult. Perennial, much-branched shrub, with scanty, irregular, rather fine brown lint which is strongly adherent to the seeds; endemic to the Galapagos Islands.

4. *G. mustelinum* Miers ex Watt, Wild & Cult. Distributed in northeastern Brazil.

5. *G. tomentosum* Nuttall ex Seemann. A densely tomentose perennial, 1-1.5 meters tall, with seeds densely covered with brownish hairs, not readily separated into two layers and strongly adherent to the seed. This distinctive species is endemic to the Hawaiian islands, where it grows on arid, rocky or clay plains not far from the sea.

6. *G. lanceolatum* Todaro. Principally a dooryard cotton in Mexico.

CHAPTER TWO

1. Dooryard cottons differ from wild cottons in having a history of casual use by local peoples. They are not grown in large populations, but occur as single plants found near habitations. Dooryard cottons have received little population selection and are thought to derive in many cases directly from local, wild progenitors. They are short-day flowering perennials.
2. Landrace cottons are cultivars grown on a commercial scale and derived from locally available cottons. They are often short-day flowering perennials, as are the wild and dooryard forms.
3. Ruminants (animals that chew for an extended period, such as cattle and deer) and nonruminants are both herbivores (animals that rely solely on plants as food). Ruminants are exemplary cases of herbivores anatomically specialized for the digestion of cellulose. They possess a highly complex digestive system consisting of a four-compartment stomach (the rumen, reticulum, omasum, and abomasum) and a long intestine. The rumen and reticulum are inhabited with anaerobic bacteria that digest cellulose. In nonruminant herbivores, such as horses and rabbits, digestion takes place in the hindgut, and even though it is less efficient, they can process large quantities of forage rapidly.
4. Self-pollination is pollination of a flower by pollen from the same flower or from another flower on the same plant.
5. Cross-pollination is pollination between two different plants of the same species.
6. Bumble bees belong to the genus *Bómbus* and are the most important bees in plant pollination. They nest in the ground, usually in a deserted mouse nest or bird nest or similar location. The fields and forests that surrounded the sea island cotton fields provided ample habitat for bumble bees, and they were the pollinators of sea island cotton.
7. Hybridization is crossbreeding between different species or varieties. For example, between *Gossypium barbadense* and *G. hirsutum*.
8. A genome is the total genetic complement of a basic diploid species. A genome group is comprised of related species whose nuclear genomes are cytogenetically more similar to each other than they are to other groups of species. Genome groups are most often recognized on the basis of comparative analysis of chromosome pairing behavior in interspecific hybrids. Hybrids between members of the same genome group typically exhibit normal or near-normal meiotic configurations and partial to complete fertility (that is, between *G. barbadense* and *G. hirsutum*); interspecific hybrids between members from different genome groups show various degrees of abnormal pairing and sterility.
9. Malvaceae is pronounced mal-VAY-see-ee
10. *Gossypium barbadense* is pronounced jos-SIP-pee-um bar-ba-DEN-see
11. *Gossypium hirsutum* is pronounced jos-SIP-pee-um hare-SOOT-um
12. Bombacaceae (the bombax family) is a family of about 20 genera and 150 species of trees in the tropics around the world. The family includes the silk-cotton tree (*Ceiba pentandra* Gaertner) from which kapok fiber is obtained. Like cotton, kapok is a seed hair of pure cellulose; however, the fiber is smooth and lends itself poorly to spinning. Instead, because of its imperviousness to water and buoyancy, it is used for life preservers and insulation in sleeping bags.
13. Conduplicate means folded in half lengthwise.
14. The explanation of an allotetraploid is given in detail in chapter 3.
15. This treatment of six allotetraploid species follows that of Fryxell (1979, 68-71).

The Science of *Gossypium barbadense* L.

Sea island cotton, one the many market classes of *Gossypium barbadense* L., had little nomenclatorial relevance to the plant described and named by Linnaeus. It did, however, have immense evolutionary, agronomic and economic significance. Sea island cotton was developed by agronomists long after Linnaeus's time. It had an extra-long, high-quality fiber, annual growth and day-neutral flowering, all developed in the late 1700s and early 1800s. These characteristics were absent in Linnaeus's *G. barbadense*. Subsequently, sea island cotton was used by plant breeders to develop other annual types of *G. barbadense* for cultivation in Peru, Egypt, the southwestern United States and elsewhere. But all these genetic variations of *barbadense* are still the same species. This chapter deals with the science of Linnaeus's *Gossypium barbadense*. Sea island cotton and the other market classes of *G. barbadense* are discussed in following chapters.

Nomenclature

Gossypium barbadense L. was originally described to the scientific world by the Swedish naturalist and classifier Carolus Linnaeus. In his *Species Plantarum* published in 1753, which the scientific field considers as the starting point for the system of priority used in present-day nomenclature of the higher plants, Linnaeus gave the following description for *Gossypium barbadense*:

2. GOSSYPIUM *foliis trilobis integerrimis.* Hort. ups. barbadense.
204.
Gossypium frutescens annuum, folio trilobo, barbadense. Pluk. alm. 172. t. 188. f. 1.
Habitat in Barbados.

The English translation is "cotton-fruited annual with three-lobed leaves met with in Barbados."

There is, however, considerable controversy in the literature over the proper validity and application of Linnaeus's description and binomial of *G. barbadense*. Paul A. Fryxell (1968b, 378-82) did an extensive study of the Linnaean binomials in *Gossypium*, including *G. barbadense*. He concluded that W. Wouters (1963) and Borssum Waalkes (1966) were correct when they stated that Linnaeus based his application of *G. barbadense* on a drawing (fig. 3-1) by Leonard Plukenet (1642-1706). The specimen used for this drawing is on deposit in the Sloane Herbarium in the British Museum of Natural History in London.[1] Fryxell disputed Prokhanov's (1959) rejection of Linnaeus's *G. barbadense* to the South American cotton. In addition, Fryxell contended that since the holotype[2] of *G. barbadense* was not extant, Linnaeus's application of *G. barbadense* based on Plukenet's figure was adequate, if not ideal, as the lectotype[3] of the South American cotton. Further, noted Fryxell, Linnaeus examined the Plukenet Herbarium in London on July 27, 1736, so he had the opportunity to have seen Plukenet's specimen.

In discussing the missing holotype, Fryxell dismissed that contention by Prokhanov (1959) and G. K. Brizicky (1967, 152-57) that Linnaeus did not see a specimen of South American cotton. They claim that a specimen grown at Uppsala, cited by Linnaeus, and labeled as "barbadense" in his collection in the Linnaean Herbarium in the British Museum of Natural History does not conform to the South American cotton, and therefore *G. barbadense* L. cannot be typified and must be rejected as a *nomen ambiguum*.[4] Fryxell agreed that the specimen cited by Linnaeus was not South American cotton, and, in fact, represented two plants, though mounted on the same herbarium sheet. Moreover, both of these have five-lobed leaves and therefore do not conform to Linnaeus's description of *G. barbadense*.[5] Fryxell concluded, then, that "there was at least one *other* plant grown at Uppsala: one which Linnaeus described both in *Species Plantarum* and *Hortus Upsaliensis* as having 'foliis trilobis integerrimus', and which is the holotype (albeit missing) of *G. barbadense*. The holotype, then, was 'a plant grown at Uppsala.'"

The author accepts Fryxell's explanation that *Gossypium barbadense* L. should be the accepted application. In addition, *Gossypium barbadense* is universally used today to refer to the long-

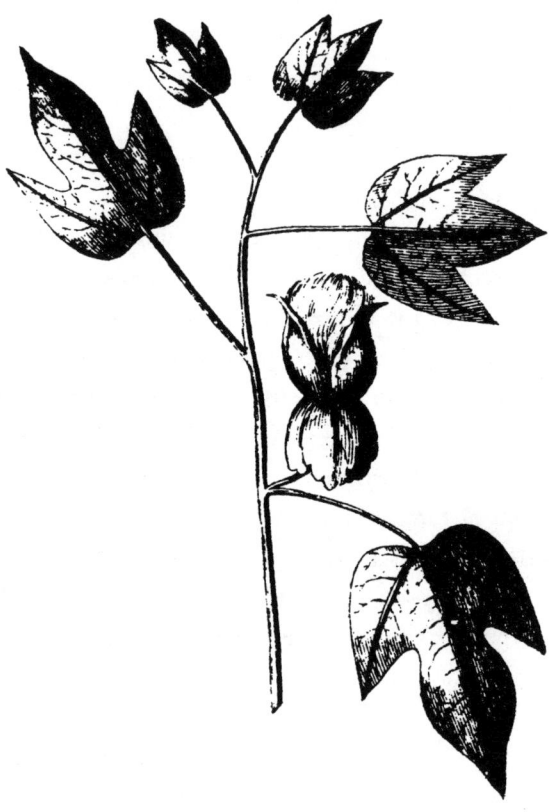

Figure 3-1. Plukenet's drawing of *G. barbadense* L.
(Leonard Plukenet, *Phytographia*, 1692, 3: t. 188. f. 1)

staple cotton that was the basis of sea island cotton and of present-day long-staple cottons. The use of any other name would lead to unnecessary confusion.

Genetics

Much of what we know about the genetics of *Gossypium barbadense*, and especially sea island cotton, was discovered in the second half of the 1900s. The evolving field of molecular genetics and cytology has allowed science to understand and explain concepts about the genetics of *G. barbadense* and its cultivars that were known only superficially or in broad terms during the early history of its culture.

Gossypium barbadense of Linnaeus, and the other major commercial species of the New World, *Gossypium hirsutum* L., upland cotton, are tetraploids. In addition, there are four other New World tetraploid species (one each endemic to Hawaii, the Galapagos, Brazil and Mexico; see figure 3-3). A tetraploid is one type of polyploid. Polyploidy[6] is manifest when a cell or individual contains three or more haploid[7] sets of chromosomes. In the case of a tetraploid, the cell or individual contains four haploid sets of chromosomes.

It has been well established on the basis of research by many geneticists and cytologists, but especially on the pioneering work by J. O. Beasley (1940a; 1940b), that the New World tetraploids have an AD constitution (fig. 3-2). That is to say, the tetraploids contain one genome that is similar to those found in the Old World A-genome diploid[8] species and one genome that is similar to those found in the New World D-genome diploid species. Since the tetraploids have whole chromosome sets from different species, they are called allotetraploids, the term that will hereafter be used to refer to the New World tetraploids. The origin of the New World allotetraploids is diagrammed in figure 3-2:

The explanation of figure 3-2 is as follows: Both diploid parents produced gametes by meiosis that contained a haploid set of chromosomes (13 chromosomes). Fertilization produced a sterile,[9] diploid hybrid (26 chromosomes) that contained a haploid set of chromosomes from each parent. Fertilization was followed by doubling of the chromosome number (polyploidy) that produced a fertile allotetraploid (with 52 chromosomes). This fertile tetraploid became the ancestral progenitor, through speciation and radiation, of the six New World allotetraploids.

Gossypium barbadense, along with the other New World allotetraploids, contains a diploid chromosome complement (with 26 chromosomes) from an Old World A-genome cotton and a diploid chromosome complement (with 26 chromosomes) from a New World D-genome cotton to form an allotetraploid with 52 chromosomes. These allotetraploid species can hybridize with each other and produce fertile offspring, but not with the diploid species.

There has been much speculation over the identity of the two parents of the New World allotetraploids. Endrizzi et al. (1985, 330) thoroughly reviewed the problem and concluded: "It is now a firmly established cytogenetic fact that the progenitor genomes of the allotetraploid species were most similar to the genomes existing in the Old World *G. herbaceum* and

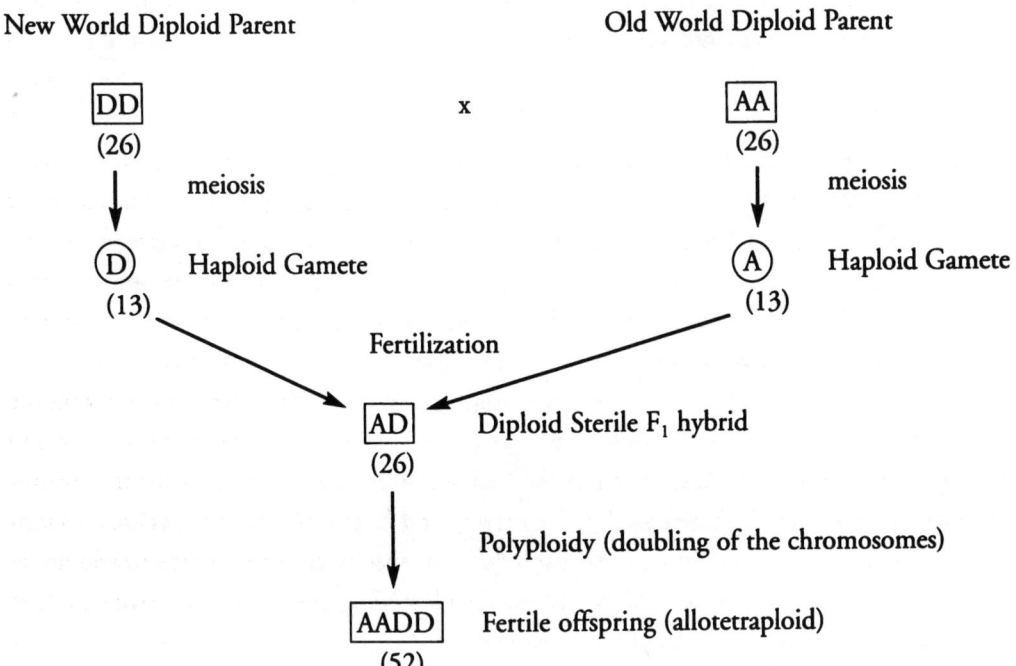

Figure 3-2. Diagram of the origin of allotetraploid in *Gossypium*. D = haploid chromosome complement (13 chromosomes) of diploid New World species; A = haploid chromosome complement (13 chromosomes) of diploid Old World species.

G. raimondii of the New World." They further stated: "Additional new diploid species have been identified, particularly in the D-genome group, but their taxonomic status does not question the current concept of the origin of the allotetraploids."

Endrizzi et al. also contended that the six New World allotetraploids had a monophyletic origin. Some scientists had proposed a polyphyletic origin of the tetraploids, the theory being that each species originated from independent hybridizations between the original AA ancestor and different New Worlds diploids (there are several New World diploid species). But based on the large body of cytological data involving the allotetraploids, most students of *Gossypium* evolution today postulate a monophyletic origin. This theory states that there was one original hybridization that produced the AADD progenitor from which the six allotetraploids originated.

Major questions that have puzzled historians about the New World cottons are: When, from where, and how many times was *Gossypium* introduced into the New World? Hypotheses range from sympaty in Gondwanaland a hundred million years ago to transport of AA cottons across the ocean by prehistoric raftsmen. Although the question may never be answered to everyone's satisfaction, the work by J. F. Wendel and V. A. Albert (1992) has added new information on these questions.

Wendel and Albert reported that the oldest malvaceous pollen (*Hibiscus* type) was from the upper Eocene, 46-38 million years before the present (mybp), in sediments from Brazil and Venezuela. In Africa, the earliest record was of Oligocene age (38-25 mybp), while in Australia there are no reports of malvaceous pollen prior to the Miocene (25-12 mybp). These data suggested to Wendel and Albert that the first, albeit tentative, estimate of the relative antiquity of *Gossypium* is that of Eocene age or younger. They then recognized that three major clades[10] among diploid species of cotton evolved corresponding to three different continents: Australia (C-, G-genomes), the Americas (D-genome), and Africa (A-, E-, and F-genomes).

The Gondwanaland supercontinent began to split by 130 mybp, when Australia, India, and Madagascar separated from Africa and South America. By 33 mybp, a paleocontinental reconstruction of the earth showed the African and Australian plates separated by several thousand kilometers of ocean. The most recent time *Gossypium* could have had a continuous Australian-African distribution was about 130-120 mybp, or about three times more ancient that the oldest recorded malvacean pollen. Wendel and Albert concluded, then, that divergence between African and Australian cottons occurred via transoceanic dispersal of seeds rather than by vicariance.[11] They noted that the seeds of *Gossypium* have been demonstrated impermeable to sea water and remain viable after prolonged immersion (Stephens 1958). They could not make a determination, however, between an African or Australian origin of cotton.

Wendel and Albert concluded that two predomestication introductions of *Gossypium* occurred to the New World. The first was a very early transoceanic dispersal of seeds from Africa of an Old World A-genome diploid species, leading to the evolution of the New World D-genome diploid species in northwestern Mexico followed by radiation outward of these species. Later, a second transoceanic dispersal occurred of an Old World A-genome diploid species from Asia[12] to the Pacific coast of Middle America or South America, which became the A-genome ancestor of the New World allotetraploids.

Hybridization of the DD diploid Old World parent and AA diploid New World parent to produce the AADD allotetraploid ancestor probably occurred only once. This hybridization (followed by polyploidy) probably occurred on the Pacific coast of either Mesoamerica or South America. From this initial hybrid stock and subsequent radiation and speciation, the six New World allotetraploids, including *G. barbadense* and *G. hirsutum*, eventually diverged during extensive natural migrations in tropical America and through widely scattered islands in the tropical Pacific. Domestication of the wild allotetraploids of *G. barbadense* and *G. hirsutum* occurred at a later date.

The times of the two dispersals of cotton to the New World are less certain. Wendel and Albert (1992) did not give or suggest times for these two dispersals. Since there is no fossil record and the archeological record is of little help, dates for these dispersals may never be fixed with certainty.

Fryxell, however, did suggest a time period for the second transoceanic dispersal. He gave convincing evidence that the allotetraploids of *Gossypium* originated independently of man, and concluded that early New World farmers *found* tetraploid cottons and domesticated them; they did not *produce* them. He gave the following reasons (1979, 164):

1. The great diversity of the allotetraploids into several species implies existence over a longer period of time than is available since the origin of agriculture in the New World.

2. The geographical dispersion of the six species of allotetraploids (fig. 3-3) argues for the evolution and dispersal of the allotetraploids over a longer period of time than is available since the development of early agriculture in the New World.

3. Certain characteristics of wild, or apparently wild, populations of *G. barbadense*, such as seed germinability and lint abundance, occur in a state similar to what one might expect in a "raw" allotetraploid.

4. The habitat of the wild allotetraploids is distinctive; they grow mostly in littoral or littoral-derived habitats, which together with their impermeable seed coats explains their wide dispersal on ocean currents. Feral cottons would not have had this distinctive ecological distribution.

From the above facts, Fryxell concluded that the origin of the allotetraploids was in the middle Pleistocene, 1/10 to 1 million years before the present, and, consequently, the second dispersal of the A-genome seeds must have occurred just prior to this period. Wendel (1989), in an earlier study, gave a possible time frame for the origin of the allotetraploids. His studies on variation in the maternally-inherited chloroplast genome suggested that the allotetraploid cotton ancestor originated within the last 1-2 million years, with subsequent rapid evolution and diversification throughout the New World tropics. Both of these dates argue for the evolution and original dispersal of the allotetraploids without the influence of man. At a later date, *G.*

CHAPTER THREE

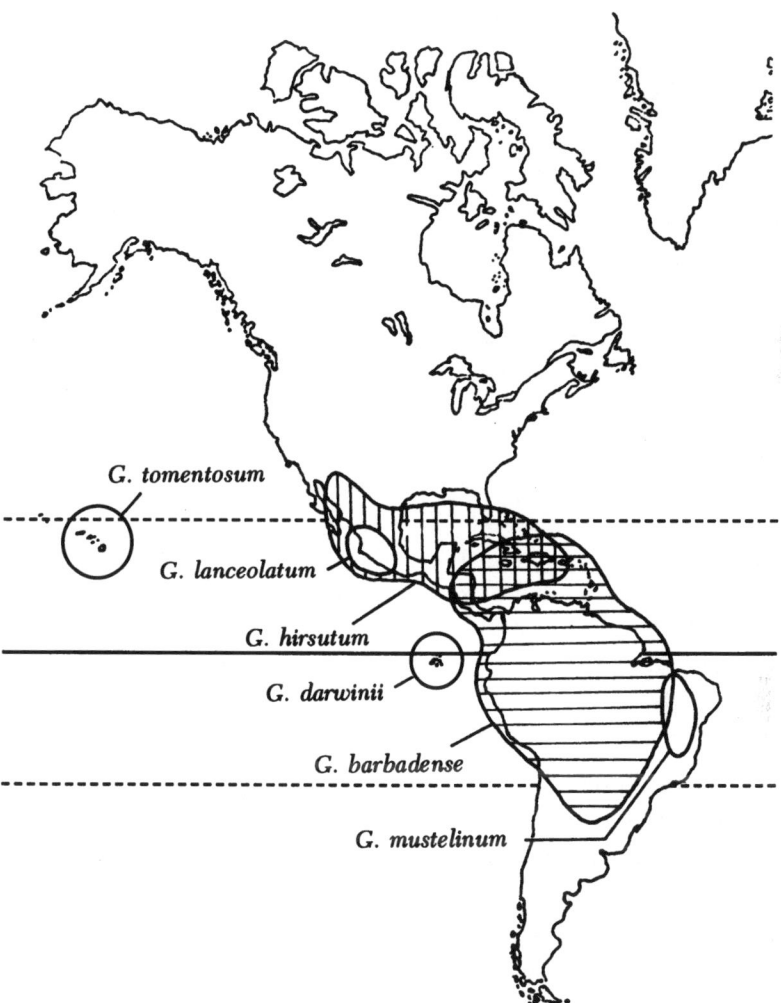

Figure 3-3. Geographical distribution of the six New World allotetraploid species of *Gossypium* prior to 1492 (Fryxell 1979, 165)

barbadense and *G. hirsutum* were carried from their indigenous habitat by Native Americans through domestication.

1. The citation for Plukenet's specimen in the British Museum of Natural History in London is: vol. 100, f. 105.
2. A holotype is the one specimen or other element used by the author or designated by him as the basis of the first published description of a taxonomic species and later designated as the type specimen. As long as the holotype is extant, it automatically fixes the application of the name concerned.
3. The lectotype is a specimen or other element selected from the original material to serve as a nomenclatural type when no holotype was designated at the time of publication or as long as the holotype is missing.
4. *Nomen ambiguum* (name ambiguous) is a name used in so many different senses that it has become a long-persistent source of error.
5. The author examined the herbarium sheet containing Linnaeus's two specimens on July 23, 2003, and concurs with Fryxell and other scientists that the two specimens are not South American cotton.
6. Polyploidy is a process in plants when a cell or organism comes to have more than two homologous sets of chromosomes. The process occurs by different methods too complicated to go into detail in this book. In the case of the allotetraploid cottons, polyploidy resulted in plants with four sets of homologous chromosomes, one diploid set from the Old World parent and one diploid set from the New Wold parent.
7. Chromosomes occur in pairs called homologous pairs. In diploid cottons, there are 26 homologous pairs. One set of the 26 pairs would be 13. When a cell or organism of cotton contains only one set of these chromosomes, it would contain 13 chromosomes. This is the haploid number of chromosomes. The haploid number, then, of all the Old World and New World cottons is 13.
8. When a cell or organism of diploid cottons both sets of chromosomes in a cell, this is the diploid condition. All the Old World and New World diploid cottons contain 26 chromosomes.
9. The hybrid is sterile because chromosome from two different genomes are incompatible as they cannot successfully pair during meiosis.
10. A clade is a group or species that includes all descendants of one common ancestor.
11. Vicariance is a process that produces vicariads, which are closely allied but allopatric taxa. Allopatry is the occurrence or origin of species or populations in different geographical regions. In layman's terms, the closely allied taxa of cottons in Africa and Australia resulted from seeds dispersed from one to the other (in which direction is not known). The populations did not arise independently in each country.
12. Whether this second transoceanic dispersal was from Asia or Africa has been subject to debate. Hutchinson et al. (1947) strongly state that it was from Asia: "Nevertheless, the distributions of the New World species together with the well-established fact that the diploid cottons are much more ancient in southern Asia than in Africa, leave no room for doubt that the migration of the diploid species was across the Pacific and not across the Atlantic." Wendel and Albert (1992) state in their abstract: "The maternal phylogenetic hypothesis and area cladogram suggest the possibility that New World allopolyploids [allotetraploids] originated following a trans-Pacific transfer of an ancestral A-genome taxon to the Pacific coast of Mesoamerica or South America." In addition to the compelling evidence cited by these scholars, Asia seems more likely as the source of the A-genome since it is difficult to hypothesize a transoceanic transfer of seeds from Africa around the tip of South America to Mesoamerica or South America.

The Worldwide Dispersal of *Gossypium barbadense* L.

This chapter traces the major dispersal routes of *G. barbadense* from its native area of speciation in Peru and Ecuador to its historical and present range worldwide.

Tracing the route of *G. barbadense* necessitates an understanding of its basic genetic groupings. R. G. Percy and J. F. Wendel (1990, 532-533) categorized these as follows:
  1. Wild Specimens. Few truly wild specimens of *G. barbadense* are thought to exist.
  2. Dooryard Cottons. These cottons differ from wild cottons in having a history of casual use by local peoples throughout South and Central America and the Caribbean. They are not grown in large populations, but occur as single plants found near habitations. Dooryard cottons have received little population selection and are thought to derive in many cases directly from local, wild progenitors.
  3. Landraces. Plants grown on a commercial scale and derived from locally available cottons. They are often short-day flowering perennials, as are the wild and dooryard forms.
  4. Improved Cultivars. These cottons display the greatest evidence of manipulation for agronomic properties and displacement from their geographic regions of origin. Although cultivation has imposed a degree of morphological and physiological uniformity on commercial *G. barbadense*, a fair amount of cultivar variation remains (e.g., in environmental adaptations and several growth and fiber characteristics). With few exceptions, modern improved cultivars are day-neutral annuals with long-staple fiber.

Ancestral Home

Gossypium barbadense is one of the two allotetraploid species (the other is *G. hirsutum*) grown commercially in the world for the production of cotton lint. It is cultivated today throughout temperate and tropical regions, with production areas in the Commonwealth of Independent States (Tajikistan, Turkmenistan and Uzbekistan, formally part of the USSR),

China, Israel, India, Egypt, Sudan, the United States, Australia, and Peru. Yet this worldwide commercial crop had its beginning as a wild, short-day flowering perennial shrub in a dry, tropical region of South America west of the Andes, in southwest Ecuador and northwest Peru. Percy and Wendel (1990) concluded that Peru and Ecuador were the ancestral home of *G. barbadense*. Their work indicated that this region of South America contained the greatest genetic variability, and is therefore the probable ancestral home of the species.

S. G. Stephens and M. E. Mosely (1974) gave earlier evidence that Ecuador and Peru were the ancestral home of *G. barbadense*. Wild forms of *G. barbadense* have been found only in a narrow zone immediately north and south of the Guayas Estuary in Ecuador and on an island offshore from Manta. Stephens and Mosely speculated that *G. barbadense* made a sudden, initial appearance around 2500 BC. Seeds, fiber samples and boll parts recovered from four preceramic sites in the Ancon-Chillon area of Peru, and from a time sequence from approximately 1750 BC, were compared with living forms of *G. barbadense*, both wild and cultivated, collected from coastal areas of Ecuador and Peru. The researchers concluded that the archeological cotton belonged to *G. barbadense*. Further, this archeological cotton exhibited morphological features transitional between the wild cottons found in the Guayas Estuary complex and the primitive dooryard forms found today in coastal Peru and Ecuador. The archeological samples, then, represented a very early stage in the domestication of *G. barbadense*.

Stephens and Mosely's research in Peru also documented that *G. barbadense* was used for primitive textiles. On the Peruvian coast, *G. barbadense* entered the archeological record as fishnets and other cordage in a pre-agricultural fishing village. Cotton bolls from around 2500 BC in northern Peru showed transitional forms between the wild plants and improved cultivars. Sometime around 1800 or 1700 BC, two important events spurred the domestication process. First was the invention of the heddle.[1] This simple technological device allowed for the mechanical manipulation of warp elements (instead of being done by hand). The heddle opened the era of mass-produced woven textiles which obviously called for more cotton production. Second was the development of canal irrigation, which replaced flood-water farming and opened large stretches of the desert to cultivation. The invention of the heddle and canal irrigation allowed for a many-fold rise in agricultural activity which combined to affect the nature of the cultural processes operating on the cotton plant, and was followed by an explosion in spinning and weaving. The pre-Inca city-states of the Peruvian oases were among the highest civilizations of the New World. Elaborate cotton textiles were found in mummy bundles and other grave goods. Weavers used cotton lint of various natural shades and often combined cotton lint with wool and other fibers.

Dispersion into the Caribbean

Pre-Columbian by Native Americans
With this early demonstration that cotton lint could be spun and woven into primitive

cloth, *barbadense* cotton domestication spread from its ancestral home into northeastern South America. Here it underwent a secondary stage of domestication that was followed by dispersal into Central America, the Pacific, and the Caribbean, where it came into contact with *G. hirsutum*. Dolores R. Piperno and Deborah M. Pearsall (1998, 150) stated:

> *We think it likely that the radiation of the species… occurred after domestication via the house gardens of tropical forest horticulturists. Although cotton would have been abundant in its habitat—the xerophytic areas of the outer coastal plain—groups occupying better watered inland valleys would have needed to grow this useful plant to ensure a supply. A rapid spread into the interior and the low-elevation Andes is likely.*

The archeological record is silent on the timing of the dispersion of *G. barbadense* into the Caribbean. However, by 1492, perennial short-day flowering *G. barbadense* was a common dooryard plant throughout the West Indies. On Columbus' first voyage, he encountered dooryard cotton, which was likely *G. barbadense*, among the Lucayo of the Bahamas and the Arawak of the Greater Antilles. He reported in his journal on October 12, 1492 that "the natives came swimming towards us, and brought us parrots and balls of cotton thread." When he landed at Cuba, he found that the natives used hammocks and other things made of cotton. He later found cotton articles in Carib gardens of the Lesser Antilles.

Samuel Wilson (1997, 135) cited a passage written by Fernando Colón in 1571 that documented the use of cotton as a wild crop in the West Indies (the brackets are Wilson's):

> *[The cotton plants grow] in the fields, like the roses, and open by themselves when they are ripe, but not all at the same time, because on the same plant one could see a small bud, and another opened, and another fallen from ripeness. From [these] plants the Indians took great quantities to the ships, and for a strap of leather they would give a full basket, although to tell the truth, none of them used them for clothing, but only to make their nets and their beds, which they call hammocks, and to weave the skirts of the women, with which they cover their immodest parts.*

Wilson also quoted Diego Alvarez Chanca (Wilson 1997, 135). There is no original date for Chanca's manuscript, but it is obviously around the same time as Colón's (the brackets are Wilson's):

> *[T]rees bearing very fine wool have been seen, such that those who know the art say that they would be able to make good cloth from it. There are so many of these trees that the caravels could be loaded with their wool, although it is laborious to pick, because the trees are full of spines; but surely some ingenious method for picking could be found. There is an infinite amount of cotton from perpetual trees as big as peach trees.*

From the description of the cotton plants by Colón and Chanca, they are most certainly referring to *G. barbadense*.

Barbados was the first West Indian colony to grow *barbadense* cotton on a commercial scale. Barbados is the most easterly of the West Indian islands, 100 miles east of the chain of islands known as the Lesser Antilles, and technically outside of the Caribbean Sea. Mainly of coral formation, Barbados was not mountainous, like most of the neighboring islands, and most of its land could be cultivated. Archeological evidence confirmed the historical evidence that Barbados was inhabited by Amerindians as late as the beginning of the sixteenth century. In 1625, the *Olive*, an English ship homeward bound from Brazil, stopped at Barbados. Captain John Powell decided to explore the island, and found it suitable for development. He claimed Barbados for the English Crown. Powell's employers were merchant brothers Sir William and Sir Peter Courteen. They decided to establish a colony on Barbados and sent the ship *William and John*, captained by John Powell's brother Henry. Henry Powell landed there in 1627, bringing ten African slaves. A series of additional settlers arrived in Barbados over the next few years. Political and social life on Barbados was in a state of flux and uncertainty during this early colonization. However, in 1641, with the appointment of Philip Bell as administrator of the island, the colony began to advance economically and socially, and became stable enough for commercial agriculture to develop.

The first commercial crops grown in Barbados were tobacco and cotton. Sugar cane production began in 1640 and quickly caused an end to tobacco planting because the value of sugar was three times that of tobacco. Exactly when cotton production began is unknown. In 1657, Richard Ligon wrote in his *History of the Island of Barbadoes* (page 40):

About a hundred sail of ships yearly visit this Island, and receive during the time of their stay in the Harbours, for their sustenance, the native Victuals growing in the Island, such as I have already named; besides what they carry away, and what is carried away by Planters of the Isle, that visit other parts of the world. The commodities this Island trades in, are Indigo, Cotton-wool, Tobacco, Sugar, Ginger, and Fustick-wood.

By the late 1700s and early 1800s, perennial *barbadense* cotton was a major commercial crop in the West Indies (fig. 4-1). The West Indies in the 1700s was the chief source from which England derived its cotton supply. The finest cotton brought to the English market at that time was raised on the island of Tobago, between the years 1789 and 1792.

Of special interest to the story of sea island cotton was the introduction of *G. barbadense* to the Bahamas. Thomas Spalding (1835, 37) gave an account of the beginning of *G. barbadense* as a commercial crop in the Bahamas:

She [England] therefore from her many colonies, selected Nova Scotia and the Bahamas Islands as the only colonies where a provision in land was to be made for the loyal men who had clung to

CHAPTER FOUR

Figure 4-1. *Barbadense* cotton in the West Indies. On the right, cotton is being picked from the tall plant. On the left, cotton is being ginned with a roller gin (note the flywheels) and the lint is being manually pressed into bags. (Diderot, *Encyclopédie*)

her fortune through blood and in ruin... and when the southern colonists were landed with their faithful slaves upon the rocks of the Bahama Islands, in looking round for something upon which might employ themselves, the new interest in which cotton had awakened, in consequence of Arkwright's machinery, reached them... There is a small island in the Caribbean sea called Anguilla, which had been long known to produce the best cotton in the West Indies. The new settlers in the Bahama Islands procured cotton seed to commence the culture with Anguilla. They had in the year 1785 introduced the culture of cotton upon several of the Bahama Islands successfully, particularly upon Long Island and Exuma.

Post-Columbian by Spanish

J. B. Hutchinson and H. L. Manning (1945) concluded that there was a second dispersal of *G. barbadense* into the Caribbean, this time by the Spanish. After the arrival of Europeans, dispersal of *G. barbadense* from its ancestral home occurred into Argentina and Paraguay. Then, Spanish carried seeds of this West Andean gene pool into the Caribbean. The significance of their conclusion will be covered in the following chapter.

Early Dispersion from the West Indies into the Southern United States

The historical record is uncertain as to who, when, where and how many times *G. barbadense* was brought into the southern states prior to 1785 when it was converted to sea island cotton. But the historical record does indicate that *G. barbadense* was introduced several times from the West Indies to the Atlantic Coast for domestic use prior to 1785. These early plants were perennial, short-day (see next chapter for discussion of short-day vs. day-neutral concept); the conversion to annual, day-neutral sea island cotton came in 1785-86.

There was certainly the opportunity for seed from the islands of the West Indies to have been carried to the southeastern seaboard. In 1668, the Lords Proprietors of England financed an expedition to establish a colony in Carolina. A fleet of three ships sailed from England in August of 1669. The ships stopped in Barbados, where a number of Barbadians joined the expedition. Only one ship, the *Carolina*, reached Carolina, landing along a bluff on the Ashley River. Although the initial colony had only a few Barbadians, over the next two years about half of the white settlers and more than half of the enslaved blacks came from Barbados. Later, more settlers came from other islands in the West Indies. Early on, then, ample opportunity existed whereby colonists could have brought seeds of *G. barbadense* from the West Indies.

In an article by Nicholas Turnbull (1917, 39-45), he accepted as true a report that *barbadense* cotton was first cultivated successfully for domestic use by John Earle of Skidaway Island, south of Savannah, Georgia, as early as 1767. Turnbull's article contains the following account from the October 15, 1799 *Columbian Museum and Savannah Advertiser*, which adds credulity to the fact that black-seed cotton (*G. barbadense*) was planted for domestic use:

CHAPTER FOUR

Cotton planting in this country is of early date; the same kind of cotton as is now cultivated on the Sea Islands, called the black seed cotton, was, in the year 1767, planted as a crop by Mr. John Earle, on the Island of Skidaway... The old inhabitants on the island always raised it to perfection, and there was hardly a family but what planted it for domestic use. It is seen in the recollection of some that previous to 1767 cotton was an article at market, and purchased by the ancient mercantile house of Smith and Gordon, and remitted to England.

In 1733, General James Oglethorpe sailed from England for the purpose of founding a colony where the oppressed and unfortunate—principally the inmates of the debtors' prisons—might find refuge and begin life anew. Seventeen miles from the mouth of the Savannah River he founded the city of Savannah, and named the colony Georgia. Records show that in the following year *barbadense* cotton was grown in the gardens of the settlers.

Mart Stewart (1996, 117) gave one account of this garden cotton:

A variety of this long-staple 'tree cotton,' which was a perennial, may have been planted as early as 1738 in Georgia by the Salzburgers in their garden, but it was killed by the cold weather in winter. It remained a garden plant, kept as a curiosity or for domestic use, until late in the eighteenth century.

Another early account that undoubtedly refers to *barbadense* cotton was given by William Bartram. In March 1774, Bartram left Savannah for Florida. He visited the islands along the Georgia coast and wrote:

The soil of these islands appears to be particularly favorable to the culture of indigo and cotton, and there are on some few large plantations for the cultivation and manufacture of those valuable species. The cotton is planted only by the poorer class of people, just enough for their family consumption; they plant two species of it, the annual and the West Indian; the former is low, and planted every year; the balls of this are very large, and the phlox long, strong, and perfectly white; the West Indian, is a tall perennial plant, the stalk somewhat shrubby, several of which rise up from the same root for several years successively, the stems of the former year being killed by the winter frosts. The balls of this latter species are not quite so large as those of the herbaceous cotton; but the phlox, or wool, is long, extremely fine, silky, and white. A plantation of this kind will last for several years, with moderate labour and care, whereas the annual sort is planted every year.

André Michaux (1805) made the following observations in his chapter on the "Low part of the Carolinas and Georgia":

The soil most adapted for the culture of cotton is in the isles situate upon the coast. Those which belong to the state of Georgia produce the best of cotton, which is known in the French trade by the name of Georgia cotton, fine wool, and in England by that of Sea Island cotton. The seed of this kind of cotton is of a deep black, and the wool fine and very long... The cotton planters have particularly to dread the frosts that set in very early, and that frequently do great damage to the crops by freezing one half of the stalks, so that the cotton has not an opportunity to ripen.

Kinsey Burden (1844a, 161; 163) gave another account of domestic use of these earlier introductions of *barbadense* cotton prior to 1785-86:

It is out of my power to say positively, who the individual was, that first introduced the black-seed cotton, or the green-seed cotton into South Carolina, but I know, that both these kinds of cotton were cultivated on my father's plantation at Burden's Island for domestic manufacture, as early as the year 1788 or 1789, and I do not know, that he did not cultivate them earlier than those year's, and I cannot say, that he was not the one to introduce them into the State.

...My father and his family partly, and his negroes entirely, were soon after he removed to the country, clad in homespuns woven in his own loom, of materials taken from the backs of his sheep, and the product of his cotton patches planted for domestic purposes.

In 1790, or 1791, I saw at the plantation of our next neighbor, Mr. Jonathan Fickling, about the eighth of an acre of black-seed cotton, which the proprietor informed me he planted to make nets, and fishing lines, and thread. From the growth, fruitfulness, and early maturity of the plants, then bent down with the load of pods, I judge that cotton to have been the same kind of common black-seed cotton, afterwards generally cultivated on the islands and seacoasts of South Carolina and Georgia. And very probably it was the same kind that my father and others cultivated during the revolutionary war, for domestic use.

From the historical record cited above, it appears clear that *barbadense* cotton was grown on the Georgia sea islands and possibly the South Carolina sea islands for domestic use before 1785. Because they were pre-adapted from the introgression of *G. hirsutum* germplasm for day-neutrality, and growing as dooryard cottons, at least some of these early introductions were probably marginally day-neutral, and, as perennials, persisted year after year, and produced some ripe fruits before frost. Although they possessed a fine fiber, they did not have the fiber quality that later came to be known as sea island cotton. There was little effort to commercially cultivate these early introductions, partly because of the Revolutionary War, but also because rice, indigo, and tobacco were already established crops; the overseas market had not fully materialized; and flower and fruit production were limited because the plants were primarily short-day flowering.

Beginning of Commercial Crops of *G. barbadense* in South Carolina, Georgia and Florida

With the Revolutionary War over, planters in Georgia and Carolina began to expand agriculture and to produce commercial crops on a more intensive scale. An expanding overseas market made cotton an attractive cash crop, and planters began to experiment with cotton production. With Whitney's invention of the wire-toothed gin in 1793, upland cotton (*G. hirsutum*) became a commercial crop throughout the South.

In 1785, seeds of *G. barbadense* were brought to St. Simons Island in Georgia from the Bahamas and led to the establishment of four market classes of *barbadense* long-staple cotton: sea island, mains, Santee long, and Georgia and Florida interior sea island cotton. At this time, overseas buyers began to show an interest in *barbadense* cotton because of its long staple and fineness.

The first market class of *barbadense* cotton established was sea island cotton. Sea island planters began its commercial cultivation and made the region one of the wealthiest plantation areas anywhere. Sea island cotton, from its initial development in Georgia in 1786, spread from the sea islands of Georgia into the sea islands of Florida and South Carolina. In South Carolina it continued to be grown until the boll weevil ended the crop in 1920.

Santee long cotton was established when seeds from the early crops in Georgia or South Carolina were carried to Berkeley County. Santee long was grown in a restricted area from the headwaters of the Cooper River across the country to the Santee River, and as high as Vance's Ferry in Orangeburg County (fig. 6-1). In 1830, the planters in the Santee long area began obtaining seed from the sea island planters. Santee long cultivation survived the Civil War, but on a very reduced scale. The few crops left were ended by the boll weevil. Santee long always sold at a discount compared to sea island cotton.

Mains was grown on the mainland of South Carolina, inland from the sea islands. Like Santee long, it always sold at a discount to sea island cotton. Hybridization with upland cottons and lack of seed selection caused a lesser-quality fiber. Little information is found in the literature on mains cotton. The author believes it was planted by sea island planters who sought to increase the size of their crops.

After the Civil War, the industry struggled in Florida, but survived, becoming concentrated in north central Florida (fig. 6-5) where it was grown as interior sea island cotton. Georgia planters by this time had abandoned sea island cotton on the sea islands and had also moved cultivation of long-staple cotton inland. The boll weevil ended the crop in 1920. However, in 1934, sea island cotton seed preserved at the Pee Dee Experimental Station in Florence, South Carolina, was sent to Florida and Georgia where it was again grown as Georgia and Florida interior sea island cotton until the 1940s.

Dispersion into Africa

Barbadense cotton was not native to Africa or Europe. However, by the close of the eighteenth century, some forms of *barbadense* cotton were growing on both of these continents. The source of the cottons is much debated and may never be known with certainty. Only two African countries, Egypt and Sudan, were/are major producers of long-staple cotton.

Both Egypt and Sudan have optimum sunshine and temperature for cotton growing; however, the lack of rainfall prevented large-scale production. The scarcity of water was overcome by irrigation from the Nile River in the last half of the nineteenth century and first quarter of the twentieth century. Afterwards, long-staple cotton flourished.

Egypt

The story of long-staple cotton in Egypt began with Jumel's tree cotton, of which S. G. Stephens (1974) gave a lengthy account. Louis Alexis Jumel, a French engineer employed by the Egyptian government, found a single plant growing in the Maho Bey garden in Cairo sometime between 1817 and 1819. The plant was a perennial, grown for decorative purposes, and was the same type that had been established in Egypt for some time but had not been developed into a crop. Jumel was impressed with the quality of the lint of the Cairo plant, and brought it to the attention of Khedive Mohammed Ali with a view to its cultivation for commercial purposes. The seeds of the original plant were saved, and the strain was multiplied and introduced into small-scale cultivation by 1820. Its cultivation was so successful that it rapidly replaced existing commercial types in Egypt. Jumel's cotton had a long, fine and strong brown lint which was readily separated from its naked seed.

Presumably, the original Jumel's tree cotton was perennial and day-neutral. According to E. R. J. Owen (1969), Jumel's cotton was planted in March-April and harvested beginning in June-July. In Cairo (latitude 30°), this would imply that Jumel's cotton was day-neutral. In regard to its perennial nature, Lasteyrie (1808) stated that in the late eighteenth century cottons were grown as annuals on some Mediterranean islands (Malta, Sicily, etc.). Most of the plants he described were probably annual forms of *G. herbacium* native to the Old World. But he did suggest that other species, some of New World origin, were also in cultivation at that time. Lasteyrie wrote: "I have not seen the annual cotton in Spain. That which is cultivated is perennial (vivace). It lasts for eight to ten years, if it is not caught by frosts."

Stephens concluded that perennial day-neutral forms of *barbadense* cotton originating in the New World were established in countries bordering the Mediterranean Sea by the close of the eighteenth century. These plants could have provided the source material for the subsequent development of Egyptian cottons. Jumel's cotton was probably one of these forms. Stephens suggested that these plants were introduced via the North Atlantic route from the Spanish Main into European ports and then into the Mediterranean, and possibly into the Levant.

Encouraged by the success of Jumel's tree cotton, Khedive Ali began to import seeds of different cottons, notably sea island from America. It is presumed that the Jumel naturally hybridized with sea island (W. L. Balls, 1912), resulting in a "medley of hybrids in the mixed Jumel stock." Selection within this medley resulted in the development around 1860 of an annual cultivar named early Ashmouni (from the valley of Ashmoun) from which all later Egyptian long-staple cottons were derived (McGowan 1961, 13). Early Ashmouni was superior to Jumel on account of its prolific and uniform lint, and had a creamy-brown color. It spread throughout lower Egypt and eventually into upper Egypt and the Sudan where it was grown under irrigation.

The outbreak of the American Civil War spurred cotton production in Egypt because cotton supplies to Manchester, England were cut off. The Egyptian government backed production of machinery for cultivation and ginning, improvements in seed quality, and sponsored irrigation projects. Consequently, the country experienced an economic revolution in the years 1861-66. The cotton industry became soundly established in Egypt and was able to insure European markets a high-quality, dependable product. Production continued in the post-war years and Egyptian long-staple cotton has been important ever since.

The next major cultivar of long-staple Egyptian cotton was Mit Afifi, which was discovered in a field of early Ashmouni in 1882. It was believed to have been a natural cross with sea island cotton. Mit Afifi soon replaced early Ashmouni in the Nile Delta.

Two more cultivars followed. Sakel was selected out of a consignment of Mit Afifi seed in 1901 by John Sakellarides (the cotton is sometimes referred to as Sakellarides), a Greek merchant who noticed a few seeds with longer and silkier lint than the bulk. Sakel was late to mature, had a low lint percentage, and was relatively low yielding; it was second only to sea island, being light cream in color, with a comparatively uniform staple of 1 1/2", and fine, strong lint. Sakel reached its peak of importance in 1922.

Giza 7 was selected in 1922 from early Ashmouni by a plant breeder working for the Egyptian Ministry of Agriculture. Giza 7 was productive, especially in high-wilt areas. The lint was nearly white, coarser and slightly shorter than Sakel, but finer and stronger than early Ashmouni. Giza 7 may have been a natural cross between early Ashmouni and Sakel, or between Ashmouni and a high-quality white cultivar.

During the period 1822-1922, the dominant cultivars in Egypt were Jumel, early Ashmouni, Mit Afifi, Giza 7 and Sakel. From 1922 onward, a bewildering array of annual cultivars emerged at Giza from a program of hybridization and selection, forming the basis of today's Egyptian long-staple cotton industry.

Sudan

Sudan became an independent nation in 1956 after 57 years of existence under the name of Anglo-Egyptian Sudan. On November 12, 1956, Sudan was admitted into the United Nations as a free independent dominion. Even though some long-staple cotton was produced earlier, Sudan became important in long-staple cotton production only in the crop year 1925-26 (while still Anglo-Egyptian Sudan) when 300,000 acres were brought into irrigation by the completion of the Makwar Dam. The dam, located 160 miles south of Khartoum on the Blue Nile River, provided water for the Gezira irrigation project, an area of about a million acres on the plain lying between the White Nile and Blue Nile rivers. Sakel was the cultivar planted in the Gezira plain, and by 1956, 585,000 bales were harvested.

Modern Dispersion into the West Indies

J. B. Hutchinson and H. L. Manning (1945) documented the introduction of the annual sea island cotton into the West Indies. They said that, in the West Indies, cotton was a major crop in the latter part of the eighteenth century and early years of the nineteenth century. This cotton was a perennial form of *G. barbadense* derived from original plants established in the West Indies prior to Columbus. Sugar cane replaced the cotton industry, and except for a short period during the Civil War, *barbadense* cotton practically vanished from the West Indies until the beginning of the twentieth century when competition from the subsidized European sugar beet industry resulted in a considerable reduction in sugar cane production. To alleviate the distress of the sugar cane producers, sea island cotton was introduced from South Carolina in 1902 as an alternative crop. Expert Carolina growers were employed to teach farmers of St. Vincent, Antigua, Barbados, and other islands how to grow sea island cotton. The seed was from the Rivers sea island cultivar. Seed selection produced numerous varieties of Barbados Rivers.

Success followed these efforts, and within a few years the Carolina farmers began to suffer from West Indian competition. The planters determined to abstain from selling their seed, not only to the West Indies, but to Georgia and Florida planters and their fellow sea islanders. As a result, much inferior sea island seed was planted, and, in addition, seed of upland varieties. Hybridization was the natural result and general deterioration of the sea island crop followed.

Another twist to the refusal of American growers to export further seed was given by Hutchinson and Manning (1945, 82):

We are indebted to Mr. Wolstwenholme for the information that the finest cotton of the Carolina Sea Islands was grown by Colonel Townsend at Bleak Hall (Edisto Island). Mr. Wolstwenholme states that the Bleak Hall crop was sold at a very high price, and no seed was sold off the plantation. A few seeds were picked out from the lint when a consignment of Bleak Hall cotton was received in Lancashier, and were sent to St. Vincent where they gave rise to BH stock. The stock was maintained by mass selection until brought into pedigree culture by Harland, and in 1915 enough was grown commercially '... to meet annually the requirements (100-120 bales of 360 lb.) of the Fine Spinners in regard to this fancy cotton.'

The growing of *G. barbadense* was discontinued in the West Indies around 1960.

American Southwest

American-Egyptian Pima long-staple cotton of the American Southwest came into existence because of the demand by manufacturers at the turn of the century that the United States Department of Agriculture develop a cotton product competitive in price and quality with

CHAPTER FOUR

Egyptian cotton. The cotton grown on the Nile around 1900 was coming into the United States at a rate exceeding 100,000 bales every year and was increasing in volume and popularity with American spinners. Since the United States grew more cotton of all kinds than the rest of the world combined, the increasing dependence on Egyptian cotton for supplies of a high-quality, high tensile strength long-staple variety was a matter of concern to the domestic industry.

Two factors were paramount in the establishment of the American-Egyptian cotton industry in the United States: the boll weevil, which ended long-staple cotton production in South Carolina, Georgia and Florida; and the need for long-staple cotton during World War I for tire cord and airplane fabric. Because warring countries were absorbing the available supplies of linen used for wing fabric, an acute shortage developed by the time the United States entered the war. A small flax crop of 1917 created an even greater shortage in the linen supply. Consequently, the government had to turn to a substitute material for linen in aircraft fabric: long-staple cotton.

Scientists in the USDA, in particular H. J. Webber, were convinced that long-staple Egyptian cotton could be produced in the irrigated valleys of the southwestern states. They reasoned that the southwestern valleys were similar to the long, hot and rainless summers of the Nile Delta, the main site of Egyptian long-staple cotton cultivation. Webber directed several unsuccessful attempts in 1901 to establish Egyptian cultivars near Yuma, Arizona. Webber's associate, Thomas H. Kearney, became involved in the experiments as well. In 1908, the Egyptian cotton project was moved from Yuma to the Gila River Pima Indian Reservation at Sacaton, Arizona. According to Smith and Cothern (1999, 159), "Kearney's initial breeding strategy was to 'acclimatize' Egyptian germplasm through single-plant selection within existing Egyptian introductions." Here, Kearney, working with E.W. Hudson, achieved success.

Once again *G. barbadense* crossed the Atlantic. The Mit Afifi variety of *G. barbadense* was brought from Egypt to the United States in 1902. In 1907, Kearney selected two exceptional plants from a row of Mit Afifi grown near Yuma, Arizona. In 1908, after several years of work, a cultivar named Yuma was segregated out. In 1912, the Yuma cultivar was released for commercial production in the Salt River Valley in Arizona and the Imperial Valley in California. Yuma became the first American-Egyptian cultivar developed in the Southwest (many more were to follow).

Kearney released his second cultivar in 1918. In 1910, an outstanding different plant of Yuma in a field had been observed and selected and a new cultivar, Pima, was developed from this single plant. This new cultivar was better than Yuma, and by 1918, it became the dominant crop in the irrigated sections of the Southwest. It was named after the Pima Indian Reservation where the research station was located. Because of the long growing season requirement of Pima, production was limited to the desert Southwest where the boll weevil had not become entrenched.

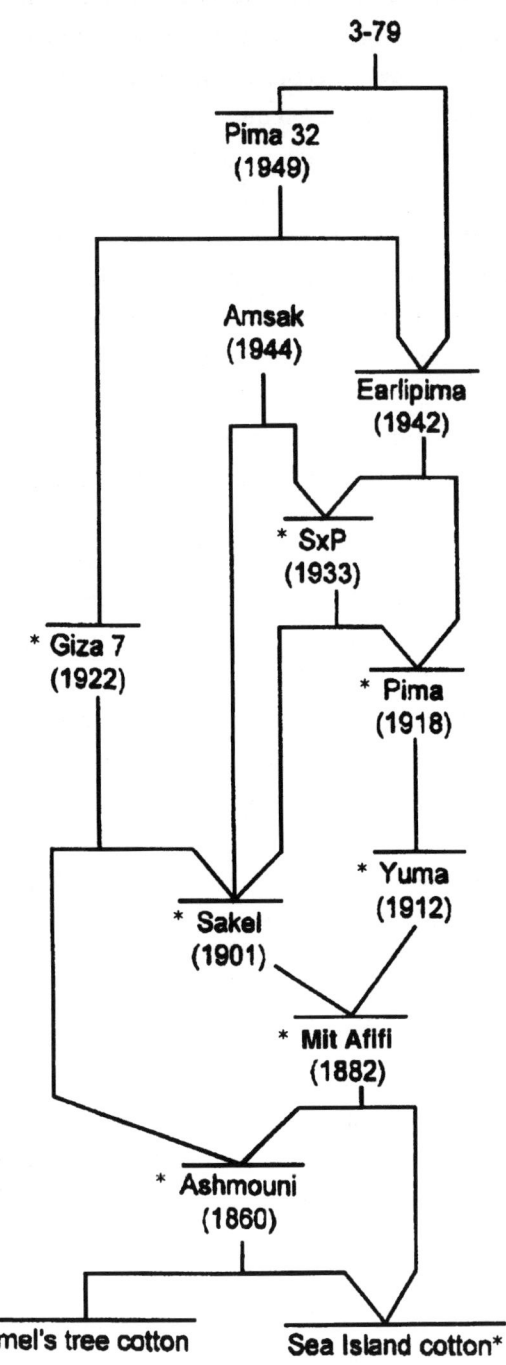

Figure 4-2. Development of Egyptian and American-Egyptian cultivars through 1949. Cultivars mentioned in the text are indicated with an asterisk.
(Adapted from Smith and Cothren 1999, 155)

The main problem to solve in the long-staple Pima and related cultivars was how to mechanically harvest the crop. *Barbadense* cottons grow so tall that machine picking was not feasible. By limiting the supply of water at a crucial time, the plant was forced into a lower growth form, and machines could harvest it like upland cotton.

Kearney's third cultivar, named SxP (the multiplication symbol representing a hybrid plant), began to replace Pima in 1935. SxP originated from a cross between Egyptian Sakel and Pima. By 1941, SxP had replaced Pima as the dominant long-staple cultivar in the Southwest.

Pima and cultivars developed from Pima represent the commercial long-staple cotton industry of the American Southwest today. From 1941, a seemingly endless number of cultivars have been developed by private and government workers. These cultivars could compete with the best Egyptian cottons because they were readily accepted by all segments of the long-staple cotton trade. All these cultivars are lumped under the heading American-Egyptian cotton. Today, the main center of long-staple cotton production in the United States is in the San Joaquin Valley of California.

Figure 4-2 is a summary of the development of Egyptian and American-Egyptian cultivars through 1949 and demonstrates sea island cotton's unique place in today's long-staple cotton industry. Sea island cotton is not grown today and the last pure strain was lost in 1934 when seeds of the Seabrook cultivar were sent to Florida and Georgia and grown as interior sea island cotton. However, sea island cotton's germplasm lives today in all the Egyptian cultivars and all the American-Egyptian cultivars since they were all derived from the cross of Jumel's tree cotton and sea island brought from America.

For the third time *G. barbadense* crossed the Atlantic. In 1918, Pima from the Southwest was returned to Egypt and from it was developed Pima/Maarad, planted on a commercial scale in 1925.

Mississippi Delta

In the first decade of the twentieth century, a "weed" cotton had seriously contaminated Egyptian long-staple, and it appeared that lean years were in prospect. Fearing a loss of Egyptian cotton, the directors of the Fine Cotton Spinners and Doublers' Association, Ltd., of Manchester, England, approved in 1911 the purchase of more than 30,000 acres in the Mississippi Delta, an area located between the Mississippi and Yazoo rivers. Ultimately, the holdings reached 45,000 acres. All the holdings came under one organization in 1919, the Delta & Pine Land Company. The company was both producer and consumer, for it sold its cotton to itself and spun the cotton in its own mills.

Shortly after the company acquired its Mississippi lands, it learned, as early experiments had proven, that *barbadense* long-staple cotton could not be grown in the area. The growing season was too short and the crop matured too late in the year to be harvested with profit. The growing of long-staple cotton was abandoned.

Gossypium barbadense Comes Home to Peru

In a somewhat ironic twist, prior to 1920, Peru imported seed of the American-Egyptian Pima cultivar. Today, cultivars developed from the Pima are the basis of the long-staple industry in Peru. It is sent to the United Kingdom for milling.

One other *barbadense* cotton is grown in Peru: Tanguis. Tanguis was developed in 1918 and in 1933 comprised 92% of the Peruvian crop. Peruvian Tanguis is a rough cotton, having a staple length of about 1 1/6", and has unique qualities required as a binder in spinning asbestos yarns and other industrial applications. Modern Peruvian Tanguis was developed from local populations of perennial *barbadense*. Annual forms were then developed from Tanguis.

Gossypium barbadense Today

Today, some form of *barbadense* long-staple cotton is grown in mainland China, Egypt, Sudan, India, Australia, Peru, Israel, the American Southwest, and in three countries that were part of the former USSR: Tajikistan, Turkmenistan, and Uzbekistan. As has always been the case, *barbadense* cotton represents only a small portion of world cotton production, averaging 3-5% annually, depending on weather and market conditions. Egypt produces about 36% of the total world market of long-staple cotton; the United States about 13%.

Long-staple cotton today is a specialty crop, just as sea island cotton was during its years of production. Long-staple cotton has its own market niche, and it appears it will keep this market for years to come.

1. The function of the heddle is covered in chapter 11.

The Origin of
Sea Island Cotton

Two aspects of the history of sea island cotton have been the subject of considerable controversy: the origin of sea island cotton in the sea islands of Georgia, Florida and South Carolina, and its subsequent geographical distribution. Even with new information obtained from the modern tools of genetics and molecular biology, historians and scientists still disagree on many facets of its origin and distribution. Future research will undoubtedly clarify many of these unknown or controversial aspects.

Sea island cotton was one of the market classes[1] of *Gossypium barbadense*. Sea island cotton was not *introduced* into the United States; it was *developed* on the sea islands of Georgia, Florida and South Carolina from seeds of West Indian *G. barbadense* plants. There was no sea island cotton until seeds of *Gossypium barbadense* were brought from the West Indies. Then, through acclimation to day-neutral flowering and seed selection that produced the exceptional extra-long fiber, sea island cotton originated.

The first scientist in modern times to present a reasonable and well-researched theory on the origin of sea island cotton was S. G. Stephens in 1976. He concluded that the West Indies was the source of the seed that was brought to the Southern states, and that its main characteristics, the fine staple and day-neutral flowering, came from introgression[2] with a *G. hirsutum* cultigen[3] that also grew in the West Indies. Stephens contended that *G. barbadense* had been carried to the West Indies from Ecuador and Peru by Native Americans prior to 1492, and it was the seeds of plants from this early dispersion into the Caribbean that were the origin of sea island cotton. These were likely the plants that Columbus discovered when he landed in the West Indies in 1492.

However, in 1990, Percy and Wendel, using statistical analysis of allozyme data, suggested that Hutchinson and Manning (1945) were correct when they concluded that the original source of *G. barbadense* plants from which sea island cotton was developed came from stock west of the Andes that was carried to the West Indies more recently by the Spanish (the second dispersal). They point out that if photoperiod neutrality and the fine staple arose via introgression from *G. hirsutum*, the most likely progenitors would have been from the areas where introgression was the highest, which they said was west of the Andes.

No matter which theory is correct, the story of the origin of sea island cotton begins in the native home of *G. barbadense*—Ecuador and Peru, on the west coast of South America. As a native plant of Peru and Ecuador, *G. barbadense* was a perennial shrub or small tree, with short, harsh, coarse lint, small, impermeable seeds, and short-day flowering. The sea island cotton developed on the sea islands was an annual[4] plant, with permeable seeds that germinated readily, and with a long, fine staple and day-neutral flowering. How each of these characteristics developed and produced sea island cotton will be considered in turn.

Perennial vs. Annual Growth

All four of today's commercial cottons had perennial antecedents that were long-lived shrubs or trees. Under cultivation, however, sea island cotton (and upland cotton) was grown as an annual. The stalks were plowed under each year after the cotton was harvested, and new seed was planted the following spring for the next crop. If left unattended in the field, the plants would have persisted through the winter and flowered the next year, and for many years. (Modern cultivars of cotton can be maintained indefinitely under greenhouse conditions.) These cultivated annuals are not true annuals in the sense that death of the plant is a natural consequence of seed ripening. Growing sea island cotton as an annual insured a more uniform crop each year. As a perennial, the plants would have grown so tall (Spalding measured plants 18 feet high) that picking by slaves would have been difficult. Even today's modern cultivars of long-staple cotton such as Pima and Egyptian and upland cotton (*G. hirsutum*) are grown as annuals. In summary, sea island cotton was a perennial cultivated as an annual.

Impervious vs. Permeable Seeds

Native, wild *G. barbadense* had small, impervious seeds that resulted in sporadic germination, a characteristic unsuited for agricultural cultivars. As cotton was changed from wild to dooryard plants, then to field cultivation, plants with large, permeable seeds that would germinate consistently were likely favored and selected for the next year's crop. The record is unclear whether this characteristic was developed in the sea islands or was already inherent in the plants that came from the West Indies. Regardless, consistency of seed germination was vital to field cultivation. The impermeable nature of the seeds was also critical to the two transoceanic crossings; however, this feature had no value in cultivated cottons.

Photoperiodism

Photoperiodism is the response of plants and animals to changes in relative duration of day and night. In some plants, flowering and fruit production is initiated by the differing lengths of day and night. Primitive forms of *G. barbadense* (including West Indian landrace and dooryard cottons) are short-day plants adapted to growth in frost-free areas; they are not frost-tolerant. They flower and fruit in the fall in response to the 12-hour-or-less short days of the tropics. The general effect of the short-day response is to restrict the reproductive period to the winter months, which in the tropics are associated with cooler night temperatures and the dry season, conditions that favored seed dispersal in wild cottons. When grown in this country, these plants do not flower before the fall equinox (the short days of fall). Instead, they become highly vegetative and produce few or no flowering branches during the long days of summer and early fall, and the branches that do fruit fail to mature seeds before the first frost.

Clearly the successful establishment of a commercial crop of *G. barbadense* on the southeastern seaboard required that the plants flower during the summer day-lengths of over 12 hours in order to produce mature fruit before the first frost. Since they were adapted to flower in the short days of the tropics, they would not flower during the longer days of the summer in the southeastern states, but much later in the fall, which would not have allowed enough time for fruit to mature before frost to produce a commercial crop. In other words, they would have to become day-neutral plants. Day-neutral plants did not require any particular photoperiod to flower and fruit; flowering and fruiting were controlled by other factors, such as moisture and/or temperature.

Stephens pointed out that no primitive forms of *G. barbadense* capable of flowering during the long summer days of temperate latitudes have been found. He refers to the results of an experimental cross between primitive forms of West Indian *barbadense* and a wild West Indian form of *G. hirsutum* as a means to bypass this problem. Plants from this cross (conducted in North Carolina in 1976) were as early maturing as standard sea island cotton. In other words, they produced flowers and set fruit under the long-day summer environment of North Carolina. Neither parent was day-neutral. A similar experiment by R. J. Kohel, T. R. Richmond and C. F. Lewis (1974) recovered a few summer-flowering plants from the F_2 generation of a cross between short-day plants of *G. hirsutum* var. *marie* and the *G. barbadense* cultivar Lengupa.

Stephens concluded, then, that day-neutral flowering resulted from introgression of germplasm from wild forms of West Indian *G. hirsutum* into primitive forms of West Indian *barbadense*. Seeds from these plants, genetically pre-adapted to day-neutral flowering,[5] established day-neutral plants when carried to the southeastern seaboard. All the periodicity controls were lost.

As plausible as Stephens's theory appears, Percy and Wendel (1990) challenged this theory, although only in part. In 1990, Percy and Wendel, using statistical analysis of allozyme data, suggested that improved cultivars of *G. barbadense* originated, at least in part, from plants west of the Andes, and not primarily from pre-Columbian West Indies plants. Most significant is the affinity of sea island accessions to those from west of the Andes. They also pointed out that if the day-neutral response arose from introgression from *G. hirsutum*, the most likely progenitors would come from where introgression was highest, which, their research indicated, was west of the Andes, in Paraguay and Argentina. Thus, Percy and Wendel's work supported Hutchinson and Manning's (1945) proposal of a west Andean parentage for sea island cotton, and not a pre-Columbian West Indian.

Since it is well established that the seeds that were brought to the southeastern coast came from the West Indies, the question then arises: How could sea island cottons have a closer affinity to west Andean stock and still come from the West Indies? Hutchinson and Manning (1945) shed light on this problem. They suggested that progenitors of sea island cotton may have been carried to the Greater Antilles by the Spanish in post-Columbian time, then carried to the southeastern seaboard. These progenitors would not have had time to diverge genetically from the west Andean stock before being introduced into the southeastern states. Like the possible early West Indian stock, because of introgression with *G. hirsutum* west of the Andes, this stock would have been pre-adapted for day-neutrality. Further research is needed to determine which of these conflicting theories is correct.

Fiber Characteristics

Regardless of the initial uses for which cotton was domesticated, all four commercial species underwent a parallel series of development under human selection. Each species was transformed from an occasional source of fiber to an industrial source of textile fiber. In the case of *G. barbadense*, by the time it had been dispersed into the West Indies in pre-Columbian times (or later by the Spanish), it had developed short, harsh and coarse fibers—the exact opposite of what would have been expected in a sea island ancestor. Stephens suggested a way around this problem. Also growing in the West Indies with *G. barbadense* were wild forms of *G. hirsutum* with very short—though fine—fibers. Stephens reasoned that sea island cotton might have acquired its distinctive fiber properties from hybridization and the resulting introgression of germplasm from short, fine-fibered *G. hirsutum* into the coarse-fibered form of *G. barbadense*. Percy and Wendel (1990) supported the hypothesis of introgression, but contended that the introgression occurred west of the Andes. A post-Columbian dispersion then occurred as Spaniards carried plants to the West Indies. More recently, Wang, Dong and Paterson (1995) supported Stephens's introgression theory. They reported that from collections of *G. barbadense* from around the world, 8.9% of *G. barbadense* alleles were apparently derived by introgression from *G. hirsutum*.

Stephens supports his theory with experimental evidence. As a result of experimental crossing of primitive forms of West Indian *barbadense* with a wild West Indian form of *G. hirsutum*, and in the absence of conscious selection during the early generations, the fiber fineness of the wild *hirsutum* parent was recovered, and fiber length was increased appreciably over all the parental materials. Later in the program, two generations of conscious selection produced a range of fiber lengths found in modern long-staple cottons. Thus, Stephens claimed, he produced experimentally what might have occurred naturally when cotton plantations of *G. barbadense* first came into contact with wild forms of *G. hirsutum*.

1786: The Origin of Sea Island Cotton

The plants of *Gossypium barbadense* that came to be called sea island cotton originated in 1786 with its conversion to day-neutral flowering. The seeds may have come from two sources. Some planters might have observed that after the mild winter of 1785-1786, some of the dooryard plants already established in Georgia set fruit the following spring earlier enough to produce ripe fruit before the first fall frost. If the planters selected seeds from the earlier-ripening pods for the next year's crop, enough plants would have become acclimated to day-neutral flowering that commercial crops were soon possible. It seems more likely, however, based on the historical record, that these seeds came in 1785 from the small Caribbean island of Anguilla, which had long been known to produce the best cotton of the West Indies.

The new settlers in the Bahamas procured cotton seed from Anguilla in 1785 and introduced cotton culture upon several of the Bahama Islands successively, particularly Long Island and Exuma Island. From the sources cited below, it is clear that seeds from these plants were sent to Georgia in 1785. Thomas Spalding (1774-1851) wrote (1831, 138): "The Anguilla seed came to us through the Bahamas, in the year 1785." These seeds were sent by Georgia and South Carolina Loyalist refugees who settled in the Bahama Islands. Spalding gave a more detailed account (1835, 36) of how this transformation to a day-neutral plant might have originated:

But the winter of 1785 and 1786 [was] fortunately mild. The cotton under experiment had generally been planted in new, and warm, and fruitful soils— frost rarely penetrates far into the earth in such situations in Georgia. The roots of the cotton had been sheltered and protected by the earth from the cold, and that life which had slumbered in the roots of the plants during the winter, was awakened into activity in the spring. The cotton stalks which had been killed in the winter were cut down to the surface of the ground. The shoots that grew up from the roots of the previous year were earlier in their growth, did not rise so high, sooner blossomed, and sooner bore fruit. The second year the cotton bore and ripened its fruit, the seed was in some degree acclimated, and the first steps taken which were to end in a few years making the United States emphatically the cotton country.

Spalding (1844a, 107) wrote from Sapelo Island in 1843, in answer to queries of W. B. Seabrook of Edisto Island, another version of this introduction. This time he identified individuals:

The first bale of Sea-Island cotton that was ever produced in Georgia, was grown by Alexander Bissett, Esq. of St. Simons' Island, and I think in the year 1778. In the winter of 1785 and 1786, I know of three parcels of cotton seed being sent from the Bahamas, by gentleman of rank there, to their friends in Georgia; Col. Kelsall sent to my father a small box of cotton-seed; the surveyor Genl. of the Bahamas, Col. Tatnall, sent to his son, afterwards, Governor Tatnall of Georgia, a parcel of cotton-seed; Alexander Bissett's father, who was commissary Genl. to the Southern British Army sent a box of cotton seed to his son, in the year 1786; this cotton gave no fruit, but the winter being moderate and the land new and warm, both my father and Mr. Bissett had seed from the ratoon,[6] and the plant became acclimatized.

A different twist to the Spalding account was given by Chalmers Murray in an unpublished manuscript entitled *Black Seed from Bahama* in the South Carolina Historical Society. The date of the manuscript was determined to be around 1940 based on a letter of rejection from a publishing company.[7] The Spalding Murray speaks of was James Spalding (d. 1794), the father of Thomas Spalding:

As soon as the winter was past, he had his slaves drop the little black seeds on the banks of an old rice field. The soil was extremely fertile and it seemed no time at all before the plants broke through the ground. Almost daily he watched their growth, from tiny little things to stalks reaching up to the waist. A little later the creamy yellow blossoms stood out against the dark green foliage. But as the weeks went by there was yet no sign of fruitage. Bitterly disappointed Spalding saw the stalks die when winter came. All seemed lost.

That year everybody was talking about how mild the winter had been. Spalding took careful note and as the days lengthened toward spring he searched his cotton field for signs of life. Somehow hope wouldn't down.

The miracle had happened! In the early spring the plants came up afresh, and this time becoming acclimated they bore firm green pods. Success was in sight. With seeds from the ratoon Spalding planted his second crop of g. Barbadense. In the meanwhile Bissett had gone through the same experience, and he too saved the seed from the volunteer plants for the second sowing.

Another account of how the day-neutral characteristic arose was given by Watt (1907, 272), who related the following story from one Mr. Wright[8]:

The former (Sea Island), indeed, could not be established until the fortunate occurrence of a very mild winter permitted the roots to live through it and produce an early crop of fresh shoots in the spring. These bore and ripened a crop, the seed of which was found sufficiently hardy to resist the cold of spring, and matured a crop of excellent cotton in the course of the succeeding autumn... The peculiar and very superior qualities of this kind are attributed to its growing in a soil highly calcareous, and strongly impregnated with salt, added by the influence of a saline atmosphere.

And Watt himself commented on its origin (Watt 1907, 278):

Many writers, for example, say that when first introduced into America the Sea Island cotton was a perennial, and that owing to the shortness of the summer in South Carolina and Georgia it rarely matured fruit. Through the accident of a mild winter and the selection of early maturing pods, when combined with more advantageous methods of cultivation, a stock had been gradually matured with an annual habit directly adapted to the climatic conditions of a limited tract of country in the United States. This new and very special stock embraces all the finest grades and the most valuable cottons of the world, and is in fact the true Sea Island.

From the above accounts, the author concludes that sea island cotton developed from seeds of perennial short-day *barbadense* cotton brought from the Bahamas that were planted on St. Simons Island in 1785. The above-ground parts of the plants froze back during the winter, but—the winter being mild—the roots were not killed. The following spring, new plants developed from the ratoons, flowered in July and produced fruit throughout the fall. Subsequent crops, grown from seeds selected each year from early-blooming plants, became acclimated as day-neutral plants. Planters then grew sea island cotton as an annual, and by the 1790s, its fiber characteristics gained a high reputation in the English market.

A few years after 1786, sea island cotton was commonly planted and exported from Georgia. By 1810, its cultivation spread to Ossabaw, St. Catherine's, Sapelo, Jekyll, and Cumberland, as well as to the mainland.

In 1790, William Elliott of Hilton Head Island grew the first commercial crop of sea island cotton in South Carolina (Seabrook 1844a:19).[9] By 1793, many coastal South Carolina planters, enticed by the high prices at Liverpool, England, began experimenting with the crop on the sea islands. Soon its production spread as far north as Bull Island in Charleston. By 1808, sea island cotton culture was regionally concentrated in the islands of James, Johns, Wadmalaw, Edisto, St. Helena, Lady's, and Port Royal.

The rapid spread and success of the crop in South Carolina is demonstrated by the export statistics in table 5-1.

Year	Pounds
Oct. 1, 1789 to Sept. 30, 1790	9,840
Oct. 1, 1790 to Sept. 30, 1791	54,075

Oct. 1, 1791 to Sept. 30, 1792	76,710
Oct. 1, 1792 to Sept. 30, 1793	93,540
Oct. 1, 1793 to Sept. 30, 1794	159,040
Oct. 1, 1794 to Sept. 30, 1795	1,109,653
Oct. 1, 1795 to Sept. 30, 1796	912,600
Oct. 1, 1796 to Sept. 30, 1797	1,108,511
Oct. 1, 1797 to Sept. 30, 1798	2,476,431
Oct. 1, 1798 to Sept. 30, 1799	2,801,996
Oct. 1, 1799 to Sept. 30, 1800	6,425,863
Oct. 1, 1800 to Sept. 30, 1801	8,301,907

Table 5-1. Exports of sea island cotton from South Carolina, 1789-1801 (*Merchants' Magazine and Commercial Review*, 1949, vol. 21)

The last step in the development of sea island cotton was the production of the high-quality, fine, long staple for which the sea islands became famous. The credit for initially developing the long staple goes to Kinsey Burden, who began growing black-seed cotton in 1798 on Burden's Island, in St. Paul's Parish, Colleton District (fig. 5-1).[10] He began his seed selection experiments on Burden's Island in 1804-05, then continued his selection at Oakvale Plantation in Johns Island, Charleston County, where he moved in 1805-06. Burden (1844a, 164) wrote: "About the year 1804 or 1805, I raised from selected seed, a pocket of fine cotton... This I believe was the first attempt in this state to improve the fineness of the black-seed cotton." Further in the article he stated: "For some years previously to 1823, I was engaged in improving the quality of my cotton..." Then, in a second article in the same year (1844b, 204), written in June, he stated: "In 1805-6, I removed [moved] to this Island..." It appears, then, that Burden began his seed selection on Burden's Island, but ultimately developed the long-staple sea island cotton for which he became famous on his plantation on Johns Island (fig. 5-2).

Burden's intensive seed selection ultimately produced a fiber from 1 1/2 to 2 1/2 inches long, strong and fine, and with a lustrous creamy tint. It was so strong that a pound could be spun into a thread 160 miles long. By all accounts, it was the finest cotton fiber ever produced, and commanded the highest price of any cotton. The impetus for improving the quality of sea island quality came from overseas, as William Elliott (1856, 70) stated: "The demand for the sea-island cottons, raised in the Southern States of America, is altogether foreign. Not a pound is manufactured in the country of production..." The total quantity of sea island cotton was never large, but its value was very high because of its marvelous spinning quality.

Gray (1958, 731) defined the staple length of sea island cotton:

CHAPTER FIVE

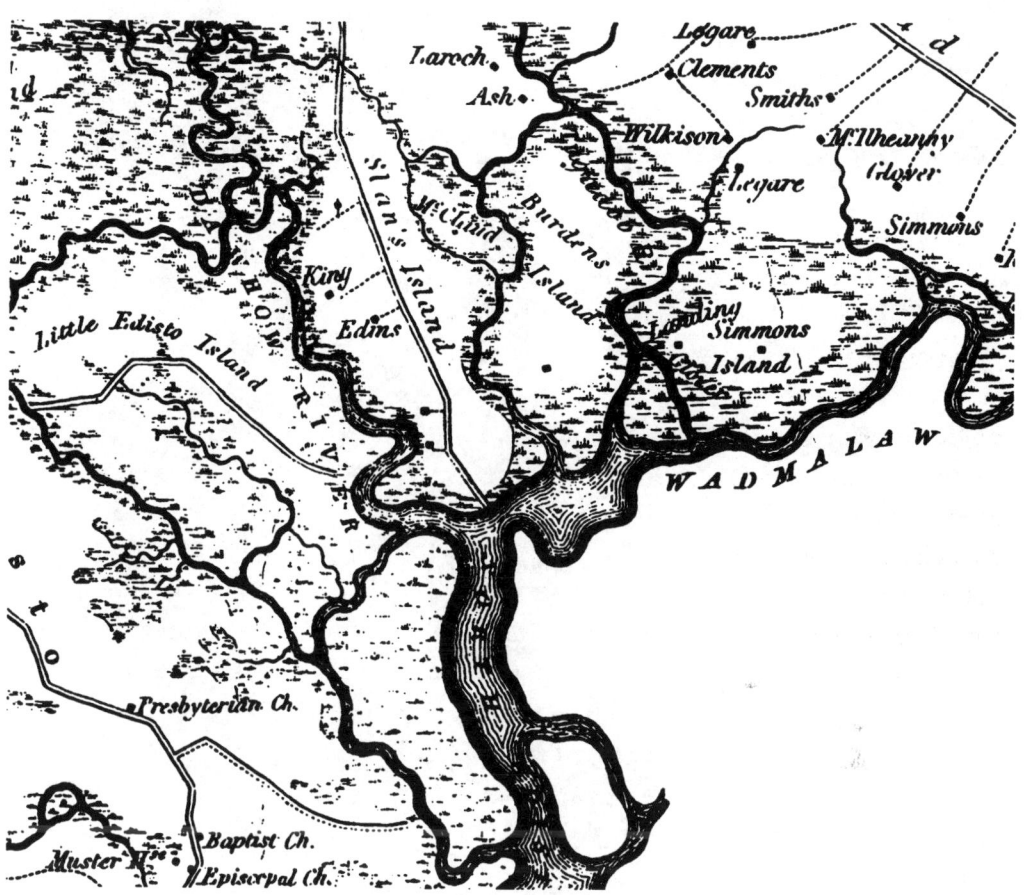

Figure 5-1. Burden's Island, St. Paul's Parish, Colleton District, 1825

Figure 5-2. Location of Kinsey Burden's plantation on Johns Island (1825 Mills *Atlas*)

CHAPTER FIVE

Fancy sea-island cotton has a length of staple of 2 inches and upwards although the bulk of the crop was probably from 1 1/2 to 1 3/4 inches, as contrasted with 5/8 inch to 1 inch for the bulk of the upland short-staple and 1 1/8 to 1 1/2 for much of the upland long-staple [Santee long and Mains].

In summary, sea island cotton began its journey as a perennial short-day wild cotton west of the Andes in Ecuador and Peru. Wild plants were carried by Native Americans to the West Indies in pre-Columbian times, and possibly again by Spaniards in post-Columbian times. In 1785, seeds from Anguilla were carried to the Bahamas, and from there sent to Georgia where they were planted. A mild winter allowed some plants to survive the winter, and they flowered the following spring in time to produce fruits before the winter frost. From introgression with wild plants of *G. hirsutum,* either west of the Andes or in the West Indies, the short, harsh and coarse fibers of *barbadense* were transformed into short, fine fibers. Thus, these plants of *G. barbadense* were converted to day-neutral plants that were able to produce abundant mature pods with fine fibers. Kinsey Burden's seed selection process then produced the long-staple that came to be true sea island cotton.

1. This book classifies sea island cotton as a market class of *G. barbadense*, not as a cultivar as in some sources. A cultivar (for cultivated variety) is a strain or genotype that is, or was, available for commercial production and has undergone intensive human selection. Within the market class of sea island cotton, planters developed their own cultivars, such as "Bleak Hall" or "Seabrook," through intensive seed selection processes. If sea island cotton is considered a cultivar of *G. barbadense*, another classification would have to be used for the cottons such as Bleak Hall and Seabrook. Likewise, American-Egyptian is considered a market class, and Pima and Yuma are considered as cultivars of American-Egyptian. Most sources list Pima and Yuma as cultivars, so the classification in this book of sea island cotton as a market class with cultivars produced by individual planters fits this concept.
2. Introgression is the incorporation of genetic material from one population into that of another through hybridization followed by repeated backcrossing; it is usually restricted to populations regarded as distinct by taxonomists.
3. A cultigen is a domesticated form of a wild species. The term is usually applied to indigenous forms that have undergone minimal human selection.
4. An annual is a plant growing from seed to fruit in one year, then dying. Wild cottons are perennial plants, living for three or more years. Cultivated cottons are grown as annuals, in that after harvest the plants are plowed under and the next year's crop comes from planted seed.
5. In more technical terms, the offspring from the crosses were genetically heterogeneous and capable of generating day-neutral segregates.
6. A ratoon is a new shoot or sprout springing from the base of a crop plant.
7. There is no citation as to where Murray obtained his information; however, the author considers it part of the historical record, and although unpublished, includes it.

8. Watt gives the citation as: [Ill. Ind. Bot I: 63. 1840]. The author was not able to find this source.

9. William Elliott is generally given credit for the first commercial crop of sea island cotton. However, as Seabook point out, sea island cotton seed was for sale in 1790, and was probably bought and planted by other planters. As their names are unknown, Elliott, whose crop was sold and recorded, is credited for the first commercial crop.

10. The Mills *Atlas* of 1825 shows the location of Burden's Island; (some sources spell the name without an apostrophe). A later map in 1862 again shows the same location and name. In 1825 and 1862, Burden's Island was located in St. Paul's Parish, Colleton district. In 1911, St. Paul's Parish was annexed to Charleston County. In maps of Charleston County today, Burden's Island is called Little Britton Island. This is also a point of confusion since James King named the island Little Britain. Confusion also occurs in the name of the creek to the west of Little Britton Island. The Adams Run Quadrangle of 1960 (U.S. Department of the Interior Geological Survey topographical map) identifies the creek on the west boundary of Little Britton Island as Tom Point Creek. In the Mills *Atlas* and on Charleston County road maps it is called McLeod Creek.

The Geographical Distribution of Long-Staple Cotton in South Carolina, Georgia and Florida

This book classifies *barbadense* cotton grown in South Carolina, Georgia and Florida into four market classes as suggested, in part, by Lewis Gray (1958, 733). The geographic distribution of these four classes is depicted in figures 6-1 and 6-5. This classification was based on the buying market and the relative quality of the fiber. The long-staple cotton grown on the sea islands of Georgia, East Florida and South Carolina is termed sea island cotton. The other three classes are termed Santee long, mains, and Georgia and Florida interior sea island cotton (often referred to as Floridas and Georgias).[1]

This latter market class was not included in Gray's classification. Gray classified Georgia and Florida interior with the mains and Santee long; however, the author includes it as a separate market class for reasons discussed below.

Marjorie S. Mendenhall (1940, 137) cited another classification for these four market classes: common, fine and superfine. Common and fine referred to mains and Santee long, while superfine referred to sea island cotton. Mendenhall did not include the Florida and Georgia interior cotton in her classification; however, it would have been grouped with the common and fine.

THE GEOGRAPHICAL DISTRIBUTION OF LONG-STAPLE COTTON
IN SOUTH CAROLINA, GEORGIA AND FLORIDA

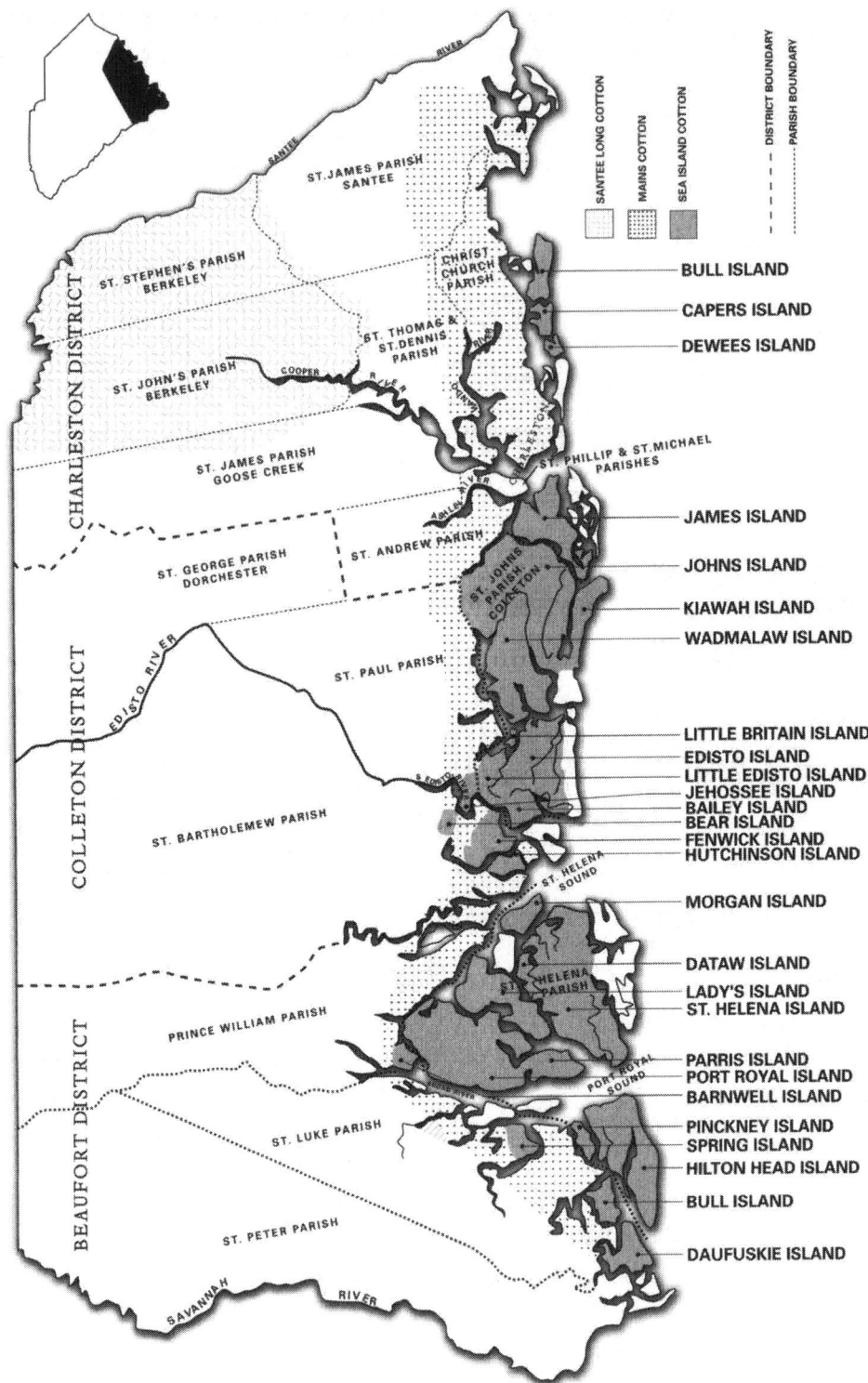

Figure 6-1. Geographical distribution of market classes of long-staple cotton

CHAPTER SIX

This chapter asks two main questions: (1) what factors were responsible for the superior quality of the fiber of sea island cotton; and (2) why did the quality of long-staple cotton degenerate when grown off the sea islands?

The discussion of the four market classes of long-staple cotton will address each of these three states in turn.

South Carolina

Sea Island Cotton

Sea island cotton was grown on a limited area in three coastal counties in South Carolina. The sea islands listed in table 6-1 were documented as having grown sea island cotton; all these islands occur in the geographical distribution depicted in figure 6-1.

Barrier Islands, by County		Erosion-Remnant Islands, by County		
<u>Charleston</u>	<u>Beaufort</u>	<u>Charleston</u>	<u>Colleton</u>	<u>Beaufort</u>
Bulls	Daufuskie	Bailey	Bear	Barnwell
Capers	Hilton Head	Edisto	Fenwick	Bull
Dewees		James	Hutchinson	Datah
Kiawah		Jehossee		Lady's
		Johns		Morgan
		Little Britain		Parris
		Little Edisto		Pinckney
		Slanns		Port Royal
		Wadmalaw		St. Helena
				Spring

Table 6-1. Major islands where sea island cotton was grown in South Carolina

Although sea island cotton was grown on the Georgia and Florida sea islands, it was on the South Carolina sea islands, through seed selection—initially by Kinsey Burden, and later by other by Carolina planters—that it reached its highest quality. Historians and agronomists have debated for years about which factors were responsible for this quality. It is unlikely that they will ever be conclusively known. There are no practical means today to conduct an experiment to try to isolate the factors responsible for the quality of sea island cotton. The conditions that existed in Burden's time would be different today. One must consult the historical record, and with today's knowledge of ecology, agronomy and genetics, make an educated guess. A starting point is to consider the array of theories that appear in the literature:

1. Thomas Spalding (1835, 39): *The only essential property that is required, is a saline atmos-*

phere; with it any soil in Georgia or Carolina may produce fine cotton — without it no soil will produce fine cotton.

2. Robert F. W. Allston (1854, 12): *Removed from the influence of a salt atmosphere, it degenerates, and the staple becomes inferior.*

3. William Elliott (1856, 68): *The enquirer will find those fortunate locations which have shown a constant tendency to improve the staple, and produce the finest sea-island cotton, on the Atlantic coast of North America, between the 32d and 33d degree of north latitude, within a few miles of the sea, enjoying a saline atmosphere, and a soil which, though rich, is dry, and in which silex is the predominant ingredient.*

4. W. A. Orton (1907, 9): *On the Sea Islands, fields having an ocean exposure are said to produce a finer and glossier staple on account of the moisture-laden ocean breezes... In the absence of sufficient moisture in the air the staple becomes harsh and shorter.*

5. William Meadows (1914, 6): *It has been the custom for years for the farmers of this section [Georgia and Florida] to renew at least once in three years their planting seed with fresh stock from Carolina. They seemingly did not rely on a seed selection from their own fields to keep up or improve the quality of their cotton, and it is even now commonly believed that 'Sea Island runs out when planted in the interior or away from the islands of Carolina.' There can be no question about the deterioration of Sea Island cotton when left alone under usual farm conditions or when no seed selections are made; but this deterioration is just about as marked on the islands of South Carolina when seed selection is neglected as it is in Georgia or Florida. Soil and climate, of course, influence the kind and amount of lint, but it seems that the chief element in determining the character of the product is the kind of seed planted. The great difference in status between the Carolina planters on the one hand and those of Georgia and Florida on the other is primarily due to the fact that the former have practiced intelligent seed selection for many years, whereas the latter have been content to buy the best planting seed that was obtainable.*

6. W. H. Johnson (1926, 66): *Atmospheric humidity appears to be an essential factor in the production of high-grade lint. Fields exposed to the moisture-laden ocean breezes produce a finer and more glossy staple; it is for this reason that a wet season is more favorable for Sea Island than for Upland cotton. In the absence of sufficient moisture, harsh and shorter staple is produced.*

7. Herbert R. Mauersberger (1947, 158): *Sea Island cotton may be cultivated in any region near the sea, the principal requisite being a hot and humid climate, but the results of acclimatization indicate that the humid atmosphere is not entirely necessary if irrigation is employed. Sea Island*

requires a great deal more moisture than the Upland cottons; in fact, moisture is an all-important factor in the quality of the staple. Dry years give a poor staple and wet years a good staple.

8. J. W. Purseglove (1968, 360): *Interspecific hybridization [between* G. barbadense *and* G. hirsutum*]: species within a section of the genus usually give fully fertile F_1's, but extensive breakdown occurs in the F_2's maintaining the species integrity.*

9. Charles F. Kovacik and Robert E. Mason (1985, 81): *The substantially longer growing season and lower rainfall on the Sea Islands may have been limiting factors in the cultivation of fine and superfine Sea Island cotton.*

From the above, it appears that three general factors have been considered important in producing the fine, long, sea island cotton staple: seed selection, preventing hybridization with upland cotton, and environmental influences. To these the author adds the methods of cultivation (see chapter 7) practiced by the sea island planters.

Seed Selection

Today's science fully understands the role of seed selection in producing superior agronomic crops. All the many cultivars of *barbadense* cotton in the world today resulted from seed selection. What is remarkable is how well seed selection was understood by the early sea island planters, especially by Kinsey Burden, who is given credit for initially producing the finest long-staple sea island cotton on Johns Island in the early 1800s. (A detailed discussion is presented in chapter 7 and diagrammed in figure 7-2.)

The importance of seed selection was demonstrated in the early 1900s when Carolina sea island planters refused to ship their seeds to the West Indies in order to curtail competition. They also refused to ship seeds to their fellow Carolina sea island planters, or to Georgia or Florida. The quality of the staple degenerated throughout the long-staple cotton growing area. As long as the planters on the Carolina sea islands maintained a strict seed selection practice and shared their seeds with others, staple quality did not suffer.

Hybridization with Upland Cotton

There is no question that hybridization between sea island and upland cotton ultimately led to degeneration of the qualities that characterized sea island cotton's market appeal. That hybridization did not occur frequently early on was serendipitous, and later purposeful. Sea island cotton brought such a high price when compared to upland cotton that sea island planters had no reason to plant upland cotton. Consequently, sea island cotton was isolated from upland cotton and no hybridization occurred. After sea island planters stopped supplying the West Indies and their fellow planters with their quality seeds, some sea island planters began planting upland cotton. Hybridization between the two resulted in a deteriorated fiber quality in the sea island cotton. Later, as agronomists came to realize that hybridization led to degeneration of the staple, care was taken to insure isolation of the sea island crop.

Environmental Influences

Numerous references, including those cited above, concluded that the "saline atmosphere" of the sea islands was responsible for the high quality of the staple. The author discounts this factor. When water evaporates from the ocean surface, the salt is left behind. The atmosphere itself does not contain salt. Only on the immediate edge of the ocean does salt occur in the atmosphere. Here, the winds blow salt water from the ocean's surface to the first few dunes, often producing a shearing effect on the immediate forest vegetation.

The sea islands are bathed in a warm, humid atmosphere that favors the growth of cotton. In the absence of sufficient atmospheric moisture, a harsh and shorter staple was produced; finer staple quality occurred in a moisture-laden atmosphere. Again, this proximity to the ocean created a high-moisture atmosphere that undoubtedly contributed to the fine fiber of sea island cotton.

The growing season on the sea islands was around 280 days (see fig. 1-10), sufficient time for a large crop of fruits to ripen and produce fiber. This long growing season spanned the last spring freeze around February 28 (see table 1-11) and the first freeze in the fall around November 25 (table 1-12).

In general, sea island cotton required warm days and relatively warm nights for optimum growth and development of the fiber, which occurred in the first 20 days after a flower bloomed. Low temperature during this period reduced the rate of elongation as well as total length. The nighttime and daytime temperature in the sea islands were in a range suited for good growth as the temperatures were modified by the islands' proximity to the ocean. Especially important were the 120 frost-free nights during the growing season that maximized the length and quality of the fiber.

Cultivation Methods

The control of soil water was paramount to producing a good crop and a resulting high fiber yield. The roots of the cotton plant could not tolerate saturated soil. If the soil around the tap root became saturated during the growing season, the flowers fell off. Early on, the planters made use of raised beds that supplemented the natural drainage of the sandy soil. Later, when low lands and salt marsh were cultivated, drainage ditches were run between the beds for drainage. After the Civil War, planters made use of subsoil drainage. These various methods reduced the level of saturation around the roots of the plants.

The first fields cultivated were in the sandy, loamy soils that supported oak and hickory forests. The soil was fertile and initially needed little amelioration. Planters simply abandoned a field after the nutrients were depleted and cleared more virgin land. Ultimately, as virgin land became scarce, the planters turned to soil amelioration, first using natural products from around the plantations (manure, leaves, salt-marsh mud); later, they used commercial fertilizers. The result was a soil base that was ideally suited for cotton production, more so than virgin soil.

The author concludes that it was the combination of these four factors—the ideal environment of the sea islands, the advanced seed selection process, isolation from upland cotton fields, and the cultivation methods practiced by the sea island planters—that resulted in Carolina sea island cotton having the finest fiber ever grown. Nowhere else in the long-staple cotton region of the pre-war South did these combinations of factors exist.

Mains Cotton

Mains (sometimes written "maines") referred to long-staple cotton grown on the mainland of South Carolina. Compared to sea island cotton, it was of moderate quality and had a staple length of 1 1/8" to 1 1/2". Mains was classed with Santee long and sold at a discount to sea island cotton. The mainland is the area just inland from the sea islands. The inland limits of mains cotton are obscure. No adequate map was found in the literature that depicts the interior extent of mains. The area of mains cotton depicted in figure 6-1 was taken from Robert E. Mason's thesis (Mason 1976, 12, figure 4).[2]

The reasons that the quality of the staple of mains long-staple cotton was inferior to sea island are summarized as follows:

Seed Selection

Seed selection does not appear to have been practiced by the planters of mains cotton; the seed source came from sea island planters. As long as fresh seeds were obtained every two or three years, the quality of fiber would have been maintained. But it appears from the literature that, during hard financial times, planters of agricultural crops would occasionally use seeds from their own crops for the next year's planting. The planters of mains long-staple cotton were probably no different.

Hybridization with Upland Cotton

Perhaps the factor most responsible for the discounted quality of the lint on the mainland was hybridization with upland cotton. In their seed selection process, sea island planters made certain that the plants they used to conduct seed selection were far removed from upland cotton fields. But this was not possible on the mainland because so much upland cotton was grown there. If the mains planters used seeds from their crops, even occasionally, hybridization would have contributed to degradation of the fiber.

Environmental Influences

It is difficult to make a case that environmental factors on the mainland varied enough from the Carolina sea islands to have been a significant cause of the differing quality of the fiber.

THE GEOGRAPHICAL DISTRIBUTION OF LONG-STAPLE COTTON IN SOUTH CAROLINA, GEORGIA AND FLORIDA

Two environmental factors, however, combined with the effects of the absence of seed selection and hybridization, probably contributed to these differences. First, the growing season was three weeks shorter on the mainland (fig. 1-10); and second, average rainfall (fig. 1-13) was about six inches more on the mainland, making it more likely that soil saturation occurred there.

Cultivation Methods

The author could not find any material in the literature that described cultivation practices of mains cotton. Whether or not it differed from sea island cotton is not known.

Santee Long Cotton

Santee long cotton was grown in the heart of St. John's and St. Stephen's parishes in Berkeley County (fig. 6-1). This was the home of noted botanists and physicians Francis Peyre Porcher, M.D., and James MacBride, M.D., and of botanists Henry William Ravenel and Thomas Walter. It was also home to the Black Oak Agricultural Society; to General William Moultrie's (of Revolutionary War fame) Northampton Plantation where the first Santee long was planted; to the rich plantation life of the descendants of the resourceful Huguenots who fled France in 1685 after the revocation of the Edict of Nantes; and to the proud descendants of other early settlers of the Carolina lowcountry such as the Cains, Sinklers and Palmers. Many of them achieved remarkable success in various agricultural endeavors. Daniel Ravenel of Wantoot gained fame for his inland swamp cultivation of rice, and William Cain of Somerset Plantation produced crops of Santee long that earned him a reputation in France. Today, most of these cotton and rice lands lie under the waters of Lake Moultrie and Lake Marion, the Santee-Cooper lakes that were created in 1940. Where Santee long cotton and Carolina gold rice once flourished, fishermen and boaters today enjoy idyllic days.

The area of Santee long cotton was outlined by Henry W. Ravenel (1843, 4):

The region of the Santee Long Cotton commences at the head of the tide-water on Cooper river, extends across the country to the Santee river, and above, as high as Vance's Ferry [in today's Orangeburg County]. Within these limits are embraced the head-waters of Cooper river, which extend to within a few miles of the Santee, intersecting the country in different directions, and forming along their courses large swamps, formerly cultivated in rice, but abandoned after the introduction of cotton, for the more profitable cultivation of the highland.

In the neighborhood of these streams are some of the best cotton lands. In their virgin state, they contain a growth of oak, dogwood, &c., generally intermixed with the short-leaf pine, indicating the proximity of lime-stone to the surface. They are well adapted to the cultivation of the black-seed cotton, and comprise the principal portion of the Santee cotton-lands.

At one time, Williamsburg County was part of the Santee long cotton region; however, the crop there was never a success. In 1812, three or four planters in Sumter District introduced

CHAPTER SIX

Figure 6-2. Plantations homes and planters of the Santee long cotton region. The Church of the Holy Trinity (Black Oak Church), an Episcopal Church that served as the chapel-of-ease for the Black Oak Community of St. John's Parish (Porcher family collection); Northampton (Porcher family collection), home of General William Moultrie (courtesy of South Carolina Historic Society collections); The Rocks (courtesy of the Charleston Museum), home of Captain Peter Gaillard; Somerset, home of William Cain (Cain's photograph and photograph of Somerset house, taken in May 1939 by Henry R. Dwight, Jr., courtesy of William Cain, Jr.); Cedar Springs (Porcher family collection), home of Frederick A. Porcher (courtesy of the College of Charleston Special Collections); Springfield (Porcher family collection), home of Joseph Palmer; Pooshee (USC Press), home of Henry Ravenel, M.D.; Belvidere (USC Press), home of Captain James Sinkler; Indianfield (Porcher family collection).

long-staple cotton into the district. The quantity and quality of the crop was initially encouraging, but the preparation of the lint was objectionable, and the growers abandoned its production because of the labor cost and time required to gin. Nothing in the literature was found to indicate that Santee long cotton was successfully established outside the area described by Ravenel.

The historical accounts of Santee long cotton are based on the works of Henry William Ravenel, Frederick Adolphus Porcher (1809-1888) and Samuel Dubose; on the plantation journals of Dr. Henry Ravenel and René Ravenel of Pooshee Plantation, and Thomas Walter Peyre of Brunswick Plantation; on the records of the Black Oak Agricultural Society; and on Peter Gaillard's planting book for the years 1803-24. These men and their families lived in St. John's and St. Stephen's parishes. They enjoyed a rich and cultured life, and built substantial plantation houses (fig. 6-2). Their accounts of all aspects of life in these parishes were recorded in numerous writings. Later accounts of long-staple cotton in the region of St. John's Parish and St. Stephen's Parish appear to have been taken from the works of these men. In addition, the records of the Black Oak Agricultural Society supplied numerous references to Santee long cotton.

Santee long cotton was grown at numerous other plantations in St. John's and St. Stephen's parishes. According to the records of the Black Oak Agricultural Society, these included Cedar Springs, Hanover,[3] Harbin, Hardput, Indianfield, Ophir, Sturaton and Walworth. Undoubtedly there were others, but no documented records were found.

According to Samuel Dubose (1858, 15), early on in the Santee long cotton region, "quantity and not quality was the aim in view; consequently, heavier yields were obtained from our lands." Accounts of the early history of Santee long cotton always stressed the amount produced per acre. Records of the Black Oak Agricultural Society contain numerous accounts of the planters experimenting with different methods to increase yield. Their experiments were extremely advanced for the times and showed a remarkable scientific knowledge. Experiments were conducted in which marl or plaster of Paris were applied to fields; other fields were used as control and no marl or plaster of Paris were added. Production results from the two areas were carefully recorded by the society and made available to planters in the area.

The cotton grown as Santee long was derived from two seed sources: (1) seeds from early crops of sea island cotton from just after 1788 (probably from Georgia); and (2) seeds obtained from the Carolina sea islands beginning around 1830. The first to plant Santee long was General William Moultrie (1730-1805), using seeds from the early crops of sea island cotton. General Moultrie planted 150 acres of long-staple cotton in 1793 on Northampton Plantation. The crop was a failure, the result of his not knowing the proper method of cultivation, of a bad growing season, and of land that was probably exhausted from previous farming. The date of this planting, 1793, was seven years after the development of day-neutral, sea island cotton on St. Simons Island, but twelve years before Kinsey Burden developed his superfine sea island cotton.

CHAPTER SIX

Although General Moultrie's attempt at planting long-staple cotton at Northampton was a failure, long-staple cotton culture from that time progressed rapidly in these two parishes. Part of the reason was that indigo ceased to be a market crop soon after the Revolutionary War. The planters looked for other crops to replace indigo, and long-staple cotton was an obvious choice. In 1799, Captain Peter Gaillard (1783-1843) of The Rocks Plantation averaged sales of $340 per hand. Gaillard purchased The Rocks in 1794, without funds, looking for nothing more than to support his family. The crop of 1799 or 1800 extricated him from debt and he became a wealthy man from his plantation crops, mainly from Santee long cotton. Twenty-two years after commencing planting cotton, he retired to Charleston and divided his lands among eight children. Peter Gaillard was called the pioneer cotton planter of the Santee long region.

In the same year that Captain Gaillard produced his first successful crop, Captain James Sinkler (1740-1800) at Belvidere Plantation produced a crop of 216 pounds per acre, for which he received seventy-five cents per pound for much of the crop. This worked out to be $509 per hand. After that year, no other agricultural crop stood in the way of production of Santee long in St. John's and St. Stephen's parishes.

Mexico Plantation, planted by Major Samuel Porcher (1768-1851), was the site of one of the most remarkable private enterprises. Mexico was located along the Santee swamp, whose lands yielded an abundance of crops until freshets[4] became so frequent that the land had to be abandoned. The increase in freshets of the Santee River was caused by the clearing of forested lands in the piedmont, after which the runoff from rain became more frequent, causing flooding of swampland downriver. Beginning in 1817, Major Porcher constructed a bank (fig. 6-3) to hold back the waters of the Santee River. For forty years, his overseer, a Mr. Foxworth, and his driver George, supervised the building and improving of the bank. When completed and perfected, Mexico became the "land of promise." The bank, four miles and a quarter in length, its base thirty to fifty feet wide, and its height nine to thirteen feet, was one of the greatest results of private enterprise in the southern country. The bank (referred to as Porcher Bank in the literature of St. John's Parish) kept Major Porcher's 1,300 acres of swampland free from flooding, and the fields again yielded an abundance of corn, oats, and other crops. The exhausted adjacent high land, fertilized by manure from cattle he raised, yielded a bountiful crop of Santee long cotton.

Robert Wilson (1907, 15) wrote of William Cain (1792-1878) of Somerset Plantation of St. John's Parish:

Like the others Mr. Cain was a successful planter of the long cotton and his crops usually brought the top of the market. I do not know any better illustration of his courteous good humor that the pleasant and unprotesting smile with which he accepted the statement of a gentleman who was credited with seeing many things and telling more, that walking through the streets of Paris he had been surprised and gratified at seeing a number of the familiar round bales of St. John's, Berkeley, all marked W. C.

THE GEOGRAPHICAL DISTRIBUTION OF LONG-STAPLE COTTON IN SOUTH CAROLINA, GEORGIA AND FLORIDA

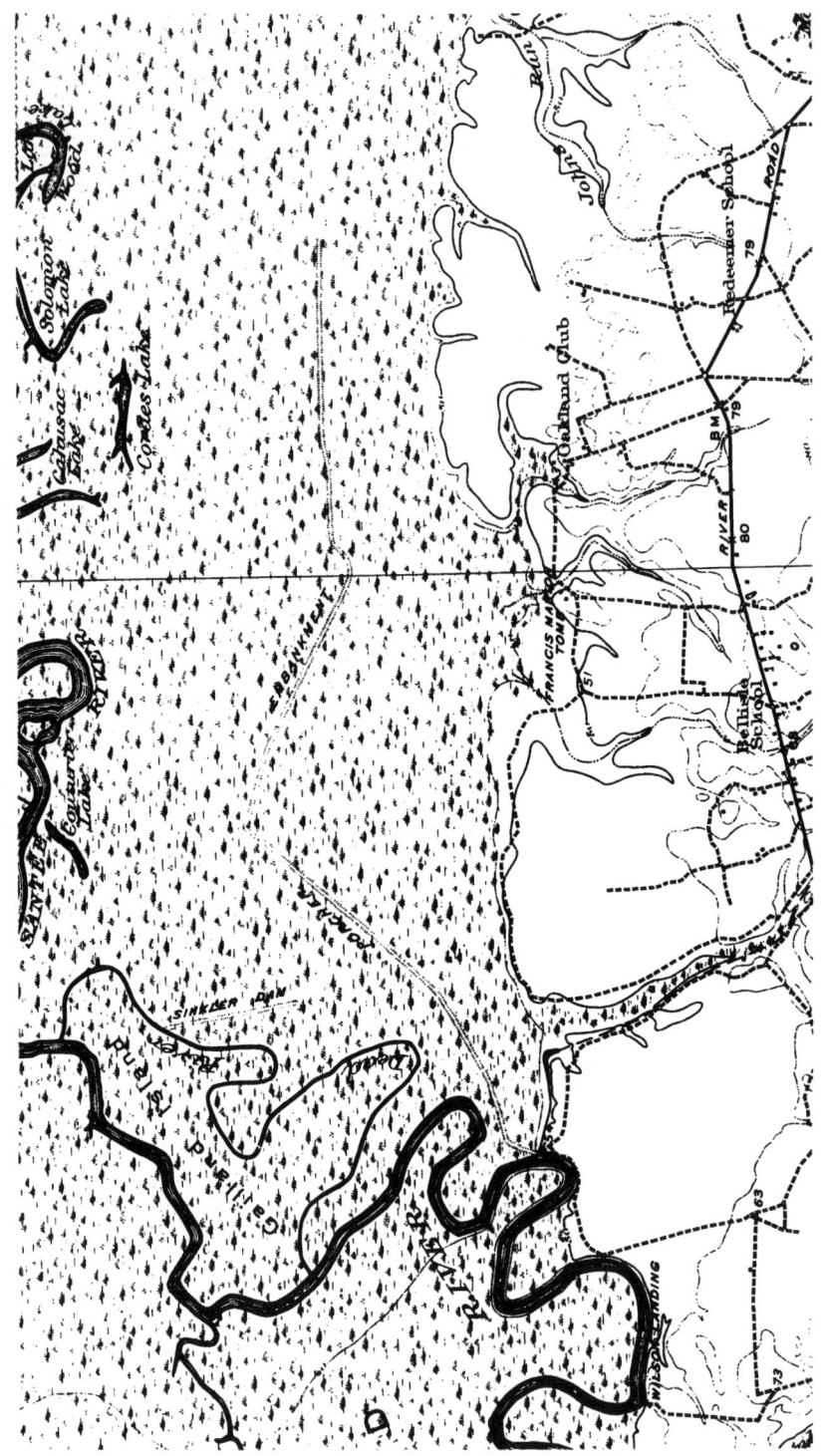

Figure 6-3. Porcher Embankment (U.S. Department of Interior Geological Survey, Chicora Quadrangle, 1921)

CHAPTER SIX

Springfield house was the home of Joseph Palmer (1770-1841), in St. John's Parish. Frederick A. Porcher (Stoney, 1945) wrote of Springfield:

The land thereabouts is some of the finest in South Carolina, and very congenial to the growth of long staple cotton... The soil is generally light, rather sandy, and to a superficial observer might appear thin and infirm, but experience has shown that it is really inexhaustible, and though it may be worn out & tired for a time with overcropping, it recovers its strength rapidly and is especially grateful for the aid of manure.

J. D. Legare's 1831 article, the "Account of the Management of Pushee, the residence of Dr. Henry Ravenel" (1790-1867), documents Pooshee[5] Plantation as a site for Santee long. Dr. Ravenel's success as a planter was noted by Robert Wilson (1907, 14): "His cropping methods and plantation economy were the outcome of his own judgement and experience and differed in many particulars from the general practice of his day, but his uniformly successful results were his ample justification and their influence is still with us." Ravenel was most noted for his cattle composting system, which influenced his fellow planters. Many cotton planters, rather than attempt to restore the fertility of old fields, simply cleared and cultivated new land until it was exhausted. Ravenel, however, freely used natural manures produced on Pooshee to restore exhausted fields. Cattle, sheep, and hogs were enclosed in moveable pens, and workers raked leaves and pine straw into the pens to mix with the manure. Ravenel's methods produced abundant vegetable crops and Santee long cotton; undoubtedly, he was ahead of his times in agricultural practices.

Around 1830, the Santee planters began buying seeds from the sea island planters and the quality of the crop became more important than quantity. Ruffin referred to seeds from the sea islands (William M. Mathew 1992, 72):

The kind cultivated is not the green-seed, but the long-staple Santee, a black seed variety which is the product of sea-island seed, but somewhat degenerated from the fine & long staple of the sea-island product.

Another source concerning seeds from the sea islands came from the records of the Black Oak Agricultural Society on April 18, 1857:

...in the climatizing if the finer qualities of cotton whether by selection of Seed grown here or by importations from the Islands - with a comparison of the productiveness of our lands at its earliest cultivation with the old "Santee Black" & that of the present time with the finer Island seed...

The most detailed account of long-staple cotton in the Santee long region was recorded by Thomas Walter Peyre (1812-51) of Brunswick Plantation in St. John's Parish. He began his plantation journal in 1834 and wrote in it until his death.[6] Peyre recorded planting times, listing times, manure methods, ginning data, thinning data, production totals, and harvest times over the period of his journal. He even recorded his seed sources. For example, on April 11, 1836, he wrote: "Planted a half acre of Sea Island seed from Hilton Head with about 3 pints of seed given to me by Mr. W. Snowden." Most importantly, his journal documented that both black-seed and green-seed cotton were grown at the same time on his plantation. Peyre recorded cotton production for 1837. Table 6-2 is compiled from his journal.

Type of Cotton	Acres Planted	Weight in Seed (lbs.)	Net Weight of Lint (lbs.)
Black Seed	29	6,700	1,833
Green Seed	40	4,670	1,390
Total	69	11,370	3,223

Table 6-2. Cotton production on Brunswick Plantation, St. John's Parish, in 1837

At least one planter in St. John's Parish continued to plant Santee long using seeds from the original source at the same time that he planted a crop using seeds from the sea islands. On April 20, 1838, Dr. Henry Ravenel of Pooshee Plantation wrote in his diary: "Sent by Deveauxs Boat—14 & 1/2 Bales of Cotton. 9 Stained & 5 & 1/2 of white. 2 of which were from Sea Island Seed. The Sea Island sold to Gourdin & Smith at 35 [cents per pound]." On June 5, 1839, Ravenel wrote: "Sent by McBeths Boat 3 & 1/2 bales Sea Island Cotton & 15 Bales Stained Santee Cotton."

Ravenel planted four plantations: Indianfield, Northampton, Pooshee, and Hardput. And, like Peyre, Ravenel planted both Santee long cotton and green-seed (upland) cotton on these four plantations. For example, on December 21, 1839, he recorded: "Sent by Clark's Boat 6 Bales of Cotton green seed, 4 white & 2 Stained."

Ravenel's diary also substantiated the monetary value of Santee long cotton to the planters of St. John's. Ravenel meticulously recorded the number and weights of bales he sold, both long-staple and short, and stained cotton, and how much he received for sales of bales. He made the distinction between the long-staple cotton derived from seed from the original source and seed from sea island planters after 1830, both crops of which in the commercial market were classified as Santee long. Table 6-3 is compiled from his diary.[7]

Date	No. of Bales		Total Weight	Price/lb	Gross ($)	2003 Value
	Sea Island	Original				
April 20, 1838	2		752	35¢	263.20	5,171.50
January 22, 1839		15	6,718	43¢	2,888.74	56,759.61
April 2, 1839	4		1,653	47¢	776.91	15,265.17

August 5, 1839	2		814	42¢	341.88	6,717.45
January 1, 1840		6	2,672	25.5¢	681.36	14,417.58
January 1, 1840	10		4,659	28¢	1,304.52	27,603.64

Table 6-3. Monetary value of Santee long cotton in St. John's Parish, 1838-40

There seems to be no question, based on the above sources, that at some time the planters of St. John's and St. Stephen's purchased seeds from the Carolina sea island planters who produced the finest quality of cotton, replacing their original seed sources. Sea island seeds were used until the end of cultivation of Santee long cotton. After the introduction of the sea island seeds, the quality of staple was higher, as Henry W. Ravenel (1843, 18) reported:

Within the past 8 or 10 years, from the introduction of the finer seeds of the Sea Islands, the Santee cotton has lost that distinctive character it formerly possessed.— Like the Sea Island Cotton, it has become more of a fancy article; dependent very much upon favorite brands and particular qualities of seed.

There is no record as to when cultivation of Santee long cotton ceased. The records of the Black Oak Agricultural Society ended in 1862, just after the beginning of the Civil War. The *News and Courier* of February 28, 1885 quoted receipts of 12 bags of Carolinas, 8 bags Santees and 19 bags of Floridas; on March 13 the same year, it quoted 44 bags Carolinas, 2 bags Santees and 4 bags Floridas. In a letter from Charles St. George Sinkler of Belvidere Plantation in Upper St. John's Parish, Berkeley County, to his fiancée Anne Wickham Porcher on September 2, 1883, Sinkler wrote: "The planters of the long staple cotton anticipate fine prices owing to the ravages of the cotton caterpillar on the coast, but unfortunately the most of my crop is in short cotton which is lower than I have ever known it."[8]

From these sources the author concludes that some Santee long cotton was indeed grown after the war. However, it is likely, in the absence of records indicating otherwise, that only minimal crops were produced at that time. This is understandable, as the war left the South impoverished, and agriculture became a matter of mere subsistence. One short paragraph in Henry Edmund Ravenel's *Ravenel Records* (1898, 113), written about his family plantations in and around Black Oak Church in St. John's Parish, gave a clue to the situation after the war:

To this day the labor of the section of country which we have in view remains completely demoralized. Not has any substitute for cotton yet appeared, nor indeed any crop which may be expected to enrich the country.

Although Santee long was a profitable crop and brought great financial rewards to its planters, it never equalled the fineness of texture and the length of sea island cotton, which always held the first rank in the markets. Santee long, grouped with mains as upland long-staple, had a fiber length of from 1 1/8 to 1 1/2 inches long (Lewis C. Gray 1958, 731). Two main factors that prevailed during the cultivation of Santee long caused it to sell at a discount to sea island (the same factors that affected mains): it was grown in the vicinity of upland cotton, resulting in hybridization; and the planters of Santee long did not practice seed selection, but instead purchased their seeds from Georgia early on and from the Carolina sea islands after 1830. This did not always guarantee that the seeds were of the highest quality, as it is possible that the sea island planters were reluctant to sell their best seeds, substituting inferior seeds unbeknownst to the planters.

The plantation journals of Thomas Walter Peyre and Dr. Henry Ravenel clearly indicate that both green-seed and black-seed cotton were planted at the same time on the five contiguous plantations they farmed: Brunswick, Northampton, Pooshee, Indianfield and Hardput. Peyre also documented that some type of cotton was planted throughout Middle St. John's, likely a mix of long- and short-staple cottons.[9] It does not appear that these planters could have successfully isolated the long-staple cotton from the short-staple crops. Brunswick, where Peyre planted, had only 630 acres of high land, not all of which was cultivated. Given the required distance of 100 meters separation to prevent hybridization, this would have been difficult to accomplish. Furthermore, in these two journals, and in those of Peter Gaillard and René Ravenel, there is no mention that they attempted to isolate long-staple and short-staple crops, or were aware of the problem of hybridization.

The author concludes, then, that the absence of significant isolation between long-staple and short-staple crops, the lack of a seed selection process for Santee long, and the slight differences in climate between the Santee long area and the sea islands (the former having a shorter growing season and higher rainfall) were responsible for the lower fiber quality of Santee long cotton as compared to sea island cotton. The cultivation methods of the Santee long planters were as advanced as the sea island planters, so this factor probably played no part in the difference.

Georgia

Sea Island Cotton

Sea island cotton began its worldwide journey in Georgia in 1785-86 when it was converted to a day-neutral plant on St. Simons Island. This new long-staple cotton spread throughout the sea islands of Georgia (fig. 1-4), East Florida and South Carolina and was a great boon to the planters suffering from the depression in the indigo industry. The first sea island cotton to reach London from Georgia was sold to Glasgow manufacturers for 4 shillings 6 pence sterling per pound. By 1789, some twenty planters on the Georgia coast were producing the new cotton. The following year, William Elliott planted the first commercial crop of sea island cotton in South Carolina on Hilton Head Island. In the Carolina sea islands, seed selection by

CHAPTER SIX

Kinsey Burden (and later by other Carolina planters) produced the superfine staple for which the islands became famous.

Georgia planters attempted to copy Burden's method of seed selection. However, by the 1850s, they became more concerned about producing a high-quality crop than they were over competition with the Carolina breeders, and simply purchased fresh seed each year from Carolina planters who had succeeded in producing top-quality seed.

The growing of sea island cotton produced great wealth along the Georgia sea islands, and as in Carolina, provided a rich aristocratic life for the most successful planters. Major Pierce Butler's (1744-1822) Hampton Plantation on St. Simons Island along the Altamaha River was a model for production of long-staple sea island cotton. Cotton from Hampton brought a premium price in the Liverpool market. On Hampton, ginning was done with a machine from Joseph Eve's design. It was powered by two horses and manned by seven slaves. A screw press compressed the ginned cotton, reducing the size of the bale, which allowed more cotton to be loaded onto a ship.[10] The high land of Hampton was well adapted to growing long-staple cotton. Even the marsh land that surrounded St. Simons was put into cotton production.

Thomas Spalding (1774-1851), who wrote extensively on long-staple cotton (see Bibliography), moved to Sapelo Island and became a successful planter of sea island cotton. He began acquiring land on Sapelo in 1802. Like the Carolina sea island planters, he was innovative in his planting methods, using salt-marsh mud to replenish the sandy soils of Sapelo. Thomas Spalding died in 1851. His grandchildren tried to revive sea island cotton after the war by renting out land and collecting a portion of the cotton crop as rent. But the problems of dealing with freedmen as a source of labor rendered the venture unsuccessful. Ultimately, the Spalding heirs turned to timbering and cattle for income. In 1873, the planting of sea island cotton on Sapelo Island was discontinued.

Jekyll Island was the site of Christophe P. DuBignon's (1739-1825) plantation chronicled by Martha L. Keber in her book *Seas of Gold, Seas of Cotton* (2002). Originally, DuBignon lived in France as a nobleman with income from land, moneylending and manufacturing. Fleeing the French Revolution, he settled in 1790 on Jekyll Island, a barrier island, among other refugees from France and the Caribbean. On Jekyll Island, DuBignon became a diligent and successful cultivator of sea island cotton despite its vulnerability to early frosts, drought, winds, and all manner of diseases and insect pests. Keber described cotton cultivation on Jekyll Island (2002, 195-96):

Life on Jekyll Island reflected the tempo of tending to the cotton, beginning with planting in mid-March. Slaves hoed the fields four to eight times in the spring and early summer to keep down weeds, but after early July, hoeing was suspended and the weeds tolerated rather than risk jostling the cotton pods. In the heat and salt air of the barrier islands, the cotton grew quickly and in August it was topped to encourage the plants to bear more. The harvest began in September and continued until December. As soon as the pods opened, slaves picked the cotton before it could be damaged by

THE GEOGRAPHICAL DISTRIBUTION OF LONG-STAPLE COTTON IN SOUTH CAROLINA, GEORGIA AND FLORIDA

dust or winds. Nine or ten or eleven times the slaves retraced their steps between the ridges, picking the silky fiber from newly opened pods. After the cotton dried on scaffolds, two revolving wooden rollers of a cotton gin separated the lint from the smooth, black seeds. Finally the cleaned cotton was packed tightly into round bags weighing three hundred pounds each.

DuBignon's crop of 1799 netted him a profit of over $30,000 ($436,135 in today's terms). But when cotton prices dropped in 1810 to about eighteen cents a pound, DuBignon and other planters had to find ways to maximize production. Improved methods of seed selection, the use of salt-marsh mud and composts, care to keep trash out of the crop during picking, and the purchase of a gin on Jekyll Island all contributed to a more efficient system and greater profits.

DuBignon's son Henry inherited Jekyll Island after his father's death in 1825 and continued to manage it for cotton and other products. Although it was still a profitable plantation, the high profits of long-staple cotton of the first two decades of the 1800s were never again equalled. Hurricanes, insect pests and diseases, and the loss of slaves during the Civil War all took a toll on Jekyll Island and other plantations on the Georgia sea islands. In 1886, Jekyll Island was sold and became an elite resort for wealthy industrialists and businessmen.

Cumberland Island,[11] the southernmost and largest (30 miles long) of the Georgia sea islands, was owned in the late 1700s by two men and their families: General Nathanael Greene of Revolutionary War fame and Thomas Lynch (1727-1776), a wealthy rice planter from South Carolina. Lynch's son, also named Thomas, inherited his father's Cumberland Island holdings, but before his father's will was probated, he was lost at sea in 1779. The Greene family fell on hard times, and in 1800 the property on Cumberland Island belonging to the heirs of General Greene and Thomas Lynch was divided into twelve tracts, beginning with tract #1, Dungeness, on the southern end and ending with tract #12, Little Cumberland Island, on the northern end.

Records indicate that Thomas Stafford and his uncle Robert resided on Cumberland Island by 1800, probably because of some permanent position with the Greene family. In 1813, Thomas's son, another Robert (1790-1877), began his quest to own all of Cumberland Island. With his sisters Susannah and Mary, and his mother Lucy (then married to Isham Spalding), he bought a 600-acre tract on Cumberland Island in 1813 as tenants-in-common. The tract was called Littlefield. In 1834, Stafford purchased Rayfield Plantation, bringing his total acreage to 1,360. Stafford acquired the Gray Field tract from John Gray through a forfeited promissory note. He added other tracts when clients secured loans from him by placing their lands as collateral, then defaulted. By 1870, Stafford had acquired the rest of his Cumberland Island holdings. Although he never owned all of Cumberland, his property extended to 8,125 acres.

Although Robert Stafford's holdings on Cumberland Island were large, lands suited for sea island cotton cultivation were small. By crop rotation, fertilization, and careful weeding,

Stafford made best use of his limited long-staple cotton land. According to Mary R. Bullard's calculations in her book *Robert Stafford of Cumberland Island* (1995, 150), he cultivated possibly 75 acres in 1850 (representing 262,500 pounds of unginned cotton) and probably 43 acres in 1860 (or 150,000 pounds of unginned cotton). Even these small acreages were significant. One hundred and fifty thousand pounds of unginned cotton in 1860 would have sold at a considerable price. Unlike the Carolina sea island planters who sent their sea island cotton to England and France, sea island cotton from Cumberland Island was sent north to Rhode Island and Massachusetts.

Stafford was able to hold onto Cumberland Island after the war. However, it does not appear that significant sea island cotton was grown after the war. Robert Stafford died in 1877 and his Cumberland Island properties were sold by his heirs in 1882 to Thomas M. Carnegie and Leander M. Morris for $40,000.

The Civil War left the sea island plantations of Georgia in ruins, both financially and physically. Labor problems prevented Georgia planters from raising long-staple cotton, and production on the islands never recovered. J. William Harris best stated the plight of the Georgia sea island cotton growers (2001, 23): "Whatever wage it might have taken to get freedmen to dig mud in the winter and haul it to the cotton lands, these planters were unable to pay." Disgruntled planters grazed cattle on their plantations, sold timber to mills, or rented land to black farmers who cultivated provision crops. By 1879, sea island cotton was grown on the sea islands and adjacent mainland only by small farmers, most of them black. Only in South Carolina was there a successful attempt to produce sea island cotton on the coastal islands after the war.

Interior Sea Island Cotton

By the early 1900s, according to Orton (1907, 8), the coastal counties in Georgia produced scarcely any cotton, owing to the unfavorable character of the country, the absence of necessary labor, and the predominance of the lumbering and trucking industries. But long-staple cotton production was not over in Georgia—it moved to the interior of south Georgia. By 1907 (fig. 6-5), an interior sea island cotton belt ran from Bullogh County southwest to Lowndes County, abutting the Florida long-staple cotton region. (These interior counties also produced considerable upland cotton.) Like the Florida interior sea island cotton, the Georgia cotton was classed with the Carolina mains and Santee long, selling at a discount to Carolina sea island. Prior to the advent of the boll weevil, interior sea island cotton was one of the most important money crops in south Georgia. From 1899 to 1918, Georgia production ranged from 21,279 to 77,961 bales, or about 50%-60% of the total long-staple crop in the United States. Production figures from 1909-18 indicate that Georgia (and Florida) greatly surpassed South Carolina in the production of long-staple cotton (table 6-4).

THE GEOGRAPHICAL DISTRIBUTION OF LONG-STAPLE COTTON IN SOUTH CAROLINA, GEORGIA AND FLORIDA

Year	Florida Interior	Georgia Interior	Carolina Sea Island
1918	20,571	21,279	10,358
1917	37,327	47,979	7,313
1916	36,092	77,981	3,486
1915	28,094	57,572	6,178
1914	33,662	42,395	5,597
1913	25,587	43,305	8,671
1912	22,334	43,736	7,707
1911	41,270	72,904	5,119
1910	29,417	47,935	13,016
1909	28,158	52,060	14,573

Table 6-4. Production in bales of long-staple cotton from 1909 to 1918 for Florida, Georgia and South Carolina (U.S. Bureau of the Census)

G. A. Gordon (1907, 8-9) outlined the reasons for the move to interior counties:

The invention of the sewing machine [in 1830] worked a revolution in the production of Sea Island cotton. It was found that thread made from upland cotton could not stand the jerk of the sewing machine, and it became necessary to find a substitute. The genuine island cotton was too expensive and yield too small a quantity for the uses of the trade. In seeking to meet this demand, it was discovered that the level, sandy pine lands of Georgia... would produce a good style of Sea Island cotton of a coarser variety. After some experiments, the Carolina planter succeeded in producing a seed known as "The Gordon C seed," or "Gordon Low Bush" seed which was very prolific; produced a staple somewhat coarser and shorter than the island cotton; gave a yield of one pound of lint to three of seed on the Georgia lands, and yielded per acre nearly as much as upland cotton. This cotton was found to meet exactly the requirement of the thread men, and as it could be produced cheaply, a large increase in the crop took place.

The effect of this cotton-thread market on the Georgia interior sea island cotton production was remarkable. In a few years, the Georgia planters rose from a state of extreme poverty to comparative independence. This period of wealth and increased production was short-lived, however, as the boll weevil reached Georgia in 1915 and cotton growing ceased soon after.

In 1936, Georgia planters became aware of the revival of long-staple cotton in Florida and wanted to commence growing long-staple cotton again. Georgia planters sought to obtain seeds from the Florida planters. However, at that time, there was an infestation of pink boll worm in Florida and a quarantine was effected against movement of cotton seeds into Georgia. In the spring of 1936, in order to prevent Georgia farmers from sneaking infested seeds through the quarantine, the U.S. Bureau of Plant Industry made available to Georgia farmers 125 bushels of sea island seeds. Seventy-five bushels (assumed to be free from disease) were shipped from Leesburg, Florida, and 50 bushels were sent from the Pee Dee Experiment Station in Florence, South Carolina. Seventy-five bales averaging about 400 pounds each were produced from these seeds. Almost all of the seeds from the 1936 crop were saved for planting in 1937.

The quarantine against the pink boll worm was lifted in 1936 and Georgia planters were again able to obtain seeds from Florida. Seeds from both of these sources were used and 4,000 acres were planted in 1937. The industry revived and expanded.

Three factors contributed to the expansion of this new production: (1) the boll weevil control methods developed in Florida and adapted in Georgia; (2) the fact that long-staple cotton was exempt from the government's cotton reduction program; and (3) a number of roller gins that had been stored in barns after the boll weevil ended long-staple production could be used again to gin the cotton.

This new period of interior sea island cotton production, however, was also short-lived. Commercial cultivation in Georgia ended in the 1940s around the same time as in Florida. W. H. Jenkins, agronomist with the Pee Dee Experiment Station in Florence, South Carolina, wrote to Chalmers S. Murray in 1950: "There were no commercial plantings of Sea Island cotton in the United States in 1950 and there have been none for many years. Efforts were made to revive the industry in Florida and Georgia and there were extensive plantings in these states from about 1935 to 1941..."[12] In Georgia, the main reason for its second demise was the lack of an adequate labor force. Long-staple cotton was still picked by hand. Mechanical pickers used in the Southwest for long-staple cotton damaged the fiber of the Georgia cotton. Pima cotton was coarser and could withstand the forces applied by mechanical pickers. Also, it had such a low yield compared to upland cotton that it became cost-inefficient to plant long-staple cotton. Timbering also became more profitable at this time.

Florida

Sea Island Cotton

Cotton was "King" in the agricultural regions of Florida from the earliest days of the state's development until the mid-1900s. When England acquired the Florida peninsula from Spain in 1763, many large land grants were made to pioneers from the British Isles who established cotton plantations on the coast of northeast Florida. During the second Spanish occupation, 1783-1819, the Spaniards, as in their previous ownership, displayed little interest in agricultural activities, but many Americans received Spanish land grants and their acreage was principally devoted to growing long-staple cotton.

James L. Watkins, in his 1908 book *King Cotton*, gave an early account of sea island cotton cultivation in Florida. As Florida was not acquired by the United States until 1819, no records of cotton production were available before that time. Watkins theorized, however, that sea

THE GEOGRAPHICAL DISTRIBUTION OF LONG-STAPLE COTTON IN SOUTH CAROLINA, GEORGIA AND FLORIDA

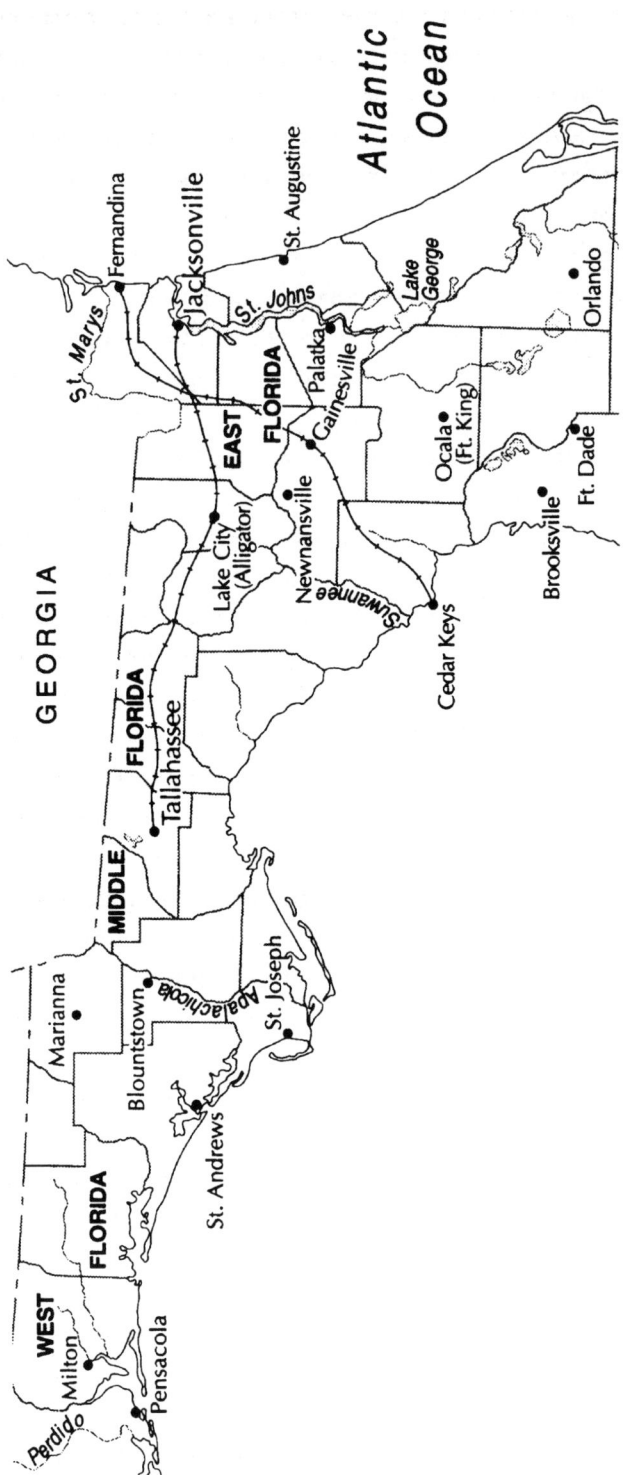

Figure 6-4. Map showing East Florida, Middle Florida and West Florida

island cotton was cultivated to some extent from the date of its development in Georgia in 1786, and that "the adaptability of the soil and climate, to the production of a superior quality of sea-island cotton, was known not many years after this variety was successfully introduced in Georgia, and it was profitably cultivated the first years of the last century by English settlers from the Bahama Islands" who had come to Florida to avail themselves of a better soil. Watkins cited planting in the Tomoca River[13] area: "...all of them have prospered, and several have become very rich by raising sea-island cotton, which for some years previous to this period (1822) well repaid their labors." Watkins also reported that in 1825, "samples of sea-island cotton of Florida grown and produced in the western portion of the State, were exhibited at Pensacola and pronounced to be equal to that produced elsewhere."

Undoubtedly, long-staple cotton was grown in Florida beginning in the early 1800s. The extent of cultivation was not well documented; production totals have not survived or were never recorded. Watkins (1908) included several tables on crop totals; however, his tables are labeled, for example, "Commercial Cotton Crops of Florida, 1820-1829." There is no way to determine whether upland cotton was included in these figures. Accordingly, the author is hesitant to use these tables to calculate sea island cotton production in Florida in the early 1800s.

A rich pre-war plantation system, similar to that of the sea islands of South Carolina, developed in East Florida (fig. 6-4) with sea island cotton a major commodity. The brief descriptions of the following two plantations in East Florida give a view of this plantation system.

Judge James Thomas O'Neill's New Hope Plantation ran along the boundary of Lanceford Creek, a tributary of the Amelia River in Nassau County. His daughter, Isabel Barnwell, related the history of the plantation.[14] His pride was the crop of sea island cotton he kept segregated from upland cotton. (It was also his main money-making crop.) Like his Carolina sea island counterparts, O'Neill practiced seed selection. When he spied an exceptionally long lint, he would tie a string around that plant to save it for seeds. Seeds to be used for planting the next year were ginned by hand and stored. There were never any plows used; all cultivation was done by hand. Under his care, New Hope Plantation produced one of the longest and finest lints in Nassau County.

Judge O'Neill and his family fled New Hope when federal gunboats appeared in Fernandina Harbor in 1862, and settled in Hamilton County. After the war, they returned to New Hope, but the judge never farmed again on a large scale. His daughter closed her story with: "We still own New Hope, the old house, rebuilt in 1884 still standing but rapidly deteriorating, and the land overgrown with scrub pines and palmettoes..."

Another East Florida plantation was Laurel Grove, chronicled by Daniel L. Schafer in Jane G. Landers's book *Colonial Plantations and Economy in Florida* (2000). Laurel Grove was located in Duval County on Fort George Island and ran along the St. John's River for two miles and west along Doctor's Lake for one mile. The plantation was owned by Captain Zephaniah Kingsley and operated from 1803 to 1813.

THE GEOGRAPHICAL DISTRIBUTION OF LONG-STAPLE COTTON IN SOUTH CAROLINA, GEORGIA AND FLORIDA

Kingsley was born in Bristol, England, in 1765 and moved with his family to Charleston in 1770. He became wealthy as a merchant and slave trader. An article in *Harper's Magazine* (S. W. G. Benjamin 1878, 845) said Kingsley "seemed to have been a man of marked originality and force of character, shrewd, canny, a law unto himself, a despot who combined the elemental traits of planter, slaver, and buccaneer, but tempered at least by certain negative virtues..." He built and often commanded his own ships, and brought his slaves directly from Africa. In 1803, he took an oath of loyalty and became a Spanish citizen at St. Augustine.

He purchased Laurel Grove that same year, and imported African slaves to operate the plantation. With additional purchases, Laurel Grove was expanded to nearly 3,000 acres. The plantation's main export crop was sea island cotton. As a planter, Kingsley understood all the mysteries connected with the culture of the best sea island cotton. He established a task system (similar to that of the Carolina sea islands) where the workers tended quarter-acre increments of cotton and other crops. Kingsley established a vast support system for the plantation, dividing the work force into three separate agricultural villages, building plantation stores, warehouses, a blacksmith shop, and cotton houses, and installing three double-sized cotton gins (roller gins) operated by water power. Laurel Grove became self-supporting, a model plantation for its time.

Schafer (Landers 2000, 104) commented on Kingsley's crop of sea island cotton in 1812:

During July 1812 there were sixty bales (21,000 pounds) from the 1811 crop awaiting export. With long-staple cotton selling for fifty cents a pound, Kingsley expected the bales to bring $10,500. An additional 30,000 pounds of 'unginned' seed cotton from the 1810 crop was on hand, estimated to be worth only $.15 a pound (or $4,500) before ginning. Only 200 acres were planted in cotton in 1812, but the predicted yield was 200-300 pounds per acre—or 40,000 pounds, worth $20,000 after ginning.

Laurel Grove experienced record profits until July 1812 when prosperous times abruptly ended. From 1812 to 1815 (Landers 2000, 106), "...hungry invaders from Georgia... brought destruction to East Florida and an end to its booming export economy... The invaders were joined by residents of the Spanish province in an insurgency aimed at annexing it to the United States." Numerous plantations were looted and destroyed, including Laurel Grove, which never was a major producer of sea island cotton again.

An interesting debate by two individuals identified as only "Verum" and "W" appeared, concerning where long-staple cotton was, or could be, grown in Florida. First, Verum commented (1844, 449):

Sea Island cotton can perhaps be cultivated on a few of the Florida Islands, and on a narrow strip of land on the Eastern coast, about Indian River. This remains to be determined. It cannot be raised in the other parts of the Territory, and least of all in the Northern portions of East Florida, which is the least adapted to the production of Florida staples. It cannot be raised in the very center of the Peninsular.

W (1844, 452) answered Verum in the same article (and gave his address as Leon County, Florida, October 6, 1844): "...I am utterly at a loss to account for the broad assertions of 'Verum,' made directly in the face of the real facts of the case." In his article, W stated:

Sea Island Cotton has been successfully raised in Jackson, Gadsden, Leon, Jefferson, Madison, Hamilton, Columbia, and Duval counties, embracing the Northern part of East Florida, the whole of the Middle District, and one county at least in West Florida, and for ten to fourteen years past.

In an article in the *National Intelligencer*, an individual identified as only "a physician" wrote (A Physician, 1843):

It is not merely in its tropical productions that East Florida possesses great advantages over every other State in the Union; it is now established, beyond a doubt, that the Sea Island or long staple cotton (the production of which has heretofore been confined to a few small islands in South Carolina and Georgia) will grow luxuriantly even in the center of the peninsula. A superior quality of this article has been produced extensively on the Suwannee, and in the very center of Alachua, as well as on the eastern coast. This important fact is no doubt attributable to the most insular portion of East Florida.

Interior Sea Island Cotton

In the last decade of the antebellum period, there was an extension and codification of cotton classed as interior sea island cotton into the interior of Georgia and Florida. About 1849, it was being grown in Bullock, Wayne and Ware Counties in Georgia, 100 miles from the coast. A little was grown on the Gulf coast. However, the main extension occurred in the interior of Florida, as well as on sea islands along the coast (fig. 6-5). The discovery that sea island cotton could be grown inland from the influence of the sea was a fact reluctantly admitted by Carolina planters since they contended that the staple degenerated when produced at a considerable distance from the sea (which it did, but not for the reasons they understood at that time).

It was with great trepidation that Florida planters brought the cultivation of long-staple cotton inland. The geographic position of Florida, however, with water on three sides, and the proximity of the Gulf Stream, provided the atmospheric moisture necessary for fine staple (just as in the sea islands of South Carolina and Georgia). Some of the inland counties became great centers of interior sea island cotton production. Alachua County became famous for its fine interior sea island cotton, as did Bradford, Marion and Levy Counties. In this climate, the staple produced was of such length and fineness that it was woven into rich laces, silks, satins

THE GEOGRAPHICAL DISTRIBUTION OF LONG-STAPLE COTTON IN SOUTH CAROLINA, GEORGIA AND FLORIDA

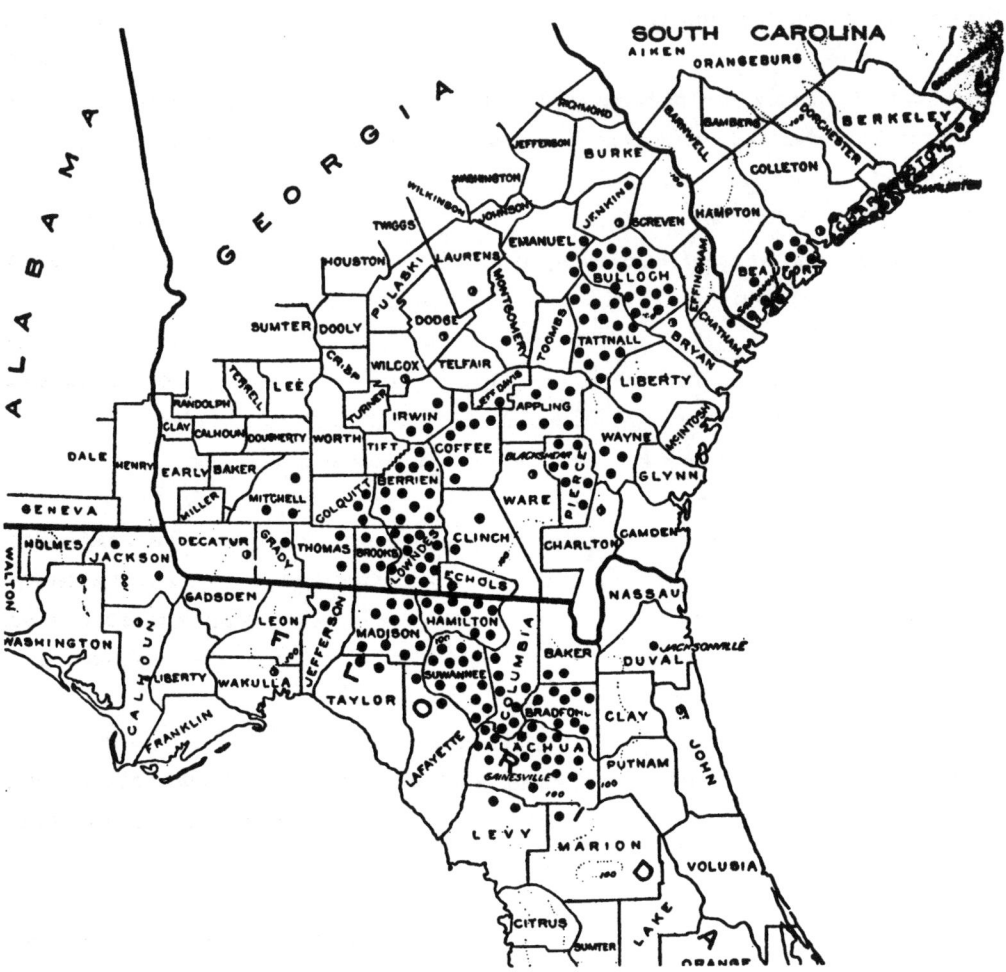

Figure 6-5. Map of Florida and Georgia interior sea island cotton and Carolina sea island cotton. Each dot represents an average production of 500 bales. (Orton 1907, 8)

and velvets. Perhaps the most important factor that produced this fine cotton was isolation from upland cotton that prevented hybridization.

Lewis Gray (1958, 734) summed up the movement into Florida:

The expansion of the industry in Florida was facilitated by the fact that Florida planters, free from the strong prejudices which bound the planters of the older region, made freer use of the plow and succeeded in making about twice as many acres to the hand as in the older region. Extension into Florida was further favored by the gradual increase in demand, especially in the sixth decade. The product was classified with the Mains and the Santee cotton of South Carolina.

By 1858, the combined Florida and Georgia industry had surpassed South Carolina, as evidenced by the following production data for the year ending August 31, 1858:[15] Florida, 25,685 bags (bales); Georgia, 10,008 bags; South Carolina, 26,663 bags.

The effect on Carolina sea island cotton of the successful Florida market was noted by William Elliott (Scafidel 1978, 862) when he wrote to his wife in 1857: "My cotton will have to be shipped—the excess of Florida cottons has destroyed the market here."

William S. Taggart (1919, 5) described Florida interior sea island cotton:

This cotton is somewhat similar to sea island, being grown from the same seed, but on the mainland of Florida and adjacent states. It has a smooth bright silky appearance, but a large percentage of immature fibers prevents it being used for the highest numbers of yarn, its limit in this respect reaching 200 [count]; unless for special purposes, it is not used for lower numbers than 140 [count] twist or weft.

One reason the Florida long-staple cotton sold at a discount to sea island cotton and was classed with the mains and Santee long through the first half of the 1800s was revealed in an article in *DeBow's Review* (July-August 1867, 134-138):

It is true that the average quality of Florida cotton is not rated so high as that of the Sea Island; but the difference in this respect is chiefly, if not entirely, attributable to the defective manner of preparing the former for market. It is a notorious fact that some of the Florida cotton has commanded the highest market price of the long staple cottons, and it is therefore a fair inference that it is owing more to a deficiency of skill, or of care in its preparation for market, than to any inferiority of texture, that the long cottons of Florida are rated lower than the Sea Islands. When the Florida planter finds that he can make an average crop of three hundred pounds of this cotton to the acre, he is not likely to bestow as much care on its preparation for market as the planter will on the Sea Islands, where one hundred and twenty pounds is a good average crop. It is in the quantity, rather than the quality, that the Florida planter finds his best remuneration.

THE GEOGRAPHICAL DISTRIBUTION OF LONG-STAPLE COTTON IN SOUTH CAROLINA, GEORGIA AND FLORIDA

By all accounts, long-staple cotton remained a dominant crop in Florida until well after the Civil War (see table 6-5). Even though the Civil War slowed agricultural progress in Florida, cotton production—mainly long-staple—continued to increase in the state during the last quarter of the nineteenth century. In the post-war era, Florida and Georgia replaced South Carolina as the main producer of long-staple cotton (see table 6-4). According to the Liverpool Cotton Association's annual circular to the cotton trade, from 1882 to 1913, Florida produced 869,362 bales of long-staple cotton of 400 pounds each, a considerable portion of the world's supply for these years. In 1902, the six counties that produced the most cotton were the north central counties of Alachua (3,462 bales), Bradford (3,224), Columbia (4,025), Hamilton (4,434), Madison (3,433), and Suwannee (5,234).

Year	Number of Bales	Year	Number of Bales
1900	28,066	1912	23,334
1901	27,765	1913	25,587
1902	31,969	1914	33,622
1903	27,840	1915	28,094
1904	39,619	1916	36,092
1905	41,531	1917	37,327
1906	23,995	1918	20,571
1907	28.935	1919	2,787
1908	34,744	1920	1,236
1909	28,158	1921	2,573
1910	29,417	1922	4,886
1911	41,270		

Table 6-5. Production of Florida interior sea island cotton from 1900 to 1922 (State of Florida 1941, 26)

By the early 1900s, Florida's cotton industry was centered in the interior counties in the north-central portion of the state (fig. 6-5). Here, the proportion of upland cotton to interior sea island cotton was much smaller. At the western coast, conditions were less favorable for long-staple cotton because upland cotton was mainly grown there, increasing the chance of hybridization between the two. Since the Florida planters did not practice seed selection as extensively as in Carolina, they secured fresh seeds every three years from Carolina planters to insure the continued quality of the crop.

But this boom period was short-lived. Several factors were responsible for the decline in Florida's interior sea island cotton industry from its peak in 1905—41,531 bales, with an estimated market return of $2,744,095 ($55,700,054 in today's currency)—to another high in 1917—37,327 bales with returns of $6,074,632 ($85,426,160), due to expanding market and higher prices—down to a low period in 1929 when only seven bales were produced in the entire coastal plain of South Carolina, Georgia and Florida. First, many of the large pre-war plantations had been divided into small farms (similar to the Carolina sea island plantations) of 50 to 100 acres; second, the Florida citrus industry, started commercially in the 1870s, and truck crops of the east coast and ridge sections of the state drew the attention of small farmers (both helped by new railways which penetrated the peninsula); third, the reduced export demand during WWI; fourth, the exodus of young men into the armed services in 1918; fifth, the sea island planters of South Carolina cut off their supply of quality seeds to the West Indies (and to Florida and Georgia as well as to their fellow sea island planters); and sixth, the arrival of the boll weevil in Florida in 1915, more insidious than falling prices or war. Florida produced 90,000 bales in 1917, but only 11 bales in 1924. By 1924, production of interior sea island cotton in Florida had virtually ceased.

Fortunately for farmers and rural merchants, a boom in the price of general farm produce took place about the time interior sea island cotton production began to decline. There were cash markets for corn, hogs, syrup, potatoes, hay, and in fact, about anything that could be produced on a north Florida farm. Many farmers started producing upland cotton, which was considerably less susceptible to boll weevil damage, and for which the market price had about doubled. Consequently, the threatening economic situation arising from the loss of long-staple cotton production was averted.

The depression of 1929-30, however, brought a decrease in the market prices of hogs, corn, and syrup, and pushed upland cotton and many other north Florida farms to a point where it was difficult or impossible to produce these products profitably. Throughout the country, various government public works programs were formed to address problems such as existed in north Florida at that time.

An attempt to revive the long-staple cotton industry was started in 1934 when the Florida Commissioner of Agriculture asked for and secured the supply of sea island seeds stored by the USDA in its Bureau of Plant Industry at the Pee Dee Experiment Station in Florence, South Carolina. These seeds, the Seabrook cultivar, came from James Island, South Carolina. When the James Island Station was closed, the Bureau of Plant Industry obtained some seeds to store in order to preserve the sea island cotton genetic source. The seeds had become old and were losing their viability. The USDA was anxious to obtain fresh seeds, and reviving interior sea island cotton in Florida afforded this opportunity. The seeds were distributed under a contract in which the government had the option of buying all the seeds from the cotton raised.

The Seabrook cultivar was originated around 1890 by Elias L. Rivers of James Island, and its selection and improvement had been carried on afterwards by its owner, F. P. Seabrook of James Island. It was a bearer of medium-quality lint and had a large proportion of lint to seed. The staple had a length of 1 1/2" to 1 7/8"; the plant had a compact habit and was resistant to disease. The seeds were initially distributed in 1901 by Seabrook.

The prospect of reviving the interior sea island cotton industry fired the imaginations of the old cotton growers, and new farmers who had come to the territory since 1920 had hopes, if not visions, of a profitably revived cotton industry.

The first crops were planted in 1934 in Gilchrist County, near Trenton. The region was chosen because it was a remote section in north Florida, a part of the old interior sea island cotton belt, where no cotton was then being planted. Fifteen bales were made and the seeds saved for planting the following year in Gilchrist County. Then, in 1935, the Works Progress Administration, seeking to put needy persons to work and looking for project operations to accomplish its objectives, volunteered to assist in the revival project. WPA took seventy bushels of seeds to Madison County to determine whether it would be possible to develop a weevil control treatment in a boll weevil area. Madison County was chosen because it had a history of boll weevils.

WPA entomologists realized that any method of weevil control would have to completely eradicate the initial infestation. All previous research on boll weevil control had ignored the thirst of the weevil. WPA researchers discovered that the application of poisoned-syrup mixtures in the afternoon—while the plants were dry and the weevils thirsty—killed all adult weevils within a few hours. The poison used was calcium arsenate. The poison-syrup was applied by brushing a wet mop through the tops of the plants. This affixed the mixture to the underside of the leaves and branches of the main stems where it was protected from removal by rain and sun. The method was sufficient to prevent damage from the midsummer migrations of the weevil, provided the cotton was planted early. It also killed all the hibernated weevils as they entered the field during May and June.

Revival of the industry was helped by the Florida Sea-Island Cotton Law passed in 1937. The main provision of the bill prohibited the planting of upland cotton in designated "cotton production control districts." This prevented hybridization with upland cotton, which normally resulted in a mongrel cotton of shorter staple and less market value. Further, interior sea island cotton was exempted from governmental restrictions on planting (unlike upland cotton, which was highly controlled under a quota system).

Production was helped as buyers came back into the market, paying an average of 30¢ a pound for the 1936 crop and 24.5¢ for the 1937 crop. They indicated that they might pay more if they could be assured of ample and uninterrupted supplies to justify manufacturers setting their spindles to use the longer staple. A major boost was the sewing thread industry. Lily Mills Company, in Shelby, North Carolina, began making sewing thread out of "home grown" long-staple cotton from Florida, stating that "the Sea Island Cotton grown the last three years is of better quality than was ever grown before—and, to date there is no other section in the world that produces cotton of equal quality." Another North Carolina mill started making sea island cotton dress socks for men, boosting them over the silk and rayon products.

After two years of successful weevil control in Madison County, a state-wide weevil poisoning program was established in 1937. With an adequate method to control the boll weevil and a plan to prevent hybridization with upland cotton, Florida once again produced interior sea island cotton. In 1937, over 20,000 acres were planted, and in 1938, nearly 40,000 acres were planted in Georgia and Florida and elsewhere.

However, the revival was once again short-lived, and ended in the 1940s. Records of the Florida State Office of Statistics in Orlando show that the state stopped recording cotton productions for all lints in 1952, and from then on recorded only production for upland cotton. (The author interprets this as meaning that not enough interior sea island cotton was produced after 1952 to justify recording it.) By 1958, acreage allotments for interior sea island cotton in Florida—formerly in the tens of thousands—totalled only 1,020 acres (USDA 1958, 8). Competition of long-staple cotton from the American Southwest and overseas; labor problems; and land more valuable for truck farming and the citrus industry ended commercial production. Finding adequate labor was a major problem during the war because of the higher wages paid for workers in the military effort. In 1942, one planter in Lake County (anonymous unpublished source) stated: "A numbers of growers paid from 3¢ to 5¢ per pound for seed cotton, to get it picked; even then, it was trashy and full of stained locks. Many of the growers stated that if they 'got after' the hands about picking the cotton cleaner, the entire force would leave the field."

No *barbadense* long-staple cotton has been planted in Florida since the 1940s.

1. Gray stated (1958, 731) that the staple length for fancy sea island cotton was two inches and upward although the bulk of the crop was probably around 1 1/2" to 1 3/4". Staple length for mains, Santee long and interior sea island cotton was 1 1/8" to 1 1/2".
2. Mason cites Henry W. Ravenel (1843, 132) and Marjorie S. Mendenhall (1940, 136) as his sources. The author has referenced both of these sources and neither includes a map of the mains cotton-growing area.
3. The house at Hanover Plantation was one of two moved and saved before the waters of Lake Moultrie inundated the St. John's Basin. It was relocated to the campus of Clemson University.
4. A freshet is a sudden overflow of a river or stream resulting from a heavy rain or thaw. It became more common on the Santee River after the clearing of the piedmont, which was part of the watershed for the Santee River.
5. In the article, the plantation is spelled Pushee. Pooshee is the correct spelling.
6. The Plantation Journal of Thomas Walter Peyre is located in the South Carolina Historical Society, Charleston, South Carolina, in text and fiche.
7. Ravenel's diary also refers to "white cotton." The author does not know what "white cotton" refers to. There are other transactions on the sales of cotton that are illegible. The quotes here are only for the sales about which the author is certain of the dates and the type of cotton.
8. The letters between Sinkler and Anne Wickham Porcher are in the possession of Anne Sinkler Whaley LeClercq of Charleston, South Carolina.
9. Peyre's journal (page 213) has this heading: "Bales of cotton produced in Middle St. Johns by." The list contains the following: Dr. H. Ravenel, Mr. William Cain, Samuel Dubose, Whitehall, Goshen, Cedar Springs, Wantoot, Wampee, Somerton, Hanover, Ophir, Brunswick, Chapel Hill, Moorfield, Sarrazins, Dubois, Hogswamp, Bunker Hill, Chelsea, H. W. Ravenel, Fairspring, Cedargrove, Fountain

Grove, Woodboo, Halls, Gippy, Dr. Theo. Gaillard, Woodlawn and Milton.

10. Carolina planters always packed their cotton by hand, saying the screw press damaged the longer-stapled sea island cotton. Georgia planters reported no damage to their long-staple fiber from the screw press.

11. Part of Cumberland Island is preserved today as the Cumberland Island National Seashore.

12. The letter from Jenkins to Murray is with the papers of Chalmers S. Murray on deposit in the South Carolina Historical Society in Charleston, S.C.

13. The Tomoca River (spelled Tomoka today) is located just inland from Daytona Beach in Volusia County and extends into Flagler County.

14. Isabel Barnwell's account of New Hope is contained in an interview on 27 July, 1940 by Rose Shephard. The manuscript is in the office of the Department of Agronomy at the University of Florida, Gainesville. The author does not have any knowledge whether the interview was ever published; no one in the department in 2003 knew anything about the manuscript. The manuscript was filed with twenty-five other manuscripts concerning sea island cotton in Florida.

15. Gray cites the following for this data: U.S. Department of Agriculture, Atlas of American Agriculture, V, Sec. A, Cotton, 20.

The Culture of Sea Island Cotton

This chapter deals with the culture[1] of sea island cotton from its establishment as a day-neutral, annual plant in the sea islands of South Carolina, Florida and Georgia in 1786 until the end of its culture in 1920. When compared to today's highly automated and mechanized culture of upland cotton and long-staple cotton in the United States and worldwide, one may be prompted to dismiss the culture methods used in the sea island cotton plantations as primitive. However, for their time, they were highly advanced. Moreover, the early sea island planters did not have a ready store of literature to draw upon since they were the first to cultivate the crop.

They had to rely on their native intelligence to determine ways to increase the crop yield and to improve the quality of the lint. Planters who were involved in rice culture when sea island cotton was developed could draw upon aspects of agronomy learned from rice planting. Only toward the latter half of sea island cotton culture did significant local, state and federal services become available.

Sea island cotton in the early days after its origin was one of the two most profitable crops ever raised in the South (Carolina gold rice being the other); however, the increase in its production and the varying fineness of the fiber caused wide fluctuations in price. While some planters realized considerable profits, others, often on adjacent plantations, were hard put to make expenses. Some planters attempted to remedy this situation so they would all benefit—

if not equally, at least collectively. From their attempt came improvements in methods of agriculture such as the careful selection of seed, soil amelioration, soil analysis and crop rotation. They organized agricultural societies, subscribed to agricultural journals, wrote articles, and sent out questionnaires. Even as early as 1828, Whitemarsh Seabrook (1828, 26) shared his understanding of the value of scientific principles:

Such a negligence of the scientific principles of Cotton-planting was easily tolerated, when the universal object was to augment the amount produced. But a very different state of things has succeeded. Every thing now depends upon the excellence of the article, and the skill employed in its preparation. To accomplish this, it is necessary that men of leisure and intelligence should devote their attention to accurate observations and well-conducted experiments.

Even with skilled slaves and the special care taken with the plants, sea island cotton was an uncertain crop, succumbing to unseasonable rains, storms, insect pests and a fluctuating market. When crops prospered, however, and prices were high, sea island cotton was a highly rewarding commodity, readily finding an overseas market, and huge profits were realized by the planters.

There was never one universally accepted method of cotton culture by sea island planters. Planters experimented with different methods to increase fiber quality and crop yield, all the time trying to decrease the cost and effort to bring the crop to market. As agricultural societies became established on the local, state and federal levels, the planters had at their disposal help with newer methods of culture. As culture developed, it reached a point where it became more standardized, and most planters adapted the better methods. Still, even at the end of the culture, planters continued to experiment on their own or with help from agencies. Of the various methods of culture experienced by the planters, many were obscure and had no impact on the broader methods that became the trend. This book addresses only the major methods of sea island cotton culture as practiced by the most successful planters.

In regard to advances in the methods of agriculture, sea island cotton culture can be divided into two broad periods: from the origin of sea island cotton up to the Civil War, and after the war until the end of culture in 1920. The period before the war did not rely entirely on established methods of culture, but rather on experimentation by individual planters. Still, it was the period in which the greatest wealth was accumulated. So esteemed was the quality of sea island cotton that prices sometimes reached $2.00 a pound, and this high price offset the non-uniform agricultural practices of this period.

William Elliott (1849, 6) best summed up the state of agriculture for the first half of sea island cotton culture:

It was observed that where water remained on the surface of the earth, there, likewise was a sickening of the plant, and then came the art of draining. It was observed that the earth sickened at the constant reproduction of the same order of plants, and thence came the rotation of crops. It was observed that with rotation and culture, the wearied earth still refused her increase, and thence came the practice of restoring the wasted fertility, by manures... From its first rude beginnings, observations and induction have established every progressive step, up to the point on which we stand, when this noble art has almost risen to the dignity of science.

After the war, however, numerous factors caused a decline in sea island cotton production. Planters had lost everything: slaves, money, tools to work crops, their fine houses and carriages, and often their farm buildings. Furthermore, the old financial system which had furnished the capital for planting and operating had vanished. To save money, some planters allowed their fields to remain untouched until the arrival of the planting season, even though field preparation should have begun months earlier. Some planters used only a plow to work the fields; however, certain aspects of field preparation were better done with the hoe instead of the plow. It became apparent, then, to some planters that the drop in demand of sea island cotton and changed social and economic conditions necessitated a change in agricultural practices if the culture were to survive. The minutes from the Agricultural Society of South Carolina dated July, 1880, and recorded by member Elias L. Rivers, explained (Gregorie and Surles, 1936b):

When the War closed, there returned from the army to James Island to engage in planting a few young men who had been educated for other vocations in life, and who, although heartily in earnest, were sadly ignorant, not only of the first principles of agriculture, but even of the merest details, of plantation management. Anxious to avoid mistakes, but having no experience to guide them, they had recourse to frequent consultations among themselves as to what was best to be done. ... As each emergency arose, unless requiring immediate disposition, it was considered in all its aspects, the views of each, were taken and as far as possible, a uniform course of action agreed upon. Thus from their ignorance began the community of thought and practice which has been perhaps, the underlying cause of whatever progress they have made. Had they been old planters, individualized by past education and confirmed in their ideas of agriculture, while they might have avoided many mistakes in the details of the plantation, they might have seen no necessity for consultation, but relied altogether upon their past experience.

The resumption of sea island cotton planting began immediately after the war in 1866. The first crop planted was a success with an excellent yield, mainly due to the fields having been fallow during the war. However, 1866 was an anomaly. Rivers pointed out that the sea island cotton crops of 1867 and 1868 were two of the most unfavorable ever known on the seacoast because constant rains saturated the soil and caterpillars attacked the cotton plants. The combination of the two completely destroyed the crops. After 1868, planters began considering the possibility of installing subsoil drainage. The first systems were installed in 1872 and subsoil drainage was generally adapted afterwards with excellent results. This is one example of the post-war planters adapting new methods to continue sea island cotton culture.

The rebirth of sea island cotton on the sea islands after the Civil War was based on advanced methods of agronomy that resulted in increased yields on smaller land holdings. Despite spending as much as $66 to raise an acre of sea island cotton, they earned a profit of about $46 per acre (from an average crop of 280 pounds per acre which sold for around 40 cents a pound). However, in spite of these advances, other events (such as the labor problem) prevented a return to the glory days prior to the war. It was more of a struggle to keep the culture alive than to reap vast fortunes. Still, sea island cotton culture became marginally profitable, but only until 1920.

Many of the culture methods used by sea island cotton planters helped deter diseases such as rust and blue cotton, as well as insect pests. Often the planters did not realize that their farming practices would result in disease and pest control, but once the lessons were learned, these methods were adapted intentionally.

Much of the information on cotton culture comes from minutes of the James Island Agricultural Society and the Agricultural Society of South Carolina. These groups tended to be more involved with sea island planters closer to Charleston, so their practices were more likely to be recorded than those of the more distant sea islands such as St. Helena Island or Lady's Island. (The records of these two islands were not available or were not located in this study.) The following descriptions are taken primarily from accounts of South Carolina sea island cotton planters. Based on the literature researched for this book, sea island cotton cultivation methods in Georgia and Florida were similar to those of South Carolina.

The Labor System

The culture of sea island cotton (and of upland cotton, as well as the other major crop of the coastal area, rice) required a large labor force. Before the Civil War, the labor force was supplied by African slaves working under the task system. After the war, the main problem that the planters encountered was how to obtain a sufficient supply of labor. Under these conditions, a system of tenant farming developed.

The Task System

A plantation system of labor management before the war was based on the task system. Each laborer was assigned a fixed amount of work for each day. When the task was completed, the slave was allowed to return to quarters and to utilize his/her time in his/her own manner. The task system was applied to all plantation activities. Slaves were divided into groups based on health, sex and strength. Men were used for heavy labor, such as ditching and digging the canals, while women performed lighter tasks such as sorting and cleaning cotton. The cotton fields were divided into squares or sections, usually in terms of acres or fractions of acres, and the slaves were assigned tasks on this basis. The work was measured in fractional figures based on one "full" task. The planter was always cognizant of how many tasks were necessary to bring a crop to market.

Thomas Spalding (1835, 45-46) gave an account of the labor required under the task system in 1835 to prepare a 300-pound bale of sea island cotton for market, calculating that it took the labor of forty persons working one day to produce one bale of cotton weighing 300 pounds:

We will now look back and collect the quantities of labour that is, or should be applied, to every bale of 300lbs. of sea island cotton, in preparing it for market. It requires 1000lbs. of seed cotton to produce 300lbs. of clean white cotton wool; fifteen persons will be required to sort and prepare 1000lbs. for the gin or machine; taking all weather, 25lbs. is the mean quantity received from gin pr day; this gives 12 days labour to each bag for ginning; and 10 women mote these 300lbs. of cotton in the day, making, for sorting 15, for ginning 12, for moting 10, for packing 1, in all 38. But, besides these 38 that must be good and steady persons, there are usually two inferior persons, young or old, to place the cotton, which is about to be ginned, upon the drying floor, or to remove or pass it about it in any change of weather, thus requiring to every bag of sea island cotton well put up, the labour of 40 persons, one day.

Kinsey Burden (1844b, 207), when asked about the daily task of a laborer, replied:

In listing land, if the land had a heavy sward, the task was one fourth of an acre; if only one year at rest, and lighter, one-third of an acre; if it had been cultivated the year before, half an acre... In ridging, one fourth of an acre was done, unless the plough was used. In hoeing half an acre.

J. A. Turner (1857, 285) included a letter from Thomas Spalding on the task system in listing:

The task in listing, the fields being previously cleared up and the remains of the former year burned off, was half an acre; the laborer was required to ridge afterwards, when carefully done, three-eights of an acre; and in hoeing, half an acre was the task, depending, however, much upon the season and the condition of the field.

Each planter worked out a task system based on his labor force, on the type of cotton he planted, and on the culture methods used. He was then able to judge how many acres of cotton he could plant in a particular year. Or, as Whitemarsh Seabrook reported, he could determine how many acres of fields could be covered with marsh grass. Seabrook determined that one task for a laborer in gathering marsh grass was three full carts. Ten laborers, in thirty days, could cut nine hundred loads, which, if applied in the summer, would cover forty acres of field.

The slaves were the main expense on a plantation, and formed a highly liquid type of investment. A plantation that suffered a financial problem could turn slaves into cash on short notice.

The Tenant System

The tenant system evolved after the Civil War and was called the "two day" tenant system. The planter provided the Negro laborer's family a house, wood gathering (fuel) rights, and from five to seven acres of land. In return, the tenant agreed to work for the planter two days a week; the rest of the week the family could work its own fields. The tenant laborer was expected to work "two tasks," or one-half acre per day. If more work was required for the crops, the planter would provide for more tenants or pay his own tenant a wage for the extra work. The agreement usually extended for a period of ten months. It was also common for the planters to make cash advances to their tenants. Nearly every planter operated a commissary store and supplied the tenants with provisions throughout the year. In short, the planter tried to offer as many inducements to the freedmen to settle on his plantation. Of the different work systems that were tried, the tenant system appeared to have been the most satisfactory to both planter and laborer.

Two other systems were also practiced on the islands, but with less success than the tenant system. In the share-cropping agreement, the planter supplied a house for the laborer and his family, as well as seed, fertilizers and farm implements; in return, the tenant furnished the labor for the planter's fields. When the crop was sold, the planter and tenant would share the profits at an agreed-upon percentage. Negroes who were not tenants or sharecroppers worked for day wages, which in 1880 averaged about fifty cents a day.

Location of Fields

Five principal environments of the sea islands were planted in sea island cotton : (1) oak-hickory forests of the erosion remnant islands; (2) maritime forests of the barrier islands; (3) salt marshes; (4) low, poorly drained soils of the swamps and low, flat woods of the erosion-remnant islands; and (5) the pine barrens. The first sites planted were the maritime forests and the oak-hickory forests. But prolonged use depleted the minerals, and the planters simply abandoned fields and cleared more forest since it was easier to do this than to fertilize the worn out fields. Also, in the early period of sea island cotton culture, the planters were not familiar with adequate methods of soil amelioration.

A point was reached when there were no more virgin oak-hickory or maritime forests left to clear; the planters then turned to the salt marsh, swamps, freshwater marshes and low, wet woods and pine barrens for cotton fields.

Oak-Hickory Forests of the Erosion-Remnant Islands

Numerous references state that the sea island planters chose the sandy, loamy soil of the erosion-remnant islands as best suited for the cultivation of sea island cotton in the beginning of the industry. The sandy loam soil had one advantage over the sandy soil of the barrier islands: being Pleistocene in nature, it had a clay content that gave it a better water- and mineral-holding capacity. Only in heavy rains was this soil bad for the cotton plants, and ridges with drainage between them easily solved this problem.

Few clues exist today to determine the original vegetation of the erosion-remnant islands. William Elliott (1828, 152) described these islands: "Such high lands of a light brown or yellow complexion, as were covered by an original growth of hickory, laurel, and red bay, interspersed with the live and white oaks, and the towering palmetto."[2] The author interprets this description as that of a transitional maritime forest occurring along the borders of the islands where they were flanked by salt marsh. In the interior, the transitional maritime forest graded into oak-hickory or pine forest. It was in these forests that planters initially produced the best sea island cotton.

Barrier Islands

The soil of the barrier islands was composed of well-sorted sands, ideal for cotton growing except that it lacked a good mineral-holding capacity and was easily depleted. But it drained well, which was ideal for the plant. Evidently only the larger barrier islands were planted in sea island cotton, including Bull, Capers, Dewees and Kiawah in Charleston County; and Hilton Head and Daufuskie in Beaufort County. In most cases, the islands were so heavily cultivated that one could see the ocean from the back of an island. However, compared to the erosion remnant-islands, the barrier islands (with the exception of Hilton Head and Daufuskie) were not the main sites for sea island cotton culture.

Swamps, Low, Flat Woods, and Freshwater Marshes

Throughout the sea islands were a variety of low, flat lands that traversed the sandy uplands. They ranged from freshwater marshes and swamps to low, hardwood flats. The soil on these lands was the most fertile in the sea islands; however, unless drained, it would not grow cotton. Even the raised beds were not sufficient to avoid the drainage problem. But as the planters understood more and more about ditching and drains, and with the addition of manures and compost, more and more of these low lands were put into cotton, until a significant portion of a plantation's cotton crop was grown on the previously wet lands.

The Salt Marsh

It is lost in history when the first planter or planters realized that the *Spartina* salt marshes[3] that surrounded the sea islands and traversed the interior of the islands via a myriad of tidal creeks could be suitable soil for sea island cotton. Before methods to restore worn-out lands were discovered, planters had to regularly seek new lands. At first, the lower-lying swamp and flatlands were used when it was realized that drainage ditches would make these lands arable. But even these lands had limitations, so the planters also turned to the salt marshes.

The first account of converting salt marsh to a cotton field was by an individual identified only as X. Y. from Beaufort (X. Y. 1828, 21):

THE CULTURE OF SEA ISLAND COTTON

The lands I have in the culture of Cotton, are situated at the heads of salt-water creeks, and commonly called coves or hard marshes... The lower parts covered by common tides, the upper, by spring tides... The soil for six inches deep, principally consists of the fibrous roots of grasses; but below this, black mud, blue, and sometimes yellow clay is found. The labor of banking in these lands must depend on their situation... They can scarce be ditched too much, as the land should be kept very dry...

Edward Barnwell (1831, 238-239) of Beaufort wrote:

In compliance with your request, and my promise, I forward you a continuation of my experience in the culture of salt-marsh lands... They [the banks] should be, at least twelve feet wide at the base, and no ditch dug inside, or not nearer than thirty feet. The fiddlers being amphibious, will make horizontal perforations from the side of the inner ditch, to the outer, if they are nearer than forty or fifty feet, that the water may, at high tide, flow through. The earth, or mud, must be well rammed when forming the bank, and the best obstruction I have yet found, to prevent this enemy from boring along side of the trunks,[4] which is their favorite place of resort, is our common green moss[5] rammed in, with still mud, or clay.

Barnwell began his reclamation of salt marsh in 1825; however, it was not until the early 1840s that the cultivation of salt marshes became common. The best salt marshes were those removed from strong tides, such as small creek coves and areas between small marsh hummocks and the mainland. (fig. 7-1 depicts both of these.) The coves were easily transformed into fields: First, a bank was constructed across the mouth of the cove to prevent salt water intrusion at high tide. Then, a series of dikes were built progressively up the creek, creating individual fields. Rains helped flush the salt from the fields; then they were made ready for planting. Some planters used the change in vegetation to determine if the salt was removed. As William Elliott (1828, 162) wrote: "I planted, during the present season, nine acres of reclaimed marsh land, whose change of growth indicated that it was sufficiently freshened."

The areas adjacent to and between the hummocks and mainland were more difficult to reclaim. An elaborate network of banks was constructed (fig. 7-1) that joined the mainland and hummock and created numerous individual fields. After rainwater flushed out the salt water, the fields were made ready for planting.

When the planters revived sea island cotton after the Civil War, they did not plant the salt marsh fields. The dikes had eroded and the fields had returned to marsh. The labor costs necessary to repair the banks were too much to justify their repair. Today, remnants of these banks and fields can be seen throughout the marshes of the sea islands (plate 7-1).

Both Barnwell and X. Y. noted that sea island cotton harvested on the reclaimed salt marshes brought higher prices than cotton from the upland fields. Consequently, most planters with salt marshes adjacent to their plantations experimented with its culture.

CHAPTER SEVEN

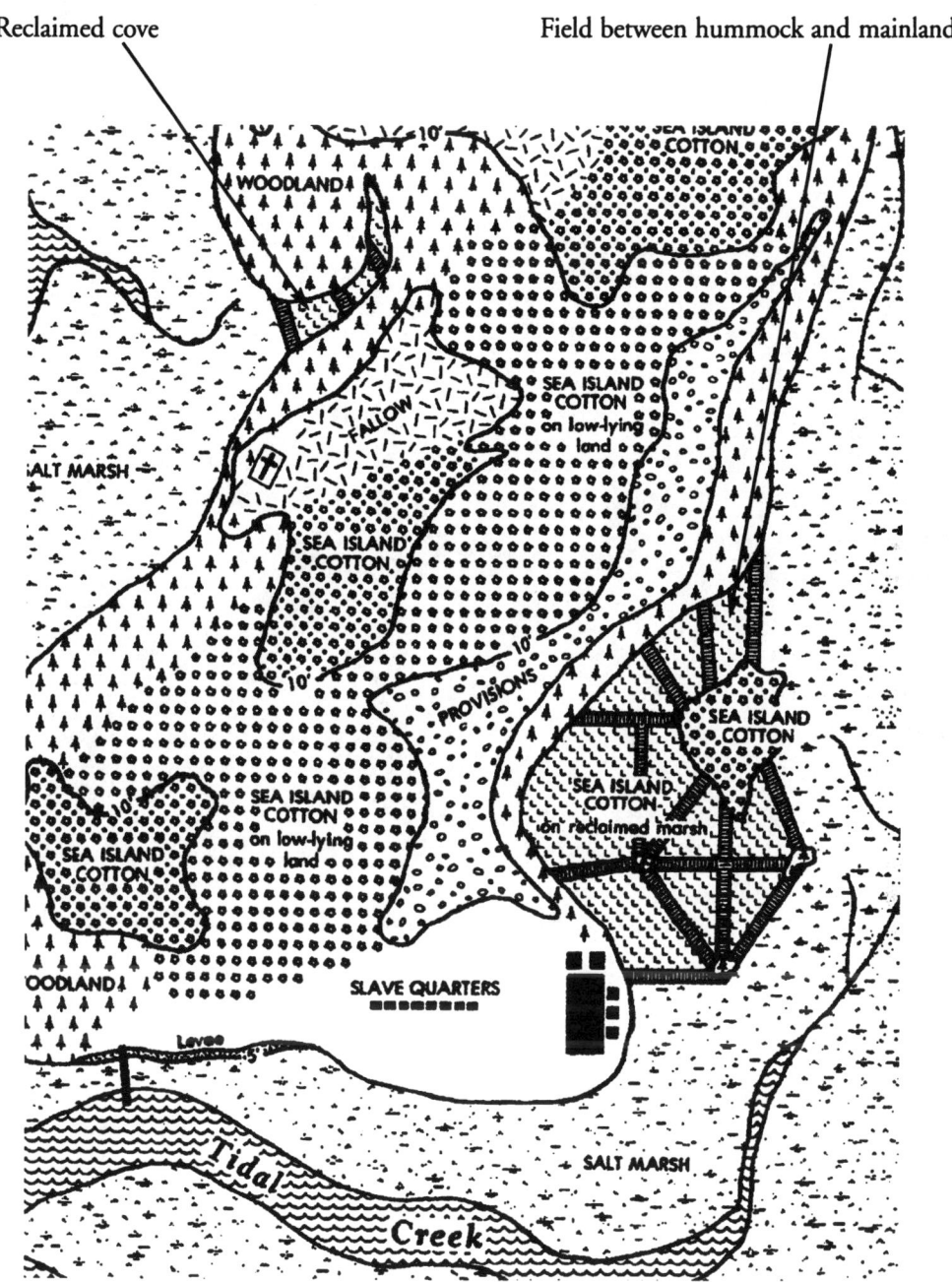

Figure 7-1. Salt marsh cotton fields (Kovacik and Mason 1985, 90)

Plate 7-1. Abandoned salt marsh fields, Prospect Hill Plantation, Edisto Island
(Photograph by author)

Pine Flatwoods

Several accounts refer to the "pine barrens" of the sea islands that were used for cotton fields. This term referred to what is today called the longleaf pine flatwoods or the pine/saw palmetto flatwoods (Porcher and Rayner 2001, 89-91).

Typical longleaf flatwoods are dominated by a canopy of tall, longleaf pines. The terrain is flat to gently rolling with a sandy soil and high water table. Although longleaf pine characterizes the community, loblolly and slash pine may occur. Where fire is infrequent, a well-developed shrub layer and understory may develop. Under higher fire frequency, the shrubs and understory species are kept in check. Because of the variation in the understory and shrub layers from site to site, pine flatwoods are difficult to characterize. Common understory trees include sweet gum, blackjack oak, and black gum; common shrubs include wax myrtle inkberry, huckleberry, running oak, sweet pepperbush, and scrubby post oak.

The pine/saw palmetto flatwood community is found in South Carolina only in Jasper and Beaufort Counties, its northern limit; it is more extensive in Florida and Georgia. The canopy consists of longleaf pine on the ridges and slash pine and/or pond pine in depressions. A subcanopy of oaks is usually sparse. Saw palmetto dominates the shrub layer. Other shrubs include hairy wicky, rusty lyonia, and southern evergreen blueberry. The latter two are confined to this community, occurring only in Beaufort and Jasper Counties. Typical pocosin and pine flatwood species such as sweet bay, inkberry, sweet gallberry, fetterbush, sweet pepperbush, and honey-cups are also part of the shrub layer. The sparse herbaceous layer is a mixture of pine flatwood species and includes galactia, vanilla plant, and Walter's milkweed. Periodic fires promote herbs and saw palmettos; an absence of fires leads to a greater dominance of shrubs.

The literature confirms that pine barrens were a component of the sea islands. Whitemarsh Seabrook (1828, 29) wrote: "Mr. William Seabrook, sen. from a steadfast adherence to the application of salt mud, has literally converted a pine barren to as fruitful a soil as Edisto Island can boast..." David Ramsay (1858, 278) reported about Edisto Island: "The more elevated parts consist of a stiff, clayey quality. It contains a less proportion of barren land, and is more generally fertile than any of the adjacent islands. About three-fourths of it are cleared. Firewood and fencing-timber are on some plantations scarce, and with difficulty procured." In an article in the April 22, 1880 *News and Courier*, the following description of Edisto Island appeared: "The more elevated parts consist of a light, sandy soil. The low grounds or bottoms are of a stiff, clayey quality. It contains a smaller proportion of barren land and is more generally fertile than any of the adjacent islands. Timber in some localities is scarce, and with difficulty procured." From the same article, about Johns Island: "It contains 40,000 acres. Out of this immense tract of land only 17,560 are arable, the balance being pine and swamp lands. The most fertile lands are on the outskirts running along the waters which surround it, and the interior is one vast and almost impenetrable swamp. Regarding James Island: "...consisting of open fields, pine land, and dense thickets and swamps."

Edmund Ruffin (William M. Mathew 1992, 122) referred to pine barrens on Port Royal Island: "The next ferry, over the Coosaw, (salt water here) took us into Port Royal Island, & 10 miles thence, mostly over pine barrens, & some inferior cotton lands, brought us to the town of Beaufort, about 4 P.M."

Undoubtedly, pine flatwoods (both longleaf and pine/saw palmetto) were part of the sea islands and were converted to sea island cotton fields. Both communities had an underlying restrictive layer that inhibited the drainage of rainwater. These lands were poor places for cotton fields as the saturated soil was not suited for cotton growing. The planters overcame this problem by using a subsoil plow to cut through the restrictive layer to allow adequate drainage. Then, by using raised beds, soil amelioration (manure, compost, cotton seed and salt-marsh mud) and drainage ditches between the beds, the pinelands were converted to excellent fields for sea island cotton.

Virtually all the original stands of pine flatwoods on the sea islands are gone. On Edisto Island, a plantation along Peter's Point Road (SC 767) went by the name Pine Barren.[6] The author drove this area and could find no trace of longleaf pine (or elsewhere on Edisto Island). James Island is totally devoid of any remnant of pine flatwoods, and Johns Island has scattered, small sites with longleaf on its northern end, but nothing on the southern end where the main concentration of sea island cotton fields were located. The eastern end of Wadmalaw where one enters the island contains remnants of longleaf pine. There are scattered stands of pine/saw palmetto stands on Port Royal Island.

In general, the pinelands that were originally part of the sea islands have long vanished, mostly replaced with secondary loblolly forests or loblolly/mixed hardwood forest where the cotton fields were abandoned.

Seed Selection

In regard to seed selection, the planters of sea island cotton had three main goals: (1) to carry on an active process of seed selection to produce new cultivars; (2) to protect cultivars already produced; and (3) to prevent degeneration of the fiber by hybridization. A field of cotton, or any crop, does not consist entirely of a pure genetic strain; rather it consists of a complex mixture of genetic strains. The interaction of these strains, accompanied by the selective action of the environment, leads to changes in the general character of successive generations. When unguided and left to itself, these changes are very likely to lead to degeneration of the quality of the fiber. However, by continued seed selection, the planter could prevent the degeneration and either increase the quality of the fiber or maintain its quality. Degeneration of the fiber quality also occurred from hybridization with upland cotton (*G. hirsutum*).

The sea island cotton market class originally came into being by seed selection (see chapter 5, the Origin of Sea Island Cotton). Just as important, seed selection from that point onward was necessary to maintain or increase the quality of the fiber or to produce new and different strains. Through seed selection, the character of the plant was radically changed from the plant first grown on the sea islands. The importance of seed selection was stressed by virtually anyone familiar with crop science, even in its rudimentary beginnings. As early as 1827, Whitemarsh Seabrook (1827, 8) wrote:

It will be readily conceded, that, in every crop, the selection of the best seed is of primary importance. The judicious horticulturist reserves the largest and the most perfect plants with a view to re-production. He pursues a principle which nature inculcates, and in daily experience confirms. To diligent and skilful cultivation, with a proper choice of seed, he confidently relies for a reward for his labour.

O. F. Cook and C. B. Doyle (1927, 2) concurred:

The selection of special strains of sea-island cotton was a highly developed art, and the precautions used by the sea-island planters have not been equaled in other parts of the world.

The planter recognized as achieving the highest position of the sea island planters in regard to seed selection was Kinsey Burden of Johns Island. Burden kept his seed selection method a secret for many years. However, a fellow planter, William Elliott, suggested to other planters that Burden's success might be in the character of his seeds. With this in mind, several planters began their own seed selection, each one having a different idea as to the best form of the plant and the most profitable type of staple. Hugh Wilson soon sold cotton for $1.25 a pound, and in 1828, two bags of extra fine cotton sold for $2.00 ($37.35) a pound, which, according to Seabrook, was the highest price paid at that time in the United States or any other country. Soon it was evident that seed selection was the key to producing the finest sea island cotton, and the market was flooded with so much high-quality cotton that prices fell to a fraction of what they were. Seed selection was an agronomic success, but not a market success.

Kinsey Burden (1844a, 164-65) gave an account of his cotton culture and mentioned his seed selection as follows:

About the year 1804 or 1805, I raised from selected seed, a pocket of fine cotton, which the merchant through whom it was shipped, informed me that one of the most distinguished spinners told him, was so superior to any cotton he had ever seen, that he would give 25 cts. per lb. for it more that any other cottons at any price...

In 1823, I sent a pocket of cotton to Manchester. After examining it, my correspondent wrote thus— "And we have little doubt that such cotton will always command three to four times the price of ordinary Sea-islands."

For some years previously to 1823, I was engaged in improving the quality of my cotton, and succeeded in doing so to a considerable extent, generally getting an advance in price upon the previous year.

Burden never revealed his method of seed selection. He even employed members of his family in moting the cotton to keep seeds from being purloined and sold or given to fellow planters. The author has not been able to find any reference to Burden's exact method of seed selection except a statement by Whitemarsh Seabrook (1828, 31) that "Mr. Burden selects his seed from the *most perfect, early stalks, produced on the best land* [emphasis original]. To an inflexible adherence to this system, it is supposed, that his pre-eminence in market, is, in a great measure, to be attributed."

The best detailed account of the seed selection practiced by sea island planters was given by Herbert J. Webber (1902), summarized and diagrammed (fig. 7-2) as follows:

A field is gone over carefully, and perhaps some 50 of the best plants selected; a second examination in the field reduces these perhaps to one half, and each plant is numbered. The cotton from each is collected and kept separately, and at the end of the season carefully examined and weighed, and a final selection is then made which reduces the number to perhaps five; the cotton from each of these plants is ginned separately and the seed preserved for sowing. The simplest case in which only one plant is finally selected is illustrated in the diagram. From the seeds of the selected plant of the first year about 500 plants can be raised in the next year. One plant is selected again from these 500, and the general crop of seed is used to sow about five acres for the third year, from which seed is obtained for the general crop in the fourth year. One special plant is selected each year from the 500 raised from the previous season's test plant, and in four year's time the progeny of this plant constitutes the "general crop."

How close Burden's seed selection practice was to Webber's description is not known. Burden left no account of his process. There is no question, however, that it was successful.

Planters had to observe certain conditions for the process of seed selection to work. First, test plots had to be isolated so that hybridization with upland cotton or undesirable plants of sea island cotton did not occur; and second, the seeds of the new cultivar had to be ginned separately to avoid contamination.

Each planter had his own ideals that represented the best form of the plant and selected a plant conforming most closely to this ideal. In general, the planter selected for five characteristics of the fiber: length, strength, evenness, fineness and freedom from knots and entanglements. A number of distinct cultivars of sea island cotton were developed. Although they were not given cultivar names, when offered for sale they were known by the name of the breeder—Hinson, Seabrook, Rivers, La Roche, etc.—or by the plantation name, such as Bleak Hall. Unfortunately, few records were kept, resulting in much confusion regarding cultivar status and characteristics. However, this system of breeding, which relied on the skill and art of each planter, created an array of distinct cultivars producing some of the finest cotton in the world (Smith & Cothern 1999, 157). Modern experimental methods could scarcely be more painstaking than the seed selection practiced by planters such as Kinsey Burden, William

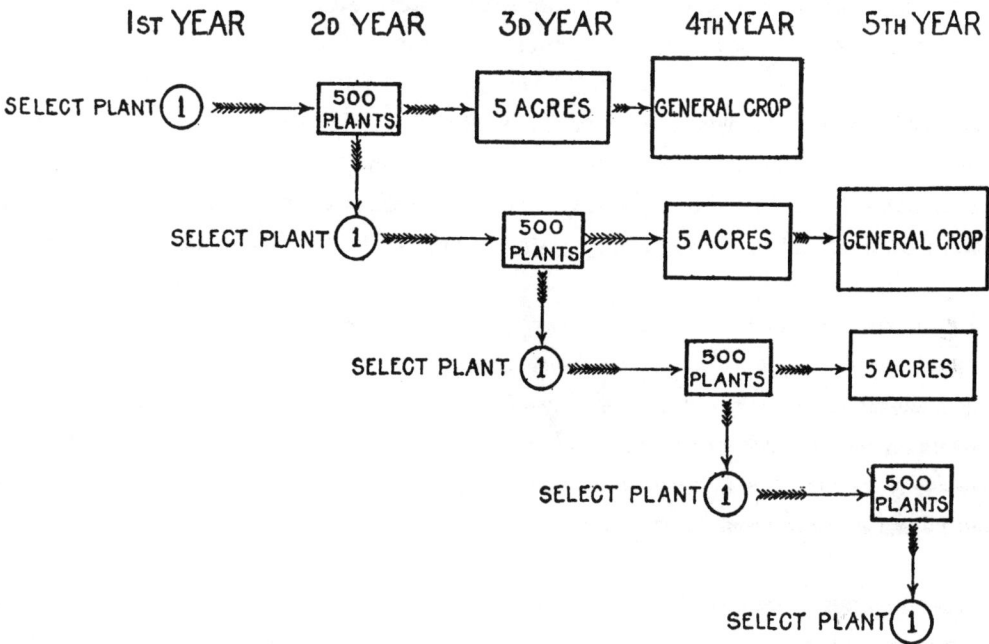

Figure 7-2. Method of seed selection as practiced on James and Edisto islands (Webber 1902, 374)

Seabrook and William Elliott. Furthermore, seed selection was also a continuous process, without which the staple degenerated with great rapidity.

This system of producing highly specialized cultivars opened the concept of "breeders' rights." The developers of the finer cultivars—the breeders—considered them their personal property, and would not part with any of their seed, even to their neighbors. To do so would likely have resulted in an overproduction of that particular cultivar and a lowering of prices. A fine cultivar of cotton was the product of many years of careful selection and could not be duplicated without long, continuous work requiring much skill and care. Since there were no laws at that time to protect the breeders' cultivars, their only protection was not to share their seeds.

Not only did the breeders go to elaborate means to protect their seeds, but other planters went to more extreme means to acquire their seeds through deceit and trickery. Chalmers Murray (1949, 191) related the following: "The tale is told of a James Islander who bribed his coachman to 'lift' a bag of seed, while he, the planter, was calling on a certain acquaintance."

He further elaborated:

If a planter had a strong suspicion that another had somehow acquired a strain of cotton from his fields, he would break off diplomatic relations at once. Members of the two families would stop speaking to each other, and more than once the offended party would change his church affiliation, rather than attend the same house of worship with "that grand rascal."

Some planters, instead of developing their own cultivars, bought the seeds of a particular cultivar either from a fellow planter or from a government agency like the Bureau of Plant Industry in Washington, DC. Their goal was then to preserve the quality of the cultivar so they did not have to buy new seeds every year. The method of selection to be followed in preserving a cultivar from deteriorating was different from that employed in the development of new cultivars. The breeder of a new cultivar looked for exceptional plants and preferred those that were unlike any cultivar previously known. To preserve the already established cultivar, planters took the following steps: (1) fields were isolated to prevent hybridization; (2) fields were selected that were surrounded by a forest; (3) before seed was gathered for the next year's crop, plants which were not true to the purchased cultivar were rogued out; (4) seeds were selected from the earliest-ripening plants; (5) seeds were selected from the largest and best-formed bolls; and (6) the cotton was ginned separately from any other cottons.

Drainage

Members of the cotton genus (*Gossypium*), and sea island and upland cotton in particular, did not tolerate saturated soils. Saturated soils prevent adequate oxygen uptake by the roots, leading to death of the plants in extreme conditions, and in less extreme conditions to premature shedding of squares and young bolls, or to blue cotton and rust. Saturated soils were not a major problem in the sandy soils where most of the cotton was grown because the cotton was planted on elevated beds that facilitated drainage from around the roots. Still, even in sandy soils with beds, heavy rains could render a field unsuitable. Lowland sites, however, were always a problem, so planters installed open drains in their low-lying fields.

The first serious mention of the value of drainage in the sea islands was by Joseph E. Jenkins (1830, 562):

What is the intention of a drain? Certainly to relieve the tap-root of cotton from superabundance of moisture— if the drain has not this effect, but on the contrary, dams the water by its improperly hauled back edges, it stands to reason that the object has not been attained...

The most complete description of the system of ditch drainage practiced by sea island planters was given by William H. Capers (1835, 402). Based on available literature, it was closest to the standard system developed by planters who used open ditch drainage. Figures 7-3 and 7-4 from his article illustrate Capers's method of drainage on either flat or hilly land.

In preparing a field where the soil is close, moist and cold, and the land low, it is all important to have it well drained: ditches must, therefore, be sunk in the most appropriate places that water may run off, and be discharged during heavy rains; and half and quarter acre drains cut leading to them, and even at shorter distances if requisite, to prevent the water from resting superficially on the land, and to keep it as dry as possible. It should first be laid out in tasks of 105 feet square, and tracked so as that the beds will run to the best advantage, and in such directions, that the water will flow with the greatest facility into the drains; which should be cut at right angles or crosswise with the beds, thus:

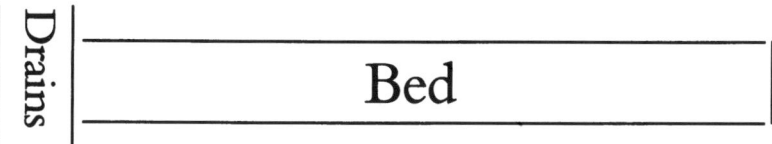

Figure 7-3. Ditch and bed system on level land (Capers 1835, 402)

or if the land be hilly; on the elevation, the beds to run diagonally with the ditch or drain thus:

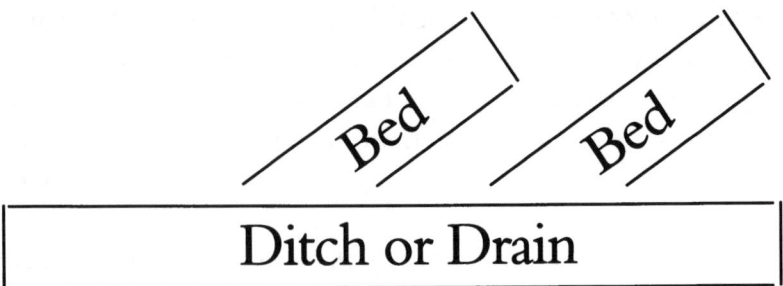

Figure 7-4. Ditch and bed system on hilly land (Capers 1835, 402)

Capers also noted that there was considerable difference of opinion among planters on whether the ditches should be wide and shallow or deep and narrow; however, no matter the type of ditch, the vent for the water had to be sufficient to remove the water from the fields and prevent reabsorption from the ditches.

An interesting note is Capers's suggestion to planters that the location of beds and drainage ditches be marked with small posts, about the thickness of one's arm, and fashioned of chinquapin (*Castanea pumila*) or cedar, cut about three feet long, and driven into the ground a foot, "whereby the labour and loss of time of every year's splitting new stakes, and running out the land afresh are profitably saved."

The most advanced planters had for some time constructed open drains through their fields. The drains were generally formed by running two furrows with a plow and afterwards hauling out the loose dirt with a hoe, thus leaving an open ditch a foot or more in depth.

After the Civil War, Elias L. Rivers gave a report for the James Island Agricultural Society, which in turn was presented to the Agricultural Society of South Carolina and included in its minute book in July, 1880 (Gregorie and Surles 1936b, 7-9):

But the seasons of 1867 and 1868 were two of the most unfavorable ever known upon the seacoast. Constant rains so saturated the soil ... to render the fields impassable to those on horse back, and caterpillars coming in August so completely destroyed the crop as to leave ... less than twenty pounds per acre for harvest... Much interest was awakened upon the subject of drainage ... It was admitted that unless better drainage could be secured no calculation could be made upon a crop in a wet season. Inquiries were made as to what methods were used elsewhere. Many doubts were entertained upon the subject, but as experiments have already been made in the low-country and elsewhere with covered drains made of boards the weight of opinion was in favor of their practicability. Unfortunately the crops of 1867 and 1868 had left us one in a pecuniary situation to experiment upon the subject, and the immediate action was necessarily postponed.

Though ditches and subsoil drains—long square wooden boxes buried underground between rows to drain water away at root level—were installed in the fields, they were not always adequate to alleviate the problem. The report of the crop of 1886 on James Island in the minutes of the James Island Agricultural Society (Federal Writers Project 1936, 65-66) stated that "the general condition of the crops are badly broken, very irregular, very small, grassy and suffering from an excess of water; in many instances ditches have been cut right through the fields to let off the water, the under-drains being totally unable to take it off with sufficient rapidity."

Still, for the most part, after the system was perfected, subsoil drainage did function adequately and eliminated the labor necessary for digging and maintenance of the elaborate ditching system practiced before the Civil War. Accordingly, the planter was able to cultivate the high-yielding lowland, increase the amount of cultivable land on his smaller post-war holdings, and help reduce crop loss from the best fields from heavy rains. Open ditches and subsoil drains made of wooden trunks, used until the late 1870s, were afterwards replaced by two- to eight-inch tile pipes (plate 7-2). Outlets of the tiles opened to the sea at the low-water mark, and the pressure of the water in the pipes preserved a constant outflow even at high tide, so that land only a foot or two above the high-water mark was drained to a depth of four, or even five feet.

Of all the islands where sea island cotton was planted after the war, it was on James Island that subsoil drainage with tile pipes reached its greatest installation. James Island had 50 miles of drains, and one 65-acre tract alone included over five miles of drains. No post-war figures are available for the other sea islands. In an article in the April 22, 1880 *Charleston News & Courier* by J. K. Blackman, the drainage situation of Johns Island was described thus: "Some little ditching is done, but not nearly enough to afford security to the planters against the ruin of their crops by heavy rains." On Edisto Island, the paper reported, "many of the most prosperous planters have adapted the system of subsoil drainage, and with those who cannot afford this improvement a thorough system of ditching is resorted to." And on Wadmalaw Island, "they have in many instances adapted the system of under-drainage..."

The state of the other sea islands was reported in the same article:

Besides the islands mentioned there are St. Helena Island, Lady's Island, Paris Island, Edings's Island, Hilton Head Island, Bull's Island, Dawfuskie Island, Spring Island, Port Royal Island, and a number of other small islands and the main land adjoining where Sea Island cotton is raised, but as the planters have not to any considerable extent adapted the new system of cultivation their improvement is not so marked. The total crop of Carolina long cotton last year is put down at 10,000 bags, of which Edisto, Wadmalaw, John's and James Islands produced about 7,850 bags.

The system of subsoil drainage perfected on James Island was described in detail by Blackman:

The fields are first ditched for the reception of the pipes. These ditches are placed at distances from each other varying from ten to twenty feet, according to the requirements of the soil, and pipes varying from two inches to eight inches are then laid, and the ditch is covered up level with the surrounding soil. Into these long drains, which generally run the whole length of the plantation, are run shorter and smaller lateral drains, and at certain intervals throughout the fields are placed brick wells, into which some of the pipes empty and from which others are kept supplied... When a plantation becomes thoroughly drained in this way a canal is then cut to the nearest creek. Into this canal is led the water from the pipes, and it in turn carries off the water from the pipes into the creek.

The subsoil drainage system has long ceased to function. Whether farmers after the end of sea island cotton culture in 1920 used the system in agricultural endeavors is not recorded. Remains of the tile system surface periodically in fields, or are seen on the edges of marshes where they drained water from the fields (plate 7-2).

Rotation of Land and Crops

Early on, the planters were aware that the light, sandy loam soils lost their fertility through continuous use. One method adapted to solve this problem was land rotation. One type of rotation was the "two field" system, practiced on soil that was light and unproductive without manure. One field was planted in cotton, corn and sweet potatoes, in a proportion of seven-twelfths cotton, two-twelfths sweet potatoes, and three-twelfths corn. The second field, the "field at rest," was pastured. As many cattle as possible were kept on the field in movable pens for the year. The pens were moved around each day. Fine straw and coarse marsh grass or weeds were laid between the old beds, and manure and salt-marsh mud were added. Grass from the beds was hoed down into the alleys. The cattle were allowed to trample the vegetation. The next year this field was planted in cotton, corn and sweet potatoes, and the field previously planted in crops was "rested."

A form of fallowing was practiced before and after the Civil War. Its value was noted by Elias L. Rivers (1896): "Old planters regarded a year's rest of the land, with cattle upon it, as the best preliminary preparation for a sea island cotton crop." Land planted in cotton one year was pastured by cattle and sheep the next year. The animal stock trampled the loose soil, compacting it to a desirable level. The growth of bushes, briers and weeds was kept down, and the dried stems of the cotton stalks were broken and trampled down. The natural manure from the stock also contributed to the fertility of the soil. The cattle were removed from the fields in November. If care had been taken so that the grass was not eaten so close as to expose the soil on the tops of the beds to the summer sun, the field was in exactly the right condition to plant the following year.

The value of rotating cotton fields with a leguminous crop is now well known, and this method is practiced worldwide today. Symbiotic bacteria in the root nodules of plants such as soybean and peas convert atmospheric gaseous nitrogen (N_2) into ammonia (NH_3), which,

Plate 7-2. Remains of subsoil tile drainage system, Dill Wildlife Sanctuary, Stono River, James Island (Photograph by author)[7]

upon decay of the plant, is released into the soil. It is not known when sea island planters or early agronomists first understood the value of annual crop rotation to enhance fertility of the soil. As early as 1842, however, there appeared mention of crop rotation as a means to restore worn-out cotton fields. The "Report of the Committee on Sea-Island Cotton" in the *Southern Agriculturist* (1842, 15) explained: "Peas, if put in the ground in the spring, and only so well attended as to insure a full supply of seed, is another decidedly meliorating process, where a subsequent growth of cotton is looked to." Obviously, the benefit of rotating with peas was understood, but the reason for the benefit was probably not known. Harry Hammond (1881, 52) stated, in reference to the Upper Pine Belt of the state, "Green manuring, especially with the cow-pea, is regarded favorably, although it is not practiced as a system. Sown broadcast, manured with the 'ash Element' (a cheap fertilizer composed chiefly of lime and potash) and turned under after the vines are wilted by frost, remarkable results have been attained."

By the time Orton wrote his paper, "Sea Island Cotton," the role of legumes in adding nitrogen to the soil was well known. He stated (1907, 17): "The culture of cowpeas, velvet beans, and other legumes adds to the soil large quantities of nitrogen drawn from the air, enabling the farmer to secure at a slight expense an element which is the most costly part of purchased fertilizers."

Available literature on sea island cotton contains little mention of planters actually using legumes in rotation of crops. Yet reports strongly suggest that the value of rotation with legumes was known, at least to agronomists. The author concludes, then, that cotton-crop land depleted through years of use was restored—at least partially—by rotation with legumes. For whatever reason, crop rotation was not well documented by planters in their journals or reports.

Seed Preparation

Sea island planters found early on that seed for planting required proper preparation. Sea island cotton was ginned on roller gins that did not clean the seed completely of coarse trash and tangled remains of lint. When planted by hand, the remnants of lint increased the difficulty of handling the seed and under some conditions caused poor germination because the matted lint prevented normal water absorption. When mechanical planters were used, the matted lint prevented uniform seed distribution. The planters developed a method called "raying" the seed which consisted of rubbing the seed through coarse screens which removed the trash and tangled lint.

Planters on large plantations did not send their cotton elsewhere for ginning. These planters maintained their private roller gins so they could insure the quality of their seed for planting the next year's crop. Many of them would not even gin the cotton of a neighboring plantation for fear of contamination of their seeds.

CHAPTER SEVEN

Preparation of the Land

On the sea islands, cotton was at first grown on ridges or beds.[8] Drayton (1802) gave the first description of cotton beds: "Or, in the first instance, beds are made rather low and flat, and the cotton is sown therein. By some they are sown in holes, at about ten inches distance; but the more general practice is to sow the cotton in a drill, along the length of the bed; after which it may be thinned at leisure according to its growth. In rich high land soils, not more than fifteen of these beds are made in a quarter of an acre; but in inferior lands, twenty-one beds are made in the same space of ground."

Michael Edwards (1967, 90) gave Thomas Spalding credit for first using the ridge method:

In 1794, a new ridge method of planting the seeds more thickly was introduced by a planter from the Bahamas. The method was first adapted by Thomas Spaulding [sic], an influential Southerner, who had been one of the first to see the possibilities of Sea Island cotton growing on a large-scale. Within a short time he had increased the yield from 100 to 340 lb. per acre, and his success encouraged others to use the new system, making possible a sharp jump in the output of Sea Islands from 1799 onwards.

The ridge method was important for several reasons: the elevated beds (generally 18 inches to two feet high) allowed better drainage; the planted seeds warmed faster in the spring (promoting germination); the ditches between the beds served as drainage ditches; ridges allowed a way to bury the previous year's growth of vegetation under the new bed for the benefit of the new cotton plants; and manures and fertilizers could be applied in the alley between each bed. But even though the completed beds were generally similar among the various plantations, the method of construction differed. Some planters continued to use the hoe and never made use of plows and other tools that became available. More progressive planters, however, made use of newly-invented plows and cultivators to make the beds, but continued to use the hoe for weeding. Throughout the culture of sea island cotton, modifications were made on the construction of the beds, and it is difficult to identify one method as the standard. Material from several sources has been combined in the following description:

Beginning in January (or according to some planters, as soon as the previous year's crop had been picked—even before the cotton had been cleaned for market), the old stalks on the previous year's bed were broken down, the limbs and trash raked into the alleys, and the coarser litter burned. Where the hoe was used, the surface of the old bed was subjected to a process known locally as "listing," that is, shaving the surface of the old bed of vegetation and hauling it into the alley (fig. 7-5a). In February or March, cotton seed (from the ginning of the previous fall) was strewn into the alleys. Then, a compost of stable manure, pine straw, marsh grass (*Spartina alterniflora*), and salt-marsh mud was added to the alleys (fig. 7-5b). After the Civil War, commercial fertilizers were added.

THE CULTURE OF SEA ISLAND COTTON

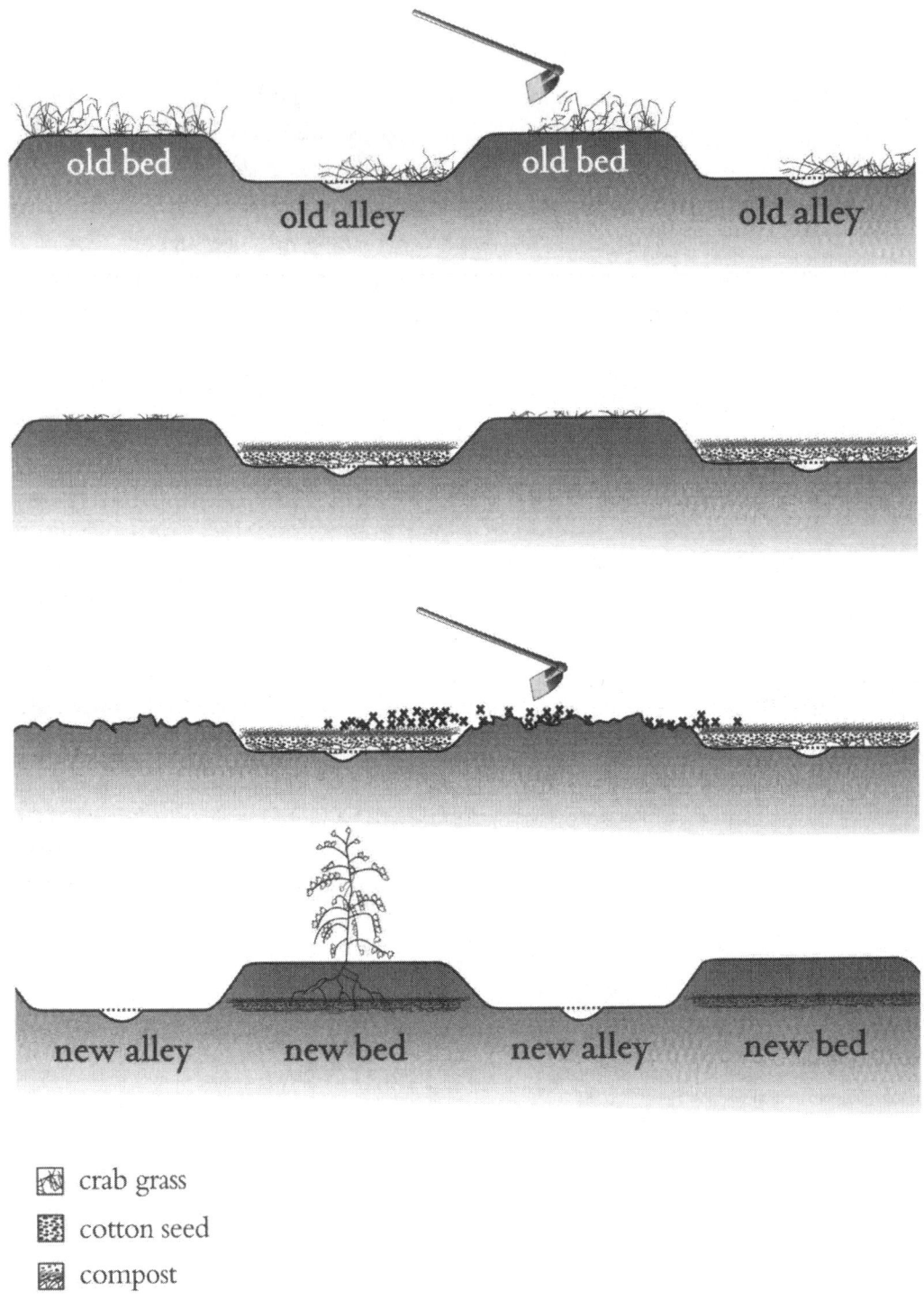

Figure 7-5a-d. Construction of beds

CHAPTER SEVEN

Figure 7-6. Double roller used on the sea islands, showing strips of wood to mark location of holes (Orton 1916, 16)

Next, the "bedding" stage was begun. The centers of the beds were made generally five feet apart, although they varied from four to six feet depending on the soil conditions. The older practice of making the new beds was done with the hoe by hauling the soil from the tops and sides of the old beds (fig. 7-5c) and making new beds of regular size and shape in the old alleys on top of the listed material (fig. 7-5d). Later, construction of the new bed was often begun with a two-horse plow. A furrow was turned in from each side of the old bed to cover the compost and seed. Then the hoe was used to haul up the remaining earth of the old bed to make the new bed. In all cases, whether just the hoe, or the hoe and plow were used, a large bed was made and a clear alley left on each side for drainage.

A double roller[9] (fig. 7-6) weighing 800 pounds was used to press together and compact the entire bed, completing two rows at a time. If seeds were to be sown in holes, strips of wood on the rollers, fixed from 12 to 18 inches apart, marked the position of the holes. Construction of the beds should have been completed by the middle of March. If all went well for the planter, the result of this preparation was that, when the cotton came up, there were no ridges between the beds to prevent adequate drainage, and the beds were free of grass. By the time the roots of the cotton penetrated into the base of the bed, they found abundant fertilizer from the decomposed vegetable matter that had been listed.

Some planters before the Civil War used the plow almost exclusively in making the beds. Robert Chisolm described his method (1872, 341), which was probably the standard:

I had given up for many years the practice of listing my cotton land with the hoe, because it was very laborious for the hands, and I found that it was much better as well as more cheaply done by running together two furrows of the two-mule plough, and the laborers employed the time usually spent in listing with the hoe in gathering material for making manure, which generally enabled me to gather enough for the year. Just before I was ready to plant, two more furrows of the two-mule plough were run in the old bed, breaking it out entirely, and the hoes followed, bedding easily an acre per day, although my lands are uncommonly heavy for Sea island soils.

One of the main problems encountered after the Civil War by planters trying to renew sea island cotton culture was preparation of the beds. In order to save money, many planters allowed their lands to remain untouched until the arrival of planting time. Just prior to planting time, one furrow was run in the center of the alley, and afterwards a plow used to turn down the sides of the beds on this furrow. A ridge was thus left between the new beds higher than the beds themselves, for the planter had no time to cut down these ridges before planting, leaving this task until after planting. The ridge prevented proper drainage. Also, the "list" had no time to decompose sufficiently. For these reasons, and others, the land was marginally suitable for planting.

Lewis Gray (1958, 735) stated that some planters practiced a method of "permanent ridges," sometimes alternating them with provision crops. This method does not appear to have been common and is mentioned only for the record.

Field Protection

Damage to the crop from wind was always a problem for sea island cotton planters. As often as possible, a natural border of trees was left around fields to block the wind. Where there was no natural stand, farmers planted a border of small trees and shrubs. They also frequently planted rows of corn between the cotton rows, alternating crops every fifth or sixth row. The corn protected the cotton from wind-blown sand and other wind damage. While traveling in the sea islands, Edmund Ruffin often wrote in his diary (Mathew, 1992) about wind damage to the cotton crop. On St. Helena he observed, "The effect of high winds on the light sandy soil is a great & general evil." Since the sea islands were mostly cultivated land with little natural vegetation to act as breaks for wind generated off the ocean, man-made wind breaks became a necessary tool to protect the crops.

An unexpected benefit of the corn plants was their absorption of excess moisture from the soil, which aided the cotton plant.

Soil Amelioration

[Note: This book does not delve extensively into the various methods and materials used by planters for soil amelioration. Articles by Seabrook, Spalding, Capers and others appear throughout the literature on sea island cotton culture, giving varying advice on when and how to apply nutrients, which materials should be used, and why different methods were preferred. It would be a lengthy and arduous task even for a modern agronomist to evaluate these practices, and—based on current knowledge—to understand why some methods worked and others were either useless or of little value.]

During the early years of sea island cotton culture, when fields first selected for cotton became exhausted, as they invariably did in a few years, planters abandoned these fields and cleared virgin land. Trees were girdled without taking the effort to remove them, so that a cotton field often resembled a cemetery of dead oaks and palmettos, which made the use of plows impossible until roots and stumps either decayed or were grubbed. As virgin uplands became unavailable, planters turned to salt marshes and lowlands. However, if sea island cotton culture was to continue, planters had to begin restoring worn-out land, and soil amelioration became a necessity.

A few planters fertilized their cotton fields soon after the introduction of long-staple cotton. In fact, all the materials used as manure in the later antebellum period were used as early as 1805 in a limited way. By 1825, methods of manuring were generally known to sea island planters, and they began serious manuring of their fields to maintain soil fertility.

From the beginning of sea island cotton culture, a variety of materials was used to ameliorate the soil. Again, there was no standard practice accepted by all the planters. Multiple materials and methods were tried, some discarded, others becoming more widespread. Early on, the planters used materials that could be obtained from their plantations and gathered by the plantation slaves. After the Civil War, a major change occurred in sea island cotton culture: commercial fertilizers became available. Although it was difficult for planters to purchase these fertilizers, they had little choice, since cotton planting after the war was done on smaller fields, and yield came to be more important than the quality of the lint.

The first amelioration each year was done during the listing process. The remains of the previous year's crop and vegetation that grew during the season on the beds was "listed in" under the new beds. This material contained a variety of minerals that were released into the soil during decomposition. For this reason, it was important to list the vegetation early enough for decomposition.

The use of salt-marsh mud[10] for soil amelioration was recommended as early 1828 by Whitemarsh Seabrook (1828, 174): "I consider salt-mud, as manure, highly valuable; it has a powerful tendency to increase the production of the Cotton plant; to hasten its maturity, and to make the fiber stronger and finer; it also gives consistency and strength to light, weak soils." Seabrook (1844a, 26) also gave an account of the early use of salt-marsh mud: "Salt mud, as a garden manure, was employed in South Carolina in 1801. Judge William Johnson states that, in that year, he commenced his experiments with it, and, after repeated trials, arrived at the conclusion, that it was a great meliorating agent."

Salt-marsh mud, readily available in the adjacent marshes of the sea islands, was a common soil ameliorate. It was first thought that its benefit to the cotton plant was from its salt content, but later it was realized that it was mainly because of its potash (potassium) content.[11] The mud was generally applied in the alleys between the beds and spread in a layer about two inches thick. About 40 one-horse cart loads were applied to an acre. Planters employed various methods of adding the mud to their fields. On Edisto Island, planters used it as soon as it was dug. Slaves went out in boats to the salt creeks, loaded their boats with the mud, and returned to empty it into ox-carts or hand-woven baskets. Other slaves hauled it to the fields. Some planters dried it before spreading it on the fields; other planters made a compost of the mud.

In Seabrook's article on salt-marsh mud (1829a, 361-365), there appears a note signed by "J. G." that described an elaborate system of planking into the marsh to gather the mud (fig. 7-7). He wrote: "Nothing can exceed the expedition with which this operation goes on, and the quantity of mud delivered by an expert gang of hands exceeds belief."

Rails or pine poles with the branches attached, laid on top of the mud, were employed to keep the planks from sinking. Plantation-made wheelbarrows with wheels made of tupelo or gum tree (*Nyssa aquatica* most likely), were used to haul the mud across the planks. Workers would proceed with the wheelbarrows from the landing onto gangway A, then to gangway E. Then, from gangway E, workers would enter any one of planks D where from each side the marsh mud was dug with the broad hoe and emptied into the wheelbarrows. Once filled, the

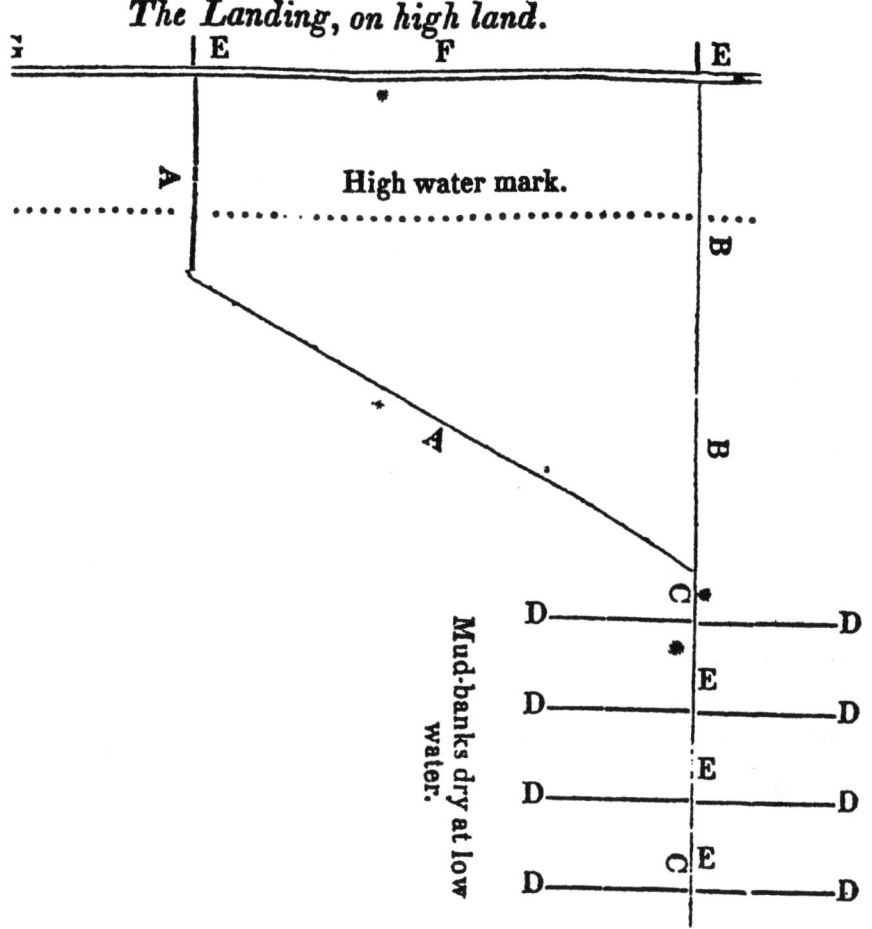

Figure 7-7. Plan of the mode of laying the planks (Seabrook 1829a, 364)

A. A.—The first gang-way of planks.
B. B.—The second do. [ditto]
C. C.—The planks beyond the junction of the gang-ways.
D. D.—The planks at right-angles, from which the mud is dug on each side.
E. E.—Corners. If any difficulty occurs with hands un-accustomed to the work, it may be necessary to have a number of short pieces, eight or ten feet long, to place to suit the negroes mode of turning the corner, which at first will be difficult.
F.—The landing platform, two planks wide, at which the mud is discharged.
G.—A slanting plank, one end resting on the ground on which the wheel-barrows are carried up or down when repaired.

Plate 7-3. Remains of Native American shell mound on Edisto Island
(Photograph by author)

workers would return to the landing via gangway B where the marsh mud was unloaded at the landing. For the most efficient operation, "The hands, *be they more or less, must all fill and start together* [emphasis original], falling into line as they reach the common path [gangway B]; on this they are to proceed to the landing, when each stopping and taking out the side of his barrow, empties his load."

Most plantations kept some combination of cattle, sheep and horses, which were a continuous source of animal manure. Planters would scatter leaves and dead marsh grass in the pens, and this was trampled and mixed with the manure to form a compost which was then liberally applied to the cotton crop.

Cotton seed was a readily available source of nitrogen as a soil ameliorate since each plantation generally ginned its own cotton. It had only to be hauled to the fields and strewn in the alleys in February or March, generally at a rate of 1,000 pounds to the acre. Since sea island cotton required less nitrogen than most crops, cotton seed was an adequate source of nitrogen.

Besides the vegetation listed into the alleys from the previous year's crop, marsh grass (*Spartina alterniflora*, harvested from the salt marsh with a scythe) and pine needles were added to the mass of material in the alleys. Seabrook (1847, 13-14) suggested that marsh grass for the following year's beds be cut after the working of the crop had been completed (in July, as a rule). Each day's cuttings should be hauled to the fields, placed in the alleys, and covered lightly by hauling a little soil from the tops of the beds. This was in contrast to the more common method of winter listing, which, explained Seabrook, did not provide the same amount of nutrients as summer listing because decomposition was not as advanced. Pine straw, although often used, was, according to Seabrook, of little value except when trampled by cattle and should be used only on the highest and driest lands, as its main role was collecting and retaining moisture.

Charles U. Shepard, reporting on the nature of the soils of Edisto Island to the St John's Colleton Agricultural Society, suggested that "the peculiar fertility of new sea-island land" may be "owing to the proportion of comminuted shells natural to such soils, and the deterioration of these lands under long culture, ascribable to the exhaustion of carbonate of lime." Where deficiency occurred, some planters used crushed oyster shells from natural shell deposits which were everywhere along the banks of the rivers and creeks of the sea islands. Another easily-mined supply of shells was the remains of Native American shell mounds (plate 7-3) along the coastal islands. An unusual source of carbonate of lime was the old indigo heaps, the refuse of the vats. The lime used in the preparation of the dye had become mixed with earthy materials and was especially beneficial to the cotton fields. Another source of carbonate of lime was the refuse lime and half-burnt shells forming the remains of old lime kilns. There were also numerous deposits of post-pliocene marl on the sea islands, as at Dalton's Swamp, Johnson's Island, Stono Creek, Edisto Island, and Distant Island, near Beaufort.

After the Civil War, modifications were made to make cotton profitable again. The main innovations were planting smaller fields (reduced from 400-500 acres to 50-60 acres), adopting the tenant system of labor, installing subsoil drainage, reducing dependence on salt marsh mud and plantation manures (because of the labor required, and due to the loss of animal stock), and using commercial fertilizers (wholly unknown before the war). On James Island the maximum production of lint cotton (that is, of ginned cotton) to the acre went from 103 pounds in 1872 to 400 pounds in 1879. On Edisto Island, ginned lint increased from 80 and 100 pounds to 300 pounds an acre. Upon a prize acre on Wadmalaw Island, the yield reached 566 pounds. Much of this increase was attributable to the use of commercial fertilizers.

The most significant event regarding fertilizers was the discovery of Carolina phosphate beds in 1869. Planters now had a ready phosphate source, and together with commercial kainit (a natural salt which replaced the use of marsh mud) and the home supply of manures, soil amelioration became more of a science than an art. Although there was much variation in how a planter improved his soil, this description by Hammond (1881, 54) can be used as a general example:

On the lines of manure thus laid down a certain quantity of commercial fertilizer is drilled. This practice, wholly unknown formerly, is very common now, even the smallest negro farmers often going heavily in debt to obtain these fertilizers... On James' Island and John's Island a mixture consisting of 250 pounds acid phosphate, 200 pounds of kainit (German potash salt) and 200 pounds calcined marl is applied per acre. On Edisto Island they use 200 pounds fish scrap (half dry in barrels), 200 pounds kainit, and 200 pounds acid phosphate per acre.

For the remaining time that sea island cotton was grown (until 1920), the aim of the planter was to apply the maximum quantity of commercial fertilizers that would return a sure profit. This varied according to circumstances (type of soil, labor force, etc.) and was determined by experiments made on each plantation. Through this judicious and scientific process, the harvest of lint was frequently 300 pounds an acre.

Planting

Time of Planting

The time of planting sea island cotton was critical. The planter had to wait until there was adequate moisture in the soil; at the same time, planting had to be done early enough to insure that the plants flowered and fruited fully before frost. Unlike upland cotton, sea island cotton needed a longer growing season to reach its maximum potential. Various planting dates appear in the literature, but are in general agreement: Elliott (1828, 152), 20th of March, extending to the 20th of April; Capers (1835, 405), about the 25th of March to the 15th of April; Turner (1857, 133), from March 20th to April 10th; Gray (1858, 735), between the last of March and the middle of April; and Orton (1916, 25), "as early as a season permits... varies in different years and sections from March 15 to April 10. Early-planted Sea-Island cotton is found to be a more compact and fruitful plant, while late cotton tends to form a larger and coarser weed… On the one hand the cotton must escape frost, and on the other the spring droughts."

A similar situation occurred with the Santee long cotton. Henry W. Ravenel, of Northampton Plantation, St. John's Parish, Berkeley County, wrote (1844, 44), "The crop of last year has fallen short of that of 1842 [because] the usually cold and late spring, which prevented the Planters from putting their seed in the ground before the 10th or 15th of April, and a continued drought from that time until the 10th of May, gave too short a season to the plant to arrive at full maturity."

The problem that sometimes arose when a late frost occurred is dramatically stated in the Report of Committee on Agriculture, July 4, 1874, of the James Island Agricultural Society (Federal Writers Project 1936, 9). The report stated that because of the cold and windy spring, which terminated in a cold frost on the 30th of April, followed by excessively cold winds in May and the early part of June, crops had to be frequently replanted. The last planting was in June, and the crop for that year (1874) had "some cotton coming up in June… At this date a very anomalous appearance generally irregular with great want of uniformity as to size and general appearance…"

Method of Planting (Sowing Seed)

In the first few years of planting sea island cotton, sowing was done on level ground. Seeds were dropped in holes dug in rows about five feet apart. The holes were from 12 to 18 inches apart. But by 1802, the use of elevated beds was established as the common method of preparing the land, and until the end of the industry, sea island cotton seeds were sown on raised beds or ridges.

Three sowing methods appear throughout the literature: drilling, long hills and short hills. But from this point on, the issue is a morass of confusion. The term "hills," according to one planter, is a misnomer, for seed was not planted in hills, but holes. The term hill may have come from the practice of hauling soil with the hoe around the base of the plant into mounds, or "hills." Then, there seems to be no clear distinction between long hills (holes) and short hills (holes). The only source that explained this difference to any degree was Seabrook (1830, 142):

There are three methods of sowing the seed, viz. in long hills, in short hills, and in shallow trenches extending the whole length of the ridge. If a planter can attend in person to the thinning of his crop, the last mode is the best on high and sandy lands; for it ensures him a regular field, and greater scope in the selection of plants. Long hills* are generally preferred in very rich grounds, where it is necessary that the stalks should be far from each other. Of the three methods, that of short hills[†] will be found to be the most useful as well as profitable.

* *Two or three times the width of the hoe, each hill being that distance apart.*
† *The width of a hoe, with a space of that width between every hill.*

The following statements on planting are drawn from the extensive literature of sea island cotton:

In America it is planted in rows [beds] five feet apart, and in holes eighteen inches apart, in each of which several seeds are deposited.

…three or four seeds were planted in holes some five feet apart.

Three hands do this work; the one in front chops a hole with a hoe on the top of the bed at intervals of from 12 to 18 inches; another hand drops 8 or 10 seed in each hole, and the third follows and covers carefully with the hoe. Three to four pecks of seed are used to the acre.
The seeds were planted upon these beds in hills from 18 inches to two feet apart…

A number of holes, four inches deep and twelve inches long, are cut by the hoe on top of the bed, leaving the space of one foot between each hole.

I plant in holes, on the beds, about three feet apart, putting into each hole, at the time of planting, a large double handful of high-ground earth… The second year, I planted in the same holes, merely pulling up the old stalks.

The trenchers open the holes for the reception of the seed, each taking a task in a line, and are followed by the planters, who throw in handful (or a lesser quantity) of seed in each hole, and it is then covered by either the foot or hoe.

[Note: In this book, the term "hills" is not used, since it is evident that it refers not to a method of sowing, but to a treatment of the soil after the plants appear. Instead, planting in "holes" is preferred, as the author has concluded that the seed was actually deposited in holes dug with the hoe on the beds (fig. 7-8).]

The difference in the long-hole method and short-hole method was in the distance between the holes. The long-hole method involved digging holes separated from each other by two or three times the width of the hoe. The roller (fig. 7-6), with strips of wood set the correct distance apart, marked the locations of the holes for planting. The long-hole method was apparently used for better land where a lesser quantity of seeds could be planted to make a good stand after thinning. In the short-hole method, the distance between the holes was the width of the hoe. In poorer land, where plant survival was less likely, planting in short holes insured that enough plants survived (after thinning) to make a good stand.

"Drilling" involved making a continuous trench in the middle of each bed. The trench was from two to four inches deep, depending on the season. When cotton was planted early in March, before the sun warmed the soil to any great depth, the trench was made two inch-

Figure 7-8. Sowing cotton seed in holes on beds (*Frank Leslie's Illustrated Newspaper*)

es deep to insure sufficient heat to germinate the seed. Later in the planting season, when there was enough solar energy to warm the soil to a greater depth, the trench was made four inches deep. This greater depth also insured adequate moisture for germination. Drilling, when done by hand, required three workers. The first opened the trench; the second dropped the seed into the trench; the third, using either a hoe or his feet, closed the trench over the seed.

The main disadvantage of the drill method was the inability of the slaves to measure a suitable distance in thinning the plants. Since the seeds were sown in a continuous line, the plants had to be thinned to a certain density. Seabrook complained (1830, 142) that the "slaves seem ignorant of the art of measurement…" An order, said Seabrook, "to leave four stalks in a hill would be well understood…" Planting in holes made the thinning process easier.

No matter how the seeds were planted, attention to one main detail was necessary: insuring that enough plants survived to the end of the growing season to produce an adequate crop. Accordingly, more seed was planted in an acre than was necessary to produce a crop. A process of "thinning" reduced a field to the desired number of plants. Again, there was no norm on the amount of seed planted per acre, although early on, a bushel and a half per acre was common. Later, it was realized that this amount was too large, and that three pecks per acre should rarely be exceeded. Each planter had to decide, based on the quality of his land and the cultivar he desired, how much seed to plant each year in a given field and in a given hole or trench. One part of a field with better soil required less seed per hole than another part of the same field with poorer soil. If the hole method was used (either the long or short), the number of holes in a bed also had to be determined. In strong land, 40–45 holes per task (105 feet of bed) were dug; in weak land, as many as 80 holes per task were planted. Furthermore, the planter never knew if unexpected bad weather would kill so many plants that not enough would be left to insure the desired number. This was especially true near the ocean where injury from winds was an annual event. Insect damage or disease might kill plants. Often an entire field had to be replanted because the crop was too thin.

From the literature, it does not appear that any one system of planting was done on all plantations, and it seems that many factors determined the method of sowing. It also appears that mechanical planters were not used for sea island cotton. Mechanical planters, drawn by an animal, had a plow in front to open a furrow, a fertilizer box to drill fertilizer, a seed box from which seeds were dropped into the furrow, and a broad wheel behind, which covered the seed and firmed the soil on top. By the time these planters were available, sea island cotton planting was nearing its end and the farms were too small to make mechanical planters cost-effective.

Thinning

The thinning (or chopping) process, done at the same time the crop was worked, had a specific goal. Planters knew that not all the cotton seeds planted would germinate, and that of those that did germinate, not all plants would reach maturity. As one planter wrote, "as the elements frequently wage war against his crop, his business is to act on the defensive." If there were no disturbing causes, one plant to the hole "would be in exact accordance with the wish of the grower, for there is no doubt that, when unchecked, its isolated position from infancy establishes a strength of constitution favorable to early vigor and maturity." But the planter did not have this luxury, since diseases and insects, strong winds from the sea, a late frost or heavy rains all reduced the number of plants. Consequently, he planted considerably more seeds than necessary to make a good stand. This necessitated the process of thinning: removing by hand the excess plants to reach the desired number. As one planter lamented, "But after all this care, you are never sure from your first sowing a sufficient number of plants will stand."

Determining the best mode of thinning sea island cotton depended almost entirely on experience. No strict rule could be followed. As one planter said, "This [thinning] is a nice point, on which nothing like uniformity of practice prevails." The character of the soil, the state of the seasons, the health of the plants and other considerations always governed how the planter thinned his crop. Not only was it an art to leave the most healthy plants, and the ideal number of plants for the crop, it was critical when the thinning was done. The thinning process also depended on the skill of the worker, so the planter always used the most skillful and intelligent hands for this job. Growing thickly, the plants served as mutual props to each other, and seldom was injury from winds so great that all the plants in a hole became affected. Thinning the plants too quickly, before they put on their coat of bark, made them susceptible to being blown over from the wind. At the same time, bottom fruit were not produced unless the crop was thinned.

Thinning generally began when the plants were five or six inches high. Ultimately, the goal was to leave one or two stalks per hole at the end of the thinning process. But where the land was very strong, if more than two stalks were left, the plants grew so thick they could not be picked. In poor land, where the cotton grew neither thick or high, three stalks were left to the hole. Consequently, there was considerable variation as to how many plants to leave per task (105 feet of bed). William Elliott (1828, 153) suggested that in high lands where fertility was impaired by frequent cropping, as many as 120 stalks could be left in a task row; in stronger land, considerably fewer plants could be left.

Another planter used the height of the plants to determine the final thinning:

In general, cotton that usually grows about three feet high should be left from one hundred and twenty to one hundred and forty stalks in a task row— four feet high about one hundred and ten— five feet high from ninety to one hundred— six feet high and upwards from sixty to eighty stalks.

In summary, the planter had three means to obtain the desired number and spacing of plants in a field: (1) by the number of seeds drilled in the furrow or sown in each hole, (2) by the distance apart the holes were located on the bed or how the seeds were spaced in the furrow that was drilled, and (3) by the thinning process. He could not, of course, control nature, and often his plan was thwarted.

Topping

Seabrook wrote about topping the cotton plants (1830b, 147):

The practice of topping cotton is not common here. I have, however, repeatedly done it with success... As the object is to check the growth of the plant with regard to height, and thereby to induce it to expand its nourishment solely to the filling of the pods, it appears to me that the plan should be adapted as soon as the cotton begins to show symptoms of maturity.

Topping was apparently not widely practiced in the sea islands and no records were found as to whether it was a viable procedure.

Roguing

W. A. Orton (1907, 28-29) called "roguing" the simplest method of seed selection because it involved merely the removal of inferior or varying plants, called "rogues," by seedsmen. All hybrid and "run-out" stalks were removed. Hybrid plants—those crossed with upland varieties—were the tall stalks, often called "male stalks" or "bull cotton." They did harm in three ways: (1) They took up too much room in the field; (2) they bore a scanty, inferior cotton that, if detected in the sample, reduced the price of the crop; and (3) every seed produced a hybrid plant the next year, compounding the problem.

Cultivation

Like all the other methods that comprise the culture of sea island cotton, there was so much variation in the cultivation process that there was never a well-established standard among the sea island planters. Early on, cultivation was done entirely with the hoe. As plows and sweeps became available, some planters used the new mechanical devices; others, however, used only the hoe even after the Civil War. It was found on the sea islands proper where the superfine cotton was grown that the delicate nature of the plant and the extreme friability and lightness of the soil made use of the plow unsuitable. Some planters used the hoe and supplemented cultivation with plows. Other planters used the plow only for breaking the soil, forming the ridges and for cultivation of provision crops. In general, in the last two decades of the antebellum period, the plow became more generally employed.

As a general rule, planters worked the crop four times, in spite of evidence that more than four workings produced a better crop. As the cultivation process became more advanced, workings increased to five to seven times, the process beginning earlier and finishing sooner.

CHAPTER SEVEN

The process of cultivating sea island cotton included the following components: thinning (done with the hoe or by hand); control of weeds; pulverizing the soil for aeration; and hauling (mounding soil around the base of the plant for support against the wind). The cultivation process generally ended in mid-July when the plant started to put out fruit. Also, by this time, the plant would have put out lateral feeder roots into the alley, and any further disturbance with the hoe or plow would cut these roots.

Following is a generalized process of cultivation on the sea islands compiled from several sources. The process will be explained as if four workings were the standard. In all workings, the planter had to insure that the alleys remained capable of free drainage.

The first working began about the first of May when the plants had attained four to six leaves. First, the soil around the plant base was loosened by hand for aeration. Then the sides of the beds were hoed, with the loosened soil and vegetation dragged into the alleys, and all grass removed from around the plant. Generally, thinning was not done at the first working, although some planters thinned slightly at this time if the plants were very thick. Some planters made use of a skimmer-plow invented by John F. Townsend[12] of Wadmalaw Island. It was a plow with a long sword on one side which shaved the sides of the beds, with the tops of the beds left untouched. The skimmer-plow also loosened the soil in the middle of the alley to be hauled to the base of the cotton plants (to make hills around the plants).

The second working consisted primarily of hauling up more soil around the base of the plants. Creating this hill around the base of a plant gave it support against the wind. Between the first and second workings, some grass may have grown around the plants; this was first removed by hand. Next, by hand, the plants were thinned down to four, five or six, depending on the strength of the land.

The third working was similar to the second as far as weeding and hauling. The plants were again thinned according to the strength of the soil, but leaving two or three plants was probably average. Again, the skimmer-plow may or may not have been used to supplement the work of the hoe.

The fourth working again consisted of weeding by hand, hoeing grass off the beds, and hauling soil up around the base of the plants. Now, the final thinning was done. In the best soil, where the plants grew high and thick, each hole was thinned to one plant. Another thinning was done, this time to the entire bed. In strong soil, 60 stalks were left in each task (105 feet along a bed). In lighter soil, 120 plants could be left to a task row, and one or two plants left to the hole. The best mode of thinning, according to one planter, was to leave the stalks wide enough apart for air to circulate freely around the stalks.

---

1. In the broadest sense, "culture" refers to all the factors involved in growing a crop, including soil preparation, fertilizers, plowing, weed removal, seed selection, etc. The term "cultivation" will be used in a strict sense to mean the hoeing and use of plows to work the soil around the planted crop to weed, thin and pulverize the soil.

2. The hickory is probably *Carya glabra* var. *megacarpa* (Sargent) Sargent; laurel is either *Prunus caroliniana* Aiton, Carolina laurel cherry, or *Magnolia grandiflora* L., which William Bartram in his *Travels* called Great Laurel; red bay is *Persea barbonia* (L.) Sprengel; live oak is *Quercus virginiana* Miller; and white oak is *Quercus alba* L.

3. The salt marshes are dominated by smooth cordgrass (*Spartina alterniflora* Loiseleur) at the lower elevations and a mix of smooth cordgrass and black needle rush (*Juncus roemerianus* Scheele) at the higher elevations. Scattered throughout the marsh at the higher elevations are salt flats formed by the evaporation of trapped salt water, leaving behind a very high-saline soil. The salty flats are dominated by two obligate halophytes, perennial glasswort (*Salicornia virginica* L.) and saltwort (*Batis maritima* L.).

4. The notation of trunks is significant. Even though Barnwell does not mention why the trunks were installed, they must have been installed to drain the banked salt marsh in times of heavy rain.

5. In the author's opinion, common green moss refers to Spanish moss (*Tillandsia usneoides* L.), a common vascular epiphyte of the coastal area. Spanish moss was often used as a binder to make bricks and walls of houses.

6. According to longtime Edisto Island resident Nick Lindsay, the terms "pine baron" and "pine barony" also appear on maps for the same area identified as Pine Barren Plantation. The author believes they are simple local terms for Pine Barren Plantation. Pine Barren was home to Joseph Seabrook Sr. (d. 1790), his son Isaac (d. 1798), to Thomas Whaley (d. 1805), and his son Joseph (d. 1872).

7. The subsoil drainage tiles were shown to the author by L. E. Cribb (b. 1919), present manager of the Dill Sanctuary. Cribb's acquaintance with the property began in 1948. He stated that at the time there were no houses or remains of houses in the fields adjacent to where the tiles drain into the marsh, so the tiles could not have been part of a septic system or other domestic structure. Tiles exactly like the one photographed were dug up when the Big Pond was constructed on the Sanctuary in one of the abandoned cotton fields. The author concludes that the tile is from the subsoil drainage used for sea island cotton and is characteristic of James Island.

8. The ridge method of cultivation was not unique to cotton, or to the United States. Agriculture worldwide for centuries has used ridges or beds to grow crops. Some aspects of the ridge system practiced by the sea island planters, however, appear to have been unique to sea island cotton.

9. No date was found when this horse-drawn roller was first used in the sea islands.

10. Three minerals—nitrogen, potassium and phosphorus—are generally the basis of modern fertilizers. These minerals are continually removed from cultivated fields, either through leaching or in the protoplasm when a crop is harvested, and must continually be replaced. Salt-marsh mud and cotton seed were good sources of potassium and nitrogen, respectively, and explain, in part, the beneficial effect of their application to cotton fields.

11. Salt-marsh mud actually contained a variety of minerals besides potash that were beneficial to the plant. F. A. Porcher (1844, 7) cited an analysis of salt-marsh mud showing it contained silica, hornblende, feldspar, alumina, iron, lime and phosphorus. The hornblende and feldspar contained potash (potassium), lime, soda, magnesia, manganese and fluorine. As Porcher explained, "...with the aid of this manure the soil is furnished with every constituent of cotton, except chlorine and sulphur."

12. The author could not find a diagram of Townsend's cultivator.

Market Preparation of Sea Island Cotton

Preparation of sea island cotton for market followed distinct steps that held throughout the industry, although changes occurred in each step with the evolution of better machinery and methods to increase the efficiency of getting the staple ready for market.

Picking (or Harvesting)

Cotton was always picked by hand during the period of sea island cotton cultivation. Even if machines had been available toward the end of the industry, most planters probably would not have had the capital to invest in them. Also, the tall growth habit of the sea island plant and its continuous blooming and fruiting through the fall would have prevented easy picking by mechanical harvesters.

The flowering and fruiting period of sea island cotton lasted from August until December. Weather conditions often extended flowering until the end of December. During this period, one could see on a single plant the flowers in bloom, the green, half-ripe pods, and the ripened pods. Since the sea island cotton plant grew to eight feet in a good season, the amount of fiber on one plant during a single growing season was impressive. From the time the first pod was ready to pick, the whole attention of the cultivator was directed to picking, as the pods opened daily. Picking was usually done as soon as the pods burst, to avoid injury from dirt and to prevent too much exposure to the sun which could damage the fiber. Frequent picking was also important because the staple was quickly damaged by bad weather. Orton (1907, 40) stated that picking was done whenever enough cotton was open, usually about every ten days, making on the average ten to twelve pickings a season.

An anonymous source gives an interesting note on the picking season:

It is the season of universal suspicion; husbands watch their wives, and wives their husbands. No one trusts anybody else. *The planter has his special watchman; and even then, he loses many pounds by what the negroes call "dem tricky members"; for they never call each other "thieves." The small stores on the island buy this stolen cotton, and very young children are experts in keeping them in stock.*

In an early account of picking, Kinsey Burden (1827, 28-29) gave an explanation of his instructions to the gatherers:

...to gather from the field, at every picking, all the cotton, good or bad, which is blown open sufficiently, to enable them to extract the wool with ease. The reasons for being so particular are these: if the bad cotton be left, to be gathered at a future period, before the gathers return through the field, it will have become so much bleached by the weather, that it cannot then be readily distinguished from the good, either by them or by the hands who afterwards sort it for the gins; and, if ginned with the good, the extreme weakness of its fibre will depreciate the value of the general crop in proportion to the quantity of it, which may be mixed with the good.

Although the process of picking with slave labor varied over time and from plantation to plantation, the following is a generalized account of the picking of sea island cotton in South Carolina: Pickers were each furnished with a picking bag and a sheet or light basket. When the bag was full, it was emptied into the basket or placed on the sheet, which was generally spread to allow some sun drying. Good pickers, when the bolls were full, could generally pick 70 or 80 pounds, and the best pickers would often pick 100 pounds.

Pickers did not enter the field until the dew on the cotton was dried by the sun; after hard rains, one day was allowed to let the cotton dry before picking. Each picker's sheet or basket was weighed separately, with its weight subtracted from the total weight. If the cotton was wet by a sudden shower while picking, it was not weighed until it dried, which may have taken two or three days. The cotton was then stored in a common house, from whence the next morning, if the weather was good, drying and sorting was commenced.

Drying

The methods of drying sea island cotton after it was picked varied greatly, as planters experimented with different procedures. There never was, it appears, a consensus on the correct or best method of drying. Spalding (1835, 43) gave a detailed account of the drying process which appeared to be close to the standard method adopted by the planters.

The day after picking, if the weather was good, the cotton was spread upon drying floors made of American pine. The drying floor was raised three feet off the ground to allow for air circulation. If it had been gathered from the field in good weather, the cotton was allowed to dry one day; if picked in wet weather, it might require two or even three days' exposure. Spalding notes that strong winds or bright sun, if continued too long, could injure the cotton.

It is believed that drying the cotton in this manner caused the fiber to absorb some of the natural oil from the seed, which increased its luster.

Seabrook (1843, 285) suggested that the drying rooms be large and airy, and kept in the neatest condition, and that only one laborer be allowed to pass the threshold of the drying-house door, to avoid every cause of contamination of dirt or other foreign matter.

A main reason that cotton had to be dried was in order for it to be ginned on a roller gin. When wet, the strong attachment of the fiber to the seed made ginning difficult. When dry, the attachment was weak, making removal easier.

Sorting (or Nubbing)

Early on, the field workers were not careful during the picking, and did not take care to remove the dead leaves and stems from the seed cotton. The ginners also allowed stained and unstained cotton alike into the gins. Many planters ginned, moted and packed cotton in the same room. Sea island cotton prepared in this manner was suited only for coarse fabrics that were woven on the plantations. However, as the demand for quality long-staple cotton became greater, beginning around 1820, planters took steps to improve the cleanliness of their staple, a practice that endured to the end of the industry.

The exact date that sorting became a distinct step in preparing cotton for the ginner is not known; however, its value became an important factor in obtaining the highest price for the cotton. Cotton was gathered as free of trash as possible. The morning after picking, each picker would sort the cotton he had picked the day before. The hand method of going over the entire bulk of picked cotton and removing all leaves and yellow cotton was tedious and expensive, but no other method was ever adapted, and until the end of the industry, it was the principal means of cleaning the bulk cotton. Haskell's painting (fig. 8-1) of women sorting white cotton from yellow is a testimony to the labor involved in preparing the cotton for market.

Yellow cotton was cotton fiber discolored in the boll by the anthracnose boll-rot. It was important that this fiber be removed before the whipping, since whipping would mix the good and yellow, making it difficult to separate during the moting.

Capers (1835, 409-410) gave comments on sorting:

ASSORTING OR NUBBING is removing all the yellow cotton, pieces of leaf, and dirt of every description. To have this operation carefully and well performed, is the grand secret of cleaning cotton properly. It is the *first cleaning process it goes through with, and the facility and despatch of all the succeeding processes, length and strength of the staple, depends in a great measure on it: for, if the cotton be free of all dirt, rotten seed, &c., it will gin easier, and be so clean as to require little handling in the moting; too much of which destroys the staple.*

Figure 8-1. Sorting sea island cotton (Haskell 1885, 569)

Whipping

The last process before ginning was to pass the cotton through a "whipper" to shake off any sand or broken leaves, short or weak fibers, and any other extraneous matter attached to the cotton that had not been removed during the sorting. Early on, whipping was done by spreading the cotton on a coarse wire screen stretched across a small box. It was then beat with smooth sticks to dislodge the sand and other foreign material. But since whipping manually with sticks injured the fiber, especially the finest sea island cotton, numerous types of whippers were developed during the history of the industry. Spalding (1835, 43) gave a general account of one such device:

The whipper, which… is made of wood, is a long barrel, slats, or reeds, (or it might be made of wire), six or eight feet in length, and two feet in diameter, with one end closed and the other open, and is supported at the two ends by feet of different lengths, so that the barrel in its horizontal position declines about one foot at the lower end; a hopper containing about a bushel rests upon the upper side of the barrel, at the upper enclosed end of it. This hopper lets the cotton that is to be cleaned fall into the barrel, through which runs in its whole length, a shaft which is turned by the hand, by a crank attached to the shaft at the end. This shaft is intersected by rods, until it escapes at the lower end of the barrel, by which time any sand or dirt, or leaves, or other matter, attached to the cotton, has escaped through the spaces intentionally left between the slat or reeds, which constitute the external rim of this barrel or whipper.

One example of a whipper appears in Haskell (fig. 8-2). Although this hand-cranked device is not the barrel device described above, it undoubtedly worked in the same basic manner to clean the cotton. A report from the Committee on Fine Sea Island Cotton (1838, 652) gave this description of a whipper, which appears to be close to the diagram in Haskell: "This machine, constructed of wood with round wooden teeth, is turned by hand. Unless the door of the whipper be closed, which is never done, the egress of the Cotton is quickly effected."

Fones McCarthy, of Demopolis, Alabama, was granted a patent (No. 3,912) in 1845 for his Endless Return Cotton-Whipper (fig. 8-3). Whether this machine was ever extensively employed in cotton whipping on South Carolina plantations is not found in the literature. In McCarthy's machine, uncleaned cotton was introduced through an opening in the frame (E). The cotton was caught by a revolving reel of beaters (C) that whipped it as it was successively returned to the beaters. The centrifugal force of the beaters threw the cotton against the curved grating of parallel bars (D) where the dirt and trash were pushed through the bars by the motion of the beaters while the cotton remained behind. The curved bars of the grating directed the cotton to an endless revolving chain of parallel slats (B) which returned the cotton to the revolving beaters where it was again struck by the beaters and driven against the

Figure 8-2. Whipping sea island cotton (Haskell 1885, 569)

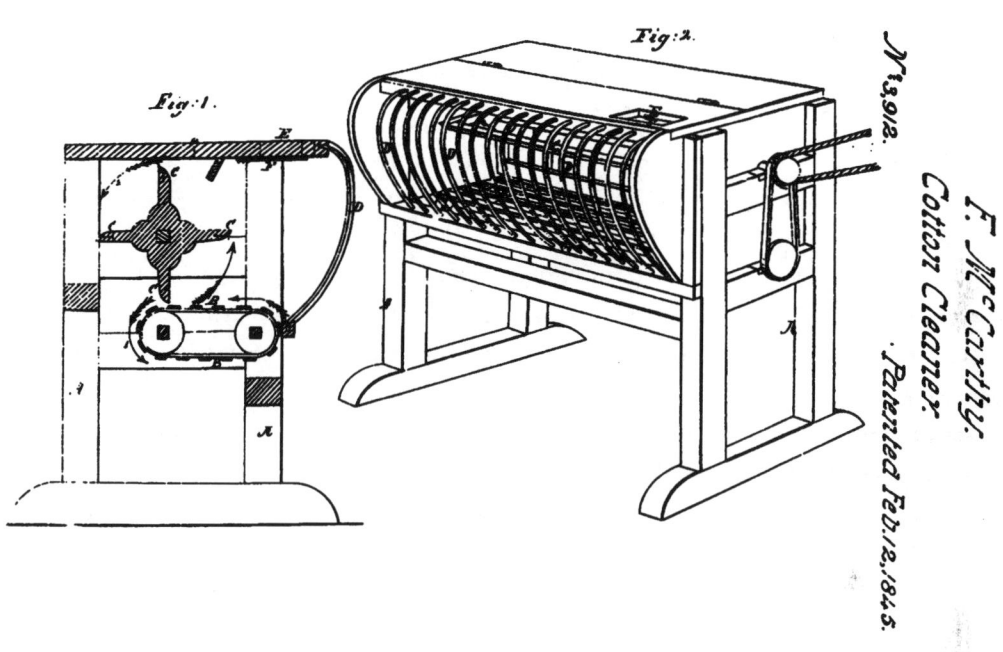

Figure 8-3. McCarthy's "Endless Return Cotton-Whipper"

grating. The cotton gradually approached the discharging end of the machine (not shown) and emerged free of dirt, having undergone a thorough whipping and beating. The machine could be powered by any of the sources available to the planter.

Capers remarked that some planters passed the cotton through the whipper before sorting, but said he always did it after, for if it was whipped before the yellow cotton was taken out, and the yellow was mixed with the white, it was difficult to sort afterwards.

After whipping, the cotton was bulked and allowed to sit from four to six weeks before ginning.

Ginning

The process of removing the fiber from the cotton seed is called ginning. The process of ginning is covered in chapters 9 and 10.

Moting

Allston (1854, 15-16) gave a definition of moting: "The cotton is 'moted' as it comes from the gin, namely: all particles of broken seed, and every speck which may have escaped detection in the 'sorting' are carefully removed." In this process, the cotton was gently shaken and opened by hand.

Turner (1857, 135) introduced a new term, the "mote-table." He wrote: "From the gins, the cotton is taken to the mote-table, where a woman looks it over very carefully and picks out every little mote or stained lock, as fast as two men gin." Haskell drew a typical mote-table (fig. 8-4).

Capers (1835, 411) warned: "Great care is necessary in this process, not to handle the cotton too much, particularly that it is not pulled or torn apart, otherwise the staple will be materially injured."

Packing

Sea island cotton was generally packed into bales manually. The screw and hydraulic presses used on upland cotton were too harsh on the sea island cotton lint, causing damage. Also, the lint was so matted that the spinners objected to cotton bagged by the screw press. A quote from Haskell (1885, 571) was quite clear in its meaning: "Packing? Yes. Sea Island cotton is not packed by screw. Hand packing is all that is allowable."

The bags in which sea island cotton was shipped were almost exclusively Scottish, were made of hemp, and measured 7 1/2 feet in length and 2 1/2 feet in diameter. The room to which the cotton was passed after moting was reserved exclusively for packing, and was kept as clean as possible. Adjoining the packing room was a small apartment under the same roof with holes in the floor. The bags were suspended from these holes (fig. 8-5), and the open

Figure 8-4. Moting (Haskell 1885, 573)

Figure 8-5. Packing sea island cotton

Figure 8-6. Bag of sea island cotton ready for shipping (Orton 1907, 12)

end of the empty bag was strongly sewn with twine around an iron hoop. A male worker would get into the bag, and other workers would throw cotton into the bag. Using a heavy wooden or iron pestle, he pressed the cotton gradually with his feet, and finally pushed it down with the pestle until the requisite quantity was in the bag. The bag was then ready for shipment (fig. 8-6).

There appears to be much variation in the literature on the weight of bales (bags) of sea island cotton. In the above-cited article by Orton, he stated the most common weight was 300 pounds a bale. Other references give around 400 pounds a bale. This book will use 333 pounds as the standard weight of a bale of sea island cotton.[1]

An interesting note by Orton relates to the bales described above: "As the use of this bag has been confined to the Sea Islands, it serves as a trademark to distinguish the crop in foreign markets."

Another mention of packing sea island cotton appeared in *Harper's New Monthly Magazine* (S. W. G. Benjamin 1878, 859):

Sea Island cotton is pressed into circular bales, and by the old method two bales per day have been the limit of one laborer's ability; but by the new and ingenious process alluded to, an active man can now press eight to ten bales a day. It is simple enough. An iron case the size of the bale is lined with the bag, and a circular plate attached to an upright bar that is by means of cogs pressed down on the cotton as it is put in by hand. When the bag is packed hard, the iron case which incloses it is opened, being in two parts, and the bale is found inside a hard and perfect cylinder.

Whether this method was common on plantations cannot be determined from the literature.

A comment by Allston (1854, 15) is noteworthy: "It requires from fifty to sixty days to prepare a bale of fine Cotton for market."

Whitemarsh Seabrook (1844a, 30) gave a summary of the improvements in the preparation of sea island cotton for market through roughly the first half of the industry:

Separate rooms for the seed and ginned cottons, as well as for the wool, which, after it is gathered, is never exposed to the sun, have long been considered necessary in the sea-board parishes to insure the proper after-handling of the crop. There are required a room for the whipper, if one be employed, which extracts the dirt and imperfect filaments; another for the assorters [sorters], who, provided with boxes for their clean cotton, perform their work before a long table, covered with wire, or wooden slats, the 1/8 of an inch apart; a third for the moters, who also stand before a latticed table, and as often as a handful of cotton is prepared, it is thrown in a wooden box, about three feet from the floor, and secured to the sides of the building immediately behind the moters respectively; a small room for the moted cotton, and one for the packer, usually adjoining it; and a house or room, proportional to the force employed, for the ginners, in which are boxes for the seed cotton in the rear of the operators, and boxes under the machines for the ginned cotton. The houses are lined on the

CHAPTER EIGHT

inside with planed boards, and the windows of the assorting and moting rooms, and the ginhouse are glazed. All of these accommodations are now to be found on nearly every plantation on the Sea Islands and the adjacent country, and, it is said, in many of the upper Parishes.

1. The author used Roberts's "The Sea Island Cotton Industry as Revealed in the McConnel-Kennedy Letters, 1819-1825" (Roberts 1965, pp. 142, 149, 178, 181, 189) to calculate the weight of an average bale of sea island cotton as 333 pounds. The firm of McConnel & Kennedy was located in Manchester, England, and was one of the leading import companies producing fine yarns made of sea island cotton.

The Ginning of Sea Island Cotton

This chapter, and the next, tell the story of the evolution of roller gins, beginning with the archaic single-roller, or foot-roller gin, through the roller gins used to gin sea island cotton, and the modern roller gins of today, including the sundry methods invented to produce "the perfect lint" for spinning. The account is, for the most part, chronological and based on advancements in the mechanical complexity of the gins. It does not follow individual plantations, but rather the industry as a whole.

On smaller plantations, for example, primitive foot gins were used long after more complex gins were invented. Planters who grew the finest grades of sea island cotton continued to use the foot gins because they felt either that their laborers did not have the ability to use the more complex roller gins, or that the foot gins did not damage the staple as much. Once the improved McCarthy gin became available in the 1850s, planters of the finest grades then switched to this gin. On plantations that produced lower grades of sea island cotton, planters quickly made use of the newer and improved roller gins to increase ginning capacity, and hence, the plantation's profits. The Civil War also influenced which ginning method was used on a plantation. After the war, many plantations were short on funds, and the planters could not invest in newer gins. They had to make use of pre-war gins.

The object of ginning is to separate the fibers from the seed, and a perfect operation would be performed if the separation were effected without the slightest injury to either. It was hopeless, however, to expect that this desirable condition would ever be attained. So many factors entered into the process through inequalities that existed in the fibers surrounding the seeds, in the seeds themselves, in the gins, and in the skill of the workers, that the degree of success of a particular ginning process could only be judged on the average result. There were always some fibers that broke into pieces before they separated from the seed; other fibers brought with them, in the separation process, portions of the seed husk; and a certain amount of the fibers were ruined by being torn or scraped. Even with the utmost care, broken seeds seemed to be a necessary evil. These and many other defects inherent in the process of ginning were and still are impediments to producing the "perfect" lint. Indeed, the entire history of the ginning process has been one of constantly trying to improve ginning in order to produce the best lint for spinning and weaving. Even with the modern gins of today, some defects are still a natural part of the process.

Two basic types of gins evolved to gin cotton: roller gins and saw gins. The saw gin had its start in 1794 when Eli Whitney was granted a patent for a wire-toothed gin consisting of coarse iron teeth embedded in a wooden cylinder.[1] Whitney, of Massachusetts, was an educated man who appeared headed to a career as a schoolmaster. But like many inventors, a chance observation and a challenge changed his life—and the cotton industry. While visiting Mrs. Nathanael Greene (wife of the war hero) near Savannah, Georgia, he became intrigued with the problem of separating the lint from the seed of upland cotton. At that time, it was separated by hand—a most laborious task. Roller gins were used for the new long-staple sea island cotton, but did not work well on the fuzzy upland cotton seeds. Whitney's saw gin consisted of a system of rollers: one roller with teeth that pulled the lint from the seeds, and a second counter-operating roller equipped with brushes that doffed (removed) the lint. As the cylinder was turned by the power source, the iron teeth rotated through a tightly-spaced metal grate. The seed cotton was fed onto the grate, and as the wire rotated through the grate, the wires pulled the fiber from the seeds (the seeds were too large to pass through the spaces of the grate). A clearer brushed the lint from the teeth of the cylinder. Whitney also included a hopper to feed the gin. The ginning teeth first pulled the seed cotton from the hopper to the grate. Only one person was needed to operate the gin, and that one simply to feed the hopper.

Two men, first John Barcley, then Hodgen Holmes, substituted circular saws for Whitney's wire teeth, and Barcley tried to patent it as a new gin. Whitney ultimately won a patent infringement suit against him, the judge determining that the saw-toothed gin was essentially the same as Whitney's wire-toothed gin, and upholding Whitney's claim for the patent. Ultimately, circular saws were substituted for the initial wire teeth, and the gin became forever known as the "saw gin."

For a time, both the roller gin and the saw gin competed for the long-staple cotton ginning market. However, when long-staple cotton was ginned on a saw gin, it had a distinctly different appearance from roller-ginned cotton because the fibers were not firmly attached to the seed. Textile mills had no standards by which to judge this different appearance. Roller gins, on the other hand, preserved the length of the staple and produced a cleaner product, both of which qualities were sought by the foreign textile market. Consequently, and in spite of the fact that the saw gin had a greater outturn of ginned lint, the saw gin was not used for long-staple cotton after the mid-1820s. The saw gin did, however, revolutionize the ginning of upland cotton (*Gossypium hirsutum* L.), and the market dominance of upland, or short-staple, cotton was and is in part a result of the saw gin.

Throughout the history of roller gin development and use, four major problems were encountered:

1. Lapping—the lint, after being pinched from the seed, stuck to the rollers and revolved with them rather than falling off.
2. Springing—springing occurred when the rollers sprung apart when the gin was loaded with seed cotton. Once this happened, seeds were carried through the rollers and the fiber was not pulled off.
3. Outturn—as long as the outturn (production) of lint depended on one ginner feeding the gin, the results were limited. Some gins like Eve's addressed this problem by having a self-feeding system independent of the ginner.
4. Power source—five sources of power were used to run roller gins: hand, animal, water, wind and steam. Steam became the fuel of choice late in the industry and increased lint outturn.

Evidence that these problems were overcome, either singly in one gin type, or in various combinations in a gin type, was exhibited by the increase in the amount of cotton that could be ginned in a day. Table 9-1, compiled by the author, shows the number of pounds of cotton ginned in a day for each type of roller gin discussed, which demonstrates the evolution of ginning outturn.

Type of Gin	Pounds Per Day
Finger ginning	1
Single-roller gin	1
Beating	4 1/2
Churkha gin	5
Tooth-geared gin	5
Double-crank hand gin	5
Foot gin (wooden fly wheels)	25-30
Foot gin (iron fly wheels)	30
Single Whittemore gin	40
One roller head (steam power)	50-75
Barrel gin (manual)	70-80
McCarthy 1840 single gin (horse or steam)	200
Whittemore (six gins run by a single horse)	240
Eve's gin	250-300

Eve's gin (altered)	600
Barrel gin (animal power)	600-800
McCarthy 1840 (one horse, three gins)	600
Foss double-roller gin (steam power)	2,000-2,200

Table 9-1. Pounds of cotton ginned a day with different types of roller gins

Finger Ginning

Ginning was first done by hand, called "pinch ginning," or "finger ginning," a practice that goes back to 4000 BC. The laborer would simply pull the fiber from the seed. Finger ginning has continued throughout the centuries in primitive areas where cotton is used for local weaving.

In early sea island agriculture, finger ginning was used on the plantations. Kinsey Burden recalled finger ginning that occurred around 1777 (Burden, 1844a, 162): "I remember well, assisting the servants in their task of separating the cotton from the seed, while at the plantation; which at first was done entirely with the fingers…"

Finger ginning was a time-consuming and labor-intensive process, and was not very efficient; one person could gin only about four pounds in a week. When cotton was used locally on the plantations to produce cloth, finger ginning was probably adequate. Once long-staple cotton culture was established in Georgia in 1786, roller gins that had previously been introduced from the Bahamas were used to gin long-staple cotton; finger ginning was virtually abandoned.

Beating

Whitemarsh Seabrook (1844a, 32) mentioned one other ginning technique—beating—which was "…still common in certain parts of India." With a smooth stick, a man could beat 4 1/2 pounds of cotton in a day. The author found no reference to whether this method was used in the sea islands.

Single-Roller Gin

The first improvement in ginning, according to Charles A. Bennett (1960, 1), was an archaic single-roller gin, or foot-roller gin (fig. 9-1), which is used to a limited extent today in India. It dates back to the fifth century and was also the original gin of India. There were two means of operation. In one, the worker sat on a stool and pushed a roller with her feet over cotton seeds placed on a flat, hard surface (called the base, and made of either wood or stone). The fiber was pinched off the seed with the roller. Or, the worker spread the seed cotton on the base, then, kneeling, leaned over and pushed the roller with her hands over the seed cotton, pinching the fiber from the seeds. The single-roller ginned about a pound a day. It is not

CHAPTER NINE

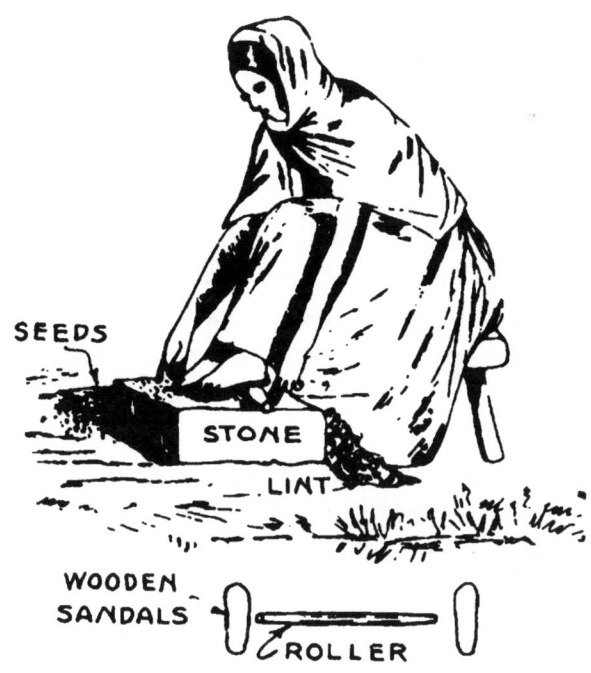

Figure 9-1. Single-roller gin (Bennett 1960, 1)

known whether this method was used on sea island plantations; available records make no mention of a single-roller gin.

Chinese Gin

The next significant advancement in roller gins appears to have occurred in China and India sometime between the twelfth and fourteenth centuries. Both utilized two rollers. The gin in China was operated by one person who turned an upper roller by a hand crank while a lower roller was rotated by a treadle in the opposite direction. The seed cotton was fed to the space between the rollers, and the fiber was drawn through, but the seeds, too large to pass between the rollers, were pinched off. The Chinese gin never reached the New World.

Churkha Gin

The churkha roller gin (figs. 9-2 and 9-3) was mentioned by explorer Marco Polo in the report of his travels in Asia and India during the thirteenth century. It is still used to some extent today in India, virtually unchanged from its original construction. The original churkha gin could produce about five pounds of lint in a day's work. This primitive roller gin was the basis for all subsequent and improved roller gins.

The churkha gin, like the Chinese gin, was operated by one person. A worker turned the crank while feeding the cotton fiber between the rollers. The two rollers turned in opposite directions because of the worm-gear mechanism (fig. 9-3), drawing the fiber between the rollers. As the fiber passed between the rollers, which were set nearly in contact, the larger seeds were pinched off without being crushed while the lint was collected on the other side of the rollers.

The churkha gin appears to have been the initial mechanical gin in the Caribbean cotton-growing areas. According to Angela Lakwete (2003, 16), despite the fact that the Chinese gin "would have allowed greater outturn and ginner productivity," it was the Indian roller gin, equipped with the worm gear, that diffused east to Southeast Asia, west to the Levant, and ultimately to the Americas on British merchant ships in the seventeenth century. This was the initial gin that was used in the West Indies in its early cotton industry, for both short-staple and *barbadense* cotton.

The churkha gin ultimately found its way to the colonies, but how and when is not recorded. Lewis Gray (1958, 674-675) reported that "There is abundant evidence of the widespread cultivation of the smooth-seed species and its separation from the seed by the 'churkha,' or roller gin, long before the invention of the saw gin or the beginning of the sea island industry." Gray also stated: "Just after the Revolution the roller gin was being used by James Kincaid, of Fairfield District, to gin green-seed cotton collected from his neighbors, and after ginning shipped to Charleston." Whitemarsh Seabrook (1844a, 33) further reported on use of the churkha gin:

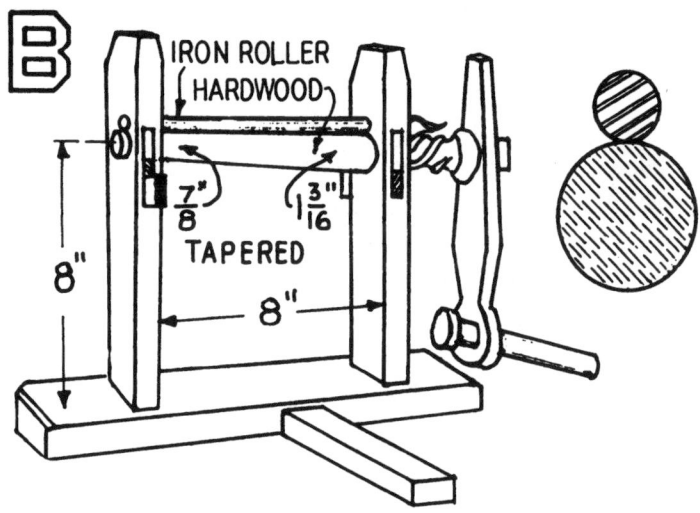

Figure 9-2. Reproduction of a churkha gin (Bennett 1960, 2)

Figure 9-3. Worm gear of churkha gin (Photograph by author)

These, and many others like them used subsequently in several parts of this State, were in part of the fashion of the cotton hand-mill of India, which consists of two rollers of teak wood, fluted longitudinally with five or six grooves, and revolving nearly in contact. The upper roller is turned by handle, and the lower is carried along with it by a perpetual screw at the axis.

It appears, then, that the churkha roller gin was in use in the West Indies and throughout the colonies from an early date to gin domestic plantings of upland cotton and *Gossypium barbadense*. But it soon gave way to four other types of roller gins, all based on the churkha: a tooth-geared gin, a double-crank hand gin, a foot or treadle gin, and the barrel gin.

Tooth-Geared Gin

The worm mechanism was difficult to manufacture on the plantations. Attempts were made to substitute a toothed gear for the worm mechanism. According to Angela Lakwete (2003, 27-28), in 1746, a French colonist in Louisiana, Moulin du Sr. Prat, replaced the worm gear with toothed gears and "separated the crank mechanism from the rollers and attached it to a large toothed gear that intermeshed with the roller gears from a position below them." But, as she relates, construction of toothed gears "presented a formidable challenge to the gin maker and ginner." Further, "[c]asting iron gears to the necessary size and tolerance would have daunted a pattern maker and founder, particularly in the colonial setting." Prat's gin was never a commercial success because of its difficult construction.

An argument can be made that Kinsey Burden, Sr., made the first attempt to construct a tooth-geared gin in the sea islands. Whitemarsh Seabrook (1844a, 32-33) described a roller gin built by Kinsey Burden Sr. that was apparently a tooth-geared gin:

Soon after the commencement of our revolutionary struggle, Kinsey Burden, deceased, late of St. Paul's Parish, constructed a roller-gin, believed to have been among the first ever made or used in South Carolina, which enabled him to clothe his negroes in garments fabricated at home. It was composed of pieces of iron gun-barrels burnished and fixed on wooden rollers, with wooden screws to secure them, and wooden cranks to turn in the manner of the steel corn-mill. It was turned by one person and fed by another.

Of this same gin, Kinsey Burden (1844a, 162) wrote:

But my father soon constructed a roller cotton-gin, with pieces of iron, gun-barrels burnished, and fixed on wooden rollers, with wooden screws to secure them—and wooden cranks to turn in the manner of the stall corn mills. With this simple gin, and one man to turn, and another to feed, he soon ginned out enough cotton for his domestic purposes. I am under the impression, this was the first cotton gin used in South Carolina, and that the present roller foot-gin is an improvement of it.

Unfortunately, no diagram survived (nor was likely ever made) of Burden's gin. But it can be inferred from the two accounts above that it must have been some type of tooth-geared gin. Both accounts state that Burden's gin was operated by one person. Like the churkha gin, a feeder was not necessary. (If a feeder was used, he could not have fed the gin and turned the crank at the same time.) Since Burden's gin was obviously not a foot gin (see next section), the author concludes it must have had a tooth-geared mechanism for there is no other way to turn two rollers by a single operator unless it used the worm gear. Whether Burden got his idea from Prat is also unknown. Since he was a carpenter by trade, he had a mechanical background and certainly could have devised the tooth-geared mechanism independently. Numerous diagrams appear in the literature of tooth-geared roller gins. The one in figure 9-4 represents the basic construction that may have been like Burden's gin.

Like Prat's gin, Burden's gin would have been difficult to manufacture on the plantation or elsewhere. Burden's gin or other tooth-geared gins apparently were never common on the sea islands.

Double-Crank Hand Gin

The double-crank hand gin did not depend on the worm mechanism or the toothed gear. Instead, each roller was turned by a crank. Charles W. Capers (1834, 73) gave an early description of the double-crank hand gin (fig. 9-5):

At the time Mr. Whitney introduced his gin into Beaufort [1793] the long-staple cotton was got out by two negroes turning a crank by hand, to which rollers were attached, the negroes being on opposite sides, and each turning in a contrary direction from the other. A third negro fed the gin.

Although the double-crank hand gin and the churkha gin had about the same outturn of lint (about five pounds a day), and the double-crank hand gin required three persons to operate while the churkha required only one operator (and if desired, a feeder), it replaced the churkha gin because it was much easier to manufacture on the plantations since it did not rely on the complicated worm gear of the churkha gin.

Foot Gin

The foot gin was the next advancement in roller gins. The foot gin was used concurrently with the double-crank hand gin in the sea islands before the development of sea island cotton

THE GINNING OF SEA ISLAND COTTON

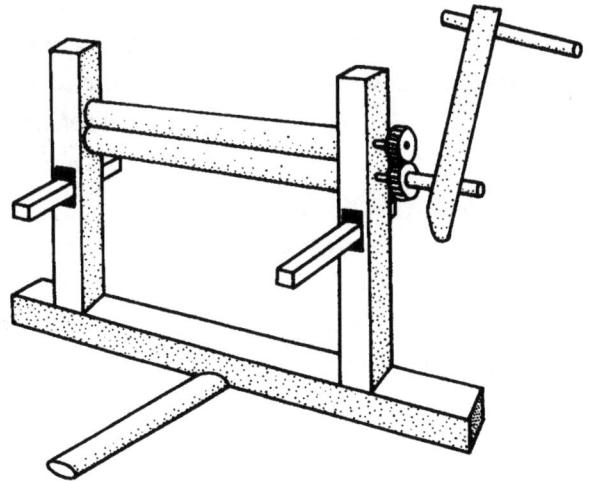

Figure 9-4. Tooth-geared roller gin

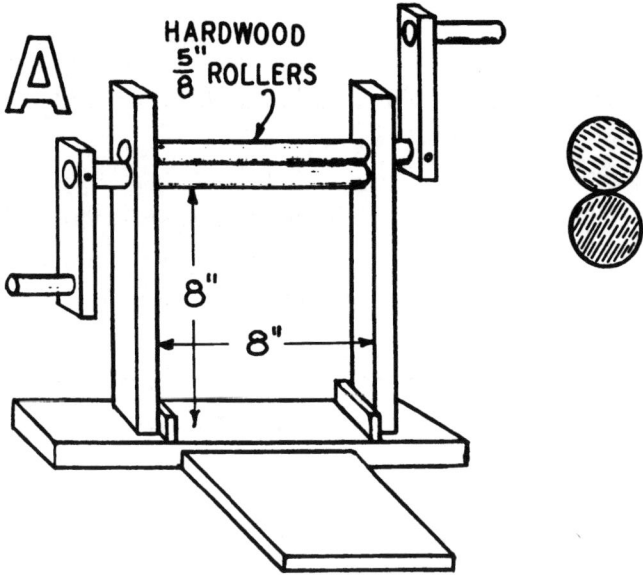

Figure 9-5. Double-crank hand gin (Bennett 1960, 2)

to gin both early plantings of short-staple cotton and early plantings of *G. barbadense*. With the arrival of commercial sea island cotton, the foot gin was more popular with the planters than the hand-cranked gin because of its greater outturn. Lint outturn with the hand-cranked gin was five pounds a day, while the outturn of the foot gin was around 25 to 30 pounds a day. The foot gin required only one plantation hand to operate, which included feeding and ginning. The operator could use either one or both feet to treadle, freeing both hands to feed the seed cotton to the gin.

The origin of the foot gin is uncertain.[2] Angela Lakwete (2003, 31) wrote: "It appeared that gin makers in the Americas eliminated the hand crank and attached both rollers to a treadle." Where in the Americas was not stated. The foot gin was known to have been used in the Caribbean as early as 1762. The *Encyclopédie* described the operation of a foot gin in San [Santo] Domingo as part of an idealized operation of cotton production. In a drawing (fig. 4-1), a slave is shown picking cotton which is probably perennial *G. barbadense*. Another slave is shown cleaning the cotton before taking it to be ginned. A woman is shown ginning the cotton on a foot gin with flywheels. Two other field hands are bagging the lint for shipment. One is inside a bag hung from the rafters of the shed trampling down the fluffy lint and tamping it with a crowbar. In the distance is a small ship that will transport the cotton for export.

One of the earliest descriptions of a foot gin in the colonies (figs. 9-6 and 9-7) was by Bernard Romans in his classic *A Concise Natural History of East and West Florida* originally published in 1775 (Braund 1999, 173): "Across this are placed two round well polished iron spindles, having a small groove through their whole length, and by means of treadles are by the workman's foot put in directly opposite motions to each other…"

The first documentation of ginning sea island cotton with a foot gin is from John Drayton (1802) where he says, "…those in present in use are foot gins, Evees's [Eve's] gins, barrel gins, and saw gins."

Both Thomas Spalding (1835, 44) and Whitemarsh Seabrook (1844a, 33) reported that the foot gin was imported from the West Indies. Spalding noted in another article on the early introduction of the foot gin into Georgia (1844b, 128):

The treadle-gin was introduced in the winter of 1788, by Alexander Bisset, at St. Simons Island; I think he took the idea from communications, from the Bahama Islands, he was an ingenious man himself, and his overseer, a mechanic; why, I remember this, is, because my father was Executor, and this overseer became mine, for the first twenty years of my being a planter.

Spalding (1835, 45-46) gave an excellent description of a foot gin, which he and Robert F. W. Allston (1854, 15) reported could gin about 25 pounds of cotton in a day:

…to wit, two wooden rollers kept together by a wooden frame and a square shaft, upon which is fixed a wooden or iron fly-wheel, from two to three feet in diameter. The iron cranks which turn

the rollers are connected with strips of wood with a treadle worked by the foot, this treadle runs under the machine, and is connected at the farther end of the floor of the house, by sockets within which it revolves; the man stands therefore in the front of the rollers, with a board between him and the rollers, upon which he holds a large handful of seed cotton, which he presents from time to time to the rollers, that are kept in motion by the presence of the foot upon the treadle,—this labour from habit becomes easy, as the feet are often changed in the operation.

Bennett (1960, 5) provides a diagram (fig. 9-6) for a foot gin with wooden flywheels that appears close to that described by Spalding.

When iron flywheels were substituted for the wooden flywheels, the machine worked more efficiently and ginned 30 pounds a day with no problem (fig. 9-7).

James Harvie's Brushes

Lapping (the lint sticking to the rollers) was always a major problem with early roller gins. Whitemarsh Seabrook, in his "Memoir on Cotton" (1844a, 33), related an early attempt to solve this problem:

To prevent the cotton from being carried round about with the rollers, Mr. Harvie of Berbice, in 1820, obtained a patent for an improvement, which consisted in the application of a thin long brush to the posterior surface of the rollers.

James Harvie was a British citizen of Berbice, a contested British colony in present-day Guyana, a small country on the northeast coast of South America. At the time he was awarded his patent he resided in Glasgow, Scotland. He was awarded a patent on August 18, 1820 for a brush "for Improvements in the Construction of Machines, commonly called Ginning Machines, and which are employed in separating Cotton-wool from the Seeds."[3] He applied "shifting brushes to the back of the rollers… by means of which brushes the cotton, on passing through the rollers,… is prevented from being carried around the rollers, whereby it has hitherto been subjected to great injury in its colour and fabric."

Each brush was attached by a pair of screws (fig. 9-8) "…[so as] the bristles may come in contact with the rollers." As the brushes wore down from friction, they could be moved closer to the rollers by loosening the screws and shifting them in.

Harvie did not indicate what the brushes were made from, except to say they "closely fill the edge of the wood with bristles, after the manner in which brushes are usually manufactured…"

Whitemarsh Seabrook noted in his "Memoir on Cotton" that the invention failed because the brushes heated up in the process. However, it appears likely that a modification of Harvie's

CHAPTER NINE

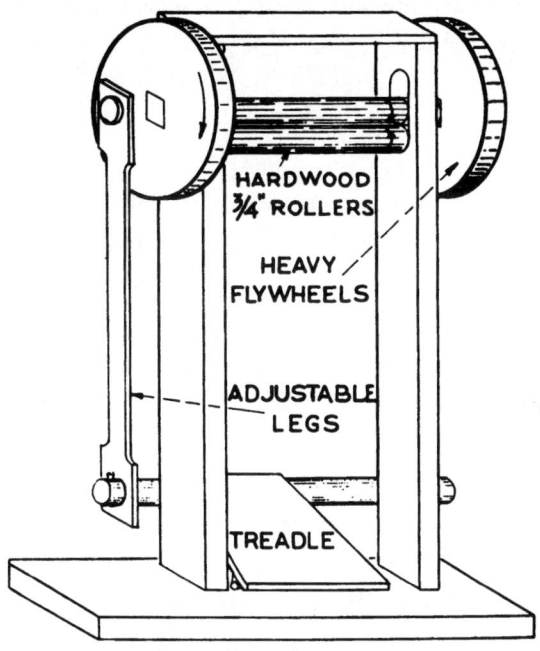

Figure 9-6. Foot gin (Bennett 1960, 5)

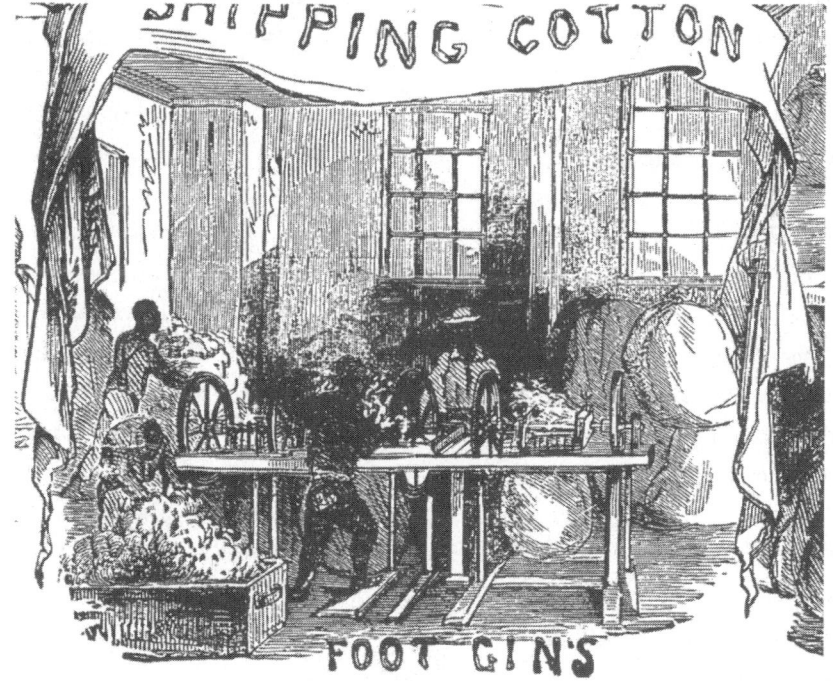

Figure 9-7. Foot gin with iron flywheels

stationary brush was incorporated into later roller gins, including the McCarthy gin. Brushes were later replaced by rotary doffers.

Barrel Gin

The barrel gin, introduced sometime in the 1770s into the colonies, made use of a cog-wheel to drive more than one roller gin. The earliest description of a barrel gin was given by Bernard Romans (Braund 1999,173-74) from his account of East and West Florida. In this primitive barrel gin, the power was supplied manually:

The French in Florida have much improved this machine by a large wheel, which turns two of these mills [roller gins] at once, and with so much velocity as by means of a boy, who turns it, to employ two negroes at hard labour to shovel the seed from under the mill... I am informed that one of those improving mills will deliver seventy or eighty pounds of clean cotton *per diem.*

In spite of the improved outturn of ginned cotton of this manual barrel gin, only after animal power was applied did the barrel gin become an efficient machine to gin cotton. The use of animal power to propel machinery is well documented for the rice culture of South Carolina. Porcher (1987) noted that animal power propelled rice mills as early as the mid-1700s. By the time gins were being used to gin cotton, the technology using animal power to drive machines would have been known to sea island cotton planters, many of whom also grew rice.

John Drayton (1765-1820), in his *A View of South Carolina* (1802, 133) described a barrel gin used in South Carolina:

Barrel gins are either worked by oxen or water; and may be said to be nothing more than foot gins, to which greater power is applied, by the complicated mechanism. This consists of a large driving cog-wheel, working a small trundle wheel. This smaller wheel, gives motion to a large cylinder, or barrel, round which, from eight to twenty-four sets of bands are passed, communicating with the pullies of as many cotton gins; which are fixed on rows on each side of it. A negro is stationed at each of these gins, to feed it with cotton; besides one who superintends the whole; and the larger kinds of these mills, will gin out from 6 to 800 weight of clean cotton in a day.

Charles Drayton (ca. 1744-1820), who owned Jehossee Island and was the uncle of John Drayton, kept a detailed diary on his agricultural practices.[4] He included a diagram of the power mechanism for the barrel gin described by his nephew John. The barrel gin is reproduced in figure 9-9.

The barrel gin operated as follows: Two animals (either horses or oxen) were yoked to a cog wheel in a room below the gins. The cog wheel, turned by the power of the animals, turned

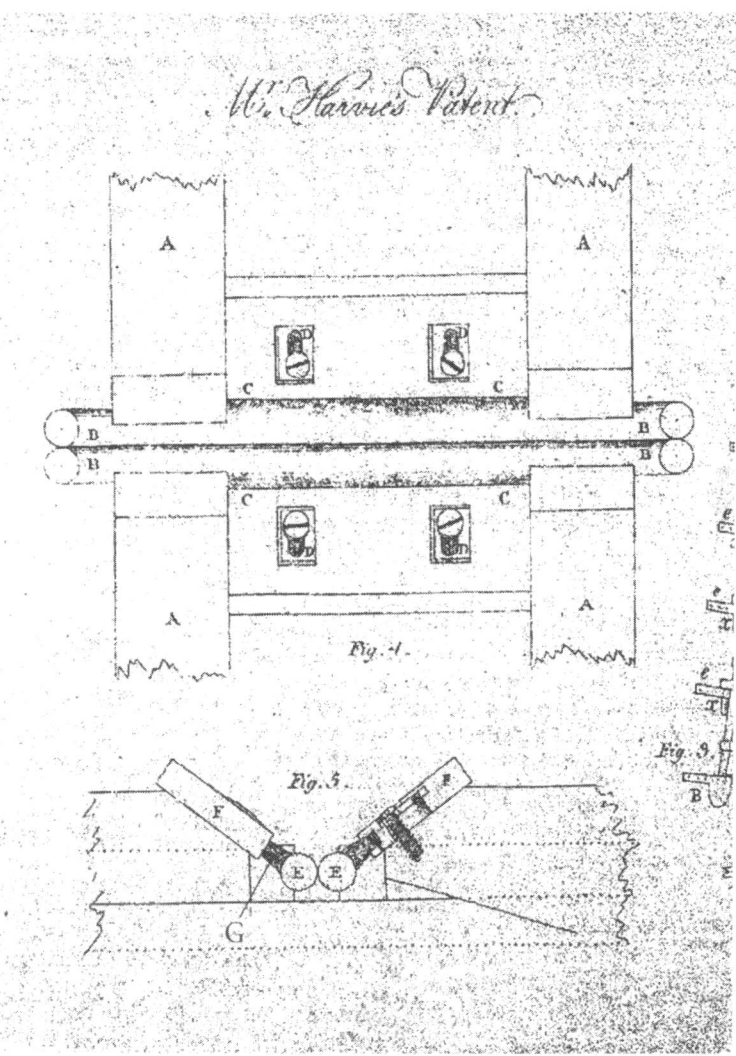

Figure 9-8. James Harvie's patent. In *Fig. 4*, ginning rollers are B, brushes are C, and screws are D; in *Fig. 5*, rollers are E, and brushes are G (G added by author).

the lantern wheel (or trundle wheel of Drayton's description) which was coupled to the barrel (a large cylinder) because they were on the same axis. The barrel consisted of a wooden framework covered lengthwise with narrow boards. Two rows of roller gins were located on either side of the barrel on the floor above. A series of belts (the number varying depending on the number of gins) ran through slits cut into the floor alternating to each series of gins. When the barrel was put into motion, the belts around the barrel would automatically align with the pulleys that ran each roller gin. The belts from the barrel drove the lower roller of each gin. The tooth-gear mechanism that connected the two rollers caused the upper roller to turn in the opposite direction. (Since the rollers were turned by belts from the barrel, the treadle or hand cranks were not needed.) A worker fed the raw cotton to the rollers which stripped the seeds from the lint.

Although the barrel gin increased production, they were not without their problems, especially in regard to safety. Angela Lakwete (2003, 8) stated:

Furthermore, it added to the danger of ginning. Metering seed cotton to the rapidly spinning rollers of a hand or foot gin was a dangerous operation, but the ginner could stop either type gin almost immediately if a finger got caught. The oxen- and water-driven barrel gins that Drayton described could not be stopped so quickly, so ginners risked serious injury.

Eve's Gin

In 1790, Joseph Eve (1760-1835) introduced a modified roller gin into Georgia that was run by animal, wind or water power (fig. 9-10). It was brought to South Carolina in 1797 or 1798 (Burden 1844b, 201). Eve was living at the time in the Bahamas (he identified himself in his patent as "Joseph Eve of Pennsylvania") and may have gotten the idea for his gin from gins used there. Eve had been encouraged to develop a gin as financial compensation was offered by the governor of the Bahamas for improvements in cotton culture. His gin proved to be an important breakthrough since it cleaned large amounts of cotton more quickly and efficiently than the traditional methods.

There is on record in the U.S. Patent Office Patent No. 502X, dated December 6, 1803, by a J. Eve for a "Machine for Separating Cotton Seed from Cotton." The description of the gin and accompanying diagram were among the many patents lost in the fire of 1836.[5] It is likely, however, that this is the gin Eve introduced in 1790, since the literature does not mention another gin by Mr. Eve. Fortunately, at least two descriptions and one diagram of Eve's gin have survived.

From Joseph Dennie (1811, 185-86) comes this explanation:

In this machine the seeds are disengaged from the cotton by rollers of wood or metal, which draw the cotton through perpendicular apertures too small to admit the seeds— these rollers are fluted

CHAPTER NINE

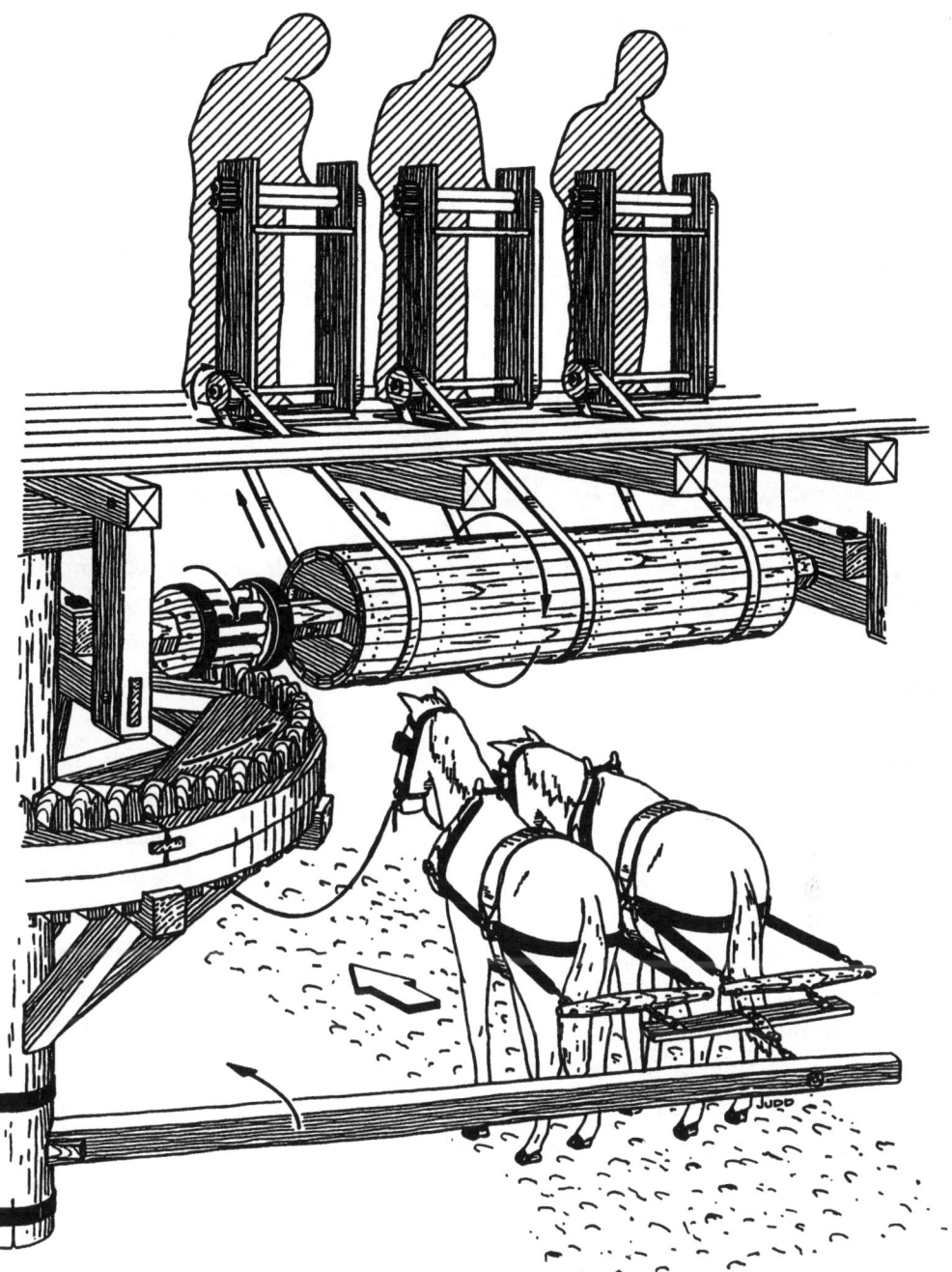

Figure 9-9. Reconstruction of a barrel gin (Courtesy of William Robert Judd)

and turn reverse-wise. There are three sets of metal combs placed before the rollers (two only of which are represented in the drawing) that feed the machine and disengage any extraneous matter; the middle set move up and down and pass between the teeth of the others. These combs are set in motion by means of a crank, and traverse on pivots, or on a slide. The rollers are impelled by bands running over pulleys on one side of the machine, and by pinions on the other, by bands, or by wheels and pinions on both sides.

The middle bar, or transverse piece that supports the boxes in which the rollers turn, has dovetail pieces in front, and tenons behind to confine the boxes. On these the sliding pieces, in which the counter set of boxes are fixed that confine the rollers, are made to move, so as to adjust the rollers; or, the sliding pieces may be made to slide on dovetails and tenons fixed in the moving bars of the machine.

There are brushes fixed behind the rollers through the whole length of the feeding spaces that prevent the cotton from wrapping round them or jamming; this may also be effected by cushions made of cloth.

Thomas Spalding (1844a, 106-107) gave this description of the operation of Eve's gin:

His gin consists of two pairs of rollers, more than three feet long, placed the one set over the other, upon a solid frame that stands upon the floor, inclined at an angle of about thirty degrees— so that the feeder may the more easily throw the cotton in the feed by the handful upon a wire grating that projects two inches in advance of the rollers, just below them; between these protecting wires, the feeding boards, with strong iron, or in preference brass teeth pass, lifting the cotton from the wire grating and offering it to the revolving rollers. The feeders should make one revolution to every four revolutions of the rollers. The rollers are carried forward by wheels supported over the gin, and upon the axle or shaft of these rollers; at the center there is a crank similar to a saw-mill crank, the diameter of whose revolvement is as one to four of the diameter of the wheels, carrying by bands the rollers.

Eve's gins were powered by "horses and oxen, or by water" according to Drayton (1802, 133), and Spalding (1844a, 107) noted that the rollers of Eve's gin "...were graduated to make 480 to 500 revolutions per minute, depending of course, upon the gait of the horses and mules, within these limits." A single Eve's gin could gin 250-300 pounds of cotton in a day. No diagrams survive for the mechanisms that supplied animal or water power to this gin.

Eve's gin, as originally sent from the Bahamas, employed rollers 5/8" in diameter, made of stopper wood,[6] and graduated to make 480 to 500 revolutions a minute within the limits of the gait of the animals. Soon after Eve sent his gins to Georgia, some of his own workers followed and began to make them on their own, presumably without Eve's consent, changing the roller size to 3/4" and the velocity of the rollers to 600 revolutions a minute. The ginning capacity of these modified gins increased to around 600 pounds a day.

Eve's gin featured advancements in all four of the problems encountered with making roller gins more effective: it automatically fed the seed cotton to the gin; greater power was supplied

Figure 9-10. The Eve gin (Courtesy of the American Antiquarian Society, Worcester, Mass.)

by animals, water or wind; brushes doffed the lint off the rollers; and it compensated for springing, or separating, of the rollers (although the literature does not reveal how).

In spite of these technical advancements, Eve's original gins (and those altered by the workmen who came to Georgia) were ultimately abandoned by the planters of the finest sea island cotton because the mechanisms that passed the cotton from the feeders to the rollers damaged the staple. Thomas Spalding (Turner 1857, 281) best stated the problem with Eve's gin for sea island cotton: "It is the crimping produced by the teeth and the wire grating, which has served as a cause for carping by the cotton-buyers, and which has gradually led to the disuse of these gins…"

Its complexity and high cost of construction also contributed to its replacement by foot gins, long the favorite of the best growers of sea island cotton. Eve's gin continued to be used for lower grades of sea island cotton until the advent of the McCarthy gin. Eve's gin was also used to gin short-staple cotton. However, in the end it lost out to the toothed gin of Whitney that had a higher ginning capacity and lower labor costs.

Eve, like other inventors of roller gins, had a Charleston connection. According to Angela Lakwete's research (2003, 79), "A newspaper notice places him in Charleston in January 1805, when Benjamin Bethel, one of his workman, reported a theft of a tool chest from the gin shop. In April of the same year, Eve announced that he had relocated to a new shop at Cochran's Ship Yard on the Cooper River near Charleston." Eve sold licenses to build his gins and offered other services to planters, as well as hiring others to make his gins. After he relocated his family to Augusta, he licensed to others until the market for his gins ended.

Reed's Gin

In 1827, Jesse Reed of Marshfield, Massachusetts introduced a sea island cotton cleaner, U.S. Patent No. 4849X (fig. 9-11). It held nine cylinders, each with metal cores to prevent springing. A hopper (A) fed the seed cotton to four spiked feeder cylinders (B) that "received, separated, and conveyed" the seed cotton to the ginning rollers which pinched off the seeds from the fiber. The upper ginning roller (C) was made of ridged steel, and the lower ginning roller (D) was wrapped "obliquely with a strip of roughened leather" to grip the fiber and pull it through the rollers. A brush cylinder (E) (perhaps adapted from Harvie) that rotated faster than the ginning rollers doffed the lint. Two spiked cylinders (F) prevented lapping.

Sea island cotton planters tried Reed's gin, for there is reference to it in the June 17, 1828 minutes of the South Carolina Agricultural Society (Gregorie and Surles 1936a, 52):

A new invented Cotton roller Gin was exhibited, accompanied by a Letter from MR Reed of Marshfield, Massachusetts, the Inventor, which was read before the Society requesting its alteration and patronage. On Motion Order'd that the following Committee be appointed to inspect it and examine into its merits and report at the next meeting. 1. William Washington 2. Francis D. Quash 3. Ed. Brown 4. James Cuthbert 5. W. M. Parker 6. Charles E. Roland-

Subsequent minutes of the society make no mention of the committee reporting on its inspection. In an article in the *Southern Agriculturist* (J. B. W. 1835, 475), the author (identified only by these initials) stated: "He [Reed] constructed several different kinds of machines, some of which were very ingenious, of superior workmanship, but too complicated and expensive for our purpose." Reed's cotton cleaner, like those preceding it and others to follow, never was successful for sea island cotton.

Whittemore's Gin

The next gin that attracted the attention of sea island cotton planters was a roller gin patented by William Whittemore Jr. of New Cambridge, Massachusetts (fig. 9-12). The first patent was granted on March 7, 1834 (No. 8,049X), and the second on May 29, 1835 (No. 8,857X). These documents appear to be copies of the original patents that were destroyed in the 1836 fire. Only Patent No. 8,857X has a description, in longhand, and it is difficult to read. Both patents have a diagram of the gin, and are most certainly for the same machine.

Whittemore's gin was propelled by horse power. However, the type of mechanism that drove the gins could run only six individual gins, severely limiting the daily output of cotton. Each individual gin could produce around 40 pounds. The reason for this is given by the same J. B. W. (1835, 476):

The machinery connected with the propelling power, consists of an ordinary cylinder or drum, which runs upon friction wheels, and a compact apparatus in a room below... The animal is without the power of locomotion, so far, at least, as his body is concerned, but propels the machinery by his feet, somewhat upon the tread-mill principle...

Since the treadmill on which the horse ran increased the friction of the machine, only a single horse—and only a horse—could be used for power, limiting Whittemore's gin to six individual gins. When six gins were used, the output was 240 pounds a day. In addition, having to install the gins in the second story of the gin house was a hindrance. Furthermore, increasing the velocity of the rollers would not appreciably increase the amount of cotton ginned. Whittemore's gin normally ran, when powered by a horse, at 250 revolutions per minute; increasing the revolutions would have damaged the staple.

Whittemore's gin never equaled its expectations, as Seabrook notes in his "Memoir on the Cotton Plant" (1844a, 34):

In Whittemore's machine, it was thought, that all the objections to the previous ones had been effectually removed. To run in the easiest possible manner, and to preserve the rollers from being heated, it was provided with friction-wheels and friction-rollers. Although, therefore, from these causes the cotton received no damage, yet, it was soon discovered, that it cut the staple, and that this irremediable defect was in proportion to the velocity of the gin. It was consequently abandoned.

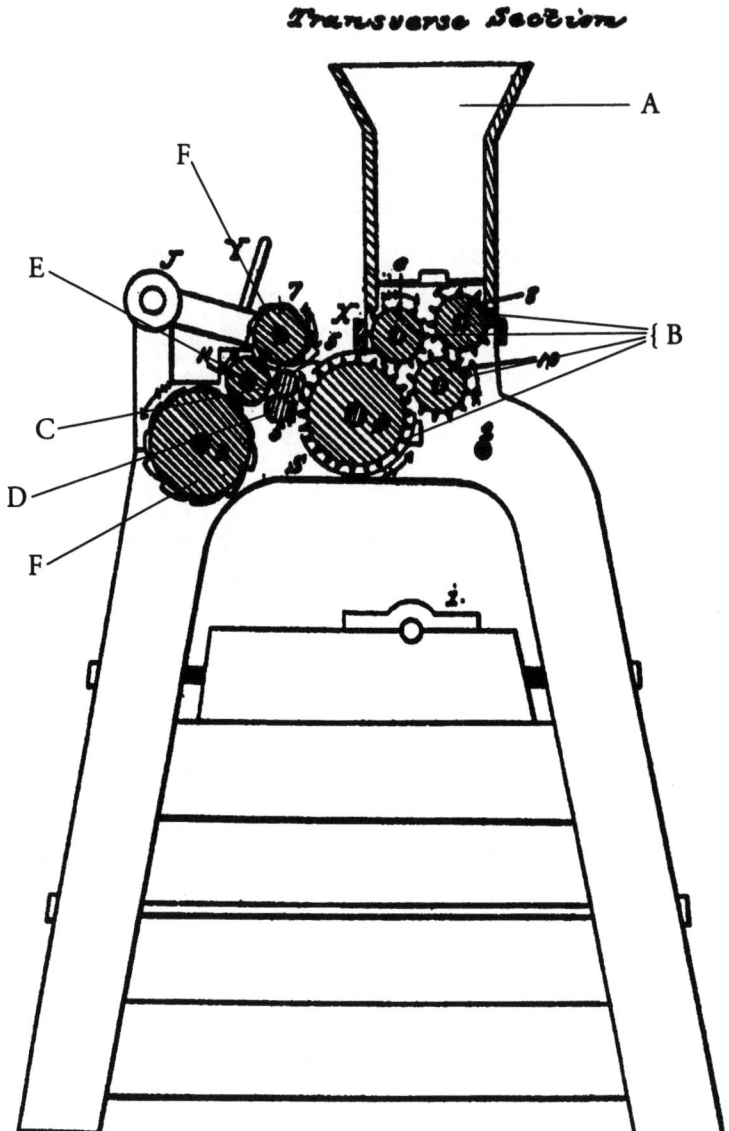

Figure 9-11. Sea island cotton cleaner by Jesse Reed, 1827

One further note on the Whittemore gin: J. B. W. (1835, 476) pointed out that if the old horizontal cog wheel and trundle had been used, the efficiency of the gin would have increased because more than one animal could have been used, including oxen.

Carver's Gin

In 1838, Eleazer Carver Jr. of Bridgewater, Massachusetts devised a machine (U.S. Patent No. 949) that used several pairs of spiralled rollers that could be fed on a flat plane (fig. 9-13). The obvious advantage of this gin was that several pairs of rollers could be included, increasing its ginning capacity. The seeds were augured to the ends of the rollers while the ginned lint went down to a moving belt. Doffers removed the lint from the rollers. Carver's machine would have been very complicated to construct in machine shops of the period, and, as noted by Bennett (1960, 6), it was never a commercial success.

Whittemore's Rollers

In 1839, William Whittemore Jr. made an attempt to improve rollers (U.S. Patent No. 1,158). He used one roller made of leather disks, and the other made of roughened metal (fig. 9-14). No record exists as to whether this system was ever commercially successful.

McCarthy's Gin

In 1840, Fones McCarthy invented a roller gin that revolutionized the ginning of long staple cotton throughout the world. It became the standard throughout the long-staple cotton industry and is still used today in some countries. (This gin is described in chapter 10.)

Reynolds's Gin

In 1844, Richard Reynolds Jr. of Beaufort, South Carolina patented (No. 3,425) a triple-roller gin operated by hand that employed two pinching rollers working ahead of a larger clearer roller (fig. 9-15). In the diagram, (B) and (C) are the ginning rollers, and (F) did the clearing by taking the cotton from roller (B). The hand crank is not shown. Nothing in the literature indicates whether Reynolds's machine was commercially used.

Ely's Gin

In 1845, Theodore Ely of New York invented a roller gin that displayed some genuine mechanical innovations (U.S. Patent No. 4,302). His gin (fig. 9-16) included both feeder and ginning rollers and a clearer (doffer) to remove the lint from the rollers. In the diagram, the

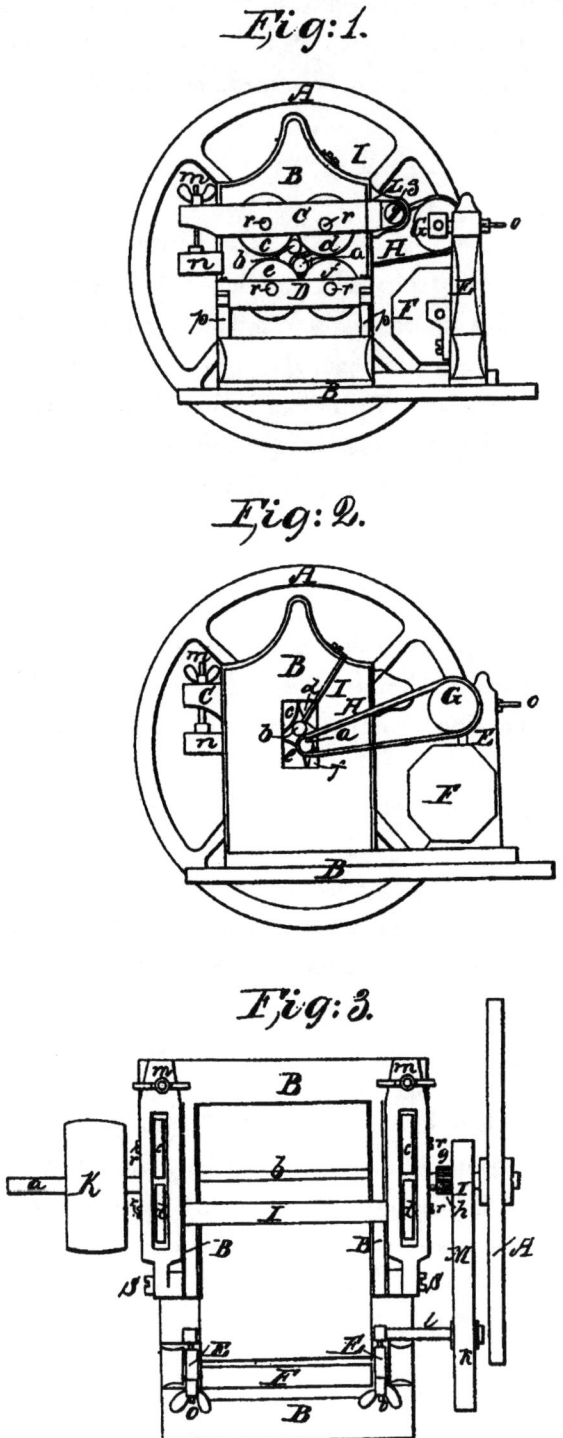

Figure 9-12. Whittemore's gin

feeding cylinder (A) fed the cotton to the two rollers (B). The lint was cleared from the rollers by the two clearers (D). A counterweight (H) provided self-adjustment of pressures between the ginning rollers. Nothing in the literature indicates whether Ely's machine was a commercial success.

Layton's Gin

On May 22, 1849, William Y. Layton of Darlington, South Carolina was granted U.S. Patent No. 6,463 for a "new and useful machine for separating the lint of cotton-wool from the seed of long-staple, sea-island, or other cotton, called 'the Self-Leveling Roller Cotton-Gin.' " Layton's gin featured adjustable bearings that set the rollers at points between the ends where the bearings were liable to wear out. By this mechanism, the operator was able to keep the rollers parallel and maintain equal pressure on the cotton, however unevenly the bearings wore out.

At a meeting of the Black Oak Agricultural Society on November 17, 1846, a committee was appointed

...to examine & report upon the capability of a Machine constructed by Wm. Layton of Darlington for ginning the long cotton, & to report at the anniversary meeting in April, as to its fitness for the proposed object— its liability to derangement & other matters pertaining to its adaptedness to the wants of the long cotton plantation,— & if defective its capability for improvement.

The committee reported back on April 25, 1848 that Layton's gin "was very unfavorable, it having ginned at most only 150 lbs. per day, & very soon got out of order. Nothing more was heard of this gin in the sea islands or in the Santee long cotton region. Since the patent was granted three years after the committee's investigation, Layton evidently went ahead with his patent request despite the negative report.

Fessenden's Gin

In 1867, two Beaufort County men received patents for roller gins. On July 9, A. Fessenden of Beaufort was granted U.S. Patent No. 66,577 for "a cotton-gin of that class in which the cotton is taken from a stationary platform and is carried between two rollers which are so close together that the seed cannot pass through between the rollers." His patent consisted of a "device for hanging the lower roller and adjusting it in the proper position; also, in connection therewith, in an adjustable feed-platform; finally, in the shape of a self-adjusting seed-clipper or knife, and the manner of hanging the same so that it will assist in separating the seed from the fibers before the cotton comes to the rollers." His machine apparently tried to improve on the McCarthy gin, but was too complicated to operate and manufacture, as there is no record of it ever having been a commercial success.

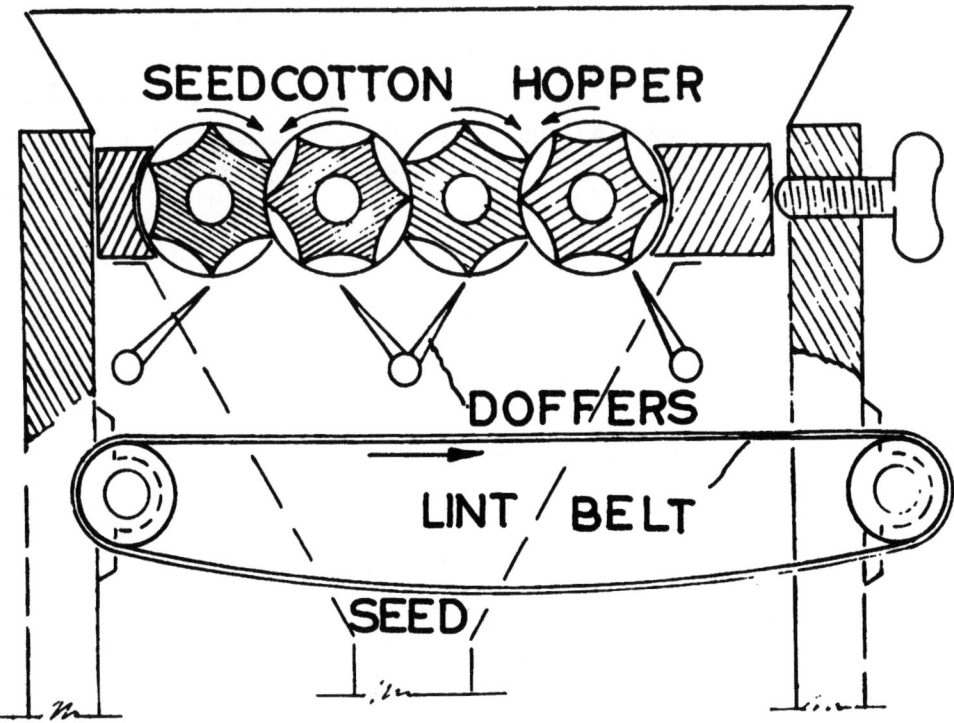

Figure 9-13. Cross-section of Model 1838 Carver roller cotton gin, which was not limited in the number of pairs of spiral meshing rollers, although only two pairs of rollers are shown (Bennett 1960, 7)

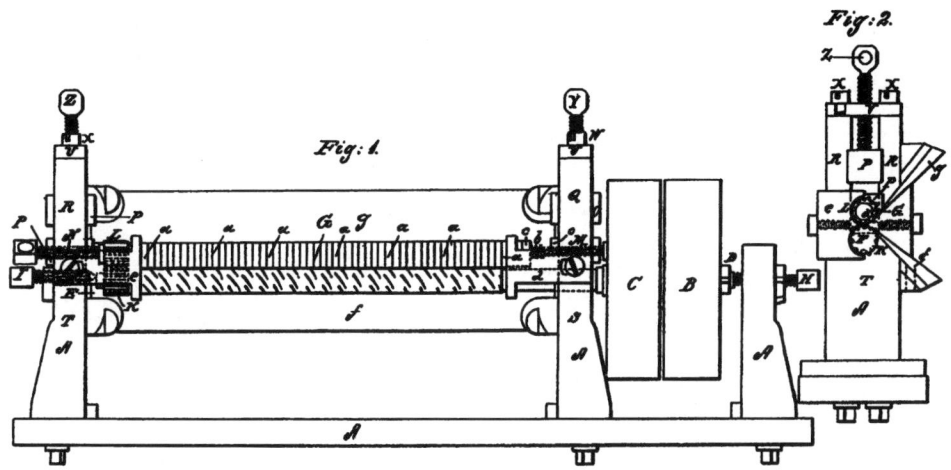

Figure 9-14. Whittemore's leather and roughened-metal rollers

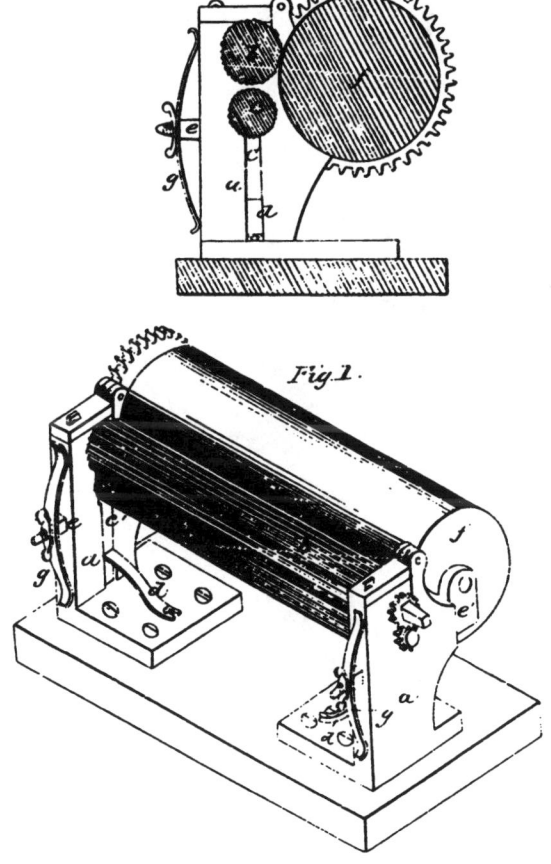

Figure 9-15. Roller gin, 1844, of Richard Reynolds of Beaufort, South Carolina

THE GINNING OF SEA ISLAND COTTON

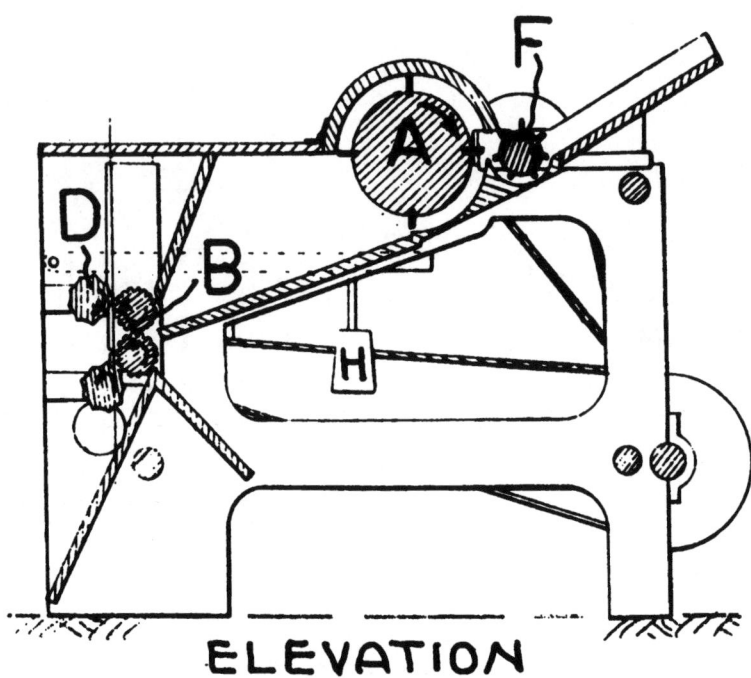

Figure 9-16. 1845 roller cotton gin by T. Ely (Bennett 1960, 7)

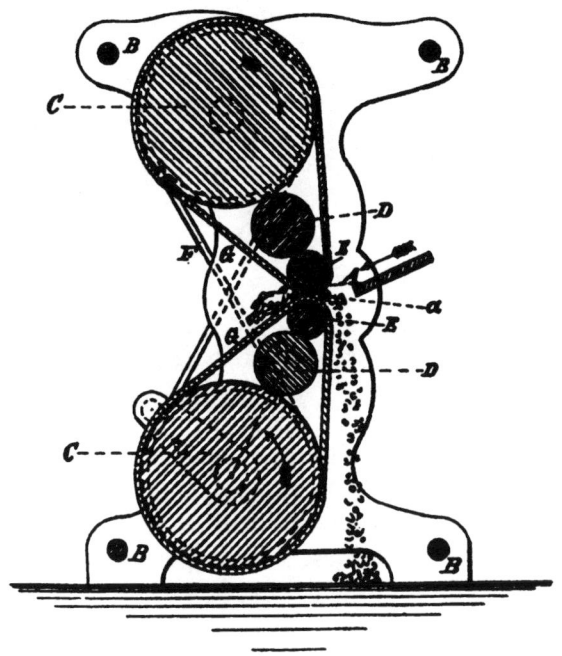

Figure 9-17. Kokemuller's gin

Kokemuller's Gin

On August 13, 1867, J. W. Kokemuller of Bluffton received U.S. Patent No. 67,773 for an "Improvement in Cotton-Gins." His invention (fig. 9-17) "is an improvement on the old roller cotton-gin, and is designed to obviate the difficulty attending the springing of rollers, a contingency due to the necessary small diameter of the latter." Springing, the separation of the rollers, was always a major problem in roller gins. In Kokemuller's gin, bearings (D) were placed on either side of the ginning rollers (E) to prevent the rollers from springing open. "[A]nd it will be further seen that the rollers *E*, in consequence of being driven by friction from *D*, in connection with the belts *G*, may be rapidly rotated without the possibility of being twisted, a contingency of frequent occurrence with the old roller-gin, in consequence of the power being applied at one end of the rollers."

In spite of the apparent "improvement" in Kokemuller's gin, it apparently had no commercial success and could not compete with McCarthy's gin.

Steam-Driven Gins

It was about this time that steam engines began to be used to drive cotton gins. Unfortunately, the record is sparse on the construction of steam-driven gins and no diagrams or artifacts have survived to help reconstruct a typical gin. Initially, steam engines were used to power a number of gins housed in one building (fig. 9-18). In 1843, Edmund Ruffin (Mathew 1992, 114) described the operation at Peter's Point Plantation on Edisto Island, owned by Isaac Jenkins Mikell:

Arrived to dinner at Mr. Mikell's beautiful residence, having the ocean in full view. Spent the afternoon in seeing his fields, & his steam cotton ginning establishment. A rotatory steam engine drives 20 of the roller gins, such as are generally used & moved by the foot for the sea-island cotton. A laborer operating alone on one of these, gins 25 lbs of cotton. But the same driven by steam, will gin 50 lbs, on an average, & a prime hand can gin lbs 75.

A sketch by Jennie Haskell of roller gins run by steam (fig. 9-18) appeared in *Frank Leslie's Popular Monthly* in 1885.[7] Although not shown, it is likely that the two workers in line past the worker operating the gin in sight are also operating gins.

With the invention of the McCarthy roller gin (see next chapter), the Foss double-roller gin, and the Boesch gin, steam power became commonly applied—especially to the McCarthy gin, which became the one most often used for long-staple cotton.

Foss Double-Roller Gin

On June 23, 1903, Leland L. Foss of Manassas, Georgia was awarded U.S. Patent No.

Figure 9-18. Steam-powered gin (Haskell 1885, 573)

730,449 for a roller gin. During the spring of 1903, the L. L. Foss Gin Manufacturing Company, of Vidalia, Georgia was formed to manufacture these gins on a large scale. The gin was advertised as the Foss Double-Roller Gin. Its basic design was, in reality, a McCarthy roller gin with two rollers instead of one (fig. 9-19) and it was touted to have a much larger ginning capacity than the McCarthy gin in use at that time. Foss's gin had other technical advancements besides the two rollers, but they are too complex to include here.

The author found no records to indicate that the Foss gin was used in the sea islands, which is understandable, as it appeared toward the end of sea island cotton culture. But it was certainly available to South Carolina planters, and it is not unreasonable to expect that a few planters might have invested in a Foss gin. It did have widespread use during the revival of sea island cotton in Georgia and Florida in 1934. M. H. Floyd wrote on January 30, 1939:

Two types of roller gins are in general use in Florida and Georgia, the single roller, 40 inch, English gins [McCarthy gins manufactured by English companies] and the 60 inch, double roller Foss gins which are made in Georgia. The former are used almost exclusively to gin Egyptian and American Egyptian crops, while the latter are preferred by many of the ginners in Georgia…

The Boesch Gin

In 1910, John C. Boesch and J. H. G. Von Oven of Charleston, South Carolina invented a gin (U.S. Patent No. 948,810) referred to as the Boesch gin (fig. 9-20). Their machine featured a metal ginning roller with diamond-grid indentations on its surface and a sliding knife that reciprocated sideways along the fixed knife. The inventors claimed that the diamond indentations readily seized the cotton fiber.

The Boesch gin came too late to be of use in the sea islands. Whether it was a commercial success elsewhere is not known.

In spite of all the "improvements" in roller gins, William Elliott of Beaufort, South Carolina stated (1828, 154) that "Eave's [Eve's] was formerly in successful use; but that, as well as the barrel gin, has been superseded by the common foot or crank gin, whose extreme simplicity of structure has given it an advantage over others more efficient, but more complicated." Charles Capers (1834, 73) wrote: "…yet in almost every instance, the planters have returned to the simple foot-gin as better adapted to the use of the negroes." R. F. W. Allston (1854, 15) noted: "The common foot gin or treadle, propelling two rollers, is the machine commonly used for separating the fiber from the seed, clearing on the average twenty-five pounds a day." And finally, J. A. Turner (1857, 135) explained: "It then goes to the gins, which are the same kinds first invented; none of the many new inventions have been found efficient, and the Whitney gin [is] totally unfit for Sea Island cotton."

It appears, then, that all the sundry improvements in roller gins that were tried prior to 1840s were abandoned in favor of foot gins by the sea island planters, especially of the

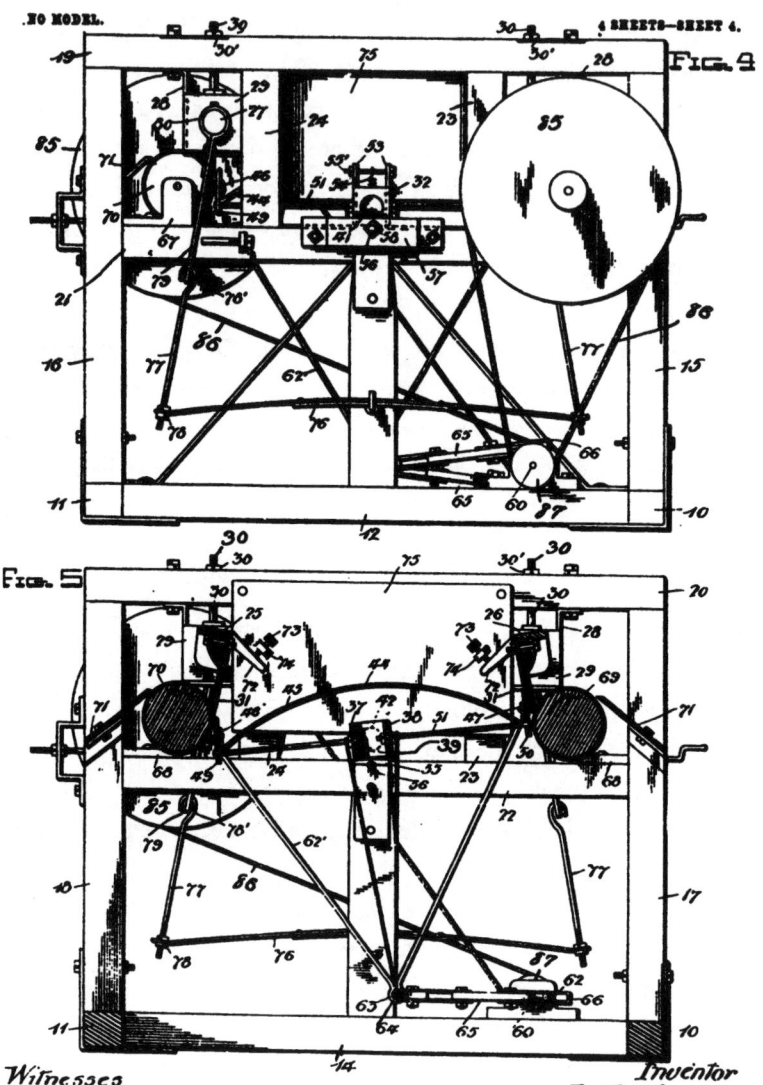

Figure 9-19. Foss double-roller gin. The two rollers are labeled 69 and 70; 31 represents the stationary blades; the moveable blades are 49 and 50.

CHAPTER NINE

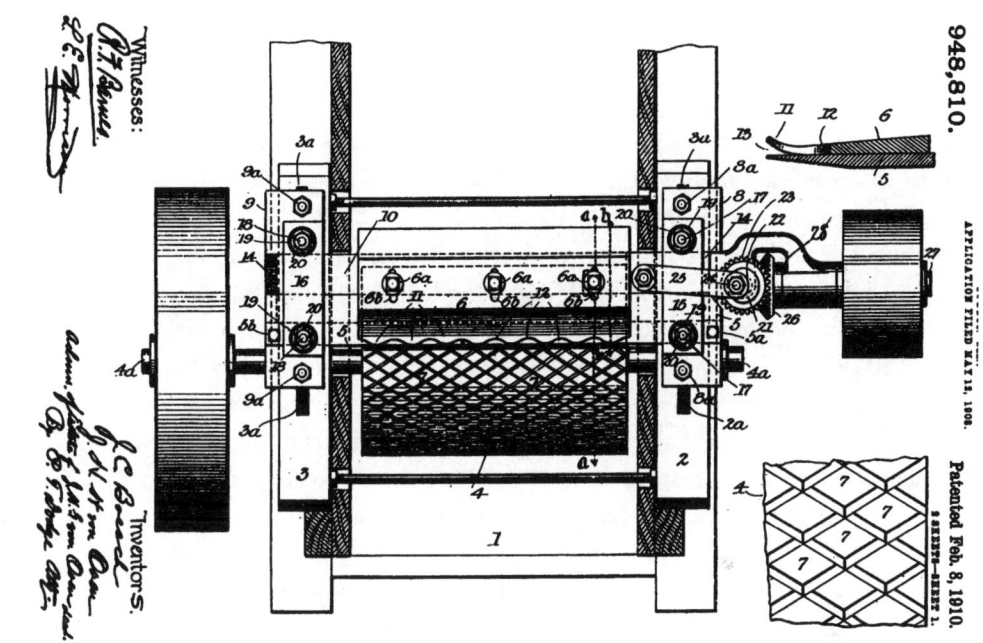

Figure 9-20. Boesch Model 1910 roller gin

Carolina sea islands where the longest and finest staples were produced. The reason appears to be fourfold: (1) the roller gins were too complex to operate, except by highly-skilled plantation hands, (2) when developed to increase outturn, they damaged the staple, (3) they were too complex to manufacture, especially locally, and (4) the foot gins could be constructed by the slave mechanics on the plantations.

After 1840, until the end of sea island cotton, the only technically advanced roller gin of consequence in South Carolina was the McCarthy gin. The gins of Reynolds, Ely, Fessenden, Kokemuller, Boesch, and others appear never to have been able to compete with the McCarthy gin. Only the Foss gin of 1903, used in the long-staple industry in Georgia and Florida, was a commercial success.

1. Angela Lakwete points out in her well-researched book *Inventing the Cotton Gin: Machine and Myth in Antebellum America* that Eli Whitney "did not invent the cotton gin." The roller gin was used to gin all types of cotton long before Whitney's invention.

2. The origin of the foot gin is unknown. Angela Lakwete (2003, 31) said it was "of uncertain origin, then, but likely an American invention…" The author found no references to support or conflict with her statement, and accepts her contention that the foot gin was of American origin.

3. The description and engraving of Harvie's patent appears in *The Repertory of Arts, Manufactures, and Agriculture* vol. 55, Second Series, published in London in 1824. Through an interlibrary search, The Citadel's Daniel Library found a copy of *The Repertory* in the Princeton University Library.

4. Charles Drayton's diaries, recorded from 1784 to 1820, are the property of Drayton Hall, a National Trust historic site in Charleston, SC. Drayton's diagram of the barrel gin is from 1808. The diagram does not show the roller gins, only the cog, lantern and barrel mechanism. William Judd, a mechanical artist from Charleston, added the gins on the second floor from descriptions and diagrams from other sources.

There certainly were other models of a barrel gin in the sea island cotton area. For example, some sources stated that the animals that drove the cog wheel were on the outside of the gin house rather than in a floor below the gins. However, the basic method was the same: animal power turning a cog wheel that turned the barrel that in turn powered the individual roller gins.

5. Appendix 2 contains a list of patents for ginning machines on file in the U.S. Patent Office in Washington, DC relating to ginning long-staple cotton. All patents by South Carolinians (even though some did not seem to have introduced significant changes in the art of roller ginning, or were not commercially successful) are included for a historical record. A Patent Office fire in 1836 destroyed the records of many patents. The Patent Office made an attempt after the fire to contact patent holders to ask them to resubmit their patent applications; some did, others did not. Patents that were resubmitted were designated with an X. The list of patents includes a note on which ones were not resubmitted; the descriptions and diagrams for these are lost to history.

6. Stopper wood belongs to the genus *Eugenia* of the myrtle family (Myrtaceae). The genus contains some 600 species of evergreen trees and shrubs in the Old and New World tropics. Many species have hard, heavy wood. Evidently, Eve used stopper wood for the rollers in order to reduce wearing and springing.

7. The author believes that the Haskell's diagram of the steam-driven gin (fig. 9-18) is highly simplified. It is unlikely that the steam engine was located in the same room as the gins.

The Fones McCarthy Roller Gin and Sea Island Cotton

The Fones McCarthy roller gin (fig. 10-1) revolutionized the ginning of all types of long-staple cotton throughout the world; sea island cotton was no exception. The McCarthy gin did for long-staple cotton what the saw gin did for upland, short-staple cotton. The McCarthy gin and its modifications came to have worldwide use because they were usually lower in cost than saw gins; they were more readily operated by unskilled labor; and they could be used on all varieties and staple lengths of cottons, including the fuzzy seeds of short-staple cotton. With the exception of the United States, countries that gin long-staple cotton still use the McCarthy gin today. It has also been the basis for improvements and modifications to other modern roller gins.

Paradoxically, McCarthy intended his gin primarily for short-staple cotton. In his first patent (July 3, 1840, U.S. Patent No. 1,675) he stated: "Be it known that I, Fones McCarthy, of Demopolis, Marengo county, Alabama, have invented a new and useful Machine for Ginning Cotton called the 'Smooth Cylinder Cotton-Gin…' " There was no mention that it was intended just for long-staple cotton. McCarthy moved to Alabama in the spring of 1840 so he could market the gin in the short-staple cotton belt. But in 1842 he began to market his gin for long-staple cotton as well. This was during a period of depressed market for sea island cotton (see table 13-6) and planters were desperate to make any change that would benefit the

Figure 10-1. Fones McCarthy roller gin

sea island market. They saw in McCarthy's gin a way to greatly increase the output of their long-staple lint. Whitemarsh Seabrook quickly touted the new gin to his fellow planters (1844b, 35): "The notice of a new and improved gin for both green-seed and black-seed cottons, recently constructed by F. McCarthy of Alabama, has been favorably received by the public." He continued:

A few pounds of the finest description of that staple ginned by this machine, and unmotted afterwards, the property of——, was sent by him in December, 1842, to Mr. Houldsworth, the eminent spinner of Manchester, who returned an answer of which the following is an extract:— "We have carefully examined the sample of Mr.——'s cotton cleaned on a new ginning machine. It is remarkably clean, and in an excellent state for our purpose as respects openness."

But the acceptance of the new gin quickly turned to rejection. Seabrook wrote (1844b, 183), "I now consider it my imperative duty to say that, *as at present constructed*, it is not adapted to the middle and finer qualities of Long Cotton," and hoped "that he [McCarthy] will soon be able to remove every difficulty" so it can be used on "both species of cotton grown in the country." The 1840 design, as pointed out by Houldsworth (1844, 185), could be used only for strong, coarse-fiber cultivars.

McCarthy redesigned his gin, and received Reissue Patent No. 262 on April 18th, 1854.[1] The improved McCarthy gin could then gin the finer staples, and sea island planters began to invest in this gin. Not all planters came on board, however; some continued to use foot gins because they were inexpensive and easy to operate. Plantation and other records from planters, factors, and industrial companies reveal that a number of new McCarthy gins were purchased. Robert F. W. Allston (1854, 15) noted in 1854: "The McCarthy, or Florida gin, with only one roller, is now attracting much attention; and the planters are putting them up as fast as they can procure them." The foot gins, once the workhorse of the sea island plantations, were soon forgotten.

In the Santee long cotton region, the redesigned McCarthy gin was also used. Henry William Ravenel (Childs 1947, 43) wrote in his diary on December 18, 1860: "Yesterday the first McCarthy cotton gin on Pooshee began to work, by steam…"

The principal elements of the McCarthy design that revolutionized roller ginning were:
1. the ginning roller covered in leather (walrus hide[2] was the preferred leather)
2. the fixed or stationary knife whose working edge bore heavily against the ginning roller
3. the reciprocating or moving knife which had an arcuate (bowed) stroke across the working edge of the fixed knife
4. the seed grate

The operation of the McCarthy gin is best understood by referring to *Fig. 5* (fig. 10-2) from Reissue Patent No. 262, 1854. Cotton was placed in the hopper (B). Immediately behind the hopper was the ginning roller, three feet in length and four inches in diameter (N). This single ginning roller was greater in diameter than churkha-type rollers and gave the McCarthy gin a greater ginning capacity. The roller was covered with coarse leather strips cut 3/4" wide and wound spirally around the roller (fig. 10-6). The grooves between the strips permitted motes and other unyielding matter to pass by the fixed knife without injuring the lint (*Fig. 3* in fig.10-2). The leather cover had a porcupine-like surface that gripped the fiber that was pushed manually from the hopper (B) toward the roller. (Walrus leather was best because it retained its rough texture even after long use. Other leathers quickly became smooth with use and would not grip the fiber.)

The roller turned in a counterclockwise direction. Held tightly against the ginning roller was a fixed knife with a rounded edge (M). As the ginning roller turned, the fibers were pulled between the fixed knife and ginning roller so that there was a constant pull against the seed in order to make a clean separation. The moving knife (C) (also called the reciprocating knife), which had fine teeth on the working edge (*Fig. 4* in fig. 10-2), was moved up and down by means of an off-center rotating shaft near the bottom of the frame. The knife moved 600-800 oscillations a minute. The moving knife traveled over the stationary knife, pushing the seed a distance of about half the staple length of the fiber. (This distance is known as the "overlap.") When the seeds were pushed upward, some of the fibers were pulled from the seed, but not all. It was important to remove the rest of the fibers. This was accomplished by the correct overlap distance.

After the first upward stroke of the moving knife, the remaining fibers were pinched between the stationary knife and the ginning roller (just as before), and the seeds were pulled back to the stationary knife. The next upward stroke of the moving knife removed these remaining fibers. If the overlap was too great, the seeds could be pushed off with the fibers still attached, and the seeds would not have been fully ginned. Obviously, the overlap had to be adjusted to accommodate cotton of significantly different staple lengths. Once the seeds were fully ginned, they fell through the slots in the adjacent seed grate (fig. 10-3) while the unginned cotton was retained on the grate.

A second diagram of just the ginning roller and knives better describes the working of McCarthy's gin. In this diagram, a reciprocating pusher board has been added to more efficiently move the seed cotton to the ginning roller (fig. 10-3) and the seeds are depicted falling through the grate.

The 1840 McCarthy gin featured a complex system to doff and comb the ginned lint from the ginning roller. His Reissue Patent in 1854 made technical improvements in the doff and combing apparatus. It appears, however, that even this improved apparatus was too complex to operate and manufacture, and was later eliminated by most manufacturers of his gin.

McCarthy's original combing and doffing system worked as follows: A small float roller and two delivery rollers were interposed between the ginning roller and a vibrating stripping comb (fig. 10-4). The upper delivery roller, called the receiving roller, was covered with cloth; the

CHAPTER TEN

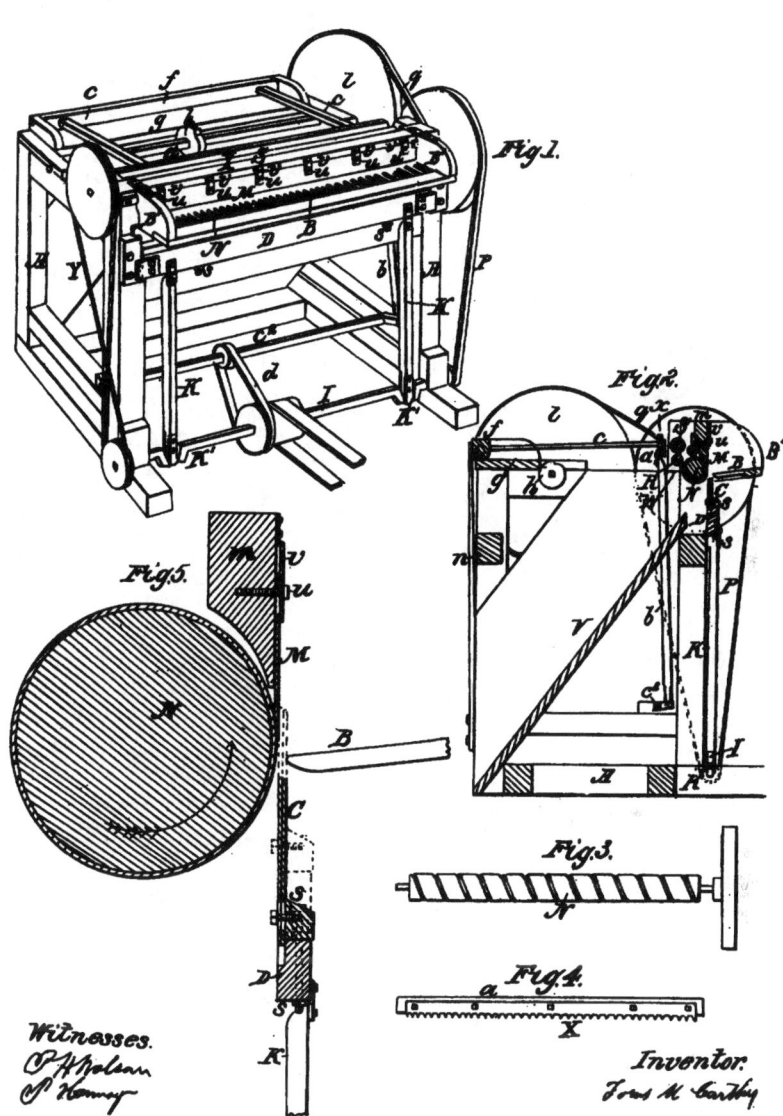

Figure 10-2. The McCarthy gin, Reissue No. 262, April 18, 1854

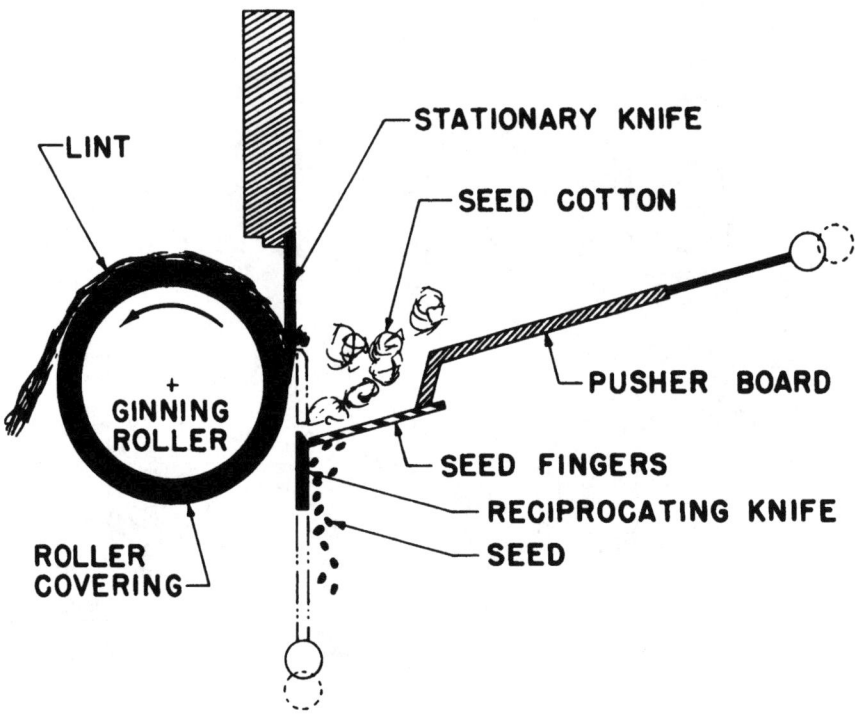

Figure 10-3. Principle of the McCarthy roller gin (M. N. Gillum 1985, 959)

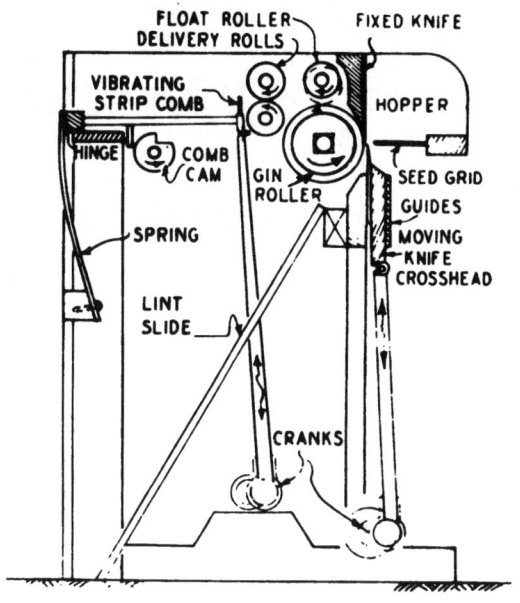

Figure 10-4. Cross-section of the 1840 McCarthy roller gin (Bennett 1960, 8)

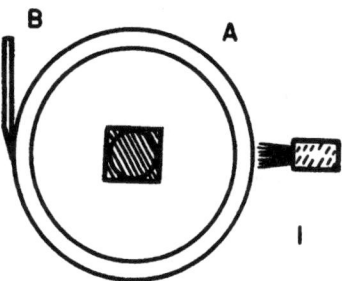

Figure 10-5. Ginning roller (A), stationary knife (B), and stationary brush doffer (I)

Figure 10-6. Roller covered with walrus hide (A) and stationary brush doffer (B)[3]

lower delivery roller was called the smooth roller. The float roller, or weighted roller, rested on the ginning roller. As the lint passed between the float roller and the ginning roller, it was pressed into a sheet. The sheet of lint passed through the receiving and smooth roller, and was wound upon the receiving roller. The lint was then stripped by the comb and discharged upon the lint slide as soon as it had taken up a sufficient quantity.

The combination of spring, comb cam and crank that ran the stripping comb allowed the comb to move forward and recede, and to move up and down. During the time that the receiving roller was taking up cotton, the comb receded. Then, in its forward movement, the comb came within reach of the receiving roller which had gathered the cotton lint. With the upward motion of the comb, the lint was stripped from the receiving roller and passed to the lint slide.

Most manufacturers discarded McCarthy's complex comb and doffer and replaced it with a stationary brush (perhaps based on the brush of James Harvie). The stationary brush (figs. 10-5 and 10-6) doffed ginned lint from the roller and was popular because of its affordability. The disadvantage of the stationary stripper was an accumulation and packing of the cotton on the brush until by its own weight and bulk it fell in a tangled mass. Much time and effort was required to untangle, straighten, and clean the fibers for proper handling in the mills.

On September 1, 1863, Israel F. Brown of New London, Connecticut, received U.S. Patent No. 39,767, for an "Improvement in Cotton-Gins." He stated in his patent that his improvement was "...especially applicable to that class known as the 'roller-gin'; and it consists in a peculiar construction of the 'doffer' or 'doctor,' which strips off the ginned cotton from the cylinder, by which construction the stripping is effected with greater certainty and with less breaking or disruption of the fiber." Brown's invention is depicted in figure 10-7.

In its operation, Brown explained, "...as the cylinder is comparatively unyielding and the plates *c* are to be made thin these plates will yield as they pass over the surface of the cylinder, thus scraping its surface [to remove the lint]." But Brown's diagram seems at odds with his description. The stationary knife must be on the side opposite from the doffer (*B*), and the ginning roller must turn counterclockwise, not clockwise as indicated by the arrow on the roller. Likewise, the doffer must turn in the opposite direction than indicated by the arrow since Brown stated that "...the doffer and the cylinder are to be so connected by a belt that both shall rotate in the same direction..." If the arrows are turned in opposite directions, the doffer would seem to function as Brown explained. Brown suggested the doffers be made of sheet zinc which would allow for slight deflection.

Numerous McCarthy gins made after 1863 supported a doffer based on modifications of Brown's invention. British manufacturers made the doffers out of leather or Indian rubber.

In 1924, James S. Townsend, residing in Charleston, South Carolina, invented a revolving rotary doffer (U.S. Patent No. 1,503,077, July 29, 1924). At that time he worked for the USDA. His invention (fig. 10-8) consisted of "attachments for use on roller cotton gins, consisting of a flapper, roller, an air current baffle, a screen, and a box-like structure, all of which

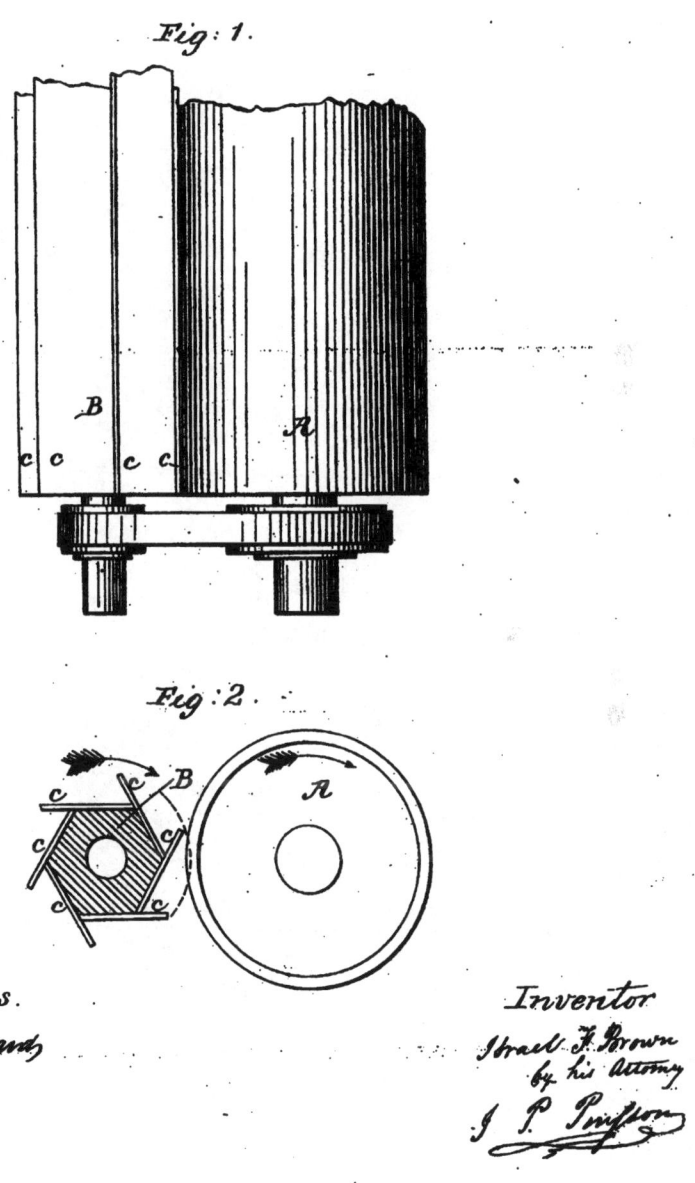

Figure 10-7. Israel F. Brown's doffer

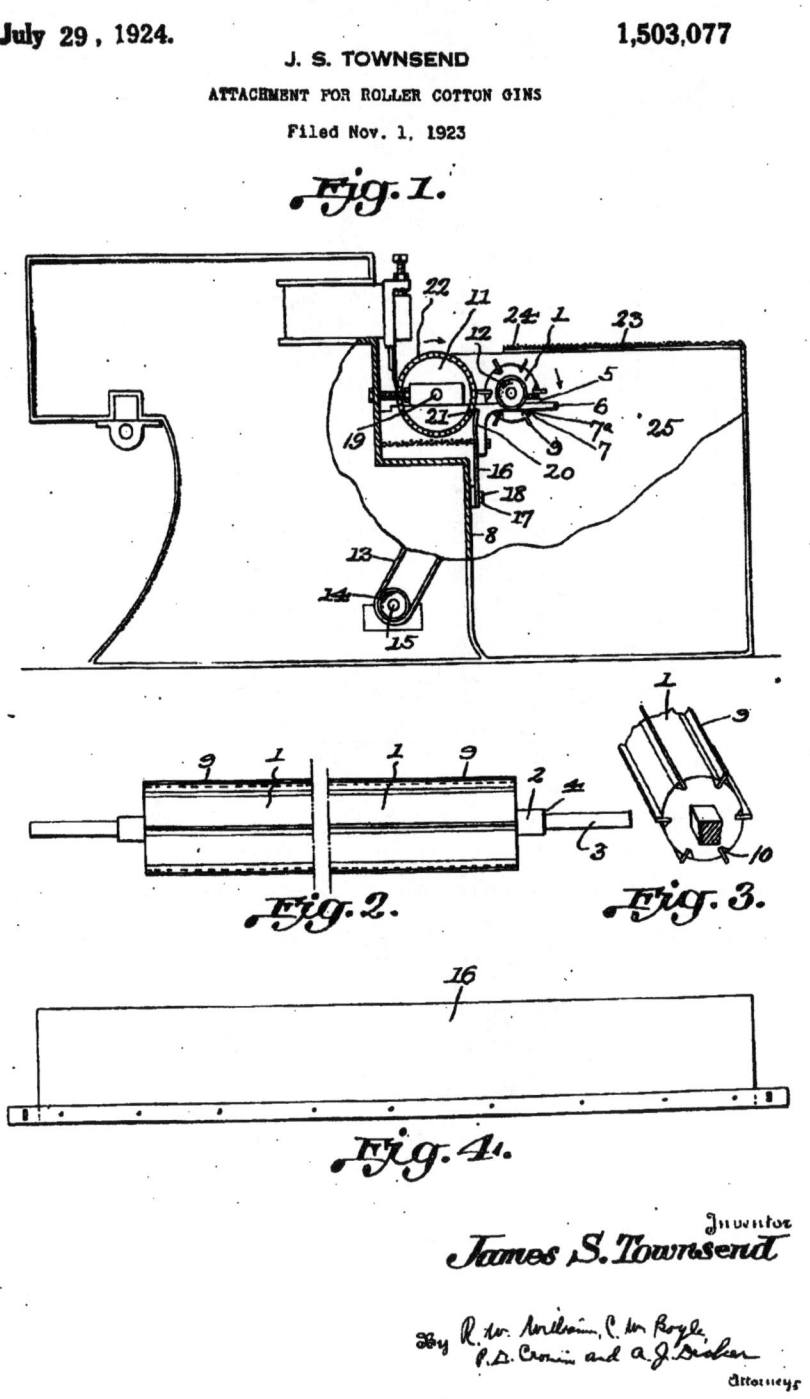

Figure 10-8. Townsend's "Attachment for Roller Cotton Gins"

are placed in a position on the cotton gin..." One of the objects of his patent was "to straighten the fiber of the cotton and prevent its folding or tangling."

The key to Townsend's invention was the "air current baffle." His flapper roller (1) was equipped with six to nine flaps made of either "rubber, leather, fabric or other suitable material, projecting preferably three-quarters of an inch from the face of the flapper roller." The flapper roller was parallel to the ginning roller (11), and both turned clockwise. As the flapper roller (1) turned, the flaps (9) created an air current that was deflected upward by the baffle (16) and was "prevented from passing beneath the cotton gin roller..." Without the air current deflection, the lint would have been carried around with the roller (lapping). The motion of the flappers and air current tended "to throw the cotton in an upward direction" and deposited it in a box (25) positioned below the flapper roller. Waste or foreign matter mixed with the lint, which was lighter, was separated from the lint by being thrown higher. It was deposited on the screen (23) above the lint box.

Townsend's rotary doffer used the same basic plan invented by Brown; however, Townsend added the baffle that separated trash and straightened the lint. Although Townsend's invention came too late for sea island cotton, it did improve roller ginning of long-staple cotton elsewhere.

McCarthy's last improvement to his gin was described in Patent No. 67,327 (fig. 10-9) dated July 30, 1867, and dealt with the problem of the mingling of the ginned seeds and the unginned cotton:

The cotton is fed to the drawing-cylinder [ginning roller] on a plane horizontal grate, and is drawn in and held by the cylinder and breast-plate [fixed knife] while the stripper [moving knife], so called, a rapidly vibrating plate, strikes it [the cotton] and takes out the seed. This stripper, which makes from six to eight hundred strokes per minute, strikes the seed with such force that a great portion of them are driven above and fall upon the unginned cotton and mingling with it, greatly retard the ginning operation, making it necessary for the attendant to be constantly shaking and opening the cotton to get the seed out of the way.

McCarthy attempted to solve this problem as follows: The feed-box (A) had an inclined feed-board (B). An immovable bar (D) was installed transversely in the front part of the feed-box, with teeth (a) inclined downward. Over the immovable bar was placed a movable bar (E), grooved so that the immovable bar fit within. Bar (E) had a series of teeth (b) that extended down directly over the teeth (a) of bar (D). Two cams vibrated bar (E) over bar (D); two springs (F) acted as a check to the momentum of the moveable bar. As seed-cotton came down the feed-board to the teeth of the immovable and movable bars, the vibrating toothed bar facilitated the descent of the seed-cotton in a vertical direction to the ginning cylinder in a small space between 1 1/2 and 2 1/2 inches. The grate formed by the teeth (a) and (b) of the two bars was too small for cotton seeds to pass through. As the seeds were stripped from the fiber by the ginning mechanism below, any seeds that might be thrown upward could not pass through the grate formed by bars (a) and (b) and into the seed-cotton above the grate, and would fall back down through the seed grate below. In this manner, explained McCarthy, the gin would do 50% more work.

Animal power was easily applied to the McCarthy gin. William Duncan, in a letter directed to H. Houldsworth in the *Southern Agriculturist* (1844, 184), commented on the McCarthy gin:

> *Mr. McCarthy's Gin is purely a Roller Gin, but the mode of operation is entirely new. The quantity that can be ginned in a day by one of those Gins is about 200 lbs., while that by one of the common Gins[4] is about 400 lbs. This apparent loss by McCarthy's Gin is more than made up to the planter by this; that one horse will turn three of McCarthy's gins a day, while it takes four horses to turn one of the common Gins a day. It is further made up by this; that the cotton is in order for being packed the moment it comes from the McCarthy Gin, while after it has left the common Gin, it has to be moted by hand, at the rate of 30 or 40 lbs. per day to the hand.*

The McCarthy gin was also able to be run by steam power. Allston (1854, 16) wrote: "Strange to say, an invention of so much value to our planters on the coast, has remained almost unknown in Carolina until a year ago, and unused by steam until the present year. A gin, costing one hundred dollars, propelled by a good horse or mule, or still better by steam, will clean from 150 lbs. to 200 lbs. a day." One reason that steam power was not used earlier by some planters was that there was not a significant difference in the lint output between using horse and steam power. However, as improvements were made to the McCarthy gin and to steam power, more and more planters converted their animal-powered gins to steam.

Numerous persons tried to improve on the rollers used on the McCarthy gins. William Wauklyn, of the Albion Mills, Bury, in Lancashire, England, obtained a patent for an improved roller in 1864 (U.S. Patent No. 45,109, November 15, fig. 10-10). His invention consisted of "…rollers of cast-iron or other suitable metal, in which fine spiral grooves are cast or cut, the edges and sides of the spiral grooves being more or less serrated or corrugated or wrinkled. By this means a greater quantity of cotton may be cleaned in a given time, and the roller is made more durable." No record was found indicating whether Wauklyn's roller was a commercial success.

A reciprocating pusher board (feeder bar) to push the cotton against the ginning roller was added by other manufacturers (fig. 10-3). The pusher worked in a reciprocating manner: with each forward motion, cotton was pushed against the ginning roller. (The McCarthy gins at the Charleston Museum and the Edisto Island Museum feature this pusher board.)

McCarthy's original gin featured a seed grate (fig. 10-2) that allowed the seeds to be separated from the fiber. McCarthy's grate was stationary and the seeds fell through it by their own

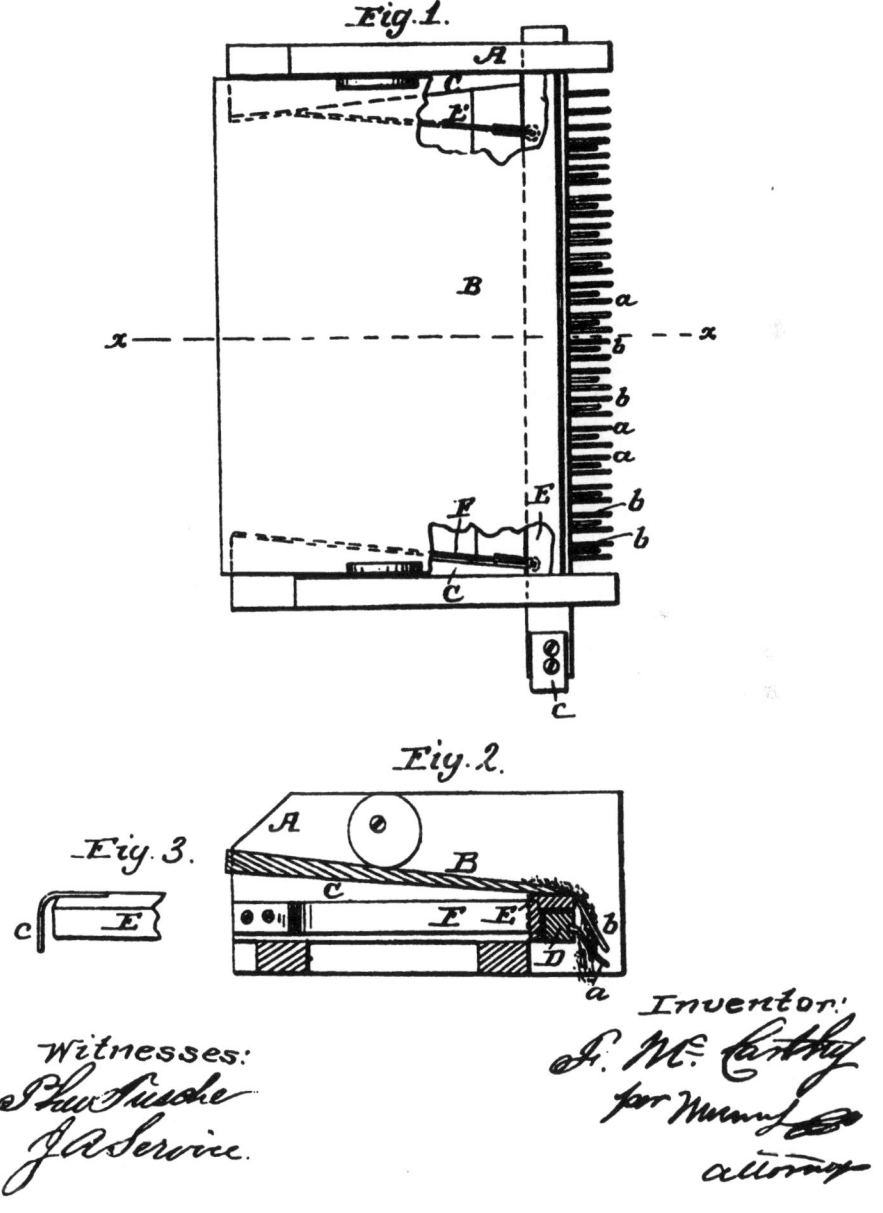

Figure 10-9. McCarthy Patent No. 67,327

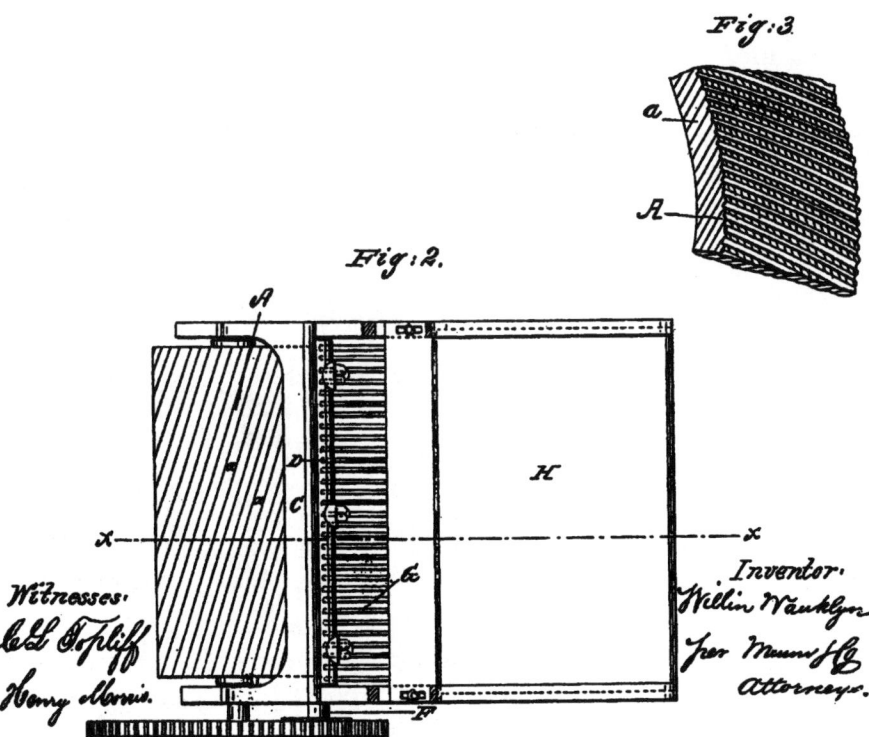

Figure 10-10. Wauklyn's roller

motion. Manufacturers added a reciprocating motion to the grate, causing the seeds to bounce around on it. The additional motion allowed the seeds to pass more effectively through the grate slots.

These modifications were incorporated into later models of the McCarthy gin as illustrated by figure 10-11. In this model, the complex stripper comb has been removed, and a pusher board (A), doffer roller, seed cotton feeder (C), and vibrating seed grate (B) were installed.

The last major modification to the standard McCarthy gin was to be found in the Double Action McCarthy Gin. In a 1928 pamphlet, Dobson & Barlow Ltd. of Bolton, Lancashire, England advertised this gin for sale. The difference in the single-action gin and the double-action gin was the application in the latter of two beater knives (fig. 10-12), which were reciprocated at equal speeds, but so arranged as to rise and fall alternately. Each revolution gave two strokes of the knives; the production of the gin was therefore greatly increased. This gin, however, came too late to have been used in the sea islands.

The most significant development in roller gins since the McCarthy gin and its improvements was the rotary-knife roller gin (fig. 10-13), developed between 1955 and 1963. Although never used in the sea islands, its discussion is a logical conclusion to the understanding of roller gins and long-staple cotton. The rotary-knife gin is the basic type of roller gin used today in the southwestern United States where Pima cotton is grown.

A major drawback of the McCarthy-type roller gin was that the reciprocating knife blocked the cotton-feed area approximately 50% of the time. When the reciprocating knife was in the upstroke to remove the seeds from the fiber, the seed cotton could not reach the ginning roller (see fig. 10-3). The rotary-knife gin retained the McCarthy gin's roller and stationary knife, but substituted a rotary knife for the reciprocating knife. The cotton-feed area was now free 100% of the time, and ginning capacity went from 1/4 bale of lint an hour per stand to 1 1/2 bales of lint an hour per stand.

The operation of this gin (fig. 10-13) was as follows: Seed cotton slid down the feeder apron and entered the gin between the ginning roller and the rotary knife. The ginning roller, which rotated constantly and was held tightly against the stationary knife pulled the lint under the stationary knife. The seeds, too big to pass under the stationary knife, were swept away by the rotary knife which spun in the opposite direction of the ginning roller, and fell onto a seed belt that delivered them to a collection bin.

The McCarthy gin became the last roller gin used in the sea islands of South Carolina. With the end of sea island cotton culture in South Carolina in 1920, many gins and other equipment were either abandoned or sold to Florida and Georgia planters to supply the revived sea island cotton culture that began in these states in 1934. Additional gins and equipment were sent to the Southwest for the American-Egyptian cotton culture. As previously mentioned, two gins have survived in South Carolina. One is in the Charleston Museum and a second is at the Edisto Island Museum.

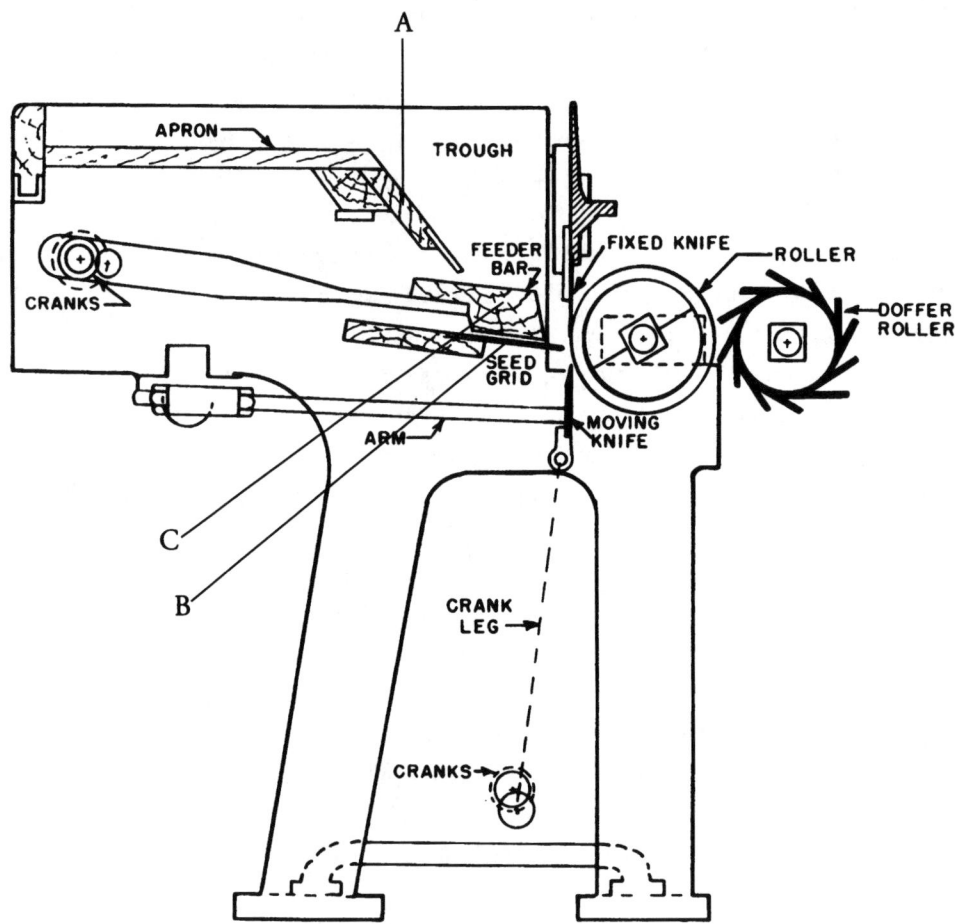

Figure 10-11. McCarthy roller gin (Anderson and Stedronsky 1964, 6)

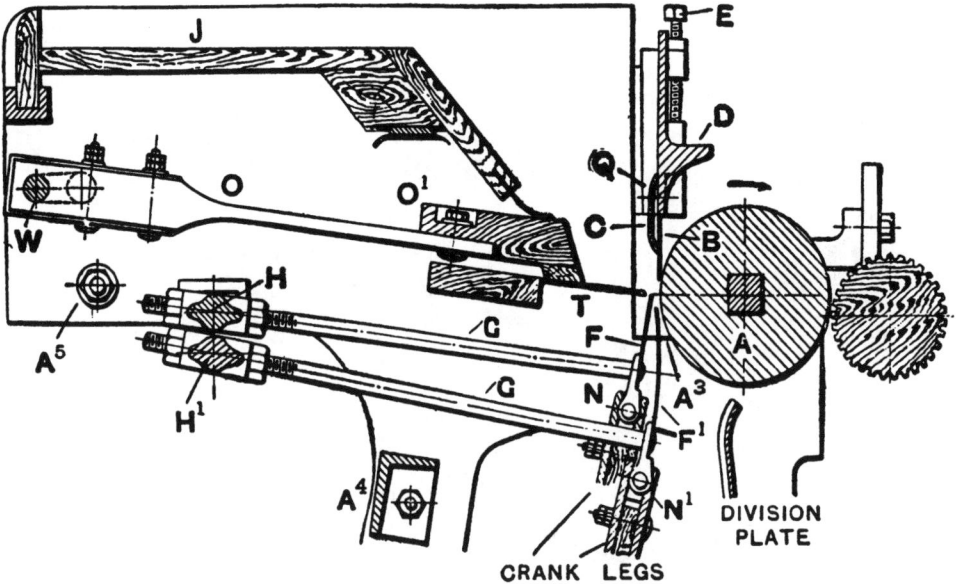

Figure 10-12. Double action McCarthy gin. (F) and (F1) are the beater knives. (Dobson & Barlow 1928)

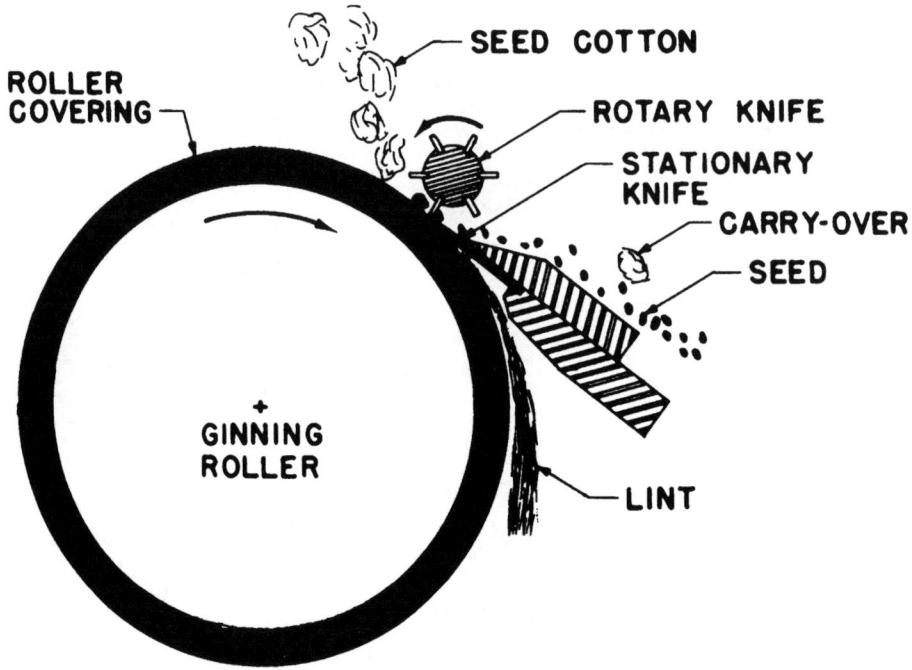

Figure 10-13. Principle of the rotary-knife roller gin (M. N. Gillum 1985, 960)

CHAPTER TEN

1. Between 1840 and 1900, a number of improvements, including ones by McCarthy himself, were made to McCarthy's original design. However, it is beyond the scope of this book to list and describe all these inventions. Most were quite technical and indeed were probably never used in the sea islands because of the collapse of the economy after the Civil War and the invasion of the boll weevil.

2. Walrus hide was used until 1938. About that time the killing of walrus for commercial purposes was barred, and it became necessary to find a substitute material. A water-pump packing type of laminated canvas and rubber was ultimately used.

3. Figure 10-6 is a photograph of the ginning roller and stationary brush from the McCarthy gin at the Charleston Museum. The brush is worn from years of use. The ginning roller is covered with strips of walrus hide.

4. The common gin referred to by Duncan was undoubtedly a barrel gin (see chapter 9) that consisted of a series of individual roller gins run by a single source of power.

The Textile Industry and Sea Island Cotton

The making of cloth is one of man's earliest industries. It is a fundamental activity: take a cluster of natural fibers (silk, cotton, flax), draw them out, and twist them to make a yarn. Then intertwine (weave) the yarn and you have cloth.[1] From these two basic concepts evolved today's worldwide textile industry.

The first coverings that the ancients used were doubtless animal skins. As time passed, they turned to lighter, cooler and more flexible clothing made from cloth. Throughout the history of the textile industry, the making of cloth first involved the spinning of yarn. In order for a fiber, either natural or synthetic, to be used as fabric yarn, certain requirements must be met. The fibers must: (1) be uniform in diameter; (2) have high tensile strength (resistance of a material to a force tending to tear it apart), durability, and pliability (flexibility); (3) have the ability to hold together when twisted; (4) be light in color and take a dye; and (5) be long enough to be twisted together. The material also must be relatively inexpensive and available. Wool meets most of these requirements, but it is not available worldwide; silk is too expensive; flax requires much labor and is expensive to produce; and synthetic fibers do not have the feel and touch of natural fibers. Enter the reign of cotton, the world's most important industrial fiber.

The story of the development of the cotton textile industry spans several thousand years, beginning in ancient India in the Old World and in Peru and Ecuador in the New World. The Hindu people began to manufacture cotton fabric around 2000 BC. From the lint of short-staple Asiatic cotton (*Gossypium herbaceum* L.), Hindu workers separated the lint from the seeds using hand-operated churkha roller gins (see fig. 9-2). They then carded[2] the lint by hand and spun it on distaffs or spindles operated with small wheels. The skillful fingers and thumbs of Indian spinners, patiently and carefully forming thread, produced yarn of exceptional quality. Weaving was done by hand-operated looms that required much skill. With these crude methods, the incredible manual dexterity of the Hindu spinners and weavers produced muslin and calico fabrics of such quality that modern equipment has been hard-pressed to duplicate them. Indeed, the development of the cotton textile industry began with an appreciation of the muslin and calico fabrics produced by Hindu weavers.

From India, cotton fabrics were introduced into Europe through trade routes established by Alexander the Great and his successors. Cotton textile production began in England around 1600. (In 1578, the will of James Billston referred to him as a cotton manufacturer and appears to be the first record of cotton manufacturing in England.) England already had an infrastructure and the expertise to manufacture woolen textiles, and these were readily applied to cotton. Improvements in spinning and weaving would contribute to the Industrial Revolution and make England for a time the center of the cotton cloth manufacturing industry.

In the New World, two centers of early cotton textiles emerged that predate the Christian era. Stephens and Mosely's research (1974) documented that early on in Peru *G. barbadense* was used for primitive textiles. They cited evidence that on the Peruvian coast, *G. barbadense* entered the archeological record as fishnets and other cordage in a pre-agricultural fishing village around 2500 BC. The pre-Inca city-states of the Peruvian oases were among the highest civilizations of the New World. Elaborate cotton textiles were found in mummy bundles and other grave goods. Weavers used cotton lint of various natural shades and often combined cotton lint with wool and other fibers. Damp and Pearsall's (1994) research dated *G. barbadense* from the Real Alto site on the coast of Ecuador from around 3500-3000 BC, the first evidence for early cotton use in the area where the crop was likely domesticated.

The Hopi Native Americans, in the region that would become the states of Arizona and New Mexico, cultivated *G. hirsutum* L. and turned it into simple textile products long before Europe began to colonize North America. Here were found archaeological remains of seeds, fibers and cloth along with simple hand looms. As advanced as both of these civilizations were, they would play little role in the development of the modern worldwide cotton industry except through the introduction of cotton germplasm into a future United States and world cotton industry (*G. barbadense* from Peru and Ecuador that produced sea island cotton and all the other extra-long staple cottons, and *G. hirsutum* that produced upland cotton).

EARLY HISTORY OF SPINNING AND WEAVING

Today's machinery for spinning and weaving cotton lint are all modifications and improvements of the primitive methods developed in the Old and New Worlds that were practiced from the dawn of agriculture. Interestingly, similar weaving methods developed independently in the Old World and New World.

Spinning

When and how spinning[3] originated no one can say for certain, though it can be traced back through many centuries. Several nations claim to have been the first to discover the art, but as for proof, the initial stages are obscured in mystery. It is not difficult to imagine that very early in the world's history the drawing out and twisting together of strands of fibers would force itself upon the attention of the ancients. Twisting together cotton lint, or any type of fiber, greatly increased the strength of the twisted strand over the loose, untwisted fibers. By twisting, the fibers are brought close together, producing a surface friction which prevents the fibers from slipping. Undoubtedly, the first type of spinning practiced by the ancients was by hand.

Hand Spinning

One can easily understand the hand spinning process through a simple experiment. In preparation for hand spinning, place some ginned cotton lint in one hand between the thumb and side of the first finger. With the other hand, grasp the cotton between the thumb and side of the first finger and gently pull, which tends to straighten the lint. Place the pulled cotton back in the first hand on top of the cotton that remains, and repeat the process. By repeating the process several times, the lints become fairly parallel. This is the process that came to be called carding. The next step consists of drawing out and twisting. Hold the straightened cotton in one hand, and with the thumb and first finger of the other hand, grasp a few of the cotton fibers and pull and (at the same time) twist the fibers. Once the fibers are twisted, yarn is formed. One can try to pull apart the yarn and see how strong it is after twisting. Ancient peoples undoubtedly produced yarn from different materials by a similar hand method.[4]

Distaff Spinning

Distaff spinning was the next step in the evolution of spinning. It involved the use of a distaff[5] and spindle.[6] In preparation for spinning, the ginned lint was first beaten with sticks until it was evenly distributed. The next step was probably folding and rolling the lint into a cylinder that was attached to a vertical post or a wooden tripod that functioned as the distaff. The spinner sat near the distaff with the spindle across his or her thigh. A stick functioned as the primitive spindle. With the left hand the spinner drew the lint from the bottom of the cylinder, twisting the lint into yarn. After a sufficient length of yarn was formed, it was wound around the spindle. Representations of spinning on pre-Columbian coastal pottery from Peru show that a similar method was used.

The next step in the evolution of spinning may have been an attempt to store yarn for possible future use by wrapping it on a stone. Sooner or later the spinner would have discovered that a stone, wrapped in a covering of yarn, if allowed to hang down and set in a twirling motion, would twist the fibers—hence, the stone became a spindle. This type of spinning was probably not used on short cotton fibers because the weight of the stone would have broken the weak yarn spun from cotton (this method was in use long before long-staple cotton and upland cotton had been developed).[7]

A modification of the above method involved a stick (as a spindle) on which the cotton was wound. A weight called the whorl[8] was added to the spindle (fig. 11-1a). A short hand-twisted segment of fiber was turned a few times around the center of the spindle, then fed to a notch at the tip of the spindle which prevented the thread from slipping off. As it hung from the thread, the spindle was sent turning and then dropped. The weighted whorl kept the spindle turning, twisting the fibers. Next, the newly-formed yarn was wound on the spindle. The spinner controlled the flow of the fibers at the point where they were drawn from the main supply (the distaff). So simple was this system that one could walk and spin yarn at the same time.

Even this method was probably not widely used for cotton because of the weight placed on the yarn by the spindle and whorl. But a modification of this process was known in the New World and the Old. The point of the rotating spindle was rested in a small bowl or vase (fig. 11-1b). The spindle was turned by hand and the fiber fed from the distaff. The partially-spun yard from the distaff was drawn out between the spindle and the hand of the spinner. In this way, the device was no longer *in* the hands—it had become a crude machine, and was finally incorporated into the spinning wheel to give greater speed to the revolutions of the spindle. This method was feasible for spinning the short fibers of cotton, and evolved independently in Peru and India. Practically all subsequent spinning has been developed on the distaff principle. The yarns of Dacha muslins, the most exquisite of cotton textures, were spun in this manner, as were those of prehistoric Peru.

The Spinning Wheel

It was in India that the spinning wheel was first used to increase the revolutions of the spindle. The spinning wheel was introduced into Europe some time in the Middle Ages and became the ancestor of all the spinning devices invented in England during the eighteenth century. There is no evidence that spinning wheels were used in the New World in pre-Columbian time. The early settlers came from England, where the arts of spinning and weaving were well known in all rural communities, and brought with them hand looms and spinning wheels with which to make warm winter clothing.

Two kinds of spinning wheels evolved through the ages: the Jersey wheel, or great wheel (fig. 11-2), and the Saxony wheel (fig. 11-4).

The Jersey Wheel

Spinning with the Jersey wheel required three steps: drafting (to draw out the lint), twisting, and winding. The Jersey wheel (fig. 11-2) used hand-drawn fibers that were twisted and wound onto the base of an open spindle. The operation of the Jersey spinning wheel was simple. After ginning, the cotton was carded by hand using a pair of rectangular wooded cards

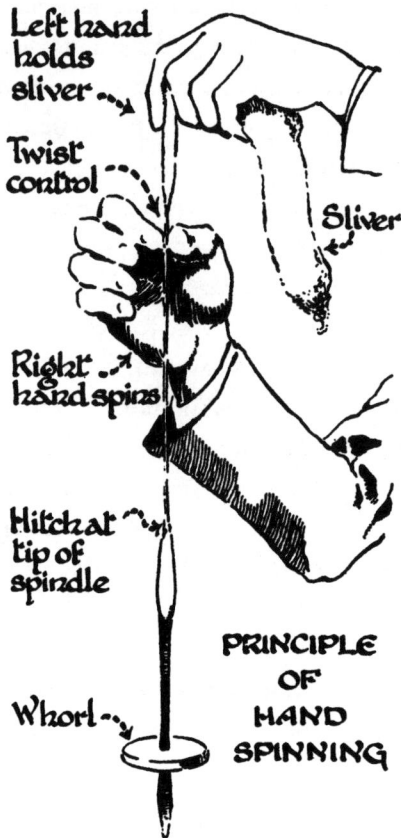

Figure 11-1a. Spindle and whorl (Ellacott 1956, 9)

Figure 11-1b. Vase spinning (Crawford 1924, plate 3)

with a handle (two cards can be seen next to the spinner in figure 11-2). Each card had wire teeth on one side. The teeth were placed together and the cotton was pulled and straightened between the teeth. The carded cotton, laid in a continuous, untwisted strand, was called the sliver (pronounced with a long i, as in diver). Then the sliver was ready to be spun.

The spinner revolved the wheel with her right hand (see woman on the right in figure 11-2). A belt ran from the wheel rim to a horizontal spindle mounted in bearings. As the wheel was turned, it gave the spindle a rapid motion. A short section of thread was first formed by hand and was turned a few times around the end of the spindle. The thread was then held with the left hand at an angle to the spindle end (the *spinning position*, figure 11-2, woman on the right, and figure 11-3), the thumb and finger controlling the amount of sliver drawn out and the degree of twist and tension. The angle of the thread caused the end of the thread to slip off the spindle end as it turned. Each turn that slipped from the spindle tip quickly travelled along the yarn, adding one turn of twist to the forming yarn with each turn of the spindle. The spinner continued to draw out (or draft) more fiber, which was then twisted.

Winding was a separate operation (see woman on the left in figure 11-2). When the desired length of fiber was twisted, the spinner stopped the turning of the spindle, then reversed the wheel to back the yarn off the tip of the spindle, and with the hand, directed the yarn to the base of the spindle. The spindle was then rotated normally to wind the yarn on to the base of the spindle. A second piece of sliver was then touched to the unspun end of the thread, which, as it revolved, caught the end of the sliver. The process of twisting, drafting, and winding was repeated many times until one continuous yarn several yards in length was formed. The obvious drawback of the Jersey wheel was that the spinning process was interrupted each time the yarn was wound onto the spindle. This type of spinning was called intermittent spinning.

The Saxony Wheel

The Saxony wheel was an improvement over the Jersey wheel. It was supposed to have originally been devised by Leonardo de Vinci in 1519, but credit is usually given to Johann Jurgen, a wood carver of Brunswick, England. The Saxony wheel twisted and wound yarn continuously. The drawn and twisted sliver, or roving, was twisted by a U-shaped flyer while being wound onto a bobbin inside the flyer, and the process did not have to stop. The flyer of the Saxony wheel lives on in the spinning machines of the modern textile industry.

The Saxony wheel operated as follows (Ellacott 1956, 24-25): A distaff was used for the roving that was attached to the wheel frame or set on a separate stand (fig. 11-4a). For short fibers like cotton, a well-teased mass was spun straight from the hand. The key feature of the Saxony wheel was the *bobbin and flyer* spindle (fig. 11-4b). The spindle had at its inner end a wharve that took the drive from the spinning wheel that was operated by a treadle. At the other end of the spindle was a fixed flyer that revolved with it. Also on the spindle shaft was a bobbin that turned on its own by a separate drive from the wheel. The sliver was fed from the spinner's hand through the hollow tip of the spindle and around one of the several *hecks* (hooks)

Figure 11-2. Spinning on the Jersey wheel
(From Guest's *Compendious History of the Cotton Manufacture*)

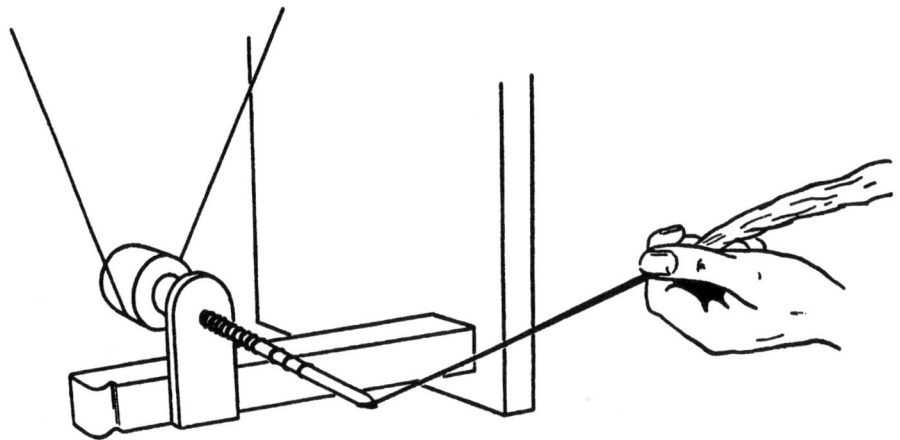

Figure 11-3. The spinning position (Catling 1970, 15)

to the winding surface of the bobbin. Each turn of the flyer gave one turn of twist to the yarn, and it was wound on a bobbin of smaller diameter than the spindle wharve so that the bobbin moved faster than the spindle. As the bobbin filled with yarn, its diameter altered, so the spinner controlled the tension on the yarn and slowed the drive by making the drive cord slip in the wharve. Spinning was continuous; twist was put into the yarn as it wound on the bobbin.

Both of these wheels were initially used for wool and flax, before the days of cotton. Once the value of cotton was understood, spinning wheels were used for cotton as well. But production was limited: both wheels employed a spinner-to-spindle ratio of 1:1. A person working a single spinning wheel produced only a pound of cotton yarn a day. The yarn was strong and coarse, with little or no yarn produced finer than 16 to 20 hanks to the pound.[9] The yarn was also subject to great inequalities and could be used only to weave coarse fabrics. It was obvious that if the amount and quality of cotton yarn production were to keep up with the increasing demand for cotton goods in England (and in the American colonies and the rest of Europe), changes had to be made.

Louis Paul's Carding Machine

For machines to spin cotton mechanically, the cotton first had to be carded. The first carding machine was Louis Paul's crude device in 1738 that separated the fibers and laid them parallel (fig. 11-5). Paul's carding machine, which was a major improvement over previous methods of carding, operated as follows: the cotton was passed between a wooden cylinder (a) covered with nails, and a semicircular receptacle (b) studded with wire points. The cylinder was turned by a hand crank (c). As the cotton passed between the cylinder and the receptacle, the pulling action of the points against the studded cylinder separated the fibers and laid them parallel, forming the sliver.

Early Mechanical Spinning

The first mechanical spinning device to make more than a single yarn was the roller frame of John Wyatt, who created a machine which would spin by means of rollers. His invention consisted of two sets of double rollers; all four rollers had a surface that would grip the fibers. The cotton, prepared by the carding machine, was passed between the two rollers of the first set, then between the second set. The second rollers operated at a faster speed than the first. Thus, the fibers were drawn out. (Had the rollers been turning at the same speeds, the cotton would have passed through the second set of rollers as it went in, unaffected.) The yarn was then twisted and wound onto bobbins by a flyer similar to the Saxony wheel. According to Anthony Burton (1984, 26), Wyatt invented the roller-spinning machine, but being short of funds, allowed Lewis Paul to patent and market it. Paul obtained a patent for the machine in 1738 and installed a full-scale version in a building at Birmingham in 1741. Donkeys were used to turn the drive shaft while the bobbins were hand-operated.

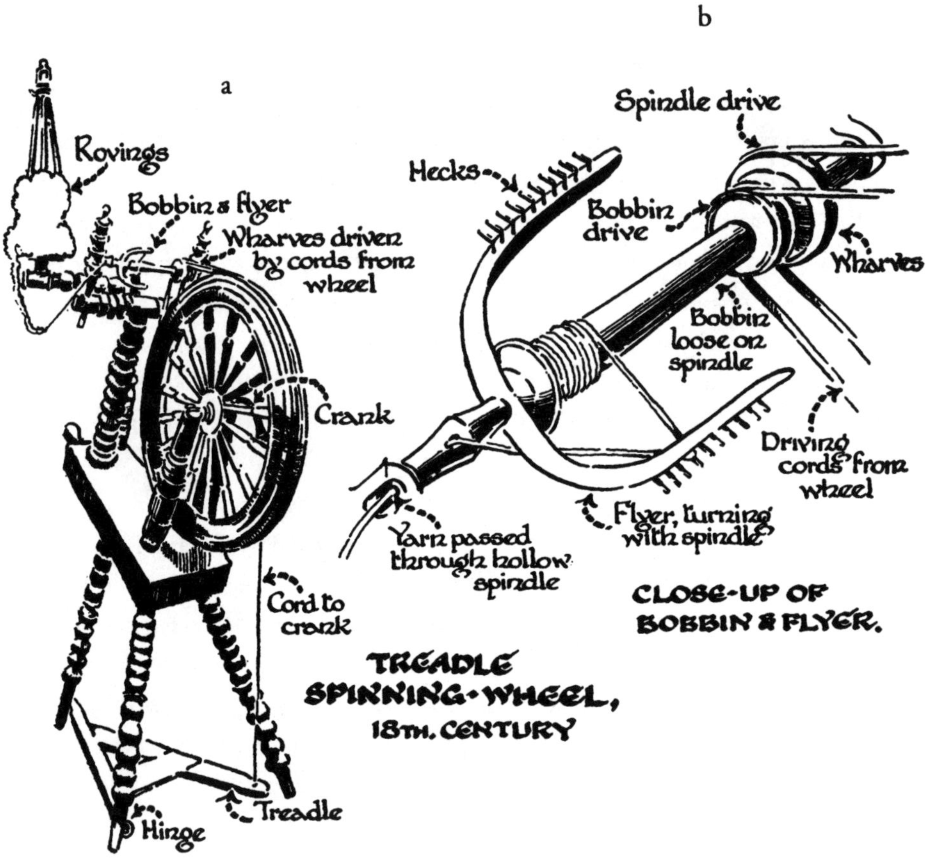

Figure 11-4a-b. The Saxony wheel (Ellacott 1956, 25)

CHAPTER ELEVEN

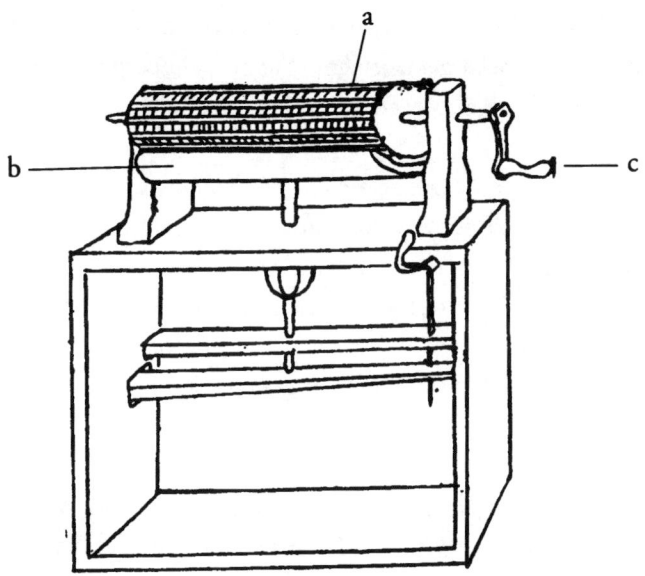

Figure 11-5. Louis Paul's carding machine (Crawford 1924, plate 16)

Figure 11-6. Spinning jenny reconstructed from James Hargreaves's patent of 1770 (Aspin and Chapman 1964)

For reasons lost to history, neither of these machines had any immediate commercial value, probably because of poor financial management. They did, however, contain the basic principles which were perfected by other inventors and incorporated into their machines.

The Spinning Machines of Hargreaves, Arkwright and Crompton

As the second half of the eighteenth century approached, and Kay's flying shuttle (see next section) came to be widely used and accepted, the demand for new spinning machines increased. In 1761, the Society of Arts advertised a prize for a machine that would "spin six threads of wool, flax, hemp or cotton at one time, and that would require but one person to work and attained [attend] it." After failure by numerous persons, enter James Hargreaves.

James Hargreaves

Hargreaves (1720-1778) was born in the semi-moorland district of Oswaldtwistle, near Blackburn, Lancashire. By 1750, he had settled half a mile away at Stanhill. Little is known about his early life except that he was a hand-loom weaver. Lancashire textile workers such as Hargreaves enjoyed a simple, independent life. By improving their machinery, they could expand upon this lifestyle. Hargreaves introduced an improvement in stock cards, used to card cotton by hand. Although his improved stock cards were unknown outside of his neighborhood, they brought his inventive talents to the attention of Robert Peel, with whom he later collaborated on the commercial production of the spinning jenny.

During this period, weavers' families could not supply themselves with enough cotton weft (because of Kay's flying shuttle—see next section), and they had to depend on neighbors' spinning to complete a day's weaving. As the story is often repeated, Hargreaves observed a spinning wheel that had overturned. The spindle, now in an upright position, was still spinning because the wheel was held off the floor by the frame and still had some momentum. From this simple observation, Hargreaves formulated his idea of the spinning jenny (probably a corruption of "spinning engine").[10]

The fundamental principle of Hargreaves's jenny was taking a number of short lengths of rovings and drawing them out steadily while continuing to introduce twist into them by the rotation of several spindles driven from a common wheel. Hargreaves's first spinning machine supported 16 side-by-side upright spindles turned by a hand-operated horizontal wheel. He based his jenny on the one-thread spinning wheel, but substituted for the spinner's left hand a draw bar made from two horizontal pieces of wood between which several threads could be clasped at the same time. A foot treadle, which required an awkward and constrained posture, was used to move a wire that lowered the thread onto the spindles for winding. The spinning jenny employed the same intermittent spinning system of the Jersey wheel. It was, in essence, an expanded Jersey spinning wheel.

According to Aspin and Chapman, who published the most comprehensive account of Hargreaves and his jenny in 1964 (*James Hargreaves and the Spinning Jenny*), no original machines survived. The writers, convinced that "some knowledge of this historic jenny was essential for any proper study of Hargreaves... ," enlisted the services of Derek Pilkington of Helmshore to construct a copy of Hargreaves's original jenny from the 1770 patent. The model was completed in 1964 (fig. 11-6).

Robert Peel, also of Blackburn, became aware of the large amount of cotton weft being produced by Hargreaves's family and apparently provided Hargreaves a place to continue working on his invention in secret. Hargreaves kept the information on the jenny to himself, presumably reasoning that he would do better by personally exploiting the machine than he would by handing it over to others. He would regret this decision later. A number of Hargreaves's jennies were built and several installed in Peel's mill. Word was circulated that one jenny could do the work of several spinners. The local cottage spinners, whose livelihood depended of the spinning wheel, feared the loss of their jobs. In 1768, they attacked Hargreaves's house and destroyed several jennies. Hargreaves fled to Nottingham, in the Midlands, where there appeared to be a more favorable attitude to textile inventors, arriving there without friends or capital.

In Nottingham, there had been numerous attempts by spinners to find an improved method of spinning. Upon learning of Hargreaves's mechanical ability, Thomas James approached him and suggested they go into business together as cotton spinners. James supplied financial support and a site for their mill; Hargreaves built the jennies. They began spinning yarn for local hosiers. Unfortunately for Hargreaves at that time, the yarn produced by the early jenny was suitable only for weft used for poor-quality hosiery, so he did not achieve great financial success in Nottingham.

But troubled again followed Hargreaves and James. Their Nottingham rivals pirated their jennies. Hargreaves, in a belated attempt to protect his invention, obtained a patent for his jenny on June 12, 1770. He then tried to enforce his patent, but his attorney learned that Hargreaves had sold some jennies before leaving Lancashire, and so gave up trying to protect the patent. Hargraves resigned himself to his loss only because of the number of those against him.

Although Hargreaves came to enjoy a lifestyle greater than that to which he had been accustomed in Lancashire, he died ill-requited by his employers, knowing that his invention had earned for others far greater fortunes than for him, and little known to his country, which reaped such important benefits from his discovery. Historians today, however, recognize the value of Hargreaves's spinning jenny to the modern cotton textile industry. Not only was it the first machine whereby cotton yarn for the weft could be mass-produced, but most notably, it was the first successful spinning device that increased the spinner-to-spindle ratio over the 1:1 employed by the spinning wheels. These concepts were further advanced in the machines of Arkwright and Crompton that were to follow.

Other people quickly made improvements to Hargreaves's jenny. Indeed, most of the descriptions by Aspin and Chapman of the operation of the jenny were based on these improved jennies, the authors not realizing they were not a part of Hargreaves's original patent. Early improvements included substituting a horizontal wheel with a vertical wheel, replacing the awkward treadle used by Hargreaves to lower a deflection wire onto the spindles for winding, and making machines that could run hundreds of spindles at one time.

Figure 11-7 shows an early "improved jenny" with the vertical wheel. It featured a series of tilted spindles mounted in a row between the rear posts of the four-posted wooden frame. A hand wheel was connected via a cord to a roller from which a smaller cord ran to sheaves connected to the base of each spindle (fig 11-7A). As the wheel was turned by hand, the spindles revolved rapidly. In front of the spindles was a movable carriage that could be slid back and forth by the spinner grasping the handle with the left hand. The carriage had wheels that allowed it to be moved to and fro on the top rails of the frame. The rovings[11] were placed on bobbins mounted on a stationary creel.

To operate, the carriage was pushed forward (fig 11-7B, position 1), and roving was drawn from each bobbin in turn. The clasp on the carriage was kept open and each roving turned around a separate peg on the carriage, and carried down to its respective spindle. The carriage was withdrawn to position 2 (fig 11-7A) to pull a length of roving from the bobbins. Next, the clasp on the carriage was closed, holding the roving tight. With the left hand the operator drew the carriage back to position 3 (fig 11-7A), and with the right hand turned the wheel to drive the roller which turned the spindles. Two events occurred as the carriage was pulled back at the same time the spindles turned. First, the roving was drawn out, or drafted. Drafting was not intended to stretch the individual fibers, but to increase the length of the roving by sliding the fibers over each other. Cotton fibers have surface irregularities that permit the fibers to slide without the roving being parted. Second, the roving was twisted into yarn in the drafting field between the spindles and the carriage. The tilt of the spindles allowed the roving coils to slip off the tip of the spindle, each turn of the spindle adding one turn of twist to the yarn (just as in the Jersey wheel).

The art in this operation was to maintain the relationship between the rate of spindle rotation and the rate of withdrawal of the carriage so that drafting proceeded smoothly. The thicker places always yielded before the thinner places, so that at the end of the draw the yarn was not only thinner but very much more uniform than the roving from which it was made.

When the carriage was stopped at position 3 (fig 11-7A), the spindles were kept running. The yarn was at the right count but it had not received sufficient twist to make it strong enough. Rotation of the spindles was continued until enough twist had been introduced. The spindles were then reversed to "back off" the few remaining loops of yarn. The carriage was then drawn back to position 4 (fig 11-7A) to take up the slack.

Next came the delicate task of winding onto the spindles the yarn that had been spun. A faller wire, operated by a control cord (fig 11-7A), was pressed down on the yarn, pushing it down onto the spindle (fig 11-7C). The carriage was pushed forward while the spindles were turned, winding the yarn onto the spindle. If the carriage moved too slowly in relation to the spindles,

CHAPTER ELEVEN

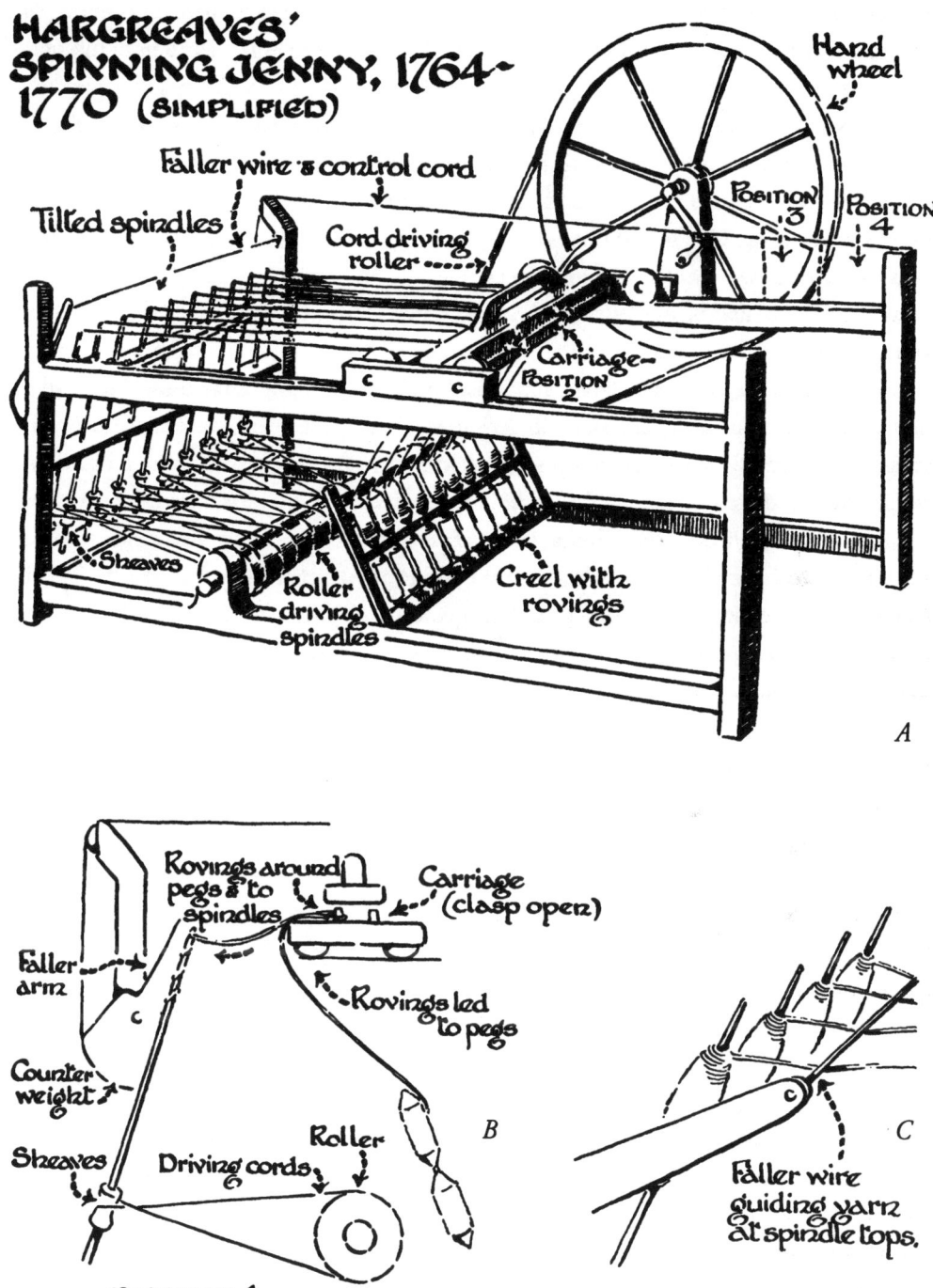

Figure 11-7A-C. Hargreaves's improved spinning jenny (Ellacott 1956, 34-35)

the yarn broke; if the carriage moved too fast, the yarn hung slack and wound poorly.

Jenny spinning of cotton reached its peak in the 1780s; after 1785, there was a more rapid adaption of Arkwright's water-frame. However, jennies were used as late as 1926 in the woolen industry of Yorkshire; even at that time, they were hand-cranked. The jenny's longevity in the Welsh woolen industry lasted even longer, one machine working in Anglesey until about 1935. Though the jenny was first mainly used in cottages, it ultimately came to be used in factories with machines of 130 spindles. Because it was hand-driven and easy to make, the jenny was chosen by those who set up business with limited capital. There was always a market for coarse yarn; there was no demand for expensive mules (see following) to spin coarse yarn.

During the first half of the 1700s, linen was spun for the warp (the yarns that run lengthwise across the loom), which had to be very strong. Cotton was used for the weft (the yarns that are woven across the warp). Manchester had always been famous for these linen and cotton mixtures (called "fustians") since the reign of Henry VII. They continued to be made because the spinning wheel could not spin a strong cotton yarn for the warp. Cotton had a shorter, weaker and more elastic fiber than flax and needed to be much more firmly twisted, which could not be done on a spinning wheel. The amount of cotton weft and linen warp the spinners produced just about equalled the amount of yarn demanded by the weavers. This balance was upset when the weavers increased the quantity of cloth they could make because they were using the flying shuttle invented by John Kay in 1738. Now the problem was how to find machines which could spin a strong cotton yarn suitable for the warp so cloth could be made entirely of cotton. Unfortunately, Hargreaves's jenny-spun cotton yarn was soft and suitable only for the weft. Linen warp continued to be spun on a hand wheel.

Richard Arkwright

In 1768, Richard Arkwright invented the water frame. Arkwright did more than any other inventor to establish the textile industry on a modern basis. Born in 1732 in the city of Preston, in Lancashire, Arkwright began his professional life as a barber, and later was an itinerant buyer of hair for wigmakers. During his travels, and listening to gossip in the barber shop, he absorbed all the talk about various mysterious machines for spinning and weaving. Unlike others, he saw these machines not as evil, but to society's advantage. In 1768, he persuaded a local clockmaker, John Kay (no relation to the Kay who invented the flying shuttle) to help him produce a working model of a spinning machine that he envisioned would spin by means of rollers. He persuaded a Mr. Smalley, a local innkeeper, to finance the project. In 1769, he obtained his first patent for spinning by means of rollers and flyers based on the machines of Wyatt and Paul. Although there were many who claimed that Wyatt and Paul were the original inventors of this method of spinning, there is do doubt that Arkwright brought these improvements to a higher state of perfection than they had attained before. Arkwright's first spinning machine was operated by horse power.

CHAPTER ELEVEN

But Arkwright met the same fate as Hargreaves. When rumors of Arkwright's spinning machines began to spread throughout Lancashire, and local spinners feared the loss of their jobs, Arkwright, being a cautious man, followed Hargreaves to Nottingham in 1769.

In Nottingham, Arkwright met two successful hosiery manufacturers, Samuel Need of Derby and Jebediah Strutt of Belfer, who were so impressed by his spinning machine that they went into partnership with him. Smalley, who had provided the initial financing, was allowed in as a junior partner. With the new partners' capital, Arkwright was at last able to try out his spinning machine. The experiment was a success, and the partners began looking for a mill site. They choose the tiny, remote hamlet of Cromford in Derbyshire, where there were no local spinners to contend with as the mill was constructed. Basically, Arkwright grouped into one unit all the most advanced devices for spinning yarn and welded them into a factory. There was no technology in the workings of mills such as Arkwright's that had not been well-known for generations in the workings of clocks and watches. The gears and ratcheting were identical. Arkwright simply applied this knowledge to wood and iron on a grand scale. In the end, the world saw a new phenomenon: the factory owner as absolute ruler over his workforce. The first mill was run by horses, but this was found to be too expensive, and a second mill, run by water power and on a larger scale, was constructed in 1771.

Arkwright's water frame was a mechanical success because it accomplished two main goals. First, the raw material was prepared free of defects and properly carded and combed. Second, the raw material for spinning was drawn out by rollers that functioned like the finger and thumb of the wheel spinner. He added the flyer and bobbin spindle, derived with little alteration from the Saxony wheel.

Arkwright's water frame (fig. 11-8) consisted of two lines of double rollers. In both lines, the lower rollers were furrowed lengthwise and the upper ones covered with leather to grasp the rovings. The first rollers (a), which received the rovings (b), slowly revolved in contact with each other. The second line of double rollers (c) was placed in front of the first and revolved at a greater velocity than the first. The second line of rollers also had the lower rollers furrowed and the upper rollers covered with leather. The first rollers pulled the rovings from the bobbins (d) which then passed to the second rollers. These rollers, revolving faster than the first, drew out the rovings in the same manner as the wheel spinner with her finger and thumb. From the second rollers, the rovings went to the spindles (e). This system was the same as the Saxony wheel and allowed for continuous spinning. Twist was put into the yarn during winding on the spindles. No hand labor was required except to join the ends of rovings that broke.

Anthony Burton best described Arkwright's mill (Burton 1984, 33):

Cromford and its mill represented something quite new. The mill itself was, by the standards of the day, enormous. It stood six stories high, with machinery filling every floor, all powered by one big water wheel. This was more than a mere change in scale from what had gone before: it forced a whole now way of working onto the industry. Men no longer began to tend the machine at their

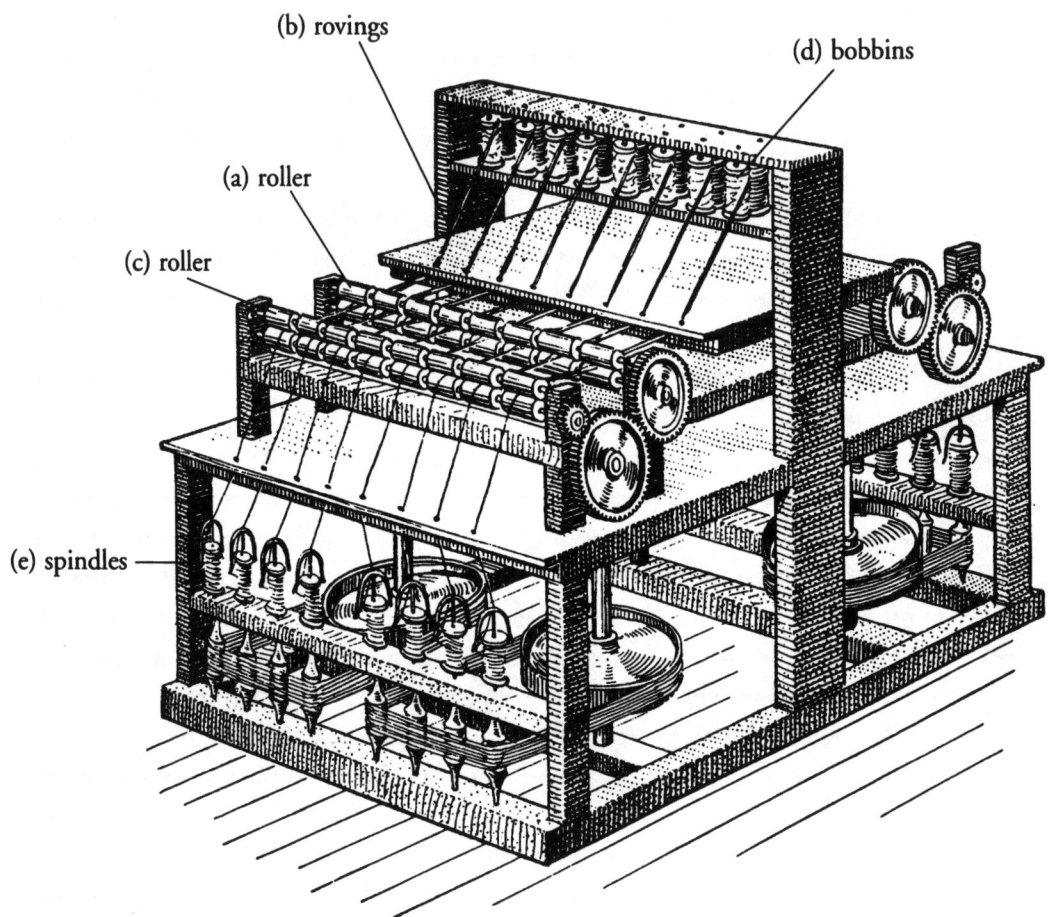

Figure 11-8. Arkwright's water frame (Turpin 1924, 55)

CHAPTER ELEVEN

convenience: the machine now demanded their presence. Once water began to flow through the sluices, turning the wheel and setting the rollers and spinners moving, then the workers had to be at their places. There they stayed, stopping only when the great wheel stopped. The factory bell rang out over Cromford announcing when work was to start. It rang again to announce the end of the working day. With the establishment of the mill at Cromford, the factory age had arrived.

Arkwright ran into trouble in Derbyshire, with personal opposition and hostility. There was a lot of money in Cromford, and Arkwright wanted a quick return from the mill. He was an overbearing and impatient person, but above all, an ambitious one. He was not interested in public acclaim, and was determined not to suffer the fate of past inventors who did not receive financial reward from their work. Trying to squeeze every cent from his operation, he employed mill children, aged seven to thirteen, as part of the work force, and paid little heed to working conditions in the mills. Within the confines of Cromford, he lived as a feudal lord.

His partner Jebediah Strutt was unlike Arkwright in every way, being calm-tempered, literate, stylish, and already a man of means. Accordingly, he was not as profit-motivated as Arkwright. Smalley, too, had difficulty with Arkwright. Strutt finally built his own mill in 1778 in Belper, and three years later, when Samuel Need died, the partnership was dissolved.

The success at Cromford encouraged Arkwright to expand his operations. He built more mills in Derbyshire and then in the textile heartland of Lancashire. But the workers of Lancashire did not accept the new mechanized mills that could do the work of many men. In October 1779, they marched on the mills and destroyed many of them. Arkwright retreated to Derbyshire and waited out the siege. But the spinners of Lancashire had no interest in marching into Derbyshire. They were content to drive Arkwright and other mill owners out of Lancashire. Arkwright was safe; he then started to expand his Derbyshire mills and to build elsewhere in England.

Arkwright received an invitation from four leading Glasgow merchants to come to that city to explore setting up his mills in Scotland. As a result of the meeting, Arkwright built a mill at Corra Linn Falls on the Clyde River. The site had plenty of water and was remote from likely arsonists. Here, Arkwright again met with success. One of the four merchants who had invited him was James Finlay, whose second son, Kirkman, was later to play an important role in the sea island cotton trade.

Arkwright died in 1792. Even though all his patent rights had eventually been overturned in the courts, he died a wealthy man. The way was now paved for anyone with capital to venture into the manufacturing business.

Arkwright's water frame produced a strong cotton yarn suitable for the warp. But neither the jenny nor the water frame could produce yarn that was fine and strong enough to make cloth garments entirely of cotton such as the exquisite muslins and calicoes made in India. This was left to Samuel Crompton. But the jenny and water frame created a greater demand for raw cotton from the States. Sea island cotton would benefit from this demand.

Samuel Crompton

When Arkwright was working as a barber, he often went to the village of Bolton, where there lived a boy who would become the greatest of the cotton-spinning inventors. This was Samuel Crompton (1753-1827). One of Crompton's household duties was to assist his mother in weaving cloth on her hand loom. He often heard her say that she could not make fine goods out of the coarse yarn made by Hargreaves's spinning jenny or Arkwright's water frame. Crompton was determined to make a machine which would spin fine and strong yarn suitable for luxurious fabrics.

Crompton was the son of a skilled craftsman, and was a man of some culture and education. He had a grasp of technology that gave him the confidence (Catling 1970, 32) "to devote all his talents to the solution of the engineering problems involved in the construction of the new machine." He did not stumble upon his machine by accident. He worked on the project for five years, succeeding in 1779. This was around the time that hand spinners of Lancashire were rampaging throughout the region, burning mills and destroying machines. Crompton dismantled his prototype to protect it, and once the turmoil was over, reassembled his machine. But Crompton was as much the victim of his own sensitive nature as of the greed of his contemporaries. His invention was stolen from him through unredeemed promises of reward, and by threats against his safety. Long after his invention had brought wealth to many others, he lived in want, trying to support his family. He did receive a belated £5,000 from Parliament, but lost this sum in a business venture, living in his old age on an annuity provided by his friends.

Crompton called his invention a "muslin wheel" because it made yarn fine enough for fine muslins. Later, it was known as the "mule" because it combined the good qualities of Hargreaves's spinning jenny and Arkwright's water frame, and did better work than either. It had rollers like the water frame to draw out the roving, a movable frame to further draw out the roving, and it twisted and wound the yarn like the spinning jenny. In other words, spinning was intermittent, as first seen in the Jersey wheel and later in the spinning jenny. Crompton's mule carried three or four hundred spindles. Now there was a spinning machine which could spin a fine, yet strong, cotton yarn suitable for both the warp and weft that could be woven into the fanciest muslins and laces.

According to Harold Catling's book *The Spinning Mule* (1970), the most difficult problem Crompton had to overcome in order to combine the operation of the jenny and the water frame was "the need, during spinning, for accurately-controlled translatory motion of the rapidly rotating spindles, relative to the precisely driven drafting rollers." To solve this problem, Crompton mounted the spindles, the bands that drove the spindles, and the drum that turned the driving bands on a wheeled carriage running on rails fixed to the floor. An ingenious arrangement of guide pulleys permitted the spindles to be coupled at all times to a stationary hand-driven fly wheel (fig. 11-10) while the carriage was moved along the rails under the control of draw bands. As Catling explained, "Both the drafting rollers and the draw bands were also coupled to the fly [a hand-driven wheel] during the draw but were disengaged from the fly during supplementary twisting, backing-off and winding."

Crompton's mule (fig. 11-9) operated as follows (Catling 1970, 34):

1. The roller and carriage drives were engaged. The fly wheel was turned by hand, which caused the rollers to turn, drawing out the roving between the rollers and roving bobbins, and delivering it to the spindles. At the same time, the fly wheel turned the spindles, twisting the roving into a soft yarn, while, by the hand or knee of the operator, the carriage (with the mounted spindles) was made to recede from the stationary rollers more rapidly than the roving was being delivered. This caused leveling of the yarn between the spindles and rollers by drawing out the thicker places.

2. Once the draw was completed, the roller and carriage drives were disengaged; however, the spindles were kept turning by the fly wheel until the required amount of twist had been inserted in the yarn. Twist was put into the yarn because the spindles were slanted, allowing each new coil to slip off the spindle tip (just as in the Jersey wheel and the jenny).

3. The fly wheel was then turned backward—which turned the spindles backward—to unwind the coils of yarn between the cop[12] and the tip of the spindle.

4. The fly wheel was next turned in the spinning direction to wind up the yarn. The right hand turned the fly wheel while the left hand guided the yarn into the form of a cop by a faller wire. Winding the yarn on the spindles tended to pull the carriage toward the rollers. The operator, to keep the proper tension on the yarn, assisted the movement of the carriage with his knees, or restrained the carriage with the hand controlling the faller wire.

5. Once winding was complete, the faller wire was raised, and the fly wheel continued to operate, laying the yarn in an open spiral from the top of the cop to the spindle tip. During this operation, the roller and carriage drives were re-engaged to prepare for the next draw.

Thus, each potion of roving was first subjected to the action of the drawing rollers, as was done in Arkwright's water frame, and then drawn still finer by the withdrawal of the moving frame, as in Hargreaves's spinning jenny. The mule differed from the spinning jenny in that the spindles traveled on the frame that ran outward on the twisting and drawing cycle, and inward on the wind. Spinning was intermittent as in the Jersey wheel and the jenny.

M. D. C. Crawford made a comparison between the water frame and mule spinning. Arkwright's water frame spun coarse and heavy yarn. According to Crawford, no record was discovered that told how many hanks the water frame spun, but models of the water frame made in America spun No. 14 and No. 20. Crawford explained (1924, 116):

Crompton himself made good even No. 80's, comparable in weight to the yarns used in fine lawns [sheer linen or cotton fabric] and nainsook [fine lightweight muslin]. The hand mule up to our time was used in the Calais lace trade and I have modern specimens as fine as 405's or 260,200 yards to the pound or approximately 150 miles. I have also a cop of No. 500 spun for the Jubilee Exposition of Queen Victoria a generation ago. These facts will prove how exquisitely perfect was the original mule for its purpose.

THE TEXTILE INDUSTRY AND SEA ISLAND COTTON

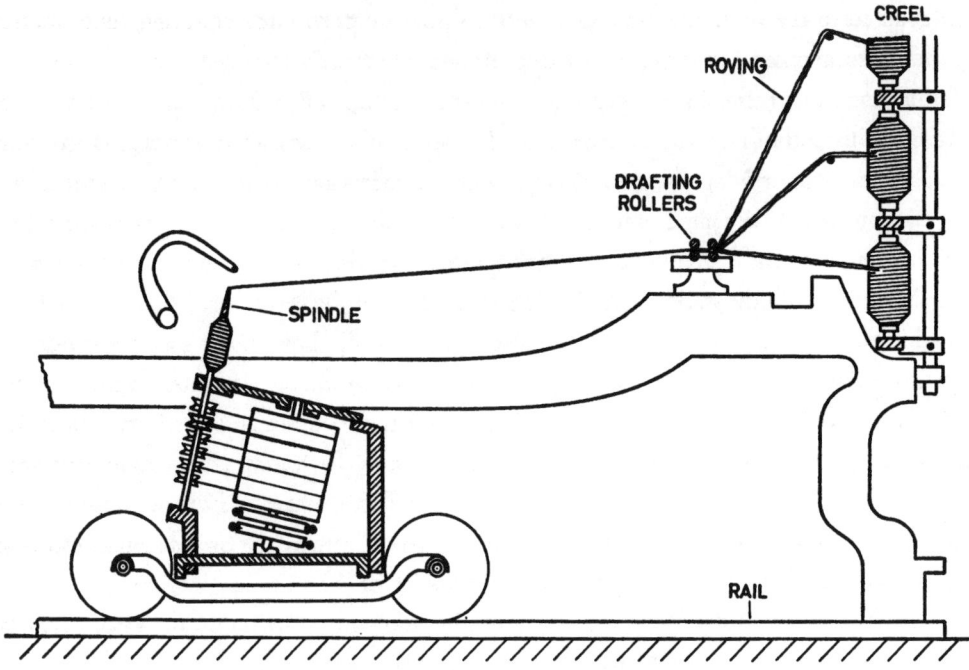

Figure 11-9. Working elements of Crompton's mule (Catling 1970, 33)

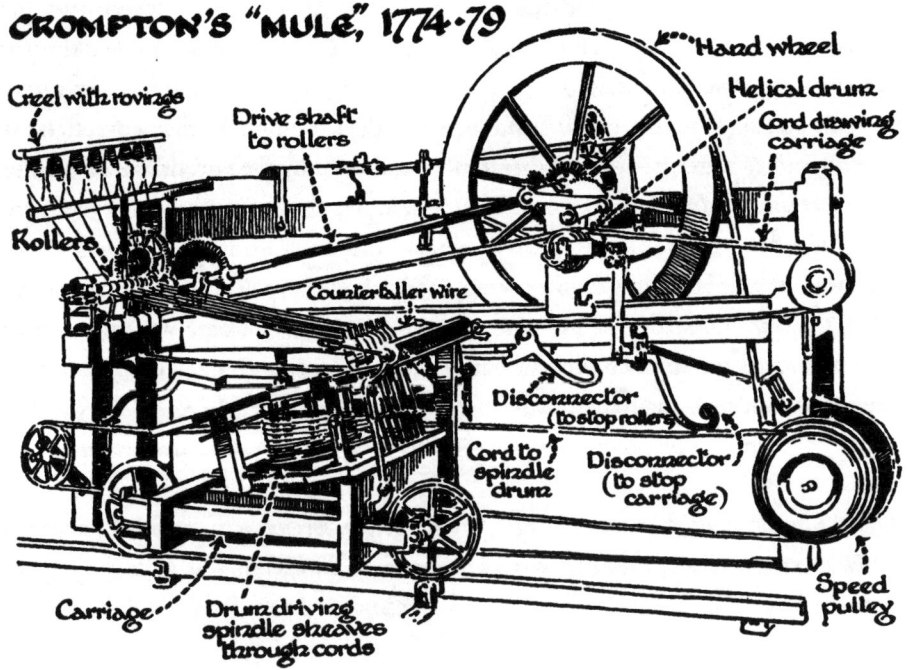

Figure 11-10. Detailed technical aspects of Crompton's mule, 1774-79 (Ellacott 1956, 39)

For all its marvelous precision of motion, Crompton's original spinning mule required skilled labor, and none knew better their value than the mule spinners themselves. These were the aristocrats of the textile trade, demanding high wages and very special privileges. Crawford (1924, 118) wrote: "It is narrated that they wore £5 notes in the bands of their hats and would neither drink nor smoke in the common rooms of inns. Worse than this in the eyes of their supposed masters, they refused to train apprentices unless at their own caprice." In 1830, Richard Roberts produced a modified self-actor mule[13] that could be operated by lesser-skilled workers, curbing somewhat the arrogance of the mule spinners.

Contributing to the demand for Crompton's yarn was the fact that most fine-count yarn prior to his machine had to be imported from India. Until the invention of the mule, Europe could not produce yarn fine enough; but with the mule, it was possible for the first time to spin yarn equal in fineness to the production of Hindu spinners. By 1811, consumer demand for cotton goods produced from fine-count yarns was so great that four million mule spindles operated in England (in contrast, Arkwright's water frame and Hargreaves's jenny spun only half a million combined). Nevertherless, the amount of yarn that could be spun on these three machines was limited when compared to the high demand for cotton cloth in England and around the world.

By the beginning of the nineteenth century, steam-powered mules and water frames were the tools of the burgeoning textile industry in England, and increasingly, abroad. In fact, modern textile spinning machines are all based on the principles of these early inventors and machines. Indeed, mule spinning became obsolete only in recent times. Today, in the two main types of spinning—ring and rotor—one still sees elements of the ingenuity of Hargreaves, Arkwright, and Crompton.

The way was now made for cotton fiber with a longer and finer staple length to be woven into yarn of the highest hanks. Sea island cotton would quickly be in high demand. Herbert Walmsley best summed up the value of sea island cotton for the spinning industry (1893, 61):

Sea Islands cotton is the most valuable of all cottons, and when seen under the microscope the fibers show themselves as twisted like a corkscrew. The more nearly cylindrical and the greater the spiral structure of the fiber the stronger and more pliant will they be found to be in spinning, readily entwining with and twisting round one another during the formation of a thread, gripping or intertwining the one with the other, and producing or giving strength, tenacity, and elasticity. There is a wide difference in the quality and value of the different varieties produced by the cotton plant. Sea Islands is the most valuable species, because it is only possible to spin the finest yarns out of a superior quality, with fine, uniform, long and perfect naturally-twisted fiber, such as Sea Islands affords.

But the second part of the textile story is yet to be told that involves sea island cotton—weaving.

Weaving

The First Weavers
It is not recorded in history by whom or where weaving was first initiated. We can only speculate. Crawford, in his classic book *The Heritage of Cotton* (1924, 17-18), supposed it was primitive man building a fish weir:

The first weaver was he who made the first fish weir. He had observed that it was a little easier to secure his prey in parts of the stream where a wind-blown tree formed an obstruction which permitted the fish to escape only in one direction. Obviously the gods of the forest sent those fortuitously fallen trees in answer to the offerings of the tribe. Still the gods were notably poor fishermen and did not send either enough trees or trees in the right place to suit the growing demand of the ravenous appetites.

This man dares to imitate the gods to improve indeed upon their careless methods. He elects a shallow ripple, between two deep pools, drives in upright sticks in a loop to suit the vagaries of the water. Between these, he intertwines saplings of pliable vines, so that the water may escape but the fish be retained. All that he thought he was doing, all that he hoped to accomplish and all so far as he ever knew he had accomplished, was to build a fish trap in imitation of wind-blown trees. As a matter of fact he is the father of weavers, and the latest, most sumptuous fabric of our times is covered by the same generic definition as this rude texture of upright staffs and intertwining withes.

As time passed, primitive peoples wove native materials by hand into baskets, thatched roofs and mats of rushes as a platform to live over water. The earliest evidence of actual weaving dates from at least 5000 BC, and it seems likely that the principles of weaving were based on these primitive methods. Consequently, it is little exaggeration to state that before the first cloth was made, the fundamental methods of fabric construction had already been developed.

Just as the idea of weaving preceded the idea of cloth making, so did the crudest cloth long precede any type of loom. The loom was only a convenient implement for weaving, not a necessity, until cloth making reached its finest state. Even today, some primitive peoples weave blankets of twisted animal fur by stretching the warp on the ground and intertwining the weft by hand. However, to make cloth, some kind of frame had to be used to hold the warp in position during weaving.

Hand Looms
Before considering the evolution of weaving implements, the general principles that characterize a weaving process must be understood. Figure 11-11 illustrates the basic components of weaving. The first step in producing a weave is the setting up of the yarn for the warp, the yarns that run lengthwise. The warp must be secured at both ends so that it can be stretched. In the diagram, one end of the warp is attached to the breast beam and the other end to the

warp beam. The warp must also be provided with a mechanical arrangement of some kind whereby the shed can be opened and closed by a movement of the hand or foot, or by the weaver's body. Weaving requires at least two sheds, resulting in a plain-weave fabric, the simplest of basic cloth. A device was needed that would part the warp-threads in the sequence of one set up and one set down that allowed the shuttle holding the weft to be passed through the shed, thus making a pick or line of weaving. The answer to the problem was the heddle, a rod placed above and across the warp, and having every second warp yarn attached to it by loops or *leashes*.[14] When lifted, the heddle raised the looped-on warp yarns all together, leaving the natural shed between these and the remaining static warp yarns (position 1 in fig. 11-11). After the weft was passed through the shed and beaten up close to the previous line of weft (called the *pick*) with a wooden sword or beater-in, the heddle was dropped (position 2 in fig. 11-11). Next, the alternate warp yarns that were not attached to the heddle were pulled down out of line with the fingers, and a thick *shed-rod* was threaded through them. This forced the yarns below the level of the others, creating a countershed. Each time the cycle was repeated and the heddle lowered, the weight of the shed-rod pressed down the warp and created the countershed. Weft yarn was then passed through the countershed, beaten up with the sword, forming another pick line.

In order to prevent the warp yarns from crossing over each other, *laze-rods* were used. At a point fairly close to the warp beam, every second warp yarn was raised and a rod passed through. The remaining yarns were then raised and a second rod was inserted, so that the warp yarns were crossed and braced on two rods. This arrangement also helped to form a clear shed opening.

Two basic types of early looms evolved: the warp-weighted loom and the two-barred loom. The warp-weighted loom was used very early in the story of weaving, but there is a body of evidence to suggest that a two-barred horizontal ground loom may have appeared first (fig. 11-11). An early diagram of a two-barred ground loom appeared on a pottery dish dated around 4400 BC, found in an Egyptian tomb.

The warp-weighted loom (fig. 11-12) was first developed in the flax area of Europe. The oldest type was discovered in the Neolythic Swiss Lake villages, and is judged to be about ten thousand years old. This loom appears in classical Greece, Scandinavia, and Iceland, and was perhaps the loom used in Britain before Caesar's time. Its latest form is found among the Haida Indians of the Alaskan Coast and is an intrusion from Asiatic migration. The simplest form of the warp-weighted loom consisted of a single, rigid horizontal bar (a), from which the warps (b) hung down with weights attached (c) to produce tension and to keep the warp yarns parallel to each other. This loom did not lend itself to the mechanical subtleties of the more highly involved constructions, and has no descendants in the machines of today. The warp loom was not used for cotton because the uneven tension of the warp weights would have broken the primitive short-length cotton threads. By the time long-staple cotton was available, more advanced weaving machines were in use.

THE TEXTILE INDUSTRY AND SEA ISLAND COTTON

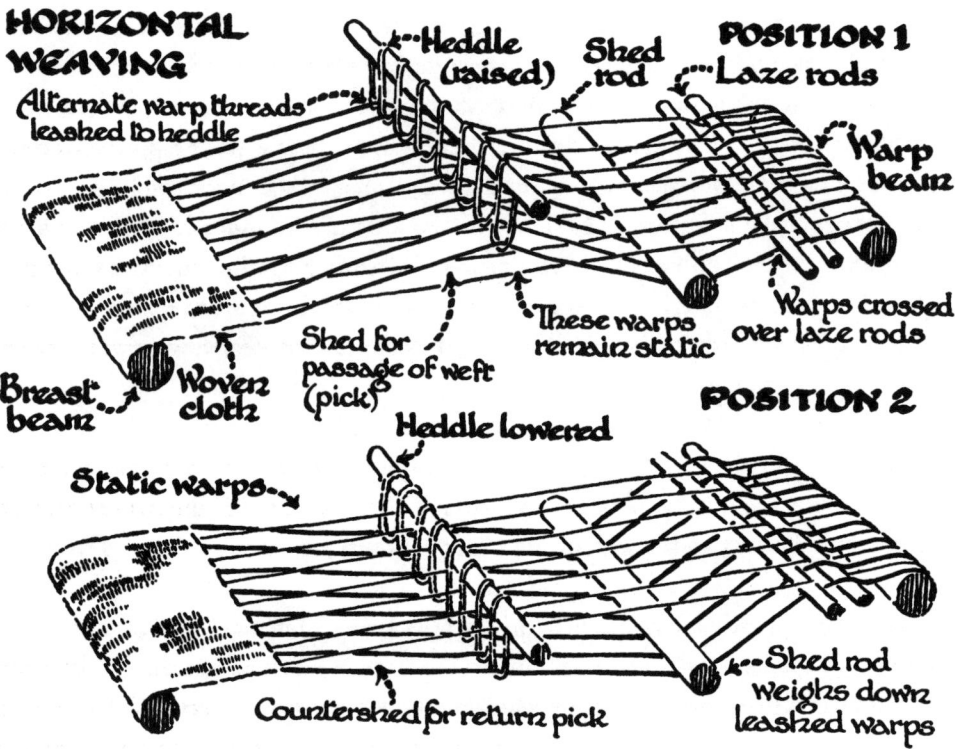

Figure 11-11. Horizontal weaving (Ellacott 1956, 4)

In both Asia and the New World, the two-barred loom was associated with the history of cotton. As Crawford stated (1924, 33), "The correspondence between the two-barred loom and cotton is absolute. Wherever this type of loom appears, there is cotton, and wherever cotton appears in ancient times, this type of loom occurs." This two-barred loom was not indigenous to Europe, but was introduced from Asia at a very early period.

Agnes Geiger (1979, 21-22) described a two-barred loom from Peru that she stated "in principle may be taken as representing the origin of all weaving devices…" Geiger continued: "Even today the same type of loom can be found in use both among the Indians of Latin America and in other parts of the world." She described its operation (fig. 11-13):

This loom… consists of two sticks with the warp stretched between them. It also includes a shed stick left in the warp to give the natural shed and a simple heddle rod for the countershed. The latter is obtained by each lower thread in the natural shed being picked up and bound by a loop (half heddle) which is generally secured to a stick, the heddle rod. When this stick is lifted, the warp threads attached to it are also lifted, to allow a pick to be inserted in the shed (= the countershed). After the rod has been lowered again, the weaver can insert a flat stick next to the shed stick and raise the latter on to one edge, thus bringing the natural shed into operation.

The woman in the diagram attached one warp beam to a tree, while the beam was secured to a belt, known as the back strap, passed around her hips. She stretched and relaxed the warp as needed by means of body tension.

The Standard Hand Loom Before the Mechanical Era

There are countless types of hand looms that appear in the literature. Ultimately, a standard hand loom developed in England that was used for cotton (fig. 11-14). The loom had a frame made of four upright posts. The two back posts were connected by a piece called the yard beam (a); around this was wound one end of the warp yarns. The two front posts also were connected by a piece of timber (f) called the cloth beam around which the newly-formed yarn was wound. After attaching the warp yarns on the yarn beam, the warp yarns were passed through a loop of wire in a frame called a harness (the two harnesses were the heddle) (c). Two harnesses were used when a piece of plain cloth was woven. The odd warp yarns were passed through the loops of one harness; the even yarns were passed through the other harness. The weaver inserted into the shuttle a quill on which the weft yarn was wound. The weaver sat on a seat that was part of the loom and pressed a treadle that raised one heddle and lowered the other, creating the shed. Through the shed, the weaver passed the shuttle containing the weft yarn, grabbing it with the other hand at the far side of the shed. The yarn was then pushed firmly against the previous weft yarn (the pick). Then, by a second motion of the foot, the lower set of yarn was raised and the upper one brought down, creating a second shed (the countershed) through which the shuttle was passed by hand. The second yarn was then

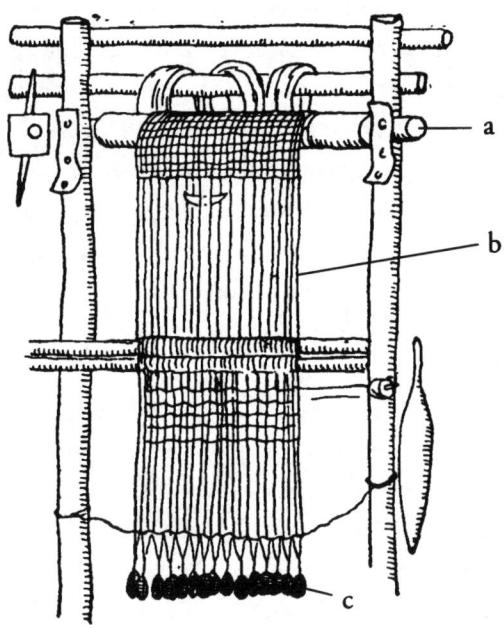

Figure 11-12. Warp-weighted loom from Iceland (Crawford 1924, plate 4, no. 4)

Figure 11-13. Primitive two-barred loom from Peru (Geiger 1979, 22)[15]

pushed firmly in place. The operations were repeated until the desired length of cloth was woven. All the cloth manufactured in England through the 1700s was made on this type of hand loom.

There were two main drawbacks of the hand loom. First, it was a very slow process. Second, if the loom was operated by just the weaver, the width of the cloth was limited to the reasonable spread between the outstretched hands of the weaver. John Kay solved these problems.

Mechanical Looms
John Kay

About the same time Wyatt and Paul were working on their roller spinning machine and carding machine, John Kay made a device that greatly increased the speed of weaving looms and was perhaps the first concrete expression of the machine age. Kay was from Bury in Lancashire and was first in a succession of men whose ideas revolutionized the industry, and who were to see others claim their profits. As a child, he was apprenticed to a reed maker. Reeds were used in looms to make the heddle, moved by a foot treadle so that alternate warp yarns were raised and lowered. Kay realized that the fragile natural reeds were not ideal for this job, and substituted durable wire, which proved successful. Next, he turned his attention to the shuttle.

During Kay's time, the shuttle containing the weft yarn was passed through the natural shed and countershed, either by the hand of the weaver, or by a second person. This was obviously a very slow process. Kay considered the problem. His solution was outlined by Burton in his book *The Rise and Fall of King Cotton* (1984, 24):

If the shuttle could be kept in a straight line then there was no reason why mechanical hands could not replace human hands. A suitable shuttle run already existed in the form of the heavy wooden batten which was used to push the weft threads close together after each throw of the shuttle. He put wheels on the shuttle and the shuttle on the batten. Now all he had to do was put little wooden boxes at the ends of the run, each containing a wire 'hand' that could be jerked by a string that dangled down in front of him to send the shuttle racing across the loom at far greater speed than the two men had ever been able to manage.

The productivity of the loom had been increased double to four-fold by Kay's "flying shuttle." The year was 1738, but Kay was never to realize his just reward for his invention. Kay's creation was pirated throughout the textile industry, as was so common in those days when patents did not provide the necessary protection for inventors. Weavers, especially the men who "threw the shuttle," broke into his house and destroyed his loom. Kay barely escaped. Throughout the manufacturing districts, mills were broken into and looms destroyed. Kay fled to France, looking for fairer treatment, but was unsuccessful, and died in 1781, poor and disillusioned.

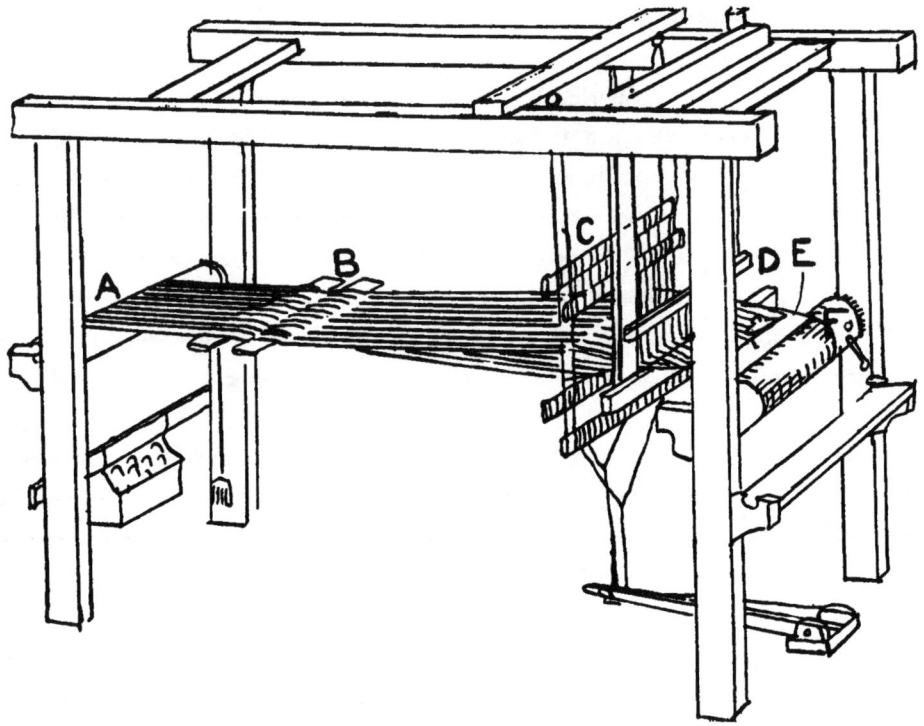

Figure 11-14. Standard hand loom (Crawford 1924, plate 16, no. 5)

During this time, there was great activity in the production of British calicoes[16] and an increasing demand for fabrics made of rough cotton and linen, all of which made Kay's improved loom of the greatest economic importance. It could not, however, reach its fullest value for cotton manufacturing until adequate supplies of cotton yarn suited for the weft were available. But the machines of Hargreaves, Arkwright, and Crompton were just in the offing that would provide the necessary yarn.

Dr. Edmund Cartwright

The next major advancement in the weaving process was the power loom invented by a man least likely of all the inventors. Dr. Edmund Cartwright was a graduate of Oxford, a clergyman, a writer, and the rector of Goadby Marwood. Cartwright took up the invention of a power loom as a challenge by guests at a dinner party who claimed that such a loom was impossible. Cartwright "was almost as ignorant of conventional weaving techniques when he completed his experience as he had been when he started." But he went to work. He examined a piece of cloth and saw that a machine must work with lengthwise and crosswise yarns; it must raise and lower the lengthwise yarns in sets; and it would have to pass the crosswise yarn (weft) through the shed and force it into place. He made a clumsy machine (fig. 11-15) with strong springs that did all three things. The warp was held in a vertical frame and the shuttle was sent across by a spring (the flying shuttle of Kay). Then he got a weaver to put in the warp and test his loom. Two men turned the hand crank for two hours before they collapsed, exhausted. But the loom worked and produced the first piece of cloth woven on a machine without the services of a skilled weaver. The year was 1785.

Up to this time, Cartwright had never seen the process of weaving on a hand loom. Once he observed how easy the operation of the hand loom was compared to his powered loom, he set about making improvements. In 1786, he obtained a patent for his improved machine, first powered by a bull on a treadmill; later, steam power was used. He went to Manchester, but failed to arouse interest. He then bought a mill at Doncaster in Yorkshire and began building his looms there. His mill drew interest, and one Manchester manufacturer built a mill with 500 steam-powered looms. No more than 20 looms had been set to working when the mill was mysteriously burned (shades of Hargreaves and Arkwright). There was no great incentive at the time to install powered looms, especially in 1793 when Cartwright's mill closed. Cartwright's mill was unsuccessful, not due to a lack of proficiency in the machines, but probably because—like most inventors—he did not have the necessary business ability to turn his invention into a profit.

But the power loom worked, and it was only a matter of time before powered looms, driven by water and later by steam, began to appear alongside spinning machines and mules in the cotton factories.

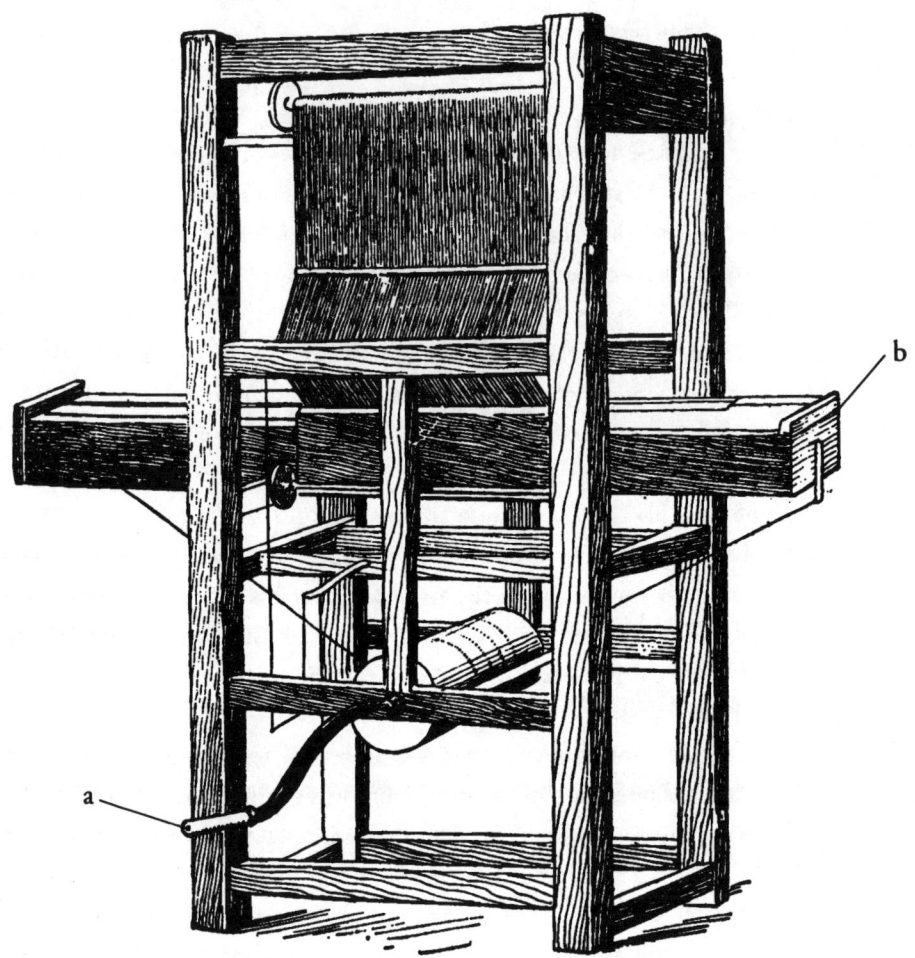

Figure 11-15. Cartwright's power loom with hand-cranked handle (a) and box (b) to hold the flying shuttle (Turpin 1924, 60)

CHAPTER ELEVEN

THE BRITISH COTTON TRADE, 1780-1815

In continental Europe, and especially in Great Britain, cotton textile production was undergoing rapid industrialization during the 1700s. As cotton does not grow well in northern Europe, buyers had to reach outward to secure a steady supply of raw cotton for the textile mills. In this process, the world of European cotton became linked to the Atlantic economy and to other semitropical and tropical regions that produced raw cotton. South America, the West Indies, the Atlantic states, West Africa and India supplied the insatiable demand for raw cotton. At the center of this demand was Great Britain and the cotton trade.

The rapid growth of the British cotton trade during the late 1700s and early 1800s has been of interest to many historians. It is of relevance to this book since the British trade had a direct influence on trade in sea island cotton. Up to 1770, virtually every operation of the cotton textile industry was performed by hand, with many people working in their homes. Around 1750, "cotton" cloth was a mixture of cotton weft and linen warp because the spinning wheel was not capable of producing a pure cotton warp in large quantities. At this time, the trade in these cotton mixtures was well established in England, and a general balance existed between weaving and spinning. This balance was upset when Kay introduced his flying shuttle, which by the 1750s had increased the output of the weavers. Now, spinners could not keep up with the demand because they were still using spinning wheels. The bottleneck was further exacerbated by an increase in home and foreign markets for cloth made of cotton and linen. The problem was obvious to manufacturers: increase the output of the spinners, and wean the market from its dependence on linen.

A major boost to the cotton industry of England and France was government restrictions on the imports of cotton cloth from India. In the latter 1600s, the East India Company began importing into Britain and re-exporting to the Continent inexpensive, brightly-colored Indian calicoes, which quickly became popular, resulting in a decline in woolen demand. The years of 1670-1700 were the boom period for Indian imports. A major appeal of cotton was its ability to take dyes, a process in which domestic workers in India excelled. As early as 1686, France prohibited the import of Indian cotton cloth. At the demand of the woolen industry, the English Parliament restricted imports of dyed calicos in 1710. However, the flow of calico, with its exotic floral designs and—especially—its bright, durable coloring, was not to be stemmed. Even as contraband, these fabrics continued to be all the rage in fashionable European circles during most of the 1700s, keeping the pressure on England to produce all-cotton fabrics.

With Kay's flying shuttle in 1738 and Cartwright's powered loom in 1785, the way was paved for an explosion in cotton manufacturing if suitable supplies of cotton yarn became available. Hargreaves's jenny, introduced in 1767, was best suited for production of cotton weft. These machines (some with eighty spindles on one machine) greatly increased the amount of weft, a valuable contribution to the expansion of the trade.

But it was Arkwright's water frame in 1769 and his carding machine in 1770 that propelled the British cotton industry onto a larger scale. The water frame could produce cotton yarn suitable for the warp. Cotton now replaced linen for the warp. Since the water frame was too large for domestic use, Arkwright and others placed them in factories. The myriad of rivers and streams provided ample water power to run the machines. By 1780, there were fifteen to twenty water-frame factories, either owned by Arkwright and his partners, or by others who paid them for the use of the water frame. Now a factory system was in place to further advance the British cotton trade. When Crompton invented his mule, English-manufactured fine muslins and laces made from sea island cotton entered the British cotton trade. The British trade never looked back.

While the improvements were being made in spinning machines and power looms, two other advances in machines were made that facilitated the burgeoning cotton industry—one local and one overseas.

There were many manufacturers ready to build and operate mills at the turn of the century; however, prime sites with available water power to turn the water wheels to drive the mills were disappearing fast. All the new inventions that seemed to point toward unimaginable prosperity were on hold. The only way to increase the supply of water power was to build new rivers, which was impossible. Enter James Watt.

Steam power had been known since antiquity. But it had never been given any practical application until it was harnessed in 1711 by Thomas Newcomen (1663-1729) to a great, clumsy engine for pumping flood water from a mine. This was his "atmospheric" steam engine, as it came to be called. Improved by the distinguished English engineer John Smeaton from the 1760s, it long provided steam power in England, where fuel was cheap. Then, James Watt was called in to repair a model of Newcomen's monster. From this encounter, Watt developed an interest in steam power. He made a major contribution to the improvement of the steam engine by adding a condenser. From his efforts, the steam engine was first used to drive a cotton mill in 1785. Arkwright replaced water power with steam in his mills in 1790, and by 1800, steam power was recognized as the most desirable source for powering cotton mills. From then on, the different sorts of machinery to which steam could be applied seemed limitless.

In the beginning, wood from the forests was used to drive the steam engines. But the forests were not an infinite supply of fuel, and without another source, the reign of steam power might have ended before it had really begun. But as is often the case, an apparently unrelated event provided an almost endless supply of fuel for steam engines. Sir Humphrey Davy invented a lamp that could be safely operated in coal mines (replacing the gas lamps that often caused explosions of the coal dust). Coal then drove the Industrial Revolution in Great Britain, carrying it to heights that had only recently been a dream.

The next step in the history of the British cotton industry occurred overseas. One reason for the American Revolution was the attempt by Britain to exclude manufactured goods from the colonies, while at the same time levying import taxes on certain goods exported to the colonies. In other words, Britain attempted to keep its American colonies as producers of raw materials (such as raw cotton) for its factories and as consumers of its finished products. But the victory at Yorktown changed this forever. The new United States was on its way to self-sufficiency in manufacturing.

The way was now paved for Eli Whitney to feed the insatiable demand for raw cotton into Britain. In 1793, the southern states produced about 10,000 bales of cotton; by 1810, 177,824 bales were produced. And that was just the beginning.

Although the saw gin did not affect sea island cotton directly, it helped create a demand for cotton goods. Although upland cotton was always the dominant cotton crop worldwide, sea island cotton was swept along with the world's insatiable appetite for pure cotton goods.

LIVERPOOL: GATEWAY TO THE AMERICAN COLONIES

Liverpool men were to be found anywhere there was a chance of trading, or buying or selling, or carrying goods across the seas. And there was a strong link between Liverpool and the United States which went back to the earliest days when the United States were British colonies. Liverpool men were involved in the slave trade, carrying Negroes from Africa to work on southern plantations and the West Indies. Sailing from the River Mersey, Liverpool ships also carried to the thirteen colonies goods such as tools, nails and other items which were not yet manufactured there. They returned to Liverpool with products of the colonies such as tobacco, Virginia pine for ship masts, live oak for ship ribs, and tar and pitch from southern pines for caulking ships and coating ropes.

Liverpool's main attraction was its docks and warehouses, the finest to be found in Great Britain. This was one of the reasons that American ships used this port more than any other. Liverpool developed a "wet dock" system. At high tide, ships sailed into the dock-basin where huge floodgates then closed the entrance. When it was low tide in the River Mersey, the ships were still afloat and could even move from wharf to wharf. The docks often had warehouses and cranes which facilitated loading and unloading. Ships departed at high tide when the water level in the dock and river were the same. In natural harbors, ships were often stranded at low tide. American captains were anxious to make full use of their ships by keeping them on the move, spending as little time as possible in port. Excessive time spent in port meant a loss of revenue.

The first lock built in Liverpool was the Old Dock completed in 1725. The second dock, opened in 1783, was called the Salt House Dock (fig. 11-16) because here ships took on salt for export to the colonies. The third dock was the George Dock, opened in 1771. The Albert Dock opened in 1846, and the Queen's Dock—the one used most frequently by American ships—in 1880. It was through these docks that sea island cotton from South Carolina found its way to the mills of Great Britain.

Liverpool was ideally suited as a port of entrance for cotton from the colonies. Even as early as the 1780s, the city had well-established links with the manufacturing districts which pro-

Figure 11-16. Salt House Dock where sea island cotton was unloaded and sent to mills

duced all the things the colonists wanted to buy. A good network of roads and canals linked Liverpool with the cotton mills of Manchester, Bolton and Glasgow, which needed the raw cotton from the colonies for yarn and cloth manufacturing. The Bridgewater Canal, opened in 1773, connected Manchester and Liverpool, as well as the Mersey-Irwell river system. By the 1840s, steamships were well established in the port and a national network of steam railways linked Liverpool with industrial areas that needed imports of raw materials or exported finished goods.

SEA ISLAND COTTON CLOTHING FOR THE RICH AND NOT-SO-RICH

The date 1790, when the first commercial crop of sea island cotton was planted on Hilton Head Island, coincided with the period in which inventions and improvements to spinning machines could produce high-count yarns. Indeed, it might be argued that if these spinning machines and mechanical looms had been developed two to three decades later, sea island cotton might never have become such an important export crop. Certainly, without Crompton's spinning mule, the demand for the long-staple lint of the sea islands may never have existed.

There is no doubt that the spinners in England knew what quality of sea island cotton they needed. Seabrook reported on a comment by a distinguished Manchester spinner (Seabrook 1827, 397):

Fineness is not the most important requisite, nor only criterion of the value of Sea-Island Cotton. Strength is a quality without which fineness is useless. Fine Cotton, if equally strong with coarse, will make better yarn even at such numbers as the coarse will spin well to, but if the fine Cotton be weak, the reverse is the case. Strong Cotton, however coarse, will make good yarn at some numbers, but weak Cotton, however fine, will never make good yarn.

At the turn of the century came the insatiable demand for the finer textile products made from cotton. Much of this demand was owed to France. When the great industrial revolution began in England with Kay's flying shuttle in 1738, the world did not tire of beauty because a few machines happened to have been invented and perfected in England, and later in the United States. With a few honorable exceptions in England and America, most of the textile designs, in one way or another, originated in France, particularly Paris. During the early years of the new machines until the French Revolution (1789-1815), France had spent her energy in other areas. France had only her craft guilds, a tradition of honest workmanship, and a love of beauty as her salvation. It was not until after 1850 that France again began to take again her place in the industrial and commercial world. Crawford aptly described France's textile industry (Crawford 1924, 196):

She had never exchanged the artisan for the mill hand, never subordinated the artist to the mechanical director. Her small, personally supervised workshops filled with skilled craftsmen, proud of their dexterity, were more flexible mediums for artistic creation than the great mills of her sister democracies.

England and America and indeed the entire industrial world would feed their hungry machines with the ideas that first saw perfection in France. So long as France created, the machines could not become sterile for ideas. France, for almost a century, has been the world's studio.

The beginning of the French Revolution, in 1789, was four years after sea island cotton was established in Georgia and one year before William Elliott produced the first commercial crop on the sea island of Hilton Head on the South Carolina coast. French women, freed from the confines of a repressive feudal system, found new freedom of expression in the thinnest muslins and laces. The demand for these materials spread quickly throughout Europe. High fashion made from fine white cotton fabrics became the vogue.

England was not under the same restraints as France. With an abundant supply of raw cotton from the States, new spinning and weaving machines, and the demand for cotton goods, England found a ready market for its cotton products and became the world's supplier of cotton goods. Upland cotton made it possible for millions of people to wear drawers and chemises where before they had worn nothing but coarse, dirty outer garments.

But it was the long-staple sea island cotton that supplied the upper classes with the finest muslins and laces made from high-count yarns. England exported finished products as well as high-count yarn spun at home to the Continent where it was manufactured into exquisite laces and muslins. Muslin, a plain-weave cotton fabric, came in many grades. But the finest muslins were made from high-count yarns spun from sea island cotton. High-count yarn spun on mules produced strong muslin with a satin-like finish, which was made into the most desirable cloth. The lower-count yarns produced muslin of a more coarse and rough nature that was more affordable for the working classes.

Early on, Whitemarsh Seabrook understood the demand for sea island cotton, and he was influential in promoting sea island planters to produce fine sea island cotton. He stated (1827, 13):

He has also a good prospect of realizing a fair profit on his outlay, from the consumers being in the opulent classes of society. Fashion and pride never undervalue the means of their gratification. The more costly a commodity, the more certain is it to command the homage of an obedient purse.

William Elliott best described the use of sea island cotton (Elliott 1856, 71): "…to be transformed into laces and muslins… clothes with rich draperies… of fashion, or, by a happier destiny, enriches with its gossamer folds the rounded forms of female loveliness, embellishing and heightening what is in itself perfect…"

Thus, the combination of England's industrial revolution, France's artistry, the desire for all-cotton cloth, and the availability of sea island cotton formed a triumphant success that fueled the rise of the plantation system of the Carolina sea islands, and clothed the European upper classes in finery.

At home, to boost the market for sea island cotton overseas, there were attempts to persuade local planters to buy French goods. The St. Andrews Agricultural and Police Society (1844, 44) stated:

A much larger quantity would no doubt be purchased by the French, if the home demand of the finer muslins and laces, manufactured by that nation, were brought back and consumed among us, instead of silk and other articles, with which the Sea-Island grower might well dispense with.

In Great Britain, Scotland quickly became a center for producing the finer counts of yarn for muslins. This was a specialization which developed naturally from the great skill of the linen weavers of Glasgow and Paisley. Accordingly, the transition to the manufacture of high-quality materials of pure cotton was not difficult. Paisley shawls made from sea island cotton acquired international fame. It was also in Paisley that the first cotton sewing thread was made. Indeed, it was in Scotland at Lanarkm in 1790 that water power was first applied to the mule for spinning. In 1778, there were 4,000 linen looms in Glasgow and vicinity, and 3,600 looms weaving silk. Towards the end of the century, there was a rapid change from these activities to the weaving of fine cottons, so that by 1838, there were 15,000 looms so occupied in the Glasgow region. Power looms were slow to spread in Scotland, partly because they were not suitable for weaving the finer yarns. But as power looms were improved to use the finer yarns, they became common in Scotland.

Into this world sprang a variety of firms specializing in the sea island cotton trade with the southern states. Some of them had Charleston connections. One such firm was James Finlay & Company of Scotland. Its role in the sea island cotton trade was outlined by Monica Clough (Clough, 1999). Traders in Scotland had long established trade with the planters of the South, supplying coarse and cheap linen to clothe plantation slaves. After Hargreaves's spinning jenny (1767), cotton weft was mixed with linen warp to produce fustian, a fabric considered inferior, but which found a market in the States. By the late 1700s, with the invention of Whitney's wire-toothed gin and the introduction of sea island cotton into the market, exports of cotton to England increased dramatically. The even power of Arkwright's water frame (1769) allowed for the spinning of yarn strong enough for the warp, and cheap cotton cloth was then produced.

By this time, James Finlay's second son, Kirkman (1772-1842), had become a business partner in the firm. Finlay & Company purchased three spinning mills in Scotland using Arkwright's water frame and the firm began to produce quantities of the highest-count yarns then possible. Then, when mule-spun yarn became available and the sea island cotton trade was established, Kirkman's company specialized in making the finest muslins. In fact, Finlay stated that his firm was one of the first to export fine yarns and cloths to Europe where they found ready markets in

Germany, Italy, France and Switzerland. So important was the supply of sea island cotton to this market that the firm sought to "tie up" imports of sea island cotton. One way for Finlay to ensure adequate supplies of sea island cotton was to establish his own factors in Charleston.

A second firm with a Charleston connection was McConnel-Kennedy and Company of Manchester, Lancashire, England. The cotton industry was already well established in Lancashire by the second half of the 1700s when the technical revolution in spinning and weaving transformed the economic and social structure of the region. By that time, the merchants of Manchester had established for themselves a dominant role in the trade through their control of the raw material and the marketing of the finished product. McConnel-Kennedy's connection in Charleston was through factors which supplied information such as price quotations, freight rates, exchange rates, production estimates, export figures, as well as purchased sea island cotton for the firm. Their factor was Trapmann, Jahncke and Company.

The Trapmann-Jahncke partnership expired in 1882. Lewis Trapmann then formed a new partnership with J. W. Schmidt. From the outset, the firm concentrated on high-count yarn made from sea island cotton; that is, numbers above 100. This was very high since as late as 1833 an estimate of the extent and value of the cotton trade took 40 as the average count. During the war of 1812, McConnel & Kennedy spun up to 200-count yarn, and soon after 1815 they produced yarn up to 250-count. At this time, McConnel-Kennedy was one of two firms that dominated the fine yarn market due to the superior quality of their product.

It was also around this time that sea island cotton planters realized that in order to get the highest price for their crop, it had to be presented much cleaner for the market. Sea island cotton not properly cleaned was suited only for coarse fabrics. As the demand for the long staple became greater, and as the highest prices went to those who carefully handled their cotton, planters were forced to use more painstaking methods. In time, they achieved this goal, and higher prices quickly followed.

DOMESTIC MARKETS FOR SEA ISLAND COTTON

Although the main market for sea island cotton was always foreign, there are early documentations of domestic commercial uses. Bagnall (1893, 273) reported on a factory in Canton, Massachusetts, that produced wickyarn in 1802:

The first work of the factory was the manufacture of wickyarn for the candle-makers. The first lot was made from Sea Island cotton, and was so smooth and handsome that Aaron Davis & Company, of Roxbury, a very prominent firm at that period, gave a large order for it at seventy-five cents per pound. The cotton, which by some means had become stained, had been bought at a low price, for Sea Island cotton, about twenty-four cents per pound. Upland cotton, from Georgia, costing sixteen to eighteen cents per pound, was afterwards used.

Another use of sea island cotton was for sewing thread.[17] In Great Britain, sewing thread from cotton was first produced in 1812 in Paisley, Scotland, the small town where Paisley shawls were made. The first account of American-made sewing thread credits the wife of Samuel Slater[18] of Rhode Island with its creation (Bagnall 1890, 48):

It is a fact, worthy of record in this history, that to Mrs. Slater was due the first suggestion of making, from the cotton fiber, thread for sewing, as a substitute for the linen thread, which had been previously in general use for most of the purposes to which cotton thread is now applied. Her husband, one day, in 1793, showed her some remarkably smooth and even yarn, which had been spun in his factory from Suriman cotton, which, in the length of its staple, and the general character of its fiber, was very similar to the Sea Island cotton of a later period. It occurred to her that it would make good sewing thread, and, with the aid of her sister, she twisted some of it on an ordinary spinning wheel, making No. 20 two-ply thread. On testing it with linen thread in making seams, the cotton thread proved to be the stronger. This, so far as there is record, was the first use of cotton for the purpose, and was the beginning of the manufacture of cotton thread, which, both in Europe and America, has become a very important and extensive industry.

Once Mrs. Slater demonstrated the use of cotton to make thread, manufacturing of cotton thread in the United States commenced. After Elias Howe invented the sewing machine in 1830 with the assistance of a Frenchman, a Mr. Thermonier, and Isaac Singer made improvements to the sewing machine, a demand was created for domestic sewing thread. Some sea island cotton was kept in the States and used to make thread. The longer staple of sea island cotton could be made into stronger thread than upland cotton. A note in the September 5, 1861 *Augusta (Georgia) Daily Chronicle & Sentinel* advertised:

Southern Made Thread.—We have been shown a sample of thread from Sea Island cotton, manufactured at the Sweet Water factory in Campbell County, W. J. Russell Agent. It is a strong, smooth, well-twisted thread, just the thing for use on army work, and will make a very good substitute for Coates' and other "contraband" made in the domestic uses of that article. A sample of this thread may be had in a few days at Gray & Turley's and may now be seen at our office.

The *Natchez Daily Courier* (October 19, 1861) followed up with this comment: "The ladies will undoubtedly find it preferable to the cheating Yankee spools with which they have heretofore been supplied, as a consequence of our unnecessary dependence on the North."

But the use of sea island cotton for sewing thread was very limited. As Robert Allston stated (1854, 18): "A few hundred bags of Sea Island Cotton are manufactured in the United States, chiefly in making spool cotton." The aftermath of the Civil War brought an end to sea island cotton being used for sewing thread.

After the war, a shift occurred in the ratio of domestic and foreign use. Data compiled by the cotton brokerage firm Henry W. Frost & Company of Charleston and Savannah showed a gradual decline in foreign use and a rise in domestic use (see table 13-15). Various factors contributed to the change in markets, of which seed quality was paramount. The war interrupted the seed selection process that had contributed so greatly to the quality of sea island cotton. After the war, fields were much smaller, and numerous planters experimented with upland cotton. Hybridization between the two species resulted in lower fiber quality and thus a lower demand from the specialty overseas market.

Other uses of long-staple cotton emerged in the late 1800s and early 1900s, keeping alive the hopes of a revived sea island cotton industry. New domestic markets developed for use in pneumatic tires, racing sails, mail bags, stockings, fishing line, electrical tape, typewriter cloth, dirigible coverings, parachute cloth, barrage balloons for national defense, and coverings for WWI airplanes. The industry might have survived a decade or two more in the Carolina sea islands, had not the boll weevil ended it in 1920.

A benefactor of the demise of sea island cotton was the Florida and Georgia interior sea island cotton industry. Now a new source of long-staple cotton was available. It was found that upland cotton could not withstand the jerk of the sewing machine, but the long-staple Georgia and Florida cotton was strong enough to withstand it. Gordon stated (1907, 3-4):

Probably every man before me today is indebted to Sea Island cotton for enabling him to maintain a decent and presentable appearance before the world. Your clothes are held together by sewing thread made from Sea Island cotton, and were it in your power at this moment to renounce all dependance upon Sea Island cotton, the stitches would part, your garments would fall from you and the members present would be placed under arrest by the police for indecent exposure.

This source of sewing thread ended in 1920 with the arrival of the boll weevil. On the revival of the Georgia and Florida interior sea island cotton in 1934, this long-staple cotton was used in thread manufacturing. In 1937, two southern mills began spinning sea island cotton: Lily Mills in Shelby, NC, and another mill at Cherryville, NC, operated by a Mr. Rudisill. The latter spun medium-grade 140-count yarn from sea island cotton.

When all is considered, it was from the manufacture of fine muslins and laces that sea island cotton gained its fame. One has only to view and feel a muslin or lace fabric made of mule-spun yarn to appreciate its quality, and to understand why Josephine and other women of the French Revolution drifted about in the finest and thinnest muslin gowns, embroidered with lace, without a stay or hooped petticoat between them.

SEA ISLAND COTTON ARTICLES

In spite of the great number of products made from sea island cotton over its time, very few articles appear to have survived today in museums or other public collections. The Charleston

Museum, the sponsor of this book, and located in the heart of the sea island cotton-growing area, has no articles made of sea island cotton. In the fall of 2003, a notice was sent to Museum members soliciting any articles they might have in their private collections. The responses were negative.

An intensive search was conducted in the United States. Two likely sources were the Smithsonian Institution in Washington and the Cooper-Hewitt National Design Museum in New York. Neither had any articles labeled as sea island cotton. Numerous mill museums in the states of Rhode Island, Connecticut and Massachusetts, the heart of the 1800s cotton mill region, were visited by the author with fruitless results.

In the summer of 2003, the author traveled to England to do research on sea island cotton. One goal of the trip was to look in museums there for articles made from sea island cotton. In London, the Victoria and Albert and the British Museum were visited. Neither of these had any articles made of sea island cotton. No organization in Manchester or Liverpool was located with articles of sea island cotton in its archives.

At the Quarry Bank Mill in Styal, Cheshire, North West England, are four cotton christening gowns that were donated to the mill. On the box was a notation that the donor believed that one of the gowns was made of sea island cotton, but there was no label inside identifying which one it was. Curator Caroline Hill showed the gowns to the machine demonstrator of the mill, who identified one that could possibly be made from sea island cotton.

At the Bolton Museum & Art Gallery in Bolton, Lancashire, England, Angela Thomas, Keeper of Egyptology & Archaeology, located three white muslin dresses and an evening gown dated to around 1820-30. There was no indication as to whether or not they were made of sea island cotton. In a following email, Thomas wrote: "My contact Allan Lord, who worked in the cotton textile industry, would certainly know raw sea island cotton, but recognizing it in a woven piece might be more difficult. A thread would be needed for microscopic examination, which one could probably get from a cloth sample, but might be harder from a made-up garment."

As the authenticity of articles from these two locations was questionable, the author decided not to photograph either for this book. At least future researchers on sea island cotton will have these sources to investigate further.[19]

One item did surface locally. Descendants of sea island cotton planter Edward Mitchell have several items from the Charleston and West Indian Exposition of 1901-02, including a piece of Valenciennes lace made in France from sea island cotton from Point of Pines Plantation, Edisto Island (Plate 11-1). The owner of Point of Pines was Julian Mitchell, son of Dr. Edward Mitchell of Frogmore Plantation; he received the following award for his sea island cotton in 1907 from which the lace was made:

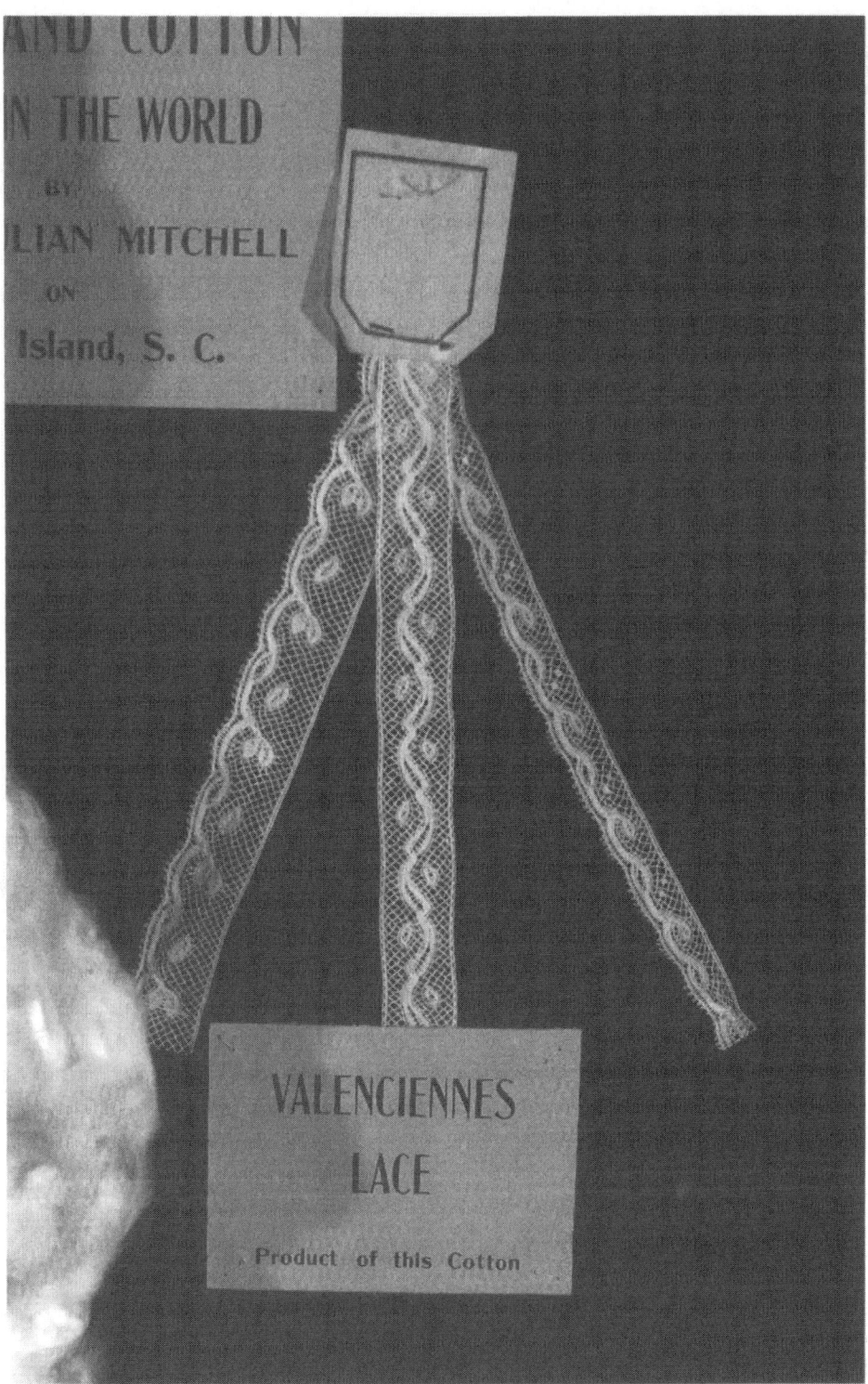

Plate 11-1. Sea Island Cotton lace

THE TEXTILE INDUSTRY AND SEA ISLAND COTTON

Jamestown Exposition
Norfolk, Virginia
Gold Medal
Awarded to Julian Mitchell
Charleston, SC
For Excellence in Long Staple Cotton
by the Jury of Awards
1907

1. Cloth is a material formed by weaving, knitting, pressing or felting of natural or synthetic fibers. If the fibers used are cotton, it is called cotton cloth.
2. Carding is the process where the staple is opened, cleaned, the fibers aligned, and formed into a continuous, untwisted strand called the sliver.
3. Spinning of yarn consists of two steps: attenuating or increasing the length per unit weight of slivers or rovings (drafting or drawing), and then twisting the drawn-out strands to produce strength to the finished yarn.
4. There is little doubt that from the literature hand spinning was done by ancient peoples. Whether that followed the method here described is speculation.
5. The distaff is a staff having a cleft end that holds the unspun fiber.
6. The spindle is the long slender pin by which its turning motion twist the thread into yarn, then onto which the yarn is wound for storage.
7. Fiber length was critically important only with the marriage of cotton to machine power. Until the end of the 18th century, while cotton was spun by simple hand- or human-powered machines, the length of fiber determined the convenience of spinning but was not critically important to the spinning process. Spinners preferred long cotton fibers because they were easier to use (Roberts 1965, 43).
8. The whorl is a small flywheel, that, once set in motion, regulates the speed of the primite spindle or a spinning wheel.
9. A hank is a unit of length. For cotton, a hank was 840 yards. Cotton yarn spun to a count of 80 (written normally as "80's, or as 80 count) meant that 80 individual hanks (or 67,200 yards of yarn) could be produced from one pound of cotton. The special qualities of sea island cotton allowed it to be spun into an individual hank extremely strong and fine; accordingly, more hanks could be produced from a pound of sea island cotton than from any other cotton.
10. Anthony Burton, for one, in his *The Rise and Fall of King Cotton* (1984) disputes this version of Hargreaves's for the inspiration for his invention. He stated that Hargreaves had already produced a successful carding machine, and with encouragement from a successful and ambitious entrepreneur (Robert Peal), "…Hargreaves needed no accident to persuade him to turn his mind to the problem of a spinning machine."
11. By the time spinning was done on machines, another step of preparing the cotton for spinning had to be developed if clothing was to be made from fine yarns. The process was called combing. Combing was just a continuation and refinement of the carding process. Short fibers were eliminated from the sliver; the sliver was drawn several times, which reduced its size; the fibers were laid more

parallel; it was given a slight twist; and it was then called the roving and wound onto bobbins. From the bobbins, the roving was fed into the spinning machine.

12. A cop is a cylindrical package of yarn on the spindle with conical ends, so constructed that the yarn may be withdrawn substantially axially from one of the conical ends without rotation of the spindle. A cop is diagrammed in figure 11-9.

13. A self-acting mule was a semi-automatic mule developed through the labour of several keen mechanics, chiefly Richard Roberts, a Manchester millwright (1789-1864). His design of 1830 found wide acceptance at the time and established the basic principles on which self-actors were to be build for more than a century. With the self-acting mule, several thousand spindles could be worked in a single room with little attention. By 1837 more than 500,000 spindles were in use. By the end of the nineteenth century highly complex self-actors were able to spin even the highest counts of yarn.

14. In the New World, according to Stephens and Mosley (1974, 111), the heddle was used as early as 1800 or 1700 BC.

15. The source of this diagram, according to Agnus Geijer (1979, 21), is from a petition to the Pope written in about 1600 by Don Felipe de Ayala, a high-ranking prince of the Incas and probably the only member of his class to have survived the cruelties perpetrated by the Spaniards during their conquest of Peru.

16. Calico (from Calicut, India) is a printed cotton fabric that originated in India. At first, London directors dared not to import calico, but from 1660 onwards, the demand for Indian calicos increased enormously, the years of 1670-1700 the boom period. Even the Act of 1707, limiting the import of Indian fabrics to protect the home textile industry, could not stop the flow of calicos into England because it entered as contraband.

17. Thread is made by twisting together several individual lengths of yarn. If a six-ply thread is to be made, six strands of yarn are twisted together. Different types of thread were made by not varying the ply, but in the methods of twisting.

18. Samuel Slater migrated from England in 1790, and built a factory at Pawtucket, Rhode Island, that embodied the coveted English inventions. It was the first in the United States; the year was 1793.

19. One area the author did not have time to investigate was Glasgow, Scotland. Sea island cotton was sent to Glasgow and nearby Paisley. Both were centers of manufacture of goods made of sea island cotton. A search of museums in these cities might turn up articles of interest to future researchers.

Insect, Pests and Diseases of Sea Island Cotton

Agricultural crops throughout history have been subjected to a variety of insect pests and diseases. Cotton grown on the sea islands of South Carolina and adjacent Georgia was no exception. Almost from the first plantings of the crop, various diseases and pests were a constant problem. Whitemarsh Seabrook (1827, 7) wrote:

The cotton crop of 1825, long before it had attained its maturity, was denuded of its foliage and tender bark, by the devastations of the caterpillar. The necessary consequence was an instantaneous cessation of its generative power.

Thomas Spalding (1835, 41) also spoke of the destruction of the caterpillar:

The full moon in the month of August too, is the time when the caterpillar is expected. We have seen four hundred acres of cotton that looked promising and well to day, that four days afterwards had not a green leaf, and scarcely a small pod remaining upon it.

And Spalding wrote of the cut-worm (1835, 40):

The cock chaffer or cut-worm is to be apprehended during the month of April, and as the cotton comes through the ground and remains for several days, like the pea or other pulse, with but two radical leaves, every one of the plants that are cut by the worm, either above or below the ground, are destroyed; so that it is not unfrequent that whole fields have to be replanted in the month of May; about which time the worms pass into their winged state.

Seabrook, in his "Memoir on the Cotton Plant" (1844a, 45-46), summed up the state of pests and diseases for the first half of sea island cotton growing:

INSECTS, PEST AND DISEASES OF SEA ISLAND COTTON

It has been well said by a judicious observer that, of all the productions to which labour is applicable, the cotton plant, more particularly the species grown on the Sea-Islands, is the most precarious. In its first stage it is attacked by the grub; it is devoured by bugs in the second; and by caterpillars in the third; it is often withered by the wind in its infancy, and by the blight in maturer age; and when the grower, excited by all the causes which hope so kindly presents to his ardent imagination, is about to reap the golden harvest, an equinoxial gale, or a few saturating showers, deprive him at once of the fruits of his labours, and bid him to reassume the toils and vexations of his vocation.

How a planter coped with these problems, either individually or collectively with other planters, determined, in part, his success. Various local, state, and federal agricultural organizations were formed that assisted the planters in all aspects of cotton growing, including the means to cope with insects and diseases. The U.S. Department of Agriculture (USDA), the Agricultural Society of South Carolina (founded in 1785 and which continues today), the Black Oak Agricultural Society of St. John's Parish, Berkeley County, and the James Island Agricultural Society all sought to inspire agriculturists of the state, among them sea island planters, to develop better agricultural practices, including confronting diseases and insect pests. It appears, however, that adequate pest and disease control methods were not available to sea island cotton planters for most of the 1800s and many crops were lost as a result.

The early planters received advice from agronomists such as Edmund Ruffin, who reported in the *Farmers Journal*:

Every plant is subject to be preyed on by its own peculiar tribes of insects, which are continued to be supplied by their proper food, and favored by the still continuing circumstances of the field, and therefore are increased continually in numbers, and in their destructive ravages, as long as the crop which fed them, and the circumstances which favored them, remained unchanged; and that these insects must be destroyed or greatly reduced in their numbers and power of mischief, by a total change of the growth, and of the treatment of the field.

Although there were many diseases and insects that caused damage to sea island cotton, the following appear to have caused the major damage. There were certainly others, but either they were not a serious problem, or they were not documented. Some of these pests and diseases still infect commercial cottons throughout the world today, but modern means of eradication or control have greatly lessened or eliminated their damage.

Insect Pests

Cutworms

The USDA *Bulletin* Number 33 (1896, 343) gave an account of cutworms that plagued cotton crops, both upland and sea island, and vegetable crops in general in the South. The

Bulletin stated: "The first insect which attacks the young cotton plant in the spring is liable to be a cutworm." The cutworms hid beneath the ground surface by day and came out at night to feed on the young plants. Normally, they cut the plant stem close to the ground. The USDA considered it likely that the species of cutworm most common on cotton crops was the larvae of *Feltia annexa* Treitschke, but reported that other species also infested cotton and other crops, all with a similar habit.

The USDA also listed remedies that could have been used against cutworms, including traps poisoned with Paris Green.[1] Nothing in the literature indicates which methods of eradication, if any, were used against the cutworms by sea island cotton planters.

Cotton Caterpillar

The cotton caterpillar (*Aletia argillacea* Hübner)[2] plagued the sea island planters from the beginning of the industry. It was also called the cotton worm or cotton leafworm. Burden (1844b, 208) reported that as early as 1802, 1804, 1822 and 1825, the caterpillar made its appearance in the sea islands. The slender, bluish-green caterpillar (fig. 12-1a) with small black spots, and often with black stripes down its back, fed voraciously on both the upper and lower surfaces of the cotton leaf. In seasons of abundance (a warm winter followed by a wet spring), plants were entirely defoliated. According to the USDA *Bulletin* Number 33 (1896, 320-328), up to the year 1881, the damage done by the cotton caterpillar far exceeded that inflicted by any other species.

The life cycle started as the female moth (fig. 12-1b) laid eggs on the underside of a leaf at night in midsummer. Three to four days after the eggs were laid, they hatched into the caterpillar (larva) stage. After five molts, which took from one to three weeks, depending on the weather, the caterpillar reached full growth. The mature caterpillar then spun a light silken web, forming an imperfect cocoon, usually within a folded leaf. This pupa stage (fig. 12-1c) lasted from one to four weeks, and at last produced an olive-gray moth. In about four days, the female commenced to lay eggs, and could lay as many as six hundred during her life. After five generations of caterpillar-to-moth in one season, untold damage was done to a single field. In the extreme southern region of the cotton caterpillar's range (which included the sea islands), the moth hibernated during the winter and remained torpid in sheltered places, ready to begin the cycle the following spring.

Planters such as William Elliott and Robert Chisolm observed that the cotton caterpillar did not visit the sea islands annually. Chisolm (1875, 7-9) wrote:

Before the [Civil] war, the appearance of the worms might pretty regularly be expected every third year, except on a few plantations on St. Helena Island, where they seemed to come every year… Every twenty-one years they prevailed extensively, and, generally, cut off our crops almost entirely. They first prevailed generally in 1804, but as they disappeared after the great gale of that year, it was generally supposed that they were either blown away or destroyed. They appeared occasionally

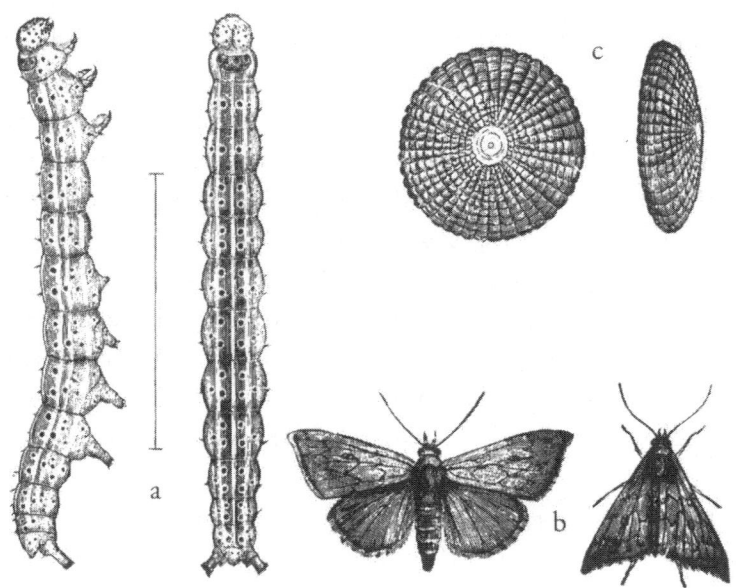

Figure 12-1a-c. Cotton caterpillar (Brooks 1898, 177)

until 1825, when they swept everything before them. From 1825 to 1846, they made their appearance pretty regularly every third year, frequently only to disappear again almost immediately; but in 1846, they came in such crowds that they swept our cotton crops just as if a fire had passed ever them.

Chisolm (and others) concluded that the reason the caterpillars occured generally every three years was that the pupa or chrysalis stage could not survive the cold winters of the sea islands. Instead, they escaped extermination by overwintering where there was not enough cold weather to destroy them. It then took three years for them to increase to such numbers as to be obliged to seek new and more northern fields for a food supply. They planters reasoned that Florida, without cold winters, was the ideal site for the moths to overwinter. It was only about a month after caterpillars were observed in Florida that the moths reached the sea islands.

The planters were accurate in observing that the caterpillar came periodically and did not overwinter in the sea islands; today, more is known about its life cycle. An essay by Leonard, Graves and Ellsworth, in Smith and Cothren (1999, 513), explains:

Cotton leafworm, Alabama argillacea Hübner, is a tropical insect that was a serious defoliating pest of cotton in the Gulf coast states of Louisiana, Texas and Mississippi until the 1940s. Outbreak populations have not occurred in several years probably due to being inadvertently controlled by insecticides used against other pests. The insect does not overwinter in the United States and immigrates to the United States annually.

Planters in the Santee long cotton region also had to contend with caterpillars. Charles St. George Sinkler of Belvidere Plantation in Upper St. John's Parish wrote to his fiancée Anne Wickham Porcher on September 20, 1883: "I am sorry to say that Mr. John Stoney's prophecy has been correct and the Caterpillars have attacked two of my fields with great ferocity and there is now hardly a leaf in one of them. I believe these terrible worms have injured the Middle St. John's planters more than they have us."[3] Although he did not state whether it was his Santee long or upland cotton that was infected (he planted both at Belvidere), it is likely that both crops suffered.

According to Seabrook (1844a, 43-44), the first recorded attempt to eradicate caterpillars by a sea island planter was employed by John Townsend of St. John's, Colleton:

By the adoption of prompt and vigorous measures, some of which are new, and a rigid perseverance in their execution, his crop escaped unscathed, while many of his fellow-labourers, who lacked faith in any remedy, suffered greatly. In the attainment of his purpose, the means resorted to by Mr. Townsend were the following:

1. His people searched for and killed both the worm and the chrysalis of the first brood.
2. On the appearance of the second brood, he scattered corn over the field to invite the notice of the

birds, and while they depredated on the worms on the tops of the stalks and their upper limbs, the turkeys destroyed the enemy on the lower branches.

3. When in the aurelia state, the negroes crushed them between their fingers.

4. Some patches of cotton, where the caterpillars were very thick, and the birds and turkeys could not get access to them, were destroyed.

5. The tops of the plants, and the ends of all the tender and luxuriant branches, where the eggs of the butterfly are usually deposited, were cut off.

Since the cotton caterpillar, unlike the bollworms, did not bore into a cotton boll where it was somewhat protected from pesticides, eradication using Paris Green was effective on the caterpillar. Johnson (1930, 66) stated that sea island cotton planters learned before 1860 that they could combat the caterpillar by dusting the plants with Paris Green, but that method was not common knowledge until much later. It was reported in the *News and Courier Book Presses* (1880) that the "Sea Island planters no longer took the caterpillar into serious account, and do not dread it coming. Thorough drainage and the application of various mineral compounds to the growing plant have reduced the injury done by the caterpillar." It appears, then, that toward the end of sea island cotton planting, methods were in place to adequately eradicate the cotton caterpillar. But the planter of the antebellum period knew little to do but curse the fate which sent the caterpillars.

American Bollworm

Kohel and Lewis (1984, 266-283) stated that the American bollworm was one of six insect species that caused the majority of losses to cotton worldwide, and that control measures against the American bollworm (*Heliothis armigera* Hübner) were being carried out in twenty-four countries worldwide in 1984. However, despite its worldwide range, no mention was found in the literature to indicate that the bollworm was known to sea island cotton planters. If it did infect sea island cotton, it was not recognized, or was mistaken for another malady. The author mentions this insect to avoid its possible confusion with the Mexican cotton-boll weevil.

Mexican Cotton-Boll Weevil

The losses caused by the boll weevil were both direct and indirect, and ultimately extended throughout the entire financial and economic structure of the United States Cotton Belt, which consisted of upland cotton (*Gossypium hirsutum*) and the various cultivars of long-staple cotton (*Gossypium barbadense*). Upland cotton recovered and is the world's major textile crop today. The long-staple cottons grown in the American southwest also recovered; however, true sea island cotton grown primarily on the sea islands of South Carolina and Georgia never recovered from the effects of the boll weevil. Planting of true sea island cotton virtually ended in 1920. Although there were attempts to revive it in the 1930s in the Carolina sea islands, they were not successful. As sea island cotton required a long growing season, matured late in the fall, and was a large plant, giving the insect many times to complete its life cycle and spread, it was especially liable to damage from the ravages of the boll weevil. Modern methods of eradication came too late to save sea island cotton.

The Mexican cotton-boll weevil is not a native of the United States. Scientifically known as *Anthonomus grandis* Boheman, its native home was the plateau region of Mexico and Central America. About 1892, the boll weevil crossed the Rio Grande near Brownsville, Texas, either by flying or in ginned cotton seed at Brownsville. At first, the advance of the insect was comparatively slow, and for the first ten years damage was practically confined to Texas. Later, however, the weevil spread rapidly, especially through the cotton-growing areas east of the Mississippi. By the end of 1922, 614,213 square miles of land in the United States had been infested by the boll weevil. Figure 12-2 shows the dramatic spread of this insect. The boll weevil reached the sea islands of South Carolina around 1917, and by 1920, sea island cotton planting ended.

The boll weevil's devastation is clearly demonstrated by the figures for the number of bales of sea island cotton produced in the 1919-20 and 1920-21 seasons. In 1919-20, 3,030 bales were produced; in 1920-21, only 265 bales were produced.

Bubberson Brown, in an interview chronicled by Nick Lindsay (2000, 121) in his book *And I'm Glad: An Oral History of Edisto Island*, lamented the arrival of the boll weevil: "The boll weevil had come in about nineteen eighteen. He bite that long staple cotton—eat him, rot him right on down. Can't nobody nor nothing stop him. The thing get bad, then it got worse, and while I was up in New York, the long cotton run out entirely. The boll weevil came in force and he prevented that crop altogether."

The adult boll weevil (fig. 12-3a) is about 1/4 inch long. The adult stage is a beetle and it passed the winter in this stage under trash in or near a cotton field, or flew into adjacent woods, hedges, farm buildings or haystacks. In every cotton field in the South, they could be seen flying about in spring. As soon as the first flower buds (squares) were formed, the beetles, using their hard snouts, bored holes into young flower buds, and deposited eggs in the cavities formed by eating into the bud.

The eggs hatched in about three days and the larva or grub (figs. 12-3c and 12-4) immediately began to feed on the interior substance of the bud. By the time the larva reached full growth, it had made a cell large enough to accommodate itself. In about 7 to 12 days, the larva passed into the pupa stage (fig. 12-3b), corresponding to the cocoon of moths and butterflies. The cell was generally made next to the outer wall of the bud so that the weevil, when transformed, had only to make its way through this thin wall to escape.

The pupa stage lasted from three to five days. Then the adult beetle emerged, and in about five days, began the production of another generation, infecting new buds and bolls that had formed. As there are three or four generations of weevils each year, one pair of weevils could produce hundreds of thousands of progeny. In issuing from the boll, it left a small hole in the wall of the boll, which marked the infected boll.

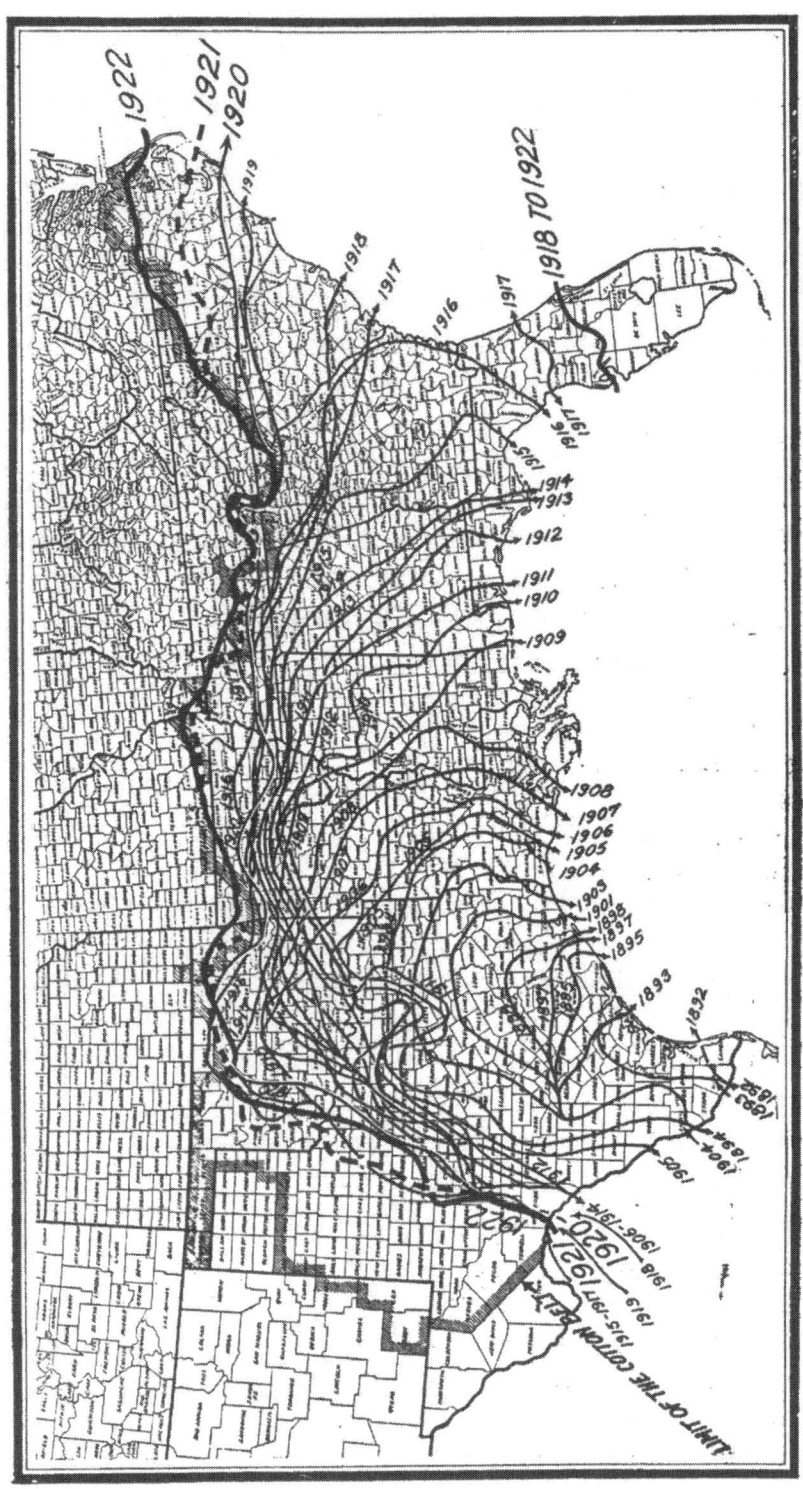

Figure 12-2. Spread of the boll weevil (Hunter 1923, 3)

CHAPTER TWELVE

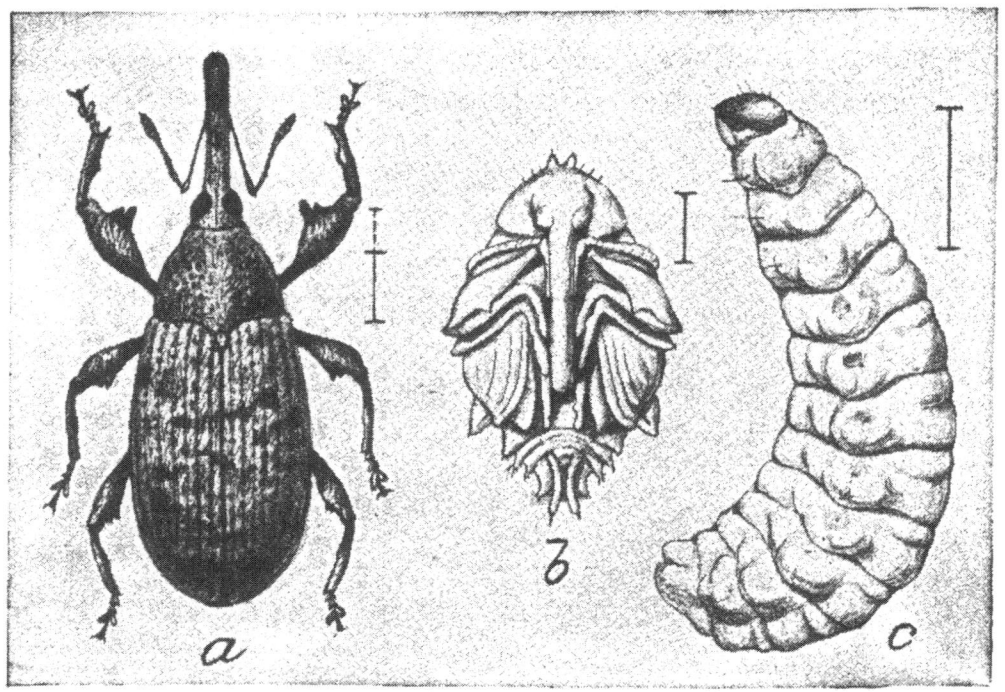

Figure 12-3a-c. Life stages of the boll weevil (Brooks 1898, 187)

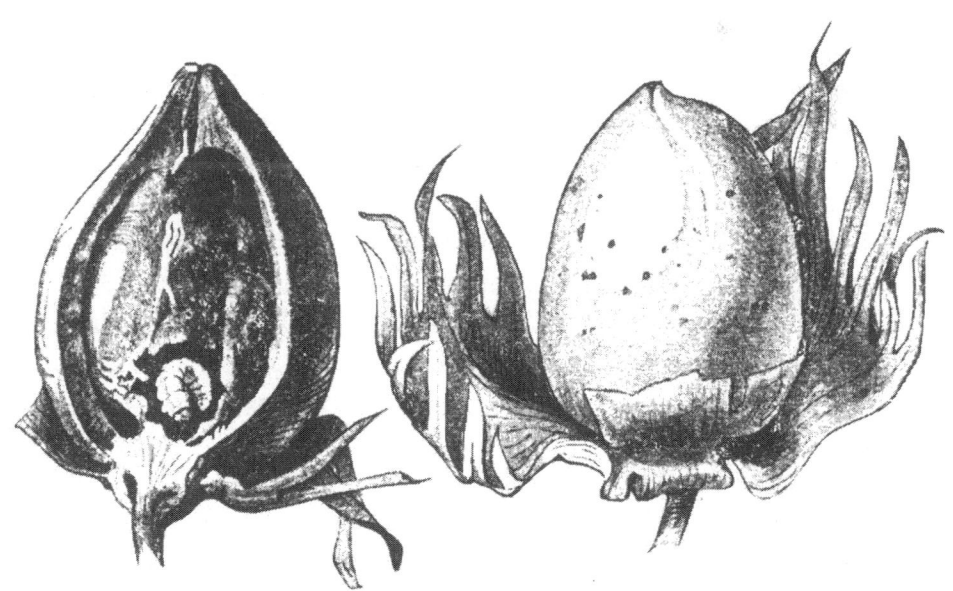

Figure 12-4 Mature boll cut open showing full-grown larva

The damage to the plant was threefold: (1) young flower buds punctured by the weevil failed to develop flowers, (2) young infected bolls dropped from the plant, and (3) some of the cotton in older bolls was badly stained and damaged and the value of the cotton fiber greatly deteriorated.

Sea island cotton was also more susceptible to damage from the boll weevil than upland cotton because of the morphology of its bolls. The full-grown bolls of some of the upland varieties have a thick wall and a tough lining of the chambers which render the adult bolls more resistant to the weevils. However, the walls of the bolls of sea island cotton are thinner and softer, and do not reach a stage of hardening that protects them from weevil injury. The sea island bolls were susceptible through their entire period of development. Furthermore, sea island cotton was more susceptible to boll weevils because of its longer growing period.

The sea islands were especially prone to the weevil for other natural reasons as well. Throughout most of the Cotton Belt, when infested buds fell to the ground, they became so hot that the larvae were killed quickly. The insect in the larval stage had no way to leave the bud since the larvae had no locomotion. However, in the sea islands, where precipitation was heavy and provided a cooling effect, many larvae survived in the fallen buds.

The Agricultural Society of South Carolina attempted to keep the boll weevil from the sea islands. In 1917, the Society offered a prize of ten dollars a bushel for the earliest ten bushels of sea island cotton seed produced in Charleston County. The idea was that early-maturing cotton would beat the boll weevil to it. It was stipulated that the seed had to be delivered before September 1. The Society's prize was won by T. J. Hamlin, who delivered his cotton seed on August 28. Hamlin's seed was distributed in half-bushel lots by the society to the planters. The experiment was ultimately futile since the boll weevil ended sea island cotton growing in 1920 despite the early-maturing cotton.

In an attempt to preserve the sea island cotton industry, the U.S. Department of Agriculture also endeavored to develop earlier-maturing strains of sea island cotton that would yield profitable crops in the presence of the boll weevil. This effort also failed. More success was attained by substituting an early-maturing upland variety known as Meade, which, under favorable conditions, produced a lint with a staple of 1 11/16 inches in length, of fine texture and quality, and closely resembling sea island cotton. As the Meade cotton had smooth seeds, it could be ginned with a roller gin. With the same care to harvesting and ginning as that bestowed by the planters on sea island cotton, Meade cotton was readily accepted on the market on a par with sea island cotton, which it resembled so closely it could be distinguished only by experts.

Meade originated from a selection made in 1912 in a field of Black Rattler cotton in Texas. Continued seed selection lead to the superior Meade cotton. Test plots of Meade were conducted on Swinton Whaley's plantation on James Island in 1916. Favorable results from this planting led to small commercial plantings the following season at several points in Georgia. For the next five years that Meade was grown in the southeastern states, it continued to demonstrate its value as a substitute for sea island cotton.

The early success of the Meade variety turned to failure, almost before it had been able to prove its value. Two scientists at the USDA laid the demise of the Meade variety on the persistent planting of sea island and short-staple cotton in the same localities with Meade. Planters never did understand the necessity of complete isolation of the fields and separate ginning of the cotton to maintain the purity of the seed stocks and the uniformity of the fiber. Careless ginning (which resulted in mixing of the seeds) and hybridization with upland and sea island cotton rendered it impossible to secure the fiber quality required by manufacturers. When spinners rejected the product, planters abandoned Meade cotton.

Fungi and Bacteria

Bacterial Blight

Kohel and Lewis (1984, 295) reported that before the development of resistant cultivars, bacterial blight, also known as angular leaf spot and blackarm, was historically the most important cotton disease in the world. This disease is still one of the most signifcant bacterial diseases of cotton today, but is rapidly declining due to modern methods of eradication and control.

Blight was known to the sea islands early in cotton culture. Whitemarsh Seabrook (1844a, 45) wrote, "The blast or blight is now, perhaps, the most common of all the diseases to which cotton is liable. Its tendency is to check or destroy the vegetative powers of the plants."

According to Orton (1907, 41-43), bacterial blight was caused by *Xanthomonas campestris* pv *malvacearum*,[4] which occurred on different parts of the plant, produced various symptoms and was identified as angular leaf-spot, black-arm, boll-spot, etc. according to the part of the cotton attacked. The earliest appearance was on the leaves, producing spots (angular-leaf spot) that were at first a water-soaked green, turning black when older. Infection of the stem and boll followed. Defoliation occurred with extensive infection. Infection of the stem weakened it so that winds or cultivation caused the plant to fall over. The most damage occurred in the summer, when the disease attacked the fruit-bearing limbs. The vitality of the plant was sapped, causing the shedding of smaller bolls. A secondary result of bacterial blight was the infection of anthracnose that gained entry through the bacterial spots.

Orton wrote that remedial measures had to be indirect. Since the bacterium survived in infested seed and in dry residues of diseased plants left on the field surface, diversification and rotation of crops would reduce infection; also, selection of seed from only healthy bolls would greatly aid in its control. To what degree sea island planters practiced remedial procedures, either early in the crop history or later when Orton and agronomists had come to understand the life cycle of the blight and suggested remedies, is not known.

Sore-Shin

Sore-shin was caused by the soil fungus *Rhizoctonia solani* Kuehn. The fungus normally infected the cotton plant after cold or wet weather had reduced growth and weakened the plant. If warm and favorable weather prevailed, the plant outgrew the disease. Symptoms included spots or cankers on the stem or root of the seedling. The spots resulted in a cessation of growth, yellow leaves, and in death if they circled the stem. It does not appear from the literature that sore-shin was a major disease of sea island cotton.

Orton (1907, 41) stated that no direct remedies were practicable, but crop loss could be minimized by thorough preparation of the land before planting, by drainage, and by thick seeding.

Anthracnose

Anthracnose (or pink boll rot) was caused by a parasitic fungus (*Colletotrichum gossypii* Southworth) first described in 1890. The greater part of loss from rotting of sea island cotton bolls was caused by this disease (also called "boll rot" by some planters). Anthracnose occurred as dark-colored spots on the bolls, which enlarged and became depressed and gray or pink in the center (fig. 12-5). The cotton fiber in the bolls became discolored and spoiled. "Yellow cotton" was cotton fiber discolored in the boll by the anthracnose boll rot. It was important that this fiber be removed before the whipping since whipping would mix the good and the yellow, making it difficult to separate during the moting. The disease was worse in wet seasons.

Orton (1907, 47) stated that no practicable remedy was available because of the expense, so sea island cotton farmers had to rely on preventive measures. Since the disease was spread in part by seed from infected plants, the seed for the next year's crop was selected from healthy plants. Also, the planters learned to avoid running the selected cotton seed through a roller gin that had just handled diseased cotton unless the gin had been thoroughly cleaned. Finally, after the crop was picked, the old cotton stalks were burned.

Fusarium Wilt or Cotton Wilt

Fusarium wilt, or cotton wilt, was caused by the fungus *Fusarium oxysporum* f. sp. *vasinfectum* (Atkinson) Snyder & Hansen.[5] Orton (1907, 43-46) gave an extensive discourse on the disease, and the following description draws from his work:

Fusarium wilt was one of the most serious diseases of sea island cotton and was characterized by the death of the plants in gradually enlarging areas in a field where the disease reappeared each year. The plants were attacked any time after being a month old; however, plants died faster in June and July. The brown or black discoloration of the stem or root interior, one of the most characteristic symptoms of the disease, gave it another name: black-root.

Fusarium wilt was most prevalent on sandy loam soils that were characteristic of the sea islands. It also affected upland cotton fields from North Carolina to Louisiana. Clay soils were relatively free of wilt, as were low spots and rich bottom lands. Orton emphasized that wilt was caused by a soil fungus, and not by unfavorable soil conditions.

The fungus entered the roots from the soil, growing upward through the xylem (water-carrying vessels) of the roots and stem and blocking the water supply to the plant, thus causing wilting of the leaves and ultimate death of the plant. The fungus spread by direct growth

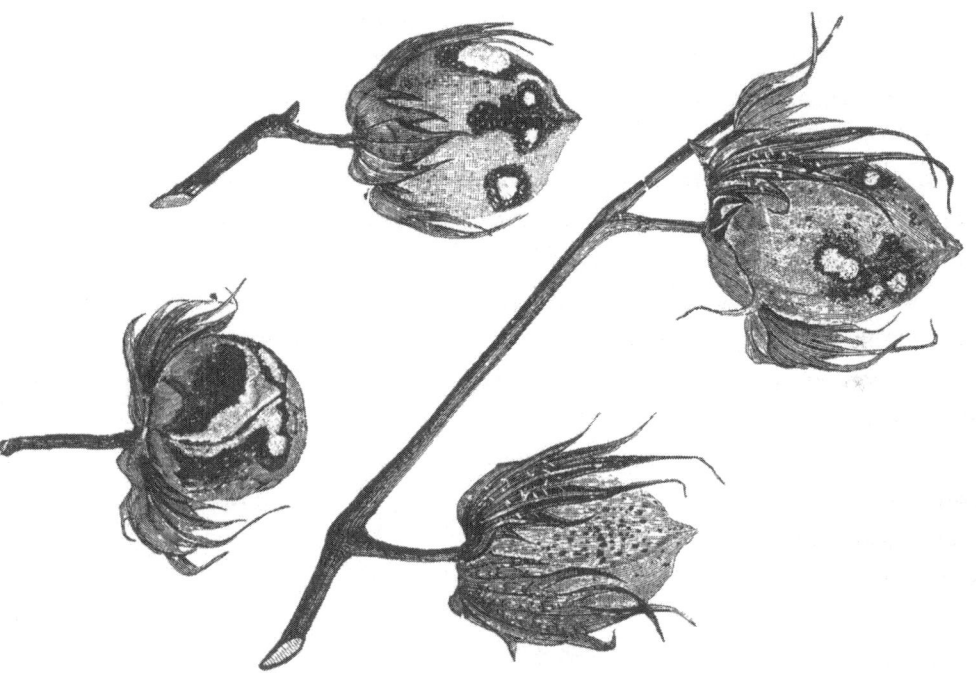

Figure 12-5. Anthracnose (Brooks 1898, 169)

through the soil and from spores. Orton indicated that it was impossible to kill the fungus in the soil by any treatment of fungicides that were known prior to 1907. Even rest or rotation of a field was not a solution, since the fungus could live in the soil for years.

Unknown at the time of sea island cotton growing was the synergistic relationship between wilt and root-knot nematodes. Wilt occurred in somewhat acid, coarse-textured soils also favored by root-knot nematodes. Scientists believe today that the most likely reason for the nematodes' enhancing wilt is a physiological interaction between the fungus, the nematode and the plant. The most important element in this interaction is the nematode; when nematodes are controlled, or nematode resistance is incorporated into cotton culture, wilt is greatly diminished.

It was found, however, that seed selection could produce varieties that were resistant to wilt. Rivers Sea Island Cotton originated in cooperation with the U.S. Department of Agriculture's Dr. W. A. Orton and Mr. Elias Lynch Rivers of James Island. In 1899, Rivers found one healthy plant in a field badly affected with wilt. He saved the seed from this plant, and planted the seeds the next year in a single row in a badly-infected area. In the resistant row not a single plant died, while the adjoining rows planted with ordinary seed were almost totally destroyed. Sufficient seed from this row was obtained and an acre was planted the next year (1901). Sufficient seed from this acre was obtained and fifteen acres were planted in 1902 which proved as resistant as the previous year.

Dr. Orton went to South Carolina and joined Mr. Rivers in the selection process, and as a result of this work, the wilt-resistant Rivers Sea Island Cotton was released. Through the auspices of the Department of Agriculture, the Rivers Sea Island Cotton seed was made available to other planters. Ultimately, however, the Rivers cultivar fell to the onslaught of the boll weevil.

Nematodes

Root-Knot

Root-knot was caused by the sedentary endoparasitic soil nematode *Meloidogyne incognita* Chitwood.[6] Orton (1907, 46-47) said that root-knot was a common and widely distributed disease in sandy soils throughout the southern tier of states. The nematode penetrated the roots and lived within, causing distortion of the cotton roots and resulting in their being covered with small swellings or knots. The effect on the plant was to lessen its vigor and dwarf its size, thus reducing yield. Root-knot was an even more deleterious organism when combined with wilt.

The only remedy apparently available to sea island cotton planters against root-knot was crop rotation.

Soil Conditions

Two ailments of sea island cotton plants, rust and blue cotton, were described by Orton (1907, 47-48). Both were caused by poor soil conditions.

Blue Cotton

Blue cotton was a condition which occurred to a limited extent in the sea islands and in Florida. It was noted early on by the sea island planters, as Burden reported (1844b, 208): "There was, however, another disease less extensive, which some planters named the 'blue rust,' and which was developed in what are called 'alum spots.'"

The leaves turned a deep-green or bluish color, the plants became prostrate, and the fruits shed. This condition was caused by poor soil, which was remedied by the use of salt-marsh mud, liming and proper drainage.

Rust

As early as 1844, rust was known to sea island cotton planters. Burden (1844b, 207-208) stated in an answer to a query: "The common rust, caused by an impoverished soil, and in some cases, by the opposite extremes of excessive hot dry [weather], or excessive wet weather, prevailed very much, and was the only formidable disease the cotton plant was subject to for many years."

Rust was not caused by a fungus, but by unfavorable soil conditions. Symptoms were the dropping of leaves and the upper bolls not opening. Lint from infected plants was weak and inferior. Three factors were mainly responsible for cotton rust in the sea islands: (1) exhaustion of soil humus by continued cultivation, (2) deficiency of potash, and (3) lack of drainage.

Rotation of crops, the addition of stable manure, and the application of potash alleviated the first two conditions. Drainage of fields by ditching and tiles had to be done in extremely wet areas. In more moderate conditions, deep plowing, rotation with leguminous crops (turned under) and the addition of stable manure conditioned the soil so that heavy rains would not cause stagnation of the soil, and the rust could thus be eliminated.

---

1. Paris Green is a poisonous emerald-green powder used as a pigment, wood preserver, and insecticide.
2. *Aletia argillacea* Hübner in today's taxonomy (Smith and Cothren 1999, 513) is *Alabama argillace* Hübner.
3. The letters between Sinkler and Anne Porcher are in the possession of Anne Sinkler Whaley LeClercq of Charleston, SC.
4. Orton (1907, 41) used the taxon *Bacterium malvacearum* Erw. Sm. for bacterial blight. Kohel and Lewis (1984, 295) use the modern taxon *Xanthomonas campestris* pv *malvacearum*.
5. The fungus that causes wilt today goes under the taxon *Fusarium oxysporum* f. sp. *vasinfectum* (Atkinson) Snyder & Hansen according to Kohel and Lewis (1984, 291), and the disease is referred to as Fusarium wilt. Orton (1907, 44) used the synonym *Neocosmospora vasinfecta* (Atkinson) Erw. Sm.
6. Orton (1907, 47) used the taxon *Heterodera radicicola* (Greef.) Mül. for the root-knot nematode. Kohel and Lewis (1984) note that the root-knot nematode was originally named *Heterodera radicola* Atkinson. The author does not know why these two older names differ, but undoubtedly both refer to the root-knot nematode. Kohel and Lewis (1984, 312) state that modern nomenclature uses the taxon *Meloidogyne incognita* Chitwood for the nematode, based on works by Triantaphyllou and Sasser.

The Sea Island Cotton Trade

The three great commercial crops in the coastal area of South Carolina from 1685 until 1920 were indigo, Carolina gold rice and sea island cotton—none native to the lowcountry. Rice was of Asian origin; one species of indigo was of Asian origin and one of African; and *Gossypium barbadense* was native to Ecuador and Peru in South America. But all three were successfully cultivated in the Carolina lowcountry.

In fact, sea island cotton and Carolina gold rice were the finest examples of these two crops grown anywhere in the world. Even today, their quality has not been equalled. These three crops, with indigo to a lesser extent, dominated the economic, cultural, social and political life of Charleston and the lowcountry. The wealth of these crops helped make Charleston one of the cultural and economic centers of the colonial period, produced a plantation aristocracy, and was the genesis of the American slave trade in the lowcountry.

Rice was introduced into the area in 1685 and quickly became a dominant export crop of the state (and of its two adjoining states, North Carolina and Georgia). Initially, rice was grown in inland freshwater swamps that were banked and then cleared of vegetation. Reservoirs held rainwater and supplied the crop in the field through a system of canals. The uncertain (because of droughts) water supply convinced the planters to seek a more dependable source of water. Beginning in the mid-1700s, planters abandoned the inland fields and turned to the tidal freshwater swamps that lined the blackwater rivers (for example, the Edisto) and brownwater rivers (for example, the Santee) that traversed the lowcountry.

Upriver from the influence of salt water, and up to about thirty miles inland where the tidal amplitude became negligible, was a freshwater tidal swamp ecosystem that was flooded and dry twice a day. The planters banked the swamps, installed trunks with gates to control the flow of water between the fields and river, and cleared the swamp vegetation. The planting of rice then commenced. All this work was supplied by slave labor. By the end of the Revolution, approximately 150,000 acres of tidal swamp and tidal freshwater marsh were converted to rice fields. This tidal system flourished until the early 1900s. The loss of slave labor after the Civil War, combined with competition (beginning around 1880) from rice cultivation in Mississippi and further west, and hurricanes along the Atlantic coast in the early 1900s, ended rice growing as a major commercial crop in 1911.

The cultivation of indigo was short-lived compared to Carolina gold rice and sea island cotton. Indigo was commercially unimportant until successful varieties and methods of cultivation were introduced, mainly from the West Indies. The first successful crop was grown by Eliza Pinckney in 1744 on her father's plantation on Wappoo Creek, near Charleston. Eliza was the daughter of George Lucas, the Governor of Antigua, a Caribbean island. She devoted this crop largely to the production of seeds which she distributed among sea island planters. The indigo plant thrived in the dry, light soil of the sea islands.

During the colonial period, indigo cultivation, subsidized by a bounty from the British Parliament, expanded greatly, but was a precarious undertaking. Improper soil preparation, weeds, caterpillars, improper fermentation, mistakenly rubbing off the bluish bloom from the stalks by the field workers, and failure to carefully regulate the addition of lime water to produce the best dye quality, all made for a "sometimes" crop. Nonetheless, because of the high price obtained for quality indigo (an acre of virgin land produced about 80 pounds which sold from 40 to 80 cents a pound), lowcountry planters were willing to take the risks as long as Great Britain was paying a subsidy.

The American Revolution, combined with the repeal of the British bounty, virtually ended the market for indigo. Its cultivation lapsed and indigo never again was a large commercial crop in South Carolina or the other colonies. Production lingered in some remote places until the 1880s.

With the decline and ultimate loss of indigo, lowcountry planters turned to long-staple (and upland) cotton to fill the economic void, either as their only commercial crop, or to supplement rice. Because lowcountry planters already had established plantations (for rice and indigo), had slave labor, and had knowledge of how to operate a plantation system, cotton culture was readily accomplished. Seed of the new product from the Georgia planters, where the long-staple cotton was first grown as a annual, day-neutral plant, soon reached the South Carolina sea islands and adjacent mainland, as well as the Santee region.

The spread of the long-staple crop was largely due to the high prices that prevailed in the English market because of the Industrial Revolution, which welcomed the new staple. In 1799, long-staple cotton sold readily in Liverpool for 5 shillings a pound. Quickly, three market classes of the new long-staple cotton were developed: sea island cotton on the Georgia, Florida, and Carolina sea islands, mains on the adjacent mainland, and Santee long. And Charleston, profiting from the trade turned her way by the European wars and the export of cotton and rice, became a port of world importance.

By 1789, some twenty persons on the Georgia coast were producing the new cotton, and it soon spread rapidly in the coastal region of South Carolina. In 1790, William Elliott of Hilton Head Island produced the first commercial crop of sea island cotton in South Carolina. The following year, planting of sea island cotton spread. John Screven of St. Luke's Parish planted about 30 to 40 acres on his May River plantation, and the next year, John Rose planted a small field on Oakatee Creek in Beaufort County. Prominent planters such as James King, Sr., of St. Paul's Parish, Col. Edward Barnwell and Captain John Joyner of St. Helena's Parish began planting sea island cotton. General William Moultrie of Northampton Plantation, Peter Gaillard of The Rocks Plantation, and James Sinkler of Belvidere Plantation in St. John's Parish, Berkeley County, began growing Santee long cotton. The struggle between indigo and long-staple cotton was over: long-staple cotton had become the main money crop of the sea islands and adjacent mainland.

The Factorage System

The economy of South Carolina, from its earliest beginnings to the Civil War, was based almost entirely on agriculture, and most of its commercial facilities were oriented to supporting this agriculture-based economy. A concentration in growing cotton, both upland and sea island, came about as a direct effect of the Industrial Revolution in England and its insatiable demand for cotton. Under this agricultural system evolved the cotton factorage system.

The very uncertainty of the sea island cotton crop, as well as its nature, tied the planter to the system of factorage so well known in England and other countries long before the settlement of the American colonies. The cotton factor was the home agent of the sea island cotton planter, as well as of planters of upland cotton. Although the factor served as the planter's banker, factorage houses were not banks in the real meaning of the word; that is, unlike commercial banks, factors did not have the power to create money, either through note issue or deposit loans. The factors owned no land or slaves, planted no cotton, limited their risks and grew rich, building great houses in Charleston and Savannah. The factor was at once a combination moneylender and buying/selling agent. Although many cotton factors were wealthy and could use their own personal resources to advance funds to their planter customers, even their wealth was not sufficient to satisfy the needs of all their customers. But the factor could tap capital resources that could be funneled into the local markets. The factor often endorsed a planter's note with a merchant who then accepted the note or draft. The factor never sold directly to mills, only to cotton buyers.

The factor was the moneylender to the planter and was indispensable when the planter was in debt or had insufficient capital for the year's needs. Since the cotton was the main crop of the sea island planter, he tended to consider acres planted in provision crops a financial loss. It was seldom that enough food crops were planted to support the work force, and the planter had to make frequent purchases of corn, rice and other provisions. Here, again, the factor came to the assistance of the planter, providing credit or cash advances to purchase goods. The factor bought products from overseas that were not available locally, which he sold to the planter. In exchange, the factor sold cotton abroad for the planter. Often the factor gave the planter an advance on the future sale of the crop. The factor might make in one year enough to pay off the debts of several year's accumulation. More importantly, he became the link in the chain between the planter and the cotton markets, both at home and overseas. Although at certain times the planter dealt directly with the buyers in Liverpool, England (the main overseas market), in essence, the factor was the principal means for marketing the sea island cotton crop for the planter. Many factors dealt with more than one crop, handling, for example, upland and sea island cotton and rice.

The price for cotton in Charleston was determined by the buyers in Liverpool, the center of the cotton trade. The prices quoted in Charleston depended on the quality and quantity of cotton and the demand of the Liverpool market. Most often, the factor in Charleston was working on his own, since slow communications between Charleston and England (four to six weeks) meant a time lapse between price quotes in Liverpool and Charleston. The factor was also expected to report back to Liverpool anything that might affect the quality and quantity of the crop. Information such as rain, insect infestations, river navigation (low water meant difficulty getting the cotton to port), time of first frost, temperature or anything else that might affect the crop was important to the buyers in Liverpool as they tried to set the price they would pay.

The cotton factorage system did not emerge fully intact; rather, it evolved gradually as a practical effort to meet certain needs. Early on, the planters of the sea islands and inland farmers hauled their cotton into Charleston and Savannah and sold it directly to local buyers or traded it for goods. These buyers then resold the cotton to representatives of shippers or to speculators. For the large planters this system was cumbersome. The main problem was that the planter had to sell the cotton immediately since he had no storage facilities to store the cotton in the port cities and therefore could not wait on a better price if the market changed. Because of this, the planters ultimately resorted to a factor. The factor would hold the cotton in a storehouse and wait on the best price during the market season. This way the planter was relieved of this obligation and could tend to duties on his plantation.

Like many other features of the antebellum agricultural economy, the factorage system was not of southern origin—it was of West Indian origin, and developed primarily with the growth of the sugar cane industry. The institution was simply adapted to each new staple as it appeared. West Indian sugar crops and southern colonial tidewater tobacco were consigned by their growers to British merchants who sold the crops, advanced credit, and purchased and shipped manufactured goods. Then, as rice became an important crop in tidewater South Carolina, British merchants handled the rice. When the Revolution destroyed the business of the British merchants, their places were taken by enterprising men in more important southern commercial towns like Charleston and Savannah. Some of these had been exporting agents and correspondents of English houses; others were attracted to the factorage business by the promise of large financial rewards and because it was viewed as an honorable business. Ultimately, the factorage system came to be the very foundation of a large-scale, slave-labor agriculture of cotton and rice. Indeed, the cotton crop, more than rice, was responsible for the factorage system. The cotton was non-perishable and early on lent itself to concentration at ports where warehouse facilities were poor, and the rough handling, exposure and long delays it endured would have destroyed the value of any other agricultural crop. Sea island cotton was usually later in reaching the market than upland cotton because it was picked later in the year and took longer to prepare for market. Often it did not reach the market until the first of the year, and it was not uncommon for a factor to hold a planter's cotton for sale until July or August.

The functions of the southern factor were generally the same as his British progenitor; however, there was one main difference. The relations between the American factor and planter were often of an intimate and confidential character. They often developed lifelong ties, and the relationship was social and personal as well as a business one. Frequently, the planter and his factor were related by blood, so that the factor had an additional incentive to treat him as a preferred creditor. Considerable sums of money were often advanced upon only the word of the planter, with no formal security and only a memorandum to witness the amounts involved. This relationship was closer between the sea island planters and their factors because they were often part of the same plantation aristocracy.

The factor system functioned in the following way for sea island cotton. A firm in England, such as McConnel-Kennedy Company of Manchester, would instruct a Charleston firm—their agent, such as Trapmann, Jahncke and Company—to purchase a certain amount of cotton of a specified grade. The purchase price was set by the English firm. The factor then purchased the cotton from the planter, paying the planter. Although most of the purchases were less than $10,000, Roberts (1965) makes note from the McConnel-Kennedy Letters of May 9, 1825, of a purchase in excess of $16,000 (equivalent to $289,291 today),[1] and from April 30 of the same year of a purchase of about $15,000 ($271,210). Based on the value of today's dollar, these were considerable sums of money for 1825. The commission rate charged for the purchase was 5%. The financial benefit to the Charleston economy from just this aspect of the sea island cotton trade, therefore, was significant.

The factors generally depended for capital on local financial institutions rather than foreign sources. By the time the factor system was in place, Charleston had no fewer than five banks (Smith 1958, 193), and by 1860 had ten (Smith 1958, 194) The money from the sea island cotton trade was a major part of the banks' business. They also provided financing for exporting.

Although the factor-planter relationship was a successful system for both parties, it was not without its problems. It was expected that there would be no conflict of interest between the factor and planter. In the perfect system, the higher the price the factor could attain for the planter's cotton, the higher the factor's commission, and, consequently, the greater the factor's reputation as a salesman. This would serve to attract more clients for the factor. However, should the factor decide to speculate in the staple, the factor's interest might not be that of the planter's. The courts were clear: the factor could not buy cotton he was hired to sell. But the factor was not barred from both buying and selling or from buying on his own account; he was merely barred from buying cotton he was hired to sell. But abuses did occur, especially when the price of cotton was fluctuating widely, and the planter had to be vigilant in inspecting the statements of his factor for possible conflicts of interest.

Often there was a feeling of resentment between the factor and planter. If the crop failed, the factor stood to lose money as well as the planter. The factor might consider that the failure was due to the planter's mismanagement of his plantation. The planter, in turn, often regarded his factor's commission as too high and felt that the factor did not obtain the high price the planter thought his crop should have brought.

There was also much consternation among planters about the differences in prices for cotton from plantations that produced a seemingly equal quality. Planter William Elliott (1828, 155) posed a question that he thought sea island planters should examine and understand: "What is the cause of the difference of price given for Cotton, grown even on adjoining plantations?" Then he expounded on the question:

Formerly a difference of a few cents in the pound, was considered as equivalent to any difference of value between the product of contiguous lands; and such a difference was, in truth, an adequate compensation for the extraordinary labour and expense incurred by the careful cultivator; but latterly, the range of price has baffled all calculation, and has expanded to such a pitch, that a favored Planter has been known to obtain for his crop, five times the price *obtained by his immediate neighbor. Is this difference real or imaginary? If real, whence has it arisen?*

Evidently, the planters could not get honest answers from the factors. At first, the factors said the lower-priced cotton had been handled too much which accounted for the difference. When these planters changed their preparation methods and handled the cotton less, and the price difference still prevailed, the factors responded that the planters had handled the cotton too little. Again, the planters changed their processes to adhere to the factors' demands. Still, the favored planters received higher prices for their cotton while the other planters "received a disproportionate reward for [their] labours." What made it so hard to accept was that the factors, when they paid a price of, say, 50 cents a pound to the favored planter, could have bought equal-quality cotton for half the price from other planters. Elliott and the planters finally realized that a system of favoritism had emerged in the trade. Elliott could not determine if the factor was at fault, buying and rejecting cotton without skill or rule, or if the factor was obeying instructions from the buyer overseas to pay the higher price to planters whose reputation for certain staples was already known. The loss of capital was obvious to the non-favored planters; the profit had gone to the foreign purchaser and manufacturer, "who obtained a superior commodity without any corresponding advance in price."

Elliott recommended that the non-favored planters strive to persevere in their efforts to approach the standards of the favored planters in hopes that finally a "gradation of prices may be established" so the planter would receive a just price for his efforts. [The author found no reference in the literature that the planters' efforts paid off to remove "favored status" pricing from the market.]

William Elliott's personal letters (Scafidel 1978, 701-705) also reveal the ill will between planters and factors that prevailed throughout the industry. He wrote twice to his mother about a factor's attempt to "break down" the market:

Oak Lawn 15th Jany 1853.

I regret to hear that Trenholm has sold Your cotton at 41 cents! Very harsh things are said of him. It is surmised that he contracted to deliver to an English house— two thousand or more bales of Sea Island cotton, at a low price— and that finding that he would lose by the very high prices at which the articles ruled in the market— he has done every thing to break down the market. It is known that he was the first to break down prices— to the extent of six cents per pound in a single day— (as I remember he did some years ago.) Now, if these things be true, you see he has an interest therefore in selling Your cotton low— or that some sleeping partner may in fact buy it for his own benefit. And to the loss of the customers who put trust in him to do the best for their interests. If these things are true— No cotton planter should place his cotton in their hands—it is absolutely suicidal—yet such is the force of habit— and the reluctance of primitive country folks to unlearn their long established favorable opinions of their agents— that they who are sacrificed— will offer themselves to be sacrificed again.

Oak-Lawn 3^d Feby 1853.

I found the cotton market depressed in Charleston. I was unable to sell some lot[s] which I had sent down. I was getting them out for the high price— but was too late— Mr Trenholm was too quick for me. There is little doubt but that he did break down the cotton market.

It appears, however, that the planters were able to have at least some influence on the price. In a June 23, 1819 letter (Roberts, 1965, 29-30) from the firm Trapmann, Jahncke & Co., in Charleston, to their buyers in Manchester, England, Messrs. McConnel & Kennedy wrote:

In Sea Island very little is doing & it would be difficult to ascertain at what price quality could be bought, our best planters marks are not in the market on account of the unwillingness of the owners to yield to the present price.

Perhaps the greatest problem the planters faced was the policy of "secret pricing." Whitemarsh Seabrook (1847, 5-6) called the secret pricing "…a disingenuous device on the part of purchasers to keep down the amount of their outlays at the expense of the planter's profits." Cotton buyers dealt individually with each of the planters, paying a special and individual price, rather than a general market price. The factors convinced the planter that it was in his (the planter's) interest to conceal from his neighbors his market transactions. As a result, the cotton was frequently sold below its real value. Although a few planters received a high premium for their cotton, most planters suffered a loss through the policy of secret prices. If a planter tried to ship his cotton directly to buyers in England to obtain an honest price, it was generally to no avail. Fortunately for the planters, once leaders like Whitemarsh Seabrook informed them that the buyers profited more than they did, the secrecy practice came to an end with no long-lasting damage to the planters.

Even the freedmen experienced problems with the factors. Freedman Sam Gadsden of Edisto Island (Lindsay 2000, 127) commented on his relationship with the factors during the 1915 season:

I couldn't take all the cotton to one place, I had to divide it out among the brokers, for if any one of them thought I was bringing in that big a load of cotton, he would cut me down. They had an allotment there for any colored farmer and if you brought in any more than that allotment, they would play a bad trick on you. They wouldn't sell your cotton, but put it back in the warehouse until it got old and rotten. We found out about this trick and the safe politics they were playing. When I divided the crop out that way, each one thought I had just an ordinary, little crop and he paid me for it.

Although the factorage system was not perfect, it served the planters well throughout the sea island cotton industry, and without it, planters would have been hard put to have operated their plantations. At least, no better system was ever substituted.

The System of Marketing in Charleston after the Civil War

The conditions in the Charleston market after the Civil War bear particular note because the city was long the center of the sea island trade. William R. Meadows, in his 1914 study of the sea island cotton industry, considered this economic market.

Before the war, the majority of sea island cotton was traded in Charleston. After the war, the structure of the marketing system remained essentially the same: the factor continued to act as the selling agent for the planter and received a commission on the sale. Some planters and factors had maintained "business as usual" relations during the war and simply continued on into the postwar period. Newcomers with any sort of wealth soon joined the factorage business. Just as before the war, the factor never sold directly to mills, but to cotton buyers. He worked with warehousemen, who simply received a storage fee and were not involved in the buying or selling.

After the war, the sea island planters continued to grow cotton, but at a reduced acreage, relying on the tenant system for labor. Meadows (1914, 9) explained: "In financing their business after the Civil War the planters naturally turned to their old friends, the factors, who continued to advance them on open account the money and supplies necessary to make the crop." During the years from 1867 to 1880, the price for sea island cotton was profitable, but not outstanding. The Carolina sea islands produced more than one-third of the country's long-staple crop—somewhat less than Florida, but far in excess of Georgia—and maintained the lead over Georgia until 1889. As long as Charleston (and Savannah, to a lesser extent) remained the primary market for long-staple cotton, prices held and remained reasonably satisfactory to the planters. However, as Georgia began to increase its production of interior sea island cotton for which domestic markets opened, and Egyptian long-staple imports increased, the importance of these ports declined and planters could no longer fix the price of long-staple cotton. Prices began to fluctuate widely. With the increase in production and decrease in prices, planters became more indebted to the factors. By 1913, fully 80% of the crop was produced on money advanced by factors.

As Meadows (1914) pointed out, the system was inflexible and often worked to the disadvantage of the planters. Most noticeable was the centralization of market control in Charleston after the war. A single firm in Charleston usually purchased over three-fourths of the sea island crop, and four firms of factors made almost all the advances on the crop. Further, these buyers and factors banked with the same institution. Even more detrimental to the planters was that the cotton-buying firm was also represented on the directorate of the bank. No matter how honest the banker-buyer relationship was, it was always a matter of suspicion to the planters.

One of the perplexing questions concerning the financial system after the war was the source of funds in Charleston to support the factor system and sea island cotton marketing. The Civil War was a struggle between the southern planter-capitalist and the northern industrial-capitalist for supremacy in national affairs. The end of the war saw the planter aristocracy crushed by the industrial giant of the North. The sea island planter had held almost all of his wealth in slaves and land, and the loss of the war wiped out most of this investment. Planters were now faced with mere survival. Many plantations were in an advanced state of decay: farm animals were gone, fields left unattended during the war were choked with weeds, buildings were destroyed, and much of the valuable seed source was gone. Many of the young men were dead or injured, and older men who had not served in the military were too feeble to do the labor. There was not enough food left to last until a new crop could be made, and a new labor system had to emerge, which would take capital. To make matter worse, many factors, merchants and banks were also ruined.

But money did become available to plant cotton after the war. The following sources were documented from the literature. Whether they all applied to sea island cotton planters is not known. Undoubtedly some did, since planting resumed after the war.

1. In August of 1861, cotton factors placed a notice in the *Charleston Mercury* suggesting that planters (both upland and sea island) not send the current season's crop to Charleston for

storage, fearing that it might fall into enemy hands, "but to make arrangements to store it carefully and properly under their own sheds and gin houses." For planters who did heed this advice, this cotton was a source of some income after the war. Records do reveal that a significant number of southern upland cotton growers did store cotton that escaped detection by Union forces, and they were able to sell it after the war. The author found no direct source to document whether any sea island planters were able to hoard some of their cotton, but it certainly was possible.

2. The first months of peace made it clear that the powers of King Cotton were ample enough to produce a rapid economic reunion between erstwhile enemies. Funds from northern banks began to flow south. Obviously the North had a vested interest in helping cotton recover because northern mills needed a new supply of raw cotton. Although this effort was made mainly for upland cotton, some of the money found its way into the sea island market because the same factors handled upland and sea island cotton. Northern merchants also scaled down the debts of pre-war obligations as a way to stimulate the recovery of cotton.

3. Planters began to sell off some of their plantation lands, both to freedmen and northern speculators. This generated enough money to begin growing cotton again, but on a smaller scale.

4. Plantation owners mortgaged their lands and promised the year's crop for interest, just to get enough money to start planting. Planters were willing to pay 20% to 30% interest. The South Carolina legislature repealed all laws regulating interest in order to accommodate the planters who were trying to obtain loans. More importantly, southern legislatures passed crop lien laws whereby the planter could give a lien on his unplanted or growing crop for credit. By advancing credit, the lender acquired first rights on all cotton produced by the borrower. The lien system was really a codification of the antebellum factorage system which had prevailed under common law and tradition between the planter and factor.

5. Some capital may have been available from southerners who had avoided the war and remained at home to make money in speculating and blockade running.

6. There were a few planters who had some holdings in Europe, and this money began to return after the war. But this was a limited amount because the amnesty proclamation excluded persons with wealth over $20,000, and these planters feared the money might be seized, so it was left overseas. Still, what little that did return was vital to get a small operation going again.

7. Since the sea islands were the major source of quality long-staple cotton in demand in England, undoubtedly some financial aid was made available to local banks.

8. Although many factorage houses were ruined by the war, many survived by obtaining capital from Northern financiers and selling stockpiled cash crops. The planters again turned to these factors, who advanced funds and supplies to those who pledged their crops as security.

9. Perhaps the most important means to resurrect sea island cotton came from the planters. They changed the method of cultivation to suit smaller landholdings and reduced capital, and employed a new system of labor.

How Sea Island Cotton was Moved to the Port Cities

Charleston served as the primary market for sea island cotton (and mains and Santee long); however, some plantations closer to Savannah used that port city as their market. The existence of large areas of marsh surrounding the sea islands, and of the swamps that traversed the islands, prevented the construction of a major road network. Fortunately, most plantations were situated adjacent to a navigable waterway which ultimately gave access to the ocean and to Charleston. Plantations located in the interior of islands had to expand the primitive road network to link producing areas with their shipping points. Some plantations maintained their own landings; other made use of public landings. Planters on St. Helena Island usually sent their cotton to Beaufort by their own sailboats which were loaded at plantation docks.

The period of greatest prosperity for sea island cotton occurred during the beginning of the steamboat era. In 1816, steam paddle wheelers made their first appearance on the Savannah River, and within three years, regular steamboat traffic connected Savannah, Charleston and Augusta. From Beaufort, the cotton was sent to Charleston via ocean steamer (fig. 13-1). In 1826, there were ten steamboats engaged in commercial trade between Charleston and the towns of Savannah, Augusta, Hamburg, Georgetown, Cheraw and Columbia. Although the main use of the steamboat trade was for getting upland cotton to the port cities, the sea island planters used the steamboats to get their crop to market. The individual plantations either had their own landing, or used a neighboring plantation's landing. Kinsey Burden at Oakvale had a landing on the Stono River which is still evident today.

One of the most innovative planters was William Seabrook (1773-1836) of Edisto Island. He established a steamboat line between Savannah and Charleston, and between the intermediate islands. Before the steamboat, the planters of the area sent their produce to market with very little certainty or dispatch in their own boats, either flats or sailboats, a mode of transport which cost four times the price of the steamboat. Steamboat Creek, on which Seabrook's plantation was situated, got its name from his line.

With the opening of the Santee Canal in 1800, Santee long cotton had a direct route via the Cooper River to Charleston. The canal ran from the Santee River through the heart of the Santee long region and joined the Cooper River at Stony Landing, providing easy access to Charleston and the world. That the Santee long planters made frequent use of the Santee Canal is documented by Dr. Henry Ravenel in his diary from the period 1835-42 when he resided at Pooshee Plantation. His entry on June 5, 1839 reads: "Sent by McBeths Boat 3&1/2 bales Sea Island Cotton & 15 Bales Stained Santee Cotton." This boat (actually, a narrow barge) was one of many that operated on the Santee Canal.

The Economic Impact of Sea Island Cotton

The economic impact of sea island cotton on Charleston and the coastal sea islands has not

CHAPTER THIRTEEN

Figure 13-1. Sea island cotton being loaded on steamer at Port Royal, *ca.* 1861

been well researched or documented. Several problems were encountered by the author in the course of research:

1. There were three market classes of long-staple cotton exported from Charleston: sea island, mains, and Santee long (see chapter 6 for a definition of the three classes). Undoubtedly, all the Santee long was exported from Charleston; there is no reason to believe that it was taken to Savannah. The most likely outlet for the majority of mains was also Charleston. However, most tables listing the exports of cotton from Charleston do not make the distinction between these three market classes; mains and Santee long were often included with sea island cotton. Not being able to remove mains and Santee long from sea island cotton export figures overestimates somewhat its economic impact to the Charleston economy. Table 13-1 from Lewis Gray (1958, 1032) emphasizes this point.

Table 13-1. Sea island cotton exported from the United States, 1805-60. Figures are for million of pounds (Gray 1958, Table 44, p. 1032)[2]

Year	Quantity	Year	Quantity	Year	Quantity
1805	8.8	1824	9.5	1843	7.5
1806	6.1	1825	9.7	1844	6.1
1807	8.9	1826	6.0	1845	9.4
1808	0.9 (Embargo)	1827	15.1	1846	9.4
1809	8.7	1828	11.3	1847	6.3
1810	8.6	1829	12.8	1848	7.7
1811	8.0	1830	8.1	1849	12.0
1812	4.4 (War of 1812)	1831	8.3	1850	8.2
1813	4.1 (War of 1812)	1832	8.7	1851	8.3
1814	2.5 (War of 1812)	1833	11.1	1852	11.7
1815	8.4	1834	8.1	1853	11.2
1816	9.9	1835	7.8	1854	10.5
1817	8.1	1836	7.8	1855	13.1
1818	6.5	1837	5.3	1856	12.8
1819	7.5	1838	7.3	1857	12.9
1820	11.6	1839	5.1	1858	12.1
1821	11.3	1840	8.8	1859	13.7
1822	11.3	1841	6.2	1860	15.6
1823	12.1	1842	7.3		

Gray did not state whether the figures for pounds per year included mains and Santee long. Even though the author concludes from the text material that the figures probably represent only sea island cotton, there is no certainty. This is an important point to understand, since the author uses this table to document the economic value of sea island cotton to the Charleston economy (tables 13-8, -9, and -10).

E. J. Donnell (1872) separated true sea island from mains and Santee long (grouped together) and short staple. The weekly quotes gave an insight into the relative prices from 1816 through 1825, and clearly showed that sea island commanded higher prices than mains, Santee long, and short staple:

Table 13-2. Weekly quotations in the Charleston cotton market for sea island; mains and Santee long; and short-staple cotton, 1816-25. Price quotations are given in cents per pound. (Donnell 1872)[3]

Week	1816			1817			1818			1819			1820		
	Sea Island	Mains and Santee	Short-Staple	Sea Island	Mains and Santee	Short-Staple	Sea Island	Mains and Santee	Short-Staple	Sea Island	Mains and Santee	Short-Staple	Sea Island	Mains and Santee	Short-Staple
1	50	0	26	39	35	26	58	0	35	55	50	27	37.5	34	16.5
10	43	0	28	39	35	26.5	56	0	33	55	45	25	35	30	16.5
20	50	0	30	45	43	30	72	60	33	37.5	33	16	35	30	17.5
30	53	0	32	45	43	29	75	0	33	40	35	18	37.5	31	20
40	43	40	27	45	40	30	65	0	32	40	35	18	34	30	20
52	37	35	25.5	58	0	35	55	50	27	37.5	34	16.5	30	25	16.5

Week	1821			1823			1824			1825		
	Sea Island	Mains and Santee	Short-Staple	Sea Island	Mains and Santee	Short-Staple	Sea Island	Mains and Santee	Short-Staple	Sea Island	Mains and Santee	Short-Staple
1	30	25	16	30	20	12.5	30	22	14.5	23	24	5
10	30	24	14	25	21	12	25	21	14.5	50	30	19
20	26	21	15	25	19	12.5	28	23	16	85	55	30
30	30	25	17	30	20	15	26	23	15.25	75	60	24
40	30	25	16.75	30	20	17	26	21	14.5	65	40	16.5
52	30	23	18	28	22	14.5	28	24	15.5	55	32	14.5

2. There are several handicaps that make it difficult for historians to establish prices of sea island cotton: (a) no standard set of classifications was accepted by all buyers and sellers of sea

island cotton; (b) the practice of secret pricing (see above) made it difficult to determine the real price; (c) the small size of the market and the large variations in qualities and prices did not lend easily to averaging; (d) the trade in sea island cotton was a specialty trade, and the quantity and quality were affected by many factors, both economic and agricultural; and (e) the price of sea island cotton was subject to wide fluctuations because there was a limited market and the market could be oversupplied by adding a few thousand bales. The problem was clearly stated by Gray (1958, 1031): "It is difficult to construct a satisfactory price series for sea island cotton because the market was extremely narrow, the variation in classes and grades was large for so small a total crop, no single class or grade was regularly reported, and many transactions were private and did not appear in market quotations." This problem of determining prices is clearly illustrated in tables 13-3, -4 and -5, where numerous grades are cited and prices fluctuated widely between grades and within grades.

Table 13-3. Prices of cotton at Liverpool, 1844 and 1845 (*Merchants Magazine and Commercial Review* 1845, vol. 12, p. 392)[4]

	1844	1845
Sea Island stained and saw ginned	4 a 9.25	3.25 a 8
Ordinary	10.5 a 11	9.75 a 10
Middling	11.25 a 11.50	10.25 a 11
Fair	12 a 13	12 a 12.5
Good Fair	14 a 15	15 a 16
Good and fine	17 a 24	19 a 25

Table 13-4. Sea island cotton prices, 1819-25, in cents (Charles A. Roberts 1965, pp. 22-23)[5]

Year	Ordinary to Good Grades			Fine-to-Fancy Grades	
	Low	High	Average	Fine	Fancy
1819	33	40	36.5	41	43
1820	25	35	30	40	43
1821	22	35	28.50	32	35
1822	22	36	29	31	40
1823	19	33	26	32	50
1824	21	35	28	27	50
1825	24	70	42	35	1.00

Table 13-5. Prices of all descriptions of cotton wool, at Liverpool, during the last week of the years 1837, 1838, 1839, and 1840. The abbreviation *d.* represents the English penny or pence. (*Merchants Magazine and Commercial Review* 1841, vol. 4, no. 3, p. 484)

Description	1837		1838		1839		1840	
	d. to d.		d. to d.		d. to d.		d. to d.	
Sea Islands	16	22	18	28	20	22	13.5	30
Stained ditto	8.5	0	7	16	6	14	6	12

The author used the following tables of Lewis Gray (1958, 1031) and Alfred B. Shepperson (1921, 123) as the primary source of prices of sea island cotton to demonstrate the economic impact of the sea island cotton trade on Charleston during the antebellum and post-war periods.

Table 13-6. Annual averages of monthly prices of sea island cotton in Charleston, 1800-1860 (Gray 1958, 1031)[6]

Year	Price (cts./lb.)	Year	Price (cts./lb.)	Year	Price (cts./lb.)
1800	44.9	1821	26.7	1842	18.1
1801	46.4	1822	24.8	1843	16.6
1802	44.2	1823	24.5	1844	18.8
1803	51.5	1824	24.6	1845	26.6
1804	38.6	1825	54.3	1846	26.6
1805	51.6	1826	32.7	1847	31.4
1806	36.7	1827	21.1	1848	19.0
1807	34.3	1828	25.6	1849	23.2
1808	24.7 (Embargo)	1829	22.9	1850	27.8
1809	25.4	1830	24.8	1851	29.3
1810	28.4	1831	20.0	1852	37.2
1811	22.5	1832	18.2	1853	41.2
1812	17.5 (War of 1812)	1833	20.2	1854	33.4
1813	19.0 (War of 1812)	1834	25.1	1855	31.6
1814	25.3 (War of 1812)	1835	34.8	1856	39.8
1815	37.9	1836	39.5	1857	38.1
1816	44.8	1837	46.0	1858	29.3
1817	43.5	1838	35.3	1859	35.2
1818	63.2	1839	38.7	1860	47.0
1819	42.1	1840	22.5		
1820	32.8	1841	26.8		

Table 13-7. Average price per pound of sea island cotton and Georgia and Florida interior sea island cotton, 1910-21. Values are expressed in cents. (Shepperson 1921, 123)

Years	Florida	Georgia	South Carolina
1909-10	27.10	27.10	32.85
1910-11	27.36	27.36	35.62
1911-12	20.41	20.41	23.73
1912-13	19.50	19.50	25.00
1913-14	19.61	19.61	23.47
1914-15	18.06	18.06	22.00
1915-16	23.00	23.00	27.00
1916-17	45.50	45.50	50.00
1917-18	72.50	72.50	80.00
1918-19	60.00	60.00	65.00
1919-20	100.25	100.25	110.25
1920-21	60.00	50.00	

3. Obviously, the value of a crop of cotton sold in 1805 was not equal to today's money. For example, 8.8 million pounds of cotton were exported from Charleston in 1805. The average price of sea island cotton in 1805 was 51.6 cents per pound, making the sale for 1805 worth $4,540,000, which was equal to $69,278,596 in 2002.

In spite of the above limitations, the economic impact of the sea island cotton trade on Charleston and the sea islands can be fairly well constructed by considering the main periods that comprised the industry.

1790-1819: Prosperity and Expansion

The beginning of the sea island cotton trade was described by George S. White (1836, 365):

Previous to the year 1790, North America did not supply England with a single pound weight of cotton; it was only after the termination of the American war that cotton began to be cultivated in Carolina and Georgia, and it has succeeded so well, that it now forms one of the staple productions of the United States. But that which was first imported into the English market was very imperfectly cleaned, and, in consequence, was for some time used only for spinning low numbers. It was soon perceived, however, that the cotton grown upon the coast, termed Sea Island cotton, had a finer and longer staple than that which was produced farther up the country, and known by the name Upland cotton. But some years elapsed before it was ascertained to be of a quality in every respect superior to that which was brought from the Isle of Bourbon, the only cotton then used for the finest qualities of yarn, but which now is entirely superseded by the former.

William Elliott, a planter on Hilton Head Island, has historically been given credit for producing, in 1790, the first *commercial* crop of sea island cotton in South Carolina. This year is considered the commercial beginning of sea island cotton culture. Elliott's success spurred others to engage in cotton culture. Table 13-6 includes the price ranges for cotton from 1800 to 1819.[7] Early prices were high, due to the generally high price level that prevailed for all cottons, but also because of the large differential in the quality of sea island cotton. The Embargo Act of 1807[8] caused a drop in price in 1808, but prices rose slightly over the next three years. From 1812 to 1814, prices again fell because of the War of 1812, but made a quick recovery after the war. Prices then rose in of a frenzy of speculation, peaking in midsummer of 1818 at about 75 cents per pound.

The sea islands during this period became a region of new and expanding wealth. With their new-found fortunes, sea island planters emulated the lifestyle of the rice planters who had amassed great wealth a century before. They became statesmen, served on boards, and held public office. They became the aristocracy of the sea islands, and took great pride in their affluence, families and social status. Their prosperity allowed them to travel abroad, often for extended periods; in fact, some planters became absentee landowners, leaving the running of the plantation to an overseer.

As did the rice-planter aristocracy, sea island planters summered in ocean or mountain retreats, or moved to pineland villages, to escape malaria. Beaufort-area planters summered in fine houses in the town of Beaufort, or at Bluffton on the May River, or at Gillisonville, Grahamville or McPhersonville; planters on St. Helena sojourned at St. Helenaville. (All of these villages exist today except St. Helenaville.) Edisto Island planters reposed in the summer winds at Edingsville, Legareville was the retreat for Johns Island growers, and Wadmalaw landowners went to Rockville. Planters on James Island went to Secessionville, so named because of the secession of planters from their plantations to this village.

Not to be outdone by the rice planters, the wealthier cotton growers of the sea islands built fine mansions in Charleston to enjoy the social season. Others of the Charleston area went to Mt. Pleasant or to Moultrieville on Sullivans Island. This new aristocracy strove to emulate the exclusiveness and social refinement of the English country gentleman. The wealth of the sea island planters is clearly evidenced by the plantation homes and infrastructure presented in Part II of this book.

Some planters who excelled at seed selection obtained prices far above other planters. For example, Kinsey Burden obtained the following for his sea island cotton: In 1826, $1.10/pound (or $19.89 today); in 1827, $1.25/pound ($22.41); and in 1828, he sold two bales at $2.00/pound ($37.75). On Edisto Island, William Seabrook and John Townsend of Bleak Hall emulated the seed selection process of Burden, and produced their own cultivars of sea island cotton known respectively as "Seabrook" and "Bleak Hall" that commanded higher prices than the average crop. These planters became icons in the industry.

From 1790 to 1819, the sea islands experienced their greatest land-use expansion. New plantations developed rapidly and new land was cleared for cotton fields. After 1824, the number of new plantations increased little because the best sites for fields had already been claimed. Figure

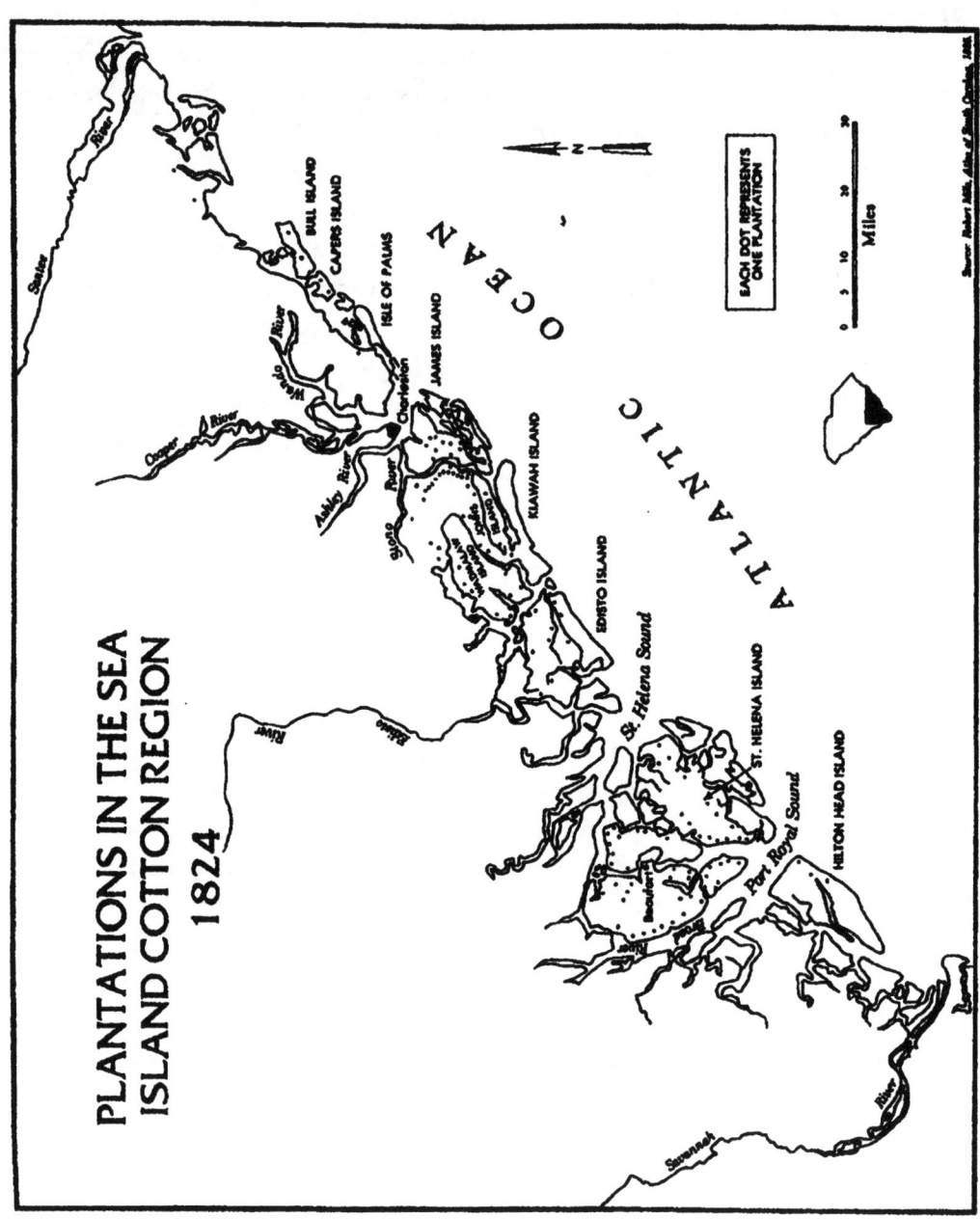

Figure 13-2. Sea island cotton plantations in South Carolina in 1824 (1825 Mills *Atlas*)

CHAPTER THIRTEEN

13-2 depicts the locations of plantations on the sea islands in 1824. Though expansion slowed after that, individual planters began to convert salt marshes and lowlands to cotton fields. The expansion into salt marsh was especially important, for as Legaré (1828, 24) noted, "there was, in one instance, a difference of 32 cents per lb. between the Cotton raised on the marsh land, and that raised on the same plantation on the high land, in favor of the marsh land." Lowlands that were drained also produced a better quality cotton than did the higher land.

For the most part, plantations were located near waterways, the lifeline of the fields. On Johns Island, plantations were strung along the Stono River; on Port Royal Island, they were distributed along the perimeter adjacent to a waterway; and at St. Helena Island, they formed a linear distribution east of Seaside Road (today SSR-17) and at Land's End on the southwest side. Besides the sea islands, there were many small plantations on such islands as Datah, Bull (Beaufort County), Barnwell and Pinckney.

The financial impact of cotton on the sea islands and the Charleston economy during this era of prosperity was significant (table 13-8). For example, the value of the sea island cotton crop of 1805 ($4,540,000) would be the equivalent of $69,278,596 in 2002.

Table 13-8. Historical values of sea island cotton exports from Charleston, 1805-18, converted to equal values for 2002[9]

Year	Quantity (millions of lbs.)	Price (cts./lb.)	Historic Value ($)	2002 ($)
1805	8.8	51.6	4,540,000	69,278,596
1806	6.1	36.7	2,238,700	32,767,318
1807	8.9	34.3	3,052,700	47,253,248
1808	0.9 (Embargo)	24.7	222,300	316,750
1809	8.7	25.5	2,218,500	32,252,254
1810	8.6	28.4	2,442,400	35,570.281
1811	8.0	22.5	1,800,000	24,511,944
1812	4.4 (War of 1812)	17.5	770,000	10,354,594
1813	4.1 (War of 1812)	19.0	779,000	8,729,684
1814	2.5 (War of 1812)	25.3	632,500	6,449,713
1815	8.4	37.9	3,183,600	37,026,197
1816	9.9	44.8	4,435,200	56,466,237
1817	8.1	43.5	3,523,500	47,382,354
1818	6.5	63.2	4,108,000	57,769,864
1819	7.5	42.1	3,157,500	44,403,200

The financial impact of sea island cotton reverberated throughout the area. Factories in Charleston supplied tools and machinery to the plantations, and a shipping business that reached across the seas provided employment. Charleston furniture manufacturers had a ready local market for their fine products. Today's descendants of these planters prize the furniture passed down through their families. The building of plantation homes and mansions in Charleston required a labor force of considerable talent and size which became an integral part of the Charleston economy. In the post-bellum era of sea island cotton, fertilizer companies sprang up and supplied goods such as phosphate to the struggling industry. And a banking and merchant industry thrived on the business derived from the sale of cotton.

1820-1834: Depression and End of Expansion

By 1820, the great wealth of the sea island planters had been achieved and few large fortunes were made after 1819. Still, sea island cotton was a highly lucrative crop and the planters continued to enjoy a rich lifestyle. The Charleston and lowcountry economy still depended on the sea island cotton trade for its continued prosperity. Table 13-9 illustrates export values for this period.

Table 13-9. Historical values of sea island cotton exports, 1820-34, converted to equal values for 2002[10]

Year	Quantity (millions of lbs.)	Price (cts./lb.)	Historic Value ($)	2002 ($)
1820	11.6	32.8	3,804,800	58,059,736
1821	11.3	26.7	3,017,100	47,732,385
1822	11.3	24.8	2,802,400	42,763,510
1823	12.1	24.5	2,964,500	50,622,460
1824	9.5	24.6	2,337,000	43,347,401
1825	9.7	54.3	5,267,100	95,232,885
1826	6.0	32.7	1,962,000	35,474,344
1827	15.1	21.1	3,186,100	57,126,879
1828	11.3	25.6	2,892,800	54,597,895
1829	12.8	22.9	2,931,200	56,310,550
1830	8.1	24.8	2,008,800	38,938,217
1831	8.3	20.0	1,660,000	34,342,910
1832	8.7	18.2	1,583,400	33,076,211
1833	11.1	20.2	2,242,200	47,765,608
1834	8.1	25.1	2,033,100	42,470,156

Gray (1958, 738) best summarized the sea island cotton industry during the 1820-34 period. From its peak in midsummer 1818, the price of sea island cotton rapidly weakened, and by the end of 1819 the price was around half of its highest price, which had been 75 cents per pound. From 1820 to 1824, prices averaged around 25 cents per pound. An artificially manipulated cotton speculation in 1825 carried sea island cotton quotations to as high as 87.75 cents per pound by June of that year. In the second half of 1825 and the first part of 1826, prices were still at remunerative levels. However, in the latter part of 1826, prices dropped, and a severe depression ensued that lasted until 1834. During this period of depression, annual prices averaged from 26 cents per pound to as low as 18 cents in 1832. The cause of the depressed prices has been the subject of much debate, which continues even today.

The reduction in the price had another effect on the planters beside reduced profits. Often a planter's status in the community was based on the reputation of his cotton crop. Sea island cotton became more than a commodity: it became an index of social standing. The planters took great pride in the quality of their sea island cotton and put their names on the best bales. Once a planter established a reputation for very fine cotton, bales stamped with his name commanded higher prices. Planters like William Seabrook and John Townsend of Edisto Island were icons in the sea island cotton culture, and their reputation as cotton planters influenced their social and political standing in the community and the state. In the sea islands, cotton was woven into the fabric of plantation society. The depression in cotton prices beginning in 1820 caused planters to feel that their reputation and status in the community was threatened.

Since 1791, the great demand and higher prices throughout the sea islands encouraged an increase in production, and most planters were rewarded by a ready sale and generous prices. But the realization by the planters that sea island cotton was in a depression was a turning point in its history. Frederick A. Porcher (1844, 4) perhaps best stated the problem in an address to the Black Oak Agricultural Society on November 19, 1844:

The cultivators of most other products, have for their guides the experience of ages and of the whole extent of civilization. We, stand as agriculturists, isolated from the rest of mankind; their practice to us is a mystery, their experience to us useless. Let us hail then, as the opening of a new era in our agriculture, the scientific discoveries which enable us to apply to practical farming the mysteries of the chemical laboratory.

Although Porcher's comments were about South Carolina agriculture in general, his comments were more applicable to sea island cotton than to other crops. Since sea island cotton was not developed until 1786, becoming a commercial crop in 1790, there was no history of its cultivation to draw upon. The sea island planters had to turn inward if they were to maintain sea island cotton as a viable commercial crop.

Initially, the planters blamed the depressed prices on a variety of factors, such as the ravages of caterpillars, untimely storms, the incompetence of their factors, and the post-1815 protective tariffs. In addition, it was suggested that the depression was partly caused by the planters' absence from the plantations during the crucial period of cultivation and market preparation. In their absence, overseers ran the plantation. The overseers of that time, however, were notorious for their incompetence and inattention to their work. These external factors may have contributed to the depression, but they were not the only reasons for the price decline. Ultimately, two prevailing explanations emerged as to why the sea island cotton market was depressed: overproduction and decreased consumption.

According to Whitemarsh Seabrook (1843, 282), the distinguishing qualities of sea island cotton fiber, in their relative order of importance, were strength, fineness, length and uniformity. In the years after Kinsey Burden's seed selection process became public knowledge, sea island planters worked mainly to increase the *fineness* and *length* of the staple. And they succeeded. In the 1830s, however, the planters realized that in their efforts to increase fineness and length to unprecedented degrees, they were sacrificing other valuable qualities of long staple cotton (that is, strength and uniformity), and decreasing the quantity produced. In effect, the planters glutted a limited market. As Seabrook (1831, 339) explained: "Of superfine Cotton so small a quantity is wanted, that a few planters could supply the world. It is believed that Messrs. Burden and Wilson do now raise enough to meet the demands of the British and French manufacturers."

It was also realized that cottons from other countries were competing favorably with the lower grades of sea island cottons, thus depressing the prices. Overproduction was not the sole cause of the decreased values—it was also a question of reduced consumption of the lower grades of the crop. This problem was clearly stated in a June 5, 1824 letter from the Charleston firm of Trapmann, Schmidt & Co. to their buyer in Manchester, England (Roberts 1965, 158):

...and on which we venture to predict an opinion that prices of fine Sea Islands will be sustained, and probably even advance, while the influx of Cotton from Egypt will tend to produce a decline in the common descriptions. We have little apprehension that the monopoly in fine Sea Islands, which this country enjoys will be interfered with by the Egyptian Cottons...

The problem realized, the wisest of the planters on the sea islands turned their efforts to producing better quality lower-grade sea island cotton and increasing their yield per acre. Seabrook (1847, 5) described the problem of the planters:

...but mischievous notion, that the seller of [sea island] cotton at 80 cents is necessarily in the receipt of more money than he who disposes of his crop at a rate of fifty percent lower cannot much longer be entertained. The inquiries of the cultivator now very properly relate to the profitableness of cotton, or, what is substantially the same thing, to the kinds best suited to his grounds.

It was only on the best land that the superfine sea island cotton could be grown, but at such a high cost that the profit margin was not great. When planters tried to produce the superfine cotton on marginal land, the resulting fiber did not command the high price (80 cents per pound) of the superfine. However, when they produced lower grades of sea island cotton, which their lands supported, even though they received a rate 50% lower (40 cents per pound), their profit margin was greater since they had produced it at far less cost. This is the message that the sea island planters finally realized.

Communicating with fellow growers became paramount if the planters were to be successful in reversing the decline in prices. In the forefront was the South Carolina Agricultural Society, founded on August 24, 1785, and based in Charleston. The Society became a place for planters to meet and share ideas on increasing crop yield and better preparing cotton for market. Another local society, the St. John's Colleton Society, began analyses of soils and plants. This scientific endeavor was carried to brilliant heights by the Black Oak Agricultural Society centered in St. John's Parish, Berkeley County, in the heart of the Santee long cotton region. Paramount in the Society were the descendants of the French Huguenots—merchants and artisans that had fled France in 1685 and settled in Berkeley County. Through the Black Oak Agricultural Society, planters could discuss elementary chemistry, including the topics of potash, phosphates, nitrogen, and organic and inorganic substances. Also important were the journals like the *Southern Agriculturist* and the *Rural Carolinian*. These publications gave the planters a medium to exchange ideas on agriculture at the local level.

The planters approached the problem of decreased prices in three ways: they produced a cleaner staple for market; they continued seed selection and produced cotton grades that were in demand; and they increased their yield per acre.

Once again, Whitemarsh Seabrook was the agriculturist who most influenced other planters. He noted in his articles that planters ginned, moted and packed cotton in the same room; that there was no reinspection of the cotton before it was bagged; and that spinners often found in the cotton leaves, crushed seeds, stained cotton and any manner of trash. The difference in prices of clean sea island cotton and stained cotton is evident from table 13-3, where the former sold for around triple the latter. The planters took notice, and preparation was improved to the point that six different rooms were used to support six different steps in the process: drying, sorting, whipping, ginning, moting, and packing by hand. The result was a noticeable increase in fiber cleanliness. Even the picking process was improved: pickers were trained to remove as much trash as possible.

That the planters acted on Seabrook's advice is seen in a letter dated August 1, 1823 from the firm of Trapmann, Schmidt & Co., a Charleston factor, to a buyer in Manchester, England (Roberts 1965, 105-106):

The promise of an abundant crop of Sea Islands is good, and from the great exertions now made by all our extensive planters to send their crops to market in the best order, we anticipate a better average quality of long staple cotton than has yet to come to market...

1835-1861: Consolidation

Gray (1958, 738-739) gave a summary of the sea island cotton trade during the 1835-61 period. In the latter half of 1834, prices climbed and peaked between 45 and 50 cents a pound by the early months of 1837. Lower prices prevailed during 1838 and 1839; however, prices for these two years were about 80% above the four years preceding 1835. In 1840, prices opened lower, and throughout the 1840s prices were depressed and shared with other southern staples the low fortunes of the period. In the years 1842-44, prices averaged around 18 cents per pound. Prices recovered somewhat in the last half of the 1840s.

It was during this period that thought was given to expanding the Carolina sea island cotton market to include China to supplement the English and French markets. Whitemarsh Seabrook wrote to the St. Andrew's Agricultural and Police Society and suggested that the Society explore the overseas Chinese market. A committee was formed to answer Seabrook's suggestion and to investigate the possibility. The committee reported (1844, 53):

In conclusion, your committee beg leave respectively, to urge upon your attention, the trial shipment of Sea Island or long staple cotton to the Celestial Empire— believing if it is attended with no immediate benefit, the amount expended on the experience will be no loss in the end. If on the contrary it should prove successful, our object will be attained, and a partial competition will be created for the article. It is very evident, that every exertion should be made by the grower of the raw material, to create a greater demand for this description of cotton, whether it be in France, China, or the United States.

The author found no reference in the literature to whether a serious attempt was made to secure the Chinese market or if a Chinese market ever developed. The issue evidently was never raised again.

The sea islands shared in the prosperity of the 1850s. Prices improved considerably in 1851; by 1852, prices reached on average 37 cents per pound and over 41 cents in 1853. For the remainder of the 1850s, prices averaged better than 30 cents per pound, except for 1858. Fear of a cut-off from sea island cotton by the coming Civil War forced prices to 47 cents in 1860.

The Charleston and lowcountry economy continued to benefit from the sea island cotton trade. Even during the depressed years, based on today's monetary value, the amount of currency pumped into the economy was significant (table 13-10). The low point was in 1844 when the value of the crop was $1,146,800 ($27,416,216); the high point came in 1860 when the value of the crop was $7,332,000 ($157,755,605).

Table 13-10. Historical values of sea island cotton exports, 1835-60, converted to equal values for 2002[11]

Year	Quantity (millions of lbs.)	Price (cts./lb.)	Historic Value ($)	2002 Value ($)
1835	7.8	34.8	2,714,400	55,097,300
1836	7.8	39.5	3,081,000	59,188,320

1837	5.3	46.0	2,438,000	45,614,004
1838	7.3	35.3	2,576,900	49,504,181
1839	5.1	38.7	1,973,700	37,912,257
1840	8.8	22.5	1,980,000	40,963,230
1841	6.2	26.8	1,661,600	34,048,621
1842	7.3	18.1	1,322,030	29,025,357
1843	7.5	16.6	1,245,000	30,098,280
1844	6.1	18.8	1,146,800	27,416,216
1845	9.4	26.6	2,500,400	59,119,457
1846	9.4	26.6	2,500,400	58,476,854
1847	6.3	31.4	1,978,200	42,992,959
1848	7.7	19.0	1,463,000	33,134,701
1849	12.0	23.2	2,784,000	65,109,408
1850	8.2	27.8	2,279,600	52,178,685
1851	8.3	29.3	2,431,900	56,874,845
1852	11.7	37.3	4,364,100	100,965,752
1853	11.2	41.2	3,507,000	81,136,292
1854	10.5	33.4	3,507,000	74,309,655
1855	13.1	31.6	4,139,600	85,642,114
1856	12.8	39.8	5,094,400	107,462,072
1857	12.9	38.1	4,914,900	100,713,509
1858	12.1	29.3	3,545,300	77,051,329
1859	13.7	35.2	4,822,400	103,758,951
1860	15.6	47.0	7,332,000	157,755,605

In 1854, Robert Allston (1854, 18) stated that reasonably good sea island cotton, though not the finest, made with the proper use of the plow and cleaned by improved machinery, yielded "a very handsome income interest upon the capital invested, say not less than from ten to twelve percent." Allston, along with Whitemarsh Seabrook, encouraged the planters to use the new McCarthy roller gin, and by the 1850s it was in common use, improving the quality of the market product. Thus, in spite of the many problems in the sea island cotton trade, planters who concentrated on growing the lower grades of cotton, and who stressed yield per acre and a clean market product, still made a "handsome income." Their attention to improved agricultural practices was rewarded.

By the end of this period, there were 359 plantations spread from Hilton Head to Bull Island in Charleston County. The industry was focused mainly on St. Helena and Edisto islands where the largest plantations were located, the most improved acreage occurred, and the highest yield per acre was made.

In 1860, exports of sea island cotton were up and the prices were highest since 1818 (63.2

cents per pound). The planters anticipated continued prosperity. This was not to be. The American Civil War brought an end to the exceptional prosperity of the sea island cotton culture, as well as all southern staples. Never again were the planters of the sea islands to enjoy the lifestyle that prevailed from 1790 until 1861.

1861-1867: The War Years and Beginning of the Demise of Sea Island Cotton

As war loomed between the South and North, the South perceived cotton as one of its greatest assets. Southerners counted on the continued dependence by Great Britain, France, and the rest of Europe, on southern cotton to feed their insatiable mills, and calculated that Europe would choose to recognize the South's independence in order to keep up their supply of cotton imports. Confederate emissaries in Europe tried to convince European governments that the Union blockade was a "paper" blockade and hence a violation of international law. If the blockade was indeed illegal, European countries would be justified in breaking it. But the goals of diplomatic recognition and intervention remained elusive. British officials were reluctant to support a principle that might backfire against them in a future war. Then, with Lee's failed Maryland campaign and Antietam, followed by Lincoln's announcement of the preliminary Emancipation Proclamation, the British cabinet decided that the time was not ripe for a decision on diplomatic recognition of the South, but instead would wait until the war took a more definite turn. Events that followed ended any possibility of European support.

Part of the southern strategy to remind Europe of its dependence on southern cotton was to put into place a self-imposed embargo on cotton to Europe (but at the same time to conceal the embargo and make it appear that the embargo was having only minimal effect). Planters burned much of their cotton and hid countless thousands of bales to keep it off the market. A law was passed to limit cotton acreage. Henry W. Ravenel (Childs 1947, 171) wrote in his diary on February 17, 1863: "The Legislature lately in session has passed an act making it penal for any one to plant more than 3 acres of upland or 1 1/2 acres of long staple cotton to the hand."

The more patriotic planters to the Confederate cause decreased their cotton acreage (both upland and sea island) to plant more corn and other provision crops to feed the Confederate Army. In the end, these measures were a mistake, since diplomatic recognition was not forthcoming and the South was denied a significant source of money to finance the early war effort. The South also did not count on the East India Company acquiring other sources of cotton (mainly Egyptian) to offset the loss from the South.

Although long-staple cotton (sea island, mains and Santee long) comprised only a fraction of the South's cotton crop, planters of these crops shared the same fate as the planters of upland cotton. They had the same hope that diplomatic recognition would come, the blockade would be broken, and an insatiable European market for their cotton would be realized. Ravenel, in his journal entry of August 6, 1861, expressed what these planters felt (Childs 1947, 86):

CHAPTER THIRTEEN

It would not surprise me to hear that England & France had recognized our Independence, & were proceeding to activate measures in concert for raising the blockade of our ports. These is no time to be lost, for millions of their people earn their subsistence by the cotton manufacture...

And on August 12, Ravenel wrote:

The cotton factors of Charleston are out in a card to Planters to keep at home their cotton until the Blockade is raised from all the Ports of the Confed. States. This will be generally adapted throughout the South; & foreign nations will get no supplies until that takes place...

As the above events were playing out, another one would shake the sea island cotton industry. On November 7, 1861, the islands of St. Helena Parish in Beaufort County were taken over by Union forces and would remain occupied until 1870. The sounds of dull explosions that rolled across Port Royal Sound and echoed up the tidal creeks on that November morning tolled the end of one way of life—the planter aristocracy—and the beginning of another—the development of a free Negro community in the parish. Port Royal served as the base of the Union fleet that blockaded Savannah and Charleston, the main ports for overseas export of sea island cotton. At once, the planters abandoned St. Helena Island, Lady's Island and most of Port Royal Island, and sought refuge inland.

Although the sea islands north of St. Helena near Charleston were not occupied by Union forces, most plantations on these islands were also abandoned as the planters were uncertain of Union intentions outside St. Helena. Safety was their primary concern. Cotton production was suspended on the sea islands except on St. Helena, where freedmen were encouraged to plant their own cotton.

Hilton Head Island became the headquarters for Union naval blockades and land operations. In the later years of the war, the base was commanded by General Milton S. Littlefield, who is credited with an attempt to establish a town on the island, named Mitchellville, for refugee slaves. He apparently planned a get-rich scheme in the hope of developing a "boon city" for the displaced Negroes, but the scheme never materialized and the town disappeared by 1870.

On August 5, 1861, Congress imposed a direct war tax of $29,000,000 on the secessionist states. South Carolina's share was $363,570 ($7,379,798). In St. Helena Parish, the lands of the planters were confiscated, subdivided, and sold to freedmen and northern speculators. Proceeds from the sales were used to help pay for the Union cost of the war. Freedmen now came to own tracts of land of about 10 acres or less; northern speculators took possession of larger acreages. The lands of the former planters were fragmented in such a manner that field boundaries, drainage patterns, and natural features were obliterated. The plantation system in St. Helena Parish was gone forever.

The only sea island cotton grown in South Carolina from 1861 to 1866 was by freedmen in St. Helena Parish. T. J. Woofter (1930, 134) described the situation:

In 1861 agents of the Treasury Department came to take up where the planters left off. The only change at first was that the Negroes were allowed wages for their work. Even before the agents came, however, and after the masters had left, the drivers were holding the hands together in the fields, partially through force of habit and partially because of the realization that the cultivation of the soil was their best chance to avoid starvation. For several years this persistence of the Negroes in working at their accustomed tasks even after their masters had left, fed them as well as produced thousands of bales of the valuable sea island cotton.

During the period of wage-earning, freedmen saved enough of their wages to purchase, at $1.50 per acre, 10-acre plots when the federal government subdivided the plantations and sold the land to heads of families. By June, 1865, there had been 347 such purchases made on St. Helena Island. But when left alone to independent farming, the freedmen experienced numerous problems. Cultivating the crop was not a problem since this was their expertise; however, independently managing financial affairs and marketing was initially beyond their capabilities.

Complicating the problem of cultivation were the disrepair of the drainage systems of the fields, poor climatic conditions, and caterpillars that ravaged the crops. But the biggest problem was the quality of the seed. The cotton crop of 1861 was confiscated and shipped north for ginning and the seed was lost for planting the next crop.[12] Afterwards, inferior seed was used, and on the sea islands, this meant degradation of the long-staple fiber.

Some freedmen overcame the problems they encountered and became reasonably successful small cotton farmers, although they never produced the high-quality fiber of their planter predecessors. Most, however, in the years just after the war, farmed on a subsistence basis, raising their own vegetable crops and planting enough cotton, both short- and long-staple, to produce a little ready cash and pay their taxes.

The author found no records on prices or exports of the long-staple cotton grown in St. Helena Parish during the 1861-67 period. It appears likely that these records were not made or kept.

1867-1920: Attempt to Resurrect Sea Island Cotton Culture

In 1865, after reaching the sea on his march through the South, General Sherman issued Special Field Order No. 15 setting aside "the islands from Charleston, south, the abandoned rice fields along the rivers for thirty miles back from the sea, and the country bordering the St. John's River, Florida," for the freedmen, excluding land sold for tax revenues. Then, two months later, on March 3, 1865, the Freedman's Bureau Act was passed which gave freedmen homestead rights on lands abandoned or confiscated during the war. This act was an attempt to legalize the decrees of war regarding the confiscated lands. Male adult freedmen were allowed to lease not more than 40 acres for three years with an option to buy. The sea island plantations, especially outside of St. Helena Parish, were subdivided and settled by these freedmen.

CHAPTER THIRTEEN

The American Civil War ended on April 9, 1865 when Robert E. Lee surrendered the Army of Northern Virginia to Ulysses S. Grant. President Abraham Lincoln was assassinated on April 17 and Andrew Johnson became president. As a preliminary to Reconstruction, President Johnson issued, on May 29, a pardon to almost all those formerly in rebellion, with restoration of all property rights, except for property sold for the war tax and certain lands under adjudication. On July 16, 1866, Congress enacted—over a veto by President Johnson—an extension of the Freedman's Bureau Act, stating that the sales by the tax commissioners were confirmed and that Negroes holding lands under Sherman's order should have six years to buy their lands at $1.50 an acre. The act also provided for the relocation of freedmen who had acquired land under Sherman's order to other lands in the sea islands confiscated by the government. Lands not included under such tenures were restored to the planters.

Because of the tax sales in St. Helena Parish, most of the land remained in the hands of freedmen. They cultivated tracts ranging from one to 20 acres, growing provision crops such as corn and sweet potatoes, and also long-staple cotton. On the sea islands of James, Johns, Wadmalaw and Edisto, freedmen came to own around ten thousand acres of land. Most of the tracts were around 10 to 60 acres in size and were planted in long-staple cotton and provision crops. They were able to harvest one bag of cotton for every three acres of land, a yield of around $500 to $800 for a typical farmer (Heamphill 1882, 13-14). By 1880, however, freedman produced more vegetable crops than sea island cotton. They viewed the provision crops as more important than cotton, and the crops they raised over their own needs could be sold, producing income.

The end of sea island cotton planting by freedmen on the sea islands was told by Willie Lee Rose in her book *Rehearsal for Reconstruction: The Port Royal Experiment* (1964, 407):

After 1870 truck farming came to be a more important economic activity. Two great calamities eventually spurred the readjustment to its final stages: a great tidal wave in 1893, which wreaked havoc upon the central islands; and the arrival of the boll weevil in 1918. Thereafter the long-staple cotton disappeared, making room for new crops better suited to the new institutions of freedom and small land-ownership.

On the islands of Edisto, Wadmalaw, James, and Johns, after planters regained their former plantations, a new period of sea island cotton cultivation began. But it was a different industry. The main difference in cotton-growing after the war was the number and size of the plantations. The era of large sea island plantations was over. Statistics cited by Kovacik and Mason (1985, 92-93) attest to this change. In 1860 the number of individual farming units was 359; in 1870 there were 2,261. In 1860, 23% of the units were 1,000 acres or larger; in 1870 only 2% were that size. In 1860 only about 5% of the farms were fewer than 100 acres; in 1870 this number had increased to 2,046, or about 90%. Improved acreage dropped from 139,000 acres in 1860 to 81,000 in 1870. Sea island cotton production declined by about 56%.

The wealth of the planters was virtually eliminated by the war. Not only did they lose the value of their slaves, which they could convert to liquid assets when necessary, they lost the value of their land. On Edisto Island, for example, lands that had been worth from $75 to $100 an acre before the war were worth less than $30 by 1867. Plantation lands on the other islands saw similar reductions.

Although the great wealth of the pre-war period was gone, and despite reduced acreage, sea island planters who could afford to and had the knowledge to change their methods of cultivation (see chapter 7) enjoyed prosperity through the 1880s. In the 1890s, however, the nationwide depression reduced this success. During this period, labor became a serious problem. Better employment for freedmen became available elsewhere, especially in cities up north, and they migrated from the sea islands, further exacerbating the labor problems that had plagued the planters since the Civil War. Although the planters had improved their methods of cultivation, only the use of a mule-drawn plow significantly lessened the use of field labor—and some growers still had not shifted to the plow. Nevertheless, for planters able to maintain a sufficient labor force, sea island cotton was profitable through the end of the century and into the early 1900s.

The situation that faced the planters at the beginning of this period was best summarized by William M. Lawton (1870, 228-229):

The growth, preparation and general management of sea island cotton is very expensive, and the selling of it is a matter of chance... The cultivation of this cotton does not yield the producer a reasonable living, and it appears almost futile to contend against its decline... The competition by other countries now producing sea island cotton at cheaper rates, similar to that of Carolina, Georgia and Florida, and the fact that the spinners are discontinuing the use of American sea island varieties, are serious admonitions and undoubted evidences to those in the trade... Growing sea island cotton appears, truly, to have ceased to afford a money profit.

H. A. Towles also expounded on the problems facing the sea island planters in his report to the Sea Island Cotton Protective Union (1891, 5):

In 1889 there was imported into the U.S. for consumption— 7,983,699 pounds of cotton valued at $1,195,368.00, brought here by manufactures and speculators from the different countries where long staple cotton is raised. The price paid for this cotton, imported that year, was, 15 1/2c per pound.

He pointed out that the sea island planters could not produce cotton at a price to compete with the foreign imports that used cheap labor. He outlined an elaborate plan to send a delegation from Florida, Georgia and South Carolina to Washington to lobby for a duty to be placed on foreign long-staple cotton to keep out all or a portion of it. He was convinced that the domestic production of sea island cotton could satisfy the markets. There is no record of

Congress ever requiring such a duty and the issue evidently was never again brought up.

Cook and Doyle (1927, 2) probably stated best the problem with growing sea island cotton in the early 1900s:

Several years before the war-time advance in the cost of production it was recognized that the growing of sea-island cotton could not be continued at prices below 30 cents a pound, whereas the market held around 23 cents, even for the best sea-island fiber.

Even in 1907, however, planters were optimistic that the sea island cotton industry could survive well into the future because of new domestic markets. Even though the quality of sea island cotton had declined considerably, it still commanded a higher price than upland cotton. The invention of pneumatic tires for a burgeoning car industry, continued demand for finer fabrics in the overseas markets, and specialized domestic uses such as racing sails, lace making, stockings, fishing line and electrical tape, gave hope to the planters that the industry could survive.

Events beginning in the early 1900s, however, signalled the final decline of profitable sea island cotton. The West Indies introduced the Rivers strain of sea island cotton in 1902 to provide a commercial crop to supplement or replace their flagging sugar cane crop. Expert Carolina planters were employed to teach farmers of St. Vincent, Antigua, Barbados and other Caribbean islands how to grow sea island cotton. Seed was provided from the best Carolina plantations. The project became so successful that within five or six years the pressure of this new competition began to be felt in the Carolina sea islands and a depression of prices followed. The James Island Agricultural Society in 1905 (1936, 111) adopted the following resolution in response to the problem:

Whereas. It is believed that the crops of Sea Island Cotton grown in Georgia & Florida and that now being harvested in the West Indies are the main causes of the depressed conditions of our local Sea Island Cotton and

Whereas. These crops have been grown mainly from seed raised upon our Sea Islands and sold to parties in these various localities and

Therefore. /be/it Resolved that in the judgement of the James Island Agricultural Society, the sale of Sea Island Cotton seed to parties beyond the limits of the State should be stopped.

Continued success of the Caribbean crop relied on seed purchased from the Carolinas. Seeking to combat this market, planters who produced the high-quality seed terminated all sales of it, even to fellow planters. But this action had devastating effects on the industry. Sea island planters who had depended on this seed now either planted inferior seed or switched to upland cotton. By 1913, James Island had more than 100 acres of upland cotton; Johns and Wadmalaw had more upland than sea island cotton; and Edisto Island had about equal amounts of each.

Switching to upland cotton resulted in hybridization if the upland cotton was planted adjacent to sea island fields, further reducing the quality of the staple. Georgia and Florida interior sea island cotton, which was produced more profitably and on a larger scale, gradually cut into the local market. Cultivars of American-Egyptian long-staple cotton grown in the American Southwest became competitors. The Yuma cultivar was introduced in 1912 and the Pima in 1918. In 1912-13, Carolina planters decided to hold their cotton off the market to try to get a higher price. This failed because other suppliers of long-staple cotton filled the gap. Great Britain exploited the long-staple cotton from India when their U.S. supply was cut off during World War I (1914-18).

Carolina sea island planters, seeking answers to the problems with their crop, forwarded through the Charleston Chamber of Commerce to the U.S. Department of Agriculture a request for an investigation of the market and economic conditions in the Carolina sea island cotton industry. The Office of Markets of the Department of Agriculture sent cotton technologist William R. Meadows to perform a study. Meadows expanded the original request to include Georgia and Florida, and presented his report on September 25, 1914. He found that the unsatisfactory condition of the sea island trade (he lumped Florida and Georgia as well as Carolina cotton as American sea island)[13] was due to underconsumption rather than to overproduction. Further, said Meadows, the loss of this market was due to the increase in consumption of Egyptian long-staple cotton. Basing his findings on a study of the 1912-13 season, Meadows gave six reasons, summarized as follows, for the decreased consumption of American long-staple cotton at the expense of Egyptian:

1. The competition of Sakellaridis. Sakellaridis was a long-staple Egyptian cotton that, although somewhat coarser than sea island, harsher and less elastic, was stronger than the lower grades of American sea island. It also had a comparatively uniform staple of 1 1/2 inches in length. Sakellaridis, then, replaced American sea island for sewing thread and tire cloth. Also, once the mills shifted to the new cotton, it was difficult to turn back to American sea island because the customer tended to be suspicious when a mill changed the appearance of its goods.

2. The deteriorated quality of sea island. Once the Carolina planters quit selling their seed to the West Indies and at home, the quality of American sea island cotton deteriorated.

3. Changes in clothing styles. Women's dress goods changed from soft, smooth, lustrous cloths composed of fine yarns and of high counts per inch of both warp and weft, to coarser, rougher effects with fewer threads per inch in the woven fabric. Accordingly, less American sea island cotton was required, once again favoring other long-staple cottons like Sakellaridis.

4. Economy of production. The introduction of advanced combers that could successfully comb upland cottons and improved cotton-mill machinery made it easy for manufacturers to switch to shorter staples and still produce an attractive article to the average consumer.

5. The tire industry. The change in the cotton fiber used in the large automobile tire industry had a dramatic effect on American sea island cotton. Early on, the best grades of sea island cotton were considered none too good for tires. Prices and quality were paramount, and tires

were sold under a guarantee as to lasting qualities. Then, demand from consumers for a cheaper tire brought about a switch to upland long-staple and lower grades of sea island or brown Egyptian. Thus, the largest market for American sea island cotton was closed.

6. The market deadlock of 1912-13. In the sea island cotton trade there was not a "futures" market as there was for the upland or Egyptian cottons. Spinners who wanted to buy their supplies against sales of yarns (which were frequently made a year in advance) had to buy sea island cotton outright, or else find a dealer who was willing to assume the risk. The dealer would sell contracts for the delivery of a definite number of bales per month during the time covered by the agreement.

In October of 1912, spinners were buying cotton at the prevailing prices. But when the planters saw a Census Bureau report that predicted the crop for 1912 would be 70,000 bales—less than originally expected by the planters—the better-informed planters decided that the crop would be short and that the price would advance, so they resolved to hold out for better prices. This resulted in an immediate advance in the primary asking price of two to three cents per pound. Accordingly, cotton buyers and exporters were unable to buy cotton at the price the spinners were willing to pay, and they refused to sell spots or make contracts with mills for future delivery at the prices which millmen offered. Spinners then turned to Egyptian Sakellaridis and brown Egyptian. They bought not only for their immediate needs, but up to twelve months in advance. Many of these substitutes were contracted for a year in advance and became permanent. This closed the market for American sea island cotton.

Meadows then discussed the situation in just the Carolina sea island cotton culture. He contended that excessive use of the hoe had resulted in higher costs in producing cotton, and pointed out that in Georgia and Florida, where all cultivation except two hoeings were done with the plow, the cost of cultivation was about two-thirds that of the sea islands. While acknowledging that conditions in the sea islands were different from Georgia and Florida, Meadows suggested it would be worthwhile for Carolina planters to make a trial of substituting horsepower for human power.

Another problem Meadows saw was the tendency to produce too great a diversity of staples. There would not be a problem with a few planters growing the highest quality staple, he counselled; however, if the planters could organize for the purpose of growing one variety on a community basis and keep the planting seed to one type, they would produce a product better suited to the needs of the mills. Meadows suggested a fiber length of 1 7/8 inches, which would remove it from competition with the 1 5/8-inch staple length grown in Florida and Georgia. But, he cautioned, the planters with the best crop must share their seeds with their fellow planters to make the process work. Meadows also pointed that there was a problem with marketing in Charleston (see the section on the factorage system at the beginning of this chapter).

World War I gave the planters one more hope for sea island cotton. Airplane wing covering had been made chiefly of linen prior to the war. With the increasing scarcity of linen, and with Egyptian cotton unavailable because of the halt in shipping, planters hoped that the government would have to depend on sea island cotton to mount a successful air campaign against Germany. Planters would have even welcomed government control over cotton-growing since they believed they would receive a better profit there than in the open market.

Sea island planters never had the time to implement Meadows's suggestions or to clothe the American air fleet. The boll weevil ended the sea island cotton industry in South Carolina in the 1919-20 growing season. Only 3,030 bales were harvested, and a crop was not planted in 1920. Along with Carolina gold rice, another crop which represented the finest of its kind ever grown, sea island cotton vanished forever as a commercial crop in the South Carolina lowcountry.

The events cited above that affected the sea island cotton industry after the Civil War can best be summarized by the figures in table 13-11. Although the Charleston economy still benefitted significantly from sea island cotton, compared to the pre-war years, the benefit was reduced.

Table 13-11. Historical values of sea island cotton crop for South Carolina, 1867-1920, converted to equal values for 2002[14]

Year	Bales	Pounds	Price (cts./lb.)	Historical($)	2002($)
1867-68	9,266	3,085,578	.8600	2,653,597.10	33,388.831.20
1868-69	7,350	2,447,550	.9800	2,398,599.00	31,468,507.33
1869-70	11,585	3,857,805	.6800	2,623,307.40	35,951,074.49
1870-71	13,049	4,345,317	.7500	3,258,987.80	47,701,028.48
1871-72	11,945	3,977,685	.8100	3,221,924.90	47,158,547.64
1872-73	17,418	5,800,194	.6400	3,712,124.20	55,465,425.54
1873-74	11,703	3,897,099	.4300	1,675,752.60	26,317,962.99
1874-75	11,223	3,737,259	.3600	1,345,413.20	21,930,275.93
1875-76	8,188	2,726,604	.3900	1,063,376.60	17,736,165.47
1876-77	11,057	3,681,981	.3800	1,399,152.80	23,892,244.14
1877-78	11,106	3,698,298	.2900	1,072,506.40	19,230,075.50
1878-79	9,419	3,136,527	.2900	909,592.83	16,309,029.76
1879-80	9,966	3,318,678	.3600	1,194,724.10	20,898,968.12
1880-81	14,868	4,951,044	.3070	1,519,970.50	26,588,411.44
1881-82	10,796	3,595,068	.3010	1,082,115.50	18,929,138.52
1882-83	16,591	5,524,803	.2800	1,546,944.80	27,507,542.31
1883-84	7,329	2,440,557	.3970	968,901.13	17,666,877.52
1884-85	12,588	4,191,804	.2870	1,203,047.70	22,314,502.10
1885-86	8,497	2,289,501	.3460	792,167.35	15,083,455.21
1886-87	8,735	2,909,421	.2450	712,808.15	13,453,340.94
1887-88	8,561	2,850,813	.2890	823,884.96	15,549,773.47

1888-89	9,618	3,202,794	.2690	861,551.59	16,700,160.79
1889-90	9,256	3,082,248	.2940	906,180.91	17,887,545.60
1890-91	16,306	5,429,898	.2160	1,172,858.00	23,151,614.35
1891-92	11,499	3,829,167	.1680	643,300.06	12,698,412.68
1892-93	7,212	2,401,596	.2510	602,800.60	12,009,149.83
1893-94	2,578	858,474	.3400	291,881.16	6,097,210.40
1894-95	5,894	1,962,702	.2400	471,048.48	10,034,750.43
1895-96	9,971	3,320,343	.2680	889,851.92	18,956,524.26
1896-97	10,701	3,563,433	.2080	741,194.06	15,947,561.04
1897-98	10,201	3,396,933	.2070	703,165.13	15,129,329.06
1898-99	5,629	1,874,457	.2470	462,990.88	9,961,730.29
1899-1900	7,810	2,600,730	.2000	520,146.00	11,080,675.39
1900-01	8,377	2,789,541	.2450	683,437.55	14,416,538.89
1901-02	8,641	2,877,453	.2330	670,446.55	14,005,198.92
1902-03	12,635	4,207,455	.2500	1,051,863.80	21,350,890.18
1903-04	9,549	3,179,817	.2840	903,068.03	18,159,297.06
1904-05	12,242	4,076,586	.2712	1,105,570.10	22,441,028.77
1905-06	13,714	4,566,762	.2638	1,204,711.80	24,000,580.81
1906-07	8,037	2,676,321	.3800	1,017,002.00	19,364,474.08
1907-08	12,727	4,238,011	.2400	1,017,122.60	19,715,721.21
1908-09	15,392	5,125,536	.3400	1,742,682.20	34,399,651.31
1909-10	14,578	4,854,474	.3285	1,594,694.70	30,097,820.13
1910-11	13,357	4,447,881	.3562	1,584,335.20	29,902,297.84
1911-12	5,140	1,711,620	.2373	406,167.43	7,469,328.78
1912-13	8,375	2,788,875	.2500	697,218.75	12,606,207.15
1913-14	8,961	2,984,013	.2347	700,347.85	12,557,260.30
1914-15	5,488	1,827,504	.2200	402,050.88	7,149,208.94
1915-16	6,212	2,068,596	.2700	588,520.92	9,740,492.04
1916-17	3,573	1,189,809	.5000	594,904.50	8,366,005.89
1917-18	7,146	2,379,618	.8000	1,903,694.40	22,755,536.03
1918-19	10,067	3,352,311	.6500	2,179,002.20	22,649,033.09
1919-20	3,030	1,008,990	1.1025	1,112,411.50	9,972,787.64

The Sea Island Cotton Market

The sea island cotton staple was, by all accounts, the finest staple of cotton ever grown. Throughout its cultivation, its silky fiber was in high demand in the overseas market for the production of muslins and exquisite laces to clothe the wealthy and middle ranks of society (upland cotton was used to clothe the common man). A quote from John Mathewes in a letter to Whitemarsh Seabrook (Seabrook 1827, 35) testified to the demand for quality long-staple cotton:

A very respectable Broker, in Glasgow, observed, "a superior cotton is much wanted, and, that price is only a secondary object to the dealers in this valuable quality of your staple produce."

The sea island cotton market was almost entirely foreign, as the United States excelled in the production of basic cloth, and short-staple cotton was adequate only for this market. A few hundred bales of sea island cotton were used in the United States, chiefly in making spool cotton. During the latter years of its cultivation, where great strength and durability were required, it was used in the United States for mail bags and pneumatic tires.

Sea island cotton was sold mainly in Charleston, South Carolina, and Savannah, Georgia. Charleston was by far more important because of its central location and its fine harbor along with its market facilities. The customary selling season ran from October 1 through September 30 of the following year. The bulk of the crop was sold from October through January. Any surplus not sold was carried over until the next selling season, but never amounted to very much.

The long-staple, sea island cotton market can be divided into three somewhat well-defined periods: (1) The market from William Elliott's first commercial crop in 1790 to the beginning of the Civil War in 1861; (2) the war years and immediately afterward, 1861-67; and (3) the post-war market after cultivation recommenced in 1867 to its end in 1920 when the boll weevil ravaged the crop.

1790-1861: Beginning of the Industry until the Civil War

The majority of the South Carolina sea island cotton crop grown during this period was shipped overseas. At that time, there was little or no competition from other long-staple cottons of the high quality of sea island cotton. The following tables show the exports of sea island cotton for two periods during this time frame:

Table 13-12. Exports of sea island cotton from South Carolina, 1790-1801 (Gray 1958, 679)

Year	Pounds	Bales
Oct. 1, 1789 – Sept. 30, 1790	9,840	30
Oct. 1, 1790 – Sept. 30, 1791	54,075	164
Oct. 1, 1791 – Sept. 30, 1792	76,710	232
Oct. 1, 1792 – Sept. 30, 1793	93,540	284
Oct. 1, 1793 – Sept. 30, 1794	159,040	482
Oct. 1, 1794 – Sept. 30, 1795	1,109,653	3,363
Oct. 1, 1795 – Sept. 30, 1796	912,600	2,765

Oct. 1, 1796 – Sept. 30, 1797	1,008,511	3,056
Oct. 1, 1797 – Sept. 30, 1798	2,476,431	7,504
Oct. 1, 1798 – Sept. 30, 1799	2,801,996	8,491
Oct. 1, 1799 – Sept. 30, 1800	6,425,863	19,472
Oct. 1, 1800 – Sept. 30, 1801	8,301,907	25,157

Table 13-13. Exports of bales of sea island cotton from the United States, 1825-57 (Donnell 1872)

Export Foreign and Coastwise	From Georgia	From South Carolina
1825	7,769	18,523
1826	6,354	12,647
1827	14,666	31,828

Export Foreign and Coastwise	From Savannah	From Charleston
1828	11,648	22,750

Export to Foreign Ports	From Savannah	From Charleston
1830	9,579	16,536
1831	7,582	18,597
1832	9,964	16,941
1833	12,168	21,787
1834	9,055	17,149
1835	8,362	15,171
1836	7,938	15,168
1837	3,906	12,154
1838	5,680	16,712
1839	4,225	9,975
1840	8,108	19,310

Export		From Savannah	From Charleston
1841	To Foreign Ports	5,100	12,991
	Coastwise	807	970
1842	To Foreign Ports	6,976	14,119
	Coastwise	674	741
1843	To Foreign Ports	6,444	16,351
	Coastwise	1,046	681
1844	To Foreign Ports	3,554	15,043
	Coastwise	2,151	1,148

Year				
1845	To Foreign Ports	6,108	20,905	
	Coastwise	1,901	423	
1846	To Foreign Ports	8,472	19,527	
	Coastwise	2,225	476	
1847	To Foreign Ports	5,665	10,869	
	Coastwise	1,530	698	
1848	To Foreign Ports	7,258	15,345	
	Coastwise	1,253	685	
1849	To Foreign Ports	10,622	18,111	
	Coastwise	938	813	
1850s	To Foreign Ports	8,603	14,366	
	Coastwise	1,839	2,071	
1851	To Foreign Ports	8,497	13,576	
	Coastwise	3,145	2,210	
1852	To Foreign Ports	7,605	19,008	
	Coastwise	3,656	3,305	
1853	To Foreign Ports	6,731	17,848	
	Coastwise	6,140	2,128	
1854	To Foreign Ports	3,861	18,154	
	Coastwise	11,667	6,612	
1855	To Foreign Ports	6,993	18,680	
	Coastwise	7,474	5,771	

Export		From Savannah	From Charleston	From Florida
1856	To Foreign Ports	8,138	18,765	
	Coastwise	7,346	9,286	10,900
1857	To Foreign Ports	6,611	16,581	
	Coastwise	10,028		

None of these tables indicates that the exports were for the total sea island crop produced. As such, it cannot be known with certainty what percentage of the total crop was exported. However, from the literature cited throughout this book, the author concludes that these export figures represent the total crop produced each year. From the records of this time period there is no mention of significant pounds or bales of sea island cotton remaining in the United States.

The years 1841-56 cite a small amount of the South Carolina crop going "coastwise." This is interpreted as the part of the crop remaining in the United States and being used in the specialty area of the burgeoning domestic manufacturing industry. No matter how the data are interpreted, certainly the greater portion of the sea island cotton was exported, and of the countries to which it was sent, Great Britain and France were the major markets.

Table 13-14 gives the breakdown of the bales exported to Great Britain and France respectively for the two years 1843 and 1844. Although the author found no statistics on the breakdown between Great Britain and France for other years, text material indicates the same export ratio existed then.

Table 13-14. Exports of sea island cotton from Charleston and Georgia to England and France, 1843 and 1844 (Lebby, Hinson and Rivers 1844, 414)[15]

	Exports 1843 Great Britain	France	Exports 1844 Great Britain	France
Georgia	6,444		3,458	62
South Carolina	15,200	1,050	12,350	2,440
Total	21,644	1,050	15,808	2,502

1861-1866: The War Years and Immediate Aftermath

The Civil War brought a total cessation of sea island cotton production except by freedmen on St. Helena Parish. St. Helena came under Union occupation on November 7, 1861, and the white planters fled the island, leaving behind their plantations and a unpicked crop in the field. According to T. J. Woofter's classic book, *Black Yeomanry: Life on St. Helena Island* (1930), the crop in the field was sent to New York to be ginned. The author found no reference to where the market was for the small amount of sea island cotton produced on St. Helena during occupation by Union forces.

1867-1920: The Post-War Years and the End of Sea Island Cotton

Great Britain and France were the major consumers of Carolina sea island cotton prior to the Civil War. That changed after the war as evidenced from the data (table 13-15) compiled by the cotton brokerage firm of Henry W. Frost & Company of Charleston and Savannah. The data shows a gradual decline in foreign use and a rise in domestic use. Various factors contributed to this change in markets. The war interrupted the seed selection process that contributed so greatly to the quality of sea island cotton. Coupled with the loss of seed selection was the effect of hybridization with upland cotton. After the war, fields were much smaller, and numerous planters experimented with upland cotton. Crossing between the two species resulted in lower fiber quality. The consequence was a lower demand for the specialty market overseas that sea island cotton had experienced before the war.

Table 13-15. Exports of bales of sea island cotton from Charleston, 1906-07 to 1919-20 (*Henry W. Frost & Co.'s Sea Island Cotton Circular*, 1907-20, Charleston Museum)[16]

Market Season	Liverpool	Manchester	Havre	Northern Mills	Southern Mills
1906-07		3,029	2,190	2,792	
1907-08		4,231	1,748	3,896	
1908-09		9,681	2,007	5,571	
1909-10	400	7,547	1,159	5,154	
1910-11	500	5,559	1,419	4,447	
1911-12		909	1,344	3,695	
1912-13		1,937	3,112	1,841	
1913-14	15	3,153	2,082	4,327	921
1914-15		1,519		2,868	707

Market Season	Liverpool & Manchester	Havre	Northern Mills	Southern Mills
1915-16	545		3,814	1,039

Market Season	Liverpool	Havre	Northern Mills	Southern Mills
1916-17	365		2,946	290
1917-18			4,619	1,186
1918-19	371	237	9,338	548
1919-20	417	460	2,002	165

Sea island cotton was only slightly affected by the fluctuations of short-staple upland cotton; however, the amount and quality of long-staple upland cotton, as grown in the Mississippi Valley, seriously affected the low grades of sea island cotton. Sea island staples less than 1 5/8 inches sold well only in a year when the long-staple upland cotton was inferior. During years when long-staple upland cotton was of high quality, since it could be produced at lesser cost than sea island, it competed well. Sea island growers had to avoid letting their staple become less than 1 5/8 inches to avoid this competition.

Also instrumental in reducing the demand overseas was the production of other cultivars of long-staple cotton that could now compete with sea island cotton. Great Britain exploited the long-staple cotton from India when the American supply was cut off by the war. In 1902, sea island cotton from the United States was taken to the West Indies where a commercial crop was established. Then, in 1908, a variety of long-staple cotton called Yuma was established in the American Southwest.

By the end of the industry, the main market for sea island cotton was domestic. The boll weevil ended the domestic trade in 1920.

---

1. The author has converted historical monetary values to today's equivalent using John J. McCusker's website www.eh.net/hmit/ppowerusd. His conversion at the time of publication was for the year 2002; accordingly, the figues quoted in this book are all converted to 2002 values. For example, $16,000 in

CHAPTER THIRTEEN

1825 was worth $289,291 in 2002. Whenever a historic monetary figure has been converted to modern currency, it is represented in the text as follows: $16,000 ($289,291). The figure in parentheses is the equivalent value for 2002.

2. Table 13-1. Gray stated his data came from the U.S. Department of the Treasury, Bureau of Statistics, *Cotton in Commerce*, page 20. Gray does not indicate whether the quotes are for true sea island cotton or include mains and Santee long. Judging from the text material, the author surmises that the figures are for sea island, and that mains and Santee long are not included.

3. Table 13-2 was compiled from Donnell's (1872) "Weekly Quotations in the Charleston Market" for the years 1816-25. He stated that he was unable to find market quotations prior to 1816. No reason was given why the weekly quotations ended in 1825. The quotations for each year included figures for all 52 weeks. For brevity the author used quotations for only weeks 1, 10, 20, 30, 40, and 52.

4. Table 13-3. The author interpret the notation "4 a 9.25" to mean a range of 4¢ to 9.25¢.

5. Table 13-4. Roberts stated that the data in this table were based on figures given in the *Letters* and tend to support figures cited in Gray (table 13-5), but are probably more accurate than Gray's as they are for classifications making up the bulk of the crop, ranging from ordinary to good. The figures indicated that a wide range of prices for sea island cotton existed among classes, with the better classes often selling for more than double the price of ordinary grades.

6. Table 13-6. Gray states that the data for this table came from the following sources: for 1800-15, mainly from the *Carolina Gazette* or *Charleston Courier*, with scattered quotes from other sources, and for 1816-60, quotes came from the *Charleston Courier*. For 1800-31 the quotes are for sea island cotton; for 1832-34 the quotes are for a mixture of mains and Santee long; and for 1845-60 the quotes are mainly for sea island cotton. Gray states that it was difficult to construct a satisfactory price series for sea island cotton because the market was extremely narrow, and the variation in classes and grades was large for so small a total crop. Furthermore, no single class or grade was regularly reported, and many transactions were private and did not appear in market quotations.

7. The author was not able to find price quotes before 1800.

8. The Embargo Act of 1807. The resumption of war between Britain and France in 1803 compromised the Atlantic trade, of which Charleston was a major participant. Both Britain and France commenced retaliatory trade restrictions, each believing its enemy was being helped by trade. The United States, a neutral country, was caught in the crossfire. Tensions escalated between Britain and the United States because the Americans maintained their rights as a neutral country with rights to trade with all countries. Britain seethed over the Americans making money via trade with its enemies. War appeared likely with Britain. Hoping to prevent war, President Jefferson declared the Embargo Act of 1807, which closed American ports to foreign ships and prohibited overseas trade. The embargo was lifted by Congress in March of 1809.

9. Table 13-8. Quantity export values for 1805-19 were obtained from table 13-1; prices were obtained from table 13-6; historic values were obtained by multiplying quantity times price; values for 2002 were obtained using McCusker (2002).

10. Table 13-9. Quantity export values for 1820-34 were obtained from table 13-1; prices were obtained from table 13-6; historic values were obtained by multiplying quantity times price; values for 2002 were obtained using McCusker (2002).

11. Table 13-10. Quantity export values for 1835-60 were obtained from table 13-1; prices were

obtained from table 13-5; historic values were obtained by multiplying quantity times price; values for 2002 were obtained using McCusker (2002).

12. Three accounts appear in the literature explaining why the 1861 cotton crop was sent to New York for ginning instead of being ginned locally. Willie Lee Rose (1964, 24) reported that Colonel William H. Reynolds, in the capacity of a Treasury agent, was sent to Beaufort to collect contraband cotton (seized after the planters fled). Reynolds chose to send the cotton to New York for ginning to help the unemployed classes of the North rather than have it ginned locally. A second Treasury agent, Edward L. Pierce, was sent to Beaufort to look after the welfare of the freedmen, and thought it best to gin the cotton on site to give the freedmen work they had been accustomed to doing. He suspected that there might have been graft in Reynolds's plan to ship the cotton to New York. But Pierce did not act on his idea, and the cotton was shipped to New York. Guion Johnson (1926, 161) reported that "The agents had expected to bale the cotton on the plantations, but the Negroes had quite generally broken up the gins so that most of it had to be sent to New York for this purpose." In any case, the good seed for the next year's crop was lost.

13. "American sea island" is used to include the Georgia and Florida interior sea island cotton and the Carolina sea island cotton. Mains and Santee long were no longer produced after the Civil War, and Georgia had abandoned long-staple on its sea islands, so these market classes were no longer used.

14. Table 13-11 has been compiled from numerous sources. The number of bales exported from 1880 until 1921 was obtained from Shepperson (1921, 55). The prices of sea island cotton for the market seasons 1880-81 to 1901-02 were compiled from weekly quotes in the *Charleston News and Courier*. The price for each year was the average for all classes of sea island cotton. The prices for the market seasons 1902-03 through 1905-06 were obtained from Meadows (1914, 17, table 3). The prices of sea island cotton from the market seasons 1906-07 through 1908-09 were obtained from Henry W. Frost & Company's Sea Island Cotton Circular on deposit in the Charleston Museum. The prices for the market seasons 1909-10 through 1919-20 were obtained from Shepperson (1921, 123). Pounds for each year were obtained by multiplying 333 times the number of bales. The pounds per bale were obtained from Roberts (1965, pages 142, 149, 178, 181, and 189). The weights of the bales cited on these pages were averaged to get 333. The historical values of the cotton were obtained by multiplying price per pound times the number of pounds. The historical values were converted to values of 2002 by using McCusker's (2002) conversions. For a particular growing season such as 1888-99, the second year was used to calculate the values for 2002 since most of the cotton was sold during the spring after the cotton was picked and baled.

15. Table 13-14. The statistics for this table were obtained from Lebby, Hinson and Rivers (1844, 414). They state that their source was the *Charleston Courier* of August 10, 1844.

16. Table 13-15. The information on the number of bales coming into the Charleston market was obtained from the Henry W. Frost & Co.'s Sea Island Cotton Circular at the Charleston Museum. The blank entries in this and other tables were original; it is unknown to the author why no data were shown.

The Kinsey Burden Family and Sea Island Cotton

The Kinsey Burden family played a significant and prominent role in the history and development of sea island cotton from its inception until the Civil War. The central figures of the Burden family were: Kinsey Burden Sr. (died 1785); Portia Ash Burden, his wife (dates unknown); their son, Kinsey Burden (1775-1859); and James King (died 1840), who married their daughter, Theodora Ash Burden.

Considerable confusion appears in the historical literature over the name Kinsey Burden. During the time that sea island cotton was planted, three men held this name. Confusion has arisen because of the sequencing of Senior and Junior among these three. Standard practice is for Senior to be applied to the older of two persons having the same name, while Junior is applied to distinguish the son from the father of the same name. In the Burden family this sequence was not uniformly followed. The first Kinsey Burden (died 1785) is referred to as Kinsey Burden Sr. His son has been referred to as both Senior and Junior, and sometimes with no designation. He was Kinsey Burden (1775-1859), who developed sea island cotton. He will be referred to in this book simply as Kinsey Burden because this is how he was most often called. The son of this Burden is referred to in the literature as Kinsey Burden Jr.[1]

Kinsey Burden Sr.'s birthdate and early history are unknown. His will read, in part: "If any property should be recovered from my parental Estate in Philadelphia, Pennsylvania, New Jersey…" From this note it appears that Kinsey Burden Sr. was originally from the Pennsylvania or New Jersey area. Prior to 1770 he married Portia Ash, daughter of Captain Richard and Martha Ash. Through Portia's inheritance, she and Kinsey came to reside at Dedcott's Island (Taylor, 1974).[2] Dedcott's was the first recorded name of the island described as "…lying and being on the west side of Edisto River, butting and bounding on the eastward on the marsh of the said river, to the southward and westward on a large creek of said river, and to the northward on 'Tubedue' Creek." The Edisto River mentioned is the North Edisto and Tubedue Creek is called Toogoodoo Creek today. Sometime before 1825 the island was changed from Dedcott's Island to Burden's Island, since it appears as such on the Mills *Atlas* of 1825 (fig. 5-2).

Kinsey Burden Sr. was a carpenter by trade, as is evidenced from this amusing notice in the August 22, 1769 *South Carolina Gazette and Country Journal*:

As Miles Brewton Esquire's dining room is of a new construction with respect to the finishing of windows and doorways, it has been industriously propagated by some, (believed to be Mr. Kinsey Burden, a carpenter) that the said Waite did not do the architecture, and conduct the execution thereof. Therefore the said Waite, begs leave to do himself justice in this public manner, and assure all gentlemen, that he the said Waite, did construct every individual part and drawed the same at large for the joiners to work by, and conducted the execution thereof. Any man that can prove to the contrary, the said Waite promises to pay him One Hundred Guineas, as witness my hand, this 22nd day of August, 1769.

Ezra Waite

There are numerous references in "The Thomas Elfe Account Book, 1768-1775," published in the *South Carolina Historical and Genealogical Magazine* (for example, see vol. 36, no. 4, 1935, p. 130) to a "Henzy" Burden and a "Kenzie" Burden, both of whom are undoubtedly Kinsey Burden Sr. The reference above contains the following notation:

Henzy Burden 24th For 4 Bal-
coney posts Turned a 5/
Sundries   D^r. To Shop

Kinsey Burden Sr. also went into partnership with Richard Muncrief, for there are references in the records of the Court of Chancery of South Carolina, 1671-1790 (Gregorie 1950, 608) regarding legal matters in dissolving their partnership.

Much of what is known about Kinsey Burden Sr. as a planter was given by his son Kinsey in an article in the *Southern Agriculturist* (Burden 1844a, 161). He stated that his father retired from the City of Charleston in 1777 and settled on Burden's Island (fig. 5-1) with his family. As early as 1778 or 1779, both black-seed cotton (long-staple) and green-seed cotton (short-staple) were cultivated by his father for domestic use. His father clothed his family partly—and his Negroes entirely—in homespuns, woven on his own loom, of materials taken from his sheep and his cotton patches.

During this period, reported Burden, he remembered assisting the servants in separating the cotton lint from the seed by hand, and that the servants preferred the black-seed cotton. It was at this time, in 1777, that his father constructed probably the first roller gin used in South Carolina. With this simple gin, enough cotton was ginned on Burden's Island for the family's domestic use.[3]

During the Revolutionary War, Kinsey Burden Sr. and his family and slaves were driven by the British from his plantation to the mainland, where they built earthen cellars in thick woods. There they remained for several months until he procured a residence at the house of an elderly physician where his family stayed while Kinsey Sr. was at the American camp.

Kinsey Burden recalled (1844a, 162):

From that sequestered spot, the faithful part of his people [Negro slaves] who were not carried off by the enemy, resorted in the day time in boats to the plantation, to cultivate the crop, having sentinels placed on the look-out to give notice of the approach of the enemy, who repeatedly plundered the plantation.

Kinsey Burden Sr. returned with his family to Burden's Island after the war, where he cultivated indigo as a crop, and stopped growing cotton. He died in 1785. His widow, Portia Ash Burden, assumed operation of the plantation, employed an overseer, and planted indigo in 1786 and 1787. Both crops were lost because of mismanagement or neglect by the overseer. After the second year, she discharged the overseer and took over the planting herself. She secured a few bushels of long-staple cotton seed from a merchant in Charleston, manured her fields, and planted cotton and corn. The cotton plants grew about six feet high, but did not bloom until the latter part of September or October, which, according to her son, did not produce ripened pods. The cause of the failure was subsequently traced to the seed, which was from Bourbon cotton first imported into Manchester, England, in 1783 (Seabrook 1844a, 21).[4]

The creditors of Burden's estate became impatient for the money owed them, sold the Negro slaves, and prevented Portia from pursuing experiments with other cotton seed. For the record, however, Portia Ash Burden was the first individual to attempt a crop of long-staple cotton in South Carolina.

James King, according to Slann Simmons (1958, 78), came to South Carolina in 1788 from Norwich, England. Kinsey Burden (1844a, 163) gives a brief account of King's early years. He reported that King came to Charleston about the year 1790[5] with an adventure of goods, sold them off, went to Georgia, invested his money in Negroes, and planted a crop of rice with success in 1791. In 1792, King moved to the Ogeechee River in Georgia and planted cotton, with the crop failing. He sold out his holdings in Georgia, moved to Burden's Island, purchased more slaves, and planted in 1793 his first crop of long-staple cotton on shares with his mother-in-law, Portia Ash Burden.

Kinsey Burden reported that James King's cotton produced well, and that he (Burden) sold it for King and his mother at "12 and 13 pence per lb. to Messrs Teasdale & Kiddle, the only purchasers of cotton in Charleston at that time." In 1794, King's crop of cotton failed, and he abandoned it, instead planting rice in 1795 and 1796. In 1797, Kinsey Burden persuaded King to again plant long-staple cotton, which he did. King continued to plant on Burden's Island until at least 1825, for there is this reference in the McConnel-Kennedy Letters (Roberts 1965, 221):

The crop of Sea islands J. King came to market only yesterday... The quality of the cottons is very superior, more especially the parcel of 27 bags at 61¢ from Burdens island...

There is no question as to the quality of King's cotton on Burden's Island. In a letter (Roberts 1965, 222) from the firm Trapmann Schmidt & Co., a factor in Charleston, to McConnel & Kennedy, their buyer in Manchester, England, the factor wrote:

Invoice of 47 Bags Sea Islands J. King amt: $11,725.95 Shipped for your account & risk by the Plutarch, Graves for Liverpool, which we hope will arrive safe & be found satisfactory the Burden's Island Cotton, we believe it almost quite equal *[emphasis original] to any made in this state.*

King was an innovative planter. Seabrook (1844a, 26) gave him credit for the discovery of the value of salt-marsh mud as a crop manure:

The merit of its discovery, however, as a fertilizer for cotton lands, seems to be due to the late James King of St. Paul's Parish. By him it was freely used before the late war with Great Britain.

Kinsey Burden (1844b, 203) also gave King credit for first employing the use of salt-marsh mud on cotton, even though the suggestion came from Burden himself:

...accordingly I found him carrying the pond-mud into his cotton field as a manure, when I remarked to him, that I considered [salt] marsh-mud better, as it contained a portion of salt and lime. Some years after he tried the marsh-mud, and was thus the first to use it as a manure for cotton. I do not recollect the year in which his experiment with it was made.

James King also experimented with applying cotton seed as a manure. In 1831, he published an article in the *Southern Agriculturist* (King 1831, 127-128) entitled "On the best mode of applying Cotton-Seed as a Manure." It was signed James King, Sen., St. Paul's, Little Britain. In the article, he cited the results of an experiment on corn manured with cotton seed which doubled the crop yield, and he had no doubt that manuring with cotton seed on long-staple cotton would yield similar results.

Edmund Ruffin (Mathew 1992, 120) related another incident about King and his progressive farming practices. Recounting a trip west through Colleton County March 2-4, 1843, Ruffin recalled:

CHAPTER FOURTEEN

Two of the gentlemen who met me were sons of an Englishman named King who was a very successful planter on Burden's island, close adjacent to this place. He applied there a cargo of lime, on some of the worst land, about 20 years ago, and the benefit still is apparent.

Before his move to Burden's Island, James King married Theodora Ash Burden on December 16, 1790. At his death in 1840, King owned all of Burden's Island.[6] He renamed Burden's Island "Little Britain," by which name it is still known today.[7] His choice of "Little Britain" recalled his native England. James King died at his plantation on Pon Pon and was buried at Rose Hill Plantation near Adams Run.

Little Britain was also known on at least one map as King's Island. A U.S. Coast Survey map dated 1851 clearly shows King's Island and a house site identified as "King" along the east side of Toogoodoo Creek.

Kinsey Burden, son of Kinsey Burden Sr. and Portia Ash Burden, played the most important role in the development of sea island cotton. Kinsey was born August 15, 1775, and died in 1859. On June 13, 1805, he married Mary Legaré, daughter of Thomas Legaré (1733-1801) and Elizabeth Bassnett (1734-1798). Prior to his marriage, he resided on Burden's Island; through his marriage settlement he took up residence with Mary on Johns Island.[8] The date of his move from Burden's Island was given by Kinsey in an article written in 1844 (Burden 1844b, 204) in the *Southern Agriculturist*: "In 1805-6, I removed [moved] to this Island..." At the beginning of the article, he gave his address as Johns Island.

There has been some uncertainty among historians about which plantation Kinsey Burden resided on after his marriage to Mary Legaré. It was generally thought to have been Oakvale along the Stono River; however, none of the family correspondences, articles written by Burden, or wills or deeds specifically mention Oakvale by name in such a manner as to definitely place Burden there. Historically, it is important to pinpoint Burden's residence after his marriage, since it was there that he lived when he planted sea island cotton and built his seed barn where he guarded his cotton seed from fellow planters.

The 1825 Mills *Atlas* (fig. 5-2) shows a "K. Burdon" along the Stono River on what is now Johns Island in Charleston County. The misspelling notwithstanding, this citation unmistakably places Kinsey Burden at this site in 1825. Kinsey Burden Sr. had died in 1785, and Kinsey Burden Jr. never resided along the Stono River in Johns Island.

A map of Johns Island (fig. 14-1) drawn by Kinsey Burden shows the location of Burden's residence and the estate of Thomas Legaré (1733-1801) along the Stono River. Burden's is number 11; the estate of Thomas Legaré is number 10, north and west of Burden's residence. Thomas Legaré was the father of Mary Legaré and owned adjoining Oakvale. Through the marriage settlement with Mary's brothers James (1762-1830) and Thomas (1766-1842), Kinsey and Mary came to reside at Oakvale. The positions of two creeks are clearly shown, surrounding a section of land on which Burden's post-marriage residence (number 11) is marked. The northernmost creek is today called Burden Creek.

A third map (fig. 14-2) clearly establishes residence number 11 on the Burden map as Oakvale Plantation, and the second home of Burden. This map, dated 1873, is labeled:

Plat of Oakvale Plantation Situated on John's Island, Charleston County, State of South Carolina. Belonging to the Est. of Charles L. Trenholm dec'd, Containing 271 Acres of High Land and 364 9/10 Acres of Marsh. Surveyed Dec. 30Th, 1873.

In a comparison of these two maps, the area surrounded by the two creeks and the Stono River on the 1873 map is undoubtedly the same area of Burden's 1826 map where residence number 11, indicating his plantation, is located.

Further evidence supporting this site as the residence of Burden is taken from his marriage settlement with Mary Legaré. The settlement refers to a tract of land identified as:

...all that Plantation or tract of land situate on John's Island containing on or about seven hundred and thirty eight acres butting and bounding to the east on Stono river to the north and west on lands belonging to the Estate of Thomas Legaré and to the south on Land belonging to William Johnson.

This tract is undoubtedly Oakvale Plantation. Reference to the Burden map (fig. 14-1) clearly shows residence number 11 to be bound on the east by the Stono River and to the north and west by the estate of Thomas Legaré. When the acreage of the tract in the marriage settlement (738 acres) is compared to the acreage in the map of Oakvale (712.37 acres),[10] although not identical, they are close enough—given the primitive state of surveying at the time—to conclude that the two tracts are the same.

Also placing Burden at Oakvale is the fact that in 1873 (the date on the map of Oakvale) Oakvale was part of the estate of Charles Louis Trenholm (1809-65) who married in 1835 Portia Ash Burden, daughter of Kinsey Burden and Mary Legaré (and named after her grandmother). In his will, Burden left one-fourth of his estate (in this case, Oakvale, although not mentioned by name) to Charles L. Trenholm "In Trust for the use and behoof of my daughter Portia A. Trenholm and her children during her natural life..."

Today, physical evidence indicates that Stono Point subdivision is the former site of Oakvale Plantation. Burden Creek Road turns off River Road (S.C. 54) and follows the road depicted on the 1873 plat of Oakvale (fig. 14-2) until it reaches the Stono Point sign. Burden Creek Road then veers right and more or less parallels the 1873 road until it dead-ends into Kemway Road. The veer was made from the original road to leave enough highland between the marsh along Burden Creek and the road to build homes. A hundred feet left (north) of where Burden Creek Road intersects Kemway, the outline of the original road can be seen running through a vacant lot and dead-ending at Kemway Road. At this location stood the house depicted in Portia Trenholm's painting of Oakvale in 1890[11] (plate 14-1). The position of the house at the

Figure 14-1. Map of Johns Island by Kinsey Burden, 1826[9]
(Courtesy of the Charleston Library Society, Charleston, South Carolina)

end of the old road is also marked on the 1873 plat. The landing shown on the 1873 plat is still present along the edge of the marsh north of the old house site, and the graveyard identified in the 1873 plat along Burden Creek is still extant. This physical evidence compellingly indicates the location of Oakvale at Stono Point. No record was found relating how or when the Oakvale house and associated buildings vanished.

Little is known of Burden's life while he resided on Burden's Island. He was thirty-one when he moved to Oakvale in 1805. He began to experiment with cotton planting on Burden's Island, according to an article he wrote in 1844 (Burden 1844a, 164):

About the year 1804 or 1805, I raised from selected seed, a pocket of fine cotton, which the merchant through whom it was shipped, informed me that one of the most distinguished spinners told him, was so superior to any cotton he had ever seen, that he would give 25 cts. per lb. for it more than any other cottons at any price...

It appears, then, that Kinsey Burden got his start as a cotton planter at Burden's Island before moving to Oakvale. It was at Burden's Island that he apparently realized the value of producing a superior variety of long-staple cotton. After his move to Oakvale, he continued the seed selection that resulted in the production of his long-staple cotton that became sea island cotton. Kinsey was recognized as initially achieving the highest position of the sea island planters in regard to seed selection and the quality of lint. Through his pioneering seed selection, later duplicated by other sea island planters, sea island cotton came to be the best long-staple cotton ever produced.

Burden also appears to have been active in gardening and horticulture while at Oakvale, and was as well-versed in these pursuits as he was in developing his exceptional cotton. In a visit to Oakvale on November 13, 1827, Abiel Abbot recorded in his journal (Moore 1967, 239):

The peach tree suffers here as well as with us, he [Burden] thinks, by a little red insect too small to be seen by glasses. With a lie of ashes he irrigated one fine tree, which perfectly destroyed them. He did it by a waterspout on the upper side of the leaves & by splashing up the water with his hand against the underside. The tree has never since been troubled.

One of the enduring legends of Kinsey Burden was his attempt to keep his seed selection method secret and his storage of seeds in a locked building to prevent theft. Frederick A. Porcher, in his memoirs published in the *South Carolina Historical and Genealogical Magazine* (Stoney, 1945), related the following:

Some years before, Mr. Burden of John's Island had succeeded in raising cotton which sold in Charleston for a dollar and upwards the pound. Every one considered the possession of this cotton desirable, and Mr. Burden might have made great deal of money by selling his seed, or his secret but he would not do neither. He endeavored to keep the secret to himself, and the cotton

CHAPTER FOURTEEN

Plate 14-1. Oakvale Plantation by Portia Trenholm (Courtesy of Annie Caroline and George Marion Reid of Blackloch Plantation, Johns Island)

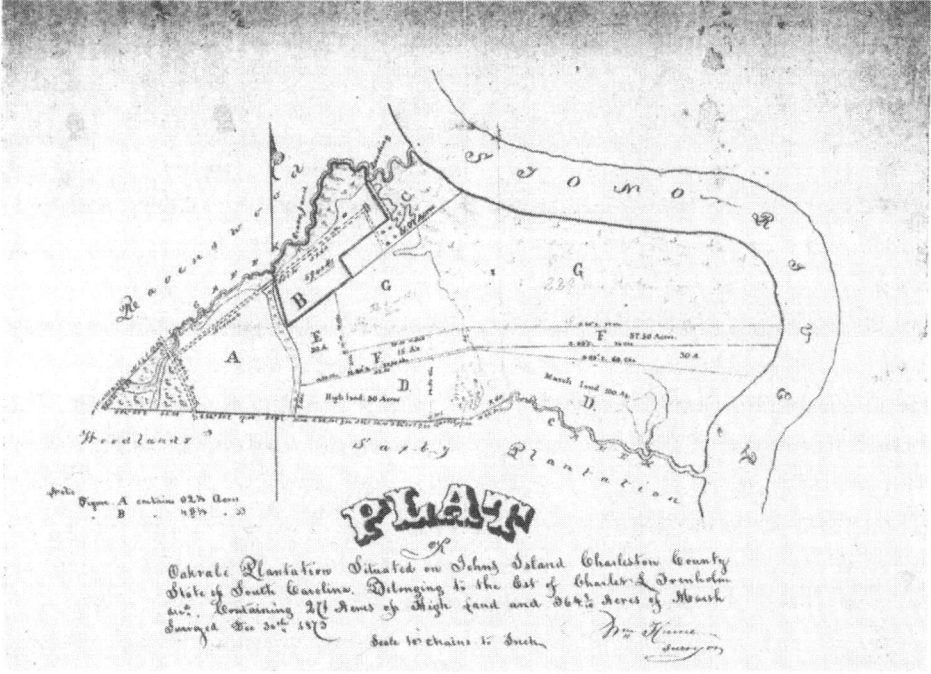

Figure 14-2. Plat of Oakvale Plantation, 1873 (Courtesy of William Lucas Gaillard Sr.)

house, which was always open to all visitors on other plantations, was on his sedulously guarded against intrusion.

An 1842 article by the Committee on Sea Island Cotton that appeared in the *Southern Agriculturist* (1842, 4) reported on Burden's seed selection secret:

For many years Mr. Kinsey Burden, of St. John's, received for his crop over $1 per lb., whilst his co-laborers were unable to obtain one-half of that sum. The collisions of mind, however, soon elicited the important secret, and as soon as it was known that the value of Mr. Burden's cotton was traceable to the seed, the task of rivalling his fame as the grower of the finest vegetable wool in the world was not a difficult one. In a short time several of the Islanders exceeded the Colleton planter in price.

Whitemarsh Seabrook (1844a, 36), in his "Memoir on the Cotton Plant," said that the planters were indebted to the "botanical skill and laudable perseverance of Kinsey Burden" for his improvement in the texture of cotton as early as 1804 or 1805. Ultimately, as William Elliott of Beaufort concluded, the result of Kinsey's success was traced to his seed selection. From Seabrook's article the following is pertinent:

Mr. Burden's discovery was held to be so valuable to the State, that he was induced to forward a memorial to the Legislature, offering to sell his secret for $200,000; he resigning all his seed, except what was necessary for his own crop, and communicating the mode of perpetuating the silky properties of the new cotton fiber. The memorial, for reasons satisfactory to the applicant, was never presented.

An article in the *Commercial Review* (1846, 305) relates this same story about sea island cotton and Kinsey Burden's seed selection secret; undoubtedly it was based, at least in part, on Seabrook's 1844 article:

The finest and best specimens of sea island [cotton] have been produced by the most finished practical skill on the part of some of the planters,... Kinsey Burden, Senr., [Kinsey Burden] of St. Johns, Colleton, S.C., occupies the first place on the list. He succeeded in producing from selected seed a parcel of fine cotton in 1805, worth 25 cents a pound more than that of any of his neighbors... Mr. Burden's wonderful success excited quite a sensation, but his secret was kept closely for many years. William Elliott suggested that it might lie in the character of the seed used; and upon the hint several set to work... Mr. Burden's secret beginning to leak out, he proposed to divulge it to the Legislature for the sum of $200,000, but afterwards changed his mind. William Seabrook, of Edisto, had designed offering $50,000 for initiation into the method, but declined afterwards, alleging that "conjecture had yielded to certainty, that to the seed solely was traceable the fine cot-

CHAPTER FOURTEEN

ton which Mr. Burden continued to grow."

Lewis Gray (1958, 732), in his extensive book *Agriculture in the Southern United States to 1860*, also mentioned Kinsey Burden's secret. Gray's material, however, was probably based on previously published material, and may not represent an independent conclusion:

He kept his methods secret, going so far as to employ members of his family in "moting" the cotton [to prevent seeds from being stolen by workers]. At one time, it is said, he offered to sell his secret to the South Carolina legislature.

Abiel Abbot disagreed with the story that Burden guarded his secret jealously, according to his journal from his 1827 sojourn to Oakvale (Moore 1967, 239):

By great attention to cotton seed he had improved the staple of his plantation, so that it secured an advanced price. He had, however, liberally distributed his seed to others. The merchants laid him under the obligation of silence as to the price he had received, but he did not hesitate to say that in some instances he had refused a dollar per lb.

[This is the only statement the author found in the literature that contradicts material claiming that Burden kept his seed selection process secret.]

The closest that Burden came to publicly discussing his seed selection was in reply to an inquiry to planters by Whitemarsh Seabrook dated August 20, 1827, and published by the Agricultural Society of St. John's, Colleton. The fifth of Seabrook's twelve questions to sea island cotton growers was: "Are you very particular in the selection of seed?"

Burden responded on October 4, 1827 (Seabrook 1927, 28):

I have generally been particular in selecting from the earliest ripe cotton, produced on the best land, the seed which has a small tuft at the point, and that which is clean and black; but neither of these will always produce the same kinds of seed only; they must be annually cleaned of their degenerated woolly associates, which sometimes produce fine long cotton; but generally, the staple is short or of an uneven length. I have found it a good rule in saving all kinds of seed, to select that portion which is most perfect and comes to maturity first...

Burden's response, however, was given about the time that his neighboring planters began their own seed selection at the suggestion of William Elliott, and may not represent a complete revelation of his seed selection process, which was much more complex than his response implied. This explanation, and his answers to the other eleven questions raised by Seabrook, revealed that Burden cooperated with his fellow planters by sharing information.

A story is told by his descendants about Burden and his seed house: A planter would visit

Plate 14-2. Ruins of tabby structure, 3405 Kemway Road, Stono Point, Johns Island (Photograph by author)

CHAPTER FOURTEEN

Oakvale and ask Burden if he could have some of his special sea island cotton seed. Burden would say: "Sure, go get it from the seed house." They did not realize that the seed house Burden sent them to was a house that contained culled seeds and not his special seeds.[12]

Historians and local Johns Islanders have speculated where Burden's seed house was located, if it indeed existed. The author suggests the following:

It seems that if Burden saw the necessity of guarding his seed house, it would probably have been located at Oakvale. Oakvale is the most likely place for two reasons: first, there the seed house would have been under his close, personal supervision; and second, he did not purchase The Hut and Blackloch, two plantations he bought on Johns Island, until after he developed his superior seed.[13] If the seed barn was in fact located at Oakvale, the ruins of a tabby structure at Stono Point[14] are a likely candidate. Reference to the 1873 plat (fig. 14-2) shows a rectangular building along the north side of the road leading to the house, located between the road and marsh of Burden Creek. The painting of Oakvale by Portia Trenholm (plate 14-1) shows a rectangular building in the same general location. Examination of the ruins today (plate 14-2), which are at the rear of 3405 Kemway Road, reveals a rectangular tabby structure measuring 30 feet x 10 feet with walls 18 inches thick. The roof and surrounding wooden structures have long since deteriorated. There is one large door in the side facing the road. (These ruins could not be of the slave cabin depicted in Trenholm's painting of Oakvale, as there is no indication of a chimney in the ruins.)

One noticeable difference between the building depicted in Portia Trenholm's painting of Oakvale and the ruins in Stono Point is that Trenholm depicted the building with three doors, while the ruins have only one door. This suggests that the two structures might not be the same. However, Trenholm painted Oakvale in 1890, which, according to family history, was after the plantation was destroyed. If she painted it from memory, she could easily have been in error on the number of doors. With this one exception, all the evidence today suggests that the tabby ruins could have been Burden's seed barn.

The role of Kinsey Burden and his family in the history of sea island cotton is not well documented. Through his research, the author has come to believe that Kinsey Burden, more than anyone else, was responsible through his seed selction process for making sea island cotton the finest long-staple cotton ever grown.

1. Kinsey Burden Jr. played no role in sea island cotton. The name appears for a fourth time in Kinsey E. Burden, the son of Kinsey Burden Jr., who died at an early age and also played no role in sea island cotton.
2. Eloise Lanier Taylor (1974) gives a detailed history of Dedcott's Island prior to its becoming Burden's Island.
3. No diagram of Burden's gin is known to exist; it is unlikely that a diagram was ever made.
4. One reference to Bourbon cotton was found in Seabrook's "Memoir of the Cotton Plant" (1844a, 15). He wrote: "…The Bourbon was brought from that Island to Charleston, through the instrumentality of James Hamilton, who was a merchant, and part owner of the only India ship at that time trading beyond the Cape of Good Hope." The Isle of Bourbon is now known as Réunion Island, situated

in the Indian Ocean east of Madagascar, 120 miles west southwest of the Isle of France. It was discovered in 1542 and was named Bourbon in 1642. At the beginning of the French Revolution it was changed to Réunion, but at the restoration of the Bourbons in 1815 it was changed back to the Isle of Bourbon. According to an article in the *Merchants' Magazine and Commercial Review* (1847, 17:63-67), raw cotton was exported from Bourbon. The author assumes that cotton seed was also exported and was the seed planted by Mrs. Burden to produce the cotton referred to in the literature as Bourbon Cotton. Rees (1822) describes this cotton: "Bourbon—the most even and uniform in quality of any other. It is a fine silky staple, and very clean. Prior to 1796, Bourbon cotton was the highest quality cotton imported into England; shortly after 1796, it was supplanted by sea island cotton." The staple was reported to be two inches long with a fineness equalling sea island cotton.

Guion G. Johnson (1926, 23) reported that Bourbon cotton was *Gossypium purpurascens* Poir, probably a cultivated form of *Gossypium taitense* Parlatore, and was carried throughout the world by French colonists. Fryxell (1979, 70) lists *Gossypium taitense* as a synonym under *Gossypium hirsutum*.

5. There is confusion as to when James King came to America. Kinsey Burden (1844a, 163) places it about 1790 and Slann Simmons (1958, 78) gives 1788. The earlier date seems more likely, since it would have been difficult for King to have arrived in 1790, married Theodora Ash Burden in that same year, and planted a crop of rice in 1791.

6. It is unclear in the literature whether King became the sole owner, or owned the island together with his wife, from whose family the land was inherited.

7. The 1960 U.S. Topographic Map, Adams Run Quadrangle, gives the name "Little Britton Island." This is obviously a misspelling.

8. In nineteenth-century South Carolina, married women could not own real property. A woman's property at marriage became the property of her husband. To circumvent this law and prevent a woman's property from being denied her children, the marriage settlement was instituted. The property was transferred to a trustee or trustees who would hold the property in trust for her. Under conditions of a marriage settlement, a wife's property could not be claimed for her husband's debts; the wife had exclusive use of income from the property; and the property reverted to her family at her death. In Mary's marriage settlement, her brothers Thomas Legaré and James Legaré became the trustees.

This document, dated August 2, 1805, is on file in the South Carolina Archives in Columbia (vol. 5, 59-67).

9. No date is given for this map. It was undoubtedly drawn by Kinsey Burden, for there was a letter signed by Burden attached to the back of the original map. The handwriting on the map and the letter are the same. The map was given to the Charleston Library Society in 1916 by E. E. Reid with this statement: "The Plat came to me with other papers of the Estate of Mr. Kinsey Burden, my grandfather, by whom it was evidently made, for I recognize the writing on it as being in his hand. To further identify the writing, a letter, written and signed by Mr. Kinsey Burden, is attached." The letter is dated 1826.

10. The acreage of 712.37 was reached by totalling the acreages of the individual tracts depicted on the map of Oakvale, which are as follows: A = 92.25; B = 49.25; C = 31.97; D Highland = 50; D Marsh = 100; E = 20; F = 15; F = 37.50; F = 30; G Highland = 57.4; G Marsh = 229.

11. On the back of the painting is the notation: Painted in 1890 by Portia Trenholm.

12. Personal communication with George Marion Reid of Blackloch Plantation, Johns Island, 2002.

13. Kinsey Burden purchased The Hut in 1828; the date he purchased Blackloch is unknown.

14. Stono Point is a private residential area and is not open to the public.

Part 2. Sea Island Cotton Plantation Architecture
by Sarah Fick

Sea Island Cotton Plantation Architecture

The Dwelling Houses

During South Carolina's colonial era, well-off planters and successful merchants joining their ranks created their country seats on the English model. Mansions as fine as Brick House and Head Quarters dotted the riverbanks of the sea islands. These early dwelling houses were constructed of brick, mostly with hipped roofs, and combined a very regular exterior design with an asymmetrical four-room hall-and-parlor plan. Large flanking buildings, likewise of masonry construction, were part of the overall designed setting.

By the time sea island cotton proved its reliability as a cash crop in the late eighteenth century, the era of the manor house had passed. When fires, hurricanes, relocations, or changing fortunes drove planters to build new houses, their design choices reflected contemporary fashion. With dwellings that were restrained in size and scale, a conservative consistency in form and detail became the hallmark of plantation architecture. Even as larger and finer edifices went up in town, ostentatious construction was out of style for the country house. Some prosperous planters found an opportunity for display in extravagant gardens and outbuildings; others satisfied themselves with travel, acquisitions, and outsized hospitality. As their means allowed, they built, not showpiece plantation seats, but second, third, and even fourth houses—in town, in summer villages, on auxiliary plantations.

Because waterfront plantations offered convenience for shipping goods in and out, they were most frequently selected for residence by the first settlers, and throughout the antebellum period. The best building sites were on higher ground, and sea island houses were usually set alongside tidal creeks. A bluff beside deep water was considered the healthiest situation, as it was elevated and exposed to salt breezes rather than swampy vapors. Beginning in the eighteenth century, sea island residents relied on roads for daily travel, so it was essential to build in a location that could be made accessible to the public roads linking plantations, churches, summer villages, and ferry landings.

At least from the early eighteenth century, when Brick House and Head Quarters were built, sea island planters generally constructed residences that faced south, more commonly toward the public roadway than toward the water. The Vanderhorst House, William Seabrook's

Vanderhorst House, 2003 *(Courtesy of Rick Rhodes)*

House, McLeod, and The Oaks all turn their rear elevations north toward a nearby river. Prospect Hill was built facing south, its left side against the bold South Edisto River; Brookland, too, fronts southward, away from the tidal creek that melts into marshes on three sides of the house. Ashe's, or Little Edisto, on the other hand, presents its welcoming south façade directly to Russell Creek only a few yards away—and from the porch, one saw the rear yard of Baynard's Old Place across the water. Dr. William Jenkins was more fortunate: the view south from the front veranda of his house on St. Helena was of Port Royal Harbor and the Atlantic Ocean.

Why build a south-facing house in the lowcountry's hot climate? One reason is that, for most planters, these were seasonal residences. Sea island cotton was picked and ginned from very late summer through the end of winter, and during these months, if at no other time, a careful planter watched his laborers daily. Winter was also thought to be the only healthy time for a family to stay in the country. Spring and fall (when children went to school) should be spent in a town house; the summer season took island families to Bluffton, St. Helenaville, Edingsville, Rockville, Legareville or Secessionville, or to more sophisticated resorts further away. Reading the plantation house as a winter residence gives a sound explanation for the southerly orientation: the porch and front rooms were warmed by the sun, leaving the chillier rear areas for storage and service functions. Turning the house away from the river and its breezes, reducing the number of windows on the waterfront side—even using the spaces beside fireplaces for closets instead of windows—does not mean that the builder forgot ventilation, but that he avoided it.

THE DWELLING HOUSES

Ashe's/Little Edisto, view north across Russell Creek, 2003 (*Courtesy of Bruce G. Harvey*)

Yet the exceptions to south-facing houses are too many to ignore, and suggest that roadways were the determining factor. The principal elevations of The Launch and Frogmore are at their north sides, in the direction of a public road. On the interior plantations whose layouts are certain, all the residences were oriented toward the main road.

Along with a southward orientation, several elements were characteristic of sea island residences. The architecture shows a consistency in material, scale, and plan, with forms first used before 1800 being favored throughout the nineteenth century. Built of wood (masonry construction was rarely seen), the rectangular house of two or more stories was raised on a brick or tabby foundation. There were clearly front and rear sides, with a porch or veranda across one or both principal elevations. Window and door openings were regularly placed, with entries at the long sides.

Only a small number of plantation residences were designed by trained architects. The skillful composition of The Launch sets it aside from its contemporaries, and it may be that other notable dwellings were professionally designed. If not taken from a pattern book, the plan for Rose Hill was certainly provided by a builder familiar with the Gothic Revival style. A handful of houses, such as those of Arnoldus Vanderhorst and William J. Jenkins, reflect the architectural tradition of the nearby city. Most plantation houses, though, were designed as rural villas whose fairly simple plans could be executed by journeyman carpenters.

Only three of the houses pictured here were built by newcomers to South Carolina: James Hopkinson (Cassina Point), Ebenezer Coffin (Coffin Point), and John Stoddard (Melrose). Each was proprietor of a plantation inherited by his wife, and all commissioned buildings in the local vernacular.

The houses can be organized into several types, according to their plan. Even in the largest buildings, interior rooms were few: the standard was six or eight "upright" rooms, supplemented by basement or attic rooms. The great majority were laid out with a central hall connecting the front and rear entries, and accommodating the stairway. Some houses had twin front parlors entered separately from the porch and opening into each other, with no passageway between. Although less popular than the central hall, this paired-entry plan was no more challenging to construct, and was used throughout the lowcountry and sea islands.

Whether built with a central hall or twin parlors, most houses had four principal rooms on the first floor. Over half of those documented here were double houses, with four rooms at both main levels, in a four-over-four configuration. A roof over the first-floor back rooms, and only two rooms upstairs, resulted in a "two-over-four" plan. With any of these plans, rooms at the front of the house were larger than those behind, continuing a custom seen in the earliest mansions. A "two-over-two" plan, with two rooms to a floor, was rarely seen.

Chimneys positioned on the lateral interior wall were characteristic of the sea island residences. This placement of the chimneys inside the back wall, as in a Charleston single house, was highly functional: whether the house was one or two rooms deep, two chimneys served fireplaces in all the principal rooms, and sometimes in the attic or basement. The preponderance throughout the sea islands of interior rear wall chimneys, which were infrequently used outside the lowcountry, might have had its origin in Charleston-trained builders.

Without taxing the competence of the builders available for work on island plantations, a rectangular structure could be modified with extensions and additions. One-story wings were incorporated as integral components, as at The Launch or Brookland, or as separate appendages like those at Melrose or Tom Fripp's House. The T-shaped plan used for The Oaks and William Jenkins's House was more widely used near Beaufort, but was seen at least once on Edisto Island, at Crawford's Plantation.

The stair was most easily located in the central passageway, where it rose along one wall to a landing and returned to the upper floor. Because of its dual use as stairhall and through-corridor, the hallway occupied a large portion of the interior space. The passage at the Vanderhorst House is twelve feet wide, but in buildings like the William Edings House, a narrow hallway reserved as much space as possible to the main rooms. Pushing the stair to the rear of the hall, squeezing it between the back rooms as at Crawford's, was a more convenient overall plan, though the stairway itself became cramped. Nevertheless, only a few sea island houses featured a rear tower to provide space for a stairway behind the core of the building. William Seabrook's impressive staircase begins on both sides of the passageway, two flights that join at the first landing and continue to the upper levels within the projecting rear tower. A stairhall projection, whether as pronounced as that at Baynard's Old House or concealed by flanking wings as at The Oaks, was an architectural solution generally atypical of sea island construction, despite its frequent use elsewhere in the lowcountry.

THE DWELLING HOUSES

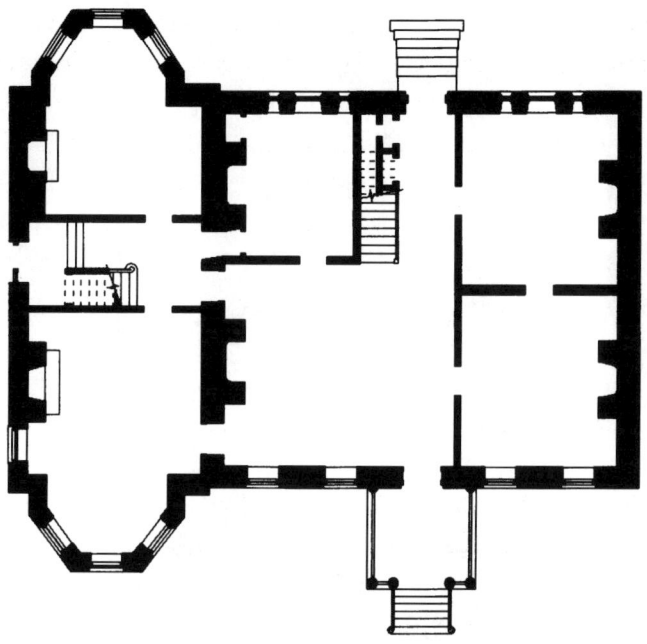

Head Quarters Plantation House, built ca. 1730, enlarged by 1805. Hall-and-parlor plan with addition *(Courtesy of Rueben J. Solar)*

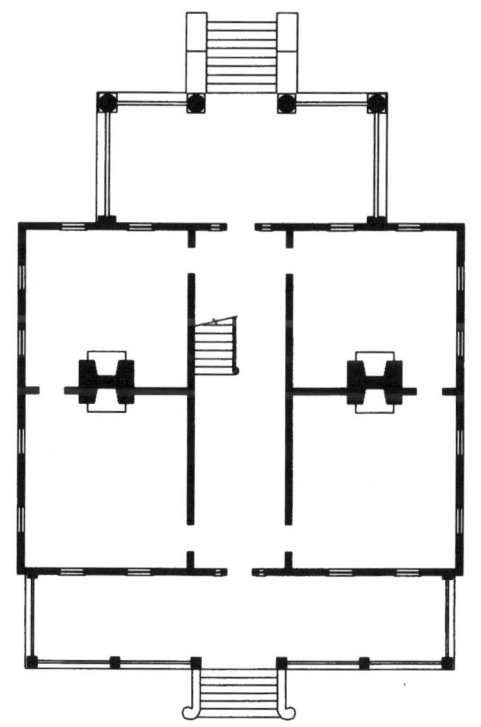

McLeod Plantation House, built ca. 1851. Four-over-four room plan with center hall
(Courtesy of Rueben J. Solar)

SEA ISLAND COTTON PLANTATION ARCHITECTURE

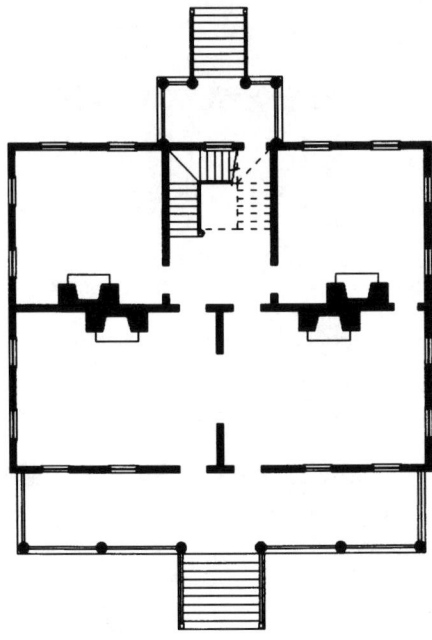

Cassina Point Plantation House, built ca. 1849. Four-over-four room plan with twin parlors and paired entry doors *(Courtesy of Rueben J. Solar)*

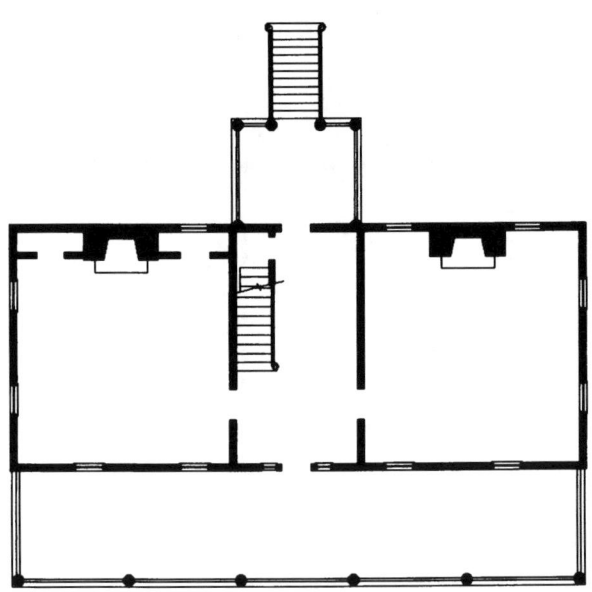

Vanderhorst House, built 1803. Two-over-two room plan with center hall *(Courtesy of Rueben J. Solar)*

THE DWELLING HOUSES

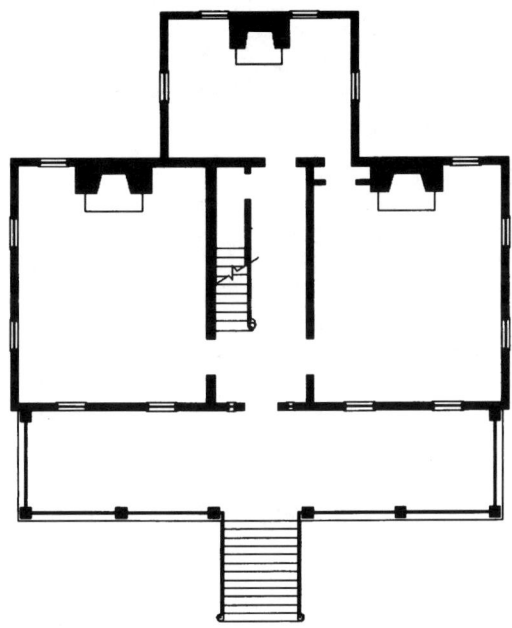

Prospect Hill Plantation House, built ca. 1827. Two-over-two room plan with center hall; rear addition made soon after first construction *(Courtesy of Rueben J. Solar)*

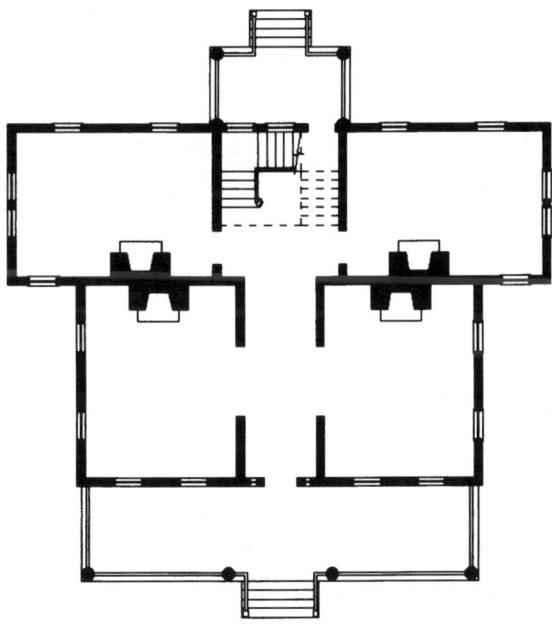

Crawford's Plantation House, built ca. 1835. Four-over-four room plan with center hall and rear T-wing *(Courtesy of Rueben J. Solar)*

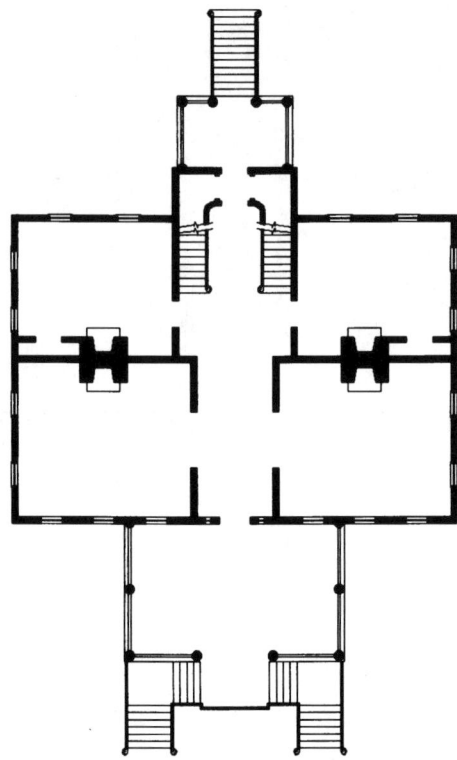

William Seabrook House, built ca. 1805. Four-over-four room plan with center hall and rear stair tower (*Courtesy of Rueben J. Solar*)

By the late eighteenth century, the sea island planters' houses always had porches. A one-story porch extending across the entire elevation usually defined the façade. Unlike the Greek Revival compositions of the interior and western south, none of the dwellings considered here had full-height pedimented porches. Although several had a two-tiered porch, only a few conform to the stereotype of a double piazza across a waterfront façade. A simple shed-roofed construction was the norm, but there are some notable exceptions. The graceful porticoes at The Launch and Oak Island and the elegant two-story veranda at William Seabrook's house enhance these mansions without obscuring their architectural cores. Upper balustrades ornamented the hipped porch roofs of Seaside, Melrose and Ashe's, and there were paneled parapets at Oak Island and the William Jenkins House.

There was usually at least a portico at the rear entry, as simple as the gabled constructions at Fish Hall and Youghal, or as stylish as the Greek Revival pediment at Woodward. At Peter's Point, a one-story porch extended across the entire rear elevation, while The Launch had rear projections sheltering a recessed porch. Coffin Point was seen in the 1920s with a two-tier porch across the inland side (which might have been a later alteration).

"Every house stands on posts so that the air can circulate under and there is not a single cellar here..."[1] Elevated buildings did escape the damp ground and bring fresh breezes indoors,

William Seabrook House, 1978. Entry hall (*Historic American Buildings Survey, Library of Congress*)

but it was the high water table and absence of below-ground stone that encouraged builders to raise houses on masonry foundations instead of excavating a basement story. The ground floor beneath the main structure was customarily finished as interior space, with the area below the deck of the primary piazza left open as a secondary porch. A few porch foundations—at Vanderhorst, Myrtle Bush, and Peter's Point—were elaborated as arcades, but very plain masonry supports were more usually employed.

Until the 1830s, hipped roof systems were used more often than gabled construction. Hipped roofs eventually fell out of fashion, and all the post-1850 houses pictured here show lateral gabled roofs. Dormers were somewhat rare, and even when finished as living space, garrets did not always have fireplaces.

Although infrequently affecting plan or form, architectural fashions popular in the cities influenced the ornamental detail of plantation houses. Adamesque elements are featured in the porch details at the William Seabrook and Mary Jenkins houses, the round-arched door surrounds of Coggins Point and Seaside, and in the interior trim of William Edings's house and the Vanderhorst House. Some exterior treatments—a central pediment, as at the Stanyarne House, or tripartite windows, used most effectively at The Launch—continued during the transition to the Greek Revival style, and both the Adamesque and Greek Revival influences can be seen at the Woodward Plantation house. The Greek Revival style, ubiquitous in the south, was particularly suited to the sea island house type, lending a refined appearance to an essentially plain farmhouse; Cassina Point is an excellent example. By the 1850s, exterior adornment was very limited, and interiors exhibited simple detail. Ornament was applied only

Oak Island Plantation House, 1978. Hallway and stair
(Historic American Buildings Survey, Library of Congress)

in the principal rooms, doors and windows were set in plain surrounds, and fireplaces were unembellished except by pilasters and flat mantel shelves.

Sea island cotton was cultivated in South Carolina into the first quarter of the twentieth century, but under circumstances very different from those enjoyed by antebellum plantation proprietors. A few notable new houses were erected on the sea islands in the late nineteenth and early twentieth centuries; however, in keeping with the focus on the residences constructed during the period when cotton dominated the sea island economy, they have not been included in this study.

The dwelling houses presented here are arranged as nearly as possible in chronological order. For many of them, an exact date is not known, and the period of construction has been estimated according to architectural detail. The results are inexact, and at times seem to contradict what is known about periods of prosperity on sea island cotton plantations. Surely, some

THE DWELLING HOUSES

William Edings House, 1978. Drawing room cornice detail *(Historic American Buildings Survey, Library of Congress)*

McLeod Plantation House, 1990. First floor drawing room
(Historic American Buildings Survey, Library of Congress)

planters were tempted to build a new house when prices and yields were high. It appears, though, that there was usually a more personal reason for building: marriage, inheritance, or the replacement of a house lost to fire or storm. The knowledge of individual planters' circumstances can explain why they built during the time period indicated by the architecture. Continuing research into the history of South Carolina's sea islands may clarify the dates, the builders, and the designers of these irreplaceable architectural resources.

The Sea Island Plantation Landscape

A sea island cotton plantation was a commercial agricultural enterprise as well as the home of a sizeable residential community. Its overall landscape plan was dictated by the geography and topography of the particular property: accessibility to water and roadways, the locations of owner's and overseer's houses, and drainage and soil conditions. Every planter dedicated some acreage to peas, corn, and sweet potatoes for plantation use, but it was a rare plantation that was completely "improved" for cultivation. Forested areas were set aside to produce firewood and, sometimes, rough lumber for construction, and to provide habitat for free-ranging cattle, sheep, and swine. Unlike the engineered fields of rice plantations, cotton fields were not permanent constructions, but with the gradual acceptance of manuring the soil, the best-drained fields remained in production year after year.

Service buildings were required for each aspect of the plantation's operation, their placement depending on their function and the planter's personal attitudes about efficiency and aesthetics. On every plantation were slave cabins, corn houses, pea houses, and blade houses (for the corn shucks used as animal fodder). There was also a variety of special-purpose buildings: chimney house, kitchen, smoke house, meat house (a locked shed to which only the owner, overseer, or a particularly well-trusted slave held keys), dairy, mill house, grist mill, store house; carriage house, wagon shed, boat house, flat house, stables and sheds for horses, cattle, mules or oxen, poultry house, pigeon house; overseer's house, hospital, chapel; cotton house, gin house, moting house, packing house. These last structures were crop-specific. Because high-grade cotton could be ruined by trash and fragments of seed, processing and storage buildings were kept free of dust and litter. The best cotton barns were two-story buildings with glassed windows to light the interior without admitting breezes.[2]

Along with its agricultural use, when chosen as the planter's principal residence, a plantation also served as a proud family seat. The setting of the house became as important as its architecture in proving the owner's position and sophistication. Most visitors arrived by land, so the designed landscape began with the plantation's entry from the road, where an avenue of mature evergreen trees spoke of ancestral position: "On every hand you see the marks of long settlement, in avenues of fine live oaks, cedars and pines, leading up to the plantation houses and bounding the roads."[3] At William Pope's plantation, "a lovely place indeed, the fine old southern mansion [probably Cotton Hope] was situated in a large grove of live oak trees,

Preparing cotton for the gin, Old Fort Plantation, 1862 *(Library of Congress)*

with ample grounds neatly fenced. Large groves of orange trees, whose fragrance filled the air, gave evidence of the home of contentment and wealth."[4]

Like the flowering orchards with fruit trees ordered from Charleston or Europe, the larger landscape of a residence plantation married beauty to practicality. Fencing of lath or rails separated the house and grounds from the entry drive, and sometimes enclosed portions of the kitchen garden and orchards. Groves of evergreen trees provided shade and grandeur, and scattered among them, a short walk from the residence, were service buildings. Privy houses were rare, but other domestic needs – kitchen, washing, storage – as well as sleeping space for house and yard slaves, were accommodated in structures close by the planter's dwelling.

Burial at the home plantation reinforced a planter's emotional claim to his land, and in the

SEA ISLAND COTTON PLANTATION ARCHITECTURE

Sorting cotton, Fish Hall Plantation, 1862 *(Courtesy of The Western Reserve Historical Society, Cleveland Ohio)*

Cotton gin building, Edisto Island, ca. 1862
(Courtesy of The Western Reserve Historical Society, Cleveland Ohio)

THE SEA ISLAND PLANTATION LANDSCAPE

Old Fort Plantation, 1862
(Courtesy of The Western Reserve Historical Society, Cleveland Ohio)

Water garden at Oak Island Plantation, 1862. Cassina Point House is seen at upper left.
(Courtesy of The Western Reserve Historical Society, Cleveland Ohio)

eighteenth century it was customary to establish a family cemetery near the house. New plantation burial grounds were rarely created after about 1800, although existing graveyards continued to be used. William Seabrook (died 1836) was buried in a plot reserved to the Lawton family and their kin in 1774,[5] Thomas Bannister Seabrook (died 1839) and his wife Elizabeth Clark (died 1817) were both buried at her family's Cypress Trees Plantation,[6] and Anna Stanyarne of Charleston (died 1836) was buried near her Freer nephews on Johns Island.[7]

Private cemeteries generally went out of use during the nineteenth century. More and more, sea island planters erected family tombs in churchyard cemeteries. They held to the practice of bringing home the remains of those who died away from the island, to inter them beside their closest relatives. The earlier burial sites were remembered and honored by later generations. When the Gibbes heirs sold Peaceful Retreat Plantation in 1826, they retained ownership of their family burial ground "in the garden by the Fish Pond next to the Stable."[8]

Saltwater ponds, large or small, were maintained on many plantations, and occasionally dominated the landscape. As photographed during the federal occupation, Oak Island seems to float above its water garden, proving the aptness of the plantation's name and bearing out I. J. Mikell's description of Peter's Point:

I must not forget the artificial fish pond, made not for beauty alone, but as a reservoir for our winter supply of fish, which occupied the time of a slave for the whole summer to keep it stocked for winter use... It combined beauty and utility in a marked degree. [Building it] required means, time, patience and unlimited command of labor...

There were several Venetian bridges thrown across it and small islands covered with fancy shrubbery scattered at intervals over its area, each island about the size of a miniature dwelling-room, on which diminutive Chinese "tea gardens" were built, reached only by a little skiff.

There was built out from the outer side of the pond, into and over the river, a small house, on palmetto logs, connected with the shore by a bridge, from the piazzas of which one might fish in the river with hand line or pole. And in the floor was a trap door, through which, in case of rain, one might catch sheepshead in satisfying quantities.[9]

Their residences were uncomplicated in plan and detail, but sea island cotton planters, like urban homeowners, employed picturesque and exotic designs for small outbuildings. The Gothic Revival embellishments on the icehouse at Bleak Hall Plantation give it the ornamental appearance appropriate to a garden folly. With its thick flushboard walls and shuttered openings, the structure would keep ice frozen for weeks, but it was essentially frivolous when constructed in the mid-1840s. For years sea island planters had enjoyed cool drinks and frozen confections year-round without stockpiling a reserve of ice. Instead, they relied on the commercial icehouses in Charleston and Savannah that received regular shipments of ice from New England, where it was cut all winter and warehoused for later delivery. Planters obtained their ice in barrels, to be kept inside or beneath the house.[10]

Outbuilding on Swallow's Bluff Plantation, Edisto Island, 1991
(Courtesy of South Carolina Department of Archives and History, Columbia)

Other service buildings at Bleak Hall were trimmed with Gothic Revival elements. A smoke house and barn, both of tabby construction, are finished with wood spires at the peaks of their roofs, and sawn wood trim beneath the eaves.

The small library building at Oak Island was highly ornamented but sensibly planned. A small portico was supported by elaborate openwork posts, and the wide wood siding was detailed to imitate the quoining of a stone building. Sidelights and overscaled windows flooded the single room with light.

Some planters erected their own billiard houses, a "useful resource for exercise in bad weather."[11] The "amusements and refreshments [Dr. William J. Jenkins] can offer" included a billiard house,[12] and Freedmen's Bureau teachers at William Seabrook's plantation found "a building once used as a billiard room, which accommodated a large number of pupils."[13] Only one billiard house on the sea islands has been investigated, and like many other plantation amenities, it was intended for winter use. In the landscaped gardens at William Aiken's house on Jehossee Island (a rice plantation) stood a rectangular structure with a well-supported floor system and a substantial corner fireplace. This is believed to have been Aiken's billiard room.[14]

In numbers, the majority of auxiliary buildings on every plantation were slave cabins. A few near the main house were reserved for slaves engaged in house and garden duties, but the more numerous domiciles of field laborers were grouped in clusters or lines, which might be set near the main house, along the entry drive, or near the working areas. Slave settlements laid out in single or double rows provided a tidy appearance while allowing convenient oversight and

Ice house at Bleak Hall Plantation, 1971
(Courtesy of South Carolina Department of Archives and History, Columbia)

The library at Oak Island Plantation, 1862
(Courtesy of The Western Reserve Historical Society, Cleveland Ohio)

THE SEA ISLAND PLANTATION LANDSCAPE

The grounds at Oak Island Plantation, 1862
(Courtesy of The Western Reserve Historical Society, Cleveland Ohio)

Gazebo at Melrose Plantation, ca. 1910
(Courtsey of Albert H. Stoddard)

McLeod Plantation, 1990 *(Historic American Buildings Survey, Library of Congress)*

supervision. The small houses had one or two rooms per family, with additional sleeping space in the low attic. Some planters constructed separate buildings as slave kitchens where food could be prepared for the entire community; others erected hospitals or sick houses for their work force.

A few slaves attended religious services in the churches of their masters, but most laborers worshipped on their own or a neighboring plantation, meeting in brush arbors, simple praise houses, or white-sponsored chapels. Some lowcountry planters are known to have erected church buildings for their slaves, but few were photographed on the sea islands. The slave chapel on Old Fort Plantation, a dignified small meeting house, may have been representative, although an 1843 missionary's description of John Joyner Smith as "one of nature's truest noblemen"[15] hints that providing such a building was unusual. On the other hand, slave cemeteries were an essential component of any plantation. Unlike the white family's burial ground, the graveyards of slaves were set apart from their residence area, often at the margin of the plantation's woodland or beside a creek.

Regardless of the practical functions of fish ponds, fruit trees, and service buildings, if a plantation was its proprietor's principal seat, the scenic qualities of the landscaping were paramount. Winding among well-tended planting beds dotted with specimen trees and flowering shrubs, pathways of sand or crushed shells led to small pavilions used as outdoor sitting rooms. These garden follies illustrate architectural design at its most whimsical. The gazebo near Dr. William Jenkins's house was thoroughly rustic, whereas neatly latticed garden houses, trellises, and bridges dressed the grounds at Oak Island.

THE SEA ISLAND PLANTATION LANDSCAPE

Slave chapel, Old Fort Plantation, 1862
Courtesy of The Western Reserve Historical Society, Cleveland Ohio

Slave cabins on unnamed plantation, Port Royal Island, 1862
(Library of Congress)

When Elizabeth Botume, a teacher for the Freedmen's Bureau, came to Old Fort Plantation in 1864, she found an avenue of magnolias, bordered with a thick hedge of "Spanish daggers," leading from the house to the river. After three years of neglect, "it was only when I walked around and saw the carefully arranged grounds, with fine shrubs and vines and graveled walks bordered with flowers, that I realized what the place had been."[16]

1. Josephine W. Martin, ed., *Dear Sister: Letters Written on Hilton Head Island, 1867* (New York: Viking Press, 1977), pp. 7-8.
2. South Carolina Comptroller/State Auditor "Claims for property lost due to the enemy" (Record Series S126189, South Carolina Department of Archives and History).
3. *Harper's New Monthly Magazine* correspondent Charles Nordhoff, quoted in Katharine M. Jones, *Port Royal under Six Flags, The Story of the Sea Islands* (New York: Bobbs-Merrill Co., 1960), pp. 256-262.
4. Charles K. Cadwell, *The Old 6th Regiment. Its War Record* (New Haven CT, 1875), pp. 29-30.
5. Thomas O. Lawton, Jr., *Upper St. Peter's Parish and Environs* (Garnett SC: privately printed, 2001), pp. 61-66.
6. Mrs. John Hanahan, "Tombstones in Cypress Trees Plantation – Edisto," in *South Carolina Historical Magazine* 40 (1939).
7. Laylon Wayne Jordan and Elizabeth H. Stringfellow, *A Place Called St. John's, The Story of John's, Edisto, Wadmalaw, Kiawah, and Seabrook Islands of South Carolina* (Spartanburg: The Reprint Company), p. 279.
8. Will of Mrs. Sarah Gibbes of Charleston, cited in Charleston County Register of Mesne Conveyance, Deed Book R9:239.
9. I. Jenkins Mikell, *Rumbling of the Chariot Wheels* (Columbia: The State Company, 1923), pp. 163-165.
10. Gavin Weightman, *The Frozen Water Trade, A True Story* (New York: Hyperion Books, 2002), pp. 77-79.
11. D. M. Reese, *An Encyclopedia of Domestic Economy* (New York: Harper and Brothers, 1847), p. 43, cited in Michael Trinkley, *Archaeological and Historical Investigations of Jehossee Island, Charleston County, South Carolina* (Columbia: Chicora Foundation Inc., 2002), p. 161.
12. Theodore Rosengarten, *Tombee: Portrait of a Cotton Planter* (New York: William Morrow and Co., 1986), pp. 114, 673.
13. Mary Ames, *A New England Woman's Diary in Dixie in 1865* (New York, 1906, rep. 1969).
14. Trinkley, *Jehossee Island*, pp. 160-163.
15. Rev. A. M. Chreitzberg, quoted in Jones, *Port Royal*, pp. 169-170.
16. Jones, *Port Royal*, pp. 275-280.

Brick House
EDISTO ISLAND

Built during the 1720s, Brick House was constructed of brick (imported from New England, according to a nephew of Paul Hamilton, the builder) laid up in Flemish bond, and detailed with quoins and banding of rusticated stucco. Its tall bellcast hipped roof emphasized the regular symmetry of the building's exterior. At the south elevation's center entry was a gabled portico. The north (riverfront) side was detailed with an oversized round-headed window that illuminated the rear hall and stair.

Brick House, 1928 *(Courtesy of Gibbes Museum of Art/Carolina Art Association, Charleston)*

In 1798, Joseph Jenkins of Edisto Island paid £750 sterling to James Rivers Maxwell and his wife Harriet Elliott Maxwell, also of Edisto Island, for a plantation that Maxwell had inherited from his father. The 230 acres of high ground was described as "bounding north on a creek commonly called Russell's Creek"; adjoining it was a 181-acre marshland tract.[1]

When Joseph Jenkins bought Brick House Plantation, he had been married for thirteen years to Elizabeth Evans, a close relative of the Chaplin and Fripp families of St. Helena Island. Already the parents of five children, they may have established a residence at Brick House. The family was nomadic, maintaining houses in Charleston and Edings Bay as well as plantation homes. Additionally, Jenkins spent a number of years in the State House and Senate,[2] and seems to have resided on St. Helena at least occasionally.

With their family connections, he and his wife moved easily among the sea islands, and in 1816 their son Joseph Evans Jenkins married Ann Jenkins Fripp of St. Helena.[3] Two years after his son's marriage, Joseph Jenkins gave him the Brick House tract. By then the plantation had been enlarged to 530 acres.[4]

Joseph Evans Jenkins planted sea island cotton on Edisto Island, but his larger landholdings were in the rich Toogoodoo Creek section of St. Paul's Parish. In 1844, he conveyed to William G. Baynard of Prospect Hill the 200-acre west part of "my present plantation, being part of a tract given to me by my father Joseph Jenkins."[5] Retaining about 325 acres with the Brick House residence, Joseph and Ann Jenkins raised their eight children on Edisto Island and at Toogoodoo.

Brick House Plantation has remained in the Jenkins family through several generations. The house burned in 1929, but the roofless exterior walls still stand.

1. Charleston County Register of Mesne Conveyance, Deed Book T6:495. For the earlier conveyances, see Mrs. E. F. Jenkins's Memo in Thomas T. Waterman, "Brick House," HABS No. SC-1, Historic American Buildings Survey, Library of Congress, 1940.
2. N. Louise Bailey, Mary L. Morgan, and Carolyn R. Taylor, *Biographical Directory of the South Carolina Senate, 1776-1995*. Vol. 2 (Columbia: University of South Carolina Press, 1986), p. 812.
3. Joseph LaRoche Rivers, *Seven South Carolina Lowcountry Families: Bailey, Clark, Grimball, Jenkins, Seabrook, Townsend, and Whaley* (Charleston: privately printed, 1997, rev. ed. 2001).
4. Charleston County RMC, Deed Book B9, p. 11.
5. Charleston County RMC, Deed Book I11, p. 521.

Head Quarters (Fenwick Hall)
JOHNS ISLAND

This much-photographed brick mansion was built by John Fenwick in about 1730. Fifty years later it was described by Captain John Peebles of the Scottish Grenadiers as "a large modern house which holds them all [British officers] and from which they see the Spires of Charles Towne."[1]

Known until the twentieth century as the Head Quarters Plantation House, Fenwick Hall was built in two stages: the original construction, and a wing, added by John Gibbes before 1805, set at right angles to the main core. The older Georgian-styled section, with two stories above the basement level, has a steep hipped roof. The rectangular addition, also with a hipped roof, is extended beyond the planes of the core by Adamesque three-sided polygonal bays with slightly lower roof systems.[2]

Head Quarters Plantation House and Outbuilding, ca. 1910
(Courtesy of The Charleston Museum, Charleston South Carolina)

The building and its setting remained attractive for decades: an 1810 newspaper advertisement described the 2,000-acre plantation "in sight of Charleston from which, by water, it is about six miles, and by land over the Ashley River Bridge, probably not more than three or four. There are on the premises an exceeding good dwelling house, containing 13 upright rooms, a large kitchen and stable all built of bricks; a machine house, cotton house, etc. The grounds around the buildings are elegantly laid out...."[3]

After the Fenwick-Gibbes tenure, Head Quarters changed hands several times: to Joseph Jenkins Sr. in December 1805,[4] to Robert Brown in March 1806,[5] and to Benjamin Reynolds in 1817.[6] Reynolds was living there at his death in 1826, and his will divided the plantation between his married daughters.[7]

Cornelia Reynolds Scott inherited the 1,300-acre tract with the house, then with her husband Benjamin Scott offered it for sale. The buyers, in 1828, were Justus and Martha Waight Angel, who financed the purchase with proceeds from their sale of a plantation on St. Helena Island to Thomas A. Coffin.[8] In 1840 the widowed Martha Angel sold the land and buildings to Daniel Jenkins Townsend, known as Jenkins.[9]

With its 1,300 acres, Head Quarters Plantation was an appropriate seat for Jenkins Townsend, the younger son of Daniel and Hephzibah Jenkins Townsend of Bleak Hall. After his education at the College of Charleston, Yale, and the South Carolina Medical College, Dr. Townsend initially took up his mother's Sharegools (Shargould) Plantation, at the landing opposite Bleak Hall. Here he lived for several years in a house his strong-willed mother had built during a period of separation from her husband.[10]

When Daniel Townsend first wrote his will, he devised Sharegools to Jenkins, his home plantation to the elder son John, and his house in Charleston and a small Edisto Island plantation to his wife Hephzibah. She, however, insisted that her widow's estate be provided at Sharegools (which had come to Townsend through her own family), and in 1839 Daniel revised his will and settled a sum on Jenkins sufficient to finance a separate plantation of his own.[11] Perhaps a suitable tract was not available on Edisto at the time; for whatever reason, Head Quarters was selected.

In 1840, Dr. Jenkins Townsend, his wife Henrietta Evans,[12] and their two young sons moved from Edisto to Johns Island. This was not strange territory for Townsend, as he had cousins on the island, and he and his family spent long periods at Rockville, where his brother also had a summer house.

After ten years of marriage, Henrietta died, leaving two sons, Daniel and John. Still only in his thirties, Jenkins Townsend married again. Susan Lavinia Swinton bore him Susan Mary in 1845, Eliza Amarinthia (1847), and James Swinton (1849).[13]

In 1849, Townsend had a total of 2,205 acres (830 improved) on Johns and Wadmalaw islands, and produced 64 bags of sea island cotton. Preparing inheritances for his children, he added to his land, and by 1860 had more than 5,000 acres, which yielded 140 bags of cotton. By this time, Daniel, the eldest son, was twenty-four years old, married, and planting the 490-

acre Cedar Springs Plantation on Johns Island. At home at Head Quarters and Rockville were Jenkins and Susan, John, Susan, Eliza, and young James.

From his Johns Island home and two houses on Wadmalaw Island (one at Rockland Plantation, one in the village of Rockville), Jenkins Townsend planted on both islands. Along with Head Quarters, in 1861 he was planting at Oakland, a former Gibbes property that had belonged to Thomas Roper.[14] In 1867, then living at Rockville, Townsend deeded Head Quarters to his son John Henry.[15] The younger Townsend sold the property in 1876.[16] For a number of years it was operated as a market farm, growing livestock and a variety of crops, and in 1922 was first called "Fenwick Hall" in a real estate transaction.[17]

1. Ira D. Gruber, ed., *John Peebles' American War: The Diary of a Scottish Grenadier, 1776-1782* (Mechanicsburg, PA: Stackpole Books, 1998), pp. 339-340
2. Robert P. Stockton, "Fenwick Hall, Stono River, John's Island, South Carolina," (MS, Charleston, 1992).
3. *Charleston Courier*, November 1810.
4. Charleston County Register of Mesne Conveyance, Deed Book R7, p. 62.
5. Charleston County RMC, Deed Book A8, p. 257.
6. Charleston County RMC, Deed Book R8, p. 349.
7. "Will of Benjamin Reynolds," Charleston County Wills, Book 37, p. 104, Charleston County Public Library.
8. Charleston County RMC, Deed Book X9, p. 423; W9, pp. 412, 443.
9. Charleston County RMC, Deed Book D11, p. 314.
10. Chalmers G. Davidson, *The Last Foray. The South Carolina Planters of 1860: A Sociological Study* (Columbia: University of South Carolina Press, 1971), pp. 255-256. Kate McChesney Bolls, "The Townsends of Edisto Island, Supplement to *The Daniel Townsends...* " (MS, 1977).
11. "Will of Daniel Townsend," Charleston County Wills, Book 42, p. 442, CCPL.
12. Brent Holcomb, *Marriage and Death Notices from the Charleston Observer 1827-1845* (Columbia, 1980), p. 93.
13. Kate McChesney Bolls, *The Daniel Townsends of the South Carolina Islands, Their Forebears and Descendants* (Verona, VA: 1975).
14. South Carolina Comptroller/State Auditor "Claims for property lost due to the enemy" (Record Series S126189, South Carolina Department of Archives and History).
15. Charleston County RMC, Deed Book F15, p. 397.
16. Charleston County RMC, Deed Book X16, p. 446.
17. Charleston County RMC, Deed Book Q33, p. 217.

Tom Seabrook's House
EDISTO ISLAND

This house, known to generations as Tom Seabrook's house, was thought to have been built about 1740,[1] a date that is supported by the unusual gambrel roofline. The building burned in the 1940s, and its original date will probably remain unknown. It is shown in photographs as a narrow two-story frame structure on foundation piers of brick, lower to the ground than was typical of later houses. In sharp contrast to Head Quarters and Brick House, which were built not many years before, this was an early example of the farmhouse style that became dominant on the sea islands. There were originally six main rooms, four on the ground floor and two above, with a center hall on each level. By the time photos were made, the rear of the house was obscured by a series of side wings, and an upper level had been added to the porch.

Tom Seabrook's House, 1930 *(From the collections of the South Carolina Historical Society)*

The name Tom Seabrook derives from Thomas Bannister Seabrook of Edisto Island and Charleston. A son of Benjamin Seabrook, Thomas married Elizabeth Clark in about 1802. Under the will of her father James, Elizabeth, who was only eleven at his death in 1790, would receive certain lands when she came of age or married.[2] Whether the T. B. Seabrook plantation was a Clark holding has not been determined, but it is certain that Seabrook himself did not build this house.

Thomas B. and Elizabeth Seabrook established their household in Charleston, where they raised three daughters. Seabrook bought a 720-acre plantation on Johns Island in 1802,[3] and in 1816 acquired another large tract on the Stono River near Rantowles.[4] In 1825 he paid taxes on 803 acres in St. Andrews Parish and 1,027 acres in St. John's Colleton, as well as on lots in town.[5] After Elizabeth Clark Seabrook died in 1817, her daughters remained distant enough from Edisto Island's circle of relatives that all three were married out of the family: Elizabeth to Andrew Milne, Sarah to Henry F. Faber, and Caroline to Gilbert Geddes.[6]

Thomas Bannister Seabrook died in 1839. His estate inventory includes the contents of a comfortable town house, but the only personal property appraised outside of Charleston was a list of 158 slaves.[7] If the dwelling on Edisto Island was furnished, the goods must have been of negligible value (it might have housed an overseer).

T. B. Seabrook's was a productive cotton plantation, and Edward C. Whaley of Old Dominion bought it in about 1840. It became home to Edward's son William Baynard Whaley and his wife Martha Mary Hanahan. Six Whaley children were born here between 1843 and 1854: William Baynard, John C. Calhoun, Arthur Murray, Josephine, James, and Percival Hanahan.[8]

The family lived comfortably, if not lavishly, at T. B. Seabrook's, where William Baynard Whaley made twenty-four bags of sea island cotton on two hundred acres in 1849. He supplemented his own workforce with some of his father's slaves, and provided much of their medical care himself. (The most valuable single item in his personal estate was a "physic chest" worth $70.)[9]

In 1857, when his youngest son was only three, William B. Whaley died. His widow and children remained in their home, their income enhanced by Martha's share of a 740-acre plantation on Johns Island, left to her and her sisters at their father John Hanahan's death in 1856.[10] The cotton yield seems not to have fallen off significantly: with the assistance of her husband's family and her own, Martha produced twenty bags in 1859.

Edward C. Whaley outlived his son by only a few years, and devised T. B. Seabrook's to William's children.[11] Not until 1881 was the property partitioned among the heirs. A narrow 63-acre tract, extending from the public road to the water's edge, with the entrance avenue and house, was the portion of Arthur Murray Whaley and his wife Susan.[12]

---

1. Samuel Gaillard Stoney, *Plantations of the Carolina Low Country* (Charleston: Carolina Art Association, 1938), pp. 62-63; Harriette Kershaw Leiding in *Historic Houses of South Carolina* (Philadelphia: J. B. Lippincott, 1921), p. 220, suggests 1780.

2. "Will of James Clark," Charleston County Wills, Book 23, p. 638, Charleston County Public Library.

3. Charleston County Register of Mesne Conveyance, Deed Book F7, p. 305.

4. "Wappoo Plantation (38CH1199/1200). Data Recovery at an 18th Century Stono River Plantation," (Mt. Pleasant: Brockington and Associates, 1992).

5. Tax Returns, 1824, South Carolina Department of Archives and History.

6. Chalmers G. Davidson, *The Last Foray. The South Carolina Planters of 1860: A Sociological Study* (Columbia: University of South Carolina Press, 1971), p. 230. *Southern Patriot* 10/25/1827. Mabel C. Webber, "Early Generations of the Seabrook Family," in *South Carolina Historical Magazine* 17 (1916).

7. "Will of Thomas Bannister Seabrook," Charleston County Wills, Book 41, p. 924. Charleston County Inventories, Book H, p. 410, CCPL.

8. James Garner Patey, *The Whaley Family and Its Charleston Connection* (Spartanburg: The Reprint Company, 1992), pp. 37-39.

9. Charleston County Inventories, Book F, p. 23, CCPL.

10. "Will of John Hanahan," Charleston County Wills, Book 47, p. 806, CCPL.

11. "Will of Edward Whaley," Charleston County Wills, Book 48, p. 601, CCPL.

12. Charleston County RMC, Deed Book A19, p. 250.

Laurel Bay
Port Royal Island

Laurel Bay Plantation was part of the Barnwell family's holdings well before the American Revolution. Robert Gibbes Barnwell inherited Laurel Bay, and by 1800 he was planting sea island cotton.

Barnwell replaced a fine brick residence burned by the British or their Tory allies, using the thick-walled ground floor of the mid-eighteenth-century dwelling as the foundation of a new building. According to Joseph Walker Barnwell, "only the roof and wood-work were injured by fire. My grandfather put a new roof on the building and fitted up the upper story, leaving the basement unfinished. My father [William Hazzard Wigg Barnwell] not long before 1860 put the basement in order, making four rooms there and a large hall."[1]

The photograph of Laurel Bay shows the grand live oak avenue more than it does the house. It is possible to make out only the deep front porch, a one-story wing, and the window and door openings. It does appear that the ground floor was masonry and the upper floor wood-frame, bearing out Joseph Barnwell's recollection. The wing at the right might have included two of the basement rooms.

Laurel Bay Plantation, 1862 *(From the collections of the South Carolina Historical Society)*

Robert Gibbes Barnwell (1761-1814) and his wife Elizabeth Hayne Wigg had eight children during the eighteen years of their marriage. Although Barnwell's will (if he left one) has not survived, it was customary for a planter to bequeath his home plantation to the youngest son, first providing a lifetime interest in the property to his widow. While elder brothers were establishing their own plantations, the younger children and their mother could remain in the family home. This was the case with Laurel Bay, which was inherited by William Hazzard Wigg Barnwell, the fifth child and youngest son of his parents.

William Hazzard Wigg Barnwell followed his brother Robert Woodward to Harvard, graduating in 1824. After further studies in law, he was admitted to the bar in 1827 and went to work with his brother's firm in Coosawhatchie. In late 1829 he married his cousin, twenty-year-old Catherine Osborn Barnwell. They divided their time between Coosawhatchie, Laurel Bay, and Beaufort, where their son Robert Woodward Barnwell, the first of twelve children, was born in 1831.

In 1833, W. H. W. Barnwell was called to the Episcopal ministry. After a brief tenure in Pendleton, he moved to Charleston where Robert Barnwell Rhett assisted his formation of a new church, St. Peter's Episcopal. He served this congregation until 1853, when poor health forced his retirement to Beaufort. Still with most of their children at home—Charles, the youngest, was barely a toddler—he and Catherine returned to their neglected house at Laurel Bay. The improvements described by his grandson must have been made before 1857 when Barnwell moved to Pennsylvania in search of medical treatment. There he died in early 1863.[2]

William Hazzard Wigg Barnwell planted at Laurel Bay throughout his life, but his active ministry interfered with his planting career. In 1850, only half of Laurel Bay's eight hundred acres was improved land, and the sixteen bags of cotton he produced in 1849 is not impressive compared to other sea island planters (at Myrtle Bush, his brother-in-law Osborn Barnwell made fifteen bags on about half the acreage).[3]

Although Stephen Elliott Barnwell gave up studies at South Carolina College to assist the management of his father's Laurel Bay, production deteriorated still further after 1850. The 1860 census lists one hundred acres of improved land, with an 1859 yield of only six bags.

During the federal occupation of Port Royal, Laurel Bay became famous for its oak avenue, longer than that at Myrtle Bush and more majestic than the comparatively new avenue at Woodward. In 1862, it was "the handsomest show of trees down here. No person is supposed to have seen the sights on Port Royal unless he has been out to Barnwell's."[4] The Barnwell house was burned while still in federal possession.[5]

---

1. Joseph Walker Barnwell, "Recollections," (MS, 1929, South Carolina Historical Society). Colin Brooker, "Tabby Structures at Woodward Plantation, Port Royal Island, Beaufort County, S.C." (MS, Beaufort County Public Library).
2. Stephen B. Barnwell, *The Story of an American Family* (Marquette, MI: 1969), pp. 116-121.
3. W. H. W. Barnwell, "Rev. W. H. W. Barnwell Plantation Book," (MS, South Carolina Historical Society).
4. Caption on "Laurel Bay," Samuel A. Cooley, photographer, #22 in Reed Collection, BCPL.
5. Barnwell, "Recollections."

Old Fort (Smith's) Plantation
Port Royal Island

Old Fort Plantation took its name from the tabby ruins of a structure known as Spanish Fort. The plantation residence was said to have been built for John Joyner, who bought the land in 1785, and became known as Smith's Plantation after it was inherited by his grandson John Joyner Smith.

In 1813, J. Joyner Smith married Mary Gibbes Barnwell.[1] Although they had no children, they lived closely surrounded by nieces and nephews. After about 1850, Bower Williamson Barnwell, one of sixteen children of Mary's brother William Wigg Barnwell, managed Smith's plantations. This arrangement appears to have continued after Mary Barnwell's death in 1853 and Smith's remarriage to Mary Duncan in 1858,[2] as it was Bower W. Barnwell, Smith's executor, who filed compensation claims in 1873 for Smith's thirteen hundred acres sold by the federal government a decade earlier.[3]

J. J. Smith held a great deal of land during his lifetime. In 1825, he paid taxes on 1,540 acres and several town lots in St. Helena Parish, and also owned three hundred acres in St. Peter's Parish. He might have sold or otherwise conveyed some of the land by 1850, when he reported owning two tracts totaling fourteen hundred acres in St. Helena. On Old Fort's seven hundred acres he had produced sixty-five bags of sea island cotton.

The few available photographs of Smith's plantation house show an avenue of magnolias leading to the front of the building, where there was a one-story shed-roofed porch. The five inner bays of the façade are symmetrical, with a low pediment centered in the lateral gable roof. The outer wings, which make of the front porch a recessed room with one open side, might have been additions.

Freedmen's Bureau teacher Elizabeth H. Botume left a description of the Smiths' home in 1864:

My location was to be at Old Fort Plantation, a place of historic renown and great beauty... The plantation house...was one of the oldest on the island. It was a low, two-storied mansion, built in a wonderful grove of live oaks and water oaks which covered an area of sixty acres.

The house contained nine small rooms. The outside door opened into a medium-sized apartment which was called "the hall" but had always been used as parlor and dining room. Out of this opened a butler's pantry and buttery, which enclosed one end of the open piazza. At the other was an office or waiting room. There was adjoining this a small room which the servants designated as the "drawing room." A door opened from this room directly upon a narrow front piazza, from which there was a pleasant view of the broad river and of the islands beyond.

A narrow flight of winding stairs led up outside from the back piazza to a small square entry, from which four doors opened into the bedrooms. The kitchen and laundry and servants' rooms were

Old Fort (Smith's) Plantation, 1862 *(Courtesy of The Western Reserve Historical Society, Cleveland Ohio)*

in separate buildings. A row of these houses faced the back entrance. Not far away and in plain sight were the "Negro quarters."[4]

This description suggests an architectural style unusual for the lowcountry, but very common along the Gulf coast, where it was customary to place the stair at one side of a porch, inaccessible from the interior of the building. A more complete understanding of the house awaits better photographic documentation.

1. Chalmers G. Davidson, *The Last Foray. The South Carolina Planters of 1860: A Sociological Study* (Columbia: University of South Carolina Press, 1971), p. 250. Stephen B. Barnwell, *The Story of an American Family* (Marquette, MI: 1969), pp. 83, 94-95.
2. Barnwell, *American Family*, p. 91. Davidson, *Last Foray*, p. 250.
3. National Archives, Record Group 58, c. 1873 petition for compensation.
4. Quoted in Katharine M. Jones, *Port Royal under Six Flags, The Story of the Sea Islands* (New York: Bobbs-Merrill Co., 1960), pp. 275-277.

Baynard's Old Place
EDISTO ISLAND

The house called "Mr. Charles Seabrook's place" survived into the twentieth century, but was rarely photographed. Considered "one of the old landmarks of the island, although of no particular significance, architecturally speaking,"[1] its design provides few clues about its history. The two-over-four plan with two chimneys, each with three flues, was used for generations.

The south elevation, with a one-story piazza, was oriented toward an oak avenue leading from Edisto Island's main public road. The back of the house stood against Russell Creek, directly opposite Ashe's Plantation on Little Edisto. We have not located a photograph of the façade; however, the rear view depicts two fairly unusual features. Unlike the integral shed-roof system that was the more typical treatment for the one-story section, here we see a hipped roof. Like the stair tower projection, also with a hipped roof, this design was not unique, but it was one of the less common aspects of sea island architecture.

The clutter of small structures visible from the Russell Creek bridge in the early twentieth century reflects a characteristic approach to locating outbuildings. Extending from both sides of the house, they appear slightly closer to the creek than was the residence, but none were placed between the house and the water. The dock was set to one side, farther from the house than were its service buildings.

Baynard's Old Place, ca. 1930. Rear of house viewed from Russell Creek
(From the collections of the South Carolina Historical Society)

The "Seabrook place" was formerly a Baynard plantation. At his death in 1772, William Baynard devised to his son Thomas "this tract of land I now live upon," leaving land "over the creek" to son William.[2] Young boys when orphaned (their mother Elizabeth died in 1773),[3] Thomas and William grew up to become planters with land on both Edisto and Hilton Head.

Thomas Baynard married Sally (Sarah) Calder of Edisto Island in 1784. There were at least six children over the next sixteen years, including William Edings Baynard of Hilton Head and Savannah. At some point between 1790 and 1800, the family returned from Hilton Head to Edisto, where Thomas died.[4]

Thomas Baynard's estate was partitioned among his wife and children, as each child came of age. Eldest son John C. Baynard received two tracts, 282 acres on Little Edisto Island and this 200-acre plantation, presumably with the family house. Much remains unknown: by early 1839, his cousin William G. Baynard of Prospect Hill had bought both tracts from the estate of J. C. Baynard, who "became of unsound mind and died" after coming into possession of them.[5]

Having paid $30,000 for the two plantations, W. G. Baynard enlarged his grandfather's home tract. In 1844, he bought two hundred acres adjoining to the east (part of Brick House Plantation) from Joseph E. Jenkins[6] and, in 1846, purchased another forty-seven acres from Whitemarsh B. Seabrook.[7]

Like other sea island fathers, Baynard bought and enlarged valuable plantations with an eye to his children's futures. This "Old Place" was the portion of his son Edward Mitchell Baynard.[8] In about 1852, when Edward was twenty-two, he married his cousin Catherine, a daughter of William Edings Baynard.[9] Their first two children were born in Savannah, but by 1856 they had settled into life on Edisto, where their two younger children were born. In 1860, Edward M. Baynard was a prosperous thirty-year-old planter with 460 acres, on which he produced sixty bags of sea island cotton in 1859. His house was not new, but it was well appointed. In 1862, he estimated the value of his furniture at $1,500, with a further $60 claim for a set of china,[10] a loss that must have been a particular irritant.

The acreage of Baynard's Old Place was gradually reduced after the deaths of Edward and Catherine Baynard. As tracts were partitioned off for their children, some being conveyed out of the family, the plantation became known as Pine Ridge. Charles and Eva Whaley Seabrook bought the parcel with the Baynard house in about 1915.[11]

---

1. Harriette Kershaw Leiding, *Historic Houses of South Carolina* (Philadelphia: J. B. Lippincott, 1921), p. 226.
2. "Will of William Baynard," Charleston County Wills, Book 15, p. 399, Charleston County Public Library.
3. "Will of Elizabeth Baynard," Charleston County Wills, Book 15, p. 525, CCPL.
4. Annie Baynard Simons Hasell, *Baynard: An Ancient Family Bearing Arms* (Charleston: privately printed, 1972), pp. 152-155.

5. Charleston County Register of Mesne Conveyance, Deed Book W10, p. 494.
6. Charleston County RMC, Deed Book I11, p. 521.
7. "Will of William Grimball Baynard," Charleston County Wills, Book 49, p. 886, CCPL.
8. "Will of William Grimball Baynard."
9. Hasell, *Baynard*, p. 179.
10. South Carolina Comptroller/State Auditor "Claims for property lost due to the enemy" (Record Series S126189, South Carolina Department of Archives and History).
11. Charleston County RMC, Deed Book S29, p. 20.

Tombee
St. Helena Island

Tombee Plantation House was built by Thomas Benjamin Chaplin, a member of the first generation to plant sea island cotton. Born in 1742, Chaplin was approaching middle age when he constructed this dwelling in about 1795.[1] By that time, the post-Revolutionary turmoil had subsided, planters and their slaves were back on the land, and the profitability of sea island cotton was becoming evident.

Given an imposing appearance by the broad two-tiered porch facing south toward Station Creek, Chaplin's frame house is elevated on a tabby foundation, with massive piers carrying the porch. The two-over-two plan of four rooms is extended by a prominent rear wing built at right angles to the main core (this might be an early addition). The wing provided two rooms, each with windows on three sides, essential ventilation for the six hot months of the year. However, placement of the chimneys outside the gable ends left the rear rooms unheated, a feature that would have been uncomfortable in a house used mainly as a winter residence. The closed gable end of the landward-facing wing is nicely detailed and the entrance is by no means a back door.

When the plantation was first called Tombee, and whether the name was taken from its builder or his grandson (both Tom B.), remain uncertain. With the lack of land records for Beaufort County, tracing antebellum property boundaries and names is difficult. However, the second Tom Chaplin's financial problems led to constant borrowing, and at least one mortgage was filed in Charleston. To secure a debt in 1845, Chaplin mortgaged the "plantation called Palmetto Point on St. Helena Island, whereon I now live, ... butting and bounding north on Mrs. I. C. Baker [his mother], south on Capt. Daniel Jenkins and Station Creek, east on Benjamin Chaplin Jr. [his uncle] and Station Creek...."[2] Later documents refer to "the T. B. Chaplin place" and "the Tom Chaplin place."[3]

The first Thomas B. Chaplin and his wife Elizabeth Fripp had ten children, beginning with William in 1770. Most of their sons were grown by the time the Chaplins moved into the new house. It was their seventh child, Saxby, who remained on his father's home plantation. Saxby Chaplin might already have been living here in about 1815 when he married the widowed Isabella Field Jenkins. There were four children.[4] The elder son, Thomas Benjamin (born 1822), who inherited the plantation, achieved a degree of immortality through the preservation of his journal, which was edited for publication as *Tombee: Portrait of a Cotton Planter* by Theodore Rosengarten.

Diarist Tom Chaplin was very young when his father died in 1828. The plantation with its 376 acres, dwelling house, slave cabins, and service buildings, was left in trust to him under the management of his uncle Benjamin Chaplin. For the next ten years it might have stood vacant or been occupied by an overseer. Tom's mother remarried within a year of his father's death, and the family moved away from St. Helena. In 1839, before he had quite reached seventeen, Tom Chaplin married Mary Thomson McDowell of Charleston, who was even younger. The teenaged couple moved to Tom's plantation, which he would legally inherit upon his twenty-first birthday. Surrounded by uncles and cousins, Chaplin settled into married life and management of his property.

Along with Mary came her half-sister Sophy Creighton, who shared the six-room house with the Chaplins. Mary was frequently bedridden—there were seven children in nine years—so Sophy acted as nurse, aunt, and director of the eight domestic slaves: seamstress, washer, cook, nurse, and one woman and three men charged with general household duties.[5]

Three of the Chaplins' daughters died between 1845 and 1851, and the four surviving children spent time away at boarding school or with their grandmother. The house was often empty except the three white adults and their servants. The diarist occasionally complains of crowds and racket ("children making a great noise"), but an entry from 1850, when the

Tombee Plantation House, 1975 *(Courtesy of South Carolina Department of Archives and History, Columbia)*

women and children were at St. Helenaville, reveals a man accustomed to his large family: "The house is so still it makes one feel lonesome."[6]

After a brief adulthood marked by constant illness, Mary Chaplin died in 1851. Tom and Sophy married within the year. Life continued much as before, except that Chaplin had matured and was becoming a responsible husband and planter. The evacuation of St. Helena in November 1861 after the Union victory at Port Royal ended any opportunity to establish himself successfully.

The Chaplin plantation was bought by the federal government in 1863 as a school farm. A succession of superintendents and tenants occupied the house after the war, while Tom and Sophy Chaplin lived in overseers' houses, first near his mother's plantation on the Combahee River and then, back on St. Helena Island, at Coffin Point. In 1890, only months before his death, title to the house and some three hundred acres was returned by the federal government to Thomas B. Chaplin.

1. William P. Baldwin, *Plantations of the Lowcountry, South Carolina 1697-1865* (Greensboro, NC: Legacy Publications, 1985), p. 137.
2. Charleston County Register of Mesne Conveyance, Deed Book T11, p. 135.
3. *Beaufort Republican*, January 10, 1863.
4. "Chaplin Family Chart" in Theodore Rosengarten, *Tombee: Portrait of a Cotton Planter* (New York: William Morrow and Co., 1986).
5. Rosengarten, *Tombee*, pp. 488, 494.
6. Rosengarten, *Tombee*, p. 500.

Unidentified House
St. Helena Island

Photographed in 1920, this house was identified only as "Old house on St. Helena Island now owned by a Colored man." Taken from the rear, the photograph tells us little about the setting of the building.

We can see, though, that this substantial dwelling, probably built in the early nineteenth century, retained its original plan of two rooms over four. Its steeply pitched hipped roof was characteristic of early sea island construction, but the exterior end chimneys were infrequently used in the lowcountry. In this respect, the house bears a close resemblance to the typical farm house of upcountry South Carolina.

The tabby foundation walls at the right side prove this to have been a sea island residence. The scale of the building and the fine brickwork at the stuccoed chimneys suggest it was among St. Helena's finer early dwellings.

Unidentified house on St. Helena Island, 1920
(Special Collections, University of Virginia Library)

Coffin Point
St. Helena Island

Ebenezer Coffin, born in Boston in 1765, moved to Charleston in his mid-twenties. In 1793, he married Mary Mathews, then twenty-two years old.[1] Thus a Charleston merchant became a St. Helena Island planter: Mary's father Benjamin Mathews of St. John's Colleton Parish gave her sixty-three slaves and a 1,120-acre plantation in St. Helena Parish, in trust for her children.[2] Although their contemporaries might have called the property Coffin's Point, our first reference to its name comes in 1862, when Coffin's son called it "the Point."[3]

Ebenezer Coffin assumed management of his wife's plantation, and by late 1800, he was ready to build a new house. He employed a "Mr. Wade" and five carpenters to erect a dwelling house, stable, and slave houses. The work expanded to include improvements to the gin house, and a new cotton house and kitchen house. Throughout 1801 and 1802, Coffin made payments for bricks, lumber, shingles and flooring.[4]

An oak avenue leads from the island road to the Coffin house, which faces St. Helena Sound. Two and a half stories above the raised basement level, the building was laid out in the familiar plan of four rooms on each level, with a central passage and stair hall. Dormers extend the hipped roof at both sides, their windows enframed by fluted pilasters. The architectural detailing of Coffin's house set it apart from its contemporaries. A hipped roof made the grand front porch appear taller. The first-floor entry had a large transom, with a Palladian window above and a lunette window at the pedimented front gable. Heavy dentil work on all sides of the main block is echoed by much narrower trim at the dormers.

Additions have obscured the original appearance of the land side, which now appears as a secondary rear elevation. However, a 1920s photograph shows this south side of the house much differently, with a stately two-tier piazza.[5] The front elevation, too, was dramatically altered with the replacement of the original porch by a flat-roofed composition with a balustrade at its upper deck.

During construction of the plantation complex, the Coffin family also bought a new town house in Charleston. Between 1801 and 1802, Ebenezer, Mary, four children, and more than a dozen household slaves moved from Tradd Street to Bull Street. The 1810 census shows the Coffins living in Beaufort District, but they kept a residence in Charleston.[6]

Although he was no longer engaged in mercantile business, Ebenezer Coffin continued to invest in Charleston real estate. He succeeded in every facet of his life—business, planting, and family. Eight children were born to him and Mary: Thomas Aston in 1795, followed by William Mathews, Francis Augustus, William Parker and Anna Sarah Smith, all born by 1804; and George M., Elizabeth Peronneau, and Harriet Mathews between 1805 and 1811.[7] In

Coffin Point Plantation House, ca. 1880 *(Courtesy of Cecily McMillan)*

Coffin Point Plantation House, 1985 *(Courtesy of Wade Spees)*

1813, in a sad and not uncommon occurrence, Mary Coffin died at the age of forty-two. Ebenezer, the "affectionate father of a numerous family" died four years later.[8]

By that time, Thomas A. Coffin had graduated from Harvard, and he took over as manager of the family property and head of the household.[9] He and his brothers and sisters had inherited the plantation in undivided portions, and making his St. Helena residence in their parents' house, Thomas planted sea island cotton on behalf of the family. The plantation was described in 1826 as 1,181.5 acres, bounded by St. Helena Sound, lands of William Fripp, a creek, and Harbor Island River.[10] The Coffin heirs had already bought Harbor Island, another four hundred acres of high land and marsh, supplementing funds from their mother's estate with a legacy from Thomas Aston Coffin of Boston.[11]

Thomas A. Coffin of Charleston and St. Helena married in 1829. Harriet, his bride, was the seventeen-year-old daughter of James Elliott McPherson of Prince William Parish and Charleston.[12] They sometimes lived at the Point, but throughout their lives they kept a house in Charleston, which allowed them to educate their children without sending them to boarding school. In 1850, Henry (14), Juliet (12), Carolina (10), and James (8) were all in school, while young Christine and Arabella were at home. (Two sons, Thomas Aston and John McPherson, had died in New York.)[13]

After Harriet Coffin's death in 1852,[14] Thomas bought a great deal of property on St. Helena Island, some for his mother's estate, some with an eye toward his own children's future. In June 1853, on behalf of the family trust, he paid John J. T. Pope $6,000 for the 255-acre Cherry Hill Plantation, and at some point bought two hundred adjoining acres from the McTureous family.[15] On his own account, he bought Frogmore, with a full complement of slaves, from William J. Grayson.[16]

In 1859, nearly sixty years old, Thomas Coffin produced 137 bags of sea island cotton. Two years later, the 1861 crop—some packed and some still in the field—was abandoned when planters were forced to evacuate the sea islands. The Coffins' fine plantation residence became the temporary dwelling of a number of northerners, including teachers attached to the Freedmen's Bureau. One of them, Miss Harriet Ware of Massachusetts, observed with some sympathy the part-time home of a cosmopolitan planter family: "[The house] was built in good style originally, but it is very old, and has been so abused... It must have been handsomely furnished, to judge from the relics, rosewood tables, sideboards and washstands with marble tops, sofas that must have been of the best..."[17]

Coffin and his second wife Sarah Cruger Creighton were in Columbia in late 1862, but managed to return to Charleston, where Coffin died in July 1863.[18] His will and inventory mention not only lots in Charleston and plantations on St. Helena Island, a pew in Charleston's Grace Episcopal Church and a plot in Magnolia Cemetery, but also 999 acres in Wisconsin and a house in Newport, Rhode Island.[19]

1. "Register of the Independent Congregational Church of Charleston SC 1784-1815," in *South Carolina Historical Magazine* 33 (1932).
2. South Carolina Marriage Settlements, Book 2, p. 143, South Carolina Department of Archives and History.
3. "Will of Thomas Aston Coffin," Charleston County Wills, Book 50, p. 119, Charleston County Public Library.
4. Ebenezer Coffin, "Coffin Point Plantation Journals, 1800-1816" (MS, South Carolina Historical Society).
5. Photograph of "Coffin Plantation," in T. J. Woofter, Jr., *Black Yeomanry, Life on St. Helena Island* (New York: Henry Holt and Company, 1930).
6. James William Hagy, *People and Professions of Charleston, South Carolina, 1782-1802* (Baltimore: Clearfield Company, 1992).
7. "Register of the Independent Congregational Church."
8. "Inscriptions from the Independent or Congregational Churchyard," in SCHM 29 (1928).
9. Chalmers G. Davidson, *The Last Foray. The South Carolina Planters of 1860: A Sociological Study* (Columbia: University of South Carolina Press, 1971), p. 185.
10. South Carolina Marriage Settlements, Book 9, p. 243, SCDAH.
11. Charleston County Register of Mesne Conveyance, Deed Book Z8, p. 300.
12. Davidson, *Last Foray*, p. 185.
13. Theresa E. Wilson and Janice L. Grimes, *Marriage and Death Notices from the Southern Patriot, 1831-1848* (Easley: Southern Historical Press, Inc., 1986), p. 131.
14. City of Charleston Death Records Index, CCPL.
15. Charleston County RMC, Deed Book P13, p. 540.
16. "Will of Thomas Aston Coffin."
17. Elizabeth W. Pearson, ed., *Letters from Port Royal Written at the Time of the Civil War* (Boston, 1906), pp. 59-60.
18. Letter, Kimball Elkins (Harvard University Archives) to Chalmers Davidson, August 4, 1961, South Carolina Historical Society.
19. Charleston County Inventories, Book F, p. 528, CCPL.

Vanderhorst House
Kiawah Island

When John Stanyarne of Johns Island died in 1772, he owned all of Kiawah Island. His granddaughter Elizabeth Raven Vanderhorst, the wife of Arnoldus Vanderhorst, inherited the island's east half.[1]

Arnoldus Vanderhorst was a Charleston resident with extensive holdings in Christ Church Parish. In 1772 he was twenty-four years old, married for a year, and newly elected to South Carolina's Royal Assembly. From that date until 1799, Vanderhorst held public office almost continuously, balancing his legislative responsibilities with service as intendant for the City of Charleston. After two years as governor of South Carolina, Vanderhorst served a final term in the general assembly.[2]

With his children growing up (Elias, the youngest, was born in 1791), Vanderhorst's political retirement at the age of fifty began a period of reorganization. No longer distracted by public affairs, between 1800 and 1810 he built two tenement houses at the foot of his downtown wharf.[3] In 1801 he directed William Nicks, the overseer on Kiawah Island, to plant cotton for the first time. Slaves began picking the first crop late that summer,[4] and in November 1801 Vanderhorst deeded his land in Christ Church Parish to his son Arnoldus.[5]

The elder Vanderhorst's Kiawah Island laborers were busy not only learning to handle a cotton crop, but also with new construction—pea house, fodder house, blade house—to store provisions. By 1802 there were ten small buildings. The following year Vanderhorst finally erected a plantation house to replace a dwelling burned in 1780.[6]

Set on the north side of the island, beside a creek out of the Kiawah River, the house overlooks a lawn and an oak avenue leading toward the ocean a half-mile away. With service buildings and slave cabins scattered to the sides of the mansion, the return from the seaside featured a long uninterrupted view of the three-and-a-half-story residence with its prominent front porch.

Carried by an arcaded foundation that creates a ground-level entry porch, the upper piazza has slim columns aligned with the brick supports. Sidelights and an oversized fanlight ornament the upper doorway. Access was not through this handsome upper porch, but through the lower level, where the entry door with its large glass transom was nearly as fine as that above.

The design of this unusual plantation house closely resembles a Charleston single house, two rooms wide and one room deep. It differs from that urban type, however, in significant ways: the principal front elevation is the long side, there are almost as many window openings at the rear wall as at the facade, and the center hall is a through-passage connecting entries at both sides. Like its plan, the decorative detail of this island mansion was squarely in line with Charleston tastes. The Adamesque design of the interior paneling and mantelpieces was the height of style in early-nineteenth-century Charleston.[7]

Vanderhorst House, 2003 *(Courtesy of Bruce G. Harvey)*

At Arnoldus Vanderhorst's death in 1815, his will directed that his sons Elias and John would jointly inherit the plantation and the wharf, Elias controlling Kiawah and John the wharf, sharing equally in the profits from both.[8] By this time Elias had finished his education at Yale and was probably managing Kiawah under his father's supervision. The senior Vanderhorst's will would seem to guarantee friction between the brothers, but John Stanyarne Vanderhorst died unmarried in 1816, leaving Elias the sole owner of the plantation and the downtown business.[9]

According to the inventory of Arnoldus Vanderhorst's estate, much of the furniture in his Kiawah Island house was mahogany and there were expensive carpets and fine brass firedogs and fenders. Vanderhorst may not have entertained lavishly (the inventory includes no wine or bottles), but the house was prepared for more sedate pleasures with two dining tables, four card tables, a bookcase, and a "hand organ." The family was obviously accustomed to serving tea in the ceremonial English fashion, with special china and silver tableware and serving pieces.

Although there were dozens of chairs, accommodation for overnight guests would have been no more private than in a roadside inn. Even counting the garret—which had no fireplaces—there were not many sleeping rooms. In 1815 the house had three bedsteads with gauze pavilions (mosquito netting). There were only two featherbeds, two sets of bed curtains for cooler weather, seven pairs of sheets, seven mattresses, and four pairs of pillows.

Unlike his parents, Elias Vanderhorst made his primary residence on Kiawah Island. In 1821, several years after he came into his inheritance, he married Ann Morris of the South Edisto River rice-planting family. During the summers, they left Kiawah for Sullivans Island or Edings Bay. After Vanderhorst built a town house in 1832, Ann and the children mostly lived in Charleston. Even then, Elias often stayed on the plantation in the summer, using instead of the big house a beachside cabin at the east end of the island.[10]

Cotton production dwindled after the Civil War, but later Vanderhorsts continued to plant the crop into the twentieth century. Kiawah Island, with the Vanderhorst Mansion, was sold in 1950 as the estate of Adele Allston Vanderhorst.

1. Michael Trinkley, ed., *The History and Archaeology of Kiawah Island, Charleston County, South Carolina*. Research Series 30. (Columbia: Chicora Foundation, 1993), pp. 56-57.
2. N. Louise Bailey, *Biographical Directory of the South Carolina Senate*. Vol. 2 (Columbia: University of South Carolina Press, 1986), p. 1643.
3. Jonathan H. Poston, *The Buildings of Charleston. A Guide to the City's Architecture* (Columbia: University of South Carolina Press, 1997), p. 98. "Will of Arnoldus Vanderhorst," Charleston County Wills, Book 32, p. 924, Charleston County Public Library.
4. Trinkley, *Kiawah*, p. 62.
5. "Will of Arnoldus Vanderhorst."
6. Trinkley, *Kiawah*, pp. 28, 258.
7. Colin Brooker, "The Architecture of the Vanderhorst Mansion," in Trinkley, *Kiawah*, pp. 321-335.
8. "Will of Arnoldus Vanderhorst."
9. Bailey, *Biographical Directory*, p. 1643.
10. Trinkley, *Kiawah*, pp. 65-66.

William Edings House (Seaside)
EDISTO ISLAND

The Edings/Eddings family were planting in the South Carolina lowcountry from a very early date. As with other sea island families, their habits of remaining close to the place of their birth, marrying relatives, and repeatedly using the same given names make it difficult to trace their land holdings.

The history of the plantation that became known as the Edings Place or Seaside begins with William Edings, who died in 1767 leaving "all my lands lying on Edisto" to his twenty-five-year-old son Benjamin, also directing that his wife would have the right to live in his plantation house.[1]

Benjamin Edings had land grants of his own in addition to the plantation he inherited. He had married Mary Baynard, the widow of Henry Bailey, in 1765, and they likely had a dwelling separate from his father's. In 1783, Benjamin conveyed to his sons "all my lands on Edisto to be equally divided ... the half that my large dwelling house stands on to William, the other half to Joseph."[2] Both sons were minors, and the reason for the gift is unclear. They would have inherited anyway (subject to their mother's rights) upon their father's death the next year.

The younger William Edings became a successful planter, and added several tracts to his father Benjamin's home place. In 1805, he paid Joseph Jenkins Sr. £3,000 for a 389-acre plantation known as Spanish Mount, which was beside Scott's Creek, southwest of land he already owned.[3] Considering his father's intriguing reference to "my large dwelling house" and the inventory of his personal goods, which included mahogany furniture and table services of queensware and pewter,[4] it seems that William Edings and his wife Sarah Evans probably lived in his father's house during their early married life, replacing it later.

Family history holds that William built the residence, but does not claim a date.[5] The period from 1800 to 1810 would be consistent with the architecture and the fine Federal-style interior trimwork. Despite the unusual masonry construction, the design is characteristic of the sea islands. Only the placement of the two chimneys inside the end walls is unique. The one-room-deep house, two-and-a-half stories high above its ground-level basement, has a hipped porch, originally with fairly heavy Tuscan columns, and bold cornices at the pedimented gable ends. Windows are regularly placed, two at each exterior wall of the four main rooms, and dormers and quarter-round end windows light two additional rooms at the wood-frame attic level.

At his death in 1836, William Edings owned a great deal of land, most of it on Edisto Island. Three tracts totaling twelve hundred acres composed his home plantation. This ("my principal Mansion house, yard and garden") he left to his widow for her lifetime. The plantation included the area that came to be called Edingsville, known to the family as Edings Bay, and he reserved to his sister Mary Chisolm and each of his daughters the right "of having a lot of land for a residence on any of my Sea Bays."[6]

William Edings House, 1978 *(Historic American Buildings Survey, Library of Congress)*

William and Sarah Edings were the parents of five known children: Eliza (born in 1799), James (1800-1818), Sarah, Mary, and John Evans Edings (born in 1808).[7] William valued the custom of inheritance through the male line, but for undetermined reasons he considered his surviving son a questionable heir. John Evans Edings had married Mary Wilkinson Mathews of Edisto Island in 1827, and was himself the father of two small boys when William Edings wrote his will. He left the home plantation to J. Evans Edings (subject to his mother's right of occupancy), but carefully made the legacy for his son's lifetime only, entailing the land to his grandsons. The terms were that if there should be any bankruptcy or foreclosure action against John Evans, his legacy would be revoked and given immediately to his sons.

J. Evans Edings outlived his father by only six months, and legends about the house are rife after 1836. Sarah (William's widow) might have exerted her right of occupancy until her death in 1857. The census for 1840 includes "Estate William Edings" with four white residents: Sarah, two other middle-aged women, and a man in his twenties, probably a relative managing the plantation. J. Evans Edings's widow Mary kept a separate household with her young sons William and John Evans Jr., who were the heirs to the property.

In 1842 Mary Wilkinson Edings took a second husband, Optimus Hughes.[8] Her sons spent time at boarding school, but they soon returned to Edisto Island, while Mary and Optimus settled in Charleston. In 1850, young William Edings was two years married,[9] claiming no occupation, and sharing a richly furnished home on Edisto with his brother, seventeen-year-old John Evans.

That year, though, William died, leaving his brother sole heir to their grandfather's house. In 1854, J. Evans Edings Jr. married his cousin Josephine Edings Seabrook[10] of Oak Island. Although he would inherit his grandfather Edings's plantation, the young couple moved into the mansion of her grandfather, William Seabrook.

From there and their house at Edingsville, Edings oversaw his cotton fields. Evacuating Edisto Island in 1861, he lost 130 bags of "fine sea island cotton," but most of his land was restored to him in 1865.[11] Edingsville Beach was lost to the hurricane of 1893.

---

1. "Will of William Edings," cited in William Garner Chisolm "Edings of Edisto Island" (MS, Leesburg, VA: 1943).
2. Charleston County Register of Mesne Conveyance, Deed Book N5, p. 496.
3. Charleston County RMC, Deed Book R7, p. 102.
4. Charleston County Inventories, Book H, p. 169, Charleston County Public Library.
5. The house has been ascribed a date of 1802, following Edings's purchase of a 150-acre tract on Edisto, but he sold that parcel in 1825: Charleston County RMC Deed Book L7, p. 85, Deed Book R7, p. 112.
6. "Will of William Edings," Charleston County Wills, Book 40, p. 400.
7. Chisolm "Edings."
8. Brent Holcomb, *Marriage and Death Notices from the Charleston Observer 1827-1845* (Columbia: n.p., 1980), p. 175.
9. He married Angelina Rivers in 1848 (Marriage Settlement recorded in Charleston County RMC, Deed Book A12, p. 219).
10. Chalmers G. Davidson, *The Last Foray. The South Carolina Planters of 1860: A Sociological Study* (Columbia: University of South Carolina Press, 1971), p. 194.
11. Freedmen's Bureau transcripts in David H. Lybrand papers, Edisto Island.

Myrtle Bush
Port Royal Island

Samuel Cooley photographed the house at Myrtle Bush in 1862 during its occupation by the Tenth Corps, U.S. Army. A note on the back of the photo comments: "Very poor house—only six rooms in it and half of those unfit to live in."[1] Like many other federal officers and civilians staying on the sea islands after 1861, Cooley noticed the condition of the house, not its architectural quality. His photographs show a substantial dwelling and its garden at the head of a shady avenue of live oak trees.

While we cannot make out the sides or what appears to be a rear porch at the right, this large structure must have been two rooms deep, with fireplaces only at the front rooms. The one-story shed porch across the first floor, its Tuscan columns placed above the pillars of the arcaded basement porch area, is quite similar to that of the Vanderhorst House on Kiawah Island. The obvious difference is that the Vanderhorst porch was inaccessible from the ground, while at Myrtle Bush the spreading front stair, with its unusual cylindrical ends, provides a welcoming aspect to the facade. This porch is the only architectural embellishment, as the entry door is set in a very plain surround.

Myrtle Bush was the home of Thomas Osborn Barnwell, the second son of Captain Edward Barnwell. Upon his graduation from West Point in 1834, Osborn received a lieutenant's commission and orders for duty in Kansas Territory. There he married the daughter of his post commander. Eight months later, his young wife died, and Osborn Barnwell resigned his commission, returning to Beaufort in the autumn of 1837. The following January, his father Edward deeded Myrtle Bush Plantation (shown as "E. Barnwell" in the 1825 Mills *Atlas)* to Osborn.[2]

Myrtle Bush may be a portion of the plantation Captain Edward Barnwell had advertised for sale as part of his father Colonel Edward Barnwell's estate in late 1816: "plantation on Port Royal Island, 4 miles distant from the town of Beaufort, containing about 800 acres of Cotton and Provision Land of the first quality, and a good pine barren. Upon the premises are a very fine two-story Dwelling House, with the customary Outbuildings. This Tract has not been much cultivated for 7 or 8 years."[3]

It was not unusual for an executor to buy a property himself once it had been fairly offered for sale. It seems that Captain Edward Barnwell had purchased Myrtle Bush from the estate of his own father Edward, who died in 1808. (Disposition of the estate was probably delayed until the younger son, William Wigg Barnwell, turned twenty-one.) Given the years of disuse before the sale, this would indicate that the house was constructed before 1808, which is consistent with its architecture.

In 1841, St. Helena Parish planter Osborn Barnwell married Jean Kerr Richardson, a daughter of Dr. Henry Richardson of Beaufort. He was then twenty-six; she was thirty. With their

Myrtle Bush Plantation House, 1862 *(Courtesy of The Western Reserve Historical Society, Cleveland Ohio)*

plantation so near town, the family lived mostly in Beaufort, where they raised four daughters (Thomas Osborn, the only son, died in childhood).[4]

T. O. Barnwell's Myrtle Bush consisted of 450 acres. In 1849, with 250 acres under cultivation, Barnwell made fifteen bags of sea island cotton. Gradually reducing the fallow and woodland areas, by 1859 he was planting three hundred acres and produced twenty bags. Although there were good harvests of corn, oats, peas, and sweet potatoes, these were for home consumption. Cotton was more important than garden produce, regardless of the market it would have found in Beaufort.

After the Civil War and Reconstruction, Thomas Osborn Barnwell reclaimed Myrtle Bush in the early 1870s. He remained in Beaufort until his death in 1879. The Myrtle Bush Plantation house burned in the 1880s.[5]

1. "Murkle Bush, Port Royal Island, Oscar Barnwell's Place," Reed Collection, Photograph #19, Beaufort County Public Library.
2. Stephen B. Barnwell, *The Story of an American Family* (Marquette, MI: 1969), pp. 81-86.
3. *Charleston Courier*, January 29, 1816.
4. Barnwell, *American Family*, pp. 81-86.
5. National Archives, Record Group 58, c. 1873 petition for compensation, cited in Beaufort County Historic Sites Survey 1997, Site #13-025-0623 (Site Form, South Carolina Department of Archives and History).

Hopkinson's
Edisto Island

Known only through photographs, this house raises more questions than it answers. With its low foundation, Tuscan columns, nine-over-nine window sash and corbelled chimneys, the house might have been built at any time from 1790 to about 1830. The hipped roof, upright scale, and paired front doors with transoms give it a strong similarity to the Santee cotton planters' houses of St. John's Parish, Berkeley, but the exterior chimneys are not characteristic of that section of South Carolina.

The angle of the view makes it impossible to read the house with any certainty. There appears to be a two-room deep core on the twin-parlor plan, with the rear rooms extended beyond the plane of the building at each side, in the manner of Beaufort houses. The most prominent feature is the broad porch that wraps around both sides.

James Hopkinson, son-in-law of William Seabrook, was a transplanted Pennsylvanian and a conspicuously capable planter. From his home at Cassina Point, he managed the Edisto and Wadmalaw plantations of two of his wife's sisters, Julia (Mrs. John Berwick Legare of Charleston) and Martha (Countess de Lasteyrie of Paris). In 1860, each had about nine hundred acres under cultivation on Edisto Island. The plantation called "Hopkinson's" by Union soldiers was more likely a Seabrook family place known by the name of its operator.

House on "Hopkinson's" Plantation, 1862 *(Library of Congress)*

Coggins Point
HILTON HEAD ISLAND

At the northeast end of Hilton Head Island, overlooking Port Royal Sound, Coggins Point's location made it a valuable lookout point for occupying Union forces, and the only photographs we have located of the house show it with the army's rooftop signal station.

The substantial frame dwelling of six principal rooms (four at the first floor, two at the second) rose above a brick ground-floor level, while a fairly steep hipped roof with dormers provided an additional half-story of living space. Across the façade was a one-story porch supported by oversized brick piers, with slender Corinthian columns centered above them. The front gable with its lunette window between the two front dormers gave a nice balance to the façade, while the handsome fanlight and sidelights brightened the long hallway. The symmetrical composition of the exterior and the structural ornamental detail indicate an early-nineteenth-century date. The house was most likely built by William Pope Jr.

Coggins Point House, 1862 *(US Army Military History Institute)*

The earliest reference found to Coggins Point is the will of Samuel Green, written in 1767. He bequeathed the tract where he lived (Fish Hall) to his son Samuel and "Colgins Point" to his daughters Susannah and Sarah. Her brother and sister having died, Sarah came to ownership of both tracts while she was the wife of Thomas Tucker. As Tucker's widow, Sarah remarried William Pope Sr., and Fish Hall and Coggins Point became Pope land.[1] William himself purchased nearby Springfield.[2]

William Pope Jr., known to local history as "Squire William," was the son of William and Sarah Green Pope. After Sarah Green's early death, William Pope Sr. took a second wife, Sarah Scott, in 1798. In 1806, the junior William also married, selecting as his wife his stepmother's younger sister, Ann Scott. Their son William John was born in 1814.[3] Ann Scott Pope died not long afterward.

Assisted by his father and by their Scott in-laws, Squire William Pope established himself as a sea island cotton planter. He entered politics as well, representing St. Luke's Parish in the general assembly for two terms between 1810 and 1813. He returned to the State House in 1816, the same year he was married for the second time, to his twenty-three-year-old cousin Sarah Lavinia Pope. (Their daughter Eliza was born about 1820.) Between 1822 and 1831, Pope served five more terms in the State Senate (there was a final term in the State House in 1850).[4]

Squire William Pope's first plantation residence was probably Coggins Point (his younger brother John Edward occupied Fish Hall). The family lived in Savannah and Bluffton much of the time, but Pope was a long-staple cotton planter, and it was island property that he wanted. In 1823, the year his father died, he bought Point Comfort Plantation from the heirs of John Davant. On the 587-acre property was a "tolerable comfortable Dwelling House, Kitchen and other outbuildings,"[5] but over half of the tract was still uncleared land. Pope enlarged Point Comfort until its 1,750 acres extended from Broad Creek to the Atlantic Ocean.[6]

Pope added to his holdings throughout his life. During the 1830s, he acquired Cotton Hope Plantation south of Skull Creek, which was more accessible to the mainland ferry than were Coggins Point and Point Comfort. In 1850, he bought Haig Point Plantation on Daufuskie Island for his daughter Elizabeth, the wife of Alsop Park Vail Woodward, rector of St. Luke's Parish.[7]

Family history holds that William Pope gave Coggins Point to his son William John, who married Hephzibah Pope, the daughter of John J. T. and Mary Townsend Pope of St. Helena.[8] The 1850 census shows four separate plantations for "William Pope," a total of some 3,050 acres, of which 1,750 were improved. Some of this acreage, and some of the eighty-four bags of cotton produced, must represent Coggins Point, the younger Pope's tract.

In 1852, William John Pope died, leaving two orphaned daughters. They went to live with their mother's parents,[9] and Joseph J. Pope Jr. of Charleston took over management of his nieces' affairs.

In early 1859, William Pope wrote to Joseph that the latter had acted well in buying Orange

Grove Plantation on Lady's Island for William John's estate, going on to say that Joseph would "succeed much better than at the old Coggins plantation—that place has been overplanted, wants rest, and is much exposed." The older man offered the use of his boat in "removing the hands and their effects... together with provisions for the people."[10] Coggins Point Plantation was "resting," the house unused, when the planters abandoned Hilton Head in 1861. It remained a military reservation until the 1920s. During this time the house, much altered for service as a signal station, was scrapped.[11]

1. David McCord Wright, "Records and Notes of the Scott Family of St. Helena Island," in *South Carolina Historical Magazine* 66 (1965). Hartridge Collection, Box 21, Folder 482, Georgia Historical Society, Savannah. Virginia C. Holmgren, *Hilton Head: A Sea Island Chronicle* (Hilton Head, 1959), p. 53.
2. Chatham County Will Book G5, Georgia Historical Society.
3. Wright, "Scott Family." Chalmers G. Davidson, *The Last Foray. The South Carolina Planters of 1860: A Sociological Study* (Columbia: University of South Carolina Press, 1971), p. 238.
4. N. Louise Bailey, Mary L. Morgan, and Carolyn R. Taylor, *Biographical Directory of the South Carolina Senate, 1776-1995* Vol. 2 (Columbia: University of South Carolina Press, 1986), pp. 1295-1296.
5. *Charleston Courier*, January 1823.
6. Carolina Archaeological Services, "Archaeological Inventory and Testing at 38BU956, Marsh Lakes Plantation Development, Hilton Head Island" (Columbia: Carolina Archaeological Services, 1989). *Southern Patriot*, February 11, 1841.
7. Billie Burn, *An Island Named Daufuskie* (Spartanburg: The Reprint Co., 1991), p. 84.
8. Wright, "Scott Family."
9. Mabel Runnette, "Tombstone Inscriptions from St. Helena Island," in SCHM 35 (1934). Population Schedules, U.S. Census, St. Helena's Parish, 1860.
10. Pope family papers, South Carolina Historical Society, Folder 11/550/5.
11. Holmgren, *Hilton Head*, pp. 130-131.

William Seabrook House
EDISTO ISLAND

William Seabrook began his planting career when he was seventeen years old. Although his father had died when Seabrook was a young boy and he had only a brief education, he became one of Edisto Island's leading sea island cotton planters. With the deaths of his brother in 1795 and his mother in 1798, Seabrook was heir to a significant portion of land.[1] He focused on careful processing to improve the quality of his finished crop, and gained respect for his seed selection. While his contemporaries "resisted the notion and the work," he seized on the practice of using salt-marsh mud as a manure. His production and his prices increased.[2]

William Seabrook married Mary Ann Mikell, and the first of their children were born in the house he later referred to as "my old Settlement."[3] There is no record of when Seabrook built his namesake house, but it was most likely between 1805 and 1810.[4]

The dominant feature of the Seabrook House is its pedimented south portico. The gabled roof and flat arches of this two-story front porch, only half the width of the façade, give it a more open appearance than the customary one-story construction. The building is detailed with nine-over-nine windows, traceried fanlights and sidelights, and dentil blocks at the upper cornices. Arched openings of the brick foundation beneath the porch echo the low arches at its second level. Approached from Steamboat Creek, the north side of the house is very much its rear elevation, ornamented only by the arched windows of the projecting stair tower.

According to a contemporary, "Mr. Seabrook's style of living corresponded with his fortune. Without ostentation, he had every thing elegant about him...."[5] His house is true to this reputation. The plan of four rooms on each floor is in the mainstream of sea island design, but the building is notable for its large scale and finely detailed trimwork. Paneled double doors under fanlights lead from the broad central hall to the main front rooms. Beyond an archway across the passage, the hallway widens to accommodate the unusual double staircase.

In this elegant dwelling the Seabrook children grew up: William (born in 1799), Ephraim Mikell, George Washington, Sarah, and Mary Ann. When Mary Ann Mikell Seabrook died in 1818, her older sons were nearly grown.

A year or so after Mary Ann's death, William Seabrook, by now in his late forties, married Emma Elizabeth Edings. She was only about six years older than his eldest son. Five children of this marriage survived: Robert Chisolm (born 1821), Joseph Edings, Carolina LaFayette, Martha Washington, and Julia Georgiana. While their father raised his new family, the sons were occupying their own plantations. In 1822, the younger William married Martha Washington Edings (sister of his stepmother Emma). Ephraim Mikell Seabrook married Margaret Wilkinson Mikell in 1825, and George Washington married Martha Abigail Clark in 1830.

William Seabrook House, 1928 *(Courtesy of Gibbes Museum of Art/Carolina Art Association, Charleston)*

The senior William Seabrook's adult life was one of success and stability centered on his planting and his family. From about 1800 until the end of his life, he purchased additional plantations, first on Edisto Island and in nearby St. Paul's Parish, and eventually on Johns, Wadmalaw, and Hilton Head islands. As his children reached adulthood, he settled them on Edisto plantations, also giving them properties to manage as absentee owners. His will provided comfortable fortunes for the younger children as each became twenty-one.

William Seabrook seems never to have kept a town house, but was as entrepreneurial as any urban merchant. Over the cautious doubts of his neighbors, he established a steam packet line to call on docks at Edisto, Rockville, and Charleston. The steamer *William Seabrook* operated for years, expanding to reach Hilton Head, Bluffton and Savannah.[6]

When he wrote his will in 1836, Seabrook was in his early sixties, blind, and in "bad health of Body but of Sound and disposing Memory and Mind." To his wife he left lifetime occupancy of "my Mansion House" and all the furniture and bedding, bed and table linen, books and pictures therein; the house servants Nancy and her son June, and Bella and her two children; a carriage and horses; and $20,000. Emma also received "all the Negroes which I got from her father Joseph Edings, with their issue and increase," and the use of "so much of the land as she can plant with the slaves being bequeathed to her."[7] Her income would be enhanced by the Seabrook plantation on Hilton Head, where a wharf had been established for the steamboat line.

William Seabrook's estate was active into the 1850s, with divisions made as his children came of age or married, and the shares of those who died—Mary Ann in 1836, Joseph Edings in 1838—reverting to the estate. In 1840, Seabrook's older sons were managing their father's estate and slaves (216 on Edisto alone). His widow, the owner of 231 slaves, remained in the "mansion house" with her three daughters, but Robert Chisolm Seabrook was away, either at school or traveling.

Although the younger Seabrook girls married and left home during the 1840s, Robert returned to live with his mother and manage her plantations. In 1850, Emma Seabrook and her son Robert (aged twenty-nine) were occupying the family residence. Robert does not seem to have been a particularly lucky planter: he made only twenty-one bags of sea island cotton in 1849, fewer than several of his peers with smaller holdings.[8]

His father's estate had not been completely settled in 1852 when Robert Chisolm Seabrook died. Although he did not have his own home, he left a large personal collection of paintings, art catalogs, engravings and books. These things were sold off in March 1853: nearly 1,100 books, 162 engravings, and two large oil paintings. His brothers and brothers-in-law bought most of the items.[9]

In the mid-1850s, with William Seabrook's widow in her sixties, and all the surviving children occupying their own properties, the family finally divided the estate. They deeded land to each other, and settled complicated finances arising from years of loans, bonds, and conveyances. In January 1857, soon after the death of Emma Seabrook, the 340-acre plantation "with mansion and other buildings" was sold to John Evans Edings Jr. for $36,500.[10]

This sale did not take the Seabrook plantation out of the family. J. E. Edings Jr. was married to Josephine Edings Seabrook, a daughter of the younger William Seabrook. Although he was heir to the nearby Edings house at the Seaside, it was the newer and larger residence of Josephine's grandfather where they chose to settle and raise their own children. The 1860 census shows them with two young sons. As did several of their well-off peers, they employed an Irish-born nursemaid in their household.

With the evacuation of the sea islands in 1861, the "beautiful Seabrook place" became headquarters for federal officials and Freedmen's Bureau teachers.[11] A little dilapidated, and marred by soldiers' graffiti, the house with 360 acres was returned to J. Evans Edings in 1865.

1. Thomas O. Lawton, Jr., *Upper St. Peter's Parish and Environs* (Garnett, SC: 2001), pp. 61-66. Mabel C. Webber, "Early Generations of the Seabrook Family," in *South Carolina Historical Magazine* 17 (1916).
2. "A Sketch of the Life of the late William Seabrook, planter, of Edisto Island South Carolina," in *The Southern Agriculturist*, February 1837 (South Carolina Historical Society).
3. "Will of William Seabrook," Charleston County Wills, Book 41, p. 536, Charleston County Public Library.
4. Harriette Kershaw Leiding, *Historic Houses of South Carolina* (Philadelphia: J. B. Lippincott, 1921), p. 218, suggests 1805; Samuel Gaillard Stoney in *Plantations of the Carolina Low Country* (Charleston: Carolina Art Association, 1938, p. 78) dated it to c. 1810 based on stylistic evidence. Seabrook might have built it on a tract he bought from Daniel Townsend in early 1805, Charleston County Register of Mesne Conveyance, Deed Book O7, p. 67.
5. "A Sketch of the Life."
6. "A Sketch of the Life."
7. "Will of William Seabrook."
8. Agricultural Schedules, U.S. Census, St. John's Colleton Parish, 1850.
9. Charleston County Inventories, Book C, p. 406, CCPL.
10. Charleston County RMC, Deed Book V12, p. 555.
11. Mary Ames, *A New England Woman's Diary in Dixie in 1865* (New York: 1906, rep. 1969).

Mary Jenkins Plantation
St. Helena Island

Sometime before 1820 Mary Sarah Chaplin married William Jenkins.[1] The census for that year shows them living on St. Helena Island with their daughter, and in 1825, William Jenkins paid taxes on 596 acres and sixty-five slaves in St. Helena Parish. He had died by 1832, when Mary S. Jenkins, as his executrix, sold fifteen slaves.[2]

For years the widowed Mary Jenkins managed her affairs successfully, and her name became firmly attached to her home and the surrounding community. In 1849, 147 acres of her land were improved, and she made eight bags of cotton. By 1859, she had improved another hundred acres, and produced twenty bags.

The Jenkinses' only daughter, Charlotte, married Dr. Randell Croft. Born in Charleston, Croft owned plantations on St. Helena Island and in Newberry District, but he and Charlotte lived in Greenville, where he had grown up.[3] In 1859, Croft's four hundred acres on St. Helena yielded seventeen bags of cotton—less than his mother-in-law's production.

In January 1863, Jenkins Neck (147 acres) and the adjacent Croft Place (150 acres) were sold for taxes and brought into the Freedmen's Bureau system.[4]

Samuel Cooley photographed the Mary Jenkins House on Jenkins Neck Plantation while it was the residence of Freedmen's Bureau school official G. M. Wells. Taken from the drive leading to the landward façade, the photo shows a two-story house on high masonry piers, with a steep hipped roof and a one-story porch with low arches between the slender columns. Close to the residence is its one-story wooden kitchen house with a large central chimney.

Mrs. Jenkins seems not to have returned to St. Helena after the Civil War. In 1876, "Mary Sarah Chaplin, wife of the late William Jenkins of St. Helena and mother of Mrs. R. Croft," was buried in Greenville.[5]

---

1. "Jenkins Family Chart" in Theodore Rosengarten, *Tombee: Portrait of a Cotton Planter* (New York: William Morrow and Co., 1986).
2. Combined Index to 30 Records Series, 1675-1929, South Carolina Department of Archives and History.
3. Obituary in *The Southern Enterprise*, March 3, 1869.
4. *Beaufort Republican*, January 10, 1863.
5. WPA Cemetery Inscriptions, South Carolina Historical Society.

Mary Jenkins House, 1862 *(Courtesy of The Western Reserve Historical Society, Cleveland Ohio)*

Seaside
St. Helena Island

There is no clarity about which member of the Fripp family built the Seaside Plantation house, or when, but based on the architecture, a date of 1810 seems reasonable. The house is best remembered as the home of Edgar Fripp and his wife (and first cousin) Eliza Fripp.[1]

"Proud Edgar" Fripp was one St. Helena Island's most successful planters, recognized not only for the high quality of his cotton, but also for his skill, and vanity, at producing award-winning quantities of more mundane crops such as corn. This competitive man kept more riding horses than most of his neighbors, and usually won the races he proposed.[2]

Well into his middle years in 1849, Fripp was the owner of 1,197 acres on St. Helena. On 847 improved acres he grew corn, sweet potatoes, and other food and livestock crops, and made fifty-five bags of cotton. His Seaside plantation, which he called Palmetto Hills, included much of his father-in-law's Parsonage Tract, an undetermined acreage formerly owned by

Seaside Plantation House, 1997 *(Courtesy of South Carolina Department of Archives and History, Columbia)*

Isaac Perry Fripp, and also 350 acres of Orange Grove Plantation, for which he had paid Thomas Fuller Sr. $6,000 in 1845.[3]

Fripp must already have been in poor health in 1859 when he wrote his will. His cotton yield that year was only thirty-eight bags, a decline larger than should have resulted from his sale of two hundred acres of land. Without children, he devised much of his land to his young relative Edgar W. Fripp, leaving Eliza a life estate in "Palmetto Hills, the adjoining 40 acres of the Parsonage, Orange Grove, and The Bluff."[4] Eliza did not survive him long. Edgar Walter Fripp, under the guardianship of his father John Edwin Fripp, came into ownership of land reported to the census as a thousand acres total.

When St. Helena Island was occupied by Union forces in late 1861, Seaside was absorbed by the Port Royal Experiment. Several northern teachers were quartered in the Fripp house. Edgar W. Fripp finally reclaimed 732 acres in 1872, and kept it as a working farm until 1920.[5]

Although additions have been made to the side and rear of the house, its original design can easily be discerned. Seaside combines several characteristic features of sea island architecture. The two-story core had four rooms on the main first floor, and two above, with a pedimented rear stair tower allowing for a roomy central hall. Three windows along the side of each main room and a low hipped roof lend the house a substantial appearance that is strengthened by the heavy surround of the front entry.

1. "Fripp Family Chart" in Theodore Rosengarten, *Tombee: Portrait of a Cotton Planter* (New York: William Morrow and Co., 1986). "Seaside Plantation (Edgar Fripp House)" National Register Nomination (South Carolina Department of Archives and History, 1979).
2. Rosengarten, *Tombee*, pp. 116, 165, 201. Agricultural Schedules, U.S. Census, St. Helena's Parish, 1850 and 1860.
3. Charleston County Register of Mesne Conveyance, Deed Book W11, p. 75.
4. Edith Dabbs Collection, Box 2, South Caroliniana Library, University of South Carolina.
5. "Seaside Plantation."

Frogmore
EDISTO ISLAND

Frogmore Plantation House on Edisto Island was built sometime between 1814 and 1820 for Edward and Eliza Mitchell. The son of a Georgetown District rice planter, Mitchell received a medical degree from the University of Pennsylvania, and, after post-graduate studies in Europe, he returned to South Carolina.[1] In 1812, twenty-five years old, Edward Mitchell married Elizabeth Grimball Baynard of Prospect Hill.[2] Seventeen years old, Eliza would soon be an heiress: when her brother William Grimball Baynard turned twenty-one in 1813, the family would partition the estate of their father, the late William Baynard.[3]

Soon after the birth of his first child, Edward Mitchell began buying land near Prospect Hill. In 1814, he paid $1,800 for fifty acres east of the Baynard family's land.[4] Three years later he bought an adjacent 190 acres from his brother-in-law William G. Baynard.[5] These tracts at the south side of Pine Landing Road, the main route for travelers using the ferry between Little Edisto and Edisto islands, became Frogmore Plantation.

Edward Mitchell was successful as a planter and as a medical doctor, and both he and Eliza came from prosperous families. Their home may not appear an architectural showpiece today, but it boasts all the elements of a planter's comfortable dwelling. With a raised foundation and broad front porch, the north-facing building was pleasant during warm spring and fall weather, and the main upstairs rooms had windows on three sides. Equally important for a year-round residence, all the primary rooms had fireplaces. When Frogmore Plantation was advertised for sale in 1857, Mitchell's residence was described as a "fine dwelling house containing nine rooms."[6]

During their early life together, Edward and Eliza alternated living in Charleston and on Edisto Island, but by 1820 the family had settled at Frogmore Plantation for good. In 1825, Mitchell paid taxes on 525 acres and eighty-four slaves in St. John's Colleton Parish, and also on fees he earned as a physician.[7]

In general, much less is known of an antebellum woman than of her husband. Her property, even if kept separate through a marital trust, was reported as his, and she had no public career. Yet it is clear how Eliza Mitchell spent her life. Mary Baynard was born in 1813, John Elias Moore in 1816, Rachel Louisa in 1818, Edward Whaley in 1820 (he died two years later), William Grimball Baynard in 1822, Anna Abigail in 1827, Esther Marion in 1829, Francis Marion in 1833, and Julian Augustus in 1838, twenty-five years after his eldest sister.[8]

Eliza Baynard Mitchell's sister Abigail lived at Old Dominion Plantation, just across the road from Frogmore, with her husband Edward C. Whaley. The sisters were close, but the relationship between Edward Mitchell and Edward Whaley was sometimes difficult. Whaley's granddaughter remembered him as puritanical, sneering at Mitchell's cultivated "bon vivant" manners and calling his brother-in-law a "frog-eater,"[9] jesting not only at his European travels but also at the name of his plantation. Mitchell was serious about his planting and his med-

Frogmore Plantation House (rear view), 1991 *(Courtesy of South Carolina Department of Archives and History, Columbia)*

ical practice, but his lighter side often dominated. While his more earnest peers, other young planters studying medicine, had chosen topics like "Congestive Typhus Fever," "Yellow Fever of Charleston," or even "Medical Effects of Light and Darkness," Mitchell wrote his senior thesis on the "Nature and Properties of Wine."[10]

Regardless of the men's feelings, Abigail Whaley's death of measles in 1830 brought the families closer. She left nine children under the age of thirteen, and their aunt Eliza, herself the mother of six, played a large part in raising them. Little Abigail, three weeks old when her mother died, lived with the Mitchell family until she was eleven.[11]

The Mitchells remained on Edisto Island until the late 1840s, when they moved to Charleston full time. In 1850, Dr. Edward Mitchell advertised in the *Mercury* that he would "attend to the duties of his profession" at his residence on Savage Street.[12] Now middle-aged, he and his wife shared their home with their children Mary and Julian, and two young relatives, Eleanor and John Elias Mitchell.[13]

William Grimball Baynard Mitchell had taken up his father's sea island cotton plantations, a total of 1,016 acres with 416 acres under cultivation. Living not at Frogmore, but on one of Dr. Mitchell's plantations on Little Edisto Island, twenty-seven-year-old William produced thirty-eight bags of cotton in 1849, a good yield for the acreage.[14] The next year, though, he died, leaving a widow, Mary Wayne, and their infant daughter.[15]

The elder Mitchells did not move back to the island, but relied on overseers to manage their plantations, always under the interested gaze of Eliza's nearby relatives. Dr. Edward Mitchell died in Charleston in 1855, and was buried on Edisto Island.[16] His will directed his executors to hold his estate together until Julian was twenty-one, keeping "one of my plantations as a residence for the family."[17] Julian was soon an adult, and his father's real estate was sold to partition the estate.

With most Edisto families tightly intermingled by blood and marriage, and very little land being sold to outsiders, the number of plantations was decreasing as adjacent tracts were consolidated. Mitchell's property, too, stayed in the family. His brother-in-law William G. Baynard paid $13,000 for the three-hundred-acre plantation at the north side of Russell Creek, just west of the Ashe tract on Little Edisto Island.[18] (Baynard in turn bequeathed it to his daughter Abbie, the wife of E. Mikell Whaley, who annexed it to Little Edisto Plantation.)[19]

In 1858, Rachel Mitchell Whaley and her husband William, a Charleston lawyer, bought her father's Frogmore Plantation, 250 acres of high land and a large body of marsh land, with about 210 acres "under a high state of cultivation." Besides the residence, there were a new gin house and cabins for fifty slaves.[20] In 1867, they sold it to Edward Charles Whaley, whose wife Abigail, the youngest daughter of Edward C. Whaley, had spent her early childhood at Frogmore.[21]

---

1. J. I. Waring, *A History of Medicine in South Carolina*. Vol. 1, 1670-1825 (Charleston, 1964), pp. 154, 388. Vol. 2, 1825-1900 (Charleston, 1967), p. 350. Alexander Moore, *Biographical Directory of the South Carolina House of Representatives*. Vol. 5, 1816-1828 (Columbia: South Carolina Department of Archives and History, 1992), pp. 187-188.
2. Brent H. Holcomb, *Marriage and Death Notices from the (Charleston) Times, 1800-1821* (Baltimore: Genealogical Publishing Co., Inc., 1979), p. 257.
3. "Will of William Baynard," Charleston County Wills, Book 15, p. 399, Charleston County Public Library.
4. Charleston County Register of Mesne Conveyance, Deed Book H8, p. 218.
5. Charleston County RMC, Deed Book X8, p. 209.
6. *Charleston Courier*, October 22, 1857.
7. Tax Returns, 1824, South Carolina Department of Archives and History.
8. Moore, *Biographical Directory*, pp. 187-188.
9. Maria Adelaide Whaley, "The Story of Maria Adelaide Whaley," (typescript, 1926, South Carolina Historical Society).

10. Vertical files, Waring Historical Library, Medical University of South Carolina.
11. *Charleston Mercury*, March 29, 1830. "The Story of Maria Adelaide Whaley."
12. *Charleston Mercury*, May 25, 1850.
13. Population Schedules, U.S. Census, St. Philip's and St. Michael's Parish, 1850.
14. Agricultural Schedules, U.S. Census, St. John's Colleton Parish, 1850. Charleston County Inventories, Book C, pp. 96, 185, CCPL.
15. Annie Baynard Simons Hasell, *Baynard: An Ancient Family Bearing Arms* (Charleston: privately printed, 1972), p. 195.
16. City of Charleston Death Records Index, CCPL.
17. "Will of Edward Mitchell," Charleston County Wills, Book 47, p. 694, CCPL.
18. Charleston County RMC, Deed Book X13, p. 295.
19. "Will of William Grimball Baynard," Charleston County Wills, Book 49, p. 886, CCPL.
20. Charleston County RMC, Deed Book E14, pp. 363-364. *Charleston Courier*, October 22, 1857.
21. Charleston County RMC, Deed Book D15, p. 171.

Peter's Point
EDISTO ISLAND

Traditionally assigned a date of 1840, and said to have been built by Isaac Jenkins Mikell,[1] Peter's Point was almost certainly constructed at an earlier date, perhaps in 1822 when Mikell's father purchased the land. The house is one of the few sea island dwellings that conform to the stereotype of a two-tier piazza across the entire waterfront façade.

Built on the plan of four rooms and a central passage/stair hall that was used in every era, the house rises two stories above a ground-level basement of brick laid in Flemish bond, with an open arcade supporting the two-tiered waterfront porch (tabby piers at the rear are a rare surviving example of this material). An early nineteenth-century construction date is suggested by the low gabled roof with its strongly detailed boxed cornice and pedimented ends, and by the use of Adamesque elements such as the slender porch columns and elliptical fanlight. Inside, the unusual main stair, composed of a straight run up to a landing, with a pair of narrower stairs from the landing to the second floor hall, seems more akin to the composition at William Seabrook's c. 1810 house than to the typical single stairway. Altogether, despite the striking appearance of the full-height piazza and the grandeur of the marble mantelpieces (lost in the 1860s), the design of the building has a less sophisticated feel than the mid-1830s Crawford's Plantation house built by I. J. Mikell's brother William Archibald.

Peter's Point was the home plantation of Christopher Jenkins, whose death in 1794 left his wife Mary with four minor children: Christopher, John, Eliza, and Susannah. Jenkins's will assured Mary of life tenancy at Peter's Point, which was devised to Christopher once he was twenty-one or married, as "the tract of land whereon I now reside called Peter's Point." John's legacy included other plantation lands and a tract at "the Seaside."[2]

An interesting clause in Jenkins's will gave to his executrix (Mary) "full power to build a large house and other outbuildings, according to the plan which I intended, on the plantation where I now reside... " His personal estate included "lumber for building a house," but it seems unlikely that his widow proceeded with the plans for rebuilding. Along with plantation goods, the inventory of his estate includes the contents of a substantial house: carpeted dining room with mahogany tables and "fourteen green chairs," mahogany bedsteads with bolsters, quilts and counterpanes, and all the looking glasses, candlesticks, pictures, and books requisite to a comfortable dwelling.[3]

In 1797, Mary Wilkinson Jenkins married again, as the fourth wife of her second husband Thomas Whaley.[4] Although he had residences on Edisto and Johns islands, they made their home in Charleston, where Whaley's death in 1805 left Mary the mother of eight (four Jenkinses and four Whaleys) and stepmother to Whaley's three older children. Lifetime owner of plantations derived from two husbands (Whaley left for her use "my Edisto plantation

SEA ISLAND COTTON PLANTATION ARCHITECTURE

known as the Old House tract"),[5] Mary remained in Charleston until her death in 1813. By that time, her son Christopher had assumed management of his own lands.[6]

Christopher Jenkins married Catherine Boone in 1815. With their four children, they were full-time residents of Charleston,[7] but Christopher planted on Edisto Island, and was a successful investor. In 1817, he paid Jeremiah Fickling $8,005 for a 236-acre plantation "at the Seaside,"[8] and just two years later sold the same tract to Christian Staley for $10,800.[9] A quarter-century after his father's death, the younger Christopher Jenkins divided and sold Peter's Point. In the winter of 1821-22, Joseph Whaley bought two hundred acres to add to his adjoining plantation, and Ephraim Mikell purchased the remaining 374 1/2 acres.[10] A few years later, Christopher Jenkins bought land on Johns Island to replace Peter's Point. The Gibbes family's Peaceful Retreat plantation, with its handsome masonry dwelling close to the Stono River,[11] was more accessible to town than was the southwestern edge of Edisto Island.

Ephraim Mikell—the purchaser of Peter's Point—and his wife Providence Jenkins had ten living children in 1822.[12] With the eldest, Isaac Jenkins Mikell, approaching maturity, they

Peter's Point Plantation House, ca. 1960 *(Courtesy of I. Jenkins Mikell, Jr.)*

were amassing the legacy of land that would be so important to the next generation's position. Unlike the Christopher Jenkins family, the Mikells were island residents.

Isaac Jenkins Mikell graduated from Princeton University in 1826. In 1828, he married eighteen-year-old Emily, daughter of the late Thomas Price, pastor of the Presbyterian Church on James Island. The 1830 census shows the Mikells living on James Island, sharing a household with Emily's mother and another young woman. In May 1835, Emily died, shortly after the birth of her fourth child. Two months later Emily's mother died,[13] and with small children in tow, Jenkins Mikell returned home to Edisto Island. It was not long before the children found a new mother. In April 1836, Mikell married Amarinthia Jenkins Townsend at Bleak Hall, her parents' home.[14]

The Peter's Point residence may have been upgraded at about the time of I. J. Mikell's second marriage. Although he did not formally inherit "all that tract of land or plantation called Peter's Point" until his father's death in 1838,[15] the intended legacy would not have been a secret, and the family must have occupied the house. They filled it with children: Sarah Margaret, born in 1837, was the first of Amarinthia's seven children; Isaac Jenkins Mikell Jr., born in 1851, was the last. In 1850, the household included Jenkins and Amarinthia, three of Emily Price's children, and four of Amarinthia Townsend's: Sarah (11), Townsend (10), Mary (8), and Amarinthia (5).

By 1849, Jenkins Mikell owned fourteen hundred acres of improved land in St. John's Colleton Parish, as well as some unimproved acreage. He produced 112 bags of sea island cotton, assuring a substantial income even in a year when prices were only moderate. Mikell acquired more land over the next few years, buying 418 acres from Whitemarsh B. Seabrook in 1852, and the 205-acre Governor's Bluff tract from his sister Mary Ann and her husband Edward Fuller in 1856.[16] In 1859, he owned a total of twenty-two hundred acres of well-cultivated land. On eighteen hundred improved acres, he produced 175 bags of cotton.

Amarinthia Mikell died in 1852, and in 1854 Jenkins again remarried. His third wife, Mary Martha Pope of St. Helena Island, was a generation younger than he, and never healthy, but family lore claims her as "the love of his life."[17] Although their first daughter died before her second birthday, Mary had three more children before 1859. The 1860 census reveals the life she had married into: at Peter's Point were Jenkins (51) and Mary Pope Mikell (30), four of his children, Townsend (19), Mary (17), Amarinthia (15), and I. J. (12), and three of theirs together, Mary Caroline (4), Virginia (3) and John (1). There was also an Irish nursemaid, thirty-year-old Bridget Fields.

Much too old to join the Confederate service, Mikell was nonetheless a firebrand. On November 14, 1861, he destroyed his own cotton crop "to prevent its being taken by the enemy: 170 bales extra fine sea island cotton worth at least $30,000." Upon evacuating, he abandoned his house and all its contents: furniture said to be worth $3,000, and a library valued at a further $1,000.[18]

The family and most of their slaves moved upcountry to Aiken County, where Mikell leased a farm with a "commodious house and tasteful surroundings."[19] Marcellus Mikell, the last of Jenkins Mikell's children, born about the time of the evacuation, died in Aiken in July 1862.

His mother died at the end of that year, and both were buried in Aiken.[20]

While still in Aiken, Jenkins Mikell was married a fourth time, to Sarah Georgiana Lee. She took over management of his household, eventually returning with him to Edisto Island, and outlived him by twenty-five years. Although it has been uninhabited since the 1960s, Peter's Point remains in the Mikell family.

1. Harriette Kershaw Leiding, *Historic Houses of South Carolina* (Philadelphia: J. B. Lippincott, 1921), p. 227. Samuel Gaillard Stoney, *Plantations of the Carolina Low Country* (Charleston: Carolina Art Association, 1938), pp. 40, 78.
2. "Will of Christopher Jenkins," Charleston County Wills, Book 25, p. 131, Charleston County Public Library.
3. Charleston County Inventories, Book C, p. 57, CCPL.
4. South Carolina Marriage Settlements, Book 3, p. 81, South Carolina Department of Archives and History. James Garner Patey, *The Whaley Family and Its Charleston Connection* (Spartanburg: The Reprint Company, 1992).
5. "Will of Thomas Whaley," Charleston County Wills, Book 30, p. 934, CCPL.
6. James W. Hagy, *City Directories for Charleston, South Carolina, for the Years 1803, 1806, 1807, 1809, and 1813* (Baltimore: Clearfield Company, 1995).
7. Mabel L. Webber, "Descendants of John Jenkins of St. John's, Colleton" in *South Carolina Historical Magazine* 20 (1919). "Register of the Independent Congregational (Circular) Church of Charleston, South Carolina," in SCHM 54 (1953). James W. Hagy, *Charleston, South Carolina, City Directories for the Years 1816, 1819, 1822, 1825, and 1829* (Baltimore: Clearfield Company, 1996).
8. Charleston County Register of Mesne Conveyance, Deed Book T8:149.
9. Charleston County RMC, Deed Book B9:255.
10. Charleston County RMC, Deed Book G9:451. K9:92.
11. Charleston County RMC, Deed Book R9:239. Charles Fraser, *A Charleston Sketchbook 1796-1806* (Charleston: Carolina Art Association, 1971), Plate 4.
12. Townsend Mikell, "The Mikell Genealogy of South Carolina" (Charleston: Walker, Evans and Cogswell, 1910).
13. Brent H. Holcomb, *Marriage and Death Notices from the (Charleston, South Carolina) Mercury, 1822-1832* (Columbia: SCMAR, 2001), p. 167. Brent H. Holcomb, *Marriage and Death Notices from the Charleston Observer 1827-1845* (Columbia: 1980), p. 98.
14. Holcomb, *Mercury*, p. 108.
15. "Will of Ephraim Mikell," Charleston County Wills, Book 41, p. 717, CCPL.
16. Charleston County RMC, Deed Book R13, p. 255.
17. Nell S. Graydon, *Tales of Edisto* (Columbia: The R. L. Bryan Co., 1955), p. 40.
18. South Carolina Comptroller/State Auditor "Claims for property lost due to the enemy" (Record Series S126189, SCDAH).
19. "Diary of John Berkeley Grimball, 1858-1865," in SCHM 57 (1956).
20. Cyril Johnson, ed., "Aiken County Cemeteries" Vol. 4 (Aiken: Aiken-Barnwell Genealogical Society of South Carolina, 1998).

The Launch/Middleton's
EDISTO ISLAND

At the end of a long drive leading from Edisto Island's main road, this well-proportioned dwelling house stands close to the bank of Store Creek. The one-room deep building has a Palladian front composed of a two-story central block with a low-pitched hipped roof and flanking wings, and an unconventional U-shaped plan. The north facade is lengthened by one-room wings that extend south toward the water, their roofs connecting to form a back porch across the center of the house. At the main façade is a hipped portico supported by Tuscan columns, its fine entrance surround with sidelights and traceried fanlight visible from the approach. Beneath the portico, the entry into the raised brick basement also has sidelights, but the doorway on the south porch is set in a very plain surround.

Judging by its style and sophistication, The Launch was designed by a highly skilled architect whose identity is so far unknown.[1] The individuality of the architecture makes it more interesting that much of the interior trim is identical to features at Prospect Hill and Oak Island. The simple ground-level mantels and stair, and trimwork at the main floors—rope molding and scrollwork along the stair, acanthus leaf corner blocks, fluted columns supporting shaped mantel shelves—all came from the same hand or the same supplier, while in design and plan the three buildings are entirely different from one another. Only The Launch, though, departs from the sea island vernacular in so many ways.

The Launch Plantation House, ca. 1930 *(Courtesy of The Charleston Museum, Charleston South Carolina)*

Like all sea island residences, this building was a product of family connections. In 1795, William Evans bought the land that became The Launch Plantation, which he bequeathed to his wife Mary Elizabeth Edings at his death in 1802.[2] Evans left no children, but Mary Elizabeth had two daughters, Susan and Julia, with her second husband, Dr. Robert Trail Chisolm. Both were underage when Dr. Chisolm died in 1821, leaving in his estate a rice plantation on Chehaw River, a house in Charleston, and The Launch.[3]

Well-born and twice a widow, Mary Chisolm was a wealthy woman. With her extended family nearby, she remained at The Launch and in her summer house on Edings Bay. There were long weeks in Charleston, where the girls began their education before traveling north to boarding school. At Julia's death in 1826, Susan Chisolm became the sole heir of both her parents: she would become the owner of 180 slaves and two large plantations.

Mary Chisolm and her daughter Susan remained in Charleston and on Edisto Island. Before she was quite twenty-one years old, Susan found a good match in Oliver Hering Middleton of Charleston. The son of Henry Middleton, he was nine years older than she, and already established as a rice planter on his family's Combahee River property. Upon their marriage in 1827, Oliver settled $200,000 on his bride and took up the role of planter on the Chisolm lands, the eight-hundred-acre tract on Edisto Island "known by the name of the Launch," and a sixteen-hundred-acre rice plantation in St. Bartholomew's Parish.[4]

There was a residence at The Launch by about 1800, apparently built for Mary Elizabeth Edings by her first husband. Whether it was lost before Oliver Middleton married Susan Chisolm, or abandoned when the young couple built their elegant country house, is not certain. Susan's mother shared the new plantation house with them, although she seems to have maintained a separate dwelling in Charleston.[5] The Middletons, too, kept a house downtown, and the family's life was one of constant motion between Charleston, The Launch, Middleton Place, Newport, Philadelphia, Sullivans Island and Edings Bay.[6] Their children (five daughters and a son) had two strong grandmothers, Mary Edings Chisolm and Mary Hering Middleton. Mrs. Middleton welcomed Susan at Middleton Place, with or without the children; Mrs. Chisolm kept the young ones when Susan and Oliver traveled. Susan relied on her mother for childcare and companionship, taking the family to the plantation during school breaks.[7]

The Launch was Oliver and Susan's house, but there was no doubt as to Mary's rights as half-owner of the plantation or as grandmother. In 1840, Oliver turned down his sister's proposal to find a northern woman to work as governess, replying that while other Edisto planters would probably be interested, it would be "impossible to have a governess while Mrs. Chisolm lives in the house." With the children, Susan's mother and two nurses, one white and one black, the building was full.[8]

Mary Chisolm enjoyed her position as a wealthy older woman. In 1845, she sent $900 each to Mary and Matilda Middleton so they could buy a piano and a harp in Philadelphia.[9] Only with her death in 1848, at the age of seventy, did Susan and Oliver Middleton find themselves in need of a governess. The 1850 census shows them living in Charleston with several of their children. Also in the household was Ann Fitzsimmons, a twenty-year-old native of Ireland.

Until the Civil War, Oliver planted in St. Bartholomew's Parish and on Edisto Island, The Launch Plantation becoming known as "Middleton's" (although Oliver himself called it Medway[10]).

Susan Chisolm Middleton died in Columbia in 1865. Oliver returned home after the war, gradually abandoning his plantation to younger family members, and died in Charleston in 1892.[11] The Launch Plantation House remained in the family until 1902.

1. According to Gene Waddell, author of *Charleston Architecture 1670-1860* (Charleston: Wyrick & Co., 2003), the design can likely be attributed to Robert Mills.
2. Charleston County Register of Mesne Conveyance, Deed Book R6, p. 93. William Garner Chisolm "Edings of Edisto Island" (MS, Leesburg, VA: 1943).
3. "Will of Robert Trail Chisolm," Charleston County Wills, Book 35, p. 602, Charleston County Public Library. Charleston County Inventories, Book F, p. 424, CCPL.
4. South Carolina Marriage Settlements, Book 9, p. 364, South Carolina Department of Archives and History.
5. Charleston County Inventory Book B, p. 477, CCPL.
6. Eliza Cope Harrison, ed., *Best Companions: Letters of Eliza Middleton Fisher and Her Mother, Mary Hering Middleton, from Charleston, Philadelphia, and Newport, 1839-1846* (Columbia: University of South Carolina Press, 2001), passim.
7. Harrison, *Best Companions*, pp. 108, 124.
8. Harrison, *Best Companions*, pp. 101, 200.
9. Harrison, *Best Companions*, p. 470.
10. South Carolina Comptroller/State Auditor "Claims for property lost due to the enemy" (Record Series S126189, SCDAH).
11. Brent H. Holcomb, *Record of Deaths in Columbia, South Carolina, and Elsewhere as Recorded by John Glass, 1859-1877* (Columbia: privately printed, 1986), p. 72. City of Charleston Death Records Index, CCPL.

Prospect Hill
EDISTO ISLAND

William Baynard of Edisto Island died in 1772, bequeathing his home plantation (Baynard's Old Place) to his elder son Thomas. To his younger son William, he left "all the rest of my lands over the creek."[1] This legacy included the land that became Prospect Hill Plantation.

The 1790 census listed Thomas and William Baynard as residents of Beaufort District. Both acquired land on Hilton Head Island, establishing a lasting Baynard presence there. In 1791, William married Sarah Black of Beaufort, and they were probably living in Beaufort District when their son William Grimball Baynard was born in 1792. Sarah Black Baynard died the next year.

William was shortly remarried, this time to an Edisto Island girl, Elizabeth Mikell. She gave William Grimball Baynard two sisters, Elizabeth Grimball (Eliza), and Abigail Mikell. At the age of thirty-six, William Baynard died, leaving his three small children and Elizabeth.[2]

Baynard's estate inventory lists the typical contents of a well-to-do planter's home: furniture, silver and china, and stocks of rum, brandy, wine, sugar and rice. His wealth is indicated by possession of nearly eighty slaves, stored cotton and provision crops worth $8,470, and six riding horses (two of them, Great Gun and the Colt, were valued at $140 and $160 respectively—at a time when ordinary horses were worth between $10 and $50). With 5,500 bricks and 1,400 cypress shingles on the premises,[3] it appears that Baynard had been preparing for additional construction.

Elizabeth Baynard was still young, and in 1804 she took a second husband, thirty-two-year-old Scotsman Mungo Mackay. Their marriage agreement placed her property, "a considerable real and personal estate, an undivided portion in six tracts on Edisto and about 150 negroes, of her late husband; and also an undivided 1/4 of Archibald Calder's real estate and 80 slaves," into a separate trust.[4] Whether Elizabeth and Mungo Mackay lived at her first husband's house or on one of Mackay's Edisto Island plantations has not been learned. She had at least two more children with Mackay.[5]

Elizabeth's father Ephraim Mikell died in 1809, bequeathing plantations to his sons and slaves to his grandsons.[6] After other legacies, one-third of his residual estate was devised to Elizabeth, with Mikell's will directing that, after her death, her portion of his estate would be equally divided among her children and her stepson William Grimball Baynard, the budding patriarch of an extended sea island family.

William Baynard had died intestate, and the family partitioned his estate after William G. Baynard turned twenty-one in 1813. The Edisto Island property remained in the possession of Elizabeth and the children, and William Baynard's land on Hilton Head was conveyed to his nephew William Edings Baynard.[7]

Elizabeth Mackay died in 1815, a forty-two-year-old wife, mother, and grandmother. Her daughter Eliza had married Dr. Edward Mitchell in 1812, stepson William married in 1814, and in 1817, with Abigail married to Edward C. Whaley, the trustees of Elizabeth's estate sold her remaining property on Edisto Island. With the proceeds they bought a 1,404-acre tract in Prince William Parish, to be used by Mungo Mackay and left to Elizabeth's children after his death.[8]

William Grimball Baynard, his father's only son, was heir to Prospect Hill. In early 1814, he married Ann Ninian Jenkins, a fifth-generation Edisto Islander. Both only twenty-one years old, they settled into adult life, and five children were born at regular intervals. The first two died quite young. Thomas Archibald, the fifth child, was born in 1822, and a few weeks afterward Ann Ninian Baynard died of typhus. By early 1824, William had buried two more children. For several years, he and little Thomas were alone.[9]

Baynard seems to have lived in his father's house during his first marriage, but he built a new Prospect Hill house about the time of his second marriage in 1827. He was thirty-five and his bride Mary Bailey Swinton was nineteen.[10]

William Grimball Baynard's dwelling is two stories of frame construction with a low-pitched hipped roof, with a verandah across the first floor above the open porch of the brick ground-floor level. The brownstone stair to the main porch conceals the ground-level entry, which has narrow sidelights. The first floor has both sidelights and a radiating fanlight. The triple window at the facade's upper level was an architectural element frequently used on the sea islands from about 1810 through the 1850s.

Prospect Hill Plantation House, 2005 *(Courtesy of The Charleston Museum, Charleston South Carolina)*

Interior doorway, Prospect Hill Plantation House, 2005 *(Courtesy of The Charleston Museum, Charleston South Carolina)*

The plan is the customary pattern of two rooms and a center hall at each level, including two finished rooms with fireplaces at the ground-floor basement. The finely detailed Greek Revival interior has ornate overdoors like those at Oak Island; the main stair and wood mantels at the basement and second floor are nearly identical to those at The Launch and Oak Island.

The Prospect Hill house was enlarged soon after its construction. What must have been an original back portico was replaced by a one-room T-wing, three stories in height. Although the projection retains the symmetry of the original design, and the dentil moldings and carved wood modillions tie them together visually, interior circulation is awkward, with doorways cut into closet walls and an inconvenient upper stair. Regency-style marble mantels on the main floor may have been added during the early renovation.

Stronger than William's first wife, Mary Bailey Baynard survived the births of thirteen children (ten lived to adulthood).[11] In 1850, the family at Prospect Hill included William and Mary, Edward (20), Susan, Abby, William, Sarah, Anna, Caroline, James, and infant Henry Hugh. Also in the house was a twenty-year-old white woman, Margaret Dibble, their governess.[12]

Like his successful contemporaries, Baynard acquired tracts of land and whole plantations whenever possible. In 1824, he had 749 acres on Edisto. By 1850, he had nearly doubled his holdings, to 1,400 acres, and reported a large sea island cotton crop: 105 bags.[13] In 1855, he was a senior citizen, his older sons settled on their own plantations, and he purchased a house in Charleston. Son William Grimball Jr. studied law, and the younger children enrolled in school.[14] Planting was left to the management of his son Edward, and production declined: for 1859, Baynard reported only sixty-eight bags of cotton.[15]

William G. Baynard lived to see the outbreak of the Civil War, but died in September 1861, just before the sea islands were evacuated. To his "beloved wife Mary Bailey Baynard" he bequeathed the "privilege of living in my Mansion house on the Prospect Hill plantation and of using the gardens and household furniture, and the liberty of planting on Prospect Hill with twelve full hands during her life; also my house and kitchen in Edingsville and my carriage and carriage horses. Also the house [in Charleston] lately purchased from Theodore Jervey, and the furniture therein." Prospect Hill was devised to William G. Baynard Jr., subject to his mother's life estate.[16]

---

1. "Will of William Baynard," Charleston County Wills, Book 15, p. 399, Charleston County Public Library.
2. Annie Baynard Simons Hasell, *Baynard: An Ancient Family Bearing Arms* (Charleston: privately printed, 1972), pp. 161-163.
3. Charleston County Inventories, Book D, p. 161, CCPL.
4. South Carolina Marriage Settlements, Book 4, p. 478, South Carolina Department of Archives and History.
5. William Greer Albergotti III, *Abigail's Story, Tides at the Doorstep. The Mackays, LaRoches, Jenkinses and Chisolms of Low Country South Carolina, 1671-1897* (Spartanburg: The Reprint Company, 1999), p. 19.
6. "Will of Ephraim Mikell," Charleston County Wills, Book 31, p. 287, CCPL.
7. Virginia C. Holmgren, *Hilton Head: A Sea Island Chronicle* (Hilton Head Island, 1959), p. 125.
8. Charleston County Register of Mesne Conveyance, Deed Book S8, p. 8.
9. Hasell, *Baynard*, pp. 164-165. Teresa Wilson and Janice L. Grimes, *Marriage and Death Notices from the Southern Patriot, 1815-1830* (Easley: Southern Historical Press, 1982), p. 23.
10. Chalmers G. Davidson, *The Last Foray. The South Carolina Planters of 1860: A Sociological Study* (Columbia: University of South Carolina Press, 1971), p. 177.

11. Hasell, *Baynard*, pp. 162-164, 178.

12. Population Schedules, U.S. Census, St. John's Colleton Parish, 1850.

13. Tax Returns, 1824, SCDAH. Agricultural Schedules, U.S. Census, St. John's Colleton Parish, 1850.

14. James William Hagy, *Directories for the City of Charleston, South Carolina, for the Years 1849, 1852, and 1855* (Baltimore: Clearfield Company, 2000).

15. Agricultural Schedules, U.S. Census, St. John's Colleton Parish, 1860. South Carolina Comptroller/State Auditor "Claims for property lost due to the enemy" (Record Series S126189, SCDAH).

16. "Will of William G. Baynard," Charleston County Wills, Book 49, p. 886, CCPL.

Oak Island
Edisto Island

Eldest of the five children born to William Seabrook and Mary Ann Mikell, William Seabrook was completing his studies at Princeton when his mother died in 1818.[1] The following year, "in consideration of natural love and affection for William Seabrook the younger, to provide for him and advance him in life...," his father deeded to him a large tract of land, consisting of much of today's Seabrook Island and a hundred adjacent acres on Johns Island, with the "Mansion House" of the late Francis Simmons.[2] At about the same time, Seabrook Sr. took a second wife, Emma Elizabeth Edings.

While the younger William was beginning his career as a planter, he spent much of his free time with his close family. In 1822, he married Edisto native Martha Washington Edings, like him about twenty-three years old, and his stepmother's sister.[3] A few years later, William and Martha built the house known as Oak Island.

Oak Island is a two-and-a-half-story wood frame dwelling on a fairly low foundation of brick piers. Small dormers pierce the gabled roof, whose broad pediments are relieved by paired quarter-round windows, and the overall design is a very nicely balanced Greek Revival composition with well-proportioned window openings and a wide front entry of double doors under a low fanlight.

The interior ornament shares Greek Revival motifs with the exterior design, and is much more interesting when compared to elements found at The Launch and Prospect Hill. These three buildings feature very similar mantels, cornices, and door and window surrounds. About the time Oak Island was built, houses at The Launch and Prospect Hill were replaced, and the three planters surely employed the same house carpenters.

The Oak Island house may have been remodeled at an early date, perhaps by rethinking the plans during construction. There are physical indications that the two-story rear wing was not part of the original composition, although its ornament is similar to that at the rest of the building. Further, while wrapping the main porch around the east elevation took maximum advantage of the setting at the confluence of two creeks, its design is awkward by comparison with the careful rhythm of the rest of the building.

William and Martha Edings Seabrook raised three children at Oak Island: William Edings (born in 1828), John Edward, and Josephine Edings. They were the contemporaries of William's five younger half-brothers and sisters. As late as 1850, all three Seabrook children lived at home: William was engaged in planting, while Edward (20) and Josephine (16) were apparently still in school. Also in the household was forty-seven-year old Phoebe Edings.

The children became independent during the next decade. In 1854, Josephine married John Evans Edings Jr., and with him occupied her grandfather William Seabrook's residence.

SEA ISLAND COTTON PLANTATION ARCHITECTURE

Oak Island Plantation House, 1862 *(Courtesy of The Western Reserve Historical Society, Cleveland Ohio)*

Interior doorway, Oak Island Plantation House, 1978 *(Historic American Buildings Survey, Library of Congress)*

William Edings Seabrook married Esther Marion Mitchell of Frogmore in 1856,[4] and soon John Edward married Esther's niece Elizabeth Baynard Whaley.[5] Afterward, William and Martha Seabrook retired from Edisto Island and moved to Charleston. There they were living when he died in 1860.[6] With his father's retirement and his own marriage, J. Edward Seabrook had taken up residence at Oak Island.

The Seabrook family's real estate transactions have not been fully explored. In 1825, William Seabrook Jr. paid taxes on 1,066 acres in St. John's Colleton Parish—much larger than Oak Island's approximately 400 acres, but smaller than his portion of Seabrook Island. (He also held land on Wadmalaw Island at the time of his father's death in 1838.) There were many intra-family conveyances, and much of Seabrook Island, along with the Simmons house on Johns Island, came to be owned by William's brother George Washington Seabrook.

By 1849, William Seabrook had a total of 1,680 acres in St. John's, about 950 acres of it improved, and produced sixty-seven bags of sea island cotton. Like his father, he accumulated land until the end of his life. In the 1860 census, taken shortly before Seabrook's death, he reported owning 1,400 acres of improved land, on which he had made seventy bags of cotton, and 1,200 unimproved acres (which could include marsh, woodlands, and uncultivated high ground).[7]

Both of William Seabrook's sons were married and living on Edisto Island in 1860, each with a son under a year old. Both owned land, but relatively small tracts—J. Edward with 177 acres (150 improved) and William E. with 195 acres (185 improved). Such minor holdings, coupled with the fact that the brothers each reported making fourteen bags of cotton, suggests that they were co-owners of a 392-acre plantation. One or both of them surely planted their father's plantations as well.

William Seabrook's inventory, taken in December 1860, is unusual in that it includes his real estate. There were 700 acres on Johns Island, appraised at $28,000, and the more valuable Edisto Island plantation, 405 acres worth $30,325. He also owned a house and lot on the Bay (Edingsville), a lot at Rockville, and a "Kiawah Place" worth $5,000. There was a dwelling house on Johns Island, with furniture appraised at only $180—not much more than the $150 worth of furnishings left year-round in the Edings Bay summer house. However, at Oak Island was furniture valued at $3,030, including the library, and a "stock of liquor" appraised separately at $500. Along with horses, carriage horses, livestock, work boats and flats, there were also three "good" boats: the *Sarah*, the *S. Decatur*, and the *Flying Cloud*.[8]

When William Seabrook's estate was settled, Oak Island was conveyed to J. Edward by his mother, brother, and sister.[9] Edward Seabrook's plantation was extensively photographed during its occupation by Union troops, leaving us powerful images of the idyllic setting of one sea island family's home.

1. Chalmers G. Davidson, *The Last Foray. The South Carolina Planters of 1860: A Sociological Study* (Columbia: University of South Carolina Press, 1971), p. 248.

2. Charleston County Register of Mesne Conveyance, Deed Book D9, p. 170.

3. William P. Baldwin, *Plantations of the Lowcountry, South Carolina 1697-1865* (Greensboro, NC: Legacy Publications, 1985), pp. 104-105.

4. Harriette Kershaw Leiding, *Historic Houses of South Carolina* (Philadelphia: J. B. Lippincott, 1921), p. 219.

5. Annie Baynard Simons Hasell, *Baynard: An Ancient Family Bearing Arms* (Charleston: privately printed, 1972), p. 197. James Garner Patey, *The Whaley Family and Its Charleston Connection* (Spartanburg: The Reprint Company, 1992), p. 33.

6. James W. Hagy, *On the Eve of the Civil War: The Charleston, SC, Directories for the Years 1859 and 1860* (Baltimore: Clearfield Company, 2000). Charleston County Inventories, Book F, p. 160, Charleston County Public Library.

7. Agricultural Schedules, U.S. Census, St. John's Colleton Parish, 1850 and 1860.

8. Charleston County Inventories, Book F, p. 160, CCPL.

9. Charleston County RMC, Deed Book Z13, pp. 466, 468.

Woodward
Port Royal Island

Robert Woodward Barnwell, eldest son of Robert Gibbes Barnwell, grew up in Beaufort and at his father's Laurel Bay Plantation. Before he was fourteen, his father died, but under the guardianship of his older cousin John Gibbes Barnwell, he completed his education at Beaufort College and Harvard College, then studied law in Charleston. Admitted to the bar in 1823, he established a practice in Coosawhatchie with Robert Barnwell Rhett.

Barnwell began a political career, and was elected to the State House in 1826. The following spring he married his cousin Eliza Barnwell, a daughter of his former guardian. Between 1829 and 1833, while Barnwell served in the United States Congress, the first three of Eliza's thirteen children were born. Congressional sessions were brief, and although Eliza was often in Washington, the family spent more time at home on Woodward Plantation and in Beaufort.

For about two years in the mid-1830s, Barnwell occupied himself with planting. Then, in 1835, he accepted the position as president of South Carolina College in Columbia. In 1841, he retired to Beaufort, citing ill health. For the next decade, the Barnwells divided their time between their house in town and nearby Woodward Plantation.[1]

Woodward seems to have been a Barnwell property by the middle of the eighteenth century, but whether the plantation came into Robert Woodward Barnwell's possession through gift, inheritance, or purchase is unknown. The design of the house indicates a likely construction date in the early 1830s, before Barnwell moved to Columbia.

The Woodward residence had two main floors raised high on brick piers. While the core of the wood-frame building was traditional—a lateral roof with a low central pediment with a lunette window, two rear-set chimneys, and a central hall leading through to a perpendicular wing—it was distinguished by two projecting wings under hipped roofs at the outer bays of the façade. Between the wings was a one-story porch, supported by slender columns, that projected forward beyond the plane of the wings.

These Adam-inspired polygonal bays would have been more fashionable during the early nineteenth century, before the Greek Revival became the dominant design influence. During the later 1800s, such projections were uncommon, but not unique. For example, the Federal-style house at The Grove (c. 1828), a rice plantation on the South Edisto River, also featured symmetrically placed projecting bays on an otherwise regular plan.

The pedimented gable rear wing of the Woodward House was thoroughly Greek Revival in design. Above the portico was a second-story window with narrow sidelights. According to captions provided with Samuel Cooley's photographs, the front of the house faced the oak-lined drive, "full one mile and a half long," and the rear wing provided the "beautiful view out onto Broad River."[2]

Woodward Plantation House, 1862 *(Courtesy of The Western Reserve Historical Society, Cleveland Ohio)*

Although Eliza Barnwell was strong, and most of her babies survived infancy, six of the children died young. Living in the town of Beaufort at the time of the 1850 census were Robert and Eliza and six children: Eliza Woodward (21), John Gibbes (18), Robert Hayne (15), Mary Gibbes (13), and twins Nathaniel Berners and James Stuart (5). Baby Eliza Howe was born later that year.

In 1850, Barnwell was appointed to the United States Senate to fill out an unexpired term. He was re-elected, and remained in the Senate until Lincoln's election. He then resigned to join the government of the Confederate States. After the evacuation of the sea islands, the family moved back and forth between Richmond, Charleston, Aiken, and Greenville. In 1865, Barnwell was named to head the University of South Carolina, and resided in Columbia until his death in 1882.[3]

Politics and college administration were not lucrative professions, and it was Robert Barnwell's sea island cotton plantations that supported the family. In 1825, he paid taxes on 300 acres in St. Helena Parish. By 1850, he owned 1,075 acres (500 improved), which produced twenty bags of cotton, and another 1,200 acres in Prince William Parish, where another forty bags had been made in 1849.[4] The plantations were supervised by one or more overseers, while Barnwell's brother William Hazzard Wigg Barnwell, whose ministry in Charleston kept him away from his own Laurel Bay, maintained the account books for his brother.[5] It is likely that John Gibbes Barnwell, who began practicing law in Beaufort in 1853, also assisted with the management of his father's plantations.

In 1859, a fourth of the eight-hundred-acre Woodward Plantation was "improved," but Robert Woodward Barnwell's home place produced only six bags of cotton. According to the United States census, he did not own other land in St. Helena Parish. He might have given land to his sons, or it could be that he had sold some tracts in order to increase his holdings in Prince William Parish, where he had amassed 2,700 productive acres on Kean's Neck. In 1859, he produced a hundred bags of cotton on those three plantations (Cotton Hope, Bulls/Ball's Point, and Straban).[6]

The Woodward Plantation house was heavily damaged in 1864 by sailors from a Union gunboat who stripped off the stairs and doors for firewood, broke windows and tore off the roofing. The building was then set on fire, but "some of the people on the place saved it."[7] Whatever survived that incident was eventually lost, and only a scatter of brick remains today.[8]

1. Alexander Moore, *Biographical Directory of the South Carolina House of Representatives.* Vol. 5, 1816-1828 (Columbia: South Carolina Department of Archives and History, 1992), pp. 13-14. Stephen B. Barnwell, *The Story of an American Family* (Marquette, MI: 1969), pp. 108-112. Chalmers G. Davidson, *The Last Foray. The South Carolina Planters of 1860: A Sociological Study* (Columbia: University of South Carolina Press, 1971), p. 176.
2. Captions on Cooley Photographs, #24 and #25, Reed Collection, Beaufort County Public Library.
3. Barnwell, *American Family*, pp. 108-112.
4. Tax Returns, 1824, South Carolina Department of Archives and History. Agricultural Schedules, U.S. Census, St. Helena's Parish, 1850.
5. W. H. W. Barnwell, "Plantation Book," South Carolina Historical Society.
6. Agricultural Schedules, U.S. Census, St. Helena's Parish and Prince William's Parish, 1860.
7. Caption, Photograph #25, Reed Collection.
8. Colin Brooker, "Tabby Structures at Woodward Plantation, Port Royal Island, Beaufort County, S.C." (MS, BCPL).

Brick House/Stanyarne Hall
JOHNS ISLAND

Brick House was a two-and-a-half-story stuccoed brick residence situated near the north bank of Abbapoola Creek. Although the eighteenth-century owner of the tract, Joseph Stanyarne, bequeathed to his wife Elizabeth Stobo the "use and occupation of my plantation where I now reside and also of the brick Messuage [residence] and other buildings thereon,"[1] photographs show a nineteenth-century building whose dominant design influence was the Greek Revival.

At the façade's strong central pediment was a lunette window above unusual round-arched openings that read as Classical niches. Four French doors opened into twin parlors; matching doors across the second level indicate a two-tiered front porch whose design has not been documented. Palladian windows at the gable ends were elegant details on the very plain side elevations.

The interior had a four-room plan, with a large sliding door in the center wall connecting the two front parlors. Smaller rear rooms were separated by the stair hall. Greek Revival door surrounds with their ornate corner blocks, and mantels with molded architraves, were decorative elements typical of the 1830s.

Exactly when Joseph Stanyarne's "brick Messuage" was replaced, and by whom, has not been learned. His son William, who lived at nearby Acorn Hill, was heir to the property after his

Brick House/Stanyarne Hall, ca. 1930 *(From the collections of the South Carolina Historical Society)*

Brick House Interior, ca. 1930 *(From the collections of the South Carolina Historical Society)*

mother, but both died in 1784.[2] Anna Stanyarne, William's daughter, inherited Brick House Plantation, and owned it during the years when sea island cotton became the primary crop on Johns Island. Miss Stanyarne might have spent some of her time on Johns Island, but her principal residence was in Charleston, and she was not actively engaged in planting.

Anna Stanyarne's brother-in-law Charles Freer, the husband of her sister Mary, seems to have planted and occupied the Brick House property, although he resided in Charleston, and also planted rice near Willtown. Freer's estate inventory, made in 1816, includes furniture and personal possessions "at the Johns Island residence of Miss Stanyarne."[3] Freer's daughter Maria Augusta was a great favorite and principal legatee of her aunt Anna, who bequeathed her much of the family silver (eighteen spoons and a ladle engraved "Stanyarne").[4] Maria Augusta Freer treated Brick House as her heritage—it was she who placed several ornate marble tombstones in the family cemetery on the property,[5] lending credence to the local tradition that her family had lived there. It could have been during the Freer tenure that the house was built.

After Anna Stanyarne's death in 1836, the Brick House was sold to make a partition among her heirs. Advertised as 891 acres "more or less,"[6] it was conveyed as 967 acres. The buyer, B. D. Roper, paid $17,200, less than $18 an acre, for the plantation with its masonry house.[7]

When Benjamin Dart Roper bought Brick House in 1837, he was sixty years old and had been planting on Johns Island for at least thirty years. Since 1824, his plantation seat had been at Rush's Plantation, south of Abbapoola Creek, but he and his wife Barbara Calder Jenkins kept a house in Charleston throughout their lives. In their later years, they often shared quarters with one or more of their children and grandchildren.[8] Theirs was a happy home: Roper's will left slaves, horses, household goods, and the "plantation called Rush's on John's Island where I usually reside… to my beloved wife with whom I have now lived forty-three years and upwards in a union of undiminished affection…"[9]

In 1850, Roper had already given plantations to his two eldest sons, but he still owned nearly 2,000 acres on Johns Island, 847 acres of it under cultivation. This land made seventy-one bags of sea island cotton in 1849. The 1850 census lists three of Roper's sons on Johns Island. At The Oaks, originally conveyed to B. D. Roper by his father-in-law Micah Jenkins, were M. Jenkins Roper and his wife Susan. Thomas and Mary Roper and their baby Julia were at Capes, also formerly owned by Micah Jenkins. Dr. William Roper and his family were at the Brick House.

William Roper had married only a few years before. His wife Mary Julia Stevens, a Stanyarne descendant, was more than a decade younger than he. During her ten years as a married woman, Mary Julia had at least four children, and died in 1856 not long after the birth of Gertrude. William Roper was married again, to the even-younger Mary Anne Mathews, also of Johns Island,[10] and for the 1860 census reported a household of daughters, the baby being one year old.

Dr. William Roper began planting the Brick House while it still belonged to his father. After their parents' deaths, the heirs divided the estate, and William continued at the Brick House, producing fifty bags of cotton in 1859.

Roper struggled financially after the Civil War and made some bad decisions about his property. Mortgages he gave were foreclosed during the 1870s, and Brick House Plantation was sold for satisfaction.[11] Decades as a farmhouse rented with the land were followed by years of vacancy, and the "very fine old house" was demolished in the 1950s.[12]

---

1. "Will of Joseph Stanyarne," Charleston County Wills, Book 14, p. 263, Charleston County Public Library.
2. "Will of Joseph Stanyarne." Laylon Wayne Jordan and Elizabeth H. Stringfellow, *A Place Called St. John's, The Story of John's, Edisto, Wadmalaw, Kiawah, and Seabrook Islands of South Carolina* (Spartanburg: The Reprint Company), p. 289.
3. Charleston County Inventories, Book E, p. 366, CCPL.
4. "Will of Anna Stanyarne," Charleston County Wills, Book 40, p. 338, CCPL.
5. Jordan and Stringfellow, p. 279.
6. *Charleston Courier*, January 27, 1837.
7. Charleston County Register of Mesne Conveyance, Deed Book Q10, p. 90.
8. James W. Hagy, *Directories for the City of Charleston, South Carolina, for the Years 1830-31, 1835-36, 1836, 1837-38, and 1840-41* (Baltimore: Clearfield Company, 1997).
9. "Will of Benjamin Dart Roper, Sr.," Charleston County Wills, Book 46, p. 201. Charleston County Inventories, Book C, p. 322, CCPL
10. Thomas W. Roper family file, Waring Historical Library, Medical University of South Carolina.
11. Jordan and Stringfellow, pp. 158-159.
12. Annie Jenkins Batson, "Jenkins Family History" (1977, South Carolina Historical Society File 43/234).

Brookland
Edisto Island

The Brookland Plantation residence is a two-story main block with one-story wings. Roofs at the main building, wings, and front porch are low and hipped. The ground-floor basement is finished as living space, with fireplaces at the main core and wings. Exterior decorative elements—Tower of the Wind columns, paneled architraves at the first-floor French doors, dentil moldings—are good examples of Greek Revival detail. However, the full-height portico at the south elevation seems incomplete. It covers only the center two bays of the façade, although the porch deck extends across all four French doors. The existing porch might be a replacement for a more traditional one-story porch across the entire entry elevation.

The interior plan is also unusual. Twin front parlors entered separately from the outside were a characteristic lowcountry design, but most often this plan included two small rear rooms with a center stair hall. At Brookland, by contrast, there are only two rooms in the main core, with a rear passage linking the two wing rooms. Interior chimneys serve the main rooms, while the wings have separate exterior chimneys at their rear walls. Along the back wall of the passage, lit by a round-headed window at its second level, a simply-detailed stair rises from east to west.

Brookland Plantation House, 2003 *(Courtesy of Bruce G. Harvey)*

The Seabrook family's ownership of Brookland Plantation began during the eighteenth century. In 1788, Joseph Seabrook gave the 220-acre "Hill Tract" to his son Gabriel, in consideration of the "natural love and affection which I bear unto my beloved son, and for making provision for his future support and maintenance."[1] Gabriel Seabrook and his wife Ann Mikell made their home at Brookland.

Five of the Seabrooks' children lived to adulthood: Elizabeth, Mary, Ephraim Mikell, John Archibald, and Abigail Mikell. All were very young when their mother died in 1809, and by the end of the next year their father Gabriel had remarried. His second wife, Ann Jenkins, was already twice a widow, having survived both James LaRoche and Edward Delegal Campbell. She had three LaRoche children, the elder two already grown men. Only the youngest, Martha Sarah, a year older than her new stepsister Elizabeth, joined the Seabrook household.[2]

Ephraim Mikell Seabrook eventually came into ownership of his father's Brookland Plantation. He probably built the house there for his wife Elizabeth Mary Hanahan and their seven children: John Gabriel, Ephraim Mikell, Edward Whaley, Joseph Whaley, Louisa Anastasia, Mary Elizabeth, and Henry.[3] (His father Gabriel is said to have occupied a former Jenkins dwelling on another section of the property.)[4]

When Ephraim Mikell Seabrook died in 1846, his eldest sons were already planting on their own, but four of the children were still underage. Their father left a large estate. Besides Brookland, there were four plantations, and personal property totaling some $69,000. This included 175 slaves and fifty bags of cotton, probably his 1846 crop.[5]

The family remained at Brookland, where Ephraim had assured his "dear wife Elizabeth Mary" lifetime occupancy, bequeathing the plantation to his youngest son Henry. To his namesake son Ephraim Mikell, Seabrook left his "Mikell plantation purchased of Mr. Josiah Smith." The legacies to John Gabriel, Joseph, and Edward were plantations on Fenwick's Island and Raccoon Island, productive sea island cotton lands but located in areas considered unhealthy for white occupancy.[6]

Elizabeth Seabrook and six of her children were living at Brookland in 1850. John Gabriel practiced medicine, while twenty-five-year-old Edward, who was establishing himself on the adjacent Laurel Hill, took responsibility for planting. Teenagers Joseph and Henry were in school, and their sisters Louisa and Mary awaited matrimony. (In 1854 Mary married Paul Hamilton Seabrook in a ceremony at Brookland.[7] Louisa seems not to have married.)

In 1860, Joseph, Henry, and Louisa Seabrook were still with their mother, enjoying life at Brookland. They kept more horses than most of their neighbors, and owned $1,500 worth of books and pictures alone.[8] After the Civil War, debt entanglements ruined Henry, and in 1874, Brookland Plantation was sold.[9]

1. Charleston County Register of Mesne Conveyance, Deed Book B6, p. 45.
2. Joseph LaRoche Rivers, *Seven South Carolina Lowcountry Families: Bailey, Clark, Grimball, Jenkins, Seabrook, Townsend and Whaley* (Charleston: privately printed, 1997, rev. ed. 2001).
3. Rivers, *Seven Families*.
4. Joseph Jenkins was buried near the earlier house site in 1789: "Brookland Plantation" National Register Nomination (South Carolina Department of Archives and History, 1986).
5. Charleston County Inventories, Book B, p. 252, Charleston County Public Library.
6. Charleston County Wills, Book 44, p. 36, CCPL.
7. Mabel C. Webber, "Early Generations of the Seabrook Family," in *South Carolina Historical Magazine* 17 (1916).
8. Agricultural Schedules, U.S. Census, St. John's Colleton Parish, 1850 and 1860. South Carolina Comptroller/State Auditor "Claims for property lost due to the enemy" (Record Series S126189, SCDAH).
9. *Record of Burials at Magnolia Cemetery, 1836-1931*, CCPL. Charleston County RMC, Deed Book P16, p. 71.

Fish Hall
Hilton Head Island

Civil War-era photographs and magazine sketches show Fish Hall as "Rebel Gen. T. F. Drayton's House." Drayton was known to federals as the loser of the Battle of Port Royal (November 1861); his brother Percival Drayton was a captain with the victorious Union navy.[1]

When Henry P. Moore photographed Fish Hall in 1862, it had been at least two decades since the house was the main residence of a planter family. The two-and-a-half-story building had an austere appearance. It had lost most of its exterior paint, and flowerbeds and borders had been transformed into a sandy yard. Yet it remained stately, and was described as "lordly" by a northern visitor.[2] An oak avenue flanked by rows of slave cabins led from the public road to the residence, which was placed in a gated enclosure and closely surrounded by ornamental trees. High on its open foundation of brick piers, the house presented an equally imposing view from the water.[3]

Fish Hall Plantation House (land side), 1862
(Courtesy of The Western Reserve Historical Society, Cleveland Ohio)

The Fish Hall dwelling seems to have faced the water, oriented either toward Port Royal Sound or Fish Hall Creek. It was designed with a center-hall plan of two rooms over four, with interior rear chimneys and a one-story porch across the front elevation. At the rear was a gabled portico with Tuscan columns to match those at the front porch. Each of the four main rooms had two windows at the end wall, and the garret was lit by a tripartite window. At the second floor rear, three windows were separated by the wide chimneys. The rear shed rooms on the first floor cannot be read with any clarity.

The early history of Fish Hall Plantation is incomplete. In 1770, Fish Haul Creek Plantation consisted of about seven hundred acres. Like the adjacent Coggins Point, it was owned by Samuel Green. When Green wrote his will in 1767, he bequeathed the tract where he lived, Fish Hall, to his son Samuel. Upon the younger Samuel's own death, his sister Sarah, devisee of Coggins Point, inherited Fish Hall.[4] Sarah married William Pope Sr., and Fish Hall eventually passed to their younger son John Edward, the likely builder of the house later referred to as "Drayton's House."

By 1838, John Edward Pope had died at the age of thirty-two, leaving his widow Mary Baynard Edings and their daughter Emma Catherine.[5] The 1850 census shows Mary Baynard Pope as the owner of a total of twelve hundred acres in St. Luke's Parish, on which twenty-two bags of cotton were produced. The land was probably being planted by her son-in-law Thomas F. Drayton.

Born in 1808, Thomas Fenwick Drayton was the son of William and Ann (Gadsden) Drayton. After schooling in Pennsylvania and England, Thomas enrolled at West Point and received an officer's commission in 1828. He was with the army surveyor's office for several years, then worked as a civilian engineer for the Louisville, Cincinnati & Charleston Railroad.[6] In 1838, Drayton married Emma Catherine Pope,[7] and changed his life. He gave up his railroad job, and bought Rephaim Plantation near Bluffton. Here he and Emma were living in 1840, along with their baby John Edward, and Emma's mother Mary Baynard Pope. By 1850 the household had grown, with four more children: Anna Maria, William Seabrook, Mary Edings, and Percival. (Not surprisingly, Mrs. Pope had moved into her own dwelling nearby.) The Drayton family lived not at Fish Hall, but on the mainland, probably in Bluffton, where there were physicians, clergymen, and a school.

Drayton was planting profitably, but in 1853 he returned to railroad management, becoming president of the new Charleston and Savannah Railroad. Emma died in 1854, not long after the birth of her last son, Thomas Drayton Jr., and eventually the family moved to Charleston. In 1860 Thomas F. Drayton was at home on Meeting Street with five of his surviving children and eleven slaves.[8]

Thomas Drayton had himself become a large landowner, significantly increasing his holdings in 1848 when he received a grant for 3041 acres in Beaufort District.[9] In about 1857 he added a four-hundred-acre pineland tract to Fish Hall's seven hundred acres.[10] By 1860, he controlled over five thousand acres in St. Luke's Parish. His 104 slaves made forty-five bags of sea island cotton; at his children's Fish Hall, fifty-two slaves produced another twenty-five bags.

Well into his fifties, Thomas Fenwick Drayton was commissioned a brigadier general in the Confederate army in September 1861. After his defeat at the Battle of Port Royal and lackluster performances at Manassas and Antietam, he was relegated to desk jobs and spent much of the war in Arkansas and Texas.[11] In his absence, Fish Hall was sold to the federal government for taxes.

1. N. Louise Bailey, Mary L. Morgan, Carolyn R. Taylor, *Biographical Directory of the South Carolina Senate, 1776-1985*, Vol. 1 (Columbia: University of South Carolina Press, 1986), pp. 421-422.
2. Quoted in Michael Trinkley, ed. "Archaeological Survey of the Proposed Barker Field Expansion Project, Hilton Head Island, South Carolina" (Columbia: Chicora Foundation, Inc., 1989).
3. Civil War artists depicted the house in several different ways. *Frank Leslie's Illustrated Newspaper* (December 21, 1861) shows a building with a hipped roof, so cannot be reliable; *Harper's Weekly* (December 7, 1861) shows a gable-roofed house at the head of its slave street, apparently with the portico at this landward elevation.
4. Hartridge Collection, Box 21, Folder 482, Georgia Historical Society, Savannah.
5. Hartridge Collection.
6. Bailey et al.
7. Chalmers G. Davidson, *The Last Foray. The South Carolina Planters of 1860: A Sociological Study* (Columbia: University of South Carolina Press, 1971), p. 192. *Southern Patriot*, March 2, 1838.
8. Population Schedules, U.S. Census, St. Philip's and St. Michael's parishes, 1860. James W. Hagy, *On the Eve of the Civil War: The Charleston, SC, Directories for the Years 1859 and 1860* (Baltimore: Clearfield Company, 2000).
9. Bailey et al.
10. Virginia C. Holmgren, *Hilton Head: A Sea Island Chronicle* (Hilton Head Island, 1959), p. 126.
11. Bailey et al.

Tom Fripp House
St. Helena Island

The Tom Fripp House stood on a 614-acre plantation sold as the "Thomas James Fripp Place" by the federal government in 1863.[1] Although the plantation had a long waterfront on Village Creek, the house was located near its north boundary, on a slight bluff overlooking Eddings Creek. Members of the extended Fripp family owned much of the land at the east end of St. Helena Island, but it is uncertain who constructed this dwelling. It can probably be attributed to Thomas James Fripp.[2] Based on architectural details visible in the only known photograph of the house, it was built sometime after 1830.

The frame building, two rooms above four with a center hall and a one-room side wing, had a shed-roofed porch with Tuscan columns across its five-bay façade, and a fairly low foundation, with masonry piers supporting the porch (there may have been usable space under the main body of the house). The principal entry is obscured in the photograph, but the six-over-six-light windows were common throughout the later antebellum period.

During the Port Royal Experiment, the Tom Fripp house was occupied by David Thorpe, a superintendent with the Freedmen's Bureau, and his wife.[3] In the twentieth century, two Penn School teachers, Rossa Belle Cooley and Grace House, gave the name N'Dulamo to the property. The Fripp house was replaced during their ownership.[4]

Tom Fripp House, ca. 1863 *(Courtesy of South Caroliniana Library, University of South Carolina)*

1. *Beaufort Republican,* January 10, 1863.
2. "Fripp Family Chart" in Theodore Rosengarten, *Tombee: Portrait of a Cotton Planter* (New York: William Morrow and Co., 1986).
3. Edith M. Dabbs, *Sea Island Diary, A History of St. Helena Island* (Spartanburg: The Reprint Company, 1983), p. 166.
4. Dabbs, *Sea Island Diary,* p. 231.

Oakley Hall (Bloody Point)
Daufuskie Island

There is no record of when the Oakley Hall residence at Bloody Point was built, but it seems likely that William Henry Mongin erected it in the 1830s.

The two-story building of wood frame construction, with chimneys centered at the side slopes of its hipped roof, was set upon a finished ground-floor basement. On each level were four rooms of equal size, divided by a center hall. Masonry piers supported the one-story shed-roof porch with fairly heavy Tuscan columns. The cornice and a broad central gable were adorned with dentil blocks, and there were narrow sidelights and a transom at the front entry.

In 1790, Sarah Watts, heir to her father Robert's four-hundred-acre Bloody Point Plantation, married John David Mongin, a Savannah merchant and Hilton Head landowner. Bloody Point was their plantation seat until Sarah's death in 1816.

Their only son, David John Mongin, who had married Sarah Irvine in 1812, eventually took up Bloody Point, perhaps when his father acquired Salt Pond (Melrose) in 1818. David and Sarah Mongin lived in Savannah and on Daufuskie with their children William Henry and Mary Lavinia. (Mary Lavinia's twin and three other children died young.)[1]

Daufuskie Island, unlike St. Helena or Edisto, was very lightly occupied by planter families, and life there must have been tedious. Our only commentary on the Mongins' home life

Oakley Hall Plantation House, ca. 1890 *(Courtesy of Albert H. Stoddard)*

comes from a religious missionary who visited in 1822, and may reflect his own straitlaced attitude as much as the enthusiastic welcome of an isolated young family. As one of several guests, Jeremiah Evarts "resided three days on a sea-island plantation, where I was treated with all the hospitality which the owner was master of. The house was large, the rooms airy, the furniture costly, the provisions of the table profusely abundant. The master of the house was incapable of society from drinking brandy, and consequent stupidity and ignorance. He had been educated at Princeton College, and is probably somewhat under 40. Every evening he is so far overcome with strong drink, as to be silly, every morning full of pain, languor, and destitute appetite... The furniture of this mansion was expensive, but was little attended to. The general aspect of things indicated slackness, and listlessness."[2] Whether he was debilitated by alcohol or illness, David Mongin died in 1823, still in his early thirties.

David John Mongin's widow Sarah, through whose family he had acquired Freeport (600 acres) and Haig Point (358 acres) plantations, took care to preserve their children's rights when she remarried in 1825.[3] Although the young Mongin children were to inherit Bloody Point, they moved with their mother and her second husband, the Reverend Himan M. Blodgett, to Freeport, Sarah's own property. The Blodgetts had several children of their own, but all of them died young,[4] and Sarah died in 1833. Blodgett then acquired Freeport and Haig Point in his own name. With his next wife Catherine, a Pennsylvania woman he married in 1837, he built a fine new house at Haig Point. (While the new house was underway, Catherine explained to her sister that, in the Freeport house she had been brought to, "I am not very much prepared for dinner parties as our cottage has but one parlor or sitting area.")[4]

In 1833, when his mother and his grandfather John David Mongin died, William Henry Mongin became proprietor of Bloody Point's 484 acres. He was seventeen years old.

The architectural style of the Oakley Hall residence suggests a mid-1830s construction date. It was probably built about the time (1836) that Mongin married Isabella Rae Habersham of Savannah. They had no children, and at his death in 1851, William provided his widow life tenure in Bloody Point. The 1860 census shows Isabella, forty-four years old, living alone on 450 acres. At her death, Bloody Point was inherited by Henry Mongin Stoddard, her husband's nephew and a great-grandson of John David Mongin. It was Stoddard who reclaimed the property from the federal government in 1867.

Last used by farmers leasing Bloody Point's agricultural fields, the Oakley Hall house was dismantled in the 1930s.[6]

1. Billie Burn, *An Island Named Daufuskie* (Spartanburg: The Reprint Co., 1991), p. 35.
2. Jeremiah Evarts quoted in Burn, *Daufuskie*, pp. 140-141.
3. South Carolina Marriage Settlements, Book 9, p. 149, South Carolina Department of Archives and History.
4. Burn, *Daufuskie*, p. 83.
5. Burn, *Daufuskie*, pp. 83-84.
6. Burn, *Daufuskie*, p. 156.

Melrose (Salt Pond)
Daufuskie Island

Surrounded by its gardens, Melrose House stood within hearing range, if not within sight, of Calibogue Sound and the sea. The two-story frame building was raised on a brick foundation, with brick piers supporting a one-story wraparound porch with dignified Doric columns and a rooftop balustrade. Above the ground-level basement with its brick flooring, the interior had a four-room plan with a center hall. Fireplaces set on the outside walls of the eight primary rooms were adorned by marble mantels. A one-story hipped structure connected to the rear of the building probably held either John Stoddard's well-respected library, or the separate billiard room "destroyed with all the billiard and pool tables" in the fire that claimed Melrose in 1912.[1]

Originally known as Salt Pond, this plantation was first cultivated for sea island cotton in the early 1800s. Richard Russell Ashe died in 1806, the owner of a "beautiful summer residence" in Charleston and hundreds of acres on Daufuskie Island. This land had recently been divided into four plantations: Oakridge, Maryfield, Newburg, and Salt Pond. In early 1807, the Ashe properties were advertised for sale as "well worth the attention of cotton planters. The land will be found on examination, of a strong and permanent quality. The average crop of the last year is fully two bales of cotton to the hand (although 1/4 was lost by the autumnal gales)."[2]

Melrose Plantation House, ca. 1894 *(Courtesy of Albert H. Stoddard)*

Oakridge, 596 acres, had been "settled" in 1802, and had new outbuildings, but no residence for a white planter or overseer. On 530-acre Maryfield, also recently settled, was a new overseer's house and outbuildings. Newburg, with 740 acres and suitable as a planter's seat, had an "entirely new" dwelling house, kitchen, washhouse, stable, carriage house and other outbuildings, while on the 770-acre Salt Pond Plantation was a dwelling house and "every other necessary outbuilding in good repair."[3]

The land was fresh and the open exposure to the sea offered "pleasant and healthy" sites for occupancy, but whether the recent plunge in cotton prices slowed planters' interest or because of Daufuskie's isolation, only Newburg sold. Maryfield, Oakridge, and Salt Pond remained in the Ashe estate for several years.[4]

Finally, in March 1818, widower John David Mongin of Bloody Point bought the three Ashe tracts.[5] Salt Pond, with its "comfortable dwelling-house" became Mongin's new home sometime before his 1823 marriage to Ann Harrison.[6] The same year that the middle-aged Mongin remarried, his only son David died. Mongin's grandchildren, William Henry and Mary Lavinia, grew up with all the privileges of wealth and their prospective inheritances. In 1836, Mary Lavinia Mongin was in Paris, where she married John Stoddard of Massachusetts.

Ten years older than his bride, Stoddard was in charge of the French trade for his family's business, but willing to adopt a sea island planter's life. After the birth of their daughter Mary Helen in London, the Stoddards returned to Savannah and Daufuskie, where they replaced her grandfather's house on Salt Pond Plantation with a large new dwelling they called Melrose.[7] In 1837, Elizabeth Anne Stiles reported to her brother John Mackay from Savannah: "Mr. Blodgett [of Haig Point] and Mr. Stoddard are both going to build houses at Daufuskie to cost each $10,000. They have bespoken bricks from Witte."[8]

John Stoddard continued his mercantile interests in Savannah, and also had some success as a planter. In 1859, he held 6,700 acres (only 1,000 improved) in St. Luke's Parish, producing forty bags of sea island cotton. Unusual for the time, he reported no working oxen on his land. All the cotton was produced by manual labor.

The Stoddards and their children (Albert Henry, Isabelle, John Irvine, and Henry Mongin were born at regular two-year intervals after Mary Helen) divided their time between Daufuskie and Savannah, where the children were educated.[9] In 1860, all five were unmarried, still in their parents' home at Melrose. Only six white households claimed Daufuskie as their principal residence that year: the Stoddards, Isabella Habersham Mongin, elderly Mary Dunn, two overseers with wives and children, and the Frazier family, headed by the Stoddards' gardener. Both born in Scotland, Alex Frazier and his wife were in their twenties, the parents of a South Carolina-born son.[10] Although he had probably not laid out the gardens at Melrose, it was Frazier's management that made the grounds a showcase.

The garden had not been long neglected when a Union officer found Melrose in early 1862:

MELROSE (SALT POND)

Garden at Melrose Plantation, ca. 1890 *(Courtesy of Albert H. Stoddard)*

Such a garden never was, I do believe. Such walks, hedges, arbors, vines, graveled walks, shade trees, flowers of every hue, and of all descriptions... grounds all laid out on a very extensive scale, winding gravel walks going in all directions divided off by neatly trimmed Hawthorn hedges, fruit trees in profusion... mighty live oaks, gum trees, tulip and other trees, with mansion and all the outbuildings completely overgrown with grape vines and hanging rose vines, ivy, etc.

Amid the blossoming stocks stands the crown-lily of the Island, a summer house of octagonal form about ten feet across, surmounted by a cupola and a weather cock. This house is built of pieces of wood, in its natural state with the bark on. The sticks are split and nailed on in such a way as to form the most pleasing figures, checks, squares, diamonds, arches, parallels, and circles... There are eight pillars around the outside, made octagonal in form, all done with those pieces of wood, then varnished, and the different colors brought out with a pleasing effect.[11]

1. Billie Burn, *An Island Named Daufuskie* (Spartanburg: The Reprint Co., 1991), p. 100.
2. *Charleston Courier,* January 1807.
3. Ibid.

4. *Charleston Courier*, November 1810.

5. Burn, *Daufuskie*, p. 8.

6. South Carolina Marriage Settlements, Book 10, p. 88, South Carolina Department of Archives and History.

7. Burn, *Daufuskie*, pp. 36-37.

8. Hartridge Collection, Box 31, Folder 477, Georgia Historical Society, Savannah.

9. Burn, *Daufuskie*, p. 107.

10. Population Schedules, U.S. Census, St. Luke's Parish, 1860.

11. Lieutenant Charles F. Monroe of the 8th Maine, quoted in Burn, *Daufuskie*, pp. 109-110.

Crawford's
EDISTO ISLAND

By his will of 1809, Ephraim Mikell left Crawford's Plantation (named for James Crawford, its owner from 1784 to 1802) to his son Ephraim.[1] This second Ephraim Mikell added adjacent property to Crawford's one hundred acres, and bequeathed the tract to his son William Archibald as 434 acres.[2]

When his father died in 1838, twenty-four-year-old William Archibald Mikell, a younger brother of I. Jenkins Mikell of Peter's Point, had been married to Hess Marion Waring Smith for three years,[3] and already had two sons. Although the house is not shown on a surveyor's plat made in 1838,[4] the young couple might have built and occupied it before William's inheritance was formal. In its design and construction the dwelling is characteristic of the

Crawford's Plantation House, 1992 *(Courtesy of South Carolina Department of Archives and History, Columbia)*

1830s. There are definite front and back sides, the Greek Revival façade featuring a prominent pedimented gable nearly the height of the main roof. The T-shaped plan of the house, most often seen in Beaufort and its environs, is an interesting variant of the four-room dwelling. The one-story porch, central hallway with the stair rising in several flights against the rear wall, larger rooms at the front of the house, and fireplaces in the eight primary rooms are firmly in the established tradition.

In 1840, young William A. Mikell died,[5] leaving his widow and three sons with Crawford's and a summer house at Edings Bay. Besides horses and other livestock, there were fifty-six slaves, and cotton worth $2,500 to be picked and ginned.[6] Hess managed the estate herself for several years before she remarried. Her second husband was William Edings,[7] whose first wife Sarah had died at about the same time as her brother William Archibald Mikell. Edings's three children came to live at Crawford's with their Mikell stepbrothers, who were their first cousins. In 1847, William and Hess Edings sold Crawford's[8] and moved to "Bayview," where they had three children together.

The buyer of Crawford's house and 456 acres was William James Whaley. While his wife Martha raised their children at Crawford's, Whaley managed cotton crops at home and on Slann's Island (a plantation left him by his grandfather William Edings),[9] and ricefields on the Chehaw River. Martha Whaley died still in her thirties; in 1859, William James married Mary Wayne Mitchell,[10] the widow of William G. B. Mitchell. In 1860, they were at home with his children William Edings (18), James (14), and Eliza (10) and her daughter Lilly (Elizabeth) Mitchell, also 10. By that time Whaley was no longer planting rice, but he produced forty-eight bags of sea island cotton.

After the Civil War, Whaley reclaimed his house, which had been occupied by Freedmen's Bureau teachers,[11] and returned to planting. Crawford's Plantation House remained in the Whaley family until 1945.[12]

1. "Will of Ephraim Mikell," Charleston County Wills, Book 31, p. 287, Charleston County Public Library.
2. "Will of Ephraim Mikell," Charleston County Wills, Book 41, p. 717, CCPL.
3. *Charleston Courier*, January 19, 1835.
4. McCrady Plat Collection, #5617, CCPL.
5. WPA Cemetery Inscriptions, South Carolina Historical Society.
6. Charleston County Inventories, Book A, p. 128, CCPL.
7. William Garner Chisolm, "Edings of Edisto Island" (MS, Leesburg, VA: 1943).
8. Charleston County Register of Mesne Conveyance, Deed Book Y11, p. 276.
9. "Will of William Edings," Charleston County Wills, Book 40, p. 400, CCPL.
10. Chisolm, "Edings."
11. Mary Ames, *A New England Woman's Diary in Dixie in 1865* (New York: 1906, rep. 1969).
12. "Crawford's Plantation" National Register Nomination (South Carolina Department of Archives and History, 1993).

William J. Jenkins House
St. Helena Island

Planter/physician Dr. William J. Jenkins and his wife Eliza Mary Chaplin were prosperous, sociable, and notable for their enjoyment of their wealth. Their dwelling house on St. Helena Island, built between 1845 and 1846,[1] was equal to any in Beaufort, and architecturally very similar to the town houses of Edward Means and John Johnson.[2] The same carpenter might have been responsible for all three.

Facing southeast toward Station Creek, the Jenkins residence appears to have been laid out with a central hall and four rooms at each level, the rear rooms extended to either side by lateral wings. The front elevation was dominated by its two-tier porch topped by a paneled parapet that gave the building a flat-roofed appearance. Wrapping around both sides of the house, the porch was adorned with columns, identical at both levels, and brackets along the upper frieze. A projecting landing with masonry knee wall and double entry steps connected the house to the walkways and formal beds of the front garden.

William J. Jenkins House, ca. 1863 *(From the collections of the South Carolina Historical Society)*

Garden at William J. Jenkins House, ca. 1863 *(From the collections of the South Carolina Historical Society)*

Both the Jenkinses were young when this dwelling was constructed, but they had already been married several years.[3] By 1850, they had four children between the ages of two and eight; by 1860, their daughters Isabella, Marceline, and Florence were teenagers, son Llewellyn was nine, and Lelia, the baby, was seven years old. Also sharing their home were two relatives in their seventies: Eliza's widowed mother, Martha Fripp Chaplin, and William's aunt Elizabeth H. Jenkins Chaplin, the widow of Benjamin Chaplin.[4] The family divided their time between houses in Beaufort, St. Helenaville, and the plantation.

Dr. Jenkins maintained his medical practice as he planted sea island cotton on an increasing scale. The plantation he had inherited from his father was augmented by tracts his wife inherited and by land he purchased.[5] In 1850, Jenkins reported ownership of 388 acres; by 1859 he was proprietor of 1,515 acres, of which 515 acres was in cultivation.[6]

The Civil War ruined William J. Jenkins's planting career. After St. Helena was evacuated in 1861, eighty-five bags of his sea island cotton were confiscated by Union troops; in 1863, all his plantations were seized for taxes and sold. After the war, while supporting his family as a physician, Dr. Jenkins spent years in unsuccessful attempts to redeem his plantations from the federal government.[7]

The "Dr. Jenkins Place," 615 acres, and his 600-acre Sandiford Place, although separated by another tract, were operated together at least into the 1870s.[8] In 1872, Henry S. Tafft offered for rent "a Plantation occupied and cultivated by him for the past seven years known as Longwood." The plantation's twelve hundred acres included "600 acres unsurpassed for sea island cotton." Fronting over one mile onto Station Creek, Longwood also claimed "one of the most comfortable and commodious mansions on the sea islands, commanding a fine view of the magnificent harbor of Port Royal and of the ocean."[9]

There is no record that the Jenkinses had called their home Longwood, but an unknown commercial photographer documented the house and garden while that name was in use.

1. Theodore Rosengarten, *Tombee: Portrait of a Cotton Planter* (New York: William Morrow and Co., 1986), pp. 365, 423.
2. Historic Beaufort Foundation, *A Guide to Historic Beaufort*, 5th ed. (Beaufort: Historic Beaufort Foundation, Inc., 1985), pp. 84, 91.
3. Chalmers G. Davidson, *The Last Foray: The South Carolina Planters of 1860: A Sociological Study* (Columbia: University of South Carolina Press, 1971), p. 214.
4. Population Schedules, U.S. Census, St. Helena's Parish, 1850 and 1860.
5. Rosengarten, *Tombee*, p. 706.
6. Agricultural Schedules, U.S. Census, St. Helena's Parish, 1850 and 1860. Rosengarten, *Tombee*, pp. 324-325, shows Jenkins the owner of 2,185 acres on four separate plantations.
7. Rosengarten, *Tombee*, pp. 60, 290-291.
8. Beaufort County Register of Mesne Conveyance, Deed Book B, pp. 91, 92; Deed Book 5, p. 570.
9. *Beaufort Republican*, January 1872.

Cassina Point
EDISTO ISLAND

The first notice of William Seabrook's daughter Carolina Lafayette (called "Lafayette") comes in March 1825. When the Marquis de Lafayette visited Edisto Island, he spent several hours at William Seabrook's house where there was "even the baptism of a charming little infant, to which the name of Lafayette was given."[1] In February 1844, barely nineteen years old, the charming and wealthy young woman married James Hopkinson of Philadelphia, soon to turn thirty-four.[2] The marriage is proof of the Seabrooks' position: Hopkinson's maternal grandfather was a governor of Pennsylvania, and his paternal grandfather Francis signed the Declaration of Independence for New Jersey.

Lafayette Seabrook was one of five children of her father's second marriage. Under the terms of his will, a portion of his estate was to be kept together until the eldest of these, Robert Chisolm Seabrook, turned twenty-one (in 1842). Seabrook left a number of slaves, a plantation on Wadmalaw Island, and $100,000 for investment in additional land and slaves, all to be divided among the heirs.

James Hopkinson married into the land and workforce Lafayette had inherited. His success as a planter and as manager of the property of other family members, including plantations owned by Lafayette's sisters, show him to have been a man his father-in-law would have approved: a careful accountant, well-informed about crop and market conditions, and willing to spend heavily on his family's domestic comforts.

Besides good business sense, James brought his own wealth and social connections to the marriage. For the first few years of their union, he and Lafayette traveled in the north and in Europe. Their first daughter Emma Edings Hopkinson was born in 1845 in Paris, and her brother Francis was born in Charleston two years later.[3] That year James paid $1,000 for a house on the bay at Edingsville, spending an additional $700 to repair it.[4]

The family was probably dividing their time between Charleston and Edisto Island during the late 1840s, with James supervising the plantation and overseeing construction of their new house. The 1850 census shows them living on Edisto, where James reported owning one thousand acres.

Cassina Point is an especially successful example of Greek Revival design. Windows and dormers are rhythmically arranged above the one-story porch with its paired entry doors. The deep side elevations terminate in pedimented gables with large tripartite windows. The four-room interior was organized on the twin-parlor plan, with separate entries into the front rooms, used together as a large drawing room, and a narrow stair hall between the smaller rear rooms.

The Hopkinsons' new house was not fully furnished until the end of 1850. During the spring of that year, James shopped for furniture in Charleston, with a dining table and chairs

Cassina Point Plantation House, ca. 1930 *(Courtesy of The Charleston Museum, Charleston South Carolina)*

particularly noted in his memo book. By summer the Hopkinsons had received the table and twelve dining chairs, fourteen more chairs (a set of ten, a pair, a sewing chair, and one very expensive single chair), a card table, and a whatnot: in all, $275 worth of chairs and tables. They added a bedstead and spring mattress, two French pillows and bolsters, and $546 worth of carpets, among them two parlor carpets, a library carpet, stair carpet and front bedroom carpet. A few months later Hopkinson took a new list to town: a dozen each soup plates and dinner plates, a large French coffee pot, cord for hanging pictures, two pairs of candlesticks for the parlor, two walnut towel racks, and a double set of buff chamber ware.[5]

Settled into her home, surrounded by relatives, Lafayette Hopkinson must have been content. Her three youngest children were all born on Edisto: Cornelia Adelaide in 1851, Martha Julia in 1856, and James in 1860.

Like most Edistonians, the Hopkinsons took little with them when the evacuation order came in 1861. James's subsequent claim for "property taken possession of and destroyed by the Yankees" included $2,000 for furniture and contents of the Cassina Point house, and $500 at Edings Bay.[6] Judging from his careful records, these high figures are probably accurate.

Hopkinson's post-war repair notes explain the family's use of the rooms. In the ground level basement were the "entry," "Faytie's room," butler's room, pastry room, and "my room" (probably his office). On the raised first floor were drawing room ("with a pair of sliding folding doors"), library, and parlor. On the second floor were "my room," "Fee's room," nursery, and "spare room."[7] The attic rooms are not defined, but the overall impression of family life is similar to that in other grand dwellings, most of the house being set aside for daytime life and entertaining, with shared sleeping quarters in two or three rooms.

After the Civil War, James Hopkinson recovered himself as a planter and merchant, and lived fairly well, if overworked, until his death in January 1875. Lafayette Seabrook Hopkinson outlived her husband by only a few years, leaving Cassina Point in the possession of their daughter Martha Julia (Mrs. J. Murray) LaRoche.[8]

1. A. Lavasseur, *Lafayette in America in 1824 and 1825, or Journal of a Voyage to the United States* (Philadelphia, 1829).
2. Brent Holcomb, *Marriage and Death Notices from the Charleston Observer 1827-1845* (Columbia, 1980), p. 200.
3. Population Schedules, U.S. Census, St. John's Colleton Parish, 1850.
4. James Hopkinson, "Plantation Memorandum Books," (MS, South Caroliniana Library, University of South Carolina).
5. Hopkinson, "Plantation Books."
6. South Carolina Comptroller/State Auditor "Claims for property lost due to the enemy" (Record Series S126189, South Carolina Department of Archives and History).
7. Hopkinson, "Plantation Books."
8. "Edisto Island Multiple Resource Area" National Register Nomination (SCDAH, 1986).

McLeod
James Island

The conservative four-over-four room plan and restrained Greek Revival design of the McLeod Plantation house, built in the 1850s, is typical of the late antebellum era. The two-and-a-half-story building on a low foundation of brick piers has a one-story porch across its south façade, with narrow transom and sidelights at the entry. The unusual wood parapets atop the shed roof of the porch and the low curved wall at the brick steps are distinctive elements on an otherwise conventional building, and the treatment of the gable ends, detailed with cornice returns rather than pediments, was to become predominant in the latter nineteenth century. The interior features a central passageway with a straight-run stair along one wall. At the ground floor rooms are deep cornices and baseboards, and oversized plaster ceiling medallions in the popular acanthus-leaf pattern. Single windows light the attic rooms, which were plastered and finished as living space, but without fireplaces.

A formal garden south of the house separated the domestic area from the working fields. Service buildings stood north, east, and west of the house, with the kitchen and dwelling houses for slaves lining an oak avenue leading west from the planter's residence.

McLeod Plantation House, 1990 *(Historic American Buildings Survey, Library of Congress)*

When William W. McLeod purchased this plantation in 1851, it had been under cultivation for generations. From an early date, its location close to peninsular Charleston had assured that it could be profitably managed for market or staple crops by a city dweller. By his marriage to Elizabeth Peronneau, Edward Lightwood controlled a 250-acre tract here until his death in 1797. Thereafter, Elizabeth Lightwood herself managed the property with the assistance of her son-in-law William McKenzie Parker, and, after his 1802 death, through overseers. In 1816, Mrs. Lightwood advertised for "An Overseer who understands Cotton Planting and Gardening, for a plantation on James Island, about 3 miles from the city; the best recommendations will be required. Apply to E. Lightwood, No. 244 Meeting Street."[1]

Elizabeth Lightwood's death in 1826 left as her heirs her two married daughters, Mary Lightwood Peronneau and Sarah Lightwood Parker. The Lightwood executors soon offered two plantations for sale. Near the Ashepoo River in St. Bartholomew's Parish was a 414-acre plantation called Oakridge. On James Island was a "valuable and well settled Plantation and Farm, 744 acres of prime cotton and provision land (also marsh land), a little over two miles from Charleston, at the mouth of Wappoo Creek and Ashley River." The main tract was just over 717 acres; there were also several small islands, "from one of which in 1826 was made upwards of one bale of white Cotton per planted acre."[2]

In 1829, William McKenzie Parker Jr. paid his grandmother Lightwood's estate $16,544 for the James Island property.[3] In 1830, he too died, leaving the plantation to his sons after his widow's life interest.[4] (She was Anna Smith Coffin, sister of Thomas A. Coffin of Charleston and St. Helena Island.)[5] To settle Parker's estate, the James Island plantation was sold at auction, and bought in by his mother Sarah Lightwood Parker for $10,000.[6] She owned it at her death in 1847. Her will, written in 1838, directed that her estate should be "divided between my grandsons William McKenzie Parker and Edward Parker when William is 21. Until then, my plantation and negroes at James Island to be kept together and worked as at present."[7]

The land was productive, its six hundred acres of improved land yielding twenty-six bags of sea island cotton in 1849. Although this provided a substantial income, the next year the family decided to sell, advertising the "valuable cotton plantation and farm" with a "dwelling house, and all necessary out buildings and accommodations for 90 Negroes. The Cotton land has undergone a general system of improvement from manuring, leveling and ditching and is now in good heart, and fine planting order. The Farm land is in the highest state of cultivation... On the tract there is a summer settlement, and a locality for building unequaled, as regards the prospects of the bay, harbor, and city."[8] W. W. McLeod paid the Parker brothers $11,000 for 914.5 acres of high land and 779 acres of marsh.[9]

William Wallace McLeod was the youngest son of Robert McLeod of Edisto Island and his second wife Mary Mikell. In 1825, Robert McLeod owned land in the parishes of Prince William's, St. Paul's, and St. John's Colleton.[10] By 1830, he had died, and Mary McLeod died in 1839. Several of the McLeod children migrated to James Island, joining and marrying into other Edisto families there—the Seabrooks, Mikells, and Lawtons. The ties grew especially thick with the children of Winborn and Margaret Frampton Lawton. Josiah McLeod (William's older half-brother) married Mary Frampton Lawton; Martha McLeod married Mary's brother James Lawton; and in late 1843, at her father's house, Susan Martha Lawton married William W. McLeod.[11]

The Lawtons were among James Island's most prosperous sea island cotton planters, and McLeod was a worthy addition to the family. In 1859 he had six hundred acres in cultivation, his sixty-four bags of cotton (more than double the Parkers' production a decade earlier) proving his skill as a planter. He also grew corn, peas, and sweet potatoes for plantation use, and garden crops worth $3,000 for the Charleston market. Only Joseph Prevost and Wallace Winborn Lawton earned more with their fresh produce.[12]

It is uncertain where William and Susan McLeod lived for the first few years of their marriage. Three daughters were born between 1844 and 1848; by 1851, all had died. The family's new home proved healthier for the next three children. William Wallace McLeod was born in 1850, Ann Mikell McLeod soon after her father bought this plantation, and Regina, the youngest, was born in 1856, perhaps in the McLeod Plantation house. All three survived into the twentieth century, and their early memories involved the house their parents built.[13]

Susan Lawton McLeod died in 1859,[14] leaving William with his small children. He was quickly remarried, to Martha Stiles Royall, the twenty-four-year-old daughter of Croskeys Royall of James Island.[15]

William McLeod was outspoken in his support for secession, and he joined the Confederate Army in 1861. His wife died in August of that year, and when James Island was evacuated, it was probably his brother John who took the family upcountry to Greenwood.[16] First Confederate and then Union forces used the McLeod House as a field hospital and officers' headquarters. W. W. McLeod died in early 1865 without returning home,[17] but eventually his children reclaimed the property.

William Wallace McLeod II took up the north portion of his father's plantation, with the dwelling. The exterior of the house was substantially remodeled in 1926 with the construction of a monumental portico at the north elevation, but the interior retains much of its original appearance. The house and a small surrounding tract of farmland remained in the McLeod family until the 1990s.

1. *Charleston Courier*, November 29, 1816.
2. *Charleston Courier*, December 1827.
3. "Proposed Restoration and Interpretation: McLeod Plantation, James Island, South Carolina" (Charleston: Sea Island Historical Society for Historic Charleston Foundation, 1999).
4. "Will of William McKenzie Parker," Charleston County Wills, Book 38, p. 762, Charleston County Public Library.
5. South Carolina Marriage Settlements, Book 5Q, p. 371; Book 6E, p. 158, South Carolina Department of Archives and History.

6. "McLeod Plantation."
7. "Will of Sarah P. Parker," Charleston County Wills, Book 44, p. 183, CCPL.
8. *Charleston Courier*, December 1850.
9. "McLeod Plantation."
10. Tax Returns, 1824, SCDAH.
11. "McLeod Plantation."
12. Agricultural Schedules, U.S. Census, St. Andrew's Parish, 1860.
13. "Family of Rev. John McLeod" in "Conservation and Development Plan, McLeod Plantation, James Island, South Carolina" (Gainesville, GA: Jaeger/Pyburn, Inc., for Historic Charleston Foundation, 1991).
14. *Charleston Mercury*, March 21, 1859.
15. Mildred Keller Hood, "Cemetery Inscriptions of Charleston County, South Carolina" (Charleston Chapter, South Carolina Genealogical Society, 1997), p. 69.
16. "McLeod Plantation."
17. Charleston County Probate Court, Inventories & Appraisements, 1864-67, p. 458, CCPL.

The Oaks
St. Helena Island

John Jeremiah Theus Pope of St. Helena and his wife, Mary Frampton Townsend of Edisto Island, spent most of their lives together in Beaufort and at Feliciana Plantation on St. Helena Island. By the mid-1850s, Mary's health had become precarious. To be closer to Beaufort, they decided to build a new house at The Oaks, a five-hundred-acre plantation between Chowan and Wallace creeks.[1] They set the building near the south bank of Chowan Creek, and raised it on a foundation of brick piers.

The Oaks Plantation House, ca. 1863 *(From the collections of the South Carolina Historical Society)*

The Oaks Plantation House is a Greek Revival sea island residence that incorporates the lateral rear wings characteristic of Beaufort construction. These two-story wings at either side of the pedimented rear stair tower each had a chimney, and enlarged the typical four-over-four room plan to ten rooms. The balanced rhythm of the five openings at the front core continues to a single window at the front of each rear wing, and the cornice of the main roof was carried around the porch. This two-tiered front porch with a nearly-flat hipped roof had heavy wood posts and a balustrade at both levels.

The Popes did not enjoy their new house long. Mary Townsend Pope died in February 1861,[2] and in the late fall of that year St. Helena Island was occupied by federal forces. The Oaks became a residence for officials of the Port Royal Experiment, an office for its chief agent, and the location of Laura Towne's first school (which became the well-known Penn Center). Miss Towne found the house "new and clean, about as nice as country-houses in Philadelphia..."[3]

J. J. T. Pope died in 1864 without returning home. The house and about half the acreage were eventually redeemed by his son Daniel Townsend Pope.[4] The hurricane of 1893 severely damaged The Oaks, and the porch was afterward rebuilt with a gabled second-level portico above a simple shed roof. The lateral wings have since been extended to each side.

1. Kate McChesney Bolls, *The Daniel Townsends of the South Carolina Islands, Their Forebears and Descendants* (Verona VA: 1975), p. 19. Bolls, "The Townsends of Edisto Island, Supplement to *The Daniel Townsends...* " (MS, 1977), pp. 15-30. Chalmers G. Davidson, *The Last Foray. The South Carolina Planters of 1860: A Sociological Study* (Columbia: University of South Carolina Press, 1971), p. 238.
2. Mabel Runnette, "Tombstone Inscriptions from St. Helena Island," in *South Carolina Historical Magazine* 35 (1934).
3. Guion Griffis Johnson, *A Social History of the Sea Islands with Special Reference to St. Helena Island, South Carolina* (Durham NC, 1930), pp. 109-110.
4. Theodore Rosengarten, *Tombee: Portrait of a Cotton Planter* (New York: William Morrow and Co., 1986), p. 290.

Youghal
Christ Church Parish

Although Youghal Plantation, north of Mount Pleasant, was not a sea island cotton plantation, the house there was built by a sea island cotton planter. In 1856, Edward Fuller, formerly of Edisto Island, bought the 876-acre Youghal from Joshua Toomer,[1] and set about constructing a house.

Fuller's residence was a two-and-a-half-story frame building with a foundation of brick piers five to six feet in height, with a one-story hipped porch across the southeast façade and tripartite window at the pedimented gable end. Built on the twin-parlor plan, the house had four French doors accessing the two front rooms, which were connected by a cased opening. The parlors each had two side windows and a doorway to the rear stair hall; the smaller rear rooms had only one side window. Trim throughout the interior was very simple, in keeping with the late-1850s construction.[2]

The builder, Edward N. Fuller, was a son of Sarah Green Porteous and Benjamin Fuller, a St. Andrews Parish planter.[3] After attending Princeton, Edward began planting on Edisto Island, and in 1839 married Mary Ann Mikell.[4] By 1850 the Fuller household included Edward (29), Mary Ann (26), Edward (8), Catherine (6), Margaret (4), Sarah (2), William (6 months), and Edward's seventy-one-year-old mother.

Fuller had brought money to the marriage, and perhaps slaves as well, but their plantation, known as Governor's Bluff, was Mary Ann's legacy from her father Ephraim Mikell.[5] Here, "although a younger man than most of his fellow planters, he soon outstripped them by the most scientific and systematic methods he employed in raising sea island cotton. He was the

Youghal Plantation House, 1952 *(Courtesy of Mrs. Judy Byrd)*

first of them to use manufactured fertilizers. This is long before the value of Carolina phosphate rock was known, but a commercial fertilizer known as Mape's superphosphate was somewhat used at the north, and Mr. Fuller introduced its use in this part of the world."[6]

In 1856, Fuller had the opportunity to become an official of a new enterprise, the Southwestern Railroad Bank. Preparing to move to Charleston, he and Mary Ann sold their Edisto Island plantation to her brother I. Jenkins Mikell. Mikell paid $13,000 for Governor's Bluff, 170 acres of high land and thirty acres of marsh.[7] Having paid only $6,000 for Youghal, Fuller had ample funds with which to build a country house.

Edward Fuller's house in Christ Church Parish is very similar in appearance to other sea island cotton planters' dwellings. He is known to have brought some of his slaves from Edisto to Charleston;[8] among them may have been carpenters and builders. Regardless of his satisfaction with the completed house, he did not hold it long. In January 1858, he sold Youghal Plantation to George Buist Lamb of Charleston for $12,000.[9] The price of the property, its acreage unchanged, had increased by $6,000—a reasonable value for a new house in the late 1850s. Edward Fuller settled in Charleston full-time, remaining there until his death in 1896.

The unoccupied Youghal house burned in 1992.

1. Charleston County Register of Mesne Conveyance, Deed Book T13, p. 95.
2. Michael Trinkley, ed., "National Register Evaluation of 38CH932, Youghal Plantation, Charleston County, South Carolina" (Columbia: Chicora Foundation, Inc., 2003).
3. "Edward N. Fuller," obituary in *News & Courier*, May 23, 1896.
4. Brent Holcomb, *Marriage and Death Notices from the Charleston Observer 1827-1845* (Columbia, 1980), p. 154.
5. "Will of Ephraim Mikell," Charleston County Wills, Book 41, p. 717, Charleston County Public Library.
6. "Edward N. Fuller."
7. Charleston County RMC, Deed Book R13, p. 255.
8. Jessie A. Butler, "Interview with Ex-Slave (Susan Hamlin), Project #1655," in George P. Rawick, *The American Slave: A Composite Autobiography* (Westport, CT, 1992), pp. 226-232.
9. Charleston County RMC, Deed Book T13, p. 241.

Ashe's/Little Edisto/Windsor
Edisto Island

The house now called Windsor stands on Little Edisto Island, facing south over Russell Creek. With its broad gabled roof and deep front porch, this weatherboarded house is an excellent example of the square-built cotton planter's residence. Above a high brick pier foundation, the building has two full stories and a finished attic level lit by tripartite windows. The ground level was originally open, and, like the attic, is without fireplaces. Four rooms on each of the main floors are separated by wide central hallways opening to the porch with double doors. The first floor entry is distinguished by unusual hexagonal-paned sidelights.

John Ashe of Charleston and St. Paul's Parish died in 1828, bequeathing rice and cotton plantations to his children, and directing his executors to sell several other tracts. Among them was a "piece of land on Edisto Island called Russell's Point, containing about 570 acres..."[1] This was advertised for sale in 1831: "...about 570 acres high land of the first quality for the cultivation of sea island Cotton, and 300 of hard Marsh. On the premises are all the necessary buildings, in good repair."[2] The advertisement did not mention a dwelling house.

Edward C. Whaley of Old Dominion Plantation bought the Ashe plantation.[3] With nine children, most of whom survived to adulthood, Whaley acquired likely plantations as they

Ashe's/Little Edisto Plantation House, 2003 *(Courtesy of Bruce G. Harvey)*

became available, while teaching his sons the essentials of sea island cotton. By 1850, his elder sons were planting on their own, but twenty-two-year-old Mikell (Ephraim Mikell Whaley) and the younger children still lived in their father's household.

In April 1857, E. Mikell Whaley married his first cousin Abigail Mikell Baynard.[4] Abbie had just turned eighteen. Just about a year later, Edward C. Whaley gave his son the "southwest corner of my plantation known as Ashe's or Little Edisto,"[5] the portion nearest Russell Creek. This parcel is evidently where the house was erected. Whaley wrote his will the next month, devising the entire Little Edisto plantation to Mikell.[6]

The Whaleys' house was nearly new in 1860, and already home to Mikell, Abbie, and baby Edward, as well as to Clarence and Sarah Whaley, the teenaged orphans of Mikell's brother Joseph.[7] E. Mikell Whaley had begun his career well. With the labor of 116 of his father's slaves,[8] and probably some of those belonging to Clarence and Sarah, he produced 112 bags of sea island cotton in 1859.

Adjacent to the land his father had given him was a 300-acre tract that came to E. M. Whaley through his wife. This well-established plantation, with 240 acres of cleared land and cabins for fifty slaves, had been purchased from Dr. Edward Mitchell's executors in 1857 by Abbie's father William G. Baynard as her marriage portion.[9] In addition to these operations, in 1860 Mikell Whaley was superintending the plantation of his brother Benjamin, a Charleston lawyer.

The Civil War erupted before the Edward C. Whaley and William G. Baynard estates had been fully settled. By the time the war ended, three more children had been born to Abbie and Mikell Whaley, but of their nine children, only four lived to adulthood. Eva, the youngest, and her husband Charles Seabrook eventually settled at Baynard's Old Place just across Russell Creek from Little Edisto Island. J. Swinton Whaley lived in his parents' home, and gained a measure of fame by planting the last crops of sea island cotton on Edisto Island.[10]

---

1. "Will of John Ashe," Charleston County Wills, Book 38, p. 453, Charleston County Public Library.
2. *Charleston Courier*, February 1831.
3. Charleston County Register of Mesne Conveyance, Deed Book I10, p. 30.
4. James Garner Patey, *The Whaley Family and Its Charleston Connection* (Spartanburg: The Reprint Company, 1992), p. 43.
5. Charleston County RMC, Deed Book L14, p. 81.
6. "Will of Edward Whaley," Charleston County Wills, Book 48, p. 601, CCPL.
7. Population Schedules, U.S. Census, St. John's Colleton Parish, 1860.
8. Charleston County Inventories, Book F, p. 36, CCPL.
9. *Charleston Courier*, October 22, 1857. Charleston County RMC, Deed Book X13, p. 295. "Will of William G. Baynard," Charleston County Wills, Book 49, p. 886, CCPL.
10. Clara Childs Puckette, *Edisto, A Sea Island Principality* (Cleveland, OH: Seaforth Publications, 1978), p. 14.

Rose Hill
St. Luke's Parish

The Gothic Revival style of Rose Hill, built about 1859 on the mainland of St. Luke's Parish, is unique in the sea island cotton area. Built close to the ground, the south-facing house with board-and-batten siding and a steeply pitched cross-gable roof shares few architectural similarities with contemporary plantation residences. Its plan is one of projections and irregularities. The principal portico, recessed beneath the prominent front gable, is extended by a very shallow shed-roofed porch along the façade. Double windows at the upper levels are set in pointed-arched surrounds or topped by peaked-gable false dormers.

Rose Hill was built for Dr. John William Kirk, a graduate of South Carolina College and the University of Pennsylvania, and his wife Caroline Kirk.[1] John William and Caroline were

Rose Hill Plantation House, 1986 *(Historic American Buildings Survey, Library of Congress)*

first cousins; their fathers were William Kirk, a Savannah River planter, and James Kirk of Kirk's Bluff, on May River near the village of Bluffton.

The father of nine, in 1849 James Kirk owned 3,000 acres in St. Luke's Parish, producing 120 bags of sea island cotton. His son-in-law John William Kirk practiced medicine in Bluffton and planted 700 improved acres in St. Luke's Parish (mostly food crops and a small quantity of rice), while Caroline raised their two children, Emily and William John.

James Kirk died in late 1850, and his widow Mary died about a year later. Married since 1836, Caroline and her husband were not young when they inherited part of James's large estate, but John William began planting cotton, and in 1859 made fifty-one bags on his 2,200 acres, 1,000 acres of which was improved land.

By now their children were nearly grown. Emily was finishing her education at Barhamville Academy, and William was being prepared for further studies by his Scots tutor, Robertson Reid.[2] Nevertheless, the Kirks set out to build this unusual dwelling on Rose Hill, a healthy and fertile tract alongside the Colleton River.

The design of the building must have been taken from a pattern book, or created by an architect. There is a tradition that it was the work of a "French architect Dimmick," who was also involved in building Bluffton's Church of the Cross, designed by Charleston architect E. B. White.[3] Dimmick was likely the builder of Rose Hill. The 1860 census shows John Dimmick, a fifty-four-year-old carpenter born in Massachusetts, living in the village of Bluffton.

The Civil War began before the house was entirely finished. When Hilton Head was captured, the Kirks evacuated to Grahamville, a slightly safer inland village, where Caroline died in 1864. Neither John William Kirk nor his son ever occupied the Rose Hill house, although it was complete enough to serve as a tenant house for years. The building remained in the Kirk family until 1928. It was restored in 1946.[4]

---

1. Chalmers G. Davidson, *The Last Foray. The South Carolina Planters of 1860: A Sociological Study* (Columbia: University of South Carolina Press, 1971), p. 217.
2. Edward Kirk Webb, "Kirk Family Letters 1803-1868" (Charleston: privately printed, 1977).
3. Beatrice St. Julien Ravenel, *Architects of Charleston* (Charleston: Carolina Art Association, 1945), p. 198. William P. Baldwin, *Plantations of the Lowcountry, South Carolina 1697-1865* (Greensboro, NC: Legacy Publications, 1985), p. 143.
4. Baldwin, *Plantations*, pp. 141-143.

SEA ISLAND PLANTATIONS

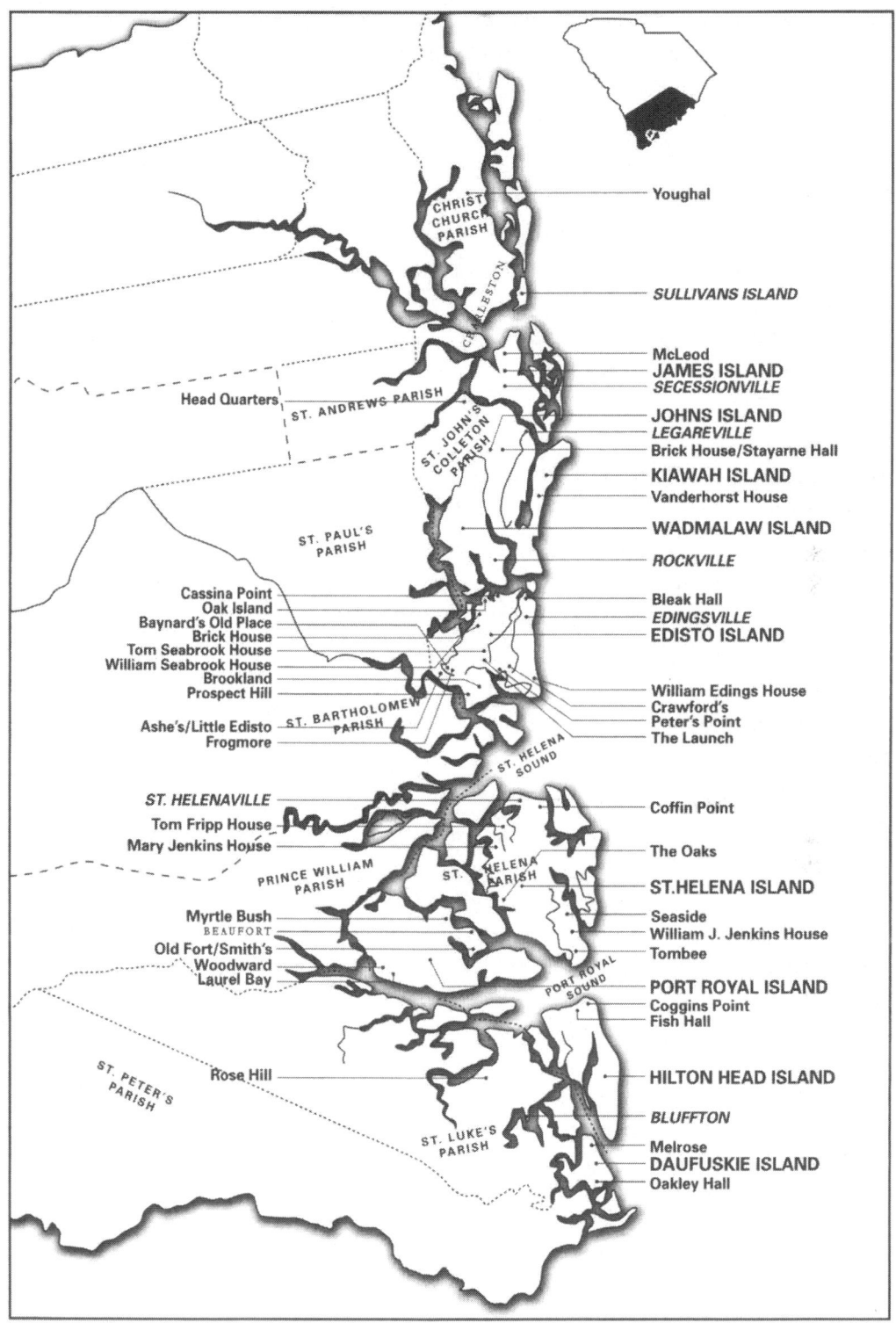

Sea Island Cotton plantation residences and planter's summer villages

Appendix I
Patents

In addition to all of the U.S. Patents mentioned in the text, the author includes other patents that may prove useful to future scholars on sea island cotton or related subjects.

Early patents were not numbered, and many were destroyed in a fire in 1836. After the fire, the Patent Office began numbering patents. The office went back through its records and assigned numbers to the pre-1836 patents, adding an X at the end to distinguish them. Unfortunately, the office could not track many inventors to obtain duplicate copies of their patents and diagrams and descriptions; these are lost forever.

December 6, 1803	Joseph Eve. MACHINE FOR SEPARATING COTTON SEED FROM COTTON. Patent No. 502X.
November 18, 1816	Englehart Cruse, Charleston, South Carolina. COTTON GIN. Patent No. 2700X.
November 6, 1826	Isaac B. Barnes, Beaufort, South Carolina. COMMON FOOT COTTON GIN. Patent No. 4559X.
August 10, 1827	J. Reed, Marshfield, Massachusetts. SEA-ISLAND COTTON CLEANER. Patent No. 4849X.
March 7, 1834	William Whittemore Jr., West Cambridge, Massachusetts. COTTON ROLLER-GIN. Patent No. 8049X.
May 29, 1835	William Whittemore Jr., West Cambridge, Massachusetts. COTTON ROLLER-GIN. Patent No. 8857X.
September 27, 1838	Eleazer Carver, Bridgewater, Massachusetts. IMPROVEMENT IN ROLLER COTTON-GINS FOR GINNING LONG-STAPLE AND OTHER KINDS OF COTTON. Patent No. 949.
May 25, 1839	William Whittemore Jr., West Cambridge, Massachusetts. IMPROVEMENT IN COTTON-GINS FOR CLEANING COTTON. Patent No. 1158.
July 3, 1840	Fones McCarthy, Demopolis, Alabama. IMPROVEMENT IN COTTON-GINS. Patent No. 1675.
January 17, 1842	Eleazer Carver, Bridgewater, Massachusetts. IMPROVEMENT IN ROLLER-GINS FOR GINNING LONG-STAPLE COTTON. Patent No. 2429.
February 2, 1844	Richard Reynolds Jr., Beaufort, South Carolina. IMPROVEMENT IN ROLLER COTTON-GINS. Patent No. 3425.
February 12, 1845	Fones McCarthy, Demopolis, Alabama. COTTON CLEANER. Patent No. 3912.
December 11, 1845	Theodore Ely, New York, New York. IMPROVEMENT IN ROLLER COTTON-GINS. Patent No. 4302.
November 14, 1848	John Schley, Columbus, Georgia. IMPROVEMENT IN ROLLER COTTON-GINS. Patent No. 5921.
May 22, 1849	William Y. Layton, Darlington, South Carolina. IMPROVEMENT IN COTTON-GINS. Patent No. 6463.
April 27, 1852	Calvin Willey Jr., Chicago, Illinois. IMPROVEMENT IN GINS FOR LONG STAPLES OF COTTON. Patent No. 8907.

APPENDIX I

April 18, 1854	Fones McCarthy, Demopolis, Alabama. IMPROVEMENT IN COTTON-GINS. Patent No. 262 (reissue).
August 14, 1855	John Simpson, Lewisville, South Carolina. IMPROVEMENT IN COTTON-GINS. Patent No. 13,441.
1856	Fones McCarthy, Demopolis, Alabama. COTTON GIN. Patent No. 1675 (reissue).
June 17, 1856	L. John Mallard and William S. Baker, Riceborough, Georgia. IMPROVEMENT IN FEEDERS FOR ROLLER COTTON-GINS. Patent No. 15,138.
March 9, 1858	Francis L. Wilkerson, Adams Run, South Carolina. MPROVEMENT IN COTTON-GINS. Patent No. 19,598.
September 1, 1863	Israel F. Brown, New London, Connecticut. IMPROVEMENT IN COTTON-GINS. Patent No. 39,767.
November 15, 1864	William Wanklyn, Albion Mills, Bury, England. IMPROVEMENT IN THE ROLLERS FOR COTTON-GINS. Patent No. 45,109.
January 3, 1865	Israel F. Brown, New London, Connecticut. IMPROVEMENT IN ROLLERS FOR COTTON-GINS. Patent No. 45,695.
July 9, 1867	A. Fessenden, Beaufort, South Carolina. COTTON-GIN. Patent No. 66,577.
July 30, 1867	Fones McCarthy, Orange Springs, Florida. IMPROVEMENT IN COTTON-GINS. Patent No. 67,327.
August 13, 1867	J. W. Kokemuller, Bluffton, South Carolina. IMPROVEMENT IN COTTON-GINS. Patent No. 67,773.
May 30, 1870	James M. Albertson, New London, Connecticut. IMPROVEMENT IN THE CONSTRUCTION OF HORSE-POWER FOR COTTON-GINS. Patent No. 103,821.
October 10, 1871	William R. Wright, Barnwell County, South Carolina, and David A. Warnock, Beaufort County, South Carolina. IMPROVEMENT IN HORSE-POWERS. Patent No. 119,909.
June 24, 1873	Thomas H. Rushton and William Dobson, Bolton, England. IMPROVEMENT IN COTTON-GIN KNIFE-ROLLERS. Patent No. 140,218.
June 9, 1903	Leland L. Foss, Manassas, Georgia. ROLLER-GIN. Patent No. 730,449.
June 23, 1903	Leland L. Foss, Manassas, Georgia. ROLLER-GIN. Patent No. 731,561.
February 8, 1910	John C. Boesch, Charleston, South Carolina, and J. H. H. Von Oven. COTTON-GIN. Patent No. 948,810.
July 29, 1924	James S. Townsend, Charleston, South Carolina. ATTACHMENT FOR ROLLER COTTON GINS. Patent No. 1,503,077.

Appendix II
Scientific Names of Plants

Taxonomy for these common plant names mentioned in the text is based on *Wildflowers of South Carolina* (Porcher and Rayner 2001).

American holly	*Ilex opaca* Aiton
Basswood	*Tilia heterophylla* Vent
Beach evening-primrose	*Oenothera drummondii* Hooker
Beach pea	*Strophostyles helvola* (L.) Elliott
Black gum	*Nyssa sylvatica* Marshall
Blackjack oak	*Quercus marilandica* Muenchh.
Bull bay	*Magnolia grandiflora* L.
Cabbage palmetto	*Sabal palmetto* (Walter) Loddiges
Camphorweed	*Heterotheca subaxillaris* (Lamarck) Britton & Rusby
Carolina buckthorn	*Rhamnus caroliniana* Walter
Carolina cherry laurel	*Prunus caroliniana* Aiton
Carolina saltwort	*Salsola caroliniana* Walter
Cedar	*Juniperus virginiana* L.
Chinquapin	*Castanea pumila* (L.) Miller
Crested coral-root	*Hexalectris spicata* (Walter) Barnhart
Devil-joint	*Opuntia pusilla* (Halworth) Nuttall
Dogwood	*Cornus florida* L.
Dune sandbur	*Cenchrus tribuloides* L.
Dunes evening-primrose	*Oenothera humifusa* Nuttall
Dunes greenbrier	*Smilax auriculata* Walter
Dwarf buckeye	*Aesculus pavia* L.
Fetterbush	*Lyonia lucida* (Lamarck) K. Koch
Galactia	*Galactia elliottii* Nuttall
Godfrey's forestira	*Forestiera godfreyi* L.C. Anderson
Groundsel-tree	*Baccharis halimifolia* L.
Hackberry	*Celtis laevigata* Willdenow
Hairy wicky	*Kalmia hirsuta* Walter
Hercules'-club	*Zanthoxylum clava-herculis* L.
Honey-cups	*Zenobia pulverulenta* (Bartram) Pollard
Horseweed	*Erigeron canadensis* var. *pusillus* (Nuttall) Ahles
Huckleberry	*Gaylussacia frondosa* (L.) Torrey & Gray ex Torrey
Indian midden morning-glory	*Ipomoea macrorhiza* Michaux
Inkberry	*Ilex glabra* (L.) Gray
Japanese honeysuckle	*Lonicera japonica* Thunberg
Laurel oak	*Quercus laurifolia* Michaux
Live oak	*Quercus virginiana* Miller
Loblolly pine	*Pinus taeda* L.
Longleaf pine	*Pinus palustris* Miller
Marsh-elder	*Iva frutescens* (L.) Augustin de Candole

Mottled trillium	Trillium maculatum Rafinesque
Needle rush	Juncus roemerianus Scheele
Perennial glasswort	Salicornia virginica L.
Poison ivy	Rhus radicans L.
Pond pine	Pinus serotina Michaux
Prickly-pear cactus	Opuntia compressa (Salisbury) Macbride
Red bay	Persea borbonia (L.) Sprengel
Rough-leaved dogwood	Cornus asperifolia Michaux
Running oak	Quercus pumila Walter
Rusty lyonia	Lyonia ferruginea (Walter) Nuttall
Salt grass	Distichlis spicata (L.) Greene
Saltmarsh aster	Aster tenuifolius L.
Saltwort	Batis maritima L.
Sand vine	Cynanchium palustre (Pursh) Heller
Saw palmetto	Sabal palmetto (Walter) Loddiges
Scrubby post oak	Quercus margaretta Ashe
Sea lavender	Limonium carolinianum (Walter) Britton
Sea oats	Uniola paniculata L.
Sea ox-eye	Borrichia frutescens (L.) Augustin de Candole
Sea rocket	Cakile harperi Small
Seabeach amaranth	Amaranthus pumilus Rafinesque
Seaside goldenrod	Solidago sempervirens L.
Seaside panicum	Panicum amarum Elliott
Seaside pennywort	Hydrocotyle bonariensis Lamarck
Shell-mound buckthorn	Sageretia minutiflora (Michaux) Mohr
Slash pine	Pinus elliottii Engelmann
Smooth cordgrass	Spartina alterniflora Loiseleur
Southern evergreen blueberry	Vaccinium myrsinites Lamarck
Southern red cedar	Juniperus silicicola (Small) Bailey
Southern sugar maple	Acer barbatum Michaux
Sweet bay	Magnolia virginica L.
Sweet gallberry	Ilex coriacea (Pursh) Chapman
Sweet gum	Nyssa biflora Walter
Sweet pepperbush	Clethra alnifolia L.
Sweetgrass	Muhlenbergia filipes M. A. Curtis
Trailing bluet	Houstonia procumbens (J.F. Gmelin) Standley
Tough bumelia	Bumelia tenax (L.) Willdenow
Vanilla plant	Carphephorus odoratissimus (J.F. Gmelin) Herbert
Virginia creeper	Parthenocissus quinquefolia (L.) Planchon
Yaupon	Ilex vomitoria Aiton
Walter's milkweed	Asclepias cinerea Walter
Wax myrtle	Myrica cerifera L. var. cerifera
White oak	Quercus alba L.
Wild olive	Osmanthus americana (L.) Gray

Appendix III
Plantation Families

Marriages among the sea island cotton families created a tightly-knit community of relatives. With so many marriages between close cousins, relationships can be difficult to chart. Early death was common, and second or third marriages routine. It was not unusual for a man to marry his deceased wife's sister (who was the aunt of his children), or for a widow to marry her husband's brother. Long-lived men and women had offspring spanning nearly a generation, so a father and son could both find appropriate mates in sisters widely separated in age.

The repetitive use of a few given names within each family is more confusing for the researcher than it must have been for the planters' contemporaries, for whom these were living people. Reference to birth and/or death dates is the modern tool for keeping individuals separate, and it reflects the nineteenth-century usage of the appellations "Sr." and "Jr." These did not consistently refer to father and son, but as often indicated the comparative ages of two men with the same name who might be uncle and nephew or fairly distant cousins.

Upon her marriage, an antebellum woman changed her name differently from today's practice, dropping her father's surname but retaining her middle name. Ann Ninian Jenkins became Ann Ninian Baynard; Mary Baynard Edings became Mary Baynard Pope.

Some families have members represented in the stories of several plantations discussed in this work. While not comprehensive (for many individuals we do not include all the children or even all the spouses), this summary of families will assist the reader who encounters duplicate names and complicated relationships. The information was drawn from a number of genealogical charts and secondary sources as well as primary documents. There are contradictions among the sources about birth and death dates (and sometimes ancestry), and we acknowledge that there are surely some inaccuracies in this document.

Properties and Their Residents

ASHE'S/LITTLE EDISTO, EDISTO ISLAND
Ephraim Mikell Whaley (1828-1900) and Abigail Mikell Baynard (1839-1905)
James Swinton Whaley (1861-1932) and Sarah Ann Seabrook (1863-1915)

BAYNARD'S OLD PLACE, EDISTO ISLAND
William Baynard (1732-1772) and Elizabeth Grimball (1735-1773)
Thomas Baynard (1763-1805) and Sarah Calder
Edward Mitchell Baynard (1830-1882) and Catherine Baynard (1831-1893)
Charles Whaley Seabrook (1876-1959) and Eva Irene Whaley (1879-1947)

BRICK HOUSE, EDISTO ISLAND
Joseph Jenkins (1761-1828) and Elizabeth Evans (1767-1826)
Joseph Evans Jenkins (1793-1874) and Ann Jenkins Fripp (1798-1878)

BROOKLAND, EDISTO ISLAND
Gabriel Seabrook (1765-1824) and Ann Mikell (1769-1809)
Ephraim Mikell Seabrook (1797-1846) and Elizabeth Mary Hanahan (1802-1888)
Henry Seabrook (1836-1872)

CASSINA POINT, EDISTO ISLAND
Carolina Lafayette Seabrook (1825-1879) and James Hopkinson (1810-1875)

COGGINS POINT, HILTON HEAD ISLAND
Sarah Green and William Pope Sr. (d. 1823)
William Pope Jr. (1788-1862) and Ann Scott
William Pope Jr. (1788-1862) and Sarah Lavinia Pope
William John Pope (1813-1852) and Hephzibah J. Pope (1824-1849)

CRAWFORD'S, EDISTO ISLAND
William Archibald Mikell (1815-1840) and Hess Marion Waring Smith (c. 1817-1904)
Hess Marion Waring Smith (c. 1817-1904) and William Edings (1809-1858)
William James Whaley (1819-1888) and Martha Mary Murray Clark (1821-1850)
William James Whaley (1819-1888) and Mary Wayne (1828-1886)

FISH HALL, HILTON HEAD ISLAND
Samuel Green (d. c. 1767)
Sarah Green and William Pope Sr. (d. 1823)
John Edward Pope (d. c. 1837) and Mary Baynard Edings (c. 1800-1856)
Emma Catherine Pope (d. 1854) and Thomas F. Drayton (1808-1891)

FROGMORE, EDISTO ISLAND
Edward Mitchell (1788-1855) and Eliza Grimball Baynard (1794-1857)
Rachel Mitchell (1818-1889) and William Whaley (1817-1879)
Edward Charles Whaley (1826-1887) and Abigail Mikell Whaley (1830-c. 1879)

HEAD QUARTERS (FENWICK HALL), JOHNS ISLAND
Daniel Jenkins Townsend (1811-1885) and Henrietta Evans (d. 1842)
Daniel Jenkins Townsend (1811-1885) and Susan Lavinia Swinton (1822-1866)

THE LAUNCH, EDISTO ISLAND
William Evans (d. 1802) and Mary Elizabeth Edings (1778-1848)
Mary Elizabeth Edings (1778-1848) and Dr. Robert Trail Chisolm (1771-1821)
Susan Matilda Harriet Chisolm (1807-1865) and Oliver Hering Middleton (1798-1892)

LAUREL BAY, PORT ROYAL ISLAND
Nathaniel Barnwell (1705-1775) and Mary Gibbes (1722-1801)
Robert Gibbes Barnwell (1761-1814) and Elizabeth Hayne Wigg (1775-1823)
William Hazzard Wigg Barnwell (1806-1863) and Catherine Osborn Barnwell (1809-1886)

MARY JENKINS PLANTATION, ST. HELENA ISLAND
Mary Sarah Chaplin (1792-1876) and William Jenkins (1782-c. 1830)

MYRTLE BUSH, PORT ROYAL ISLAND
Col. Edward Barnwell (1757-1808)
Thomas Osborn Barnwell (1815-1879) and Jean Kerr Richardson (1811-1888)

OAK ISLAND, EDISTO ISLAND
William Seabrook Jr. (1799-1860) and Martha Washington Edings (1799-1892)
John Edward Seabrook (b. 1830) and Elizabeth Baynard Whaley (1837-1895)

THE OAKS, ST. HELENA ISLAND
John Jeremiah Theus Pope (1799-1864) and Mary Frampton Townsend (1804-1861)

APPENDIX III

OLD FORT, PORT ROYAL ISLAND
John Joyner Smith (1790-1872) and Mary Gibbes Barnwell (1795-1853)
John Joyner Smith (1790-1872) and Mary D. B. Duncan (1829-1861)

PETER'S POINT, EDISTO ISLAND
Christopher Jenkins (1769-1794) and Mary Wilkinson (1770-1813)
Isaac Jenkins Mikell (1808-1881) and Amarinthia Jenkins Townsend (1810-1852)
Isaac Jenkins Mikell (1808-1881) and Mary Martha Pope (1829-1862)
Isaac Jenkins Mikell (1808-1881) and Sarah Georgiana Lee (1824-1905)

PROSPECT HILL, EDISTO ISLAND
William Baynard (1766-1802) and Elizabeth Ann Mikell (1773-1815)
William Grimball Baynard (1792-1861) and Ann Ninian Jenkins (1792-1822)
William Grimball Baynard (1792-1861) and Mary Bailey Swinton (1808-1890)

SEASIDE, ST. HELENA ISLAND
Edgar Fripp (1806-1860) and Eliza Fripp (1810-1860)
Edgar Walter Fripp (1857-1920)

TOM SEABROOK'S HOUSE, EDISTO ISLAND
Thomas Bannister Seabrook (1765-1839) and Elizabeth Clark (1779-1817)
William Baynard Whaley (1821-1857) and Martha Mary Hanahan (1823-1870)
Arthur Murray Whaley (1847-1926) and Susan Providence Bailey (1855-1931)

TOMBEE, ST. HELENA ISLAND
Thomas Benjamin Chaplin (b. 1742) and Elizabeth Fripp (1750-1790)
Saxby Chaplin (1780-1828) and Isabella Field (1785-1864)
Thomas Benjamin Chaplin (1822-1890) and Mary Thomson McDowell (1822-1851)
Thomas Benjamin Chaplin (1822-1890) and Sophy Creighton (d. 1891)

WILLIAM EDINGS HOUSE, EDISTO ISLAND
William Edings (1766-1836) and Sarah Evans (d. 1857)
John Evans Edings (1808-1836) and Mary Wilkinson Mathews (b. 1809)

WILLIAM J. JENKINS HOUSE, ST. HELENA ISLAND
Dr. William J. Jenkins (1818-1883) and Eliza Mary Chaplin (1825-1894)

WILLIAM SEABROOK HOUSE, EDISTO ISLAND
William Seabrook (1773-1836) and Mary Ann Mikell (1779-1818)
William Seabrook (1773-1836) and Emma Elizabeth Edings (1793-1856)
John Evans Edings, Jr. (1832-1883) and Josephine Edings Seabrook (c. 1834-1883)

WOODWARD, PORT ROYAL ISLAND
Robert Woodward Barnwell (1801-1882) and Eliza Barnwell (1807-1891)

YOUGHAL, CHRIST CHURCH PARISH
Edward Nathaniel Fuller (1820-1896) and Mary Ann Mikell (1822-1899)

Family Names

BARNWELL

John "Tuscarora Jack" Barnwell died in 1724 leaving six daughters and two sons: Nathaniel Barnwell (1705-1775) and John Barnwell (1712-1782).

I. Nathaniel Barnwell (1705-1775) and Mary Gibbes (1722-1801) were the parents of John Barnwell (1748-1800), Edward Barnwell (1757-1808), and Robert Gibbes Barnwell (1761-1814).
   A. John Barnwell (1748-1800) married Anne Hutson (1755-1817).
      1. John Gibbes Barnwell (1778-1828) of Coosaw Island married Sarah Bull (1782-1862).
         a. Eliza Barnwell (1807-1891) married Robert Woodward Barnwell (1801-1882).
   B. Col. Edward Barnwell (1757-1808) was first married to Mary Bower Williamson (1762-1789).
      1. Capt. Edward Barnwell, Jr. (1785-1860) of Keans Neck married first Elizabeth Osborn (1789-1824).
         a. Catherine Osborn Barnwell (1809-1886) married William Hazzard Wigg Barnwell (1806-1863).
         b. Thomas Osborn Barnwell (1815-1879) of Myrtle Bush Plantation married Jean Kerr Richardson (1811-1888).
      1. Capt. Edward Barnwell, Jr. (1785-1860) married second Eliza Zubly Smith (1803-1846), sister of John Joyner Smith (1790-1872).
   B. Col. Edward Barnwell (1757-1808) married second Mary Hutson Wigg (1774-1854).
      2. William Wigg Barnwell (1793-1856) married Sarah Reeve Gibbes (1796-1858).
         a. Bower Williamson Barnwell (1825-1895)
      3. Mary Gibbes Barnwell (1795-1853) married John Joyner Smith (1790-1872) of Old Fort Plantation.
   C. Robert Gibbes Barnwell (1761-1814) of Laurel Bay Plantation married Elizabeth Hayne Wigg (1775-1823).
      1. Robert Woodward Barnwell (1801-1882) of Woodward Plantation married Eliza Barnwell (1807-1891).
         a. John Gibbes Barnwell (1831-1888)
      2. William Hazzard Wigg Barnwell (1806-1863) of Laurel Bay Plantation married Catherine Osborn Barnwell (1809-1886).
         a. Stephen Elliott Barnwell (1842-1923)
         b. Joseph Walker Barnwell (1846-1930)

II. John Barnwell (1712-1782) married Martha Chaplin (1720-1792).
   A. Catherine Barnwell (1740-c. 1785) married Andrew DeVeaux (1736-c. 1785).
      1. Catherine DeVeaux (1759-1829), widow of Nicholas Lechmere, married John Ashe (d. 1828).
      2. Martha DeVeaux (b. 1763) married Joseph Seabrook (1750-1831).

BAYNARD

William Baynard (1732-1772) and Elizabeth Grimball (1735-1773) were the parents of two sons, Thomas (1763-1805) and William (1766-1802).

I. Thomas Baynard (1763-1805) of Baynard's Old Place married Sarah Calder.

A. John C. Baynard
B. William Edings Baynard (1800-1849) of Hilton Head married Catherine Adelaide Scott (1812-1856).
   1. Catherine Baynard (1831-1893) married Edward Mitchell Baynard (1830-1882).
C. Ephraim Mikell Baynard (1797-1865) of Rabbit Point Plantation, known as Edisto Island's "millionaire miser."
II. William Baynard (1766-1802) of Prospect Hill married first Sarah Black (1772-1793).
   A. William Grimball Baynard (1792-1861) of Prospect Hill married first Ann Ninian Jenkins (1792-1822).
      1. Thomas Archibald Baynard
   A. William Grimball Baynard (1792-1861) married second Mary Bailey Swinton (1808-1890).
      2. Edward Mitchell Baynard (1830-1882) of Baynard's Old Place married Catherine Baynard (1831-1893).
      3. Abigail Mikell Baynard (1839-1905) married Ephraim Mikell Whaley (1828-1900).
II. William Baynard (1766-1802) married second Elizabeth Mikell (1773-1815).
   B. Elizabeth Grimball Baynard (1794-1857) married Edward Mitchell (1788-1855) of Frogmore Plantation.
      1. Rachel Louisa Mitchell (1818-1889) married William Whaley (1817-1879).
      2. Esther Marion Mitchell (1829-1910) married William Edings Seabrook (1828-1889).
      3. William Grimball Baynard Mitchell (1822-1850) married Mary Wayne (1828-1886), who became the second wife of William James Whaley (1819-1888).
   C. Abigail Mikell Baynard (1797-1830) married Edward Charles Whaley (1790-1860).

CHAPLIN

John Chaplin (1682-1752) married Phoebe Ladson (1691-1764).
I. Phoebe Chaplin (1717-1794) married Joseph Jenkins (c. 1714-1770).
II. Martha Chaplin (1720-1792) married John Barnwell (1712-1782).
III. Elizabeth Chaplin (b. c. 1721) married John Evans (d. 1768).
   A. John Evans (1747-1775) married Sarah Fripp (1752-1846).
      1. Elizabeth Evans (1767-1826) married Joseph Jenkins (1761-1828).
IV. William Chaplin (1722-1779) married Sarah Saxby (1728-1765), widow of James Reynolds.
   A. William Francis Chaplin (1744-1795) married Martha Fripp (b. 1747).
      1. Thomas Chaplin (d. 1815) married Mary Jenkins.
         a. Mary Isabel Chaplin (1807-1837) married Benjamin Jenkins (1806-1836).
   B. Thomas Benjamin Chaplin (b. 1742) of Tombee Plantation married Elizabeth Fripp (1750-1790).
      1. John Fripp Chaplin (1765-1817) married Mary Fripp (b. c. 1769).
         a. Eliza Chaplin (1796-1842) married William Benjamin Fripp (1792-1853).
         b. Mary Sarah Chaplin (1792-1876) of Mary Jenkins Plantation married William Jenkins (1782-c. 1830).
      2. William Chaplin (1770-1818) married Sarah Jenkins (1766-1809).
      3. Benjamin Chaplin (1776-1851) married Elizabeth Hann Jenkins (1785-1867).
      4. Saxby Chaplin (1780-1828) of Tombee married Isabella Caroline Field (1785-1864).
         a. Thomas Benjamin Chaplin (1822-1890) of Tombee married Mary Thomson

McDowell (1822-1851) and then Sophy Creighton (d. 1891).
  5. Archibald Chaplin (1783-1849) married Martha Fripp (b. 1788).
    a. Eliza Mary Chaplin (1825-1894) married William J. Jenkins (1818-1883).
  C. Sarah Phoebe Chaplin (1778-1816) married Col. John J. Jenkins (1772-1822).
V. Sarah Chaplin (b. 1726) married William Field.
  A. John Cato Field married Elizabeth Perry.
    1. Isabella Caroline Field (1785-1864) married first Daniel Jenkins, and second Saxby Chaplin (1780-1828).

EDINGS

Benjamin Edings (1742-1784) and Mary Baynard (d. 1792) were survived by three children: William (1766-1836), Joseph (1770-1857), and Mary Elizabeth (1778-1848).
I. William Edings (1766-1836) of the William Edings House married Sarah Evans (d. 1857, sister of William Evans).
  A. Eliza Edings (1799-1823) married Benjamin Seabrook Whaley (1791-1832).
  B. John Evans Edings (1808-1836) married Mary Wilkinson Mathews (b. 1809).
    1. William M. Edings died in 1850.
    2. John Evans Edings, Jr., (1832-1883) married to Josephine Edings Seabrook (c. 1834-1883), owned the William Seabrook House.
II. Joseph Edings (1770-1857) married Sarah Scott (d. 1833).
  A. William Edings (1809-1858) married in turn Sarah Ann Mikell (1810-1838) and Hess Marion Waring Smith (c. 1817-1904), widow of William Archibald Mikell (1815-1840).
  B. Emma Elizabeth Edings (1793-1856) married William Seabrook (1773-1836) as his second wife.
  C. Martha Washington Edings (1799-1892), married William Seabrook Jr. (1799-1860).
  D. Mary Baynard Edings (c. 1800-1856) married John Edward Pope (d. c. 1837).
III. Mary Elizabeth Edings (1778-1848) of The Launch Plantation, widow of William Evans (d. 1802), married Dr. Robert Trail Chisolm (1771-1821).

FRIPP

John Fripp (1704-1739) of St. Helena Island had at least seven children, including John (1729-1781), William (1732-1794), and Paul (1737-1800).
I. John Fripp (1729-1781) married Elizabeth Hann (1725-c. 1775).
  A. Elizabeth Fripp (1750-1790) married Thomas Benjamin Chaplin (b. 1742).
  B. Sarah Fripp (1752-1846) married John Evans II (1747-1775).
    1. Elizabeth Evans (1767-1826) married Joseph Jenkins (1761-1828).
  C. Mary Fripp (1754-c. 1848) married John Jenkins (1750-1814).
  D. Paul Fripp (1762-1810) married Elizabeth Jenkins (1764-1837).
    1. Martha Fripp (b. 1788) married Archibald Chaplin (1783-1849).
    2. Ann Jenkins Fripp (1793-1878) married Joseph Evans Jenkins (1793-1874).
  E. Archibald Fripp (1766-1835) married Elizabeth Scott (1771-1849).
    1. Thomas James Fripp (1808-1840) of the Tom Fripp House was the father of Thomas James Fripp (1829-1862).
II. William Fripp (1732-1794) was first married to Tabitha Edings (1735-1769).
  A. Isaac Perry Fripp (b. c. 1766) married Mary Pope.

APPENDIX III

  1. Eliza Fripp (1810-1860) married Edgar Fripp (1806-1860).
 B. Mary Fripp (b. c. 1769) married John Fripp Chaplin (1765-1817).
II. William Fripp (1732-1794) married second Magdalene Meggett (1748-1794).
 C. James Fripp (1777-1811) married Mary (1778-1817, surname unknown).
  1. Edgar Fripp (1806-1860) of Seaside Plantation married Eliza Fripp (1810-1860).
III. Paul Fripp (1737-1800) married Amelia Reynolds (1752-1822).
 A. William Benjamin Fripp (1792-1853) married Eliza Chaplin (1796-1842).
  1. John Edwin Fripp (1831-1906) married Isabella Phoebe Jenkins (1833-1883).
   a. Edgar Walter Fripp (1857-1920) inherited Seaside Plantation.

JENKINS

John Jenkins (d. c. 1735) was married twice and the father of at least ten children. Among them were William (c. 1704-1758), Joseph (c. 1714-1770), Christopher (1716-1760), and Richard (1728-1772).

I. William Jenkins (c. 1704-1758) of Edisto Island married first Phoebe Clark.
 A. John Jenkins (1736-1764) married second Providence Grimball (b. 1738).
  1. Isaac Grimball Jenkins (1762-1794) married Margaret Wilkinson (1763-1823).
   a) Providence Jenkins (1784-1846) married Ephraim Mikell (1773-1838).
   b) Ann Ninian Jenkins (1792-1822) married William Grimball Baynard (1792-1861).
II. Joseph Jenkins (c. 1714-1770) of St. Helena Island married Phoebe Chaplin (1717-1794).
 A. John Jenkins (1750-1814) married Mary Fripp (1754-c. 1848).
  1. Daniel Jenkins (b. 1776) was the first husband of Isabella Caroline Field (1785-1864).
  2. Benjamin Jenkins (1778-1819) married Elizabeth Perry (b. 1782).
   a. Benjamin Jenkins (1806-1836) married Mary Isabel Chaplin (1807-1837).
    1. Isabella Phoebe Jenkins (1833-1883) married John Edwin Fripp (1831-1906).
   b. William J. Jenkins (1818-1883), builder of the William J. Jenkins House, married Eliza Mary Chaplin (1825-1894).
  3. William Jenkins (1782-c. 1830) married Mary Sarah Chaplin (1792-1876) of the Mary Jenkins Plantation.
   a. Charlotte Jenkins (1820-1892) married Randell Croft (1808-1869).
  4. Phoebe Waight Jenkins (1782-1843) married Richard Jenkins (1780-1823).
  5. Elizabeth Hann Jenkins (1785-1867) married Benjamin Chaplin (1776-1851).
III. Christopher Jenkins (1716-1760) of Edisto Island
 A. Christopher Jenkins (1738-1774) married first Mary Weatherly and second Providence Grimball (b. 1738), widow of John Jenkins (1736-1764).
  1. Christopher Jenkins (1769-1794) of Peter's Point Plantation married Mary Wilkinson (1770-1813), who became the fourth wife of Thomas Whaley (1750-1805).
   a. Elizabeth Caroline Jenkins (1788-1860) married second John Raven Mathews (1788-1867).
    1. Mary Wilkinson Mathews (b. 1809) married John Evans Edings (1808-1836) then Optimus Hughes.
   b. Christopher Jenkins (1790-1830) of Peaceful Retreat Plantation married Catherine C. Boone (d. 1865)
IV. Richard Jenkins (1728-1772) of Edisto Island married first Abigail Townsend (c. 1724-1753).

A. Daniel Jenkins (1751-1801) married first Hephzibah Frampton (d. 1780).
  1. Hephzibah Jenkins (1780-1847) married Daniel Townsend (1759-1842).
A. Daniel Jenkins (1751-1801) married second Martha Emma Seabrook (1758-1802).
IV. Richard Jenkins (1728-1772) married second Martha Rippon (c. 1739-1809).
  B. Micah Jenkins (1754-1830) of Johns Island married Mary Fickling (d. 1784).
    1. Richard Jenkins (1780-1823) of Bugby Plantation married Phoebe Waite Jenkins (1782-1843).
      a. Mary Caroline Jenkins (1813-1889) of Bugby Plantation married John Ferrars Townsend (1799-1881).
    2. Barbara Calder Jenkins (1784-1855) married Benjamin Dart Roper (1776-1852) of Rush's Plantation.
      a. Dr. William Roper (1816-1877) of Brick House/Stanyarne Hall married first Mary Julia Stevens (1829-1856) and second Mary Anne Mathews (1837-1887).
  C. Joseph Jenkins (1761-1828) of Brick House married Elizabeth Evans (1767-1826).
    1. Joseph Evans Jenkins (1793-1874) of Brick House married Ann Jenkins Fripp (1798-1878).
  D. Elizabeth Jenkins (1763-1837) married Paul Fripp (1762-1810).
    1. Ann Jenkins Fripp (1798-1878) married Joseph Evans Jenkins (1793-1874).
  E. Ann Jenkins (c. 1765-1846) married third Gabriel Seabrook (1765-1824) of Brookland Plantation.
  F. Sarah Jenkins (1766-1809) married William Chaplin (1770-1818).

MIKELL
Ephraim Mikell (1741-1809) of Blue House Plantation married Mary Ann Calder (c. 1741-1807), the second marriage for both.
I. Ephraim Mikell (1773-1838) married Providence Jenkins (1784-1846).
  A. Isaac Jenkins Mikell (1808-1881) of Peter's Point Plantation married first Emily Price (1809-1835) of James Island.
    1. Emily Hayes Mikell (1829-1870) married Joseph James Pope Jr. (1826-1872).
  A. Isaac Jenkins Mikell (1808-1881) married second Amarinthia Jenkins Townsend (1810-1852).
    2. Sarah Margaret Edings Mikell (1837-1906) married Daniel Townsend Pope (1837-1909).
  A. Isaac Jenkins Mikell (1808-1881) married third Mary Martha Pope (1829-1862) and fourth Sarah Georgiana Lee (1824-1905) of Edgefield District.
  B. Sarah Ann Mikell (1810-1838, died in the explosion of the steamship Pulaski) married William Edings (1809-1858).
  C. Mary Ann Mikell (1822-1899) married Edward Nathaniel Fuller (1820-1896) of Youghal Plantation.
  D. William Archibald Mikell (1815-1840) of Crawford's Plantation married Hess Marion Waring Smith (c. 1817-1904); she married second William Edings (1809-1858).
  E. Edward Wilkinson Mikell (1816-1839) married Elizabeth Meggett Seabrook (1817-1878).
II. Ann Mikell (1769-1809) married Gabriel Seabrook (1765-1824).
III. Elizabeth Ann Mikell (1773-1815) married first William Baynard (1766-1802) of Prospect Hill Plantation, second Mungo Mackay (1772-1824, widower of Ann Chisolm).
IV. Mary Ann Mikell (1779-1818) married William Seabrook (1773-1836) as his first wife.

POPE

William Pope Sr. (d. 1823) married Sarah Green, heir to Coggins Point and Fish Hall plantations. There were two sons, "Squire" William Pope Jr. (1788-1862) and John Edward Pope (d. c. 1837). In 1798 William Pope Sr. married his second wife, Sarah Scott. She and several children survived him.

I. William Pope Jr. (1788-1862) married Ann Scott, sister of his father's wife.
  A. William John Pope (1813-1852) of Coggins Point married Hephzibah J. Pope (1824-1849).
I. William Pope Jr. (1788-1862) married second Sarah Lavinia Pope.
  B. Elizabeth Catherine Pope (c. 1818-1904) married Rev. Alsop Park Vail Woodward (1804-1858).
II. John Edward Pope (d. c. 1837) of Fish Hall married Mary Baynard Edings (c. 1800-1856).
  A. Emma Catherine Pope (d. 1854) of Fish Hall married Thomas Fenwick Drayton (1808-1891).

Two daughters of James Theus and Theodora Ashe became part of the Pope family.
I. Theodora Theus (d. 1832) married Joseph Pope (1764-1818).
  A. Joseph James Pope (1792-1864) married Sarah Jenkins (d. 1857).
  B. John Jeremiah Theus Pope (1799-1864) of The Oaks Plantation married Mary Frampton Townsend (1804-1861).
    1. Hephzibah J. Pope (1824-1849) married William John Pope (1813-1852).
    2. Joseph James Pope Jr. (1826-1872) married Emily Hayes Mikell (1829-1870).
    3. Mary Martha Pope (1829-1862) married Isaac Jenkins Mikell (1808-1881) as his third wife.
    4. Daniel Townsend Pope (1837-1909) married Sarah Margaret Edings Mikell (1839-1906).
II. Elizabeth Catherine Theus married John Pope.
  A. Sarah Lavinia Pope married William Pope Jr. (1788-1862).

SEABROOK

Three brothers, Joseph Seabrook, Jr. (d. 1790), Benjamin Seabrook (c. 1724-1780), and John Seabrook (1731-1783), were the ancestors of many Edisto Island planters.

I. Joseph Seabrook, Jr. (d. 1790) of Pine Barren Plantation married Elizabeth Bailey (1730-1790).
  A. Joseph Seabrook (1750-1831) married Martha DeVeaux (b. 1763).
    1. Louisa Barnwell Seabrook (1782-1822) married Joseph Whaley (1788-1872).
      a. John Seabrook (d. 1807) married Ann Smelie.
        1. Henry Seabrook (1782-1846) married two of Gabriel Seabrook's daughters.
  B. Gabriel Seabrook (1765-1824) of Brookland Plantation married first Ann Mikell (1769-1809).
    1. Elizabeth Seabrook (1794-1846) married Henry Seabrook (1782-1846).
    2. Mary Ann Seabrook married Henry Seabrook (1782-1846).
    3. Ephraim Mikell Seabrook (1797-1846) of Brookland married Elizabeth Mary Hanahan (1802-1888).
      a. Ephraim Mikell Seabrook (1820-1895)
      b. John Gabriel Seabrook (1821-1903)
      c. Edward Whaley Seabrook (1824-c. 1882)

d. Joseph Whaley Seabrook (1835-1906)
   d. Mary Elizabeth Seabrook (1831-1896) married Paul Hamilton Seabrook (1827-1862).
   f. Henry Seabrook (1836-1872) of Brookland
 B. Gabriel Seabrook (1765-1824) married second Ann Jenkins (1765-1846) as her third husband.
 C. Mary Ann Seabrook (d. c. 1792) married Thomas Whaley (1750-1805) as his third wife.
II. Benjamin Seabrook (c. 1724-1780) married Martha May (c. 1728-1766).
 A. Martha Emma Seabrook (1758-1802) married Daniel Jenkins (1751-1801) as his second wife.
 B. Benjamin Seabrook (c. 1763-1825) married first Elizabeth Margaret Meggett (1769-1795).
   1. Whitemarsh Benjamin Seabrook (1793-1855) of Gun Bluff Plantation married Margaret Wilkinson Hamilton (1796-1839).
     a. Elizabeth Meggett Seabrook (1817-1878) married first Edward Wilkinson Mikell (1816-1839) and second Josiah Smith of Columbia.
     b. Paul Hamilton Seabrook (1827-1862) of Bluffton married Mary Elizabeth Seabrook (1831-1896).
 C. Thomas Bannister Seabrook (1765-1839) of Tom Seabrook's House married Elizabeth Clark (1779-1817).
 D. Joseph Baynard Seabrook (1768-1820) married third Martha Beckett (1787-1837).
   1. Rev. Joseph Baynard Seabrook (1809-1877) married sisters Sarah Ann Bailey (1819-1850) and Lydia Bailey (1822-1858).
     a. Martha Sarah Seabrook (1837-1922) married William Seabrook (1836-1878).
     b. Ephraim Baynard Seabrook (c. 1843-1887) married Harriet Rachel Whaley (b. c. 1849).
       1. Charles Whaley Seabrook (1876-1959) of Baynard's Old Place married Eva Irene Whaley (1879-1947).
   2. William Benjamin Seabrook (1813-1870) of Secessionville
III. John Seabrook (1731-1783) married Sarah Lawton (1739-1798).
 A. William Seabrook (1773-1836), builder of the William Seabrook House, married first Mary Ann Mikell (1779-1818).
   1. William Seabrook Jr. (1799-1860) of Oak Island Plantation married Martha Washington Edings (1799-1892).
     a. William Edings Seabrook (1828-1889) married Esther Marion Mitchell (1829-1910).
     b. John Edward Seabrook (b. 1830) of Oak Island married Elizabeth Baynard Whaley (1837-1895).
     c. Josephine Edings Seabrook (c. 1834-1883) married John Evans Edings, Jr. (1832-1883).
   2. Ephraim Mikell Seabrook (1803-1861) married Margaret Wilkinson Mikell (1806-1837).
   3. George Washington Seabrook (1808-1866) of Johns Island married Martha Abigail Clark (1808-1899).
     a. William Seabrook (1836-1878) married Martha Sarah Seabrook (1837-1922).
       1. Sarah Ann Seabrook (1863-1915) married James Swinton Whaley (1861-1932).

APPENDIX III

   4. Sarah Ann Seabrook (1812-1864) married James Christopher Wilkinson Legare (1805-1883) as his third wife.
      a. Ellen Mary Legare (1849-1888) married John Ferrars Townsend (1845-1914).
   5. Mary Ann Seabrook (d. 1836)
A. William Seabrook (1773-1836) (William Seabrook House) married second Emma Elizabeth Edings (1793-1856).
   6. Robert Chisolm Seabrook (1821-1852)
   7. Joseph Edings Seabrook (1823-1838, died in the explosion of the steamship Pulaski).
   8. Carolina Lafayette Seabrook (1825-1879) of Cassina Point Plantation married James Hopkinson (1810-1875).
      a. Martha Julia Hopkinson (1856-1946) of Cassina Point married Joseph Murray LaRoche (1858-1913).
   9. Martha Washington Seabrook (b. 1828) married Count Ferdinand de Lasteyrie (1810-1879).
   10. Julia Georgiana Seabrook (1829-1852) married John Berwick Legare (1819-1856).
      a. Joseph Seabrook Legare and Thomas Legare

TOWNSEND

Daniel Townsend (1759-1842) of Bleak Hall Plantation married Hephzibah Jenkins (1780-1847).
I. John Ferrars Townsend (1799-1881) of Bleak Hall married Mary Caroline Jenkins (1813-1899).
   A. John Ferrars Townsend (1845-1914) of Bleak Hall married Ellen Mary Legare (1849-1888).
II. Mary Frampton Townsend (1804-1861) married John Jeremiah Theus Pope (1799-1864).
III. Amarinthia Jenkins Townsend (1810-1852) married Isaac Jenkins Mikell (1808-1881) as his second wife.
IV. Daniel Jenkins Townsend (1811-1885) of Head Quarters married first Henrietta Evans (d. 1842), then Susan Lavinia Swinton (1822-1866).

WHALEY

Thomas Whaley (1750-1805) of Old House Plantation married four times. With his third wife Mary Ann Seabrook (d. c. 1792):
I. Joseph Whaley (1789-1872) of Pine Barren Plantation married Louisa Barnwell Seabrook (1792-1822).
   A. William Whaley (1817-1879) married Rachel Louisa Mitchell (1818-1889).
      1. Elizabeth Baynard Whaley (1837-1895) married John Edward Seabrook (b. 1830).
      2. Edward Mitchell Whaley (1840-1915) married three times, finally to Maria Adelaide Whaley (1849-1931).
      3. Harriet Rachel Whaley (b. c. 1849) married Ephraim Baynard Seabrook (c. 1843-1887).
II. Edward Charles Whaley (1790-1860) of Old Dominion Plantation married Abigail Mikell Baynard (1797-1830).
   A. Joseph Baynard Whaley (1821-1846) of Cedar Hall Plantation married Lydia Bailey (1822-1858).
      1. Clarence Whaley (1843-1919)
      2. Sarah A. Whaley
   B. William Baynard Whaley (1821-1857) of Tom Seabrook's Plantation married Martha Mary Hanahan (1823-1870).

1. Arthur Murray Whaley (1847-1926) of Tom Seabrook's Plantation married Susan Providence Bailey (1855-1931).
2. Percival Hanahan Whaley (1854-1915)
C. Benjamin Joseph Whaley (1824-1900)
D. Ephraim Mikell Whaley (1828-1900) of Ashe's/Little Edisto Plantation married Abigail Mikell Baynard (1839-1905).
   1. James Swinton Whaley (1861-1932) married Sarah Ann Seabrook (1863-1915).
   2. Eva Irene Whaley (1879-1947) married Charles Whaley Seabrook (1876-1959).
E. Abigail Mikell Whaley (1830-c. 1880) married Edward Charles Whaley (1826-1887).
III. Benjamin Seabrook Whaley (1791-1832) married first Eliza Edings (1799-1823).
A. William James Whaley (1819-1888) of Crawford's Plantation married Martha Mary Murray Clark (1821-1850), and then Mary Wayne (1828-1886), widow of William G. B. Mitchell (1822-1850).
B. Benjamin Seabrook Whaley (1821-1893)
III. Benjamin Seabrook Whaley (1791-1832) married second Maria Adelaide Fernalde (1802-1889).
C. Edward Charles Whaley (1826-1887) of Frogmore Plantation married Abigail Mikell Whaley (1830-c. 1880).

Bibliography

Albergotti, William Greer. *Abigail's Story, Tides at the Doorstep. The Mackays, LaRoches, Jenkinses and Chisolms of Low Country South Carolina, 1671-1897.* Spartanburg, SC: The Reprint Co., 1999.

Allston, R. F. W. *Essay on Sea Island Crops.* Charleston: A. E. Miller, 1854.

Ames, Mary. *A New England Woman's Diary in Dixie in 1865.* New York, 1906, Reprint, 1969.

Aspin, Christopher, and Stanley D. Chapman. *James Hargreaves and the Spinning Jenny.* Great Britain: The Guardian Press, 1964.

Bagnall, William R. *Samuel Slater and the Early Development of the Cotton Manufacture in the United States.* Middletown, CT: J. S. Stewart, Printer and Bookbinder, 1890.

———. *The Textile Industries of the United States: Volume 1 1639-1810.* Cambridge: The Riverside Press, 1893.

Bailey, N. Louise. *Biographical Directory of the South Carolina House of Representatives.* Vol. 2. Columbia: University of South Carolina Press, 1977.

———. *Biographical Directory of the South Carolina House of Representatives.* Vol. 4. Columbia: University of South Carolina Press, 1984.

Bailey, N. Louise, and E. I. Cooper. *Biographical Directory of the South Carolina House of Representatives.* Vol. 3. Columbia: University of South Carolina Press, 1981.

Bailey, N. Louise, Mary L. Morgan, and Carolyn R. Taylor. *Biographical Directory of the South Carolina Senate, 1776-1985.* Vol. 1. Columbia: University of South Carolina Press, 1986.

———. *Biographical Directory of the South Carolina Senate, 1776-1985.* Vol. 2. Columbia: University of South Carolina Press, 1986.

Baldwin, William P., Jr., and N. Jane Iseley. *Plantations of the Low Country: South Carolina 1696-1865.* Greensboro, NC: Legacy Publications, 1985.

Balls, W. L. *The Cotton Plant in Egypt.* London: MacMillan, 1912.

Barnwell, Edward. "On the Culture of Cotton on Reclaimed Marsh Land." *The Southern Agriculturist* 4 (1831): 238-239.

Barnwell, Joseph Walker. "Recollections." MS, Charleston: South Carolina Historical Society, 1929.

Barnwell, Stephen B. *The Story of an American Family.* Marquette, MI: privately printed, 1969.

Barnwell, W. H. W. *Rev. W. H. W. Barnwell Plantation Book.* Charleston: South Carolina Historical Society.

Batson, Annie Jenkins. "Jenkins Family History." MS, Charleston: South Carolina Historical Society, 1977.

Beasley, J. O. "The Origin of the American Tetraploid *Gossypium* Species." *American Naturalist* 74 (1940a): 285-286.

———. "The Production of Polyploids in *Gossypium*." *Journal of Heredity* 74 (1940b): 39-48.

Beaufort County Register of Mesne Conveyance, Deed Books.

Benjamin, S. W. G. "The Sea Islands." *Harper's New Monthly Magazine* 57 (1878): 839-861.

Bennett, C. A. *Roller Cotton Ginning Developments.* Dallas: The Texas Cotton Ginners Association, 1960.

Bierer, Bert W. *South Carolina Indian Lore.* Columbia: Bert W. Bierer, 1972.

Blackman, J. K. *The Sea Islands of South Carolina: Their Peaceful and Prosperous Condition, A Revelation in the System of Planting.* Charleston: News and Courier Book Presses, 1880.

Black Oak Agricultural Society Minute Book, 1842-1862. Ravenel Family Papers, 1695-1915. Charleston: South Carolina Historical Society.

Bolls, Kate McChesney. *The Daniel Townsends of the South Carolina Islands, Their Forebears and Descendants.* Verona, VA: privately published, 1975.

———. "The Townsends of Edisto Island, Supplement to *The Daniel Townsends*..." MS, 1977.

Bolster, W. Jeffrey, and Hilary Anderson. *Soldiers, Sailors, Slaves and Ships: The Civil War Photographs of Henry P. Moore.* Concord: New Hampshire Historical Society, 1999.

Borssum Waalkes, J. Van. "Malesain Malvaceae Revised." *Blumea* 14 (1966): 1-251.

Braund, Kathryn H., ed. *A Concise Natural History of East and West Florida*, by Bernard Romains. Tuscaloosa: University of Alabama Press, 1999.

Brewster, Lawrence Fay. *Summer Migrations and Resorts of South Carolina Low-Country Planters.* Durham, NC: Duke University Press, 1947.

Brizicky, G. K. "Nomenclatural Notes on *Gossypium* (Malvaceae)." *Journal of the Arnold Arboretum* 48 (1967): 152-158.

Brockington and Associates. *Wappoo Plantation (38CH1199/1200). Data Recovery at an 18th Century Stono River Plantation.* Mt. Pleasant, SC: Brockington and Associates, 1992.

Brooks, C. P. *Cotton.* New York: Spon & Chamberlain, 1898.

Bullard, Mary R. *Robert Stafford of Cumberland Island: Growth of a Planter.* Athens: University of Georgia Press, 1995.

Burden, Kinsey. Letter to Whitemarsh Seabrook. In Seabrook, Whitemarsh B. *A Report accompanied with sundry Letters of the causes which Contribute to the Production of Fine Sea-Island Cotton.* Read before the Agricultural Society of St. John's Colleton on March 14, 1827. Charleston: A. E. Miller, 1827

———. "Introduction of Black and Green Seed Cotton into South Carolina." *The Southern Agriculturist* IV, no. 5 (1844a): 161-166 (New Series).

———. "On the Cotton Gin, and Introduction of Cotton." *The Southern Agriculturist* 4, no. 6 (1844b): 201-208 (New Series).

Burn, Billie. *An Island Named Daufuskie.* Spartanburg, SC: The Reprint Co., 1991.

Burton, Anthony. *The Rise and Fall of King Cotton.* London: British Broadcasting Corporation, 1984.

Cadwell, Charles K. *The Old 6th Regiment: Its War Record.* New Haven, CT, 1875

Capers, Charles W. "Remarks on the origin and introduction of Whitney's saw gins into Southern States, with a notice of some errors in the life of Eli Whitney, by Professor Olmsted, contained in Sulliman's Journal." *The Southern Agriculturist* 7 (February 1834): 70-76.

Capers, William H. "On the Culture of Sea-Island Cotton." *The Southern Agriculturist* 8 (August 1835): 401-412.

Carolina Archaeological Services. *Archaeological Inventory and Testing at 38BU956, Marsh Lakes Plantation Development, Hilton Head Island.* Columbia, SC: Carolina Archaeological Services, 1989.

Carse, Robert. *The Department of the South: Hilton Head Island in the Civil War.* Columbia, SC: State Printing Co., 1961.

Catling, Harold. *The Spinning Mule.* Newton Abbot: David & Charles, 1970.

Charleston County Register of Mesne Conveyance, Deed Books and Plat Books.

Childs, A. R. *The Private Journal of William Henry Ravenel.* Columbia: University of South Carolina Press, 1947.

Chisolm, Robert. "Sea Island Cotton Planting." *The Rural Carolinian* 3 (1872): 341-343.

———. "Where Does the Cotton Caterpillar Hibernate?" *The Rural Carolinian* 6 (1875): 7.

Chisolm, William Garner. *Edings of Edisto Island.* Leesburg, VA: privately printed, 1943.

Clough, Monica. "Links of a Glasgow Cotton-mill Owner with South Carolina in the Early Nineteenth Century." Lecture, The Historic Charleston Foundation, March 9, 1999.

Coffin, Ebenezer. *Coffin Point Plantation Journals*, 1800-1816. Charleston: South Carolina Historical Society.

"Commercial Statistics." *The Merchants' Magazine and Commercial Review* IV, no. 3 (March 1841): 484.

"Commercial Statistics." *The Merchants' Magazine and Commercial Review* XII (January to June 1845): 392.

Committee on Sea Island Cotton. "To the Growers of Fine Sea-Island Cotton." *The Southern Agriculturist* 11 (1838): 650-656.

———. "Report of the Committee on Sea Island Cotton." *The Southern Agriculturist* 2 (1842): 1-17 (New Series).

Committee of the St. Andrew's Agricultural and Police Society. "On the Introduction of Sea-Island Cotton into the Chinese Market." James Island, SC: Proceedings of the Society, October 1, 1844.

Connor, Amy S., and Sheila L. Beardsley. *Edisto Island, A Family Affair*. Dover, NH: Arcadia Publishing Co., 1998.

Cook, O. F., and C. B. Doyle. *Sea-Island and Meade Cotton in the Southeastern States.* U.S. Department of Agriculture Circular 114, Washington, DC, May 1927.

Copp, Elbridge J. *Reminiscences of the War of the Rebellion, 1861-1865.* Nashua, NH, 1911.

The Cotton Plant: Its History, Botany, Chemistry, Culture, Enemies, and Uses. U.S. Department of Agriculture *Bulletin* no. 33. Washington, DC: Government Printing Office, 1896.

Crawford, M. D. C. *The Heritage of Cotton: The Fibre of Two Worlds and Many Ages.* New York: Grossett & Dunlap, 1924.

Dabbs, Edith M. *Sea Island Diary, A History of St. Helena Island.* Spartanburg, SC: The Reprint Co., 1983.

Damp, Jonathan E., and Deborah M. Pearsall. "Early Cotton from Coastal Ecuador." *Economy Botany* 48, no. 2 (1994): 163-165.

Davidson, Chalmers G. *The Last Foray. The South Carolina Planters of 1860: A Sociological Study.* Columbia: University of South Carolina Press, 1971.

Davis, Richard A., Jr., and Duncan M. Fitzgerald. *Beaches and Coasts.* Malden, MA: Blackwell Publishing Co., 2004.

Dennie, Joseph. "Description of a Cotton Gin, Invented by Joseph Eve of Pennsylvania." *The Port Folio* 5, no. 3 (March 1811): 185-86 (New Series).

Donnell, E. J. *Chronological and Statistical History of Cotton.* Published by the author. New York: James Sutton & Co., Printers, 1872

Drayton, John M. *A View of South Carolina as Respects Her Natural and Civil Concerns.* Charleston: W. P. Young, 1802.

Dubose, Samuel. Address delivered at the seventeenth anniversary of the Black Oak Agricultural Society on April 27, 1858. In: *A Contribution to the History of the Huguenots of South Carolina*, published for private circulation by T. Gaillard Thomas. New York: The Knickerbocker Press, 1887.

Duncan, William. "Mr. McCarthy's Cotton Gin." *The Southern Agriculturist* 4, no. 5 (1844): 184. (New Series)

Edwards, M. Michael. *The Growth of the British Cotton Trade.* New York: Augustus M. Kelly, Publishers, 1967.

Ellacott, S. E. *Spinning & Weaving.* London: Methuen & Co., Ltd., 1956.

Elliott, William. "On the Cultivation and Prices of Sea Island Cotton." *The Southern Agriculturist* 1 (1828): 151-163.

———. Anniversary address of the State Agricultural Society of South Carolina, November 30, 1848. Published by the Society. Printed by Miller & Browne, Charleston, SC, 1849.

———. "Sea-Island Cotton." *The South Carolina Agriculturist* 1, no. 3 (July 1856): 67-73.

Encyclopédie. 1765. Reprint, Stuttgart: Friedrich Frommann Verlag, 1967.

Endrizzi, J. E., E. L. Turcotte, and R. J. Kohel. "Genetics, Cytology, and Evolution of *Gossypium.*" *Advances in Genetics* 23 (1985): 271-375.

The Extra-Long Staple Cotton Situation. U.S. Department of Agriculture Statistical Bulletin no. 234, July 1958.

"Florida: Variety of Products." *DeBow's Review* 4 (July 1867): 134-139.

Fraser, Charles. *A Charleston Sketchbook 1796-1806.* Charleston: Carolina Art Association, 1971.

Fryxell, Paul A. "A Redefinition of the Tribe Gossypieae." *Botanical Gazette* 129 (1968a): 296-308.

———. "The Typification and Application of the Linnaean Binomials in *Gossypium.*" *Brittonia* 20 (1968b): 378-386.

———. *The Natural History of the Cotton Tribe.* College Station: Texas A&M University Press, 1979.

Gaillard, Peter. *Daily Plantation Journal, 1803-1825.* Peter Gaillard Papers, 1811-1847. Charleston: South Carolina Historical Society.

Geijer, Agnes. *A History of Textile Art.* London: Pasold Research Fund, Ltd., in association with Sotheby Parke Bernet Publications, 1979.

Gibbes, Lewis R. "Botany of Edings Bay." *Proceedings of the Elliott Society of Natural History* 1, no. 4 (1857): 241-48.

Gillum, M. N. "High Speed Roller Ginning." *Transactions of the ASAE* 28, no. 3 (May-June 1985): 959-968.

Gordon, G. A. "Sea Island Cotton." From the transactions, no. 82, of the National Association of Cotton Manufacturers. Boston, April 24-25, 1907.

Gray, Lewis Cecil. *History of Agriculture in the Southern United States to 1860.* 2 vols. Gloucester, MA: Peter Smith, 1958.

Graydon, Nell S. *Tales of Edisto.* Columbia, SC: The R. L. Bryan Co., 1955.

Grayson, William J. *Autobiography of W. J. Grayson.* Columbia: University of South Carolina Press, 1990.

Gregorie, Anne K., and Flora B. Surles. *South Carolina Agricultural Society: 1825-1860 Minute Book,* copied by Works Project Administration no. 65-33-118, Federal Writers Project, The Library of Congress Project, 1936.

———. *South Carolina Agricultural Society: 1880-1936 Minute Book,* copied by Works Project Administration no. 65-33-118, Federal Writers Project, The Library of Congress Project, 1936.

Gruber, Ira D., ed. *John Peebles' American War: The Diary of a Scottish Grenadier, 1776-1782.* Mechanicsburg, PA: Stackpole Books, 1998.

Guest, Richard. *Compendious History of the Cotton-Manufacture; with a Disproval of the Claim of Sir Richard Arkwright to the Invention of its Ingenious Machinery.* Manchester: Joseph Pratt, Chapel Walks, Printer, 1823. Reprint, Frank Cass & Co., Ltd., 1968.

Hagy, James W. *Charleston, South Carolina, City Directories for the Years 1816, 1819, 1822, 1825, and 1829.* Baltimore: Clearfield Co., 1996.

———. *City Directories for Charleston, South Carolina, for the Years 1803, 1806, 1807, 1809, and 1813.* Baltimore: Clearfield Co., 1995.

———. *Directories for the City of Charleston, South Carolina, for the Years 1830-31, 1835-36, 1836, 1837-38, and 1840-41.* Baltimore: Clearfield Co., 1997.

———. *Directories for the City of Charleston, South Carolina, for the Years 1849, 1852, and 1855.* Baltimore: Clearfield Co., 2000.

———. *On the Eve of the Civil War: The Charleston, SC, Directories for the Years 1859 and 1860.* Baltimore: Clearfield Co., 2000.

———. *People and Professions of Charleston, South Carolina, 1782-1802.* Baltimore: Clearfield Co., 1992.

Hammond, Harry. "Report on the Cotton Production of the State of South Carolina." In Eugene W. Hilgard, ed., *Report on Cotton Production in the United States Part II.* Washington, DC: Department of the Interior, Census Office, Government Printing Office, 1881.

Harris, J. William. *Deep Souths: Delta, Piedmont, and Sea Island Society in the Age of Segregation.* Baltimore: The Johns Hopkins University Press, 2001.

Harrison, Eliza Cope, ed. *Best Companions: Letters of Eliza Middleton Fisher and Her Mother, Mary Hering Middleton, from Charleston, Philadelphia, and Newport, 1839-1846.* Columbia: University of South Carolina Press, 2001.

Hasell, Annie Baynard Simons. *Baynard: An Ancient Family Bearing Arms.* Charleston: privately printed, 1972.

Haskell, Jennie. "Cotton, in the Coast and Upland Fields of South Carolina." *Frank Leslie's Popular Monthly* (May 1885): 567-576.

Hemphill, J. C. *Climate, Soil and Agricultural Capability of South Carolina and Georgia.* U.S. Department of Agriculture Special Report no. 47. Washington, DC: Government Printing Office, 1882.

Higginson, Thomas Wentworth. *Army Life in a Black Regiment.* Boston: 1900. Rev. ed. Boston: Beacon Press, 1962.

Hill, Albert F. *Economic Botany*. New York: McGraw Hill Book Co., 1952.

Historic Beaufort Foundation, *A Guide to Historic Beaufort*. 5th ed. Beaufort, SC: Historic Beaufort Foundation, Inc., 1985.

Holcomb, Brent H. *Marriage and Death Notices from the Charleston Observer 1827-1845*. Columbia, SC: privately printed, 1980.

———. *Marriage and Death Notices from the (Charleston) Times, 1800-1821*. Baltimore: Genealogical Publishing Co., Inc., 1979.

———. *Marriage and Death Notices from the (Charleston, South Carolina) Mercury, 1822-1832*. Columbia: SCMAR, 2001.

———. *Marriage, Death and Estate Notices from Georgetown, SC, Newspapers 1791-1861*. Easley, SC: Southern Historical Press, 1979.

———. *Record of Deaths in Columbia, South Carolina, and Elsewhere as Recorded by John Glass, 1859-1877*. Columbia, SC: privately printed, 1986.

———. *South Carolina Marriages, 1688-1789*. Baltimore: Genealogical Publishing Co., Inc., 1983.

———. *South Carolina Marriages, 1800-1820*. Baltimore: Genealogical Publishing Co., Inc., 1981.

Holmgren, Virginia C. *Hilton Head: A Sea Island Chronicle*. Hilton Head, SC: 1959. Reprint, Easley, SC: Southern Historical Press, 1986.

Hood, Mildred Keller. *Cemetery Inscriptions of Charleston County, South Carolina*. Charleston: Charleston Chapter, South Carolina Genealogical Society, 1997.

Houldsworth, H. "Mr. McCarthy's Cotton Gin." *The Southern Agriculturist* 4, no. 5 (1844): 185 (New Series).

Hunter, W. D. *The Boll-Weevil Problem*. U.S. Department of Agriculture Farmers Bulletin no. 1329. Washington, DC, 1923.

Hutchinson, J. B., and H. L. Manning. "The Sea Island Cottons." *Empire Journal of Experimental Agriculture* 13 (1945): 80-92.

Hutchinson, J. B., R. A. Silow, and S. G. Stephens. *The Evolution of* Gossypium *and the Differentiation of the Cultivated Cottons*. Final report of the Genetics Department, Cotton Research Station, Trinidad, B.W.I. London: Oxford University Press, 1947.

Jaeger/Pyburn Inc. *Conservation and Development Plan, McLeod Plantation, James Island,*

South Carolina. Gainesville, GA: Jaeger/Pyburn Inc. for Historic Charleston Foundation, 1991.

James Island Agricultural Society. *Minute Book* 1 (1904-1935). Copied by Works Project Administration, Federal Writers Project, The Library of Congress, 1936.

J. B. W. "Whittemore's Cotton Gin." *The Southern Agriculturist* 8, no. 8 (September 1835): 473-480.

Jenkins, Joseph E. "On the necessity of a more extensive system of draining, in the cultivation of the sea-islands." *The Southern Agriculturist* 3 (November 1830): 561-566.

Jenkins, Sophia Seabrook. *Rockville, Wadmalaw Island, SC.* MS, Charleston: South Carolina Historical Society, 1957.

Johnson, Cyril, ed. *Aiken County Cemeteries.* Vol. 4. Aiken: Aiken-Barnwell Genealogical Society of South Carolina, 1998.

Johnson, Guion G. *A Social History of the Sea Islands.* Chapel Hill: University of North Carolina Press, 1930.

Johnson, W. H. *Cotton and its Production.* London: MacMillan and Co., Ltd., 1926.

Jones, Katharine M. *Port Royal Under Six Flags.* New York: Bobbs-Merrill Co., 1960.

Jordan, Laylon Wayne, and Elizabeth H. Stringfellow. *A Place Called St. John's, The Story of John's, Edisto, Wadmalaw, Kiawah, and Seabrook Islands of South Carolina.* Spartanburg, SC: The Reprint Co., 1998.

Keber, Martha L. *Seas of Gold, Seas of Cotton.* Athens: The University of Georgia Press, 2002.

King, James. "On the best mode of applying cotton-seed as manure." *The Southern Agriculturist* 4 (March 1831): 127-128.

Kish, Alex J., Wayne L. Ogle, and Joe E. Toler. *Agricultural Growing Degree Days in South Carolina.* Bulletin 595, South Carolina Agricultural Experiment Station, Clemson University, 1976.

Kohel, R. J., and C. F. Lewis, eds. *Cotton.* Madison, WI: Soil Science Society of America, Inc., 1984.

Kohel, R. J., T. R. Richmond, and C. F. Lewis. "Genetics of Flowering. VI. Flowering behavior of *Gossypium hirsutum* L. and *Gossypium barbadense* L. hybrids." *Crop Science* 14 (1974): 696-699.

Kovacik, Charles F., and Robert E. Mason. "Changes in the South Carolina Sea Island Cotton Industry." *Southeastern Geographer* 25, no. 2 (November 1985): 77-104.

Landers, Jane G. *Colonial Plantations and Economy in Florida.* Gainesville: University of Florida Press, 2000.

Lakwete, Angela. *Inventing the Cotton Gin: Machine and Myth in Antebellum America.* Baltimore: The Johns Hopkins University Press, 2003.

Lavasseur, A. *Lafayette in America in 1824 and 1825, or Journal of a Voyage to the United States.* Philadelphia, 1829.

Lawton, Thomas O., Jr. *Upper St. Peter's Parish and Environs.* Garnett, SC: privately printed, 2001.

Lawton, William M. "The Sea Island Cotton Question." *The Rural Carolinian* 1 (1870): 228-229.

Lebby, Robert, J. B. Hinson, and W. H. Rivers. "On the Introduction of Sea-island Cotton into the Chinese Market." *The Southern Agriculturist* 4, no. 11 (1844): 410-420 (New Series).

Leiding, Harriette Kershaw. *Historic Houses of South Carolina.* Philadelphia: J. B. Lippincott, 1921.

Legaré, J. D., ed. "Account of the Management of Pushee, the Residence of Dr. Henry Ravenel." *The Southern Agriculturist* 4, no. 6 (1831): 360-369.

LeGrand, H. E. "Summary of the Geology of the Atlantic Coast Plain." *The Bulletin of the American Association of Petroleum Geologists* 45, no. 9 (September 1961).

Lennon, Gered, et al. *Living with the South Carolina Coast.* Durham, NC: Duke University Press, 1996.

Ligon, Richard. *History of the Island of Barbadoes.* London: Frank Cass and Co., Ltd., 1657.

Lindsay, Nick. *And I'm Glad: An Oral History of Edisto Island.* Charleston: Tempus Publishing, Inc., 2000.

Lounsbury, Carl R., and Vanessa Elizabeth Patrick. *An Illustrated Glossary of Early Southern Architecture and Landscape.* University Press of Virginia, 1999.

Martin, Josephine W., ed. *Dear Sister: Letters Written on Hilton Head Island, 1867.* New York: Viking Press, 1977.

Mason, Robert E. *A Historical Geography of South Carolina's Sea Island Cotton Industry.* Master's thesis, Columbia: University of South Carolina, 1976.

Mathew, William M., ed. *Agriculture, Geology, and Society in Antebellum South Carolina: The Private Diary of Edmund Ruffin, 1843.* Athens: University of Georgia Press, 1992.

Mauersberger, Herbert R. *Matthew's Textile Fibers: Their Physical, Microscopical, and Chemical Properties.* 5th ed. New York: John Wiley & Sons, Inc., 1947.

Mauney, Jack R., and James McD. Stewart, eds. *Cotton Physiology.* Memphis: The Cotton Foundation, 1986.

McGowan, Joseph C. *History of Extra-long Staple Cottons.* El Paso: Hill Printing Co., 1961.

Meadows, William R. "Economic Conditions in the Sea Island Cotton Industry." *Bulletin* 146 (1914), U.S. Department of Agriculture. Washington, DC: Government Printing Office.

Mendenhall, Marjorie S. *A History of Agriculture in South Carolina, 1790-1860.* Unpublished Ph.D. dissertation. Chapel Hill: University of North Carolina, 1940.

Mikell, I. Jenkins. *Rumbling of the Chariot Wheels.* Columbia, SC: The State Co., 1923.

Mikell, Townsend. *The Mikell Genealogy of South Carolina.* Charleston: Walker, Evans and Cogswell, 1910.

Moore, Alexander. *Biographical Directory of the South Carolina House of Representatives.* Vol. 5, 1816-1828. Columbia: SC Department of Archives and History, 1992.

Moore, John Hammond, ed. "The Abiel Abbot Journals: A Yankee Preacher in Charleston Society, 1818-1827." *The South Carolina Historical Magazine* 68 (1967): 238-39.

Murphy, William S. *The Textile Industries.* London: The Gresham Publishing Co., 1910.

Murray, Chalmers S. *Black Seed From Bahama.* Unpublished manuscript. Charleston: South Carolina Historical Society, n.d.

———. *This Our Land.* Charleston: Carolina Art Association, 1949.

Orton, W. A. "Sea Island Cotton: Its Cultivation, Improvement, and Diseases." *Farmers' Bulletin* 302. Washington, DC: Government Printing Office, U.S. Department of Agriculture, 1907.

———. "Sea Island Cotton." *Farmers' Bulletin* 787. Washington, DC: Government Printing Office, U.S. Department of Agriculture, 1916.

Owen, E. R. J. *Cotton and the Egyptian Economy, 1820-1914: A Study in Trade and Development.* Oxford: Clarendon Press, 1969.

Patey, James Garner. *The Whaley Family and Its Charleston Connection.* Spartanburg, SC: The Reprint Co., 1992.

Pearson, Elizabeth W., ed. *Letters from Port Royal Written at the Time of the Civil War.* Boston, 1906.

Percy, R. G., and J. F. Wendel. "Allozyme Evidence for the Origin and Diversification of *Gossypium barbadense* L." *Theoretical and Applied Genetics* 79 (1990): 529-542.

Peyre, Thomas Walter. *The Plantation Journal of Thomas Walter Peyre, 1834-1851.* Charleston: South Carolina Historical Society.

(A) Physician. *National Intelligencer* 4 (July 31, 1843). Florida.

Pilkey, Orrin H. "Barrier Islands: Formed by Fury, They Roam and Fade." *Sea Frontiers* December 1990, 30-36.

Pilkey, Orrin H., and Mary Edna Fraser. *A Celebration of the World's Barrier Islands.* New York: Columbia University Press, 2003.

Piperno, Dolores R., and Deborah M. Pearsall. *The Origins of Agriculture in the Lowland Neotropics.* San Diego: Academic Press, 1998.

Porcher, Frederick A. *Report on Manures.* Proceedings of the Black Oak Agricultural Society, November 19, 1844. Charleston: Miller & Browne.

Porcher, Richard D. "Rice Culture in South Carolina: A Brief History, the Role of the Huguenots, and Preservation of Its Legacy." *Transactions of the Huguenot Society* 92 (1987): 1-22.

———. *Wildflowers of the Carolina Lowcountry and Lower Pee Dee.* Columbia: University of South Carolina Press, 1995.

Porcher, Richard D., and Douglas A. Rayner. *A Guide to the Wildflowers of South Carolina.* Columbia: University of South Carolina Press, 2001.

Posselt, E. A. *The Structure of Fibers, Yarns and Fabrics: Being a Practical treatise for the Use of All Persons Employed in the Manufacture of Textile Fabrics. Volume 1: Being a description of the growth and manipulation of Cotton, Wool, Worsted, Silk, Flax, Jute, Ramie, Chinagrass and Hemp.* Philadelphia: E. A. Posselt, Author and Publisher, 1891.

Poston, Jonathan H. *The Buildings of Charleston. A Guide to the City's Architecture.* Columbia: University of South Carolina Press, 1997.

Prokhanov, Y. I. "What is *Gossypium barbadense* Linnaeus?" *Taxon* 8 (1959): 41-46.

Puckette, Clara Childs. *Edisto, A Sea Island Principality.* Cleveland: Seaforth Publications, 1978.

Purseglove, J. W. *Tropical Crops: Dicotyledons.* New York: John Wiley & Sons, Inc., 1968.

Ramsay, David, M.D. *History of South Carolina.* Newberry, SC: W. J. Duffie, 1858.

Ravenel, Beatrice St. Julien. *Architects of Charleston.* Charleston: Carolina Art Association, 1945.

Ravenel, Dr. Henry. *Diary 1836-1841.* Thomas Porcher Ravenel Collection, box 1. Charleston: South Carolina Historical Society.

Ravenel, Henry Edmund. *Ravenel Records.* Printed for private distribution, 1898.

Ravenel, Henry William. *A Memoir from the Black Oak Agricultural Society.* The State Agricultural Society, December 1842, at Columbia. Charleston: Miller & Browne, 1843.

——. "On the Santee Long Cotton Crop." *The Southern Agriculturist* 4 (1844): 43-44 (New Series).

Rawick, George P. *The American Slave: A Composite Autobiography.* Westport, CT, 1992.

Rheder, John B. *Delta Sugar: Louisiana's Vanishing Plantation Landscape.* Baltimore: Johns Hopkins University Press, 1999.

Rivers, Capt. Elias L. "Sea Island Cotton: An Eminent Planter Gives its History and Cultivation." *The News and Courier*, Charleston: February 10, 1896.

Rivers, Joseph LaRoche. *Seven South Carolina Lowcountry Families: Bailey, Clark, Grimball, Jenkins, Seabrook, Townsend, and Whaley.* Charleston: privately printed, 1977, rev. ed., 2001.

Rivers, Larry Eugene. *Slavery in Florida.* Gainesville: University Press of Florida, 2000.

Roberts, Charles Arthur. *The Sea Island Cotton Industry as Revealed in the McConnel-Kennedy Letters, 1819-1825.* Unpublished master's thesis, Columbia: University of South Carolina, 1965.

Rose, Willie Lee. *Rehearsal for Reconstruction: The Port Royal Experiment.* London: Oxford University Press, 1964.

Rosengarten, Theodore. *Tombee: Portrait of a Cotton Planter.* NY: William Morrow and Co., 1986.

Rowland, Lawrence S., Alexander Moore, and George C. Rogers, Jr. *The History of Beaufort County, South Carolina. Vol. 1, 1514-1861.* Columbia: University of South Carolina Press, 1996.

Scafidel, Beverly Robinson. *The Letters of William Elliott.* Unpublished Ph.D. dissertation, Columbia: University of South Carolina, 1978.

Sea Island Historical Society. *Proposed Restoration and Interpretation: McLeod Plantation, James Island, South Carolina.* Sea Island Historical Society for Historic Charleston Foundation, 1999.

Seabrook, Whitemarsh B. *A Report accompanied with sundry Letters of the causes which Contribute to the Production of Fine Sea-Island Cotton.* Read before the Agricultural Society of St. John's Colleton, on March 14, 1827. Charleston: A. E. Miller, 1827.

———. "A report accompanied with sundry letters of the causes which contribute to the production of fine sea-island cotton." *The Southern Agriculturist* 1 (April 1828): 171-177.

———. "Remarks on the advantage of marsh mud as a manure for cotton." *The Southern Agriculturist* 2 (August 1829a.): 356-365.

———. "Remarks on the advantage of marsh mud as a manure for cotton." *The Southern Agriculturist* 2 (September 1829b): 395-400.

———. "On marsh mud, in reply to a Georgia planter." *The Southern Agriculturist* 2 (December 1829c): 545-547.

———. "On the preparation of sea-island cotton for market." *The Southern Agriculturist* 3, no. 8 (August 1843): 281-291 (New Series).

———. *A Memoir on the Cultivation and Uses of Cotton, from the Earliest Ages to the Present Time, with Special Reference to the Sea-Island Cotton Plant.* Charleston: Miller & Browne, 1844a.

———. "Mr. McCarthy's cotton gin." *The Southern Agriculturist* 4, no. 5 (1844b): 183 (New Series).

———. *Memoir on Sea Island Cotton.* Supplement to the proceedings of The State Agricultural Society of South Carolina. Columbia: Summer & Carroll Publishers, 1847.

Shepperson, Alfred B., and C. W. Shepperson. *Cotton Facts.* New York: Cotton Exchange Building, Shepperson Publishing Co., 1921.

Shiver, F. S. "A Chemical Study of the Sea Island Cotton Seed." *Bulletin* 68 (February 1902). Clemson: South Carolina Agricultural Experiment Station, Clemson Agricultural College.

Simmons, Slann L.C., ed. "Diary of Abram W. Clement, 1865." *The South Carolina Historical Magazine* 59 (1958): 78-95.

Simpson, Beryl B., and Molly C. Ogorzaly. *Economic Botany: Plants in Our World.* New York: McGraw-Hill Book Co., 1986.

Sinkler, Charles St. George. *Letters dated 1883 to Anne Wickham Porcher.* Private collection, Anne Sinkler Whaley LeClercq, Charleston.

Smith, Alfred G., Jr. *Economic Readjustment of an Old Cotton State: South Carolina, 1820-1860.* Columbia: University of South Carolina Press, 1958.

Smith, C. Wayne, and J. Tom Cothern, eds. *Cotton: Origin, History, Technology, and Production.* New York: John Wiley & Sons, Inc., 1999.

Spalding, Thomas. "On the introduction of sea-island cotton into Georgia." *The Southern Agriculturist* 4 (March 1831): 131-132.

———. "Cotton—its introduction and progress of its culture, in the United States." *The Southern Agriculturist* 8 (January-February 1835): 35-46 and 81-87.

———. "On the cotton gin, and introduction of cotton." *The Southern Agriculturist* 4 (1844a): 106-111 (New Series).

———. "On the cotton gin, and introduction of cotton." *The Southern Agriculturist* 4 (1844b): 128-132 (New Series).

State of Florida. *The Story of Sea-Island Cotton.* Tallahassee: Department of Agriculture, New Series, no. 113, 1941.

Stephens, S. G. *Factors Affecting Seed Dispersal in* Gossypium. Technical bulletin no. 131 (March 1958): 1-31. Raleigh: North Carolina Agricultural Experiment Station.

———. "The use of two polymorphic systems, nectary fringe hairs and corky alleles, as indicators of phylogenetic relationships in new world cottons." *Biotropica* 6, no. 3 (1974): 194-201.

———. "The origin of sea island cotton." *Agricultural History* 50 (1976):391.

Stephens, S. G., and M. E. Moseley. "Early domesticated cottons from archeological sites in central coastal Peru." *American Antiquity* 39 (1974): 109-122.

Stewart, Mart A. *What Nature Suffers to Groe.* Athens: University of Georgia Press, 1996.

Stockton, Robert P. *Fenwick Hall, Stono River, John's Island, South Carolina.* MS, Charleston, 1992.

Stoney, Samuel Gaillard. *Plantations of the Carolina Low Country.* Charleston: Carolina Art Association, 1938.

Taggart, William Scott. *Cotton Spinning.* London: MacMillan and Co., Ltd., 1919.

Taylor, David. *South Carolina Naturalists.* Columbia: The University of South Carolina Press, 1998.

Towles, H. A. *Minutes of the Sea Island Cotton Protective Union.* Charleston: Walker, Evans & Cogswell Co., Printers. 1891.

Trinkley, Michael, ed. *Barker Field Expansion Project, Hilton Head Island [Fish Hall 38BU805].* Chicora Research Series 17. Columbia: Chicora Foundation, Inc., 1989.

———. *Haig Point, Webb Tract and Oak Ridge, Daufuskie Island [Haig Point 38BU591].* Chicora Research Series 15. Columbia: Chicora Foundation, Inc., 1989.

———. *The History and Archaeology of Kiawah Island, Charleston County, South Carolina.* Research Series 30. Columbia: Chicora Foundation, 1993.

———. *National Register Evaluation of 38CH932, Youghal Plantation, Charleston County, South Carolina.* Columbia: Chicora Foundation, Inc., 2003.

Turnbull, Nicholas. "The beginning of cotton cultivation in Georgia." *Georgia Historical Quarterly* 1 (1917): 39-45.

Turner, J. A. *The Cotton Planters Manual.* New York: C. M. Saxton and Co., 1857.

Turpin, Edna. *Cotton.* New York: American Book Co., 1924.

Verum. "Florida, its climate, soil, production, &c." *The Southern Agriculturist* 4, no. 2 (1844): 444-449 (New Series).

Vlach, John Michael. *Back of the Big House: The Architecture of Plantation Slavery.* Chapel Hill: University of North Carolina Press, 1993.

W. "Sea island cotton in Florida." *The Southern Agriculturist* 12, no. 12 (1844): 449-452 (New Series).

Waddell, Gene. *Charleston Architecture 1670-1860.* Charleston: Wyrick & Co., 2004.

Walmsley, Herbert E. *Cotton Spinning and Weaving.* 3rd ed. Manchester, England: Abel Heywood & Son, 1893.

Wang, G. L., J. M. Dong, and A. H. Paterson. "The distribution of *Gossypium hirsutum* chromatin in *G. barbadense* germ plasm: molecular analysis of introgressive plant breeding." *Theoretical Applied Genetics* 91, no. 6/7 (November 1995): 1153-1161.

Waring, J. I. *A History of Medicine in South Carolina. Vol. 1, 1670-1825.* Charleston, 1964. *Vol. 2, 1825-1900.* Charleston, 1967.

Watkins, James L. *King Cotton: A Historical and Statistical Review, 1790 to 1908.* New York: James L. Watkins & Sons, 1908.

Watt, Sir George. *The Wild and Cultivated Plants of the World.* London: Longmans, Green, and Co., 1907.

Webb, Edward Kirk. *Kirk Family Letters 1803-1868.* Charleston: privately printed, 1977.

Webber, Herbert J. "Improvement of Cotton by Seed Selection." *Yearbook* of the U.S. Department of Agriculture. Washington, DC: Government Printing Office, 1902.

Weightman, Gavin. *The Frozen Water Trade, A True Story.* New York: Hyperion Books, 2002.

Wendel, J. F. *New World tetraploid cottons contain Old World cytoplasm.* Proceedings of the National Academy of Science 86 (1989): 4132-4136.

Wendel, J. F., and V. A. Albert. "Phylogenetics of the cotton genus (*Gossypium*): Character-state weighted parsimony analysis of chloroplast-DNA restriction site data and its systematic and biogeographic implications." *Systematic Botany* 17 (1992): 115-143.

Whaley, Maria Adelaide. *The Story of Maria Adelaide Whaley.* MS, Charleston: South Carolina Historical Society, 1926.

Whaley, Edward Mitchell. *A Short Account of the Experiences of Edward Mitchell Whaley of Edisto Island, SC.* MS, South Carolina Historical Society, n.d.

White, George S. *Memoir of Samuel Slater.* Philadelphia: At No. 46 Carpenter Street, 1836. Reprint, New York: Augustus M. Kelley Publishers, 1967.

Wilson, Rev. Robert. *An Address Delivered before the St. John's Hunting Club at Indianfield Plantation, St. John's, Berkeley, July 4, 1907.* Published by the St. John's Hunting Club; printed by Walker, Evans, and Cogswell, Charleston, 1907.

Wilson, Samuel M., ed. *The Indigenous People of the Caribbean.* Gainesville: University of Florida Press, 1997.

Wilson, Teresa, and Janice L. Grimes, *Marriage and Death Notices from the Southern Patriot, 1815-1830.* Easley, SC: Southern Historical Press, 1982.

———. *Marriage and Death Notices from the Southern Patriot, 1831-1848.* Easley, SC: Southern Historical Press, 1986.

Woofter, T. J. *Black Yeomanry: Life on St. Helena Island.* New York: Henry Holt and Co., 1930.

Wouters, W. "Au sujet de binôme *Gossypium barbadense* L." *Bulletin du Jardin Botanique,* Bruxelles 33 (1963): 511-523.

Wrenn, Lynette B. *Cinderella of the New South.* Knoxville: University of Tennessee Press, 1995.

X. Y. "On the cultivation of reclaimed salt marshes." *The Southern Agriculturist* 1 (1828): 20-24.

Zeigler, John M. "Origin of the sea islands of the southeastern United States." *Geographical Review* 49 (1959): 222-237.

Index

Abbot, Abiel, 348, 351
Acorn Hill Plantation, Johns Island, 448
Africa (African), 3, 58, 61, 62, 69, 72, 81, 124, 136, 269, 271
African slaves, 76, 78, 90, 94, 117, 118, 124, 134, 135, 136, 137, 160, 168, 275, 300, 306, 325, 328, 343
aggrading barrier island, 15
Agricultural Society of St. John's Colleton, xxviii, 163, 351, 505, 515
Agricultural Society of South Carolina, xxvi, xxxiii, 135-36, 150, 204, 284, 292, 321, 507-08, 151-16
Aiken, South Carolina, 446
Aiken County, South Carolina, 431, 432
Aiken, William (1806-1887), 375
airplane fabric, 85
Alachua County, Florida, 125, 128
Albert, V. A., 61, 69, 70, 72, 519, xxxv
Alexander the Great, 239
Ali, Khedive Mohammed, 82
allotetraploid, 63, 67, 70, 72, *68*, 71
Allston, Adele Petigru (1840-1915), 406
Allston, Robert F. W. (1801-1864), xxix, 104, 180, 183, 295, 215, 221, 230, 277, 323, 503
Amazon Basin, 62
American colonies, 245, 271
American-Egyptian cotton, 85, 87, 233
American Revolution, xviii
American Southwest, xxxiv, 88, 131, 288, 330, 338
Ancon-Chillon, Peru, xi, xviii, xxiv, xxxiv, xxxv, 56, 61, 62, 64, 73, 74, 88, 89, 90, 99, 238-41, 263, *264*, 282, 298, 517
Andes (mountains), 74, 75, 90, 92, 99
Angel, Justus, 384
Angel, Martha [née Waight], 384
Anguilla (Caribbean island), xxvi, 78, 93, 99
animal manure, xxviii, 107, 111, 113, 114, 144, 155, 158, 159, 160, 163, 164, 172, 297, 344, 511, 516
animal power (for gins), 188, 198, 218, 230
annual growth (of cotton), 64, 90
Antigua (Caribbean island), 84, 299, 329
Appalachian Mountains, 4
Arawak (Greater Antilles), 75
Arcuate Section, 8
Argentina. 78, 92
Arizona, xxxii, xxxiii, 61, 85, 239
Arkwright, Richard (1732-1792), xi, xxv, xxxvi, 78, 248-49, 252-53, *254*, 255-57, 259, 267, 270, 275, 509
Ash, Captain Richard, 341
Ash, Martha, 341

Ashe, John (d. 1828), 481
Ashe, Richard Russell (d. 1806), 461
Ashe's (Little Edisto) Plantation, Edisto Island, 103, 360-61, 366, 395, 427, 481-82, 491, 502
Ashley River, 78
Asia, xxiv, 58, 61, 72, 190, 263
Asiatic cotton, 55, 238, 261
Atlantic Coast, 30, 62, 78, 104, 299, 512
Atlantic Coastal Plain, 3, 4, 8
Atlantic Ocean, 3
atmospheric steam engine, xxvi, 218, 270
Augusta, Georgia, 204, 277, 308
Augusta Daily Chronicle & Sentinel, 277
Australia, 56, 61, 69, 72, 74, 88
Bagnall, William R., 276-77, 503
Bahamas, xxv, 75, 76, 81, 93, 94, 95, 99, 155, 188, 200, 202
Bailey, Henry (1734-1764), 407
Bailey Island, St. John's Colleton Parish, 103
Bailey, Mary [née Baynard] (d. 1792), 407, 496
Bailey, Susan Providence (1855-1931), 387, 493, 502
Baker, Isabella Caroline [née Field] (1785-1864), 396, 493, 495-97
bale(s) of cotton, 94, 117, 137, 183, 184, 233, 340
Barbados, 65, 76, 78, 84, 329
Barcley, John. 186
Barnwell, Bower Williamson (1825-1895), 391, 494
Barnwell, Catherine Osborn (1809-1886), 390, 492, 494
Barnwell, Edward (1757-1808), 410, 492, 494
Barnwell, Edward (1785-1860), 410 , 494
Barnwell, Eliza (1807-1891), 445-46, 493-94
Barnwell, Elizabeth Hayne [née Wigg] (1775-1823), 390, 492, 494
Barnwell, Isabel, 123. 132
Barnwell Island, St. Helena Parish, 103, 317, 488
Barnwell, Jean Kerr [née Richardson] (1811-1888), 410-11, 492, 494
Barnwell, John Gibbes (1778-1828), 445, 494
Barnwell, John Gibbes (1831-1888), 446, 494
Barnwell, Joseph Walker (1846-1930), 389, 494
Barnwell, Mary Gibbes (1795-1853), 391, 493-94
Barnwell, Robert Gibbes (1761-1814), 389-90, 445, 492, 494
Barnwell, Robert Woodward (1801-1882), 390, 445-47, 493-94
Barnwell, Stephen Elliott (1842-1923), 390, 494
Barnwell, Thomas Osborn (1815-1879), 390, 410-11, 492, 494
Barnwell, William Hazzard Wigg (1806-1863), 389-90, 447, 492, 494
Barnwell, William Wigg (1793-1856), 391, 410, 494
barrier islands, ix, 3, 8, 9, *10*, 11, *13*, 14, 15, 18, 19,

INDEX

21, 24, 25, 26, 29, 30, 31, 57, 103, 117, 138, 139, 514
Bartram, William (1739-1823), xxvi, 79, 172
Bassnett, Elizabeth (1734-1798), 345
Baynard, Abigail Mikell (1797-1830), 425-26, 436-37, 495, 501
Baynard, Abigail Mikell (1839-1905), 427, 439, 482, 491, 495, 502
Baynard, Ann Ninian [née Jenkins] (1792-1822), 437, 491, 493, 495, 497
Baynard, Catherine (1831-1893), 394, 491, 495
Baynard, Edward Mitchell (1830-1882), 394, 439, 491, 495
Baynard, Elizabeth [née Grimball] (1735-1773), 394, 491, 494
Baynard, Elizabeth Ann [née Mikell] (1773-1815), 436-37, 493, 495, 498, 501
Baynard, Elizabeth Grimball (1794-1857), 425-27, 436-37, 495
Baynard, John C., 394, 495
Baynard, Mary (d. 1792), 407, 496
Baynard, Mary Bailey [née Swinton] (1808-1890), 437-39, 493, 495
Baynard, Sally [née Calder], 394, 491, 494
Baynard, Sarah [née Black] (1772-1793), 436, 495
Baynard, Thomas (1763-1805), 394, 436, 491, 494
Baynard, William (1732-1772), 394, 436, 491, 494
Baynard, William (1766-1802), 394, 425, 436, 493-95
Baynard, William Edings (1800-1849), 394, 436, 495
Baynard, William Grimball (1792-1861), 382, 394, 425, 427, 436-9, 482, 493, 495
Baynard's Old Place, Edisto Island, 360, 362, 393-95, 436, 482
Bayview Plantation, Edisto Island, 466
beach-ridge barrier islands, 3, 15, 18, 29
beach-ridge relict islands, 9, 11, 14, 28
beach ridges, 18
Beasley, J. O., xxxiv, 67, 504
Beaufort, South Carolina, x, xxviii, xxix, xxx, 139, 140, 144, 163, 193, 207, *211*, 215, 340, 350, 487-88, 510
Beaufort County, South Carolina, xxi, xxxi, 3, 14, 24, 30, 31, 103, 139, 143, 209, 325, 488, 504, 515
beds (for planting), x, 75, 106, 139, 144, 149, 150, 152, 155, *156*, 158, 160, 163, 164, 165, 166, *167*, 171, 172
Belvidere Plantation, St. John's Parish, Berkeley, 109, 111, 115, 287, 300
Bennett, Charles A., 188, *189, 191, 194*, 196, *197*, 210, *212, 224*, 504
Berkeley County, South Carolina, xxvii, 81, 111, 115, 108, 165, 300, 321
Bird Key, Charleston County, 21

Bissett, Alexander, 94
Blacklock (or Blackloch) Plantation, Johns Island, *349*, 353, 354
Blackman, J. K., 151, 504
Black Oak Agricultural Society, 108, 110, 1135, 115, 209, 284, 319, 321, 504, 507, 514-15
Black Oak Church, 115
black-seed cotton, 78, 80, 96, 108, 116, 342
Black, Sarah (1772-1793), 436, 495
Black Yeomanry: Life on St. Helena Island, xxxiii, 337, 519
Bleak Hall Plantation, Edisto Island, 374-76, 384
Blodgett, Himan M., 460, 462
Blodgett, Sarah [née Irvine] (d. 1833), 459-60
Bloody Point (*see* Oakley Hall), 459-60
blue cotton, 136, 149, 296, 297
Bluff Plantation, The, St. Helena Island, 424
Blue Nile River, 83
Bluffton, St. Luke's Parish, 360, 415, 418, 455, 484
bobbin, 243, 245, 250, 253
Boesch, J.C., x, xxxii, 213, 215, *217*, 218, 488
Bohicket Creek, 11
Bolton, England, xxvi, 233, 256, 273, 279, 488
Bolton Museum, 279
Bombacaceae family, 58, 63
Bómbus, 63
Boone, Catherine (d. 1865), 430
Botume, Elizabeth H., 380, 391
Bourbon cotton, xxvi, 343, 353, 354
Bradford County, Florida, 125, 128
Brazil, 62, 67, 69, 76
breeders rights, 148
Brewton, Miles, 342
Brick House Plantation, Edisto Island, 359, 381-82, 386, 394
Brick House (Stanyarne Hall) Plantation, Johns Island, 367, 448-50, 498
British colonies, 271
British cotton trade, 269, 270, 507
British Museum of Natural History, London, 65, 72, 279
Broad Creek, Hilton Head Island, 9, 19
Broad River, 4
Brookland Plantation, Edisto Island, 360, 362, 451-53
Brown, Bubberson, 289
brown Egyptian cotton, 53, 331
Brown, Robert, 384
Bullard, Mary R., xxxv, 119, 505
Bull Island, Beaufort County, 95, 103, 151, 317, 323
Bull Island, Christ Church Parish, 3, 8, *17*, 18, 95, 103, 139, 323
Bullogh County, Georgia, 119
bumble bees, 63

INDEX

Burden Creek, Johns Island, 345-46, 348, 353
Burden, Kinsey (1775-1859), vi, ix, xi, xix, xxi, xxiii, xxvii, xxviii, xxix, 81, 96, *98*, 99, 103, 105, 110, 117, 145, 146, 174, 188, 192, 193, 200, 297, 285, 308, 315, 320, 341, 342, 343, 344, 346, 348, 350-51, 353-54
Burden, Kinsey, Jr., 345, 353
Burden, Kinsey, Sr. (d. 1785), xxvi, xxviii, 192, 342, 343, 345, 350
Burden, Portia Ash, xxvi, 343, 348, 353
Burden, Theodora Ash, 341, 354
Burden's Island, St. Paul's Parish, ix, xxvi, xxvii, 80, 96, *97*, 100, 342-45, 348, 353
Bureau of Plant Industry, U.S., xx, 121, 129, 148
Bureau of Statistics, U.S., 339
Burton, Anthony, 245, 253, 265, 281, 505
Bury, in Lancashire, xxv, 230, 265
Butler, Major Pierce (1744-1822), 117
buyers (of cotton), 81, 130, 204, 269, 300, 301, 304, 305, 306, 311, 331
Cain, William (1792-1878)
Cairo, Egypt, 82
calcicoles, 28, 37
calcium arsenate, 130
Calder, Sally, 394, 491, 494
calico. 239, 269, 282
Campbell, Edward Delegal, 452
canal irrigation, 74
Cape Cod, Massachusetts, 8
Cape Henry, 8
Cape Lookout, 8
Cape Romain, South Carolina, 8
Capers, Charles, 193, 215, 505
Capers Island, Christ Church Parish, 3, 9, 18, 31, 103, 159
Capers, William H., xxviii, 175, 180, 505
Capes Plantation, Johns Island, 450
carding, 240, 265, 270, 281
carding machine (of Lewis Paul), xxv, 245, 265, 270, 281, 247
Carib gardens (Lesser Antilles), 75
Caribbean, xix, xxiv, xxvi, 62, 73, 74, 76, 78, 89, 93, 117, 190, 195, 299, 329, 519
Carolina gold rice, xvii, 108, 133, 298, 299, 332
Carolina (the ship) 78
Carolina Gazette, 338, 342
Cartwright, Dr. Edmund (1743-1823), xxvi, 267, *268*, 269
Carver, Eleazor, Jr., x, 207, *210*, 487
Cassina Point Plantation, Edisto Island, 361, *364*, 367, 373, 413, 470-72, 492, 501
Catawba River, 4
Catling, Harold, 256-57, *244*, *258*, 505

Cedar Springs Plantation, Johns Island, 385
Cedar Springs Plantation, St. John's Parish, Berkeley, 109-110, 131
cellulose, *1*, 53, 63
Census Bureau, U.S., 120, 331, 416, 420, 424, 428, 440, 444, 447, 453, 456, 464, 469, 472, 476, 482, 509
Central America, 62, 73, 75, 289
Chanca, Diego Alvarez, 75-76
Chaplin, Benjamin, 396, 468, 495, 497
Chaplin, Eliza Mary (1825-1894), 467-69, 493, 496-97
Chaplin, Elizabeth [née Fripp] (1750-1790), 396, 493, 495-96
Chaplin, Isabella Caroline [née Field] (1785-1864), 396, 493, 495-97
Chaplin, Martha [née Fripp] (b. 1788), 468, 496
Chaplin, Mary Sarah (1792-1876), 421, 492, 495, 497
Chaplin, Mary Thomson [née McDowell] (1822-1851), 397-98, 493, 495-96
Chaplin, Saxby (1780-1828), 396, 493, 495-96
Chaplin, Sophy [née Creighton] (d. 1891), 397-98, 493, 496
Chaplin, Thomas Benjamin (b. 1742), 396, 493, 495-96
Chaplin, Thomas Benjamin (1822-1890), 396-98, 493, 495
Charleston Courier, 339-40, 385, 412, 416, 427-28, 450, 463-64, 466, 475-76, 482
Charleston economy, 113, 298, 302, 314, 318, 322, 332
Charleston Exposition, 279
Charleston Harbor, 9, 21
Charleston Library Society, xxiii, 354
Charleston Mercury, 306, 426, 428, 432, 476, 510
Charleston Museum, xv, xxiii, 109, 2230, 233, 237, 278-79, 337, 340
Charleston News and Courier, 115, 143, 288, 340, 504, 515
Charleston, South Carolina, xv, xxi, 204, 218, 275-76, 299, 302, 305-06, 308, 310, 314-15, 318, 334, 339
Cherry Hill Plantation, St. Helena Island, 402
China, 60, 74, 88, 190, 322
Chisolm, Mary Elizabeth [née Edings] (1778-1848), 407, 434, 492, 496
Chisolm, Mary Julia (1807-1826), 434
Chisolm, Robert, 158, 285, 287, 417, 506
Chisolm, Robert Trail (1771-1821), 434-35, 492, 496
Chisolm, Susan Matilda Harriet (1806-1865), 434-35, 492
Chisolm's Plantation (*see* The Launch)
chopping cotton, 168
Christ Church Parish, South Carolina, 404, 479-80, 493

INDEX

Church of the Cross, Bluffton, 484
Churkha roller gin, 187, 190-93, 222, 238
citrus industry, Florida, 129, 131
Civil War, xvii, xviii, xxi, xxx, xxxi, 50, 81, 83-84, 106, 115, 118-19, 128, 134-36, 138, 140, 150-52, 155, 158, 160, 163, 170, 185, 237, 277, 299-300, 305-06,, 322, 324, 327-28, 332, 334, 337, 340-41, 406, 411, 421, 435, 439, 444, 450, 452, 454, 456, 466, 468, 472, 482, 484, 504-05, 509, 513
Clark, Elizabeth (1779-1817), 374, 387, 493
Clark, James (1744-1790), 388
Clark, Martha Mary Murray (1821-1850), 466, 492, 501, 502
clay, 4, 8, 11, 21, 25, 62, 138, 294
cloth, xvii, xiv, xxvi, 75, 188, 202, 222, 238-39, 252, 256, 259-61, 263, 265, 267, 269, 274-75, 278, 281, 330, 334
Clough, Monica, 275, 506
coastal plain, 3-4, 8, 21, 75, 129
Coffin, Anna Sarah Smith (1804-1868), 400, 474
Coffin, Ebenezer (1765-1817), 361, 400-03, 506
Coffin, Harriet [née McPherson] (1812-1852), 402
Coffin, Mary [née Mathews] (1771-1813), 400-02
Coffin Point Plantation, St. Helena Island, 361, 366, 398, 400-03, 506
Coffin, Thomas Aston (1795-1863), 384, 400-02, 474
Coggins Point (Colgin's Point) Plantation, Hilton Head, 367, 414-16, 455
Colleton County, South Carolina, 25, 27, 103, 344
Colón, Fernando, 75-6
colonial period, 78-9
Columbian Museum and Savannah Adviser, 78
Columbia, South Carolina, 37, 50, 308, 354, 402, 435, 445-46
Columbus, Christopher, xxv, 75, 84, 89
combing, 202, 222, 226, 253, 281, 330
composite barrier island, 9
Connecticut, xxx, 226, 279, 488
continental shelf, 4, 8
continuous spinning, 253
Cook, O. F., 145, 5066
Cooper River, 9, 81, 108, 204, 308
Coosawhatchie, St. Luke's Parish, 390, 445
corn, 111, 129, 152, 159, 287, 300, 324, 327, 343-44, 370, 411, 423, 475
Cothern, J. Tom, 85, 146, 516
Cotton Hope Plantation, Hilton Head Island, xxi, 370, 415, 447
Cotton Island, 11
cotton seed, xix, 48-50, 70, 72, 78, 80, 93-4, 100, 120, 144, 155, 163, 165-66, 168, 172, 180, 186, 188, 200, 230, 289, 292, 296, 329, 343-45, 351, 353, 487, 516
cottonseed oil, 50, 54, 60
cotton seed permeability, 69, 70, 90-1
countershed (in weaving), 261-62, 264
Crawford, James, 465-66
Crawford, M. D. C., xxxiii, 257, 259-60, 263, 273, 506
Crawford's Plantation, Edisto Island, 362, 429, 465-66, 492, 498, 502
Creighton, Sophy (d. 1891), 397-98, 493, 496
Cretaceous Period, 4, 37
Croft, Charlotte [née Jenkins] (1820-1892), 421, 497
Croft Place (*see* Mary Jenkins Plantation)
Croft, Randell (1808-1869), 421, 497
Crompton, Samuel (1753-1827), xix, xxvi, 248-49, 255-59, 267, 270, 273
crop rotation, 118, 134-35, 152, 154, 293, 296-97
cross-pollination, 46, 63
Cuba, 75
cuesta(s), 21, 37
cultivar, xxxii, xxxiii, xxxiv, 40, 49, 53-54, 56, 62-3, 221, 288, 293, 296, 315, 330, 338
cultivars of *G. barbadense*, xxiii, xix, xx, xxiv, xxv, xxvi, xxxii, xxxiv, xxxv, 41, 43, 45, 46-7, 49-50, 56, 58, 61-63, 64-68, 70, 72-78, 80, 82, 84-95, 99, 101, 105, 131, 190, 192, 195, 239, 288, 298, 511, 514, 518-19
  Barbados Rivers, 84
  Bleak Hall, 99, 146, 315
  Bourbon, xxvi, 314, 343, 353-54
  brown Egyptian, 53, 331
  early Ashmouni, xxix, 82-3
  Gordon C, 120
  Giza 7, xxxiii, 83
  Jumel, xxvii, 82-3, 87
  Meade, xxxiii, 292-3, 506
  Mit Afifi, xxxi, xxxii, 83, 85
  Peruvian Tanguis, 88
  Pima, xxxii, xxxiii, xxxiv, 56, 62, 84-88, 90, 99, 233, 330
  Rivers, xxxii, 84, 296, 329
  Sakellaridis (=Sakel), xxxii, xxxiv, 83, 87, 330-31
  Seabrook, xxxiii, xxxiv, 87, 99, 129, 315
  SxP, 87
  Yuma, xxxii, xxxiii, 85, 99, 330, 338
Cumberland Island, Georgia, xxxv, 8-9, 118-19, 132, 505
Cypress Trees Plantation, Edisto Island, 374, 380
Dacha muslins, 241
Damp, Jonathan E., 239, 506
Datah Island, St. Helena Parish, 103, 317
Daufuskie Island, St. Luke's Parish, 3, 18, 31, 102, 139, 415-16, 459-64, 505, 57

524

INDEX

see named plantations:
    Freeport
    Haig Point
    Maryfield
    Melrose (Salt Pond)
    Newburg
    Oakley Hall (Bloody Point)
    Oakridge
Davant, John, 415
day-neutral flowering, xxvi, 39, 57, 62, 64, 73, 78, 80, 80-95, 99, 110, 116, 133, 299
DeBow's Review, 127, 508
Dedcott's Island, South Carolina, 341-42, 353
de Lasteyrie, Countess [Martha Washington Seabrook] (b. 1828), 413, 501
Delta & Pine Land Company, 87
Dennie, Joseph, 200, 507
Department of Agriculture, U.S., 84, 1332, 284, 292, 296, 330, 506-07, 509-10, 513, 517-18
Department of Agronomy, University of Florida, 132
Dewees Island, Christ Church Parish, 9
diamondback rattlesnake, 11
Dimmick, John, 484
diploid cells, xxiv, 61, 63, 67-70
diseases of cotton, common names
    angular leaf spot, 293
    anthracnose, 175, 293-95
    bacterial blight, 293, 297
    blackarm, 293
    cotton wilt, 294
    Fusarium wilt, 294, 297
    pink boll-rot, 294
    root-knot, 296-97
    sore-shin, 293-94
diseases, scientific names
    Bacterium malvacearum, 297
    Colletotrichum gossypii, 294
    Fusarium oxysporum f. sp. *vasinfectum,* 294, 297
    Heterodera radicicola, 297
    Meloidogyne incognita, 296-97
    Neocosmospora vasinfecta, 297
    Rhizoctonia solani, 293
    Xanthomonas campestris pv *malvacearum,* 293, 297
distaff, 238, 240-41, 243, 281
distaff spinning, 240
Dobson & Barlow Ltd., England, 233, *235*
docks, of Liverpool, 271
doff (doffer), xxxiii, 186, 198, 204, 207, 222, 225-27, 229, 233
domestication (of cottons), 54, 62, 69-70, 72, 74-5
Doncaster, in Yorkshire, 267
Donnell, E. J., xxxi, 311, 335, 339, 507

dooryard cottons, xxiv, xxv, 39, 62-3, 73-75, 80, 90-1, 93
Double Action McCarthy Gin, 233, *235*
double roller (to make beds), *157*
Doyle, C. B., 145, 329, 506
drainage (of fields), xxxi, 46, 106, 135, 139, 144, 149-53, 155, 158, 164, 171-72, 288, 294, 297, 325-26, 370
drawing rollers, 257
Drayton, Charles (c. 1744-1820), 198, 200, 202, 218
Drayton, Emma Catherine [née Pope] (d. 1854), 455, 492, 499
Drayton, John M. (1765-1820), 195, 198, 507
Drayton, Percival (1812-1865), 454
Drayton, Thomas Fenwick (1808-1891), 454-56, 492, 499
DuBose, Samuel, 110, 131, 507
DuBignon, Christophe P. (1739-1825), 117-18
Duncan, Mary D. B. (1829-1861), 391, 493
Duncan, William, 230, 237, 507
Dunn, Mary [née Martinangele] (1785-1878), 462
Duval County, Florida, 123, 125
Earle, John, 78-9
East Florida, 101, 116, *122,* 123-25
East India Company, 269, 324
ebb-tidal delta, 19-21
Ecuador, xviii, xxiv, xxxv, 62, 73-4, 89-90, 99, 238-39, 298, 507
Edings Bay, Edisto Island, 15, 18, 37, 382, 406-07, 434, 443, 466, 471-72, 508
Edings, Benjamin (1742-1784), 407, 496, 498
Edings, Emma Elizabeth (1793-1856), 417-19, 441, 493, 496, 501
Edings, Hess Marion Waring [née Smith] (c. 1817-1904), 465-66, 492, 496, 498
Edings, John Evans (1808-1836), 408-09, 493, 496-97
Edings, John Evans, Jr. (1832-1883), 409, 419, 441, 493, 496, 500
Edings, Joseph (1770-1857), 407, 419, 496
Edings, Josephine Edings [née Seabrook] (c. 1834-1883), 409, 419, 441-43, 493, 496, 500
Edings, Martha Washington (1799-1892), 417, 441-43, 492, 496, 500
Edings, Mary [née Baynard] (d. 1792), 407
Edings, Mary Baynard (c. 1800-1856), 455, 491-92, 496, 499
Edings, Mary Elizabeth (1778-1848), 407, 434, 492 496
Edings, Mary Wilkinson [née Mathews] (b. 1809), 408-09, 493, 496-97
Edings, Sarah [née Evans] (d. 1857), 407-09, 493-96
Edings, Sarah Ann [née Mikell] (1810-1838), 466, 496, 498

INDEX

Edings, William (d. 1767), 407-09
Edings, William (1766-1836), 407-09, 466, 493, 496
Edings, William (1809-1858), 466, 492, 496, 498
Edings, William (d. 1850), 409, 496
Edings, William, Plantation, Edisto Island, 362, 367, 369, 407-09, 419, 493, 496
Edingsville Beach, Edisto Island, 15-16, 18, 37, 409
Edingsville (village), Edisto Island, *16*, 18, 37, 315, 360, 407, 409, 439, 443, 470, 472
Edisto Beach, Edisto Island, 9, *16*, 18, 37
Edisto Island Museum, 230, 233
Edisto Island, St. John's Colleton Parish
see named plantations:
    Ashe's (Little Edisto)
    Baynard's Old Place
    Bayview
    Bleak Hall
    Brick House
    Brookland
    Cassina Point
    Crawford's
    Cypress Trees
    Edings, William
    Chisolm's (*see* The Launch)
    Frogmore
    Governor's Bluff
    Gun Bluff
    Hill Tract (*see* Brookland)
    Hopkinson's
    The Launch
    Laurel Hill
    Little Edisto (*see* Ashe's)
    Medway (*see* The Launch)
    Middleton's (*see* The Launch)
    Oak Island
    Old Dominion
    Old House
    Peter's Point
    Pine Barren
    Pine Ridge (*see* Baynard's Old Place)
    Point of Pines
    Prospect Hill
    Russell's Point (*see* Ashe's/Little Edisto)
    Seabrook, William
    Seaside (*see* William Edings)
    Sharegools (Shargould)
    Spanish Mount
    Swallows Bluff
    Windsor (*see* Ashe's/Little Edisto)
Edisto River, *23*, 37, 342, 360, 406, 445
Egypt, xxiv, 82-88, 261, 279, 306, 513
Egyptian cotton, xxvii, xxix, xxi, xxxii, xxxiii, 53, *55*, 56-7, 64, 74, 81-8, 90, 99, 215, 233, 320, 324, 330-31, 503

Elliott, William, xxiii, xxvi, xxvii, xxviii, xxx, 93, 96, 100, 14, 114, 127, 134, 139-40, 145, 148-49, 215, 274, 285, 300, 303-04, 324, 334, 350-51, 515
Ely, T., *212*
Emancipation Proclamation, 324
Embargo Act of 1807, xxvii, 315, 339
Embayed Section, 8
Endless Return Cotton-whipper, 177, *179*
Endrizzi, J. E., xxxv, 67, 69, 507
endochrome, 53
English Parliament, 269
Eocene Epoch, 69
epicalyx (of the flower), *47*
erosion (eroding), 11, 15, 18-19, 21, 29, 31, 34, 37
erosion-remnant islands, 3, 8-9, 11, 21-22, 24-26, 30-31, 34, 38, 57, 103, 138-9
Europe, xvii, xxv, 3, 58, 60, 81, 239, 241, 245, 259, 261, 243, 249, 274-75, 277, 299, 307, 324, 371, 425, 470
Evans, Elizabeth (1767-1826), 382, 491-93, 495-96, 498
Evans, Henrietta (d. 1842), 384, 492, 501
Evans, Mary Elizabeth [née Edings] (1778-1848), 407, 434, 492, 496
Evans, Sarah (d. 1857), 407-09, 493-496
Evans, William (d. 1802), 434, 492, 496
Eve, Joseph (1760-1835), xxvi, xxvii, 117, 200, 487, 507
Extra-long-staple cotton (ELS), 56, 239, 507, 513
Exuma (Caribbean island), 78, 93
Faber, Henry (d. 1827), 387
factors (companies)
    Henry W. Frost & Company, 278, 337, 340
    Trapmann, Jahncke & Company, 276, 302, 304
    Trapmann, Schmidt & Company, 276, 320-21, 344
    Teasdale & Kiddle, 343
factorage system, 300-02, 305, 307, 331
fall-line sandhills, 4
fallow (fields), 60, 135, 152, 411
Feliciana Plantation, St. Helena Island, 477
Fenwick, John (d. 1745), 383
Fenwick Hall (*see* Head Quarters)
Fenwick Island, St. Bartholomew Parish, 452
fiber classification
    absence of faults, 54
    fiber strength, 54, 56
    length, 56
    fineness, 54, 56
    maturity, 54, 56
    uniformity, 54
    yarn strength, 54
Fickling, Jeremiah, 430
Fickling, Jonathan, 80
Field, Isabella Caroline (1785-1864), 396, 493, 495-97

INDEX

field rotation, 152, 296
finger ginning, 187-88
Finlay & Company, 275
Finlay, James, 255, 275
Finlay, Kirkman (1772-1842), 255, 275
Fish Hall (Fish Haul) Plantation, Hilton Head Island, 366, *372*, 415, 454-56, 492, 499, 517
Fish Haul (*see* Fish Hall)
fish weir, 260
flax, 39, 85, 238, 245, 248, 252, 261, 514
floodplain, 8-9
flood-tidal delta, 15, 19, *20*
Florida, xvii, xx, xxxii, xxxiii, 3, 8, 79-81, 84-5, 87, 89, 101, 103-05, 115-16, 119-33, 136, 143, 195, 198, 215, 218, 221, 233, 278, 287, 297, 299, 306, 313-14, 326, 328-31, 336, 340, 488, 504, 508, 512, 514-15, 517-19
Florida interior sea island cotton, xx, xxxiv, 81, 101, 119, 125, 127-28, 278, 313, 340
Florida Sea-Island Cotton Law, 130
flower(s) (of cotton), xxvi, 39-40, 43, *44-5*, 46, *47*, 49, 56-58, 62, 64, 73-5, 80, 89-91, 93, 95, 99, 106, 164, 173, 289, 292, 511
Floyd, M. H., 215
flyer (for twisting yarn), 243, 245, 252-53
flying shuttle, xxv, 248, 252, 265, 267-69, 273
Folly Beach, South Carolina, 14, 18-9
Foss, Leland L., xxxii, 213, 488
Frampton Creek, 18
Frampton, Margaret (1786-1830), 475
France, xvii, 108, 117, 119, 265, 269, 273-74, 276, 279, 321-22, 324-25, 337, 339, 354
Frank Leslie's Popular Monthly, xxxi, 213, 509
Frazier, Alex, 462
freedmen, xxx, xxxi, 117, 119, 138, 305, 307, 325-28, 337, 340, 375, 380, 391, 402, 409, 419, 421, 457, 466
Freedmen's Bureau, xxxi, 380, 391, 402, 419, 421, 424, 457, 466
Freedmen's Bureau Act, xxx, xxxi, 326-27
Freeport Plantation, Daufuskie Island, 460
Freer, Charles (1760-1809), 449
Freer, Maria Augusta (1793-1839), 449
Freer, Mary [née Stanyarne] (1764-1812), 449
French Revolution, 117, 273-74, 278, 354
freshet, 111, 131
Fripp, Ann Jenkins (1793-1878), 382, 491, 496, 498
Fripp, Edgar (1806-1860), 423-24, 493, 497
Fripp, Edgar Walter (1857-1920), 424, 497
Fripp, Eliza (1810-1860), 423-24, 493, 497
Fripp, Elizabeth (1750-1790), 396, 493, 495-96
Fripp Island, South Carolina, 14
Fripp, John Edwin (1831-1906), 424, 497
Fripp, Martha (b. 1788), 468, 496

Fripp, Thomas James (1808-1840), 457, 496
Fripp, Tom, Plantation, St. Helena Island, 362, 457-58, 496
Frogmore Plantation, Edisto Island, 279, 361, 425-28, 443, 492, 495
Frogmore Plantation, St. Helena Island, 402
fruit (of cotton plant), 39-40, 43, 46, 49, 56-8, 65, 80, 91, 93-5, 99, 106, 165, 169, 171, 173, 284, 293, 297
Fryxell, Paul A., xxxiv, 58, 61-3, 65, 70-2, 354, 508
Fuller, Benjamin, 479
Fuller, Edward Nathaniel (1820-1896), 431, 479-80, 493, 498
Fuller, Mary Ann [née Mikell] (1822-1899), 431, 479-80, 493, 498
Fuller, Sarah Green [née Porteous] (1778-1850), 479
fustian, 252, 275
Gadsden, Sam (1882-1981), 305
Gaillard, Captain Peter (1783-1843), xxvii, 109-11, 116, 300, 508
Galapagos Islands, 61-2, 67
Geddes, Gilbert (1806-1848), 387
Geiger, Agnes, 263
genome, xxiv, xxxv, 49, 61, 63, 67, 69-70, 72
genome group, 49, 61, 63, 69
Georgetown, South Carolina, xxix, 308, 425, 510
Georgia, xvii, xix, xx, xxiii, xxvi, xxvii, xxviii, xxxii, xxxiii, xxxiv, 3, 6, 8-10, 62, 78-81, 84-5, 87, 89, 93-5, 99, 101, 103-5, 110, 116-21, 123-25, 127-33, 136, 143, 186, 188, 195, 200, 202, 204, 213, 215, 218, 233, 274, 276-78, 283, 288, 292, 298-99, 306, 314, 328-31, 334-35, 337, 340, 343, 416, 456, 464, 487, 488, 505, 509, 511-12, 516-18
Georgia interior sea island cotton, xxxiv, 56, 81, 87, 101, 120, *126*, 278, 313, 329-30
Gezira Plain, Sudan, 83
Gibbes, John, 383
Gibbes, Lewis R., 18, 37, 508
Gila River Pima Indian Reservation, 85
Gilchrist County, Florida, 130
Gillisonville, St. Luke's Parish, 315
gin house, xxix, 205, 218, 307, 370, 400, 427
glacial cycles, 4
glaciation, 4, 37
glaciers, xxiv, 4-5, 8
Glasgow, Scotland, 116, 196, 255, 273, 275, 282, 334, 506
Gondwanaland, 69
Gordon C seed, the, 120
Gordon, G. A., 120, 278, 508
Gossypium, genome groups, xvii, xxiv, xxxiii, xxxiv, xxxv, 3, 39-40, 46, 57-8, 60, 65, 69-71, 148, 504, 507-08, 510, 516, 518

INDEX

gossypol, 48, *48*, 50, 58
gossypol glands, 40
Governor's Bluff Plantation, Edisto Island, 431, 479-80
Grahamville, St. Luke's Parish, 315, 484
Gray Field on Cumberland Island, Georgia, 118
Gray, Lewis Cecil, xxxiv, 56, 96, 101, 116, 127, 131-32, 158, 190, 310, 312-13, 318, 321, 334, 339, 351, 508
Grayson, William John (1788-1863), 402, 508
Great Britain, xvii, xix, xxiii, 269-71, 275, 277, 299, 324, 330, 337-38, 344, 503
Greater Antilles, xxvi, 75, 92
Green, Samuel (d. c. 1767), 415, 455, 492
Green, Sarah, 415, 455, 492, 499
green-seed cotton, 80, 113-14, 116, 190, 221, 342
Greene, General Nathanael, 492
Greene, Mrs. Nathanael, 492, 499
Greenville, South Carolina, 421, 446
Greenwood, South Carolina, 475
Gregorie, Anne K. (1887-1960), 135, 150, 204, 342, 508
Grimball, Elizabeth (1735-1773), 394, 491, 494
The Grove Plantation, St. Paul's Parish, 445
growing season, length of, *32*, 36, 60, 85, 87, 105-06, 108, 116, 164, 173, 289
Guayas Estuary, Ecuador, 62, 74
Gulf of Mexico, 31, 62, 125, 287, 392
Gulf Stream, 125
gumbo, 60
Gun Bluff Plantation, Edisto Island, 500
Habersham, Isabella Rae, 460, 462
Haig Point Plantation, Daufuskie Island, 415, 460, 462, 517
Hamilton County, Florida, 123, 125, 128
Hamilton, James, 353
Hamilton, Paul (d. c. 1738), 381
Hamlin, T. J., 292
Hammond, Harry, 154, 164, 509
Hampton Plantation, St. Simons Island, Georgia, 117
Hanahan, Elizabeth Mary (1802-1888), 452, 491, 499
Hanahan, John (1797-1856), 387-88
Hanahan, Martha Mary (1823-1870), 387, 493, 501
hand ginning, 187, 192-94
hand loom, 239, 241, 248, 256, 260, 263, 265, 267
hand loom, standard, 263, *266*
hand spinning, 240, 256, 281
hank, 245, 257, 259, 281
Hanover Plantation, St. John's Parish, Berkeley, 110, 131
haploid cells, 67-8, 72
Harbor Island, St. Helena Parish, 19, 402
Hardput Plantation, St. John's Parish, Berkeley, 110, 114, 116

Hargreaves, James (1720-1778), xxv, 247-53, 256-57, 259, 267, 269, 275, 281, 503
Harper's New Monthly Magazine, 124, 183, 380, 504
Harris, J. William, 119, 509, 462
Harrison, Ann (d. 1850), 462
Harvie, James, xxvii, 196, *199*, 204, 218, 226
Haskell, Jennie, xxi, 175-78, 180-81, 213-14, 218, 509
hauling (soil around cotton base), 165, 171
Hawaiian Islands, 62, 67
headlands, 15
Head Quarters Plantation, Johns Island, 359, *363*, 383-86, 492, 501
heck, 243
heddle, xxiv, 74, 88, 261, 263, 265, 282
Heritage of Cotton, xxxiii, 260, 506
high-count yarns, 273-74
Hill Tract (*see* Brookland Plantation)
Hilton Head Island, St. Luke's Parish, 274, 300, 314, 323, 325, 380, 394, 414, 416, 418-19, 436, 439, 456, 459, 484, 492, 495, 505, 510, 512, 517
  See named plantations:
    Coggins (Colgins) Point
    Cotton Hope
    Fish Hall
    Point Comfort
    Seabrook
    Springfield
Hindu (Hindus), 238-39, 259
History of the Island of Barbadoes, 76, 512
hoe (for cultivation), 117, 135, 137, 150, 152, 155, 158, 160, 165-66, 168, 170-71, 331
Holmes, Hodgen, 186
Holocene Epoch, 8-10, 14, 37
holotype, 65, 72
Hopi (Native Americans), 239, 339
Hopkinson, Carolina Lafayette [née Seabrook] (1825-1879), 417, 470-72, 492, 501
Hopkinson, James (1810-1875), 361, 413, 470-72, 492, 501
Hopkinson, Martha Julia (1856-1946), 471-72, 501
Hopkinson's Plantation, Edisto Island, 361, 413, 472
horizontal flowering interval, 43
horse power, 205, 252, 331, 488
Hortus Upsaliensis, 65
Howe, Elias, 277
Hudson, E.W., 85
Huguenots, 108, 321, 507, 514
Hughes, Mary Wilkinson [née Mathews] (b. 1809), 408-09, 493, 496-97
Hughes, Optimus, 409, 497
hull (of cotton seed), 31, 49
Hunting Island, St. Helena Parish, 19

INDEX

Hurricanes, xxxi, 14, 18, 29, 31, 118, 299, 359, 409, 478

The Hut Plantation, Johns Island, 253-54

Hutchinson Island, St. Bartholomew Parish, 25, *27*, 103

Hutchinson, J. B., xxxiv, 72, 78, 84, 90, 92, 510

hybridization, 46, 49, 63, 69-70, 81, 83-4, 92, 99, 105-08, 116, 127-28, 130, 144, 146, 148, 278, 293, 329, 337

Ice Age, xxiv, 4-5, 9

Iceland, 261, 264

ice sheet, 4-5

Imperial Valley, California, xxxii, 85

improved cultivars, 62, 73-4, 92

India, 188, 190, 192, 238-39, 241, 255, 259, 269, 282, 324, 330, 338, 353

Indianfield Plantation, St. John's Parish, Berkeley, 109-10, 114, 116, 519

indigo, 76, 79-80, 111, 116, 163, 298-300, 343

Industrial Revolution, xvii, xviii, xix, 62, 239, 270, 273-74, 299-300

inlets, 9, 14, 18-9, 21, 25-6, 37

insecticide, xx, 46, 287, 297

insect pests, common names
American bollworm, 288
boll weevil, xviii, xxxiii, 81, 85, 119-21, 129-30, 237, 278, 288-92, 296, 327, 332, 334, 338, 510
caterpillar, 135, 150, 283-85, 287-88, 299, 319, 326
cock chaffer, 283
cotton caterpillar, xxvii, 115, 285-86, 288, 506
cotton leafworm, 285, 287
cotton worm, 285
cut-worm, 283
Mexican cotton-boll weevil, xxxi, xxxiii, 288-89
tobacco budworm, 40

insect pests, scientific names
Alabama argillacea, 287
Aletia argillacea, *2*85, 297
Anthonomus grandis, 289
Feltia annexa, 285
Heliothis armigera, 288

inter-glaciation, 4

intermittent spinning, 243, 248

introgression, 80, 89-92, 99

Irvine, Sarah (d. 1833), 459-60

Isle of Bourbon, 314, 353-54

Isle of Palms, Christ Church Parish, 18

James Finlay & Company, 275

James Island Agricultural Society, xxxi, 136, 150-51, 165, 284, 329, 511

James Island Experiment Station, 547

James Island, St. Andrews Parish, 12, 129, 135-36, 143-44, 148, 150-51, 153, 164-65, 172, 284, 292, 296, 315, 329, 431, 474-76, 498, 506, 510-11, 515, xxxi, xxxii, xxxiii

Jasper County, South Carolina, 30, 143

Jehossee Island, St. John's Colleton Parish, 198, 375, 380

Jekyll Island, Georgia, 95, 117-18

Jenkins, Ann (1765-1846), 452, 498, 500

Jenkins, Ann Jenkins [née Fripp] (1793-1878), 382, 491, 496, 498

Jenkins, Ann Ninian (1792-1822), 437, 491, 493, 495, 497

Jenkins, Barbara Calder (1784-1855), 449-50, 498

Jenkins, Catherine [née Boone] (d. 1865), 430

Jenkins, Charlotte (1820-1892), 421, 497

Jenkins, Christopher (1769-1794), 429, 493, 497

Jenkins, Christopher (1790-1830), 429-31

Jenkins, Eliza Mary [née Chaplin] (1825-1894), 467-69, 493, 496-97

Jenkins, Elizabeth [née Evans] (1767-1826), 382, 491, 495-96, 498

Jenkins, Hephzibah (1780-1847), 384, 498, 501

Jenkins, Isabella Caroline [née Field] (1785-1864), 396, 493, 495-97

Jenkins, John Sr., 432, 497

Jenkins, Joseph (1761-1828), 381-82, 384, 407, 453, 491, 495-96, 498

Jenkins, Joseph Evans (1793-1874), 382-394, 491, 496, 498

Jenkins, Mary [née Wilkinson] (1770-1813), 429-30, 493, 497

Jenkins, Mary, Plantation, St. Helena Island, 367, 421-22

Jenkins, Mary Sarah [née Chaplin] (1792-1876), 421, 492, 495, 497

Jenkins, Micah (1754-1831), 450, 498

Jenkins Neck (*see* Mary Jenkins Plantation)

Jenkins, Providence (1784-1846), 430, 497-98

Jenkins, William (1782-c. 1830), 421, 492, 495, 497

Jenkins, William J. (1818-1883), 467-69, 493, 496-97

Jenkins, William J., Plantation, St. Helena Island, 360, 361, 362, 366, 375, 375, 467-69, 493, 497

Jeremy Inlet, 18, 37

Jersey wheel, 241, 243-44, 248, 250, 256-57

Johnson, Guion G., 340, 354, 487, 511, xviii, xxxiii

Johns Island, St. John's Colleton Parish, xix, xxvii, 96, 98, 105, 143-45, 151, 315, 317, 345, 347, 349, 352-54, 374, 384-85, 387, 404, 429-30, 441, 443, 449-50, 492, 498, 500

See named plantations:
Acorn Hill
Blacklock/Blackloch
Brick House
Capes
Cedar Springs

Fenwick Hall (*see* Head Quarters)
Head Quarters
The Hut
Oakland
The Oaks
Oakvale
Peaceful Retreat
Rush's
Stanyarne Hall (*see* Brick House)
Johnson, President Andrew, 327, 545
Johnson, John, 467
Johnson, Judge William, xxvii, 346
Johnson, W. H., 511
Joyner, John (d. 1796), 300, 391
Jumel, Lewis Alexis, xxvii, 82-3, 87
Jumel's tree cotton, xxvii, 82, 87
kainit, 164
kapok, 63
Kay, John (1704-1781), xxv, 252, 265
Kean's Neck, Prince William Parish, 447, 494
Kearney, Thomas H., 85, 87
Keber, Martha L., xxxv, 117, 511
Kemway Road (Stono Point), 346, 352-53
Kelsall, Col., 94
kernel (of seeds), 40, 49-50
Kiawah Island, St. John's Colleton Parish, xxx, 3, 8, 18, 103, 139, 380, 404-06, 410, 450, 511, 518
Kidney Seed Cotton, 62
King Cotton, 121, 265, 281, 307, 505, 518
King, James (d. 1840), xxix, 100, 300, 341, 343-45, 351
Kingsley, Captain Zephaniah (1765-1843), 123-24
King's Island, Florida, 345
Kirk, John William (1803-1868), 483-84
Kirk, Caroline (1817-1864), 483-84
Kirk, James (d. 1850), 484
Kirk, Mary (d. c. 1851), 484
Kirk, William, 484
Kirk's Bluff, St. Luke's Parish, 484
Kohel, R. J., xxxv, 91, 288, 293, 297, 507, 511
Kovacik, Charles F, xviii, xxxv., 105, 141, 327, 511
lace, xix, 125, 256-57, 270, 274-75, 278-80, 329, 333
Lady's Island, St. Helena Parish, 3, 21, 95, 103, 136, 151, 325, 416
Lafayette, Marquis de, 470, 472, 512
Lake Marion, South Carolina, 9, 108
Lake Moultrie, South Carolina, 108, 131
Lamb, George Buist, 480
Lancashire, England, xxv, xxvi, 230, 233, 248-49, 252-53, 255-56, 265, 276, 279
Landers, Jane G., 123-24, 512
landforms, 3, 9, 25
landrace cottons, 39, 63, 73, 91
land rotation (for crops), 152

lapping (in gins), 187, 196, 204, 229
LaRoche, James, 452
LaRoche, Joseph Murray (1858-1913), 472, 501
LaRoche, Martha Julia [née Hopkinson] (1856-1946), 471-72, 501
Late Archaic, 24
Late Pleistocene, 5
The Launch Plantation, Edisto Island, 361, 362, 366-67, 433-35, 438, 441, 492, 496
Laurel Bay Plantation, Port Royal Island, 389-90, 445, 447, 492, 494
Laurel Grove Plantation, Florida, 123-24
Laurel Hill Plantation, Edisto Island, 452
Lawton, James M. (1817-1877), 475
Lawton, Margaret [née Frampton] (1786-1830), 475
Lawton, Martha [née McLeod] (d. 1840), 475
Lawton, Mary Frampton (1807-1850), 475
Lawton, Susan Martha (1821-1859), 475
Lawton, Wallace Winborn (1837-1906), 475
Lawton, William M., 328
Lawton, Winborn (1782-1861), 475
laze-rods (in weaving), 261
leaf (leaves), 8, 29-30, 41, 43-44, 46, 54, 58, 60, 65, 107, 113, 130, 163, 171, 175, 177, 283, 285, 287, 293-94, 297, 321, 348, 433
Legaré, J. D., 113, 317, 512
Legaré, James (1762-1830), 345, 354
Legaré, John Berwick (1819-1856), 413, 501
Legaré, Julia Georgiana [née Seabrook] (1829-1852), 413, 417, 501
Legaré, Mary, xxvii, 345-46
Legaré, Thomas (1766-1842), 345, 354
Legaré, Thomas (1733-1801), 345-46
Legareville, Johns Island, 315, 360
Lesser Antilles, 75-6
Levy County, Florida, 125
Lewis, C. F., 91, 288, 293, 297, 511
Lightwood, Edward (1740-1797), 474
Lightwood, Elizabeth [née Peronneau] (c. 1748-1826), 474
Lightwood, Mary (1771-1847), 474
Lightwood, Sarah Peronneau, 474, 476
Ligon, Richard, 76, 512
Lily Mills, of Shelby, North Carolina, 130, 278
lime-kilns, 163
limestone, 4
Lincoln, Abraham, 324, 327, 446
Lindsay, Nick, 172, 289, 305, 512
linen, 39, 85, 252, 257, 267, 269-70, 275, 277, 331, 419
Linnaean Herbarium, London, 65
Linnaeus, Carolus (1707-1778), xxv, xxxiv, 60, 64-5, 67, 72, 514
lint (of cotton), xx, 39, 53-4, 57, 61-2, 70, 73-4, 77,

INDEX

82-4, 90, 104, 107, 110, 114, 118, 120, 123, 129, 131, 133, 154, 160, 164, 180, 185-87, 190, 193, 195-96, 200, 204, 207, 209, 221-22, 226, 229-30, 233, 238-41, 273, 292, 297, 342, 348
linters, 54, 62
listing, 114, 137, 155, 158, 160, 163, 310
Littlefield, Milton S., 325
Littlefield Plantation, Cumberland Island, Georgia, 18
Little Britton (or Britain) Island, St. Paul's Parish, 100, 103, 304, 345, 354, 542
Little Edisto (*see* Ashe's) Plantation
Little Edisto Island, St. John's Colleton Parish, 393-94, 425, 427, 481-82
Liverpool, England, 95, 117, 128, 271, 273, 279, 299, 301, 312, 338, 344
loam(y) soil, 106, 138, 152, 294
Long Island (Caribbean island), 78, 93
Long Island, Charleston County, *12*, 14
Longwood (*see* William J. Jenkins Plantation)
loom, hand, 239, 241, 248, 256, 260, 263, 265-67
lowcountry (of South Carolina), xv, xvii, xviii, xxii, xxiii, 25, 31, 108, 298-99, 318, 322, 332, 360, 362, 378, 382, 392, 398-99, 407, 444, 451, 453, 484, 514-15
Loyalists, 93
longshore currents, 19
Louisiana, xxv, 60, 192, 287, 294, 515
Lowndes County, Georgia, 119
Lucas, George, 299
Lucayo (of the Bahamas), xxv, 75
Lynch, Thomas, 118
Mackay, Elizabeth Ann [née Mikell] (1773-1815), 436-37, 493, 498, 501
Mackay, John (1805-1848), 462
Mackay, Mungo (1772-1824), 436-37, 498
Madagascar, 69, 351
Madison County, Florida, 125, 128, 130
Maho Bey Garden, Cairo, 82
mail bags, 278, 334
Makwar Dam, 83
malaria, 18, 315
mallow family, 57-60
Malta, 82
Malvaceae family, xxxiv, 57-58, 63, 504
Manchester, England, 83, 87, 145, 184, 221, 252, 267, 273, 276, 279, 282, 302, 304, 320-21, 338, 343-44, 509, 518
Manning, H. L., xxxiv, 77, 84, 90, 92, 510
manure (for fields), xxviii, 107, 111, 113-14, 135, 139, 144, 152, 154-55, 158-60, 163-64, 172, 297, 343-44, 417, 511, 514, 516
Marion County, Florida, 125
marl, 4, 110, 163-64

marshes, tidal, 8, 60
marsh hummocks, 9, 11, 14, 24-26, 28-30, 140-41
marsh islands, 9, 11, 24-25, 57
Maryfield Plantation, Daufuskie Island, 461-62
Mason, Robert E., xviii, xxxv, 105, 107, 131, 141, 327
Massachusetts, xxviii, 119, 186, 204-05, 207, 276, 279, 402, 462, 484, 487
Mathews, Benjamin, 400
Mathews, Mary (1771-1813), 400-02
Mathews, Mary Anne (1837-1887), 450, 498
Mathews, Mary Wilkinson (b. 1809), 408-09, 493, 496-97
Mathewes, John, 334
Mauersberger, Herbert R., 104, 513
May River, Beaufort County, 315, 484
McCarthy, Fones, xxix, 487-88, 507, 510, 516
McCarthy gin, operation of, xix, xxiii, xxix, 323
McConnel-Kennedy & Company, 184, 276, 302, 344
McConnel-Kennedy Letters, 184, 302, 304, 344, 515
McCusker, John J., 338-40
McDowell, Mary Thomson (1822-1851), 397-98, 493, 495-96
McLeod Creek, 100
McLeod, John (b. 1810), 475
McLeod, Josiah Mikell (1811-1852), 475
McLeod, Martha (d. 1840), 475
McLeod, Martha Stiles [née Royall] (1835-1861), 475
McLeod, Mary [née Mikell] (c. 1790-1839), 474
McLeod, Mary Frampton [née Lawton] (1807-1850), 475
McLeod Plantation, James Island, 360, 363, 369, 378, 473-76, 510, 515
McLeod, Robert, 474
McLeod, Susan Martha [née Lawton] (1821-1859), 475
McLeod, William Wallace (1820-1865), 474-75
McLeod, William Wallace (1850-1919), 475
McPherson, Harriet (1812-1852), 402
McPherson, James Elliott (1769-1834), 402
McPhersonville, Prince William Parish, 315
Meadows, William R., xxxii, 104, 305-06, 330-32, 340, 513
Means, Edward, 467
Mediterranean, 82
Mediterranean Sea, 82
Medway (*see* The Launch Plantation)
Melrose (Salt Pond) Plantation, Daufuskie Island, 361-62, 366, 377, 459, 461-64
Mendenhall, Marjorie S., 101, 131, 513
Merchants' Magazine and Commercial Review, The, 96, 354, 506
Mexico, 61-62, 67, 69, 239, 289, xxiii
Mexico Plantation, St. John's Parish, Berkeley, 111

Michaux, André, 79
Middle District (of Florida), 122, 125
Middleton, Henry (1770-1846), 434
Middleton, Mary [née Hering] (1772-1850), 434
Middleton, Oliver Hering (1798-1892), 434-35, 492, 509
Middleton Place Plantation, St. George Parish, Dorchester, 434
Middleton, Susan [née Chisolm] (1807-1865), 434-35
Middleton's (*see* The Launch Plantation)
Mikell, Amarinthia Jenkins [née Townsend] (1810-1852), 431, 493, 498, 501
Mikell, Ann (1769-1809), 452, 491, 498-99
Mikell, Elizabeth Ann (1773-1815), 436-37, 493, 498, 501
Mikell, Emily [née Price] (1809-1835), 431, 498
Mikell, Ephraim (1741-1809), 436, 439, 465, 498
Mikell, Ephraim (1773-1838), 429-30, 465, 479-80, 497-98
Mikell, Hess Marion Waring [née Smith] (c. 1817-1904), 465-66, 492, 496, 498
Mikell, Isaac Jenkins (1808-1881), 213, 374, 380, 429-32, 465, 480, 493, 498-99, 501, 513
Mikell, Mary (c. 1790-1839), 474
Mikell, Mary Ann (1779-1818), 417-19, 441, 493, 498, 500
Mikell, Mary Ann (1822-1899), 431, 479-80, 493, 498
Mikell, Mary Martha [née Pope] (1829-1862), 431-32, 493, 498-99
Mikell, Providence [née Jenkins] (1784-1846), 430, 497-98
Mikell, Sarah Ann (1810-1838), 466, 496, 498
Mikell, Sarah Margaret Edings (1837-1906), 431, 498-99
Mikell, William Archibald (1815-1840), 429, 465-66, 492, 496, 498
Milne, Andrew (1783-1857), 387
Mills, Robert, 435 (fn)
Miocene, 69
Mississippi, 87, 287, 299, 338
Mississippi Delta, 87
Mississippi River, 87, 289
Mitchell, Edward (1788-1855), 279, 425-28, 437, 482, 492, 495
Mitchell, Elizabeth Grimball [née Baynard] (1794-1857), 425-27, 436-37, 495
Mitchell, Esther Marion (1829-1910), 425-27, 443, 495, 500
Mitchell, Julian, 279, 281
Mitchell, Mary [née Wayne] (1828-1886), 427, 466, 492, 495, 502
Mitchell, Rachel Louisa (1818-1889), 425-27, 492, 495, 501
Mitchell, William Grimball Baynard (1822-1850), 425-27, 466, 495, 502
Mongin, Ann [née Harrison] (d. 1850), 462
Mongin, David John (1791-1823), 459-60, 462
Mongin, Isabella Rae [née Habersham], 460-462
Mongin, John David (1763-1833), 459, 462
Mongin, Mary Lavinia (1819-1865), 459, 462
Mongin, Sarah [née Irvine] (d. 1833), 459-60
Mongin, Sarah [née Watts] (d. 1816), 459
Mongin, William Henry (1816-1851), 459-60, 462
monopodial branching, 42-3
Morgan Island, St. Helena Parish, 103
Morris, Ann Elliott (1795-1879), 406
Morris Island, St. Andrews Parish, 15, 19
Mosley, M. E., 282
mote-table, 180
moting cotton, 54, 137, 175, 180, 183, 222, 230, 321
Moultrie, General William (1730-1805), xxvii, 108-11, 300
mountains, 4, 8, 76, 315
Mount Pleasant, Christ Church Parish, 479
mule, Crompton's spinning, xxvi, 256-58, 270, 273, 533
mule-spun yarn, 256-59, 267, 274-75, 278, 282, 505
Murphy Island, South Carolina, 18
Murray, Chalmers S., 94, 99, 121, 132, 148, 513
muslin, xix, 239, 241, 255-56, 270, 274-75, 278-79, 333
muslin wheel, xix, 256
Myrtle Bush Plantation, Port Royal Island, 367, 390, 410-412, 492, 494
Nassau County, Florida, 123
Natchez Daily Courier, 277
National Intelligencer, 125, 514
Native Americans, xxiv, 9, 11, 21, 24, 28-9, 31, 70, 74, 89, 99, 162-63, 239
N'Dulamo (*see* Tom Fripp Plantation)
nectary, 43, 46, 517
Need, Samuel, 253, 255
Negroes, 80, 138, 161, 164, 174, 192-93, 198, 215, 288, 325-27, 340, 342-43, 392, 419, 436, 474
Negro slaves, xvii, xviii, xx, xxi, xxx, xxxi, 76, 78, 90, 94, 117-18, 124, 134-36, 160, 168, 174, 195, 218, 271, 275, 298-300, 302, 306, 325, 328, 343, 353, 370-71, 374-75, 378-79, 387, 396-97, 400, 402, 404, 419, 421, 425, 427, 431, 434, 436, 450, 452, 454-56, 466, 470, 473, 479-80, 482, 504, 515, 518
Newburg Plantation, Daufuskie Island, 461-62
Newcomen, Thomas, xxv, 270
New Hope Plantation, Florida, 123, 132
New Mexico, xxiii, 239
News and Courier, 115, 143, 288, 340, 504, 515
New World, xxiv, xxv, xxxv, 37, 39, 57, 60-1, 67-72,

INDEX

74, 82, 190, 218, 238-39, 241, 263, 282, 517, 519
New World D-genome, xxxiv, xxxv, 61, 67, 69
New York, 207, 279, 289, 337, 340, 402, 487
Nicks, William, 404
Nile River, 82-3, 85
Nile watershed, upper, 60
nitrogen (for crops), xx, 49-50, 57, 154, 163, 172, 321
nomen ambiguum, 65, 72
nonruminant animals, 40, 63
North Carolina, xxiii, 8, 29, 91, 130, 294, 298
Northampton Plantation, St. John's Parish, Berkeley, xxvii, 108-11, 114, 116, 165, 300
Norwich, England, 343
Nottingham, England, xxvi, 249, 253
nubbing cotton, 175
Oakatee Creek, Beaufort County, 300
Oak Island Plantation, Edisto Island, 366, 368, 373-78, 409, 433, 438, 441-44, 492, 500
Oakland Plantation, Johns Island, 385
Oak Lawn Plantation, St. Paul's Parish, 304
Oakley Hall (Bloody Point) Plantation, Daufuskie Island, 459-60, 462
Oakridge Plantation, Daufuskie Island, 461-62
Oakridge Plantation, St. Bartholomew's Parish, 474
The Oaks Plantation, Johns Island, 450
The Oaks Plantation, St. Helena Island, 360, 362, 477-78, 499
Oakvale Plantation, Johns Island, xix, xxi, xxiii, xxvii, 96, 308, 345-46, 348-49, 351, 353-54
ocean(s), xxiv, 3-4, 8-9, 14, 18-9, 26, 29-30, 36-7, 57, 69-70, 72, 91, 104, 106, 139, 159, 168, 213, 308, 315, 354, 360, 404, 415, 469
Oglethorpe, General James, 79
Old Dominion Plantation, Edisto Island, 387, 425, 481, 501
Old Fort (*see* Smith's Plantation)
Old House Plantation, Edisto Island, 429-30, 501
Old World, xxxv, 57-8, 61, 67-8, 70, 72, 82, 238-39
Old World A-genome, xxiv, xxxv, 61, 67, 69
Oligocene, 69
Olive (English ship), 76
O'Neill, Judge James Thomas, 123
Orangeburg County, South Carolina, 81, 108
Orange Grove Plantation, Lady's Island, 415-16
Orange Grove Plantation, St. Helena Island, 424
origin (of sea island cotton), xviii, xix, xx, xxxiv, xxxv, 68-70, 72, 82, 84, 89-100, 517
Orton, W. A., 44, 104, 119, 121, 154, 157, 164, 170, 173, 182-83, 293-94, 296-97, 513
Ossabaw Island, Georgia, 95
Otter Island, South Carolina, 18
overseer (of a plantation), xxvii, 111, 195, 315, 319, 343, 370, 387, 397-98, 404, 427, 462, 474
overwash, 15, 18

Owen, E. R. J., 82, 513
oxen, 198, 200, 202, 207, 370, 462
oyster shells, 18, 24, 163
packing (sea island cotton), 137, 180, 182-83, 226, 237, 321, 370
Paisley, Scotland, 275, 277, 282
Paisley shawl, 275, 277
Palmer, Joseph (1770-1841), 109, 113
Palmetto Hills (*see* Seaside Plantation)
Palmetto Point (*see* Tombee Plantation)
Pangaea, 3
Paraguay, 78, 92
Paris, 111, 273, 413, 462, 470
Paris green, 285, 288, 297
Parker, Anna Sarah Smith [née Coffin] (1804-1868), 474
Parker, Edward Lightwood (1828-1892), 474
Parker, William McKenzie (1762-1802), 474
Parker, William McKenzie (1800-1830), 474
Parker, William McKenzie (1825-1860), 474-75
Parker, Sarah Peronneau [née Lightwood], 474, 476
Parris Island, St. Helena Parish, 103
Parsonage Tract, St. Helena Island, 423-24
Patent Office, U.S., xxix, 200, 218, 487
Paul, Lewis, xxv, 245
Pawtucket, Rhode Island, xxvi, 282
Peaceful Retreat Plantation, Johns Island, 374, 430, 497
Pearsall, Deborah M., 75, 239, 507, 514
Pee Dee Experiment Station, Florence, South Carolina, xx, xxxiii, 121, 229
Peel, Robert, 248-49
Pendleton, South Carolina, 390
Penn School, St. Helena Island, 457, 478
Percy, R. G., xxxv, 62, 73-4, 90, 92, 514
perennial growth (of cotton), xxv, xxvi, 39, 56-7, 61-3, 73-6, 78-80, 82, 84, 88, 90, 95, 99, 195
Peronneau, Elizabeth (c. 1748-1826), 400, 474
Peronneau, Mary [née Lightwood] (1771-1847), 474
Peru, xxiv, xxxiv, xxxv, 53, 56, 61-2, 64, 73-4, 88-90, 99, 238-41, 263-64, 282, 298, 517
Peter's Point Plantation, Edisto Island, 213, 366, 367, 374, 429-32, 465, 493, 497-98
Peter's Point Road, Edisto Island, 144
Peyre, Thomas Walker (1812-1851), 110, 113-14, 116, 131, 514
piedmont, 4, 8, 111, 131, 509
phosphate beds, 164
phosphorus, as fertilizer, 50, 57, 172
photoperiod (photoperiodicity), 39, 56, 90-1
pick (in weaving), 261, 263
picking (sea island cotton), xxx, 75, 77, 87, 90, 117-18, 121, 131, 155, 169, 173-75, 195, 294, 302, 321, 327, 340, 360, 404, 466

533

INDEX

Pig Island Shell Complex, North Edisto River, *23*, 37
Pilkey, Orrin H., 9, 10, 14, 514
Pima cotton, xxxii, xxxiii, xxxiv, 56, 62, 84-5, 87-8, 90, 99, 121, 233, 330
pinch ginning, 188
Pinckney, Eliza (1722-1793), 299
Pinckney Island, St. Luke's Parish. 1-3. 318
Pine Barren Plantation, Edisto Island, 144, 172, 499, 501
Pine Ridge (*see* Baynard's Old Place)
Piperno, Dolores R., 75, 514
pitch (from southern pines), 271
Plant communities
    beach forests, 36
    coastal beaches, 4, 29
    coastal dunes, 29
    freshwater marshes, 138-39, 299
    longleaf pine flatwoods, 143
    longleaf pine savannas, 60
    low, wet woods, 138
    maritime forests, 18, 26, 28-31, 138-39
    maritime shell forests, 27-9, 37
    maritime shrub thickets, 29-30
    oak-hickory forests, 26, 138
    pine barrens, 138, 143-44, 410
    pine/saw palmetto flatwoods, 143-44
    salt flats, 26, 28, 172
    salt marshes, xxviii, 25-26, 28, 31, 37, 46, 106, 138-42, 163, 172, 519
    salt shrub thickets, 26, 28-9, 31
    tidal freshwater marshes, 299
    tidal freshwater swamps, 298
plant names, common
    American holly, 30, 489
    basswood, 28-9, 289
    beach evening-primrose, 30, 489
    beach pea, 30, 489
    black gum, 143, 489
    blackjack oak, 143, 489
    black needle rush, 172
    bull bay, 30, 489
    cabbage palmetto, 30-1, 489
    camphorweed, 30, 489
    Carolina buckthorn, 28-9, 489
    Carolina cherry laurel, 489
    Carolina saltwort, 29, 489
    China jute, 60
    chinquapin, 150, 489
    crested coral-root, 29, 489
    devil-joint, 30, 489
    dogwood, 29, 108, 489-90
    dune sandbur, 29, 489
    dune evening-primrose, ???
    dune greenbrier, 30
    dwarf buckeye, 28-9, 489
    fetterbush, 143, 489
    galactia, 143, 489
    Godfrey's forestiera, 29, 489
    great laurel, 172
    groundsel-tree, 28, 30, 489
    hackberry, 28-9, 489
    hairy wicky, 143, 489
    halberd-leaved marsh mallow, 60
    Hercules'-club, 30, 489
    hickory, 106, 139, 172
    high mallow, 58
    hollyhock, 58
    honey-cups, 143, 489
    horseweed, 30, 489
    huckleberry, 143, 489
    inkberry, 143, 489
    Japanese honeysuckle, 30, 489
    kenaf, 60
    laurel oak, 30, 489
    live oak, 30-1, 172, 271, 370, 389, 391, 410, 463, 489
    loblolly pine, 28, 30, 143-44, 489
    longleaf pine, 60, 143-44, 489
    majagua, 60
    marsh-elder, 26, 31, 489
    needle rush, 31, 490
    okra, 58, 60
    perennial glasswort, 26, 31, 172, 490
    pineland hibiscus, 60
    poison ivy, 30, 490
    pond pine, 143, 490
    prickly-pear cactus, 30, 490
    red bay, 30, 139, 172, 490
    Rose-of-Sharon, 58
    roselle, 60
    rose mallow, swamp, 59-60
    rough-leaved dogwood, 28-9, 490
    running oak, 143, 490
    rusty lyonia, 143, 490
    salt grass, 31, 490
    saltmarsh aster, 26, 490
    saltwort, 26, 172, 490
    sand-vine, 31, 490
    saw palmetto, 30, 143, 490
    scrubby post oak, 143, 490
    seabeach amaranth, 29, 490
    sea lavender, 26, 31, 490
    sea oats, 29, 490
    sea ox-eye, 26, 28, 31, 490
    sea rocket, 29, 490
    seashore mallow, 58-60
    seaside goldenrod, 26, 31, 490
    seaside panicum, 29, 490

INDEX

seaside pennywort, 30, 490
shell-mound buckthorn, 28-9, 490
shortleaf pine, 108
silk-cotton tree, 63
slash pine, 30, 143, 490
smooth cordgrass, 25-6, 37, 172, 490
southern evergreen blueberry, 143, 490
southern red cedar, 30-1, 490
southern sugar maple, 29, 490
Spanish moss, 172
sweet bay, 143, 490
sweet galberry, 143, 490
sweetgrass, 30, 490
sweet gum, 143, 490
sweet pepperbush, 143, 490
tough bumelia, 28-9, 490
trailing bluet, 30, 490
tupelo, 160
wax myrtle, 28, 30-1, 143, 490
white oak, 139, 172, 490
wild olive, 30, 490
vanilla plant, 1443, 490
Virginia creeper, 30, 490
Virginia pine, 271
Walter's milkweed, 143, 490
yaupon, 28, 30-1, 490
plant names, scientific
  Abutilon theophrasti, 60
  Althaea officinalis, 60
  Althaea rosea, 58
  Batis maritima, 172, 490
  Carya glabra var. *megacarpa*, 172
  Ceiba pentandra, 63
  Hibiscus aculeatus, 60
  Hibiscus cannabinus, 60
  Hibiscus esculentus, 58
  Hibiscus militaris, 60
  Hibiscus moscheutos, 60
  Hibiscus sabdariffa, 60
  Hibiscus syriacus, 58
  Hibiscus tiliaceus, 60
  Juncus roemerianus, 172, 490
  Kosteletskya virginica, 58, 60
  Magnolia grandiflora, 172, 489
  Malva sylvestris, 58
  Modiola caroliniana, 60
  Quercus alba, 172, 490
  Quercus virginiana, 172, 489
  Salicornia virginica, 172, 490
  Sida rhombifolia, 60
  Spartina alterniflora, 11, 25, 155, 163, 172, 490
  Tillandsia usneoides, 172
Pleistocene Epoch, 5, 37, 70
plow (for cultivation), 90, 99, 123, 127, 135, 150, 155, 158-9, 168, 170-71, 297, 323, 328, 331
Plukenet, Leonard (1642-1706), xxv, 65-6, 72
Plukenet Herbarium, London, xxv, 65
pneumatic tires, 278, 329, 334
Point Comfort Plantation, Hilton Head Island, 415
Point of Pines Plantation, Edisto Island, 279
poisoned-syrup mixture, 130
polar ice caps, 4-5
pollination, 46, 57, 63
Polynesia, 62
polyploid (polyploidy), xxxiv, 67-8, 70, 72, 504
Pooshee Plantation, St. John's Parish, Berkeley, 109-10, 113-14, 116, 131, 221, 308
Pope, Ann [née Scott], 415, 492, 499
Pope, Daniel Townsend (1837-1909), 478, 498, 499
Pope, Elizabeth Catherine (c. 1818-1904), 415, 499
Pope, Emma Catherine (d. 1854), 455, 492, 499
Pope, Hephzibah J. (1824-1849), 415, 492, 499
Pope, John Edward (d. c. 1837), 415, 455, 492, 496, 499
Pope, John Jeremiah Theus (1799-1864), 402, 415, 477-78, 492, 499, 501
Pope, Joseph James, Jr. (1826-1872), 415-16, 498, 499
Pope, Mary Baynard [née Edings] (c. 1800-1856), 455, 491-92, 496, 499
Pope, Mary Frampton [née Townsend] (1804-1861), 415, 477-78, 492, 499, 501
Pope, Mary Martha (1829-1862), 431-32, 493, 498, 499
Pope, Sarah [née Green], 415, 455, 492, 499
Pope, Sarah [née Scott], 415, 499
Pope, Sarah Lavinia, 415, 492, 499
Pope, William (d. 1823), 415, 455, 492, 499
Pope, William (1788-1862), 370, 414-15, 492, 499
Pope, William John (1813-1852), 415-16, 492, 499
Porcher Bank, 111
Porcher, Frederick A. (1809-1888), 109-10, 113, 319, 348, 514
Porcher, Major Samuel (1768-1851), 111
Port Royal Experiment, xviii, xxx, 327, 424, 457, 478, 515
Port Royal, South Carolina, xxix, *309,* 325, 360, 380, 390, 392, 398, 403, 454, 456, 469, 511, 513
Port Royal Island, St. Helena Parish, 3, 21, 95, 103, 144, 151, 317, 325, 379, 390, 410, 412, 447, 492-93
  See named plantations:
    Laurel Bay
    Myrtle Bush
    Smith's/Old Fort
    Woodward
Port Royal Sound, Beaufort County, 19, 21, 24, 325, 414, 455
Porteous, Sarah Green (1778-1850), 479

INDEX

Posselt, E. A., 514
potash, 49-50, 57, 154, 160, 164, 172, 297, 321
potassium, as fertilizer, 50, 160, 172
Powell, Captain John, 76
power loom, xxvi, 267-68, 270, 275
pre-Columbian, 74, 92, 99, 240-41
Price, Emily (1809-1835), 431, 498
Price Inlet, Charleston County, 9
Price, Thomas (1773-1816), 431
Prince William Parish, South Carolina, 402, 437, 446-47, 474
Pritchard's Island, South Carolina, 18
prograding barrier islands, 15, 18-9, 29-30
Prospect Hill Plantation, Edisto Island, 142, 360, 365, 382, 394, 425, 433, 436-41, 493, 495, 498
Purseglove, J. W., xxxiv, *41, 47,* 54, 60, 105, 514
Quaternary Period, 4-5, 37
Raccoon Island, St. John's Colleton Parish, 452
Ramsay, David, 143, 514
ratoon, 94-5, 99
Raven, Elizabeth (c. 1753-1808), 404
Ravenel, Dr. Henry (1790-1867), 113-14, 116, 131, 308, 512, 515
Ravenel, Henry Edmund, 115, 515
Ravenel, Henry William (1814-1887), xxix, 108-10, 115, 131, 165, 221, 324-25, 505, 515
Ravenel, René, 110, 116
Rayfield, on Cumberland Island, Georgia, 118
raying seed, 154
Real Alto (Ecuador), xxiv, 239
red Peruvian cotton, 53
Reed, J., 104-06, 487
Rees, Abraham, 354
Reid, Annie Caroline, xxiii
Reid, E. E., 354
Reid, George Marion, xxiii, 354
Rephaim Plantation, St. Luke's Parish, 455
retrograding barrier islands, 15, 18, 31
Réunion Island, 353-54
Revolutionary War, xviii, 80, 108, 111, 118, 190, 270, 298-99, 301, 343, 389, 396
Reynolds, Benjamin (1750-1826), 384-85
Reynolds, Richard, Jr., xxiv, 207, 211, 218, 487
Rhett, Robert Barnwell (1800-1876), 390, 445
Rhode Island, xxiii, xxvi, xxvii, 119, 227, 279, 282, 402
rice, 80, 94, 108, 133, 136, 198, 298-302, 315, 326, 332, 343-44, 354, 370, 475, 406, 425, 434, 436, 445, 449, 466, 481, 484, 514
rice, Carolina gold, xvii, 108, 133, 298-99, 332
Richardson, Jean Kerr (1811-1888), 410-11, 492, 494
ridges (for planting), 11, 137, 139, 155, 158, 165, 170, 172
ring spinning, 259

Rise and Fall of King Cotton, 265, 281, 504
Rivers, Elias Lynch (1838-1911), 296
rivers. *See also* specific rivers, 4, 8-9, 11, 19, 21, *23,* 29, 37, 78-79, 81-3, 85, 87, 108, 111, 117, 123-24, 131-32, *153,* 163, 204, 255, 270-72, 273, 298, 300-01, 308, 315, 317, 326, 342-43, 345-46, 360, 374, 380, 384-85, 387-88, 391, 398, 402, 404, 406, 430, 434, 445, 466, 474, 484, 517
   blackwater, 8-9, 298
   brownwater, 8, 298
River Mersey, England, 271
river valleys, 4, 8, 13, 15, 21
Roberts, Charles Arthur, 184, 281, 302, 304, 312, 320-21, 339-40, 344, 515
Rockland Plantation, Wadmalaw Island, 385
Rocks Plantation, St. Johns Parish, Berkeley, xxvii, 109, 111, 300
Rockville, Wadmalaw Island, 11, 315, 360, 384, 385, 418, 443, 511
roller gins, types of
   barrel, xxiii, xxv, 187-88, 192, 195, 198, 200-01, 215, 218, 237
   Boesch's, xxxii, 213, 215, *217,* 218, 488
   Carver's, 207, 210, 487
   Chinese, 190
   churkha, 187, 190-93, 222, 238
   double-crank hand gin, 187, 192-94
   Ely's, 207, 209
   Eve's, 117, 187-88, 195, 200, 202, 204, 215
   Fessenden's, 209, 218, 488
   foot or treadle, xxvi, 192, 195-96, 215
   foot-roller, 185, 188
   Foss Double-Roller Gin, xxxii, 188, 213, 215-16, 218, 488
   Kokemuller's, 212-13, 218, 488
   Layton's, 209
   McCarthy, xix, xxiii, xxix, 185, 187-88, 198, 204, 207, 209, 213, 215, 218-19, *220,* 221-24, 226, 229-31, 233-35, 237, 323, 487-88, 507, 510, 516
   Reed's, 204-05
   Reynolds's, 207
   rotary-knife, xxxiv, 233, 236
   tooth-geared, 187, 192-94, 200
   Whittemore's, 205, 207-08, 211, 511
roller-spinning machine, xxv, 245, 265
root(s), 18, 25, 40, 60, 79, 93-5, 106, 140, 148-50, 158-59, 171, 294, 296
Roper, Barbara Calder [née Jenkins] (1784-1855), 449-50, 498
Roper, Benjamin Dart (1776-1852), 449-50, 498
Roper, Mary Anne [née Mathews] (1837-1887), 450, 498
Roper, Mary Julia [née Stevens] (1829-1856),

450, 498
Roper, Micah Jenkins (1812-1859), 450
Roper, Thomas (1820-1861), 385, 450
Roper, William (1816-1877), 450, 498
Rose Hill Plantation, St. Luke's Parish, 345, 361, 483-84
Rose, John, 300
Rose, Willie Lee, xviii, 327, 340, 515
rotor spinning, 259
roving, 243, 248, 250, 253-54, 256-57, 281-82
Royall, Croskeys (1799-1877), 475
Royall, Martha Stiles (1835-1861), 475
Ruffin, Edmund (1794-1865), 113, 144, 159, 213, 284, 344, 512
ruminant animals, 40, 63
Rural Carolinian, The, 321, 506, 512
Rush's Plantation, Johns Island, 449-50, 498
Russell's Point (*see* Ashe's/Little Edisto Plantation)
rust, 136, 149, 296-97
Sacaton, Arizona, 85
St. Andrews Agricultural and Police Society, 275, 322, 506
St. Andrews Parish, South Carolina, 387, 476, 479
St. Bartholomew Parish, South Carolina, 434-35, 474
St. Catherine's Island, Georgia, 95
St. Helena Island, St. Helena Parish, xviii, xxx, xxxiii, 3, 21, 95, 103, 136, 151, 159, 285, 308, 315, 317, 323, 325-26, 337, 360, 382, 384, 396-400, 402-03, 415-16, 421, 423-24, 431, 456-59, 467-68, 474, 477-78, 492-93, 496-97, 506, 519
See named plantations:
    The Bluff
    Cherry Hill
    Coffin Point
    Croft Place
    Feliciana
    Fripp, Tom
    Frogmore
    Harbor Island
    Jenkins, Mary (Jenkins Neck)
    Jenkins, William J. (Longwood)
    Longwood
    N'Dulamo (*see* Tom Fripp)
    The Oaks
    Orange Grove
    Palmetto Hills (*see* Seaside)
    Palmetto Point (*see* Tombee)
    Parsonage Tract
    Sandiford Place (*see* William J. Jenkins)
    Seaside
    Tombee
St. Helena Parish, South Carolina, xxiv, xxx, 300, 325-27, 337, 391, 400, 410, 416, 421, 424, 446-47, 469

St. Helena Sound, 19, 21, 400, 402
St. Helenaville, St. Helena Island, 315, 360, 398, 468
St. John's Colleton Agricultural Society, xxviii, 163, 321
St. John's Colleton Parish, South Carolina, 287, 350-51, 387, 400, 420, 425, 428, 431-32, 440, 443-44, 453, 472, 474, 482, 505, 515
St. John's Parish, Berkeley, South Carolina, xxvii, 108-11, 113-16, 131, 165, 284, 287, 300, 321, 380, 413, 450, 511, 519
St. John's River, Florida, 123, 326
St. Luke's Parish, South Carolina, 300, 415, 455, 462, 465, 483-84
St. Paul's Parish, South Carolina, xxvii, xxviii, 96-7, 100, 192, 300, 344, 382, 418, 474, 481
St. Peter's Parish, South Carolina, 380, 390-91, 420, 512
St. Phillips Island, South Carolina, 31
St. Simons Island, Georgia, xxvi, 81, 94-95, 110, 116-17, 195
St. Stephen's Parish, South Carolina, 108, 110-11, 115
St. Vincent (Caribbean island), 84, 329
saline (salt) atmosphere, 95, 103-04, 106
salinity, 26, 57
Salt House Dock (in Liverpool), 271-72
salt-marsh mud, xxvii, 11, 107, 117-18, 144, 152, 155, 160, 164, 172, 297, 344, 417
salt marsh reclamation, xxviii, 140
Salt Pond (*see* Melrose Plantation)
Salt River Valley, Arizona, xxxii, xxxiii, 85
Salzburgers, 79
Sakellarides, John, 83
sand, 4, 8-9, 11, 14-15, 18-19, 21, 25, 29-30, 139, 159, 177, 378
Sandiford Place (*see* William J. Jenkins Plantation)
Santee Canal, 308
Santee Delta, 19
Santee long cotton, xviii, xxvii, xxviii, xxix, 36, 49, 56, 81, 99, 101, 107-11, 113-16, 119, 127, 131, 165, 209, 221, 287, 299, 300, 308, 310-11, 321, 324, 339-40, 515
Santee River, 8-9, 19, 81, 108, 111, 131, 298, 308
San Joaquin Valley, California, 87
Sapelo Island, Georgia, 94-5, 117
Savannah, Georgia, xvii, xxi, 78-9, 186, 278, 300-01, 306, 308, 310, 325, 334-37, 374, 394, 415, 418, 455, 459-60, 462
Savannah River, 48, 8, 308, 484
saw gin (for upland cotton), 186-87, 190, 195, 219, 271, 312, 505
Saxony wheel, xxv, 241, 243, 245-46, 253
scarp, 4
Schafer, Daniel L., 123-24
Scotland, 196, 255, 275, 277, 282, 462

INDEX

Screven, John, 300
screw press (for cotton bales), 117, 132, 180
Scott, Ann, 415, 492, 499
Scott, Benjamin, 384
Scott, Cornelia [née Reynolds], 384
Scott, Sarah, 415, 496, 499
Seabrook, Ann [née Jenkins] (1765-1846), 452, 498, 500
Seabrook, Ann [née Mikell] (1769-1809), 452, 491, 498-99
Seabrook, Benjamin (c. 1724-1780), 387, 499, 500
Seabrook, Carolina Lafayette (1825-1879), 417, 470-72, 492, 501
Seabrook, Charles Whaley (1876-1959), 393-94, 482, 491, 500, 502
Seabrook, Edward Whaley (1824-c.1882), 452, 499
Seabrook, Elizabeth [née Clark] (1779-1817), 374, 387, 493
Seabrook, Elizabeth Baynard [née Whaley] (1837-1895), 443, 492, 500-01
Seabrook, Elizabeth Mary [née Hanahan] (1802-1888), 452, 491, 499
Seabrook, Emma Elizabeth [née Edings] (1793-1856), 417-19, 441, 493, 496, 501
Seabrook, Ephraim Mikell (1797-1846), 452, 491, 499
Seabrook, Ephraim Mikell (1803-1861), 417, 500
Seabrook, Ephraim Mikell (1820-1895), 452, 499
Seabrook, Esther Marion [née Mitchell] (1829-1910), 425-443, 495, 500
Seabrook, Eva Irene [née Whaley] (1879-1947), 394, 482, 491, 500, 502
Seabrook, F. P., 129

Seabrook, Gabriel (1765-1824), 452, 491, 498, 499, 500
Seabrook, George Washington (1808-1866), 417, 443, 500
Seabrook, Henry (1836-1872), 452, 491, 499
Seabrook Island, St. John's Colleton Parish, 8, 18, 380, 441, 443, 450, 511
Seabrook, John Edward (b. 1830), 441-43, 493, 500-01
Seabrook, John Gabriel (1821-1903), 452, 499
Seabrook, Joseph (d. 1790), 172, 452, 499
Seabrook, Joseph Whaley (1835-1906), 452, 500
Seabrook, Josephine Edings (c. 1834-1883), 409, 419, 441-43, 493, 496, 500
Seabrook, Julia Georgiana (1829-1852), 413, 417, 501
Seabrook, Martha Washington [née Edings] (1799-1892), 417, 441-43, 492, 496, 500
Seabrook, Martha Washington (b. 1828), 413, 417, 501

Seabrook, Mary Ann [née Mikell] (1779-1818), 417-19, 441, 493, 498, 500
Seabrook, Mary Ann (d. 1836), 417-19, 501
Seabrook, Paul Hamilton (1827-1862), 452, 500
Seabrook Plantation, Hilton Head Island, 419
Seabrook, Robert Chisolm (1821-1852), 417-19, 470, 472, 501
Seabrook, Sarah Ann (1812-1864), 417, 501
Seabrook, Thomas Bannister (1765-1839), 374, 387, 493, 500
Seabrook, Tom, Plantation, Edisto Island, 386-88, 493, 500-02
Seabrook, Whitemarsh Benjamin (1793-1855), xviii, xxviii, xxix, 134, 137, 143, 145-46, 159-60, 163, 168, 170, 175, 183, 188, 190, 192, 195-96, 205, 221, 273-74, 283, 287, 293, 304-05, 320-23, 334, 343-44, 350-51, 353, 394-431, 500, 505, 515
Seabrook, William (1773-1836), 143, 146-48, 308, 315, 319, 350, 359-60, 362, 366-67, 374, 409, 413, 417-19, 441, 470, 493, 496, 498, 500-01
Seabrook, William (1799-1860), 417-19, 441-43, 492, 496, 500
Seabrook, William, Plantation, Edisto Island, 308, 359, 362, 366, 367, 375, 409, 417-20, 429, 493, 496, 500-01
Seabrook, William Benjamin (1813-1870), 94, 394, 500
Seabrook, William Edings (1828-1899), 441-43, 495, 500
sea islands, xvii, xviii, xix, xx, xxi, xxvii, xxix, xxx, xxxi, xxxiii, 3, 7-9, 11, 15, 18, 21, 24-6, 36-8, 57, 60, 79-81, 84, 89-90, 95-6, 101, 103-07, 110, 113-19, 123-25, 127, 133, 136, 138-40, 143-45, 149, 151, 155, 157, 159-60, 163, 170-72, 183-84, 188, 192-93, 209, 215, 218, 233, 237, 259, 273, 275, 278, 283-85, 287-89, 292-94, 297, 299-301, 306-08, 313-15, 317, 319-22, 324-29, 331, 340, 359, 362, 368, 270, 375, 378, 380, 382, 386, 392, 402, 407, 410, 419, 437, 439, 446, 469, 478, 504, 511, 519
sea level, 4-5, 8, 11, 14-5, 18-9, 21, 25-6
Seaside (*see* William Edings Plantation)
Seaside Plantation, St. Helena Island, 366, 367, 423-24, 497
Secessionville, James Island, 315, 360, 500
secondary (forests, growth), 25, 31, 36, 38, 75, 144
secret pricing (of cotton), 304-05, 312
seed coat (of cotton seed), 48-50, 53-4, 70
seed hairs (of cotton), 50, 53, 62-3
seed house, Burden's, 351, 353
seed preparation (for planting), 154-59
seed selection, xix, xxvii, 3, 81, 84, 89, 96, 99, 103-05, 107-08, 116-18, 123, 128, 144-48,

INDEX

170-71, 278, 292, 296, 315, 320-21, 337, 348, 350-51, 417, 518
self-pollination, 46, 63
Sewee Shell Ring, 28
sewing machine, 120, 277-78
sewing thread, xxvii, 130, 275, 277-78, 330
share-cropping, 138
Sharegools (Shargould) Plantation, Edisto Island, 384
shed (in weaving), 261, 263, 265, 267
shedding (of cotton bolls), 39-40, 46, 149, 293
shed-rod (for weaving), 261
shell deposits, natural, 9, 21, 24, 28, 163
shell middens, Native American, 23-5, 28-9
shell mounds, Native American, 21, 23-4, 28-9, 163, 490
shell rings, Native American, 21, 23-5, 28
Shepard, Charles U., 163
Shephard, Rose, 132
Shepperson, Alfred B., 313, 340, 516
Sherman, General William Tecumseh (1820-1891), xxx, 326-27
Shiver, F. S., 49-50, 516
short-day flowering, 63, 73-5, 80, 90
short-staple cotton, xv, xxvii, 55, 58, 62, 99, 116, 187, 190, 195, 204, 219, 293, 311, 334, 338
shuttle (in weaving), xxv, 248, 252, 261, 263, 265, 267-69, 223
Sicily, 82
silk, xv, 125, 130, 238, 275, 514
Simmons, Francis (c. 1765-1814), 441
Simmons, Slann L. C., 343, 354, 516
Singer, Isaac, 277
Sinkler, Captain James (1740-1806), 109, 111
Skidaway Island, Georgia, 9, 78-9
skimmer-plough, 171
Slann's Island, St. John's Colleton Parish, 103, 466
Slater, Mrs., 277, 541
Slater, Samuel, 277, 282, 503, 519, 540
slave trade, 124, 271, 298
sliver, 243, 245, 281
Sloane Herbarium, London, 65
Smalley, Mr., 252-53, 255
Smeaton, John, 270
Smith, C. Wayne, 42, 44, 79, 85-6, 146, 287, 297, 302, 516
Smith, Hess Marion Waring (c. 1817-1904), 456-66, 492, 496, 498
Smith, John Joyner (1790-1872), 378, 391, 493-94
Smith's (Old Fort) Plantation, Port Royal Island, 371, 373, 378-80, 391-92, 494
Smith, Mary D. B. [née Duncan] (1829-1861), 391, 493
Smith, Mary Gibbes [née Barnwell] (1795-1853), 391, 493-94

Smithsonian Institution, 279
soil amelioration, xxvii, 11, 106, 134, 138, 144, 159-60, 163-64
Somerset Plantation, St. John's Parish, Berkeley, 108-09, 111
sorting cotton, 54, 136-37, 174-77, 180, 183-84, 321, 372
sounds, 8, 11, 19, 25
South Carolina Heritage Trust Program, 24-5, 37
South Carolina Historical and Genealogical Magazine, 342, 348
Southeast Georgia Embayment, 6, 8
Southern Agriculturist, xxviii, xxix, 154, 205, 230, 321, 342, 344-45, 350, 420, 503, 505-07, 510-12, 515-19
sowing cotton seed, 94, 146, 154-55, 158, 165-69
  drilling, 155, 164, 166, 168-70
  in short holes (hills), 165
  in long holes (hills), 165
Spain, 82, 121
Spanish, 78, 90, 92
Spanish Fort, Port Royal Island, 391
Spanish Main, 82
Spanish Mount Plantation, Edisto Island, 407
Spanish occupation (of Florida), 121, 124
Spalding, James (d. 1794), 94
Spalding, Thomas (1774-1851), xxviii, xxix, 76, 90, 93-94, 103, 117, 137, 155, 159, 174, 177, 195-9, 202, 204, 283, 517
Special Field Order No. 15, xxx, xxxi, 326
species of cotton, scientific
  Gossypium arboreum, 58, 61
  Gossypium barbadense, xviii, xix, xx, xxv, xxvi, xxxii, xxxiv, xxxv, *41, 43, 45, 46, 47,* 49-50, 56-8, 61-7, 70, 73-82, 84-5, 87-95, 99, 101, 105, 131, 190, 192, 195, 239, 288, 298, 511, 514, 518-19
  Gossypium barbadense var. *brasileinse*, 62
  Gossypium darwinii, 62
  Gossypium herbaceum, xxxv, 58, 61, 67
  Gossypium hirsutum, xxxv, 40, *41, 43,* 46, 49-50, 56-8, 62-3, 67, 70, 73, 75, 80-1, 89, 90-3, 99, 105, 144, 187, 239, 288, 354, 511, 518
  Gossypium hirsutum var. *marie*, 91
  Gossypium lanceolatum, 62
  Gossypium mustelinum, 62
  Gossypium raimondii, xxxv, 61, 67
  Gossypium tomentosum, 62
Species Plantarum, xxv, 64-5
spindle (to wind yarn), 238, 240-43, 245, 248-50, 252-54, 256-57, 259, 269, 281-82
spinning jenny, xxv, 247-52, 255-57, 259, 269, 275, 503
spinning wheel, xxv, 241, 243, 245, 248-49, 252, 269, 277, 281

INDEX

spits, 13, 15, 25
Springfield Plantation, Hilton Head Island, 415
Springfield Plantation, St. John's Parish, Berkeley, 109, 113
springing (in gins), 187, 204, 213, 218
Spring Island, St. Luke's Parish, 151
square (flower bud), 43, 46, 149, 289
stable manure, 155, 297
Stafford, Robert (1790-1877), xxxv, 118-19, 505
Stafford, Thomas, 118
Staley, Christian, 430
Stanyarne, Anna (d. 1836), 449-50
Stanyarne, Elizabeth [née Stobo] (1709-1784), 448-49
Stanyarne, Mary (1764-1812), 374, 449
Stanyarne, John (c. 1695-1772), 404-05
Stanyarne, Joseph (d.c. 1772), 448, 450
Stanyarne, William (1736-1784), 448-49
Stanyarne Hall (*see* Brick House)
steam power, xxv, xxvi, 187-88, 213-14, 218, 221, 230, 259, 267, 270
Steamboat Creek, Edisto Island, 308, 417
steamboat(s), 273, 208-09, 418-19
Stephens, S. G., xxxiv, 69, 74, 82, 89, 91-3, 239, 282, 510, 517
Stevens, Mary Julia (1829-1856), 450, 498
Stewart, Mart, 79, 517
Stiles, Elizabeth Ann [née Mackay] (1810-1867), 462
Stobo, Elizabeth (1709-1784), 448-49
Stoddard, Henry Mongin (1846-1905), 460
Stoddard, John (1809-1879), 361, 461-62
Stoddard, Mary Lavinia [née Mongin] (1819-1865), 459, 462
Stono Point, 346, 348, 352-54
Stono River, 153, 308, 317, 345-46, 385, 387, 430, 517
Strutt, Jebediah, 253, 255
subsoil drainage, xxxi, 106, 135, 51-52, 164, 172
subtropics (subtropical), 36, 39
Sudan, 56, 74, 81, 83, 88
sugar beet, 84
sugar cane, 76, 84, 301, 329
Sullivans Island, Christ Church Parish, 18, 315, 406, 434
Suwannee County, Florida, 125, 128
Swallow's Bluff Plantation, Edisto Island, 375
Sweet Water factory, 277
Swinton, Mary Bailey (1808-1890), 437-39, 493, 495
Swinton, Susan Lavinia (1822-1866), 384-85, 492, 501
sympodial branching, 42-4, 57
Tafft, Henry S., 469
Taggart, William S., 127, 517
Tajikistan, 56, 73, 88
tap root, 40, 106, 149

tar (from southern pines), 271
task system (of labor), 124, 136-37
Tatnall, Col., 94
Taylor, Eloise Lanier, 341, 353
tenant system (of labor), 164, 305
tenant system ("two-day"), 138
terraces, 8-9
tetraploid, xxxiv, xxxv, 61, 67, 69-70, 504, 519
Texas, xxxi, 287, 289, 292, 456
textile industry, 238-39, 243, 249, 252, 259, 265, 269, 273, 279, 282
thinning (of cotton), 43, 114, 165-66, 168-71
thread, xxvii, 75, 80, 96, 120, 130, 238, 241, 243, 248, 259, 261, 263, 265, 275, 277-79, 281-82, 330
tidal flats, 14
tobacco, 76, 80, 271, 301
Tom Point Creek, 100
Tombee Plantation, St. Helena Island, xxxv, 396-98, 421, 424, 458, 469, 478, 493, 495, 515
Tomoca River (Tomoka), Florida, 123, 132
Toogoodoo Creek, St. Paul's Parish, 342, 345, 382
Toomer, Joshua (1810-1893), 479
topping (of cotton), 170
Towles, H. A., 328, 517
Towne, Laura (1825-1901), 478
Townsend, Amarinthia Jenkins (1810-1852), 431, 493, 498, 501
Townsend, Daniel (1759-1842), 384, 498, 501, 504
Townsend, Daniel Jenkins (1811-1885), 384-385, 492, 501
Townsend, Henrietta [née Evans] (d. 1842), 384, 492, 501
Townsend, Hephzibah [née Jenkins] (1780-1847), 384, 498, 501
Townsend, James S., xxxiii, 488
Townsend, John, xxi
Townsend, John Ferrars (1799-1881), 384, 498, 501
Townsend, Mary Frampton (1804-1861), 415, 477-78, 492, 499, 501
Townsend, Susan Lavinia [née Swinton] (1822-1866), 384-85, 492, 501
treadle, 190, 195-96, 200, 215, 243, 248, 250, 263, 265
treadmill, 205, 267
Trenholm, Charles Lewis (1809-1865), 303, 346
Trenholm, Portia Ash Burden, 346, *349*, 353-54
tropics (tropical), xxxiv, 39, 57-8, 60, 63, 70, 73-5, 91, 125, 218, 269, 287, 514, 517
truck crops, 129
Tubedue Creek (*see* Toogoodoo Creek)
Tucker, Thomas, 415
Turkmenistan, 56, 73, 88
Turnbull, Nicholas, xxxiii, 78, 518
Turner, J. A., 137, 164, 180, 204, 215, 518

INDEX

twisting (of fibers), 53, 240-41, 243, 257, 259, 281-82
two-barred loom, xxiv, 261, 263-64
Union blockade, 324-25
Union Forces, xxix, xxx, 307, 325, 337, 414, 424, 475
upland cotton, xv, xxvii, xxxi, xxxiii, 39-40, 43, 46, 49-50, 54-6, 62, 67, 81, 84, 87, 90, 99, 104-05, 107, 114, 116, 119-21, 123, 127-31, 133, 136, 140, 144, 148, 164, 170, 180, 186-87, 192, 219, 239, 241, 271, 274, 276-78, 284, 287-88, 292-94, 299, 300-02, 306-08, 314, 324, 329-31, 333, 337-38, 509
Uzbekistan, 56, 73, 88
Valenciennes lace, 279
Vance's Ferry, South Carolina, 81, 108
Vanderhorst, Adele Petigru [née Allston] (1840-1915), 406
Vanderhorst, Ann Elliott [née Morris] (1795-1879), 406
Vanderhorst, Arnoldus (1748-1815), 361, 404-05
Vanderhorst, Elias (1791-1874), 404-06
Vanderhorst, Elizabeth [née Raven] (c. 1753-1808), 404
Vanderhorst Plantation, Kiawah Island, 359, *360, 361*-62, *364,* 367, 404-06, 410
vase (for spinning), 241-42
Venezuela, 69
vertical flowering interval, 43
"Verum", 124-25, 518
Victoria and Albert Museum, London, 279
Virginia, 8
Von Oven, J. H. G., xxxii, 215, 488
"W", 124
Wadmalaw Island, St. John's Colleton Parish, xxxi, 3, 21, 25, 95, 103, 144, 151, 164, 171, 315, 327, 329, 380, 384-85, 413, 418, 443, 450, 470, 511
Walmsley, Herbert, 259, 518
walrus hide, 221-22, 225, 237
War of 1812, 31, 276, 310, 313, 315, 317
war tax, xxix, xxxi, 325, 327
Ware, Harriet, 402
Waring, Benjamin, 50
warp-weighted loom, 261, 264
warp yarn, 261, 263, 265
Wassaw Island, Georgia, 9
water frame (of Arkwright), xxv, 252-57, 259, 270, 275
Watkins, James L., 121, 123, 518
Watt, Sir George, xxxii, 60, 62, 94, 99, 518
Watt, James, 270
Watts, Sarah (d. 1816), 459
Wauklyn, William, 230, 232
Wayne, Mary (1828-1886), 427, 466, 492, 495, 502
weave (weaving), 74-5, 238-39, 245-48, 252, 260-62, 263, 265, 267, 269, 275

Webber, Herbert J., 85, 146, 518
weft yarn, 127, 248-49, 252, 256, 260-62, 263, 265, 267, 269, 275, 330
Wells, Gideon M., 421
Wendel, J. F., xxxv, 61-2, 69-70, 72-4, 90, 92, 514, 519
West Africa, 62, 269
West Florida, *122,* 125, 195, 198, 504
West Indies, xxv, xxxii, 56, 62, 75-8, 84, 89-90, 92-3, 99, 105, 129, 190, 192, 195, 269, 271, 299, 329-30, 338
wet dock (for ships), 271
Whaley, Abigail Mikell (1830-c. 1880), 426-27, 492, 502
Whaley, Abigail Mikell [née Baynard] (1797-1830), 425-26, 436-37, 495, 501
Whaley, Abigail Mikell [née Baynard] (1839-1905), 427, 439, 482, 491, 495, 502
Whaley, Arthur Murray (1847-1925), 387, 493, 502
Whaley, Benjamin Joseph (1824-1900), 482, 502
Whaley, Clarence (1843-1919), 482, 501
Whaley, Edward Charles (1790-1860), 387-88, 425-27, 437, 481-82, 495, 501
Whaley, Edward Charles (1826-1887), 427, 492, 502
Whaley, Elizabeth Baynard (1837-1895), 443, 492, 500-01
Whaley, Ephraim Mikell (1828-1900), 427, 482, 491, 495, 502
Whaley, Eva Irene (1879-1947), 394, 482, 491, 500, 502
Whaley, James Swinton (1861-1932), 482, 491, 500, 502
Whaley, Joseph (1788-1872), 172, 430, 499, 501
Whaley, Joseph Baynard (1821-1846), 482, 501
Whaley, Martha Mary [née Hanahan] (1823-1870), 387, 493, 501
Whaley, Martha Mary Murray [née Clark] (1821-1850), 466, 492, 501, 502
Whaley, Mary [née Wayne] (1828-1886), 427, 466, 492, 495, 502
Whaley, Mary [née Wilkinson] (1770-1813), 429-30, 493, 496-97
Whaley, Percival Hanahan (1854-1915), 387, 502
Whaley, Rachel Louisa [née Mitchell] (1818-1889), 425-27, 492, 495, 501
Whaley, Susan Providence [née Bailey] (1855-1931), 387, 493, 502
Whaley, Thomas (1750-1805), 429, 172, 497, 500-01
Whaley, William (1817-1879), 427, 492, 495, 501
Whaley, William Baynard (1821-1857), 387, 493, 501
Whaley, William James (1819-1888), 466, 492, 495, 502
whipping cotton, 175, 177-80, 183, 294, 321
White, Edward Brickell (1806-1882), 484

INDEX

White, George S., 314, 519
White Nile River, 83
Whitney, Eli (1765-1825), xxvii, 50, 81, 186, 193, 204, 215, 218, 271, 275, 505
Whittemore, William, Jr., xxviii, 187, 205, 207-08, 211, 487, 511
whorl, 241-42, 281
wickyarn, 276
Wigg, Elizabeth Hayne (1775-1823), 390, 492, 494
wild cotton, 39, 53, 56-7, 60-3, 70, 73-5, 90-3, 99
Wildflowers of South Carolina, 25, 38, 489, 514
Wildflowers of the Carolina Lowcountry and Lower Pee Dee, 25, 514
Wilkinson, Mary (1770-1813), 429-30, 493, 496-97
William and John (English ship), 76
Willtown, St. Paul's Parish, 449
Wilson, Robert, 111, 113, 519
Wilson, Samuel, 75, 519
Windsor (*see* Ashe's/Little Edisto Plantation)
wire-toothed gin, xxvii, 50, 81, 186, 275
Wisconsinan glacier, xxiv, xxix, 5, 8
Woodward, Alsop Park Vail (1804-1858), 415, 499
Woodward, Elizabeth Catherine [née Pope] (c. 1818-1904), 415, 499
Woodward Plantation, Port Royal Island, 366, 367, 390, 445-47, 493-94
Woofter, T. J., xvii, xxxiii, 326, 337, 403, 519
wool, xxv, 50, 75-6, 79-80, 137, 175, 183, 196, 209, 238, 245, 248, 252, 269, 312, 350, 514
Works Progress Administration, 130
World War I (WWI), xviii, 85, 129, 278, 330-31
Wyatt, John, xxv, 245, 252, 265
xerophyte, 39
yarn, xix, xxv, xxvi, 54, 88, 127, 184, 238, 240-41, 243, 245, 249-50, 252-53, 255-57, 259-61, 263, 265, 267, 269-70, 273-78, 281-82, 314, 330-31, 514
Yazoo River, 87
yellow cotton, 175, 180, 294
Youghal Plantation, Christ Church Parish, 366, 479-480, 493, 498, 518
Yuma, Arizona, 85

Printed and bound by PG in the USA